GEORGE WASHINGTON

THE SAVIOR OF THE STATES

1777-1781

GEORGE WASHINGTON
Painted by C. W. Peale
(By permission of ex-Senator Joseph S. Frelinghuysen)

GEORGE
WASHINGTON
The Savior of the States
1777-1781

RUPERT
HUGHES

1930

NEW YORK

WILLIAM MORROW & COMPANY

PRINTED IN THE U. S. A. BY
QUINN & BODEN COMPANY, INC.
RAHWAY, N. J.

"A man never mounts so high as when he does not know where he is going."

OLIVER CROMWELL, to the French minister, M. Bellièvre, 1647.

CONTENTS

vii

ILLUSTRATIONS

GEORGE WASHINGTON

The Savior of the States

I

THE DAWN OF '77

"THE year 1776 is over. I am heartily glad of it, and hope you nor America will ever be plagued with such another."[1]

So Robert Morris wrote to Washington on January first, 1777, and his letter shows how different, to the eyes of the time, that year was from what it is in retrospect. In American ears it has an epic sound, and the people who ennobled it are revered as demigods. But it was a year of plague to those who had just lived through it and who looked forward to its successor with little hope of improvement.

It had begun brightly with Washington's announcing on New Year's day the realization of his lifelong dream, a regular army, the Continentals. With this and the militia he was keeping the whole British force locked up in Boston. But by January 14th only half of his army was recruited and the militia began to disband. He had to call them out again to take possession of the town when the British evacuated it March 17th, 1776.

From that moment he watched his power and his prestige decay. He marched to New York and found it such a nest of Tories that late in June one of his own bodyguard joined a plot to assassinate him and seize the city.

Having declared that Canada was necessary to the success of the Union and having sent thither troops that he could ill spare from his own poor ranks, he received nothing but reports of wholesale desertion, smallpox and disaster ending in defeat on defeat and, in June, the flight of "the last man to leave Canada," Benedict Arnold.

The only good news fell to other officers: the repulse of a

(For all footnote references, see Appendix I, pp. 689-772.)

British attack on Charleston, South Carolina, by troops under the nominal command of General Charles Lee. The Declaration of Independence was hardly passed on July 2nd (not 4th) when a British armada took possession of New York harbor with Lord Howe's fleet, bringing 10,000 Hessians on transports, Sir William Howe's army and fleet from Halifax, and Sir Henry Clinton's expedition returning from South Carolina —32,000 soldiers in all, besides 10,000 seamen, and many big guns.

Against these Washington had about eighteen thousand soldiers, mainly militia. On the very day set apart by Congress for fasting and prayer, he saw his men slaughtered and captured and pursued in the disgraceful Battle of Long Island.

He withdrew the remnants to New York, lingered there overlong, and witnessed, on a September Sabbath, one of the most shameful panics in history, a stampede so frantic that he rode into the mob and whipped with his cane men and officers, including a brigadier general; then he longed to die and would have let the Hessians take or kill him if an aide had not dragged him away.

At White Plains, in fifteen minutes one October morning Howe chased his men off a hill and pushed him back into the high ground, then turned and in a few hours of a November day captured Fort Washington in a whirlwind assault with 3,000 men, 12,000 shell, 400,000 cartridges and other precious munitions. Washington himself escaped in a rowboat only a quarter of an hour before the fort was surrounded. A few days later Howe crossed the river and descended on him so unexpectedly that he could not finish a letter he was writing to Congress, and the garrison at Fort Lee barely escaped capture by leaving its tents standing and its provisions and artillery for the British. Washington's army melted away as he fled across New Jersey, and he got over the Delaware with only three thousand men. In natural contempt for troops that Washington himself called "sheep," the British scattered a few outposts through New Jersey, and devoted themselves to recreation and the taking of oaths of allegiance from thousands of repentant rebels.

Congress had fled from the very menace of Howe's approach and abandoned Philadelphia, after voting Washington dictatorial powers over an army most of which would go home January first on account of the expiration of enlistments. General Charles Lee was captured by the British and there was nobody else of importance to supplant Washington, who resigned himself to a further flight across Pennsylvania and prepared for an outlaw existence in the back mountains and the wilderness beyond. His few troops were so naked in the cold that he was glad to accept old clothes gathered for them by a few charitable people in Philadelphia.

Wondering why he was not pursued, he noted that the outpost at Trenton was made up of about a thousand Hessians, under a commander who had promised to capture Washington as soon as the river froze over, but neglected to throw up even an earthen breastwork for his own defence.

Then the impetuous, headstrong, fearlessly rash Virginian (who had been called "Fabius" because that was the only polite name to give one who was forever on the retreat) succeeded at last in persuading his officers to make an attack. On the night of December 26th, 1776, he attempted to push three bodies of troops across the Delaware, to arrive simultaneously at dawn and crush the outpost. Two of the bodies could not make it, and the one he led himself was so delayed that it did not reach Trenton until eight o'clock. Fortunately for him, the Hessian patrols just missed discovering his army and the Hessian commander was asleep in a drunken stupor. The attack was a dazzling success and only a few of the Hessians escaped.

To Washington, the victory had none of the immortal splendor it later acquired. It was the desperate lashing out of a beaten fighter, who would die fighting. He wanted to push on, but New Jersey was a frozen waste, across whose snows he could foresee a rush of British troops, to gobble up his own army before it dissolved. He had nothing to do but turn back

across the river with his booty and his captives, less in a mood
of triumph than of sardonic frenzy at the thought of what he
might have achieved if his people had but done their duty.

So the year 1776 ended for him as a twelvemonth of almost
unrelieved heartbreaks, for which he could blame only his fellow citizens.

John Adams, who had, so to speak, invented Washington,
by forcing his nomination to the post of Commander-in-Chief,
was as bitter as he about the maddening poltroonery of the
people. To John Adams the glorious forefathers of '76 were
effeminate, luxurious, and corrupt! He bewailed "the gloomy
cowardice of the times" and uttered this apostrophe:

"Posterity! you will never know how much it cost the present generation to preserve your freedom! I hope you will make a good use
of it. If you do not, I shall repent it in heaven that I ever took half
the pains to preserve it." [2]

Adams knew all too well that only a minute portion of his
fellow citizens did any public service, and he expressed to his
wife a dismal hope that defeat might "cure Americans of their
vicious, and luxurious, and effeminate appetites, passions, and
habits, a more dangerous army to American liberty than Mr.
Howe's." [3]

The creative genius of John Adams has been far too well
forgotten and a recent biographer has thrown into the scales
a valuable counterweight, calling him, not altogether whimsi-
cally, "the man who never died," and piling up striking arguments for the claim that "if anyone is to be called 'The Father
of His Country,' and 'The Founder of the Republic' it is he." [4]

Even if those names belong to Washington irretrievably,
still Adams has a share in them, for, as he wrote later:

"We owe no thanks to Virginia for Washington. Virginia is
indebted to Massachusetts for Washington, not Massachusetts to Virginia. Massachusetts made him a general against the inclination of
Virginia. Virginia never made him more than a colonel . . . I was
subjected to almost as bitter exprobrations for creating Washington
commander-in-chief, as I had been, five years before, for saving Pres-

ton and his soldiers [the British participants in the Boston 'Massacre']
from an unrighteous judgment and execution." [5]

A few hard-working statesmen, a few hard-fighting soldiers
did all the work, suffered all the peril, all the malice of conditions. But in the hearts of posterity they now divide the
glory and the reverence with the indifferent, the cowardly,
the treacherous and selfish multitude whom they hated almost
more than the open enemy. Lieutenant-Colonel Ebenezer
Huntington, once, after forty-eight hours of lying out in the
rain, hungry, ragged and filthy, and long unpaid, contrasted his
lot with the comfort of the stay-at-homes who were in general
prosperous and cheerful, but would neither fight nor be taxed:

"I despise my Countrymen, I wish I could say I was not born in
America . . . My Cowardly Countrymen . . . hold their Purse
Strings as tho' they would Damn the World, rather than part with a
Dollar to their Army." [6]

Washington knew that if the Americans had risen as a
nation, raised and supported the army of which it was capable,
and had done the few wise, brave things he asked, he could
have freed them almost immediately from the invader. Perhaps that is why he revealed no word of elation or of pride
in his new power as dictator. First he had no desire for the
honor and had entered into no deal, no conspiracy, to gain it.
He was such a reluctant ruler as Plato spoke of when he said:
"No man governs well who wants to govern." [7] In acknowledging the power imposed upon him by Congress he wrote with
his usual modesty that he might fail, but added:

"I trust the failure will be imputed to the true cause, the peculiarly
distressed condition of our affairs, and the difficulties I have to combat, rather than to a want of zeal for my country, and the closest
attention to her interest, to promote which has ever been my study." [8]

To the Congressional committee of three that brought the
word of his new honors and powers from Congress he was inspired to express himself with a classic purity of diction as of
thought:

"They have done me the honor to entrust me with powers, in my military Capacity, of the highest nature and almost unlimited in extent. Instead of thinking myself freed from all civil obligations, by this mark of their confidence, I shall constantly bear in mind, that as the sword was the last resort for the preservation of our liberties, so it ought to be the first thing laid aside, when those liberties are firmly established." [9]

Sometimes, in the bitterness of his trials, he must have felt that he was not so much the foremost citizen of a great people as what a fellow-countryman of Tory convictions called him: "the first simpleton of consequence."

"The Congress . . . find themselves in a slippery situation, and are glad to throw their burden upon the first simpleton of consequence that would take it. Washington has now no mean character to support. He must be the *first* or *last* of men, who would accept power upon such terms. But as the Congress are desperate, so is this gentleman." [10]

Ragged soldiers shivering in the sleet need the blur of years to look their best. Posterity finds them both majestic and piteous. But to their contemporaries they were a pack of snivelling vagabonds in the snow and little more. The English ridiculed them and despised them, and Captain Smythe of the Royal Army set it down in his diary that even Washington could hardly keep his breeches on:

"A deserter . . . says that the Congress troops are suffering extremely for food and rum; that there is not a whole pair of breeches in the army, and that the last news from Mr. Washington's camp was, that he had to tie his up with strings, having parted with the buttons to buy the necessaries of life." [11]

Washington found most of his men poor in spirit and in flesh and as frayed in patriotism as in breeches. It was this infinitely confirmed opinion that gave him pause when he had his first sip of victory and looked on the first real array of prisoners he had ever beheld. For he had begun his military career by surrendering his command of three hundred to the French at Fort Necessity on July 4th, 1754; a year later he had barely escaped death or capture with Braddock; he had seen only hardship, humiliation and the taking of a deserted fort with Forbes in 1758. And that was all the military service he had ever known, except some Indian fighting, until in July, 1775, he took command at Boston. He made no prisoners worth mentioning there in the nearly nine months of siege, and in the subsequent battles it was nearly always Washington's men who were captured, often in droves.

But now, after the battle of Trenton, in his forty-fifth year, he could feast his eyes on his first prisoners: 868 wretched Hessians in thin and ragged uniforms surrounded by twenty-five hundred of his own ragamuffins. That little gulp of glory must have stirred him deeply and created an appetite for more. He sent his Hessian prisoners on to Philadelphia, whence most of the Whigs had fled and where the Tories were already preparing to seize the town in expectation of Howe's presence.

The confounding of these Tories by the victory at Trenton was an act of heaven, and Washington its direct agent, according to the Reverend Wheeler Case, a Presbyterian minister. This was strange, too, for John Calvin had written with all the horrible chastity of his logic that magistrates and monarchs were selected by God and must be obeyed:

"Those who rule in an unjust and tyrannical manner are raised up by him to punish the iniquity of the people; they all equally possess that sacred majesty with which he has invested legitimate authority. If we have this constantly present to our eyes and impressed upon our hearts, that the most iniquitous kings are placed on their thrones by the same decree by which the authority of all kings is established, these seditious thoughts will never enter our minds."

According to Calvin, Washington was a rebel against heaven. The Episcopalian clergy and John Wesley the Methodist said much the same thing. But all religions have always adapted themselves to all wars, and this Presbyterian preacher lauded the Episcopalian Washington for defying the anointed King and turning the sacrilege into a sacrament:

> "When these affairs are view'd and duly scann'd,
> He's blind that does not see JEHOVAH's hand.
> See Washington thro' Jersey State retreat,
> His foes rejoice—they thought that he was beat . . .
> A storm of snow and hail the LORD sent down,
> A blessed season this for Washington:
> He now return'd, and thro' the storm he press'd,
> And caught twelve hundred Hessians in their nest." [12]

The Hessians found Washington "a good rebel" and were astounded when he did no more harm to them than to take away and restore to the owners the loot they had been so assiduously compiling. They suffered horribly in their passage across the Delaware—Lieutenant Wiederholdt stated that he had to wade seventy paces through water breast-deep and break through the ice to get to shore.[13]

Washington invited several of the officers to dinner and Lieutenant Wiederholdt describes him graphically:

"General Washington is a courtly and elegant man, but seems to be very polite (*polie*) and reserved, speaks little, and has a sly expression (*listige Physiognomie*). He is not very tall yet also not short, but of medium height, and of a good figure and has some resemblance in the face to Captain von Bieserod of the Knyphausen Regiment." [14]

It is strange to hear Washington described as "sly." Yet a relation of Martha Washington's later commented on Gilbert Stuart's familiar portrait as giving too "soulful" a look to the eyes, in which she saw rather a look "not exactly of cunning but very quick and Knowing." [15]

Busy as Washington was and concerned about so many things, he took time to renew his efforts to persuade the Hessians to desert. He advised the Council of Safety to separate the soldiers from their officers, and canton them in the German counties.[16]

The effort was vain. The statistics give an unsuspected dignity to these greatly maligned victims of the cruel times. The number of Hessian deserters was less than that of either the English or the Americans.[17]

The day after the Trenton victory, Congress having no telegraphic news of it in Baltimore, had despondently resolved to make a further grand surrender of its useless military powers.

Believing the rumor that Howe had actually taken Philadelphia, Congress enlarged and particularized on December 27th the grant of December 12th by vesting Washington "with full, ample, and complete powers" to raise "from any or all of these United States" sixteen battalions of infantry, 3,000 Light-Horse, three regiments of artillery, and a corps of engineers; to call for the militia, form magazines of provisions, displace and appoint all officers under the rank of Brigadier-General, fill up all vacancies; "to take wherever he may be, whatever he may want," if the inhabitants would not sell what the army needed, allowing a reasonable price for it, "to arrest and confine persons who refuse to take the Continental currency, or are otherwise disaffected to the American cause." [18]

All this absolutism was to last for six months, unless sooner revoked. At the same time a committee was appointed to prepare a letter of explanation to the public, requesting cooperation. Also it was ordered that "Five Millions of Dollars be now emitted on the faith of the United States."

This final resounding phrase, "the faith of the United States," was taken with little seriousness by the public and with less seriousness later by Congress when it came to the matter of making good the pledge. To compel people to accept fiat money at its face value has always been as vain an effort as the hunt for perpetual motion. Penalties make no difference at all. Tyranny and prayers both fail, and one might as well issue an edict that mud is bread and people must both eat it and thrive on it.

Washington, however, accepted the fallacy and denounced as unreasonable and treasonable any refusal to accept Continental money at par. He approved the cruel and spasmodic measures taken for singling out unfortunate individuals as the victims of the laws. But he could not even force his own soldiers to accept the bad money, and later he evaded his own ruin by various devices.

In Washington's hands, the usually fatal loan of the dictatorship was accepted as a responsibility, not an opportunity for self-aggrandizement. John Adams later denied that it was even a nominal power and wrote to his wife:

"Congress never thought of making him dictator or of giving him a sovereignty. I wish I could find a correspondent who was idle enough to attend to every report and write it to me. Such false news, uncontradicted, does more or less harm. Such a collection of lies would be a curiosity for posterity." [19]

When the British failed to appear on the other side of the Delaware river and Trenton lay empty waiting for somebody to come and take it, Washington was consumed with an eagerness. Yet he could not fight without soldiers and his soldiers would not fight without pay. They could be no longer decoyed by thirst for glory or stamped paper or promises. They wanted "hard money," something that they could feel in their pockets and buy things with. The Pennsylvanians were willing to remain, for their state had given them a bounty of ten dollars each and an assurance of their wages. But the Easterners were filled with a homesickness. In the breasts of some of them this was doubtless due to the new gold rush that had set in throughout New England. The success of the patriot privateers on the ocean was costly to the British supply fleets, and the prize money was so magnificent that at one time there were said to have been ninety thousand patriots at sea, while the armies languished between three and twenty thousand. The results of privateering were dubious in many ways, for, though the Americans took and sent into port 559 British ships, the British took to port 904 American vessels.

It is not generally remarked that Washington himself felt the lure of privateering and before this year was out went in with Jacky Custis, Lund Washington and Baylor as part owner of a privateer and a sharer in the profits. [20]

Benjamin Rush, however, was alive to the peril of this lust for piratical gold and wrote to R. H. Lee:

"Many of the Continental troops now in our service pant for the expiration of their enlistments, in order that they may partake of the spoils of the West-Indies. . . . New-England and the Continent cannot spare them. They have a right at this juncture to their services and to their blood. We must have an Army; the fate of America must be decided by an Army. It must consist of seventy or eighty thousand men, and they must all be fit for the field before the first day of May next." [21]

If by the first of May Washington had found himself with half that number he could probably have ended the war. He had now less than one tenth and by June 1st only 8,000, but he decided to begin his fourth crossing of the Delaware on December 29th, 1776, a Monday. He had to leave behind most of Captain Forrest's battery because the men had neither shoes nor overcoats.

General Cadwalader with eighteen hundred men was already over. He had tried to join the battle at Trenton on Christmas night but had been unable to cross until the 27th. Then he could not get back. After waiting anxiously at Bordentown for news, he moved to the village of Crosswicks. At the same time Mifflin had brought over about eighteen hundred volunteers from Philadelphia and they were gathered at Bordentown.

Washington, being dictator now, did not have to ask Congress for permission to act. He simply wrote to the President and told him where he was going.

Having ceased to expect either help or hindrance from the remote and resourceless Congress, he threw himself on that inexhaustible worker of miracles, Robert Morris, frankly confessing that he had promised the soldiers money he did not have:

"Tomorrow the Continental Troops are all at Liberty—I wish to push our Success to keep up the Pannick & in order to get their Assistance have promised them a Bounty of 10 Dollars if they will continue for one Month.

"But here again a new Difficulty presents itself. We have not Money to pay the Bounty, & we have exhausted our credit by such frequent Promises that it has not the Weight we could wish. If it is possible, Sir, to give us Assistance do it—borrow Money when it can be done we are doing it from our private Credit—every Man of Interest and every Lover of his Country must strain his Credit upon such an Occasion. No time, my dear sir, is to be lost.

"The bearer will escort the money." [22]

That postscript was as neat a tribute to Morris as was paid to heaven in the old story about the congregation that gathered to pray for rain and was amazed to find in its midst an innocent child who had actually brought along an umbrella.

While waiting to see if his faith in Morris were justified Washington paraded the regiments whose term had now expired and bombarded them with oratory and prayers and pledges of money. Colonel Knox pleaded. Even Washington grew eloquent. General Mifflin, a famous roarer, thundered at them. John Howland describes Mifflin as "seated on a noble looking horse, and himself clothed in an overcoat made of a large rose blanket, and a large fur cap on his head." [23] He made promises of land; they were not kept. But at last Washington could write to Congress on New Year's day:

"After much persuasion, and the exertions of their officers, half or a greater proportion of those from the eastward have consented to stay six weeks on a bounty of ten dollars. I feel the inconvenience of this advance, and I know the consequences which will result from it; but what could be done? Pennsylvania had allowed the same to her militia; the troops felt their importance, and would have their price. Indeed, as their aid is so essential, and not to be dispensed with, it is to be wondered, they had not estimated it at a higher rate." [24]

Nearly half of those who accepted the bounty and promised to stay changed their minds and set out for home—and took the bounty with them. [25] When Washington crossed December 26th he took 2,500 men. When he crossed January 1st he had sixteen hundred men. He had as usual an ingrowing army.

He ordered Mifflin and Cadwalader to march to him in Trenton with what men they had, and posted an advance guard under the Frenchman, General Roche de Fermoy.

It might seem that he had learned nothing from his disaster on Long Island, for now he was in a worse trap with only five thousand men, and back of him a river that could not be crossed at all.

But, again, the fault was not his. He knew better but could not do better. When he planned to push forward and attack the British, his men would not budge until he put money into their hands. His poverty and not his will consented. In criticizing his generalship, his ineluctable fetters should always be recalled. His men were not skilled in maneuver, nor was he; else he could have marched east away from the river to where he might have had elbow room, but now he was nailed to the cross and, before he could free himself, the British had broken through his outguards, and were hastening to put back to his lips the bitter and apparently inescapable cup of defeat.

The irony of it was that on the day after New Year's day, 1777, he must accept this sour wine on the very ground where he had been granted a brief and unusual taste of victory the day after Christmas.

II

THE SECOND BATTLE OF TRENTON

WHAT had the British been doing all this while? On
Christmas day, 1776, Sir William Howe and his
officers had been congratulating themselves, and
with good reason, on the profitable business they had done since
they landed on Long Island on August 22nd. In four months
they had won battle after battle and had captured 4,430
prisoners, including 304 officers, among them three Generals,
Sullivan, Lord Stirling and Charles Lee. They had taken
from the hard-pressed Americans 12 pieces of brass ordnance,
235 iron cannon, 23,979 shells, 17,122 iron shot, 2,684 double-
headed shot, 140 grape quilted, 2,800 muskets, 400,000
cartridges, 16 barrels of powder, 500 intrenching tools, 35
breast plates for engineer armor, 4 covered wagons, 200 hand
barrows, 52 mantelets, 81 chevaux-de-frise complete, 4,000
barrels of flour, baggage, tents, long pikes, ammunition carts
and a large quantity of stores.[1]

This was a grievous loss to the poor young republic dependent now largely on supplies smuggled from France or
captured by privateers.

The loss in territory was great also, for Rhode Island was
occupied, New York largely free of alarm, New Jersey clear,
and Congress in disgraceful flight from Pennsylvania into
Maryland. Besides Washington's men, the Americans had
troops at various points in New England, New York, upper
New Jersey and elsewhere, but these were hardly more than
recruiting stations.

Lord Cornwallis had packed his things for a visit to England during the season of hibernation, and General Howe, having left the hired men from Hesse out in the cold along the

14

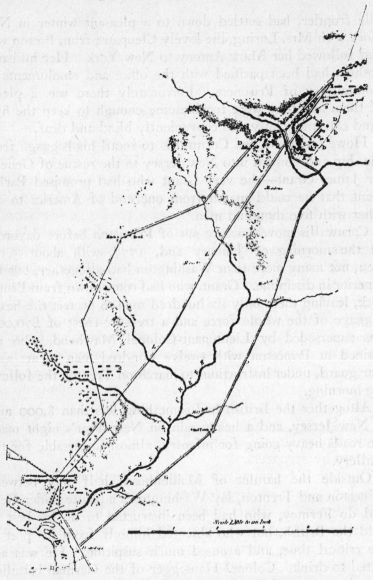

The Battles of Trenton and Princeton.

Washington's night march was along the road to the right.

(From Wilkinson's *Memoirs*.)

idle frontier, had settled down to a pleasant winter in New York with Mrs. Loring, the lovely Cleopatra from Boston who had followed her Mark Antony to New York. Her husband, Joshua, had been pacified with the office and emoluments of Commissary of Prisoners. Fortunately there was a plenty of them and they were troublesome enough to keep the husband extremely busy and conveniently blind and deaf.

Howe ordered Lord Cornwallis to recall his baggage from the ship and go back into New Jersey to the rescue of General Sir James Grant—the very Grant who had promised Parliament that he could march from one end of America to another with five thousand men.[2]

Cornwallis moved warily out of Princeton before daybreak on the morning of January 2nd, 1777, with about 5,500 men, not many more than Washington had altogether, but far superior in discipline. Grant, who had come down from Brunswick, leaving there only six hundred men to protect the heavy baggage of the whole force and a treasure-chest of £70,000, was superseded by Lieutenant-Colonel Mawhood, who remained in Princeton with twelve hundred men to act as a rear guard, under instructions to march on Trenton the following morning.

Altogether the British had something less than 8,000 men in New Jersey, and a heavy rain on New Year's night made the roads heavy going for infantry, almost impassable for the artillery.

Outside the hamlet of Maidenhead, half way between Princeton and Trenton, lay Washington's advance under General de Fermoy, who had been instructed to do his best to hold the British, but who absented himself from his post at the critical time, and aroused much suspicion. He was addicted to drink. Colonel Hausegger of the German battalion was also suspected because of the ease with which he let himself be captured and his conduct afterward as a prisoner.[3]

At ten o'clock in the morning of January 2nd, 1777, the British light infantry and Hessian Jägers who made up the advance party of Cornwallis' force struck rebel riflemen at Five Mile Run just outside Maidenhead and paused for a time to bring up the main force. The check was not serious though the British column was nagged by snipers posted in the woods along the road. There is no record of their hitting anybody.

At one o'clock the advance was held up again at Shabbakonk creek. The column deployed into line, fired a few cannon at the forest, formed into column again, and pushed on for Trenton, where Washington waited in the position he had selected: the high ground outside the town on the southeastern side of the Assunpink creek. The stream was high and swift with melted snow and only one bridge crossed it along the three miles occupied by his troops.

During the early afternoon Washington rode far up the creek with Knox to inspect his outposts. General Greene, who was in command of them, assured him that they would put up a stiff opposition to the British advance.

Washington rode back, encouraged, only to be followed shortly by his outposts, who came tumbling after him in a confusion rivalling the waters of the Assunpink. He tried to calm his men by posting himself at the end of the bridge; but they swarmed past in such a mob that John Howland long afterward remembered being crowded so hard against Washington's big white horse that he gouged his arm on one of the general's spurs. He described how "the noble horse of Gen. Washington stood with his breast pressed close against the end of the west rail of the bridge, and the firm, composed, and majestic countenance of the general inspired confidence. . . . The horse stood as firm as the rider, and seemed to understand that he was not to quit his post and station." [4]

By four o'clock Washington could see the enemy at the point where King and Queen streets then met, and from across the creek he reviewed some fifteen hundred British and Hessians taking possession of the town he could not hold with five thousand.

Washington dared not hurl his undisciplined troops across

that bridge to overwhelm the British advance, small as it was, and he had to sit still in his saddle and watch the arrival of four thousand more marching in from Maidenhead.

The second battle of Trenton was hardly worthy of the name of skirmish. In his own words, it was only a matter of "cannonading the enemy, and receiving the fire of their field-pieces, which did us but little damage." [5]

"Little damage" was the word. The list of American casualties on that day reads more like a Hessian report, for the only man killed was private John Goebel of Captain Woel-pepper's company. Besides three officers the only men wounded were named Jacob Bottamer, George Filsin, and Wender Fort-ney, all but one of the German battalion. [6]

The Hessians had eleven wounded and four killed, including Lieutenant von Grothausen, who had escaped from the first battle of Trenton only to be more or less assassinated at Shabbakonk creek. A party of six men from Colonel Hand's regiment amused themselves by pretending to be deserters, waited till the lieutenant came up to accept their surrender and then shot him down and ran. Robust humorists, those early patriots!

Perhaps it was in reprisal for this that the Hessians on over-taking a fleeing Presbyterian chaplain, the aged Reverend John Rosborough, cut him almost to pieces with their bayonets and sabers, and stripped his body. This was the extent of the "carnage" referred to by many historians, and the contemporary statements that "the creek was nearly filled" with British dead are typical of the reliability of rumor. [7] The British reports, ignoring the slight Hessian loss, do not mention a single man killed or wounded.

When night fell, the British and Americans lighted their supper fires and the cannonade ceased, except for a few shells, which, as Knox wrote to his wife, "we now and then chucked into town to prevent their enjoying their new quarters securely." [8]

Washington had arranged his troops in successive lines,

massed forty guns to sweep the bridge and set guards at all the spots where he imagined the British might attempt to ford the swollen waters. But his right flank was in the air out along the banks of the Assunpink.

Cornwallis, however, was probably so eager to enter Trenton for the moral effect of its reoccupation that he never thought of looking at his map or turning off the road at Phillips' Mill and fording the creek where it was shallow. If he had done that he might easily have smashed Washington's line in upon itself like a closed telescope and crowded among the ice floes all who did not surrender or stampede. He might in a swift round-up have annihilated the army, and ended the Revolution. As the Reverend Mr. Gordon put it:

"The fate of the continent seems suspended by a single thread." Wilkinson credited the salvation of the army to "the obstinate resistance of a handful of brave men, and the workings of Heaven in the breast of Lord Cornwallis." [9] He and others gave Cornwallis the "dreadful odds" of 8,000 men to 6,000, but the British had no appreciable superiority in numbers and they had to fight on Washington's choice of a battlefield. Yet he had to fight with soldiers whose ideals of liberty were individual rather than national. [10]

Washington seems to have had no more idea of the open door to his position than Cornwallis had. It must have been a shock to him when the bad news was brought to him at dusk by his Adjutant-General Joseph Reed, who had gone out with a few light-horse from Philadelphia to examine the raging creek and make sure if its crossings had all been guarded as Washington supposed. In a fragment of manuscript that breaks off short, Reed tells what word he brought to Washington concerning the fords:

"At Phillips's mill, about one mile higher, the ford was in very good order; and had the enemy taken the opportunity of passing it, the consequences would probably have been fatal—" [11]

What Washington must have thought of this information is found in the words of Reed's grandson and biographer:

"The night of the 2d January, 1777 . . . was, perhaps, the most gloomy and anxious that our revolutionary soldiers knew." [12]

There was a military maxim that the stronger army ought not to attack toward night. The British regulars loved maxims, loved to work out a good literary battle. And they loved hunting foxes to their holes. Cornwallis was sure that he had Washington cornered and promised his officers that they would "bag the old fox" on the morrow. The promise was not extravagant.

Sir William Erskine, quartermaster of Cornwallis' army, said: "If Washington is the general I take him to be he will not be found there in the morning. If your lordship does not attack, throw a large body of troops on the road to your left." [13] He begged Cornwallis to finish the battle that night, and other officers joined him in pointing out the lack of courage and discipline of the Americans, but Cornwallis would not be hurried. He had, as Belcher says, "imbibed much of the spirit of Howe. . . . It was a question of one hour's fighting, and the storming of the entrenchments would have certainly ended the war." [14]

It must have been the climate that dulled these brilliant British generals one by one and made them all Mañana men. In India later Cornwallis did magnificent things.

On the American side there was little doubt that the army was in a sack. Among the troops was young Major Wilkinson, who was destined to become one of the most puzzling and sinister figures in later history. He allotted Washington just half the life that Belcher gave him:

"If ever there was a crisis in the affairs of the revolution, this was the moment; thirty minutes would have sufficed to bring the two armies into contact, and thirty more would have decided the combat; and covered with wo, Columbia might have wept the loss of her most beloved chief and most valorous sons. In this awful moment, the guardian angel of our country admonished Lord Cornwallis that his own troops were fatigued, and that the Americans were without retreat." [15]

There is dispute as to who inspired Washington. To somebody in that hopeless band came one of the prettiest inspirations in all military history. No wonder so many people claimed it. Washington was content to take the advice and let the credit go as he carried out a maneuver that owed its astounding results to a recognition of the principle that Stonewall Jackson was always hammering into his staff:

"Mystery, mystery is the secret of success." [16]

III

THE "OLD FOX" IN THE TRAP

"TO give his military character, in the most sublime moment of its exertion . . . when viewing the vast superiority of his approaching enemy, and the impossibility of again crossing the Delaware, or retreating down the river"—that was the avowed motive of Colonel John Trumbull in painting the familiar full-length portrait of Washington facing the Assunpink creek—Washington as an almost effeminately elegant *poseur*, a fieldglass extended gropingly in his right hand, his other hand draped daintily over his left hip. Behind him a soldier in a feathered bonnet admires an effeminate hobby horse rearing impossibly. The broken cannon and the gnarled tree only prettify the general by contrast.

Yet Trumbull says of the picture that Washington, who posed for it in 1792, gave him expert advice.

"He entered into it warmly, and, as the work advanced, we talked of the scene, its dangers, its almost desperation. He *looked* the scene again, and I happily transferred to the canvas, the lofty expression of his animated countenance, the high resolve to conquer or to perish. The result was in my own opinion eminently successful, and the general was satisfied."

Washington may have been chiefly "satisfied" with getting the posing over with. It is refreshing to learn that, even in those days when painting was generally done with the same bombastic grandiloquence as history, Mr. Smith, who had ordered the portrait for Charleston, S. C., politely declined to buy it because "he thought the city would be better satisfied with a more matter-of-fact likeness."[1] Whereupon Trumbull, with perhaps some slight satirical intention, painted another picture in which about half the canvas is filled with the very lofty rear end of the horse.

WASHINGTON AT PRINCETON
(From the portrait by Trumbull)

A "matter-of-fact likeness" was the last thing anybody seemed to want of Washington for a century or more. A camera, had there been one, would surely have shown him at something less than his best in his impotent bewilderment outside his easily won, easily lost Trenton; and there is no reason to believe that the idea for his escape came to him in any such moment or any such posture as Trumbull shows.

The scheme seems to have been worked out gradually by a collaboration of his officers in a long and dismal night conference. The brilliance of the result and the audacity of the conception startle and delight the dramatic sense. And there was need of something unusual, for the plight of the American army was dire.

This fateful council was held at the headquarters of St. Clair in the Alexander Douglass home on Greene street to which Washington had been driven from his own earlier headquarters at Jonathan Richmond's tavern, "The True American." Washington must have looked into a sombre ring of faces gathered about the table in Mr. Douglass' two-story frame shanty, in whose combined parlor, dining room and kitchen the future existence of innumerable capitols, palaces of justice, buildings of state and monuments was being unwittingly considered.

Above the room's one candlestick fluttered a little flame that wavered with the minds of those fagged, dirty, muddy, distraught generals and colonels, certain of only one thing: that after their little glimpse of what it meant to capture and kill, they were about to be captured or killed. The one thing to do was to run for it—but which way?

Outside, the raw night was turning sharper, to the more bitter distress of soldiers fighting for sleep now on the freezing ground where the mud congealed on their tattered clothes and their half-naked feet. They must have glanced miserably at headquarters and wondered what new misery was being concocted for them.

To move off to the left was impossible. The Delaware was there. To move off to the right was to move into British territory, leaving Cornwallis in the rear and confronting Leslie at Maidenhead and Mawhood at Princeton. The south was the only way open. They might fall back hugging the river until they reached a possible crossing into Pennsylvania. But the British would follow hard, overtake their mired wagons and guns, strike the fleeing brigades in the back and capture them, slaughter them or scatter them to the four winds. General Greene's own grandson gives this detailed story of the council:

"Meanwhile, Washington summoned his officers to council, at the head-quarters of St. Clair, his own being now in the hands of the enemy.

"'What shall we do? Shall we retreat down the Delaware, on the Jersey side, and cross it over against Philadelphia; or shall we remain where we are, and try the chances of a battle?'

"Each course had its advocates, when a voice was heard, saying,

"'Better than either of these, let us take the new road through the woods, and get in the enemy's rear by a march upon Princeton, and, if possible, on Brunswick even.'

"From whom did this bold suggestion come? St. Clair claimed it as his; and why should the positive assertion of an honorable man be lightly called in question? But whose ever it was, it was the inspiration of true genius, and was promptly accepted by all." [2]

Both of these statements seem to be true and St. Clair deserves the gratitude of his adopted country, but there has been such fierce and complex controversy on the point that a full discussion of it is deferred to the second Appendix.

In any case, whipped, trapped, with an army made up of homesick soldiers and raw recruits, Washington was forced to outrage the fundamental rules of tactics: march by the flank along the enemy's front, then throw himself into the midst of the enemy between the main body and the rear guard, and crush the rear guard at Princeton before the main body could turn about and overtake him. Then if he were not destroyed he might even push on eighteen miles further and capture the enemy's magazines at Brunswick, where there was incidentally that treasure of $350,000, and where General Charles Lee was held in captivity and might be released as the final fillip to the triumph. The distances were great, the roads abominable, the maneuvers would test the skill of trained veterans, and the least failure would mean ruin. But he was ruined anyway and there was something dazzling about the opportunity to rescue the spirits of his men and his people from the collapse that would be the greater for the recent uplift. As he wrote to Congress:

"One thing I was certain of, that it would avoid the appearance of a retreat (which was of consequence, or to run the hazard of the whole army being cut off), whilst we might by a fortunate stroke withdraw General Howe from Trenton, and give some reputation to our arms." [3]

By Howe he meant, of course, Howe's army, for Howe himself was still in New York.

The chief difficulty in the way of Washington's plan was the woeful state of the roads from the recent thaw and the hard rains. The downpour had filled the Assunpink to its banks and kept Cornwallis from wading over, under fire, but it had also turned the highways and the fields into bogs.

Once more Washington's tantalizing friend "Providence" came to his rescue. Even while the council pondered, the temperature fell so rapidly that the ground froze hard in two hours. The roads would carry the guns.

He gave his orders. The council broke up. The officers dispersed in such haste that they forgot to blow out the candle. It burned itself out and left wax drippings on the table. The very stains were long preserved as a memorial of the time when American independence flickered, and might have burned out in a night like another solitary candle.[4]

The officers dispersed to the double duty of lulling the British to sleep and waking the Americans to action. The orders were passed in whispers. The captains and sergeants and corporals were wakened or were visited at the blazing fires where they collected. No one was told what was to be done, where to go.

Some of the minor officers had stolen away to farm houses for better beds than the ground afforded and they could not be found. Their companies had to march without them. They must have been amazed when they woke.

Only those who have taken part in night maneuvers can imagine what it means to wake up a family of 5,000 drowsy soldiers, push them into line, keep them awake and in line and lead them off into dense night. It is bad enough in sham battle, but when the life of the army depends upon making no noise to awaken the suspicions of the outnumbering enemy, the achievement is a triumph in itself.

The horses were certainly troublesome. They never want to be harnessed, especially at night, and they could not have welcomed the prospect of being hitched to the lurching cannon and the heavy wagons. They doubtless bucked and squealed, but the British would be having the same racket in their own camp, for army horses are forever rioting.

The British sentinels would perk their ears at the first rumble of wagons or guns and on this cold night the wheels would ring out like chimes in the frosty ruts. The rims must be wound with rags. There were rags enough, but they were on the soldiers. There must have been a scurry to find a supply not in use. Everywhere men with frost-bitten hands were kneeling and bandaging wheels, while the soldiers in line leaned on their muskets and slept or stared and blew on their fingers.

Four hundred men were selected for the uncomfortable honor of staying behind to keep the fires blazing all night by piling fence rails on them, and to deepen the trenches guarding the bridges and the fords, until just before dawn. Then they were to steal away and try to overtake their comrades. They were instructed to maintain blinding non-transparent fires, multiply their numbers by bustling about, relieving sentinels and making all the noise they could. Two cannon were sacrificed and left behind "to amuse the enemy." [5]

There is a tradition that Washington had one hearty laugh before he left Trenton. Having stationed the Virginian Colonel Scott to defend the bridge to the last, he lingered long enough to hear the Colonel rebuke his men for the usual soldierly fault of shooting too high, and add:

"Boys, whenever you see them fellows first begin to put their feet on this bridge, shin 'em!"

Washington laughed and vanished in the dark.

Speed was so important that he resolved to rid himself of three of his biggest guns and all his baggage and stores. He started them off after midnight under escort to Burlington. The Philadelphia troops were ordered to lighten their burdens for the march by putting their overcoats in their baggage wagons. In consequence they went without them for ten days.

It is heartrending to read throughout the war the countless references to bare feet trudging over ice, to backs and thighs so naked in the edged winds that they were indecent, to blanketless men lying out on snow without even straw for their comfort. There seems to be a special excruciation in the plight of those Philadelphia volunteers who owned good overcoats but had unwittingly shipped them off.

It was a little after midnight when at Washington's orders Reed sent Putnam an order to find the baggage train and take care of it. [6]

Then the march began with Patrick Lamb, tavern keeper, and Ezekiel Anderson and Elias Phillips, farmers of that neighborhood, as guides over the invisible side roads. According to one story, a woman was the guide but her name is not given. [7]

Along a vague farmroad that is now Hamilton Avenue in Trenton the soldiers moved under the strictest command to keep their mouths shut and their equipment silent. The way led across a creek called Muddy or Miry Run, then into a forest in whose night-within-night many a sleep-walker fell over a sharp stub in the new-cut road and tore his ill-shod feet. The path was afterwards traced for miles by the blood on the snow. The cannon wheels were checked and wrenched by old stumps and the men waiting for the guns to be yanked along fell asleep standing up; only to be knocked over by other stumbling wretches when the march was resumed.[8] Captain Rodney of Delaware described their mood:

"The van moved on all night in the most cool and determined order, but on the march great confusion happened in the rear. There was a cry that they were surrounded by the Hessians and several corps of Militia broke and fled towards Bordentown, but the rest of the column remained firm and pursued their march without disorder, but those who were frightened and fled did not recover from their panic until they reached Burlington."[9]

This throws a vivid side-light on the quality of the army with which Washington must defeat the British Empire. A large part of his force was so frightened by merely having to march through dark woods that it bolted and ran away from itself. At Germantown later they would run away from each other and from men trying to surrender to them. Excellent runners and ever willing.

Contempt is changed to pity when one happens upon a reference to some of these fugitives in the diary of an elderly Tory woman who looked upon them as they slept in Burlington:

"At noon upwards of one thousand men came into town in great confusion, and were quartered on the people. Several went into my next neighbour's (Colonel Cox's) house, where I went to see them, and my heart was melted to see them, lying on the floor fast asleep, although many were without blankets to cover them. I had my suspicions that they had fled the field when they should have remained, and it proved so. Among them were several innocent-looking lads, and much I sympathized with their bereaved mothers."[10]

Of the very opposite sort was young Captain Daniel Neil, a New York Presbyterian, who had moved to New Jersey with his wife and two little children and bought a mortgaged farm at Passaic where he sold imported "patent machines for dressing wheat and flour." He had joined the militia, but bad luck had only heartened him, and on the very day after Washington began his retreat across the Jerseys, Neil offered to join the Continentals, and wrote the following letter to a man of influence:

"Dr Sr the Raising of the Standing Army I sepose will Prevent the Rising of any more Troops for the Imeadiate Service of this State— Therefore I woud beg your Intrest in my behalf for a Birth in the Standing Army as I am Determined to Continue in the Artillery or other Service Dureing the Warr." [11]

When Washington had fallen back through Passaic, Neil and his artillery company had joined him, shared his disgrace and the glory of both Trentons. Neil now marched on high-hearted to an unforeseen death.

On the way north Washington's already diminished army encountered the upper waters of the Assunpink creek, and again crossed them on the Quaker Bridge. They threaded a moor of stunted oaks called the Barrens. As they sogged through Bear Swamp, they were now only four miles east of Maidenhead, where General Leslie's troops were said to be asleep. [12]

Washington's men were drawing near Princeton, but, in spite of all his efforts, he was turning up late, as at the first battle of Trenton. He had hoped to surprise whatever troops he might find and sound his own reveille to them. The British, however, were already on the march after a good sleep and a good breakfast, while his men were jaded with hours of march, and would have been the better for hot coffee or a swig of something hotter. But, as Knox wrote to his wife, they were in want of both "rum and clothing." [13]

A cold January dawn groped through a sky frosted with stars and lighted up the rime-covered foggy ground as Washington's congealing men ended their fourteen-mile trudge and emerged from the long back road into the main highway.

At Trenton in the same dawn, the yawns of the British and the Hessian sentinels were widened further by the emptiness of the heights where the only evidence that the Ameri-

cans had ever been there was the mockery of lonely camp fires
still blazing high with no other company than two abandoned
cannon.

The sentinels called their officers and the alarm was given.
Cornwallis rushed from his tent to gape and curse and register
his lifelong regret that he had not finished his military chores
before he went to bed. His fellow-officer, and later his sharpest
critic, Sir Henry Clinton, made this comment on his immortal
blunder:

"From such a situation he [Washington] could not possibly have
escaped with Impunity, had only a single Patrole been sent to feel for
him . . . for his Lordship holding the String of the Bow could have
easily met Mr. Washington before he finished his circuit." [14]

While Cornwallis was wondering what genie had lifted up
Washington's army and flown off with it, and where, he heard
thunder in the north. That was odd in winter. His quartermaster Erskine taunted him:

"Thunder? Those are Washington's guns at Princeton.
He has outgeneralled us! To arms, to arms, my lord!" [15]

Cornwallis did not linger over his repentance. He ordered
his troops into line in all haste and set out as fast as his men
could leg it. He "marched to the guns."

Washington was now in the jaws again. The British were
converging on him from both directions. And he had to meet
them in the open with a worn-out, haggard army that he had
not dared to fight with in his own entrenchments.

IV

THE TWO BATTLES OF PRINCETON

ABOUT two miles south of the village Washington halted to assemble his far-strung weary column and assign its elements to the plan he had devised for drawing a net around Princeton.

He ordered certain infantry to file off to the side of the highway and wait. Then he despatched General Sullivan along a woodcutters' road through the forest to flank the town on the east while two brigades flanked it on the west by marching up the turnpike. He planned to avoid the old road as being out of his way, but he instructed General Mercer to go over with his advance guard, including Captain Neil's two guns, and break down the bridge there so as to delay Cornwallis when he came up. Having destroyed this bridge, the advance guard was to act as a rear guard and detain Cornwallis as long as possible if he arrived during the attack on Princeton.[1]

The sun was rising the treetops by the time this elaborate rearrangement was under way with its inevitable entanglements, and Washington had hardly set his elements in motion when all of his strategy was thrown into the discard and into disarray by the premature energy of the British Colonel Mawhood, who was not only not asleep but had already marched several miles on the old road towards Trenton. Colonel Mawhood had left the 40th regiment of about two hundred men in Princeton to guard the stores and had crossed the western bridge over Stony Brook with two-thirds of his force, the 17th and the 55th regiments, two guns and some cavalry.

He was riding a little brown pony and was attended by two pet spaniels.[2] On a rise called Millet's Hill he caught sight of troops to the west of him. He could not make out how many

31

rebels there were over there below him. But the Americans were all sheep to the British, and there is an old saying that "the wolf is never frightened by the size of a flock of sheep." [3]

Mawhood's first glance selected the Clark farm as the strategic point to seize, and, whirling his column, he led it across the bridge. When his scouts ran into Mercer, Mawhood left the road, deployed in double time, ordered his wagons back to Princeton, despatched a swift rider to bring down the 40th regiment, and rushed his troops across the field, hoping to reach Clark's orchard ahead of Mercer's men and hold them in the low ground by the creek.[4]

But by this time Mercer had descried him, or had been warned by a messenger from Washington, and tried to head him off at the bridge. Realizing the impossibility of this he thought he could join General Sullivan's advance guard or at least support it by breaking the force of Mawhood's attack.[5]

Mawhood brought up the rear of his troops and passed the head of Washington's column so closely that he might have been checked if the Americans had not been too befuddled to act.[6]

Mercer was mounted on a gray horse, but his three hundred and fifty were mainly Delaware foot, under Colonel Haslett. He had also some Maryland and Philadelphia gentlemen and the two cannon in charge of Captain Neil. Mercer's brigade, already in Indian file, scrambled up the ridge, streamed through a gate into the orchard and, running down to a hedge fence, lined up behind it on their knees, while Mawhood was still on the slope.

Mercer got in the first volley with good effect, but the British light horse dismounted and opened fire from a ditch and a fence. A bullet shattered the forefoot of Mercer's horse and he had to dismount, finding Colonel Haslett dead with a bullet in the temple and his men panting from the run and panting to be gone.

The British light horse opened out to let their main body through, but Mercer held his men for two more quick volleys.

In fact the breathless Americans accomplished what was then the miracle of firing three volleys in less than five minutes, the smokes rising with the British smoke "in one beautiful cloud," says Wilkinson, while Captain Neil's two small cannon barked at the British right wing where Mawhood's two brass cannon overpowered them.

Mawhood did not pause to exchange volleys, but ordered his men forward to the charge. The Americans had no bayonets, or few, and those greedy blades of the British set up such a yearning in their bowels that they left the orchard in a wild stampede up the slope. Mercer darted here and there trying to check the rout and was knocked down with the butt of a musket. As he rose, he was quickly surrounded. The British thought they had overtaken Washington himself and encircled him shouting:

"The rebel general is taken!"

But Mercer refused to surrender and struck away their bayonets. They begged him to surrender: "Call for quarter, you damned rebel!" The brave doctor who kept the drugstore in Fredericksburg shouted back, "I am no rebel!" and slashed furiously at the eager faces behind the muskets.

So they naturally stabbed him down, and have been slandered ever since for wantonly murdering an officer who had given up his sword. The legend persists, though Mercer on his deathbed protested that it was false and claimed the honor of wielding his sword till he had seven deep wounds. Then he sank, closed his eyes, and pretended to be dead.[7]

Captain Neil was killed and his deserted cannon were turned about by the British and fired into the rebels who had only one field officer left standing—Lieutenant-Colonel Stone of Maryland.

In the meanwhile, though Washington had learned of Mawhood's presence before Mercer, he had been too far away to save him. On hearing the firing, Washington made frenzied efforts to bring up his men, but there was a long delay in getting his troops into motion. The militia were doubtless hard to manage. There was a gap of at least a thousand yards to close up.[8]

The nearest troops he found to hand were Cadwalader's untrained militia. There was a devil of a time getting them forward, and deploying them was still worse, though Captain Henry handled one little group of a hundred well enough to drive off fifty British advance guards. Cadwalader hurried a ragged line up the ridge and Washington sent along two cannon from Moulder's Philadelphia battery, also what little was left of the First Virginia regiment in command of the twenty-one-year-old Captain John Fleming and eighteen-year-old Lieutenant Bartholomew Yeates. Washington rode along with Captain Moulder and saw the cannon posted on the right of the Clark house. He saw the Pennsylvania militia run into the fleeing remnants of Mercer's brigade, take one look at Mawhood's advancing regulars and join the flight.

Captain Fleming, trying hastily to align his men near the Clark house, had just time to shout:

"Gentlemen, dress the line before you make ready."

The British closed in and mocked him:

"We'll dress you, damn you!"

They killed young Fleming and in their frenzy mangled Lieutenant Yeates so brutally that Washington sent his death-bed affidavit to General Howe with a protest. The boy lived six days with a bullet hole in the breast, a skull fractured with the butt of a musket and thirteen bayonet gouges in his flesh.[9]

Moulder's artillery from Philadelphia escaped capture by pouring in grape, and drove the British back for a time; but they formed again and pressed forward through the panic, bayoneting all who resisted until they came to the crest of the hill. There, as the fog lifted, Mawhood looked down upon an army ten times the size of his own, but in greater confusion.

As he stared, his spaniels probably yipped their contempt, for dogs despise ragged men running and Washington's army must have resembled startled hoboes. The spaniels probably took credit for the panic they were in. But Mawhood on his brown pony studied the tall man on the white horse. Washington was everywhere in a whirlwind of fury, trying to shame the fugitives, swing his column left into line and surround the insolent British few before they completely dispersed his terrified, weary, hungry irregulars. Dashing from regiment to regiment, dragging his horse back on his haunches to rebuke some skulking soldier, waving his hat to rouse his men to a cheering assault, he rode bareheaded through the crisscross of bullets.

One of Mercer's men told that he heard Washington cry to the fugitives:

"Parade with us, my brave fellows, there is but a handful of the enemy, and we will have them directly." [10]

According to a contemporary collector of anecdotes, at one moment, Washington led forward in person a shaky pack of militia and, seeing Mawhood's line about to deliver a volley, set his people an example of steadiness by halting thirty yards from the British, reining his horse's head to the front and calmly facing the blazing muskets.

He then took the perhaps greater risk of ordering his own men to fire. They did, "without their adverting to the position of the general, who is providentially preserved from being injured either by foe or friend." [11]

One of his aides-de-camp, a young Irishman, Colonel John Fitzgerald, having been sent to the rear to hustle along some laggards, returned just in time to see Washington, posing as statuary for once in his life, waiting for the volleys to cross. Fitzgerald gave him up for lost, laid his reins on his pommel and drew his hat over his eyes to hide the vision.

The smoke obliterated Washington but before it cleared he came out of it on the gallop waving his hat and cheering his men forward. Fitzgerald spurred to his side to shout:

"Thank God! your excellency is safe!"

"Away, my dear colonel," Washington howled back. "Bring up the troops—the day is our own." [12]

Washington once more, as always, terrified his bravest officers by his incredible indifference to peril. But he was in a frenzy now for the victory that belonged to him. He had brought the greater number to the point of contact. He had all the advantages, but not a moment to lose, for Cornwallis was certainly hot on his trail. If the Americans would not stand up to this little British detachment, what would they do when a British army poured in?

So he swung his great white horse this way and that, stretched him out on a lope, bridled him in to a halt, whirled him high and brought him down to a swift run again. He sent Cadwalader forward in a charge with cannon, but saw the line halt within fifty yards of the British, refuse the chance, break and fall back. Cadwalader formed them in line again and they made another try, but they could not face it. They collapsed and ran to a forest a hundred and fifty yards in the rear.

Captain Rodney's men took post behind haystacks and buildings with two cannon. Only a few of his men would stay with him, but he kept up a continuous fire that galled the British.

Washington began at last to spread a line around the ridge and envelop Mawhood's men so well that the 40th regiment rushing down from Princeton could not get to him. In fact it ran into General Sullivan, who handled it roughly and flung it back in disorder.

Gradually Washington closed in on Mawhood's little band, fighting grimly, though their excited artillery men fired over the heads of the Americans. Washington sent Colonel Hand's riflemen to turn the British left and ordered Colonel Daniel Hitchcock of Yale to turn their right.

Hitchcock was suffering from dysentery, and in just such a high fever as had racked Washington when he took part in Braddock's Defeat long before, but he led forward his regiment, now reduced to less than six hundred men, with such courage, and his men took the British fire so well that the redcoats recoiled and left their two brass cannon, all they had, in Hitchcock's possession.

Washington later took Hitchcock by the hand and thanked him and his regiment publicly and Greene took off his watch and made him a present of it. Then Hitchcock staggered away to die of his fever ten days later.[13]

The British, hopelessly outnumbered, held their ground with such magnificence that Washington is said to have exclaimed to his staff with bitter envy:

"See how those noble fellows fight! Ah! gentlemen, when shall we be able to keep an army long enough together to display a discipline equal to our enemies?"[14]

The language as reported is probably too turgid for him, but in his letter to Congress he spoke of the enemy's "gallant resistance."[15] The British properly said of Mawhood that "the brave commander, and his equally brave regiment, have gained immortal honor."[16]

Having lost his only cannon to Hitchcock and seeing Hand closing in, Mawhood fell back to the crest of the hill, where he could survey the twenty-five-to-one odds against him, for he was by now cut off from the 55th, and the 40th was lost to sight. He might have surrendered without disgrace, but he remembered his orders to join Cornwallis. He wheeled his line and, with what remained of the noble little 17th regiment, bayoneted his way through the multitudes crowding around him. Those who survived then broke into a wild run and scattered across the fields. Though his spaniels are not mentioned in the chronicles, it may be hoped that they were not left dead or wounded on the gory snow.

Strange to say, the picturesque Mawhood rides out of American history. He reappeared for a day in an obscure indecisive action a year later, then was called to England as an aide to his grateful King.[17]

His one regiment had lost sixty-six killed and wounded and thirty-five captured, out of a total of about two hundred.

Howe thanked Mawhood and Scott in his General Orders, and the historian of the British army, Fortescue, pays a double compliment to Mawhood and his opponent:

"In the circumstances he can hardly be blamed for risking an action; for it was difficult for a man to divine that Washington, who was credited with the glaring blunders of the past campaign, could be capable of movements so brilliant and so audacious." [18]

Pursuit of the fugitives was hastily organized by Washington, who gathered what riflemen he could and led them himself, forgetting all about the rest of his army in the zest of the hunt. He was having his revenge for the sickening humiliation he had endured when, on Harlem Heights, he had heard the British bugles blow the fox-hunt call as they rode down the panic-stricken rebels.

He was in high feather now and Captain Harris of Baltimore heard him cry out:

"It's a fine fox chase, my boys." [19]

"Such was the impetuosity of the man's character, when he gave rein to his sensibilities," says Wilkinson.

A squad of the Philadelphia gentlemen who had recently joined Washington accompanied him in the round-up. One of them was Mr. John Donaldson, who had a brisk morning. He rode so far ahead of the footmen that any straggler might have killed him. But he took Lieutenant Simpson in the saddle with him, and Simpson, says Wilkinson, "whenever a fugitive threatened to be refractory, jumped off and shot him, and in this manner three men, whilst taking aim at Mr. Donaldson, were knocked down and his life saved, but he made a score of prisoners, whom he sent to his rear after disarming them."

The fugitives were so widely scattered and Washington so headlong in his gallopade that he seems to have gone quite blind with joy. Again an aide saved him from capture or death. He was accompanied now by the devoted Colonel Stephen Moylan, who had been his secretary during the siege of Boston, had served as quartermaster-general until relieved by General Mifflin, and had now returned to Washington's side.

Remembering the fear and hatred of the papacy that had so inflamed the colonists and their rage at the tolerance shown to the Catholics by the Quebec Act, which was one of the important causes of the Revolution, it was odd to see Washington cantering along in warm friendship with a brother of the Roman Catholic Archbishop of Cork.[20] But it showed how little Washington cared for the fierce sectarian wars. Today he was unconsciously earning the renewed interest of His Most Catholic Majesty, the King of France.

Blindly eager to add Mawhood to his other prisoners Washington was outlining to Moylan just how he would surround the fugitives when Moylan suddenly asked:

"But where are your troops?"

Washington turned in his saddle, and saw that he and Moylan were alone on the road.[21]

He turned and galloped back, passing a few who had followed him and ordering them to return. He might easily have been captured, for Colonel Potter, who followed Mawhood too closely, was taken along prisoner.

If Washington had gone a little farther he would have run into the whole British army pressing north, since General Leslie's troops had already been ordered forward by couriers from Cornwallis, whose men had left Trenton, says Knox, "in a most infernal sweat,—running, puffing, and blowing, and swearing at being so outwitted." [22]

Realizing that the British would soon be dashing in to rob him of his success, Washington remembered the bridge that he had ordered Mercer to destroy at daybreak. Encountering Captain Varnum of the Massachusetts line, he ordered him to take a detail and break down the bridge. The captain touched his hat and asked:

"Are there enough men?"

Washington answered with blood-curdling calm:

"Enough to be cut to pieces."

The captain turned so white that, as he rejoined his troops, he pinched his cheeks for fear that they should see his pallor.[23]

The danger was real enough, for the British came up soon after the demolition began and opened fire on the detachment, several of whom had to work in the icy stream or tumbled into it.

Among these was Major Kelly, who was on the wrong end of a timber that he was hacking at when British soldiers came dashing down to the creek. One of them plunged into the icewater just as Major Kelly fell into it. As was to be expected of a Kelly, he came up clutching by the collar the impetuous Britisher. Dripping and shivering, the Major ran with his soppy prisoner while Leslie's men hesitated to breast the torrent until their commander came up and drove them through.[24]

Meanwhile, Washington paused on the corpse-littered battleground to see to his wounded. In the ploughed field where Haslett lay dead, he saw some British captives supporting a bleeding officer. Washington paused to ask who he was and was told that he was Captain Leslie, twenty-six years old. Doctor Benjamin Rush, who had accompanied Washington from Trenton and joined him now, exclaimed:

"A son of the Earl of Levin?"

On being answered Yes, Rush begged to be allowed to give the young man special care as his father had been very kind when Rush was a student in Edinburgh. Captain Leslie was taken along with the troops, but died that night and was buried with the honors of war by his weeping fellow prisoners.[25]

General Mercer had been carried into the riddled home of the Quakers. The house was crowded with wounded and dying as were other houses thereabout. Washington rode up to Thomas Olden's house and asked the farmer to make room for some British wounded and look after them.[26] He believed that Mercer was dead or dying, but could not carry him off and had to leave him for the British to bury when they came up. He lived till January 12th and was buried in Philadelphia.

In the meanwhile there was a tremendous flurry in the American army. The troops were well on their way north when somebody remembered that Washington had last been

seen galloping south.   Firing was heard in that direction.
General St. Clair and the others were sure that he had been
killed or taken prisoner, and went on about their business in
dismay.[27]

It was because of terrors such as this that Washington's
officers protested loudly against his recklessness.   Benjamin
Harrison wrote to Robert Morris:

"Every officer complains of his exposing himself too
much." [28]

The defeat of Mawhood, which is really the first battle of
Princeton, has taken a long telling, yet it was all over in twenty
minutes.   It was, however, "for the time it lasted and the
numbers engaged, the most fatal to our officers of any action
during the whole of the Revolutionary war." [29]

The defeat of the British was still to be completed.   The
majestic solidity of Mawhood's line had not been rivalled by
the 55th and the 40th, some of whom had flung away their
arms and vied with the American militia in panic.   During
Washington's absence, the braver among them had drawn up
in line at a ravine half-a-mile below Nassau Hall, where General St. Clair attacked them and drove them in flight.   Most
of them struck out for Brunswick and did not halt till they
reached there.   But a few of them crowded into Nassau Hall
with a portion of the 40th that had not responded to Mawhood's summons.   They knocked out the windows and made
ready for a desperate resistance.

Captain Alexander Hamilton is said to have commanded the
light cannon run into position here.   It sent through a window
a six-pound shot that passed through the chapel and neatly
decapitated a portrait of George II.   It fired again and the
shot glancing from the outer wall nearly killed the horse on
which Major Wilkinson was mounted.   Captain Moore with
some militiamen then dashed into the building and the inmates
surrendered, 194 in all.

And now Washington reappeared on the scene.   There was

pleasure in the knowledge that he had escaped annihilation at Trenton and had annihilated the British power at Princeton, but the job had taken an alarming amount of time.

He had lost about forty killed and wounded, the exact number being uncertain. Seven of the dead or dying were officers, and among his best.

The British loss was about four hundred, of whom perhaps a hundred were killed, and fourteen officers and two hundred and sixteen men prisoners.[30]

Washington had captured some cannon but had no horses to carry them off, except that he shifted the teams from two of his six-pounders and swapped them for Mawhood's two superior brass cannon.

Never dreaming how great his triumph would be in its effect and how glorious at a distance, he regarded it as a petty byblow, an unforeseen interruption of his original plan and a disruption of it. He was still eighteen miles from his goal at Brunswick, and once more on the defensive, for Cornwallis was actually on the outskirts of the town. Everywhere he looked he saw most of his troops scattered on the ground as if slain. They were fast asleep where they fell on their faces.

"Marching in the frigid cold without proper nourishment and uniform, the soldier's sufferings were possibly greater than those at Valley Forge," says Major Ganoe, and adds: "It was estimated by eyewitnesses that the ill-fed, ill-clothed, ill-supplied and exhausted American army could then have been put to flight . . . by one well-equipped and drilled battalion." [31]

Washington's heart was full of disappointment. If he had had a few fresh troops he could have accomplished miracles, but he lacked even cavalry enough to pursue the shattered British. He had with him only those twenty-two Philadelphia gentlemen, and he could not expect them to destroy the British infantry in Brunswick. He gave up with a sigh all hope of those precious three hundred and fifty thousand dollars. He was so pushed that he could not write his report to Congress until three days later and then it is more tinged with what might have been than with the unsuspected glory that was.[32]

Relinquishing his dreams of capturing the rich loot at Brunswick, he was so far from daring to try conclusions with Cornwallis, that he dared not stop to pick up his wounded prisoners. He had to leave his own wounded in Princeton to British mercy. His men had been without food since the night before.

At the order to march, the dead arose and pounded their red soles on the icy road again. At Kingston they turned off to the left from the Brunswick highway that was to have led to riches. Arriving at Somerset Court House, they made bivouac in the field with the sky for their blanket.

Cornwallis went puffing on to Brunswick expecting to find Washington ahead of him. But Washington pushed on to the hamlet of Pluckemin and spent his Sunday writing letters and accepting the advice of his council to seek a safety in the mountains.

The next camp was made at Morristown in the Short Hills of New Jersey. And this proved to be one of the most astonishingly happy strategical positions in all history. He was doing a better thing than he knew and he had done a luckier thing. In the words of the historian of the American army:

"Washington's daring and skill had caused his little force to outnumber that part of the enemy he had attacked. Had he failed in any part of his plan he would have been annihilated and gone down into history as a fool." [33]

But history is full of fools who might have been immortal heroes if their adversaries had been a little less acute. Washington's fame and his success in building a nation depended all too often on his genius for selecting adversaries who ignored the plainest laws of common sense and military practice. If Howe had followed the motto, "Never put off till tomorrow what can be done today," he would have put off the United States to a far tomorrow.

V

LAURELS RAIN

ACCORDING to the anecdotards, Washington's mother was the only one who begrudged him praise for the skill with which, in two moves, he shifted his army from a position of disaster to a position of checkmate. There are few stories told of her conduct during the war. It is to be hoped that they are all libels.

According to the tradition, when her Fredericksburg neighbors rushed to her with the news of the two Trentons, the two Princetons and the inspired occupation of Morristown, Mary Washington rebuked them with a priggish soul-quenching egotism:

"But, my good sirs, here is too much flattery; still George will not forget the lessons I early taught him—he will not forget himself, though he is the subject of so much praise." [1]

This is given as a proof of her "preternatural serenity," [2] and of the distressing account Lossing gives, that "she never betrayed any uncommon emotion."

But surely emotion is not a crime and a good deal of delight and less self-satisfaction would be pardonable in the mother of a Washington. The denial of a trace of elation after such a crisis amounts almost to denying that Washington had a mother at all. It orphans him.

Whether or not Mary Washington was a Tory at heart, as has been affirmed and denied, she unquestionably abhorred war, and her son's military predilections. She can be as easily forgiven and loved for trying incessantly to dissuade her son from fighting as he can be forgiven for disobeying her, but it seems too cruel that she should be accused of unwillingness to rejoice in his escape from calamity to glory. Almost more

44

heartless is the silence she is said to have slapped him in the face with when he visited her himself after his Yorktown triumph, for which he waited four whole years.

The worst of it is that these grim stories are related in alleged praise of Mary Washington. If they are true, it is well that such icy tactlessness skipped the generation of her son, who was singularly liberal in praise and parsimonious of censure.

Whimsical legend, after making Washington's mother indifferent to his welfare, has turned the indifferent Frederick of Prussia into his warmest admirer. The story is forever repeated that Frederick the Great said of Washington's battles between December 25th and January 4th:

"They are the most brilliant recorded in the annals of military achievement." Also it is insisted that he sent to Washington a noble sword on which was engraved: "From the oldest soldier in Europe to the greatest soldier in the world." [3]

Also, he denounced the rental of the Hessians and forbade their passage through his country, thus foiling Howe's hope of overwhelming reinforcement.

Frederick did denounce the rental of the Hessians, but it was because he objected to anything that helped England. He had hired them himself previously. His refusal to let them cross his realm was only temporary and he shanghaied the deserters into his own army. [4]

Frederick loathed the English whom he called "diese Goddams," and the ministry, which he called "die Goddam-Regierung," but he did not love the Americans, especially not the republicans. He refused to admit to Berlin the American representative, Arthur Lee, unless he came secretly: *S'il vient inconito, bon, mais pas en déployant son caractère.* [5] Frederick usually wrote and spoke French in preference to his own language. When Lee arrived Frederick refused to see him and teased him frantic with evasions. When Lee's papers were stolen and copied by the British minister, Hugh Elliot, whom Frederick called "goddam Elliot!" [6] the King made no protest and it was Lee instead of Elliot who lost prestige at Berlin.[7]

Frederick refused to admit American privateers into his ports. Evasively he promised to recognize American independence when France did, then declined to keep his word since the outbreak of the war of the Bavarian Succession in 1778 made him eager for the sympathy of England. When the American Revolution was over he actually urged the English not to withdraw their troops too quickly as he doubted that the republic would remain independent long.

The only sword Washington received from Germany was one sent to him in 1795, nearly ten years after Frederick's death, by a Prussian cutler who entrusted it to his son to deliver; the son pawned it in a tavern for thirty dollars; an unknown admirer redeemed it and left it at Alexandria with a friend of Washington's who paid the thirty dollars and carried the sword to Mount Vernon.[8]

The sword story may have started from a mythical tale (published in the New Jersey *Journal* of August 9, 1780) that Frederick had sent his portrait to Washington. But he did not do even this.

Washington always revered Frederick the Great, and immediately after his marriage he ordered Frederick's bust for his library, in which he kept a 13-volume edition of Frederick's works, but there is not a single hint in the voluminous records of Frederick that he ever said a kind word or cherished a kind thought of Washington. He did refer once to Washington's laughable stupidities, but even then bracketed him with others as an object lesson. He wrote to his brother:

"We study the Washingtons, Howes, Bourgoynes and Carletons in order to learn from them this great art of war wherein man can never learn enough, in order to laugh at their stupidities (*um über ihre Dummheiten zu lachen*) and to approve what they carry out in unison with the rules of the art." [9]

Frederick also wrote to his friend Voltaire a word about General Howe, "whose name every dog pronounces when he barks."

The real Frederick was within his rights and acting reasonably enough for his own people's interests, but the legendary Frederick will probably always pursue the legendary Washington with his legendary superlative and his legendary sword, which will flash as long as Excalibur and live the better for its glittering untruth.

The praise accredited to Frederick was none the less deserved and was really uttered by another Prussian, von Bülow, who wrote:

"The surprise of Trenton was . . . one of the best planned and boldest executed military movements of our century. It was, however, excelled by the Attempt upon Princeton, and both events are sufficient to elevate a General to the temple of immortality." [10]

Botta, the Italian historian, writing in 1809, was moved to this well-earned exordium:

"Thus, by an army almost reduced to extremity, Philadelphia was saved, Pennsylvania protected, New Jersey nearly recovered, and a victorious and powerful enemy laid under the necessity of quitting all thoughts of acting offensively, in order to defend himself. Achievements so astonishing acquired an immense glory for the captain-general of the United States. All nations shared in the surprise of the Americans; all equally admired and applauded the prudence, the constancy, and the noble intrepidity of general Washington. An unanimous voice pronounced him the savior of his country; all extolled him as equal to the most celebrated commanders of antiquity; all proclaimed him the Fabius of America." [11]

In England there was the typically British admiration for a brilliant enemy. Twenty-two years before, Horace Walpole had written of Washington as a swaggerer, a *"fanfaron,"* [12] again as a "brave braggart." [13] He lived long enough to confess the splendor of the Princeton climax: "Washington the dictator has shown himself both a Fabius and a Camillus. His march through our lines is allowed to have been a prodigy of generalship." He dubbed him "Caius Manlius Washingtonius Americanus, the dictator." [14] The English exile, young Nicholas Creswell, marooned in Virginia, wrote in his Journal:

"Six weeks ago this gentleman [a Mr. Kirk] was lamenting the unhappy situation of the Americans and pitying the wretched condition of their much-beloved General, supposing his want of skill and experience in military matters had brought them all to the brink of destruction. In short, all was gone, all was lost. But now the scale is turned and Washington's name is extolled to the clouds. Alexander, Pompey and Hannibal were but pigmy Generals in comparison. . . . It is the Damd Hessians that has caused this, curse the scoundrel that first thought of sending them here." [15]

Robert Morris, without whose money Washington would have been perhaps an almost unaccompanied fugitive or a prisoner, wrote of him: "He is the greatest man on earth." William Hooper, congressman from North Carolina, repeated the phrase:

"Will posterity believe the tale? . . . how often America has been rescued from ruin by the mere strength of his genius, conduct, and courage, encountering every obstacle that want of money, men, arms, ammunition, could throw in his way, an impartial world will say with you that he is the greatest man on earth. Misfortunes are the element in which he shines; . . . He rises superior to them all; they . . . bring into view those great qualities which his modesty keeps concealed." [16]

The poets, of course, leapt at this chance to celebrate themselves; and one of the pæans, called "The Jerseys" and issued with great promptness, certainly shows no lack of warmth or of classic elegances:

"As Mars, great god of battles! lay,
In dalliance soft and amorous play,
   On fair Bellona's breast;
Surpris'd he rear'd his hoary head,
The conscious goddess shook with dread,
   And all her fears confess'd.

"Loud thunder roll'd through Heaven's domain,
The Ethereal world was wrapt in flame,
   The god amazèd spoke:
Go forth, ye powers, and make it known,
Who dares thus boldly shake my throne,
   And fill my realms with smoke . . .

"The god with wonder heard the story,
Astonish'd view'd Columbia's glory,
   Which time can ne'er subdue,
Great Warren's deeds, and Gates's fame,
Join'd to great Lee's immortal name;
   And cried, Can this be true?

"Britain shall cease to plague mankind,
With sister tyrants strive to bind,
   And check the free-born soul;
To Washington her trophies yield,
Freedom shall triumph in the field,
   And rule from pole to pole." [17]

It is not even laughably bombastic to represent Washington's foxy escape with 5,000 ragged starvelings from 5,500 Hessian and British hirelings as a heaven-shaking cataclysm that frightened the god of war out of the lap of the goddess of war, and filled Bellona's bedroom with smoke.

Time has dealt as roughly with "Gates's fame" and "great Lee's immortal name" as with the proclamation that Britain would "cease to plague mankind" and that Freedom would "rule from pole to pole."

The tribute that Washington undoubtedly appreciated most of all at the time was the one paid him by Cornwallis, who had naturally little to say of praise in his despatches but proceeded to abandon all of New Jersey except what he could protect from New York, whither he hastened with his rescued treasure chest.

VI

HE DISCOVERS MORRISTOWN

ALL this while Washington was a man who stands in a rainbow, seeing none of the radiance, and feeling only the rain. To people at a distance he was, and is, enaureoled in beauty; but he was aware only of his bewilderment and the bedraggled despondency of his companions. He had his courage and little else for his comfort.

Morristown turned out to be a position of amazing strategic felicity, but he took to it on the advice of others at a time when he did not know where else to turn.[1] Whoever advised him to hide there might have used the words of Bairnsfather's Old Bill to 'Erbert:

"If you know a better 'ole go to it."

It seems that Washington had no knowledge of Morristown and was inclined to march back to the Delaware by way of Cranbury and cross to Philadelphia, when somebody persuaded him to file to the left and stay in New Jersey. St. Clair probably deserves the honor of proposing this move as well as the escape from Trenton.[2] In any case, Washington accepted the counsel, and gave up with regret his dream of taking Brunswick. As he wrote to Congress in the report previously cited:

"My original plan, when I set out from Trenton, was, to push on to Brunswic; but the harassed state of our troops, many of them having had no rest for two nights and a day, and the danger of losing the advantage we had gained by aiming at too much, induced me, by the advice of my officers, to relinquish the attempt. But, in my judgment, six or eight hundred fresh troops upon a forced march would have destroyed all their stores and magazines, taken (as we have since learned) their military chest, containing seventy thousand pounds, and put an end to the war."[3]

50

Harsh things are generally said of councils of war, but they have often justified themselves. Washington was saved from self-destruction more than once by his willingness to listen to reason. It is plain that in this case he surrendered with reluctance, still half unconvinced. But if he had had the six or eight hundred fresh troops he longed for, what could he have done with them, even if he had accomplished the capture of the six hundred soldiers at Brunswick? He could hardly have set the magazines on fire before Cornwallis would have been on him with the very 5,500 men whom Washington had run away from at Trenton with his 5,000 then fresh troops.

As it was, Washington barely got out of Princeton in time, and he would not even have made Morristown if the bridges behind him had not been demolished under British fire. At Brunswick he would have been only a short distance from Perth Amboy where the British could have landed thousands more. In fact, reinforcements had already been started for Brunswick on January 1st. The British Lieutenant-Colonel Markham described in his Journal the forced march he made through knee-deep mire, over mill-dams and ice, to reach Brunswick with General Mathew, a regiment, two battalions of British regulars and a number of cannon.[4]

In a short while Howe had ten thousand men concentrated at Brunswick and Perth Amboy.

Washington in all probability would have been crushed. He might indeed have "ended the war," as he wrote, but not as he hoped.

With fewer men than Mawhood had how could he have crushed as many British regulars as Mawhood had; then have faced eight times his force under Cornwallis?

When he learned that Cornwallis had left no troops in Trenton or Princeton, he began to realize a little of what he had accomplished, though he did not yet understand what a stronghold he would have in Morristown, and expected to halt there only briefly. He was already planning new and daring uses for the army he had hired for only six weeks longer.

From Pluckemin he wrote to Putnam a letter of considerable guile:

"I shall remove from hence to Morristown, there shall wait a few days and refresh the troops, during which time I shall keep a strict watch upon the enemy's motions. They appear to be panic-struck, and I am in some hopes of driving them out of the Jerseys. . . . You will give out your strength to be twice as great as it is." [5]

Though he expected to leave Morristown within a few days,[6] he did not leave the town for nearly five months. Every one of his innumerable letters was written at Morristown, from January 7th to May 28th. The advantages of the place were described by Major Wilkinson:

"This position, little understood at the time, was afterwards discovered to be a most safe one for the winter quarters of an army of observation, and such was General Washington's; the approach to it from the sea-board is rendered difficult and dangerous by a chain of sharp hills, . . . it is situate in the heart of a country abounding with forage and provisions, and is nearly equidistant from New York and Amboy, and also from Newark and New Brunswick, with defiles in rear to cover a retreat should circumstances render it necessary." [7]

Washington took up his headquarters in the old Freeman Tavern kept by Captain Jacob Arnold. The troops built themselves huts to replace their tents. To keep them out of mischief he set them to erecting what was known as Fort Nonsense.

Washington had had to leave fifty-six wounded and sick British prisoners under parole at Princeton. Cornwallis could not carry them away when he abandoned the town and Washington got them back since he at once established an outpost there. But when he consented to Cornwallis' sending a surgeon to look them over, he ordered Joseph Reed to be careful that the surgeon should not "convey a true account of your numbers (which ought to be a good deal magnified)."

Following this advice, Putnam had the rooms in the college and other buildings all lighted up, and his few men were paraded about in such a manner that the Englishman returned to his camp with the report that Putnam had at least five thousand men.[8]

In a recent biography of Captain Neil, who was killed at Princeton, Edwin Knott Hopson, Jr., reveals, in a hitherto unpublished letter, another of the countless instances of Washington's goodness of heart. Captain Neil left two small children and a widow, who wrote to Washington in February:

"The unhappy situation in which I am left by the late Catastrophe of my Husband, . . . induces me to apply to your Excellency, Who's known Benevolence & politeness emboldens the most diffident."

She asked Washington to help her obtain the relief promised in a supposed resolution of Congress. Washington sent her letter to John Hancock, still President of Congress, with a recommendation of his own, but confessing: "If any provision is made, I do not recollect what it is."

Congress waited two months and answered that there was no provision for widows, though the war had gone on now for nearly two years. Washington wrote a letter of regret:

"Madam, I hoped to have given you a more favourable acc^t of my application to Congress, in your behalf, than the Inclosed resolution will convey,—but that Honble body have, I presume, thought it rather too early to adopt a measure of this kind yet—what they may do hereafter, I cannot undertake to say.—In the meantime, as I sincerely feel for your distress, I beg your acceptance of the Inclosed, as a small testimony of my Inclination to serve you upon any future occasion."

The postscript notes "Fifty Dollars sent."

Mrs. Neil appealed then to the state of New Jersey, but it was not until June, 1781, that she was awarded "a certificate of half pay," for three years at twenty-five dollars a month.[9]

Congress completely ignored the widows and children of its slain soldiers, leaving them to the care of their states. In June 1777 when General Sullivan appealed for money to replace his lost baggage, John Adams wrote frankly:

"I can only say, that Congress have hitherto refused to grant any Compensation to Sufferers of any kind. . . . Several Officers Widows, in deplorable Circumstances, have petitioned and been refused."[10]

The following winter when officers were resigning unusually fast, the problem of caring for widows was discussed and deferred. Washington pleaded in vain and the question, becoming involved with a plan to give officers half-pay for life, was tossed to and fro till 1780 when widows and motherless children were granted half-pay for seven years. The creation of a new government involved so many details and difficulties that the sins of omission were inevitably numberless and some of them cruel.

Washington was about to enter upon a campaign against obstacles countless and immovable. For the next few months the waging of battle was of necessity almost entirely ignored so far as he was concerned, except for the raiders he sent out to nag the British on the Raritan and shut off their supplies, and the vain and frequent efforts of the British to tease him down from his high fortress to some ambush in the plains,— except also for the disgusting outcome of his hopes for capturing New York.[11]

From Pluckemin he had written to General Heath on that busy Sunday, outlining a campaign of vaulting ambition that seems from this distance bound to have overleapt itself and landed on the other side. He counted on the reinforcements that were reported to be pouring in—but were not. He began by describing his success at Princeton; then went on:

"It has been determined in council, that you should move down towards New York with a considerable force, as if you had a design upon the city. That being an object of great importance, the enemy will be reduced to the necessity of withdrawing a considerable part of their force from the Jerseys, if not the whole, to secure the city. I shall draw the force on this side of the North River together at Morristown, where I shall watch the motions of the enemy, and avail myself of every favorable circumstance." [12]

The instructions he sent to General Lincoln two days later actually anticipated the capture of New York: "in all probability." [13]

Receiving Washington's orders with alacrity but realizing with dismay that he had only militia to command, Heath marched his army against New York in three divisions: all on

the night of January 17th.   By some miracle they struck the
outposts at Kingsbridge simultaneously before sunrise on the
18th; but patrols discovered them and fled giving the alarm.
Heath drew up his army before Fort Independence and
sent in word: "Twenty minutes only can be allowed the garrison to give their answer; and should it be in the negative, they
must abide the consequences."

The garrison replied verbally with a refusal to surrender
and emphasized it with cannon, of whose presence the Americans were ignorant.   Eleven days of burlesque siege followed
during which a crowd of rebel generals with a handful of privates quarreled and resigned while rain and snow added to
their misery.

On January 29th, General Lincoln went back to Dobb's
Ferry, General Wooster to New Rochelle and General Scott
to White Plains.[14]

Washington was on the butt end of the joke and he was
furious.   On the 17th and 19th he had actually written to
Heath, in the belief that New York contained only a thousand
men, and was perhaps "left so destitute of troops as to afford
you an easy conquest of it." [15]   On January 22nd he was writing
Congress that he had such well-authenticated accounts of the
capture of Fort Independence "that I cannot doubt it.   It is
said that he took 400 prisoners in that Fort; and that he invested Fort Washington." [16]

This was confirmed by three officers and a spy, and one can
imagine his joy in the thought.

On January 27th he was still in high hope enough to write
to Heath:

"If you can take possession of the country round about the city,
or the city itself, I do not desire you to desist.   I have not been favored
with a line from you since the 19th, and that never reached me till
this evening." [17]

It shows the fog of uncertainty that surrounded all communication.   He was just thirty miles from Heath as the crow
or an airship flies, yet it took eight days for a message to reach

him. Only then he learned to his chagrin that Heath was so far from conquering New York or besieging Fort Washington that he had been driven off. On February 3rd Washington received two letters from Heath dated January 30th, and confessed his disappointment, though for publication he belittled his hopes. He wrote to Heath:

"I never was very sanguine, as to any thing more being effected, than to oblige the garrison either to surrender or evacuate Fort Independence and retire within the Island. As neither has been done, I wish your summons had never been sent, as I am fearful it will expose us to the ridicule of our enemies." [18]

After writing Heath this mild letter for the general eye, he wrote a private letter in which his wrath is tempered with mercy and courtesy and even a hint of further hope:

"This letter is in addition to my public one of this date. It is to hint to you, and I do it with concern, that your conduct is censured. . . . Your summons, as you did not attempt to fulfil your threats, was not only idle but farcical, and will not fail of turning the laugh exceedingly upon us. These things I mention to you as a friend, for you will perceive that they have composed no part of my public letter. . . . Upon the whole it appears to me from information, that, if you had pushed vigorously, upon your first going to Fort Independence, the post would have been carried; and query may it not yet be taken by surprise?" [19]

To this Heath replied with a long letter of self-defence, denying the bombast of the summons.[20] He had studied tactics as a boy, had become a captain at eighteen, and had taken a brave and important part in the pursuit of the British after Lexington.[21] It would have been pitiful if he had been laughed out of the army.

Eventually he won back Washington's confidence so well that he was put in command of West Point after Arnold's treason.

Of Washington it can be said, as of few other generals, that no officer ever suffered from his greed for power, his jealousy, or his revenge.

VII

THE PENALTY FOR TREASON

THE year 1777 "had three gallowses in it, meaning the three sevens," wrote John Adams,[1] quoting a Tory prophecy, only one of many that nearly came true. Adams would have dangled from one of those gallowses unquestionably for he had been especially omitted from the amnesty offered by Lord Howe in 1776. What third neck would have been stretched is uncertain, but there can be no doubt that the first gibbet would have displayed George Washington as the chief traitor.

The hanging would have been the mildest detail of the ghastly business. The logical and historical intention of executing the leading rebels had been expressed when Washington was besieging the British in Boston, and it could not have been changed by the humiliation the royal troops had suffered there:

"As every rebel who is taken prisoner in America has incurred the pain of death by the law martial, it is said government will charter transports . . . to convey the culprits to the East Indies . . . it is the intention of the government to punish only the ringleaders and commanders *capitally*, and to suffer the inferior rebels to redeem their lives by entering into the East India Company's service."[2]

A noble lord in 1774 had declared that the best way to treat the rebels was to "hang, draw, and quarter fifty of them," and the phrase was meant literally.[3]

The penalties for treason were hideous in Washington's day and there is every reason to believe that he would have paid them in full if he had fallen into the hands of the British, in whose eyes he was certainly a rebel and a traitor.

He was not only deluding multitudes and seducing them from their loyalty, but he was causing great slaughter among the British, compelling them to hire foreign soldiers, stirring up foreign nations to renewed hostility, and reducing the Empire to such straits that financial ruin impended. "The tradesmen who supplied the palaces with common necessaries were reduced to great straits for want of their money . . . the coal-merchant dunned in vain for his bill, amounting to £6000." [4]

Even while Washington was executing his dazzling flareback at Trenton, King George and Lord North were pushing through Parliament a bill to deprive American rebels of the immemorial advantages of the sacred Habeas Corpus Act, to permit the King to imprison them when he pleased without bail and bring them to trial at his pleasure. His Majesty's own letter gloating over his success with the bill is still extant. [5]

Washington's discomfiture of the royal troops could not have diminished his liability to the penalties for high treason, and if he had been taken there at Princeton where he rode so far in his pursuit of Mawhood—or if he had been taken on any of the other occasions when he came so near capture—he would have been hurried to England on the first transport, with no protection from that cornerstone of English freedom, the Habeas Corpus Act. He would have been thrown into the dismal Tower of London, tried for high treason and unquestionably found guilty.

We are so used to seeing him as lofty statuary in an attitude of supreme power or as portraiture in a mood of serene dignity that we can hardly conceive of him shackled, stretched out on a low sledge and drawn feet foremost over the cobbled streets of London, paraded as a felon through jeering mobs. He is all but unimaginable in the grotesque indignity of being suspended "between heaven and earth as being worthy of neither." [6]

Yet he must have often and vividly imagined himself undergoing the tortures inflicted on many Englishmen of equal sincerity before his time, as afterward. He, too, might have been let down from the gibbet still alive so that he might see his own bowels torn out and his heart wrenched forth to be exhibited to his eyes and to the rabble, then thrown into the flames. He was so powerful of frame that he might well have survived long enough to feel the ax cleave his neck, before his head was lifted by the hair and held aloft in the hands of an executioner, who would have walked to the right of the platform and cried:

"This is the head of a traitor, George Washington!"

Then he would have walked to the left of the platform, lifting the white face high and crying again:

"This is the head of a traitor, George Washington!"

Next, his ghastly reliques would have been cut into four parts, parboiled for preservation against the rough weather, and exposed in various conspicuous places. In time the wind might have blown his head from the pole where it was stuck, and rolled it along the gutter into oblivion.

Such an end for such a man may seem unthinkable now, but just thirty years before the outbreak of the Revolution in America, Robert Watt suffered it for being one of a few who had conspired to overthrow the English rule in Edinburgh, and had been caught with fifty-five pikes of home manufacture. A year later, in 1746, when the followers of "darling Charlie," the bonny Prince of Scotland, were defeated at Culloden, the few who were not slaughtered on the field or hanged or transported were taken to England to be tried for treason, and no less than eighty men, including earls, lords, soldiers of all ages and ranks, were found guilty. Lord Mahon describes "the barbarous ceremony" done to them, and adds:

"Nor did it fail—such is the vulgar appetite for the horrible!—to draw forth exulting shouts from the spectators." [7]

Washington was already fourteen years old when these executions took place, and he must have learned of them, must have had them vaguely in mind as he made his first outcry against the English blockade of Boston, and offered to raise, subsist at his own expense, and lead against the King's troops a thousand men.

When John Adams was ordered to France as a commissioner in 1777, he took into consideration what he called "the consequence of a capture."

"As their Act of Parliament would authorize them to try me in England for treason, and proceed to execution too, I had no doubt they would go to the extent of their power, and practice upon me all the cruelties of their punishment of treason." [8]

In 1778 Washington wrote of himself as "a man who fights under the weight of a proscription." [9]

When Henry Laurens of South Carolina, for some time president of Congress, was sent as an envoy to Holland in 1780 and captured by the British he was thrown into the Tower under charges of high treason. [10] Circumstances saved him from death, but François de la Motte, a French resident of London during the Revolution, was found guilty of high treason for giving information concerning the armies and the fleets. On July 27, 1781, he paid the price of his devotion to his native land, and was hauled on a sledge to Tyburn hill. He read a book of prayers until the moment when he must fulfill his hideous sentence. Also his heart was torn out and shown to the mob, then thrown into the flames. [11]

Americans make a national saint of Nathan Hale, and properly, but there was almost a mercifulness in the way he was hanged, compared to what young de la Motte endured, and what Washington might have had to endure.

In 1793 an Irish protestant clergyman named Jackson was sentenced to all the torments but killed himself before execution. Several other convicted Irishmen escaped in the same manner, notably Wolfe Tone. In 1820, eleven leaders of a conspiracy to seize the Tower of London were hanged, beheaded and quartered. It was 1870 before drawing, quartering and beheading were erased from the law. By 1903 humanity had grown so tender that Arthur Lynch, a member of parliament, sentenced to death for aiding the enemy in the

South African War, was pardoned after a year of imprisonment.

But in Washington's day the savage rites of ancient codes were still in vogue, and two years after his death, that is, in 1802, George III approved the infliction of the full penalty on seven Irish patriots whom he called traitors. If his troops had succeeded in trapping "the old fox," Washington, what could he have done but make an equal example of him? Since the judicial utterances tended to be standardized, Washington would almost certainly have been denounced in just about the words that Lord Ellenborough pronounced in 1802 upon the seven Irishmen:

"The objects of your atrocious and traitorous conspiracy were to overthrow the Government, . . . to overthrow that constitution, its established freedom and boasted usages, which have so long main tained among us that just and rational equality of rights, and security of property, which have been for so many ages the envy and admiration of the world; and to erect upon its ruins a wild system of anarchy and bloodshed. . . . It has, however, pleased that Divine Providence, which has mercifully watched over the safety of this nation, to defeat your wicked and abominable purpose, by arresting your projects in their dark and dangerous progress. . . .

"The only thing remaining for me is the painful task of pronouncing against you . . . the awful sentence which the law denounces against your crime, which is, that you . . . be taken from the place from whence you came, and from thence you are to be drawn on hurdles to the place of execution, where you are to be hanged by the neck, but not until you are dead; for while you are still living your bodies are to be taken down, your bowels torn out and burned before your faces, your heads then cut off, and your bodies divided each into four quarters, and your heads and quarters to be then at the King's disposal; and may the Almighty God have mercy on your souls!" [12]

The knowledge of what Washington constantly risked enhances his own valor and furnishes perhaps a partial excuse for those less dauntless colonists who deserted in droves on the eve of a battle or thronged to accept the amnesties frequently held out by British commanders. With these unfortunate waverers Washington now prepared to deal and with a severity that brought upon him unstinted abuse as an incredible criminal.

VIII

HE CONFOUNDS THE TORIES

THE sharpest sarcasm of Washington's victory at Trenton and Princeton was that it encouraged the Congressmen to resume the reins they had flung at him so hastily when they abandoned the car of state, thinking that the British would soon take Philadelphia.

They passed no official decree rescinding the grant of dictatorial powers, but simply began to meddle and give orders again, and prepare to return to Philadelphia from their exile in Baltimore and "the Extravagant price of Living here, the poorest of board without any Liquor, a Dollar a day horse keeping 3 shillings sixpence or four shillings Wine twelve shillings a bottle, Rum thirty shillings per Gall. and everything else in proportion." [1]

Washington, like a faithful servant left on guard, meekly accepted the restoration of the old tone in his masters' voices. But he woke many vigorous rebukes from all sides by one of his earliest proclamations, and some of the Congressmen also rebuked it as an act of usurpation and tyranny.

If he had been fighting in a foreign country he could have taken precautions against the natives as inevitably loyal to their own ruler. If he had been resisting an invasion by men of alien speech he could have relied fairly well on the loyalty of those who spoke his own tongue. But his nation was not established yet and the invaders did not call themselves foreigners. They all spoke the same language or mixed the same dialects.

When Washington had wavered backward across New Jersey with every look of a final defeat, and Howe followed him with amiable proclamations of amnesty to all who hastened to ask pardon of their offended but benignant monarch, thousands of prodigal sons forswore the husks of independence.

When Washington recaptured New Jersey, to the exquisite dismay of these bad guessers, he thought it both natural and necessary to offer a proclamation and an amnesty of his own, calling for a definite making up of minds on the part of the waverers. So on January 25th he put forth an edict addressed to those who had been "intimidated," "deluded," or "so lost to the interest and welfare of their country, as to repair to the enemy," explaining that "it has become necessary to distinguish between the friends of America and those of Great Britain," and adding:

"I do therefore, in behalf of the United States, by virtue of the powers committed to me by Congress, hereby strictly command and require every person, having subscribed such declaration, taken such oath, and accepted such protection and certificate, to repair to Head-Quarters, or to the quarters of the nearest general officer of the Continental army, or militia, until further provision can be made by the civil authority, and there deliver up such protection, certificate, and passports, and take the oath of allegiance to the United States of America; nevertheless hereby granting full liberty to all such as prefer the interest and protection of Great Britain to the freedom and happiness of their country, forthwith to withdraw themselves and families within the enemy's lines. And I do hereby declare, that all and every person, who may neglect or refuse to comply with this order, within thirty days from the date hereof, will be deemed adherents to the King of Great Britain, and treated as common enemies to these American States." [2]

Abraham Clark, Congressman from New Jersey, wrote twice to his State Assembly asking it to refuse obedience to the proclamation:

"I am much alarmed with Gen^{al} Washington's Procl^n. of the 25th Janry. he hath assumed the Legislative and Executive powers of Government in all the states. I hope our Legislature will . . . not tamely Submit their Authority to the Controul of a power unknown in our Constitution; We set out to Oppose Tyranny in all its Strides, and I hope we shall persevere. . . .

"I think the Genrl⁵ Proclamation a Violation of our Civil Rights and Ventured to call it in question in Congress . . . he requires an oath of Allegiance to the United States when such an Oath is Absurd before our Confederation takes place." ³

It naturally excited black wrath among the Tories. The New York *Gazette* published it as an emanation of "the Lord Protector, Mr. George Washington," accusing him of "moral turpitude" and giving so vivid a statement of the case against him that it is worth quoting at some length as an example of the abuse Washington had to endure from some of his fellow-countrymen:

" 'Tis hardly possible to read over this miserable proclamation without pity and astonishment. That Mr. Washington, who *once* was esteemed a gentleman . . . should be so contaminated by the vice of his associates as to lose all regard to the common forms of morality, all dignity of sentiment, and decency of conduct, was not to have been expected. . . .

"His desperate situation may be his apology, but it cannot be his excuse. He might have been mistaken in respect to his notions of civil polity; but he could not have been deceived in those actions and ideas of moral turpitude, which is the disgrace of human nature. . . .

"The next material circumstance in this Proclamation, is sufficient to make an honest man shudder. It may be styled, a Proclamation for the encouragement of Perjury. Mr. Washington 'strictly commands and requires every person,' who has taken a solemn oath of Allegiance to the King, and called God to witness the truth and sincerity of it, to repair to him or his officers, and take another solemn oath, and call God to witness the sincerity and truth of his adherence to the cause of rebellion. Such an impious disregard, such a flagrant violation of all that is serious and sacred among men, has rarely been seen in any age, country, or profession." ⁴

General Mifflin wrote to him advising him that he thought it "bad policy to confine persons, who will act the part of martyrs." Washington answered approving caution in "the treatment proper to be observed to Martyrs," and agreeing that "Lenity will operate with greater force, in such Instances, than rigor. 'Tis therefore my first wish to have our whole conduct distinguished by it. Still it is not my desire, neither indeed is it within my power, to release any man from a confinement imposed upon him by the Civil power." [5]

It is not the prettiest phase of Washington's conduct that, knowing and saying what he did about his army and his adherents, he should issue a proclamation ordering confiscation and exile for fellow-citizens, turn them over to the civil Administration, and then say that he had no right to intervene for their protection. This was exactly the procedure of the Spanish Inquisition. The English historian Belcher puts briskly the case of the Tories:

"They were offered the alternative of submissive allegiance to the United States of America, or of withdrawal within the lines of the British occupation. The alternative was embarrassing. There were no United States of America, and within a very short time there were no lines of British occupation. The Thirteen Colonies were independent powers severally, and Congress was, during the Revolutionary War, nothing better than a central committee of advice, or of grievances, or a committee of public safety. . . .

"The Union of States and the confirmation of Congress as a Legislature did not take place till 1789. Consequently Washington, in demanding of a New Jersey man allegiance to any one of the twelve States of which a New Jersey man was *not* a subject or citizen, went a long way beyond the powers vested in him as dictator. . . .

"Congress or any deputy of Congress had no more power in New Jersey without the concurrent consent of the Legislature of New Jersey than it might pretend to exert in Alaska. . . . Hence the miserable Tory had to make his profession of allegiance to an authority quite nebulous, or to seek the protection of an equally nebulous defender." [6]

There is, in the Huntington Library, a mutilated and unpublished letter of Washington's, written February 14, 1777, to an unknown person, that states his views upon the proclamation. In part it says:

"It is not within the scan of human Wisdom to devise a perfect Plan—In all human Institutions—In the accomplishment of all great events—In the adoption of any measure for general operation, Individuals may, and will suffer; but in the case complain'd of, the matter may, I think, be answered by propounding a few questions.—

"Is it not a duty Incumbent upon the Members of every State to
defend the rights & liberties of that State?—If so, is an
[oath ex] torted from them to observ
　　　　trary conduct, obligating
　　　　If such Oath was not e
　　　　but the effect of a volunta
　　　　can the person taking of
　　　　considered in any other light than as an Enemy to his
　　　　　　Country?
"Is a neutral character in one of the United States . . . a justifiable
one?"

He goes on to say that the Proclamation offends two kinds
of people:

"namely those that are really disaffected; and such as want to lay
by and wait the Issue of the dispute—The first class cannot be pleased;
the next are endeavouring to play a dble. game, in which their present
protections may eventually become a sure card."

That sums up his justification. In such a struggle a neutral
character was not a justifiable one, and he would not aid those
who tried to "lay by" and "play a dble. game" to find "a
sure card."

ANOTHER TRY FOR AN ARMY

THE peculiarly maddening thing about Washington's war experience was that he was always finding himself right back where he started from. He walked in circles and stepped anew into his old footprints.

Prayer followed prayer for an army enlisted for the war, a regular army, the ideal Continentals. For all the good his petitions did, he might almost as well have pasted them on a cylinder and had them run round and round and round by water power like the prayer-wheels of the Orient. There was nobody to answer them—at least nobody with the power.

This was the inevitable result of the strong states' rights spirit of the time. In the southern part of the country the feeling against a national army was so strong that South Carolina was not really brought to the belief in independence until after the British mistakes and excesses in 1780 drove the people desperate.

Edward McCrady, indeed, criticizes Washington for insisting on a regular army, and holds it so contrary to the American spirit that the ideal has never succeeded in this country.[1] This doctrine springs naturally from the South Carolinian spirit, and the same jealousy of the parts for the whole had far more to do with wrecking the Confederacy than is generally known.[2] It was this centrifugal pride that split the Union in 1861, and kept it split for four years owing to the military genius of Robert E. Lee, who was hampered by his Congress as Washington was by his.

If the British had had a great general in America the Confederacy of 1776 might have been another Lost Cause. Eventually America must inevitably have won free, but nearly everything was done to make it impossible for Washington to free it, and he frankly divided the honor of his success between Providence and the equally dilatory tactics of the British generals.

Congress has been accused of opposing the long term enlistments that Washington implored; yet, as Dr. Herbert Friedenwald asserts, Congress favored them, "but the adoption of such a policy was wrecked by the opposition of the people." [3]

Congress had a multitude of theories and problems but no authority and no weapons. Its internal jealousies and mutual suspicions were inevitable and too well justified, for the Congressman from Massachusetts felt—he knew!—that he had occasion to keep a careful eye on the Congressman from Virginia. Little Rhode Island had eminent excuse for watching big Pennsylvania. And the citizens were wise to withhold omnipotence from their representatives, whom they knew to be only politicians after all. The war was fundamentally a business and commercial war. The people were fighting against taxation and greed, and they were canny enough to know that they were in danger of a mere exchange of despots. Nobody trusted anybody and the machinery had not yet been invented for supplying power without destruction.

Now and then Washington's exceeding bitterness moved him to a form of dour humor as on January 31, '77, when he wrote of the plethora of desertions: "We shall be obliged to detach one half the army to bring back the other." [4] He is said to have written a clever Irish bull to Governor Johnson of Maryland:

"The men with me are too few to fight, and not enough to run away with."

But in general he ranged from solemn to morose. In Boston he had faced the necessity for disbanding one army and organizing another in the presence of the enemy. Now, nearly two years later, he had the very same thing to do all over again. Then the enemy was besieged and outnumbered. Now the enemy was at large and Washington hopelessly outnumbered.

Furthermore he had now less than a third of the men he had had before Boston, and practically all of these were soon to be released from their terms of enlistment, while great numbers were walking off without waiting, without even leaving their weapons behind, "in opposition to all my orders, and notwithstanding my utmost vigilance." [5]

Congress had written a fine cure for the old evils when it had authorized 88 battalions, then added 16 more. At 680 men to a battalion, this meant, together with the three battalions of artillery and three thousand cavalry, a grand army of 75,760 men. [6]

No wonder Washington dreamed dreams. He had driven the British out of Boston with 8,797 men fit for duty against their 5,000 effectives. He had captured Trenton and 868 Hessians with 2,500 men. What could he not do with seventy-five thousand?

Eighty-eight of the hundred and four battalions had been apportioned among the states, which were to commission the officers as well as provide the men. Sixteen battalions were to be enlisted by Washington, who was to name the officers below the grade of brigadier-general. There was much magniloquence about liberty and love of country, but bounties had to be offered and peddled. To secure commissions officers had as a rule to procure their own men and bribe them to serve.

Consequently the high-powered salesman prospered better than the military genius. It had seemed to Washington that no officers could have been worse than those he found when he reached Boston in 1775. Now he found that many of the new officers were "not fit to be shoeblacks." He was an aristocrat and it disgusted him to write:

"The officers are generally of the lowest class of the people; and, instead of setting a good example to their men, are leading them into every kind of mischief, one species of which is plundering the inhabitants, under the pretense of their being Tories." [7]

"Take none but gentlemen; let no local attachments influence you; do not suffer your good nature, when an application is made, to say yes, when you ought to say no; remember, that it is a public, not a private cause, that is to be injured or benefited by your choice; recollect, also, that no instance has yet happened of good or bad behavior in a corps in our service, that has not originated with the officers. Do not take old men, nor yet fill your corps with boys, especially for captains." [8]

"Take none but gentlemen," he could urge, but he found that numbers of the officers were not even honest. The service was thronged with grafters and plain thieves.

"Soldiers are sacrificed for the private emolument of Commissaries, Q^r Masters, Surgeons, Phisicians, barrack masters and Captains. The low pay of officers first led them to fraud, in order to support themselves," wrote Colonel John Taylor, and added: "The armies of the northern states are really mercenaries, and being foreigners, have no attachment to the country." [9]

Nobody has yet attempted a history of the corruption, political, military and financial, of the Revolutionary War. It stank to heaven then but historians have preferred to leave it under the smothering mantle of laurels and immortelles that have been heaped to heaven by the orators and prose-poets.

There is a noble opportunity here for some fanatic lover of the truth to do a vast amount of research and bring on himself a vaster avalanche of abuse for traducing the Fathers. The work ought to be done, however, in order to bring forth in shining contrast the tremendous sacrifices of the amazing few who really did all the work. Many of the officers were devoted patriots and paid large sums out of their own pockets, bankrupting themselves while others grew rich or at least fat. But the crisis fairly spawned criminals and traders of the lowest sort. Take Washington's own words:

"There have been horrid abuses in this way; it has been heretofore customary to see almost as many officers as men in the pay abstracts, that have been brought before me. And what is, if possible, a still greater enormity I have reason to believe it is too often a practice for officers who command parties to assume the rank of their superior officers, who happen to be absent, and to draw pay equivalent to it, under the absurd idea of their acting in their stead & capacity." [10]

In Boston a captain was "tryed for enlisting a number of men that were before enlisted by Capt. ——, . . . and for infamous and ungentlemanlike conduct." [11] He was sentenced to repay the money and leave the army.

In Putnam's Orderly Book one finds, in the writing of his Sergeant Ware (who was the unbeaten champion of all bad spellers), the case of a captain who was:

"Tryd for ye following Charges first for Disurting to the Enemy While a Capt in y^e Continental Service & after he had Rc^d 500 Dollars Recruiting money and taking with him to y^e Enemi Secondly for forfiting y^e Confidence Placed in him by Colo —— for his going to y^e Peekskill 3^d for Disarting the gentlemen under Confidence he was Put in order to be Conducted to $Genr^l$—4^{ly} for Forging a Pass . . . as to the first Charge of Disarting to y^e Enemy y^e Court is of Appinan that the Prisoner is guilty. as allso Appears by his own Confession the Court therefore order & adgudg that y^e S^d —— be Dismissed from y^e army y^e general approoves the Sentance." [12]

Washington found that the embezzlements of the officers were to blame for some of the abscondings of the men and exclaimed:

"The scandalous loss, waste, and private appropriation of public arms . . . are beyond all conception. I am well convinced, that the amazing desertions, which have of late prevailed among our troops, proceed entirely from their not being regularly paid. . . . I have in vain endeavored to make the officers bring in their pay-Rolls and draw, their money. . . . But there is a Cause, which, I fear, will be found upon examination too true, and that is, that the officers have drawn large Sums, under pretence of paying their Men; but have been obliged, from extravagance and for other purposes, to appropriate this money to their own use." [13]

To Congress he described "the base frauds practised by Several of our officers. . . ." [14] His gloomy disappointment is shown in his letter to his brother:

"I thank you for the visit to Mrs. Washington. . . . Your remark 'that you cannot depend upon the Reports of our Strength' is most litterally true . . . it depends upon Militia, who are here to-day and gone tomorrow—whose way, like the ways of [Pr]ovidence are almost inscrutable . . . it is our Interest however much our characters may [su]ffer by it, to make small numbers appear large, . . . for in order to deceive the Enemy effectually, we must not communicate our weakness to any body. . . . Desertion is a growing evil—it is become a kind of business, under the present bounty—to Desert one Corps to enlist in another." [15]

The fury for desertion and reenlistment was an inevitable result of a system that Washington had denounced from the first. To encourage quick mobilization of the new army, Congress had allowed twenty dollars for a three-year enlistment. With the amiable intention of quickening their quota the New England states added a bonus of $33.33. In a noble spirit of emulation, Massachusetts doubled this. The soldier who joined a Massachusetts battalion received therefore $86.66. Which was much money then—and real money.

The other states had to fall into line. In a fine frenzy the towns went still higher. Before long Washington was writing that in Massachusetts one hundred pounds per man had been paid for soldiers who joined for only fifteen months.[16] This naturally retarded the Continental enlistments and drew in more short-term men. The bounties ran so high that two hundred dollars became a normal bonus for a recruit. In paper money a soldier demanded $1,000 and the time came soon when "in Virginia even twelve thousand dollars could not always buy a soldier." [17]

While the states were paying such premiums to fill up their 88 battalions, they left almost no chance for Washington to recruit his 16 unless he bid higher. The states went further, passed draft laws to fill their militia, imposing fines and imprisonments, penalties which Washington could not inflict.[18]

In Maryland the authorities actually arrested one of his recruiting officers for enlisting two men to serve in the artillery.[19]

Even Virginia failed him. Patrick Henry was Governor then and Washington wrote to him begging that Virginia at

least should hasten on her quota and well equipped.[20]   Henry
wrote that there was little prospect of that.[21]   He suggested
filling the gaps with short-time volunteers, an odious phrase.
Washington answered woefully that the slow recruiting "in
Virginia affects me in a peculiar manner."   He added a violent
denunciation of the whole volunteer system:

"To the short engagements of our troops may be fairly and justly
ascribed almost every misfortune, that we have experienced.   To that
cause, and that alone, have the liberties of our country been put in
question, and the most obvious advantages lost. . . . Those who engage in arms, under that denomination, let them agree upon what conditions they may, are uneasy, impatient of command, ungovernable;
and, claiming to themselves a sort of superior merit, generally assume
not only the privilege of thinking but to do as they please." [22]

In January, 1777, he says that "reinforcements come up so
extremely slow that I am afraid I shall be left without any
men before they arrive." [23]   By February 20th his original
5,000 had grown to 4,000, and, as he wrote to Gates "under
the rose," he had hardly anybody but militia, "and what kind
of troops ours are, you need not be informed . . . most of
those that could be depended upon, are down with the small
pox." [24]

On March 6th he taxed himself with "imprudence in committing the secret to paper" that he would soon have only 500
Virginians and "parts of two or three other Continental battalions, all very weak." [25]   On March 14th he has "but a handful" and only "adequate to the least valuable purposes of
war." [26]   On April 3rd he writes, concerning the British:

"How I am to oppose them, God knows; for, except a few hundred
from Jersey, Pennsylvania, and Virginia, I have not yet received a man
of the new Continental levies." [27]

On May 17th he feels that a Draft is necessary.[28]
The desertions of soldiers are rivalled now by the desertions
of officers.

"If I send an Officer to collect the sick or scattered of his Regiment,
it is ten to one that he neglects his duty—goes home on pleasure or

Business, and the next that I hear of him, is, that he has resigned." [29]

"It seems next to impossible to make our officers in any of the States exert themselves in bringing in their men to the field, as if it were a matter of moonshine whether they come to-day, to-morrow, a week, or a month hence. The campaign will I expect be opened without men on our side." [30]

The ill health and bad morals of the army were added grievances to the much-suffering Washington. In August, 1776, out of 17,000 troops, 7,000 were sick at once and thousands died.

Having been rendered immune to smallpox as a boy by his narrow escape from death in Barbados, Washington was one of the staunchest advocates of inoculation, not by vaccine virus but by the actual human germ. Jenner did not seriously begin his immortal study of cow-pox until 1775. Washington had persuaded Martha to "take smallpox" in 1776, and he now made the heroic resolve to inoculate everybody, and get it over with.[31] His own camp was at once turned into a hospital and since he refused to accept any soldiers who had not undergone the mild form of the disease, all the recruiting camps became hospitals. The result was grave delay in building an army, but when he got his man he had one less assurance of losing him in a crisis.

What he prescribed for his army he urged upon his family and all his slaves, and he was so little alarmed by the bugaboo that he wrote to his brother John Augustine (when he refers to "my own People," he means, of course, his slaves):

"One of the best Physicians in this Army has assur'd me, that the great skill which many of the faculty pretend to have in the management of this disorder, and the great Art necessary to treat the patient well, is neither more nor less than a cheat upon the world, that in general an old woman may Inoculate with as much success as the best Physician. The whole art lying in keeping the Patient rather low in diet, and cool, especially at the period of the eruptive fever. . . . That this is truely the case, I firmly believe, and my own People (not less I suppose than between two and three hundred), getting happily through it by following these directions, is no Inconsiderable proof of it—Surely that Impolitic Act, restraining Inoculation in Virginia, can never be continued—If I was a Member of that Assembly, I would rather move for a Law to compel the Masters of Families to inoculate every child born within a certain limitted time under Severe Penalties.—" [32]

His proclamation demanding that the New Jersey people take the oath or exile caused even less excitement than his orders that not only the soldiers but the families they came from or lived with should have the smallpox forced into them. He was perhaps the first dictator to take so drastic a liberty with the people's liberties. Catherine the Great of Russia in attempting the same rescue aroused the ferocious opposition of prelates and people.

Living near Morristown in 1777 was Ashbel Green, later president of Princeton and chaplain of Congress. He was a boy of fourteen then, but afterwards described the consternation of the people when Washington and his army suddenly arrived and announced an intention not only to remain but to spread the smallpox:

"My father, I well remember, went in a sleigh to Morristown, accompanied by some of the most respectable men of his congregation, to confer with General Washington on the subject. . . .

"The General said to them in reply, that their apprehensions, he was confident, were altogether groundless; . . . that they would all be carried through the small pox without charge, and with very little danger—the surgeons of the army affording them the exercise of their best skill and attention. . . . On the other hand, that if an attempt were made to separate the soldiers from the mass of the inhabitants, . . . the natural small pox would be spread through the whole population, producing effects infinitely more to be dreaded. . . . My father and his friends came back perfectly reconciled to the measure. . . .

"It was remarkable that in our whole family there was not a single pock that filled. . . . The whole army had the disease so lightly, that I really believe there was not a day while they were under inoculation, in which they might not, with a few exceptions, have marched against the enemy, and would actually have done so if necessity had required it. For a short time my father's church was made a hospital for the reception of those on whom the natural small pox had appeared before they could be inoculated; and more frightful and pitiable human beings I have never seen. The heads of some of them were swelled to nearly double their natural size, their eyes were closed, and their faces were black as a coal. The most of these died." [33]

The colonies must have presented to the enemy such a face as was enough in itself to keep Howe at a distance. Nicholas Creswell, the Englishman marooned in Virginia, describes the look of Washington's neighbors in Alexandria:

"Got to Alexandria to dinner. All the townspeople and a Regiment of soldiers that are quartered here all innocculated for the Smallpox and I believe there is a great number that has the Greatpox along with them. Such a pock-eyed place I never was in before." [34]

Though Washington tried to keep his soldiers busy by constructing Fort Nonsense purely for exercise, Ashbel Green tells how the officers at Morristown passed their time in gambling, never read a book and

"were the most shockingly profane in their common conversation of any men I have ever known. Their language, at times, was absolutely horrifying to any ear not accustomed to blasphemy." [35]

In December Congress, probably at the behest of President Witherspoon, had "in the most earnest manner" recommended to all citizens and soldiers not only "the exercise of repentance and reformation," but also an avoidance of the "profane swearing, and all immorality." [36] In April, 1777, Samuel Adams was writing how much he was "regreting the abominable Practice of prophane Swearing in our Army. It is indeed alarming." [37]

Washington always threw his weight against interference with religious liberty, but he always paid the highest deference to religious earnestness. Though he both gambled and swore in moderation, he realized that a military campaign was no time for wasting precious hours that might better be employed in neglected military pursuits, and he knew that money was too scarce to be thrown away while many officers bankrupted themselves in mind and purse:

Throughout 1776 he had denounced gambling. Throughout 1778 he would still be thundering against it without effect. He felt apparently no inconsistency in the issuance of an order reminding the soldiers that a few tickets in the Continental Lottery were still on sale.[38]   It made all the difference in the world who was gambling.

Washington's crusade brought on him some ridicule for hypocrisy:

"The American republicans, like the rebels of all ages, from their *justice, peaceloving, and mercy,* pretend to have the especial favors of God, and none of the devil's, on their side, and for this reason we rarely see a proclamation from the rebel camp, without a pious sentence bringing up the rear.   The late orders given by the head rebel at Morristown, in the Jerseys, a copy of which is printed in all the rebel prints, is a greater illustration of this Yankee piety than any yet come out.   In it Mr. Washington forbids card playing under the penalty of a court-martial, ostensibly for the reason that it is wicked and brings a disgrace on the officers, but in reality to enlist the parsons and other old women stronger in the cause of rebellion. . . . However easily he may bait old Witherspoon, Billy Livingston, Jacky Jay, and some of the other pious ones, who are hanging on the rear of his *moral* forces; when the time comes, he'll find he can't 'fool the Lord' with pretended piety or Presbyterian general orders." [39]

He continued to deplore the vicious tendency of his men to loot the farms of sympathizers, rob fields, gardens, houses, and exceed the Hessians or the British in their ravages.

Weapons, also, were being stolen or wrecked faster than Washington could renew them.[40]

In March, 1777, two ships arrived from France with 23,000 rifles.   But at this time he had no men to use them.   Uniforms also began to pour in, but there were no men to fill them.[41]

It is a little too easy to grow sick with nausea at the revelations of these bleak days.   Public affairs were in a state of inconceivable bewilderment.   Hot-headed radicals had run away with slow thinkers, had seized power with no shadow of legal reason, had reviled the multitude who did not understand or agree with them, and terrorized the mild and the contented as well as the hostile. Soldiers came home, if at all, half-mad with the itch and the lice and full of stories of nakedness in the snow, chilblains from the cold, rags, hunger, sleep on frozen ground without tents or blankets, panics, eternal trudges for no appreciable reason to no perceptible benefit. The grog gave out. The only thing that kept them warm was the lash. Those who were wounded were often left to rot. Those who were sick were treated with an inefficiency and greed that Washington denounced as infamous.

They were sent against the British regulars under officers who had learned nothing and taught nothing. They had few bayonets to match those lines of British steel. Many of those who were captured were forgotten. Congress wrangled over fine points of "honor" while they died of famine, vermin, cruelty, disease. The farmers at home were left short-handed in harvest time or in winter. The money the soldiers received was promises on paper that could not buy anything.

"Their shirts being worn out their backs and hips were galled very sorely—and what mortified them beyond everything they were getting lousy and therefore would go home," wrote one colonel.[42]

Suppose the soldier lived to win the war, what good would it do the common man? Nobody dreamed of giving him a vote unless he had property, and the one way to get that was to stay home and grow rich and let somebody else be the fool. It is hard for latterday citizens to realize that in 1776 the thought of giving every grown white man the vote without regard to property, had hardly been imagined. When it was broached it horrified no one more than Washington, whose own state of Virginia did not permit the landless citizen to vote until 1850—three-quarters of a century after the Declaration of Independence! It was nearly half a century before white manhood suffrage was permitted in half the states. One might well ask what the poor soldier was fighting for.

If a man must be fool enough to be a soldier, let him take the best offer he could get. It would be paid him by the stay-at-homes. Why should he enlist for nothing to save their hides and rescue them from paying their taxes to the mother country? And who knew how the war was coming out? Nearly everybody ran away in battle, or deserted in times of peace. There were widowed mothers hungering, and anxious wives and impatient sweethearts courted by the slackers. Why stay?

These arguments always haunt the soldier in any army. When he is hungry, ragged, ill-equipped, ill-drilled, sick and forlorn they become a mania, if it is a mania. For that reason some form of conscription has always had to be invoked in every prolonged war. The longer it is delayed, the more scandalous is the result and the greater the waste of lives and opportunities.

After every war there has been an after-war against the "profiteer"—a name of obloquy often visited unjustly on honorable patriots who have done necessary work at home because their age, their infirmities, or their special abilities kept them from the field. The Revolution had its invaluable patriots like Robert Morris, without whose aid the army would have perished. Even he was accused of growing rich by thievish speculation, and he all but starved to death in a debtor's prison.

There is pathos in the very shiftiness of the majority and their reluctance to take a definite or a permanent stand, as in the case of the New Jersey people who had flocked to Howe and now flocked to Washington and took the oath of allegiance to the imaginary United States, "not however omitting to keep their certificates of loyalty to King George in their pockets," says Fortescue, and adds: "Herein doubtless they displayed strong common sense, for they cared very little about the quarrel though a great deal about their farms, and were quite ready to swear allegiance to any one for the sake of peace." [48]

If they had all been Washingtons, then he would not have been Washington. Yet, even he, the man who has been praised for never despairing, grew so famous in that day for his pessimism that his guardian angel, Robert Morris, felt called on to rebuke him gently and implore him to pretend a little hope at least.[44] Nothing could have been more exquisite than his appeal, but Washington answered it with even more despondency, adding Congress to his grievances:

"Genl Howe cannot, by the best Intelligence I have been able to get, have less than 10,000 Men in the Jerseys and on board the Transports at Amboy,—Ours does not exceed 4,000—His are well officerd, well disciplined, and well appointed—Ours raw Militia, badly officered, and ungovernable—His numbers cannot, in any short time be augmented—Ours must, very considerably (and by such Troops as we can have some reliance on) or the game is at an end. . . .

"Nor is it in my power to make C——ss [Congress] fully sensible of the real situation of our affairs, and that it is with difficulty (if I may use the expression) that I can by every means in my power keep the life and soul of this Army together—In short when they are at a distance they think it is but to say—Presto begone—and every thing is done—or in other words to resolve without considering, or seeming to have any conception, of the difficulties & perplexities attending those who are to carry those Resolves into effect.—Indeed Sir, your observations on our want of many principal characters in that respectable Senate, are but too well founded in truth— . . .

"I have wrote you a much larger Letter than I expected when I sat down to it; and yet if time would permit I could enlarge greatly on the subject of it." [45]

Never was there more conflict, more contradiction, more uncertainty in every phase of any war than in the American Revolution. Its immortal magnificence was in the aftermath, far beyond the vision of the wretched victims who agonized in the muck of its foundation.

X

THE "BUSINESS" OF DESERTION

THE British offered sixteen dollars, and later twenty-four for every deserter who brought along a musket.[1] The drain was serious, though there were also many deserters from Howe's starvation camps to the American lines.

The desertions of the patriots to the invaders were numerous enough, but they did not compare with the desertion of the Americans to the Americans. This became, as Washington said, "a kind of business." It was made profitable for the soldier to enlist, to pick up a bounty and a suit of clothes, desert, sell the clothes, and enlist again and again.

All this mounting bribery exerted an irresistible suction on the men at camp. Why should a soldier re-enlist in the field when he could go home and make a fortune by re-enlisting? Even a soldier feels that he must live. Otherwise he cannot die for his country.

One can form no conception of the extent to which bounty-grabbing was carried without reading the numberless cases in the Orderly books. The whole nation seems to have seethed with corruption and hilarious perjury ending often at the whipping-post, the gallows or before the firing-squad.

In Putnam's Orderly Book[2] one day's grist contains sentences to 500 lashes. The lash having failed signally, Old Put tried eloquence, and he was very eloquent, though Sergeant Ware plays havoc with his phrases:

"More than a Sentury & half ago our fore fathers fled from the Island of great Britan Crostd the atlentick to avoid the Cruel Persecution & oppresion of unrelenting British Tereny and Sought an assilleam a Place of Security then a habitation of wild Beasts and Savages Determined to bare the Fatigues & Dangers of their Interprises Magnimimity & fortetude in order to Procure their own Liberty and to Prepituate a unhampord to us their Posterity . . . when the Invious Eye of Parsecution Hereditery to Tirents Grew Jellous of growing Posterity Race and Liberty of the United States of America Began Many years ago to Prepare Chanes for America and to Presue us with Intolerable oppresion in their Exorbitant Demands upon us from time to time and now at Length have Drawn their Swords and Like outdatious Robers thretten to take away our Lives unless we will Surender our Libertys and Propertys which By the Laws of god & man we have the greatest Right to Injoy the activity & Motive is great."

In spite even of that they continued to desert!

To this generation the knowledge of what a flogging meant is lost to imagination as well as memory. Those of us who have not enjoyed a taste of the cat may gain a picture of an important phase of the soldier's life in our Revolutionary army from an Englishman who gave this account:

"At the first blow I felt an astonishing sensation between the shoulders under my neck, which went to my toenails in one direction, my finger-nails in another, and stung me to the heart as if a knife had gone through my body. The Serjeant-Major called in a loud voice, 'One.' " [3]

General Sir Charles Napier wrote:

"I declare that, accustomed as I was to such scenes, I could not on these occasions bear to look at the first blows; the feeling of horror which ran through the ranks was evident, and all soldiers know the frequent faintings that take place among recruits when they first see a soldier flogged." [4]

William Cobbett, later an ardent pamphleteer in Washington's defence, was a British soldier in his youth and had vivid stories to tell of starvation, the graft, and poor pay—he managed to save a halfpenny one week and counted on buying a red herring for his Saturday treat, but he lost the halfpenny, and—"I buried my head under the miserable sheet and rug, and cried like a child." [5]

Of army punishments he wrote:

"At the flogging of a man, I have frequently seen seven or eight men fall slap upon the ground, unable to endure the sight, and to hear the cries, without swooning away. These were as stout, hardy, and bold men as anywhere to be found." [6]

In 1809, Cobbett lost his temper when German mercenaries in England flogged a number of English militiamen for mutiny against having the cost of their knapsacks deducted from their little pay. Each of the ringleaders received 500 lashes from the Germans and Cobbett broke forth in protest at the sacrilege. For this he was accused of sedition, tried before Lord Ellenborough, fined a thousand pounds, thrown into Newgate for two years and put under bond for seven years.

The career of the philanthropist in those good old days was a little more dangerous and odious than that of a pirate.

There was no check to flogging in the American army until 1813 when "stoppage of pay, confinement, and deprivation of part of the rations" were substituted "in lieu of whipping." Yet in 1833 the lash was still in use, though one officer was court-martialled for having a private whipped till he was disabled.[7] In 1861 flogging was "abolished" again.[8] In the American navy flogging continued for years after it had been stopped by other nations.

It would have surprised and delighted Washington to suspect it possible to keep an army together without literally whipping it into line. From his earliest days as the young Commander of the Virginian troops he had flogged even before he secured authority.[9]

The Continental Congress in 1775 limited whipping in all cases to thirty-nine lashes. Failure to curb desertions led to the amendment of September 20, 1776, raising the limit to "not exceeding 100 lashes." [10] In spite of a liberal use of both corporal and capital punishment, Washington saw such traffic in bounties and such desertion to secure them that in baffled desperation he gave gentleness a trial. He issued a proclamation April 6, 1777, addressed to the growing army of repeaters. Feeling that they might be sorry for "the enormity of their crimes" and afraid to return because of the severity of punishments lately inflicted for desertion, he offered "free pardon" to all who voluntarily surrendered themselves before the 15th of May.[11]

But the heavenly dew-droppings of mercy did not prevail against the tinkle of hard money. There is no record of any penitent hastening to the seat of pardon. Washington returned to the whip, increasing the doses as far as he dared. Yet the whip did no better than no whip and he reverted to proffers of pardon on various occasions, with no success. He alternated these with appeals to Congress for an increase in the limit: "To give only a hundred lashes to such criminals is a burlesque on their crimes rather than a serious correction." He asked for "a gradual scale of punishments; in order to which, whipping should be extended to any number at discretion, or by no means, limited lower than five hundred lashes." [12]

His heart was less ruthless than these grim words imply today, for he was really seeking some means of avoiding too many executions. So he asked for five hundred lashes—to save lives. But Congress would not grant him permission.

Washington did his best with his limitations. At Valley Forge he ordered that one private who attempted to desert should "be well washed with salt and water after he has received his last fifty." [13] And a little later he managed 300 lashes for one luckless Virginian by dividing his offence into three different crimes, deserting, forging a discharge, and re-enlisting, then giving him 100 lashes for each.[14]

He made another effort to persuade Congress to extend the power of the whip to at least 500 lashes.[15]

To prove that his purpose was wholly disciplinary he mentioned with regret the fact that officers were substituting arbitrary punishments often excessive, which would not be resorted to if there were more rigor in the military laws. By "arbitrary punishments" he doubtless referred to such devices as compelling a deserter to run the gauntlet naked through the brigade. Sometimes they set a soldier in front of him to hold a bayonet to the deserter's breast and back slowly through the lines so as to give plenty of time for a terrific drubbing.

Riding the wooden horse often involved permanent mutilation even to the point of emasculation. On one occasion three deserters were made to draw lots; the loser's head was cut off and hung over the camp gallows.[16]

Washington was entangled, as humanity has always been, in the riddle of punishment. He was himself tortured by the tortures it seemed to him necessary to inflict and, to the end of the war, his orderly books continued to carry such red pages as these:

"The Commander-in-Chief is pleased to approve the following Sentences of a General Court Martial, held the 6th Inst. . . . William ―― of the 15th Virg'a Reg't, Charged with desertion, to receive 25 Lashes. Markham ―― of the 15th Virg'a Reg't, Charged with Desertion, to receive 25 Lashes. John ―― of the first New Jersey Reg't, charged with desertion, to receive 50 Lashes. Thomas ―― of the 15th Virg'a Reg't, Charged with Desertion, to receive 20 Lashes. Anthony ―― of the 15th Virg'a Reg't, Charged with desertion, to receive 20 Lashes. John ―― of the 9th Virg'a Reg't, Charged with damning the General & his orders, to receive 39 Lashes. James ―― of the 3d New Jersey Reg't, Charged with deserting, to receive 100 Lashes. Daniel ―― of the 3d Virginia Regim't, Charg'd with deserting from his own Reg't & Enlisting into another, to receive 25 Lashes. Samuel ―― of the said Regiment, Charg'd with the same, to receive 20 Lashes. John ―― of the German Battallion, Charg'd with Deserting & Enlisting into Another Reg't, the Sentence postponed for further Evidence . . . the prisoners under Sentence of Death to prepare for Execution." [17]

In his own general orders between June 9th and June 23rd, he himself approves a total of a thousand two hundred and thirteen lashes across the bare backs of his men. Putnam in the month of July, 1777, ordered a total of one thousand six hundred and fifty lashes and several executions.

A century and a half earlier Gustavus Adolphus had developed a superb army though he forbade flogging,[18] but it is hardly too much to say that the American army was bloodily lashed along the path of glory. The vanity of the incomputable pain and shame is the worst of it, for the generals never learned that the soldiers never learned anything from the tongue of the thong.

The reasons for the desertions were many and complex. Sometimes they reflected no discredit on the deserter. The causes were economic, social, and not to be escaped by the individual. The revolutionary army as a part of the revolutionary populace was a mixture of all sorts of people with all sorts of motives. The mercenary deserters are described by General Jedediah Huntington as "Transient Fellows . . . for the Sake of a Little ready Money they will risque the Smart of a few Lashes (Shame they have none)." [19]

But his half-brother, Ebenezer, who rose from lieutenant to lieutenant-colonel, wrote of another sort of soldier, the unpaid wretch who did not always resist another sort of appeal:

"Not a Day Passes my head, but some Soldier with Tears in his Eyes, hands me a letter to read from his Wife Painting forth the Distresses of his family in such strains as these, 'I am without bread, and Cannot get any, the Committee will not Supply me, my Children will Starve, or if they do not, they must freeze, we have no wood, neither Can we get any. *Pray Come home.*' These Applications Affect me, my Ears *are not*, neither *shall* they be shutt to such Complaints. they are Injurious, they wound my feelings, and while I have Tongue or Pen I will busy myself to stir up my Countrymen to act like *men*, who have all at Stake, and not think to enrich themselves, by the Distresses of their brave Countrymen, in the Field. It hath been practiz[d] too long. Dont drive us to Despair, we are now on the Brink." [20]

And, of course, there were fields going unplowed and parents appealing for the return of their sons. There must have been countless letters of the sort that Ebenezer's elder brother, Captain Joshua Huntington, received from a lonely father:

"I Hope you are well Thow I am Sencibell you Hav ben Threw Hard Seans Sence I Saw you; I Hope also my pore boy in your Company is Still a Live pray Sir as he murst be Very Much worne out if a Live Dow Let Him Com out awhile for a Recrute and if He is so unwell as not Likely to be fit for Duty pray get Him Discharg'd or Som How Let him Com home which will Give Grate Satisfaction to my family I Shall Estame it a Grate favour Sir I am Senceble you Have much Grater Things to attend to pray Let this Have a place in your Generos mind. you Will Much Oblige your Most Obediant Humble Sarv't." [21]

In the Civil War "bounty-jumpers" became a household word for the man who took a bounty, deserted, and reenlisted for another. There were even bounty-workers. Neither executions nor amnesties checked desertion. Officers deserted. Hunger, nakedness, pay deferred and in depreciated money exerted baleful and cruel influences. Out of 1,556,678 enrolled in the Union Armies, 278,644 deserted—one in seven, according to Dr. Ella Lonn.[22] Seventy-seven thousand one hundred and eighty-one were recaptured. Out of 1,082,119 Confederate services there were 103,400 desertions—one in ten. Twenty-one thousand and fifty-six were recaptured. Finally the Confederate armies fairly melted away, 70,000 deserting in four months. Possible victories were lost to Union commanders by the defection of important numbers, but Dr. Lonn believes the failure of the Confederacy was largely due to desertion. She finds the whole subject shocking and repellent, but what is one to do with the truth?

No such figures are available for Washington's army, but it probably suffered an even greater proportion of defection. His ability to keep it from disintegration, to say nothing of destruction, was almost miraculous, an unsurpassed evidence of his amazing genius in one of the most vital phases of generalship.

XI

THE PROBLEM OF OFFICERS

"I WAS told about a Month ago by a member of Congress & several principal officers, and others, that the Continent had in pay 10,000 officers, when at the same time Gen¹ Washington had not 3,000 men."

So wrote James Allen in his Diary for June 6, 1777.[1] This was hearsay, but not a gross exaggeration.

Washington's officers, who should have relieved him of anxieties, and multiplied his efficiency, chiefly relieved him of efficiency and multiplied his anxieties. It would be hard to say which was harder for him: selecting them, getting Congress and the States to agree on those they imposed on him, pacifying the jealousies of those he got, or keeping the bad ones from robbing the men, the treasury and the inhabitants, and keeping the good ones from resigning out of pique. The number of resignations was ridiculously enormous.

Washington's suggestions were largely ignored. The sacred principle of promotion by seniority was tossed aside. John Adams described "this delicate point of honor" as "really one of the most putrid corruptions of absolute monarchy." He actually advocated annual elections of all generals by Congress.[2]

The matter of decision on the new generals was put off and put off while the Congressmen bickered and traded. Washington begged for decision repeatedly: "We have very little time to do a very great work in."[3] He asked for 3 lieutenant-generals, 9 major-generals and 27 brigadiers. Congress refused him his lieutenant-generals altogether and on February 19th gave him only five new major-generals, Lord Stirling,

88

Mifflin, St. Clair, Stephen, and Lincoln. Ten new brigadiers were elected on the 21st of February, two of whom declined to serve.

Washington had to exercise his patience, his delicacy, his eloquence on the disappointed officers. He scorned the easy way of blaming Congress for its partiality and set up a model for all time to warriors for a republic.

To Colonel Woodford, incensed at being named after Muhlenberg and Weedon, who were junior to him, Washington wrote:

"If trifles, light as air in comparison with what we are contending for, can withdraw or withhold gentlemen from service, when our all is at stake and a single cast of the die may turn the tables, what are we to expect? . . . Consider twice, therefore, before you refuse." [4]

Woodford consented to stick, but he bided his time to cause worse trouble. Benedict Arnold's case was the one that most acutely distressed Washington. Arnold was the senior brigadier and his record was unequalled for brilliance. Not to promote him was to degrade him. It was a mad folly, too, since it showed all the other officers that the place to win promotion was in the anterooms of Congressmen and not on the bullet-swept battlefield.

Congress had previously ignored Arnold when in July, 1776, it made Heath, Spencer, Sullivan, and Greene major-generals. A partial excuse now was the fact that charges had been made assailing Arnold's honesty, but that excuse was rendered inexcusable by the investigation when at last it was granted. A further reason, and probably the controlling one, was the fact that Connecticut already had two major-generals, Putnam and Spencer, while the other states were clamoring for their share of the laurels. [5]

Washington could hardly believe that Arnold had been denied the place he had earned so well and would so adorn. Though he was still dictator nominally, the list of the officers had not even been submitted to him for advice or approval. When some of the newspapers announced that Arnold had received the honor they all felt inevitable, Washington made use of this as a device for breaking Arnold's heart gently and forestalling a rash outburst on the part of that impetuous hero, who was even then working on a plan to recapture Newport from the British by a surprise assault:

"We have lately had several promotions to the rank of major-general, and I am at a loss whether you have had a preceding appointment, as the newspapers announce, or whether you have been omitted through some mistake. Should the latter be the case, I beg you will not take any hasty steps in consequence of it, but allow proper time for recollection, which I flatter myself will remedy any error, that may have been made. My endeavours to that end shall not be wanting." [6]

To this Arnold replied with a Washingtonian dignity.[7] He consented to remain in the service, but resolved to secure an investigation of the charges against him and left Providence for Philadelphia. With his usual luck in finding the thick of things, he stopped at New Haven to visit his sister and his children, who were in her care, and thus was at hand when the British governor Tryon made a raid on Danbury with two thousand men and burned the stores collected there, including more than sixteen hundred much-needed tents. Arnold dashed into the fray, had a horse killed under him and managed his troops so well that Tryon's men barely made the ships under the protection of marines landed to relieve them.

And now Congress did the proper thing belatedly yet handsomely, and not only commissioned Arnold a major-general but resolved that the quarter-master general be directed to procure a horse properly caparisoned and present it to "Major-General Arnold." The congressional Board of War further announced that, after examination of all the papers and a conference with Arnold, it was agreed that the charges against him were worthless and his character and conduct had been "cruelly and groundlessly aspersed."

Still, there was trouble; for Congress still left him junior to five major-generals who had been junior to him as brigadiers. This meant more worry for Washington, and more vain appeals to Congress.[8]

Another general was on Washington's hands, that strange and tragic buffoon, General Charles Lee, who had won the confidence of so many Americans away from Washington. The British planned to hang him as a deserter, but Washington and Congress, having no British major-general to swap for him, offered five or six of the Hessian officers taken at Trenton and Washington wrote to Howe threatening bloody retaliation if Lee were harmed.[9]

Men of more ambition and less patriotism than Washington might have been glad to be so prettily rid of so formidable a rival, but Washington did everything in his power to recover Lee. He tried to mitigate his sufferings in captivity, sent him money and every comfort he could afford. Lee was a querulous person, bemoaned his hardships, and made repeated requests:

"I am likewise extreamly desirous that my Dogs should be brought as I never stood in greater need of their Company than at present. God bless you, my dear Sir, and send you Long Life and Happiness."[10]

To this Washington replied:

"Your dogs are in Virginia. This circumstance I regret, as you will be deprived of the satisfaction and amusements you hoped to derive from their friendly and companionable dispositions."[11]

Even in captivity Lee managed to stir up strife and he had been in the British hands hardly more than a month when he joined with the Howes in another of their efforts to bring about a cessation of war. He wrote to Washington asking him to transmit an enclosure to Congress in which he pleaded for the sending of two or three gentlemen from Congress through Washington's camp to Howe's, there to discuss a matter "of the Greatest consequence to me, & I think of no less to the Public."[12]

Nothing is so startling in war as a suggestion of peace, and Lee's letter threw Congress into a panic. The proposal was rejected.[13] Washington wrote to Robert Morris:

"I wish with all my heart that Congress had gratified Gen¹ Lee in his request—If not too late, I wish they would do it still—I can see no possible evil that can result from it—Some good I think might." [14]

Morris agreed with him, but Congress would not be moved. Lee was a man of such strange eccentricities, such flashes of intellectual and strategical brilliancy alternating with such eruptions of wrath and imbecility, that Elias Boudinot, who knew him peculiarly well, was finally convinced of his insanity. Assuming that he was on his way thither would explain many baffling problems in his behavior.

Boudinot's interview seems to have been overlooked by most of the historians and it is worth quoting in part. Boudinot asked him why he wanted to meet the three Congressmen, and Lee replied:

"Sir, said he, I had discovered the whole plan of the Summer's Campaign on the part of the British, and would have disclosed the whole to the Committee, by which Congress might have obviated all their Measures, for Mr Boudinot it is in vain for Congress to expect to withstand British Troops in the Field. . . .

"He then read his manuscript, which was a laboured Argument to prove . . . that in the next Campaign we must be compleatly defeated—He therefor urged. that congress would immediately have a strong fortress Built at Pittsburgh and also several hundred Boats, that they would order all the Riches of the Country to be sent there with the Old Men. Women. & Children, and that when they found themselves driven there. that Congress &c &c might take Boat & go down the Ohio to the Spanish Territory. for Protection—

"The whole of this plan struck me in so absurd a light, added to the impropriety of reading such a thing to me who he knew was on my parole of honor. within an Enemys Lines.

. . . that I could not but entertain the greatest Jealousy of the Integrity of Genl Lee—I answered without hesitation that I could not take any such message to Congress from him; or any other, without the knowledge of the British Generals. . . . That I wondered at his prudence. in keeping such a writing in his pockett, as the Discovery of it in his Pockett & in his hand writing might cost him his life—He then. waived the Business & I left him." [15]

Having failed to persuade Congress either to treat with him and surrender or to transport the entire population to Pittsburg for a trip to Spanish territory, the distracted genius seems to have determined on a desperate drive for peace at all costs.

He despaired of independence and apparently believed that it was his duty to mankind to commit what was to him a "brave, virtuous kind of treason." The Howes were liberals and Whigs and eager to protect the Americans as well as the English from King George's attack on human rights, so he sat him down and composed an elaborate "Scheme for Putting an End to the War, submitted to the Royal Commissioners, 29th March, 1777." The "Royal Commissioners" was still the style and title of the Howe brothers.

To justify himself to himself and his captors, Lee begins this strange thesis by stating that his first reason was the hopelessness of America's struggle: "She must in the end, after great desolation havock and slaughter, be reduc'd to submit to terms much harder than might probably be granted at present." He saw also that Great Britain must lose though she won, "evry life lost and evry guinea spent being in fact worse than thrown away." Relying, therefore, on the Howes for moderate terms, he felt himself "bound in conscience to furnish all the lights, I can," cautioning them that the more moderate the terms the more solid and lasting would be the union.

Assuming that Howe had 20,000 effectives, he insisted that the taking of Philadelphia would do no good:

"In my opinion the taking possession of Philadelphia will not have any decisive consequences—the Congress and People adhering to the

Congress have already made up their minds for the event . . . it is necessary to unhinge or dissolve . . . the whole system or machine of resistance."

His scheme was to reduce Maryland, as this would prevent Virginia from helping Pennsylvania. The fear of an invasion from Canada would "keep the New Englanders at home." He proposed, therefore, that 4,000 men should be put on transports, one half to go up the Potomac and seize Alexandria, the other half to go up "Chesepeak Bay" and seize Annapolis. From there proclamations of pardon should be issued and, he said, "I will answer for it with my life—that all of the Inhabitants of that great tract . . . will immediately lay down their arms." The Germans, though Anglophobes, would fear the ravages of war on their property and would yield. In closing he pledges his life that "in less than two months . . . not a spark of this desolating war remains unextinguished in any part of the Continent." [16]

This intelligent and promising scheme was excellent as grand strategy and virtuous for one who opposed independence, but it was never put to the test. The paper was apparently turned over to the secretary of the Royal Commissioners, Henry Strachey, who endorsed it, "Mr. Lee's Plan, 29th March 1777," filed it and took it to England. Oblivion swallowed it for seventy-nine years when it was somehow abstracted or stolen from the Strachey papers, and eventually reached Nova Scotia among other papers of Howe's. A manuscript collector found it and offered it to the historian Benson J. Lossing, who saw its importance but found the price too high. [17] He referred the dealer to the librarian of the New York Historical Society, Dr. George H. Moore, who bought it and published it in a volume called "The Treason of Charles Lee." [18] Dr. Moore naturally dramatized every act of Lee's into a consistent and malevolent treachery. At the cost of anticipating matters, however, it is only fair to confess that when Lee was finally restored to the Americans and resumed his post as second in command, he warned Washington in a memorandum that the British were not going to operate against Boston, as some thought, but would act by way of Chesapeake Bay, stating twice that he had "the strongest reason to think" that Howe's intention was to attack in "the Middle Colonies . . . establishing themselves about Annapolis, Baltimore or even Alexandria." [19]

Justice does not require one to defend Lee's actions in any or all cases, but it is dishonest to traduce even a Judas. When the Howes failed to leap at his brilliant plan, Lee seems to have turned against them in turn, swung back to the rebel cause, and served it as best he could with the soul he had.

Two exceedingly important facts in the case seem to have quite escaped the attention of the historians. In the first place, the Chesapeake Bay plan of March 29, 1777, was by no means the novelty that Lee and his denouncers evidently thought it to be, for there is a letter (written by the Virginian, Richard Henry Lee, to George Washington, a month before) which makes Lee's treason, or his effort at it, a sad farce.[20] He was captured by the British on December 13th, 1776, and on March 29th, 1777, developed a dazzling scheme for a British cleavage of the colonies by way of Chesapeake Bay. But, on February 27th, 1777, R. H. Lee had already mentioned a letter from London dated October 9th, 1776, saying that this very plan had already been laid before Lord Germain and approved. Still more striking is the fact that, while Lee, on March 29th, was advising Howe to strike Maryland, Washington himself knew all about the scheme and on March 31st, wrote to Congress a warning (which Congress forwarded on April 2nd, to the Governor of Maryland) "that our Enemies are meditating an Invasion of the State of Maryland." Congress earnestly requested him to "take such Measures, as will have a Tendency to Defeat their designs, should any Attempts be made in Consequence of this Intelligence." [21]

The Maryland attack was plainly a matter of considerable general discussion long before it occurred to Lee in his close confinement. The fact that Howe never acted on it reduces the whole matter to a bugaboo.

As if the thirteen colonies had not been able to manufacture enough trouble with their greedy candidates for commissions, the nations of Europe began to empty on Washington all their adventurers. They came speaking any language but English. They were all heroes and all zealots for liberty—with a commission. Anything less than a generalcy was an insult.

Most of them were sent over from France by Silas Deane and the other American commissioners there. Their number and their pretensions grew until Washington appealed to Congress to dam the flood. Congress wrote to France. But nothing could stem it. Many of these foreigners rendered superb service. Some of them died brilliantly. Others of them were almost as difficult for everybody as the American officers.

Washington tried to meet their foreign courtesies with elaborate grace, to repay them somehow for their long voyages across the sea, to use their abilities, and separate the frauds from the honest men; but he could not. He saw a fatal consequence: "the driving of all our own officers out of the service, and throwing not only our army, but our military councils, entirely into the hands of foreigners." He gave warning that Americans would not "submit much if any longer to the unnatural promotion of men over them, who have nothing more than a little plausibility, . . . men, who, in the first instance, tell you they wish for nothing more than the honor of serving so glorious a cause as volunteers, the next day solicit rank without pay, the day following want money advanced to them, and in the course of a week want further promotion, and are not satisfied with any thing you can do for them." [22]

Silas Deane promised the supreme command of the artillery to Tronson du Coudray, who brought with him a number of cannon and, on landing in Boston, let it be understood just who he was and what he was going to be. Incidentally, he would outrank General Henry Knox, whose adoring wife wrote to her husband:

"He says . . . he is a major-general and a deal of it. Who knows but I may have my Harry again? This I am sure of, he will never suffer any one to command him in that department. If he does, he has not the soul which I now think him possessed of." [23]

Her Henry would never disappoint his Lucy to that extent and he was not alone in his plight. The report was spread that du Coudray's commission was to be dated back to August 1st, 1776, which would give him seniority over Greene and Sullivan as well as Knox. These three officers from Rhode Island, Maine, and Massachusetts did not linger to verify the gossip, but sat down together, wrote simultaneous and exceedingly curt threats of retirement, and flung them at Congress.

Congress denounced their menacing tone as "an infringement on the liberties of the people, as tending to influence the decisions of Congress."

Influencing the decisions of Congress was, of course, a horror unheard-of before or since. Congress passed a resolution sending the three letters to Washington and demanding an apology from the officers or their prompt resignation.[24]

Washington had now to soothe Congress, the Frenchman, and three of his favorite officers. He managed it, too, and earned from Charles Francis Adams this tribute for holding in bounds such jealousies and discontents by his "impassible moderation":

"Herein it was that he saved the country, far more than by any act of his military campaigns." [25]

XII

JUGGLING THE PRISONERS

"I WISH to God he would repair hither immediately—I want a shrewd sensible man exceedingly for this business." [1]

Washington was referring to Colonel Coxe, whom he was trying to engage as commissary of prisoners to handle one of the most harrowing of all his concerns. Congress and the Americans in general were insisting that Washington should force the British to release all their captives on the American terms and treat them delicately in the meanwhile.

To Robert Morris he wrote of the balance against him:

"Does Congress know how much the Ball^c of Prisoners is against us?—that the Enemy have, near, if not quite, 300 Officers of ours in their possession, & we scarce Fifty of theirs?" [2]

Howe had sent to Washington a summary of the prisoners he had taken during the year 1776 up to December 1st, in five battles. They made a sad array:

Commissioned Officers		Staff		Privates
Generals	3	Chaplains	1	4,101
Colonels	8	Adjutants	3	
Lieut. Cols.	10	Quartermasters	4	
Majors	11	Surgeons	11	
Captains	69	Commissaries	2	
Lieutenants	160	Engineers	1	
Ensigns	43	Wagon-masters	1	
		Volunteers	2	
Total	304	Total	25	

These 4,430 did not include 431 taken at the Cedars, nor 424 officers and men, taken in other Canadian battles. But the

98

result was that the British had taken 5,285 Americans; the Americans had taken some 2,860.[3]

The four hundred and thirty-one prisoners taken at the Cedars had been released on an agreement that Congress would release an equivalent number of British prisoners. Congress refused to keep the pledge and disgraced the name of American honor as it did even more shamefully with Burgoyne's men later.

When he lost his senior major-general, Charles Lee, Washington offered half a dozen minor officers for him, but the British had other plans for General Lee. Though they kept him most luxuriously housed, the rumor spread that he was being treated harshly and Congress precipitately ordered reprisals, meaning to frighten the British, but succeeding only in embarrassing Washington.

For its victim Congress made a most unfortunate choice, a Scottish chief, Lieutenant-Colonel Sir Archibald Campbell of Inverneil, a wealthy member of parliament, who had been captured June 16th, 1776, in a transport overtaken off Boston by one of the swarming privateers of "Washington's fleet."[4]

Campbell, enjoying the comparative comfort of a distinguished prisoner, was on parole and scheduled for exchange when Congress, fearing that Lee might be executed, lumped the Scotchman with five Hessian officers as hostages to be "sacrificed," wrote Samuel Adams, "as an Atonement for his Blood should the matter be carried to that Extremity."[5]

Colonel Campbell wrote to Washington and to Sir William Howe describing all too graphically the abominable treatment he received as the innocent victim of a vicious revenge for a deed that the British had not yet committed. His letter to Howe is worth quoting as a glimpse into the period:

"I am lodged in a dungeon of twelve or thirteen feet square, whose sides are black with the grease and litter of successive criminals; two doors, with double locks and bolts, shut me up from the yard, with an express prohibition to enter it, either for my health or the necessary calls of nature: Two small windows, strongly grated with iron, introduce a gloomy light to the apartment, and these are at this time without a single pane of glass, although the season of the frost and snow is actually in the extreme.

"In the corner of the cell, boxed up with the partition, stands a necessary-house, which does not seem to have been emptied since its first appropriation to this convenience of malefactors. A loathsome black-hole, decorated with a pair of fixed chains, is granted me for my inner apartment, from whence a felon was but the moment before removed, to make way for your humble servant, and in which his litter and excrement remain to this moment.

"The attendance of a single servant is also denied me, and every visit from a friend positively refused: In short, sir, was a fire to happen in any chamber of the gaol, which is all of wood, the chimney-stacks excepted, I might perish in the flames before the gaoler could go through the ceremony of unbolting the doors." [6]

Washington was so incensed by Campbell's letter that he threw off his usual deference to Congress and wrote at once to the Council of Massachusetts Bay quoting Campbell's appeal to him and saying that the severity of his confinement was such "as is scarcely ever inflicted upon the most atrocious criminals . . . shocking to humanity, and not to be justified upon the most strict interpretation of the Resolve of Congress." He pointed out that General Lee was "only confined to a commodious house, with gentile accommodations," and urged that Colonel Campbell be immediately put into a house where he might live comfortably.[7]

He wrote to Congress, sending a copy of Campbell's letter and pleading with all his power against a cruelty that was also suicidal folly:

"Can we imagine, that our enemies will not mete the same punishments, the same indignities, the same cruelties, to those belonging to us, in their possession, that we impose on theirs in our power? Why should we suppose them to possess more humanity than we have ourselves? Or why should an ineffectual attempt to relieve the distresses of one brave, unfortunate man, involve many more in the same calamities?" [8]

Without waiting to hear from Congress Washington wrote also to Colonel Campbell, a gracious letter frankly stating that

he believed his treatment "the result of misconception" and
expressing the hope that the letter he had written to the
authorities would "procure a mitigation of what you now
suffer." [9] Campbell was taken from his filthy cell but merely
transferred to the jailor's house.

Congress, however, would not yield to Washington's first
letter, nor to his second pointing out that Campbell's treatment
violated the cartel and would release Howe from his obligation
—an impolitic thing in view of the fact that "the proportion
of officers in their hands is at least six to one in ours." [10]

Congress wrote coldly to Washington, "they decline making
any Alteration in the Resolve." [11] Colonel Campbell continued to suffer his peculiarly unmerited hardship for ten weeks
when Washington must have winced to receive from Howe
another protest at his continued ill-treatment.[12]

Two weeks later Howe wrote again, pressing his request for
an answer and a decision. Five days later Washington had
to confess in answer his own inability to secure decent treatment for a prisoner of his own army.[13]

The stubborn brutality of Congress, which would not yield
to all his high appeals, was suddenly whiffed away by a casual
word from General Lee, that Howe was treating him with
"kindness, generosity and tenderness." [14]

Aside from the wantonness of Congressional "reprisal"
without an effort to prove its justification, the stubbornness of
Congress prolonged and aggravated the miseries of thousands
of American captives.

It was not until April, 1777, that Washington found a fit
person to serve as commissary-general of prisoners. Then
Elias Boudinot took the heart-breaking job, with the additional
duty of superintending the intelligence department.[15] He
held it for a year and a half and sank his personal fortune in
the Samaritan work. In his Journal he describes Washington's
appeal to him and reveals some of Washington's finest moments:

"I waited on him and politely declined the task urging the wants of the Prisoners & having nothing to supply them—He very kindly objected to the conduct of Gentlemen of the Country refusing to join him in his Arduous struggle,—That he had nothing in View but the Salvation of his Country, but it was impossible for him to accomplish it alone. That if Men of Character & Influence would not come forward & join him in his Exertions all would be lost— . . .

"Affected by this address, . . . I consented to accept the Commission on the Generals assurance that I would be supplied by the secret Committee of Congress with hard Money for the relief of Prisoners, . . . I exerted every nerve to obtain Supplies but in vain. The General appeared greatly distressed & assured me that it was out of his power to afford me any supplies. . . . I told him I knew of no means in my Power but to take what Monies I had of my own, & to borrow from my friends in New York, to accomplish the desirable purpose—

"He greatly encouraged me to the attempt, promising me that if I finally met with any loss, he would divide it with me." [16]

To the well-realized fact that Washington served without pay, and the less-realized fact that he pledged his personal funds to bribe the soldiers to stay for the battle of Princeton, should be added the generally ignored fact that he offered to pay half the expense of charity to the prisoners.

Boudinot found horrible cases of persecution and neglect. The British officers corrected such evils as Boudinot brought to their attention and tried to win him over to working for peace, offering him "anything from a Dukedom to Ten Thousand Sterling pr annum."

After doing his utmost for the relief of the miserable victims of captivity, Boudinot, finding himself unable "to obtain hard Money from Congress for the Cloathing of our Prisoners," went to Washington and offered his resignation. Washington wept and again pledged his own funds:

"In much distress & with tears in his eyes; he assured me that if he was deserted by the Gentn of the Country, he should despair. He could not do every thing, He was Genl. Quarter Master & Commissary. Every thing fell on him & he was unequal to the task. He gave me the most positive Engagement that if I would contrive any mode for their support & Comfort. he would confirm it as far as was in his

Power—On this I told him that I knew of but one way. & that was to borrow money on my own private Security He assured me that in case I did. and was not reimbursed by Congress. he would go an Equal sharer with me in the loss." [17]

Boudinot fed and clothed the prisoners and advanced nearly $30,000 on his own personal security. Learning that he was totally ruined, Washington found a way for him to get the money repaid by Congress and further money advanced for relief out of a large sum the British turned in for the care of their own prisoners in the American lines.

The worst of it is that all too often the patriot soldiers were treated with hardly more tenderness in their own camps. In both places, the privates were apt to be starved, left naked, flayed raw, and in their sickness denied the simplest mercies. While Washington was berating Howe for not giving his prisoners proper medical attention, he was denouncing his own surgeons for thievery and neglect. Many of them, he said, were "very great rascals." [18]

Dr. Rush said that there were "two armies lost in the hospitals." [19] He made the gravest charges against Dr. Shippen, the Director General. Dr. Rush himself is accused of having been "too much of a politician to render himself amenable to discipline." Dr. Tilton actually charged Shippen with being so mercenary as to the sale of supplies that he was "in the fatal year, 1777, . . . interested in the increase of sickness, and consequent increase of expense." [20]

It is interesting to note that venereal disease was a crucial problem with the soldiers of that day, and an effort to profit by their bad luck was made in a resolution "that the sum of ten dollars, shall be paid by every officer, and the sum of four dollars, by every soldier, who shall enter, or be sent into any hospital to be cured of the venereal disease; which sum shall be deducted out of their pay." As Surgeon Brown remarks, the most probable result was "that the soldiers so affected would conceal their disease rather than pay a tax on the confession." [21]

The civilization of the time was still overwhelmingly aristo-cratic and in the American army as well as the British there was little mercy for the humbly born and the poor. Now and then the most delicately bred were caught in the herd of the unfortunates, but, in general, the poor were subjected to in-dignities and brutalities that are illegal now in the shipment of cattle for slaughter.[22]

Much is said about the British prison ships, but little about the American prison ships at Boston, New London, and else-where.[23] At Esopus Landing on the Hudson river was a group of boats called the "Fleet Prison" on which conditions were appalling for overcrowding, cruelty, filth and starvation, as shown by the reports to the provincial congress of New York.[24] On land, the management was often no better. The prisoners in the Court House at Kingston, New York, for in-stance, were so badly kept that when the New York convention met in the second story, Gouverneur Morris, who did not enjoy tobacco, put in a resolution which was carried permitting the members to smoke in order to disguise the sickening stench from the captives below.[25]

It is not quite honest to ignore the American prison at the Simsbury mines in Connecticut. This has hardly been rivalled in the whole history of human barbarity. There exists a description of this subterrene Gehenna seventy feet deep in an abandoned mine as it appeared to two men captured by American privateers and consigned to its gloom:

"In approaching this horrid dungeon, they were first conducted through the apartments of the guards, then through a trap-door down stairs into another upon the same floor with the kitchen, which was divided from it by a very strong partition door. In the corner of this outer room, and near to the foot of the stairs, opened another huge large trap-door, covered with bars and bolts of iron, which was hoisted up in two guards by means of a tackle, whilst the hinges grated as they turned upon their hooks, and opened the jaws and mouth of what they call Hell, into which they descended by means of a ladder about six feet more, which led to a large iron grate or hatchway, locked down over a shaft of about three feet diameter, sunk through the solid rock, and which they were told led to the bottomless pit.

"Finding it not possible to evade this hard, cruel fate, they bid adieu to the world, and descended the ladder about thirty-eight feet more, when they came to what is called the landing; then marching shelf by shelf, till descending about thirty or forty feet more, they came to a platform of boards laid under foot, with a few more put over head to carry off the water, which keeps continually dropping. Here, say they, we found the inhabitants of this woeful mansion. . . .

"They were obliged to make use of pots of charcoal to dispel the foul air, which in some degree is drawn off by the means of a ventilator or auger hole, which is bored from the surface through at this spot, said to be seventy feet perpendicular." [26]

These men escaped in a sudden outbreak. Most of the prisoners there were Tories, that is to say, fellow citizens of the Connecticut men who thrust them in. Among them was one clergyman. It is comforting to know that the souls of the prisoners were not neglected; for every Sabbath they were brought up to the nail-shop, the most refractory being chained, of course, and allowed to listen to doctrines of brotherly love under the long guns of the guards.

This prison gains especial interest since Washington, as early as December 7th, 1775, had a number of men sent there from outside Boston. He described them as "having been tried by a court martial and deemed to be such flagrant and atrocious villains, that they cannot by any means be set at large, or confined in any place near this camp." [27] A bill for their care was sent to him in March, 1777, but he objected to a charge of nine pounds six shillings for the Committee's time and trouble. [28]

It is amazing to realize how long it was before a system of exchanging prisoners could be reached in the Revolution. It was a matter of years.

Congress authorized Washington in 1776 to propose "Continental officers for those of equal rank either in the land or sea service, soldier for soldier, sailor for sailor, and citizen for citizen." [29]

Howe accepted the terms, but the pledges were not kept. Howe rebuked Washington severely, and Washington appealed to Congress without success for relief from the charge of broken faith.[30]

January 13th, 1777, he wrote to Admiral Howe from Morristown a politely acrid letter concerning the cruelty on the prison-ships and in New York:

"You may call us rebels, and say that we deserve no better treatment; but, remember, my Lord, that, supposing us rebels, we still have feelings equally as keen and sensible as loyalists, and will, if forced to it, most assuredly retaliate upon those, upon whom we look as the unjust invaders of our rights, liberties, and properties. I should not have said thus much, but my injured countrymen have long called upon me to endeavor to obtain a redress of their grievances; and I shall think myself as culpable as those, who inflict such severities upon them, were I to continue silent." [31]

The sight of a number of the redeemed captives was too much for Washington. They were described in a letter written by Colonel John Chester:

"The inhuman treatment our prisoners met with while in New York is beyond all description. Humanity cannot but drop a tear at sight of the poor, miserable, starved objects. They are mere skeletons, unable to creep or speak in many instances. One vessel lost 27 in her passage from York to Medford, and 7 died the night they were put ashore; and they are dying all along the roads." [32]

The dreadful parade of his returned soldiers so affected Washington that he not only threw off diplomatic formalities but made a grim resolve to permit no more such spectacles. He wrote indignantly to Howe and explained that the last batch of prisoners turned over to him by the British "from the rigor and severity of their treatment, were in so emaciated and languishing a state, at the time they came out, as to render their death almost certain and inevitable; and which, in many instances, happened while they were returning to their homes."

Though they were not fit for exchange, "yet our humanity required that they should be permitted to return among us."

He more than hinted that they had been hurried out because they were expected to die, and unless speedily exchanged could not be counted. Therefore he hotly refused to deliver healthy British prisoners in return for them.[33]

General Howe answered his heat with chill politeness, on April 21, 1777, defending his treatment of the captives, and saying:

"All the prisoners were confined in the most airy buildings, and on board the largest transports in the fleet, which were the very healthiest places of reception, that could possibly be provided for them. They were supplied with the same provisions, both in quantity and quality, as were allowed to the King's troops not on service, some accidental instances excepted." [34]

After a long delay Washington answered in a tone of levity:

"That airy buildings were chosen to confine our men in, is a fact I shall not dispute. But, whether this was an advantage or not, in the Winter Season, I leave it to you to decide. I am inclined to think it was not, especially as there was a General complaint, that they were destitute of fire the greater part of the time, and were only prevented from feeling the inclemency of the weather, in its extremest rigor, by their crowded situation." [35]

Since Howe would not admit mistreatment and starvation of prisoners and Washington would not surrender the prisoners claimed by Howe in return for the sick and dying he had released, the remaining captives were left to their own devices and the varying idiosyncrasies of their keepers on both sides.[36]

What it meant to be in the hands of the immortally infamous provost marshal, Conyngham (or Cunningham), Graydon reveals in one brief flash:

"In the evening, he would traverse his domain with a whip in his hand, sending his prisoners to bed, with the ruffian like *Tattoo* of, *Kennel ye sons of bitches! Kennel, G—d damn ye!*" [37]

It was to such guardians that thousands of patriots were left for what seemed an eternity while matters of policy and mathematics and etiquette engaged the opposing generals. It was not until far-off November, 1777, that Washington could bring himself even to initiate a proposal for a mutual release of officers on parole.

And by November, many things had happened, and many more American prisoners were in Howe's ungentle keeping.

XIII

HIS FAMILY

THROUGHOUT the war Washington was kept desperate for personal help. He had trouble not only in finding and keeping adjutants-general, but aides-decamp and secretaries as well. Almost all of them grew restless for military activity or for escape from the apparently somewhat oppressive atmosphere about the commander-inchief. Many of them quarreled with him and wounded him in various ways, either at once or in after years.

His first adjutant-general was Gates, who became one of his most dangerous rivals. His first aide was Major Mifflin, who, when promoted, joined the cabal against him. His old friend, Joseph Reed, of Philadelphia, served at the same time and was so restive that when he escaped to Philadelphia to finish some law suits, he would not return for all of Washington's prayers. He consented, finally, to become adjutant-general, only to write a letter to Lee criticizing Washington as hopeless. Lee's answer fell into Washington's hands and, though he was magnanimous in the extreme, Reed was so ashamed of himself that a full reconciliation was not effected until June 23, 1777, when Washington put him in command of the cavalry.[1]

John Trumbull, son of the Governor of Connecticut, was another aide, and he so disliked the social duties and the southern hospitality that he was glad to be relieved by Edmund Randolph when George Baylor of Virginia relieved Mifflin. In later years Randolph published an attack on Washington that drove him to violent profanity in the presence of several women. Baylor was no penman and asked for active service. Stephen Moylan and Palfrey served for a time. R. H. Har-

rison stuck till 1781, and Tench Tilghman served without pay
or rank from 1776 to 1780, when he received both and remained till 1783. Washington wrote to Tilghman:

"There are few men in the world to whom I am more attached
by inclination than I am to you. . . . I shall never be more happy
than in your Company at Mt. Vernon. I shall always be glad to hear
from, and keep up a corrispondence with you." [2]

Tilghman was one of the few men whom Washington
seemed able to keep in a state of unbroken friendship, though
he was generally warm and spontaneous in his expressions of
affection. In February, 1777, Tilghman wrote to his father,
who was a Tory, concerning the hope of freedom:

"If it pleases God to spare the life of the honestest man that I believe ever adorned human nature, I have no doubt of it." [3]

At times Washington, almost rivalling Julius Cæsar, was
able to keep five men busy writing letters at his dictation, or
suggestion, or for his approval. These made up his "family."
His secretaries received "Sixty dollars and four Rations a
month." [4]

One of his aides, McHenry, described the usual procedure.
First Washington gave notes:

"Having made out a letter from such notes, it was submitted to the
General, for his approval and correction—afterwards copied fair when
it was again submitted & signed by him." [5]

Suddenly there came to him what promised to be, and what
has often been indicated to have been, a gift from heaven direct. On March 1, 1777, the orderly book contained this
phrase:

"Alexander Hamilton Esqʳ is appointed Aide de Camp to the Commander in Chief, and is to be respected and obeyed as such." [6]

Hamilton was then just twenty. Born out of wedlock in the
West Indies, he came to America at fifteen and the next year
entered King's College (now Columbia University) in the au-

tumn of 1773. He probably knew Jacky Custis, for Washington left him there in May, 1773. Hamilton was a busy pamphleteer, though only a boy, and an ardent young soldier. He left college to join the artillery, took part in the Battle of Long Island, and the retreat from New York, owing his escape largely to the masterly work of Aaron Burr, who was not quite a year older and was already a veteran of splendid record. At Harlem Heights, Washington is said to have talked to Hamilton for the first time. He followed Washington to Trenton and fought at Princeton.

General Greene learned to admire his courage and his military lore and recommended him to Washington. According to A. H. Vandenberg this was "the most momentous juncture in the story of the nation." [7]

But then Mr. Vandenberg calls Hamilton "The Greatest American," which would never have satisfied John Adams, who called him "the bastard brat of a Scotch pedlar." And Adams knew him all too well, though it is still uncertain just whose "brat" Hamilton was.

Burr also, strange to say, was a member of Washington's family for a while, having been invited to enter it after the magnificent bravery he displayed in Arnold's attack on Quebec. He joined Washington in May, 1776, at New York, but lasted only six weeks, some say because Washington objected to his morals, others because Burr objected to the drudgery of secretarial work and had little respect for Washington's military ability. In any case, Burr wrote to his father's friend John Hancock that he was so disgusted that he was inclined to resign the service. Hancock secured him the post of aide to General Putnam.[8] Parton says of Burr:

"The prejudices against the general, imbibed during his short residence with him at Richmond Hill, were strengthened by subsequent events into a settled dislike, which he carried with him through life. He thought George Washington was a bad general, and an honest, weak man. He said he knew nothing of scientific warfare, and could therefore give no instruction of any value to a young soldier burning to excel in his profession.

"He thought the general was as fond of adulation as he was known to be sensitive to censure, and that no officer could stand well with him who did not play the part of his worshiper. . . .

"Burr always asserted that it was *not* an amour, nor any thing of that nature, but his independent manner of enforcing opinions, to which time added the sting of proved correctness, that made General Washington his enemy." [9]

It is questionable that Hamilton ever liked Washington, or did more than merely endure him for the sake of patriotism and ambition. The best authority for this is Hamilton himself and, while it violates chronology, it gives the reader a truer insight into their subsequent relations to quote at this point a letter Hamilton wrote to General Schuyler when he broke with Washington in 1781:

"I always disliked the office of an aid-de-camp as having in it a kind of personal dependence. I refused to serve in this capacity with two major-generals at an early period of the war. Infected, however, with the enthusiasm of the times, an idea of the General's character which experience taught me to be unfounded, overcame my scruples, and induced me to *accept his invitation* to enter into his family. It was not long before I discovered he was neither remarkable for delicacy nor good temper. . . .

"For three years past I have felt no friendship for him and have professed none. The truth is, our dispositions are the opposites of each other, and the pride of my temper would not suffer me to profess what I did not feel. Indeed, when advances of this kind have been made to me on his part, they were received in a manner that showed at least that I had no desire to court them, and that I desired to stand rather upon a footing of military confidence than of private attachment. You are too good a judge of human nature not to be sensible how this conduct in me must have operated on a man to whom all the world is offering incense." [10]

The coincidence of Burr's complaining of Washington's greed of "adulation," and Hamilton's of his need for "incense," may be explained by the limitless ambition of both men for supremacy. But David Meade, elder brother of

Washington's aide, R. K. Meade, and a lifelong acquaintance of Washington's, says that he was "deficient in personal suavity and address. . . .

"Of a saturnine temperament, he was reserved and austere, and better endowed by nature and habit for an Eastern monarch, than a republican general." [11]

Washington certainly earned his incense, as the best of the gods have done, by self-sacrifice. Whenever he could he went back to his farm, while Burr wrecked his dazzling career by trying to be an emperor, and Hamilton split and wrecked the party with which he hoped to crush the democratic spirit.

From the start, Lieutenant Hamilton, who became a lieutenant-colonel as Washington's aide, lost no time in demonstrating his great intellect, his high literary skill, and his domineering disposition. He became in a sense a tutor to Washington; and Colonel Pickering, the new adjutant-general, who also acquired a poor opinion of Washington's abilities, said that Washington was at this time "defective in grammar, and even in spelling, owing to the insufficiency of his early education; of which, however, he gradually got the better in the subsequent years of his life, by the official perusal of some excellent models, particularly those of Hamilton; by writing with care and patient attention; and reading numerous, indeed multitudes of, letters to and from his friends and correspondents." [12]

Against Pickering's condescending implications, one should place the fact that, before he ever added Hamilton to his staff, Washington had already reached such peaks of glory that he was being widely regarded as almost a divinity, and had written some of his loftiest utterances. John C. Fitzpatrick, who knows more perhaps about Washington manuscripts than anybody else ever did, scouts Pickering's statements and says:

"The greater number of these drafts are in the handwriting of the various aides, but the alterations, suppression, and additions in Washington's handwriting are numerous, and in every instance the change strengthens and improves the aide's composition."

He includes Hamilton's letters with the rest. Even if Pickering's criticism were true, it would have been a creditable thing that Washington was never unwilling to learn about the grammar of English or the grammar of war.

In his early career he knew at least Bland's Military Discipline, which he recommended with "other treatises" to his junior officers in 1756.[13] Though Hamilton is said to have accused him of never having read "any book upon the art of war but Sim's Military Guide," [14] he seems to have learned from General Forbes, in 1758, of Crissé's *Art de la Guerre* through Otway's translation. In 1774 he bought Webb's "Military Treatise." In 1775, at Boston, he recommended to an enquirer for useful books Bland and four others. In 1777 he received from France a book of regulations for engineers. His close associates, Greene and Knox, were well-read in military science, Greene having studied the works that Knox had imported when he kept a bookstore in Boston. Both were familiar with Cæsar's Commentaries and Turenne's Memoirs.[15]

Even Bishop Meade, son of R. K. Meade, quotes Colonel Meade, whom Washington called "Friend Dick," as always saying "that Hamilton did all the head-work for the General." [16]

Washington was not the only great man whose sorrow it was to be surrounded by men who secretly looked down upon him but found it to their interest, or their country's, to pretend to look up. Altars seem to make skeptics out of priests.

Early in March Congress straggled back to Philadelphia to Washington's regret, and Philadelphia grew gay again. So did Morristown, for on the 15th Martha arrived. Washington had just recovered from a severe fever, said to have been an attack of quinsy, so dangerous that he made ready to die and asked that General Greene succeed him in command.[17] Paymaster Palfrey wrote: "We are all under great concern for poor General Washington . . . Last night he was cupped in the head, and is something better today." [18] The flow of letters did not cease.

It was Washington's habit to send for his wife at the close of a campaign and return her to Mount Vernon at the opening of one, according to her grandson, who quotes Martha as saying that she always heard the first cannon on the opening, and the last at the closing, of all the campaigns.[19]

On this occasion Washington rode down to Pluckemin to meet her. A woman at whose house she waited was surprised both by the plainness of Martha's garb and the tenderness of Washington's welcome. His first questions after the usual first questions concerned the health of his horses at Mount Vernon.

There were many officers' wives in camp or near it, and the country people made much ado over Lady Washington, but were startled by her simple dresses, her checked aprons, her industry in knitting stockings for herself and the general.[20]

At length the time came for the first gun of the campaign and Martha was bundled off to the South again. As she passed through Philadelphia on June 13th, the Pennsylvania Assembly appointed a committee "to purchase a coach and present the same to the Honorable Mrs. Washington, the worthy lady of his Excellency General Washington, as a small testimonial of the sense the Assembly have of his great and important services to the American States." Later she visited her old home in Williamsburg and there she was presented with "a golden emblematical medal" and the freedom of the city, as well as a salute of "cannon and small arms." [21]

XIV

THE CAMPAIGN OPENS

"THERE is something prophetic and important in the number seven—else why do the holy scriptures hold out the number seven so frequently, and so remarkably? . . .

"A tradition hath been handed down from the first settlement of New England: that when three sevens should meet in the date of the year, the American colonies would become independent States; and . . . in the year 1777 there would be war throughout Europe. . . . An eminent Scotch divine, not more remarkable for his piety and sufferings than his spirit of prophecy, hath left it on record, that when three sevens should meet, a star of the first lustre and magnitude would fall from the crown of Great Britain. . . . May He that holdeth the seven stars in his right hand accomplish the prophecy!" [1]

To these gleaming omens, published in the *Freeman's Journal* of March 15, 1777, some of the patriots were contributing their best collaboration with the stars. Washington had begun the year with glittering victory. A number of Americans in France were doing their utmost to upset the stubborn truce in Europe; the devils who make men mad had already driven George III out of his mind, and would again.

But, unlike so many ancient warriors, Washington never consulted the auguries. He neither investigated the liver of a chicken nor opened battle with a prayer. His chief dissatisfaction with prophecy was probably the willingness of the bulk of his countrymen to sit back and let the stars and the sacred number Seven do all the work. He seems to have had no superstitions whatsoever, no belief in lucky days, lucky numbers, or talismans.

About this time a still easier method of ending the conflict was broached. Richard Rigby of the British Cabinet, Paymaster of the British forces, and as witty as he was unscrupulous, offered himself as the champion of England and proposed to decide the war in the Early Roman manner by single combat. He challenged Washington to box it out with him; or failing Washington, he would take on Lee or Putnam. He thought his scheme as likely to bring on peace as any the Howes had proposed.[2]

Lee was a prisoner and Putnam was in his sixtieth year, so this left it to Washington. Though he was forty-five, he was enormously strong with an extraordinary reach and hands like boxing-gloves, and he could doubtless have handled with ease Mr. Rigby, who was ten years older and addicted to all-night bouts with the bottle.

But the Howes would not retire from the ring and Washington must rely on his soldiery. Rigby had said that none of the Americans had the prowess of a militia drummer and his friend, the Earl of Sandwich, had wished that they would "put into the field not forty thousand, but two hundred thousand, so-called soldiers; as the greater their numbers, the easier would be the conquest." [3]

By this mode of reckoning, Washington seemed bound to win, for his army was growing smaller and smaller.

A picturesque table drawn by the British historian Stedman reviews the slump in patriotism and the gradual increase of British power:

BRITISH and REBEL FORCE in 1776

Dates	British	Rebel troops
August	24,000	16,000
November	26,900	4,500
December	27,700	3,300
In 1777		
March	27,000	4,500
June	30,000	8,000[4]

Washington's own statement of his condition as of April 12th, 1777, was made in a dismal report to Congress whose

disappointment he foresaw.[5]   His rosy publicity may or may
not have fooled the enemy, but it certainly duped his own
countrymen.

Plainly the inevitable step had to be taken and the awful
word Draft uttered.   On May 17, 1777, he wrote to Governor
Patrick Henry of Virginia that the situation was "perhaps more
critical now than ever," that a draft would enable "the Timid,
the Rich and the Tory to furnish soldiers at their own expence," and that they should be prevented from substituting
convicts or foreign indented servants.[6]

The Virginia Assembly promptly accepted the hint and
passed a draft law,[7] one result of which was to awaken an intense interest in the beauties of Kentucky and set on foot an
increasing hegira to people its hitherto uninviting wilderness,
for even though the Indians were making trouble here and
there, many of the Virginians preferred them to the patriots.
Other states drafted their own militia to fill the gaps in their
continental quotas.   The drain grew so serious that it was difficult to harvest the crops.   Some of the communities, as James
Truslow Adams[8] points out, raised money by taxation and
hired men to fill their quotas at town expense.   This started a
new rivalry, and auctioneering; and encouraged bounty jumpers
to enlist, desert, and reenlist.   Rich men when drafted hired
substitutes and the familiar protests against making the poor
carry all the burdens were loud in the land.

Of course, Washington did his best to hoodwink the British
as to his nimiety of men and their paucity of enthusiasm, but
his success is doubtful since swarms of spies served both sides
at once.

One of these suspected of doing double duty was employed
in a ruse that may or may not have deceived Howe.   Washington had false returns made out showing that he had an army
of twelve thousand men, though he really had hardly three
thousand.   Seeing the spy in Greene's office, Alexander Hamilton laid the document on a table, and stepped out for a moment.   On his return he found both paper and spy missing, and

"it was supposed that this trick did much to preserve the army at Morristown from attack that winter." [9]

We can see Washington's own mind at work in a more elaborate deception. Learning that one of his own spies had been arrested as a spy by one of his generals and sent to Philadelphia for trial, he wrote to Colonel Reed in haste to save him from death and use him: "make him a handsome present in money to secure his fidelity to us; and contrive his releasement, in such a manner, as to give it the appearance of an accidental escape from confinement." [10]

After the war, when there was such merciless proscription of loyalists, many persons escaped utter ruin by claiming that they had really been spies for Washington all the while, and publishing their proofs in the newspapers. [11]

It seems not to be generally known even among historians that Rivington, the best-abused Tory of the war, who lived in New York and published the newspaper that best abused the rebels, had all the time been a well-paid spy of General Washington, while employed in abusing him, and had imparted useful information, which could not otherwise have been obtained. [12] Nothing that Washington accomplished in the secret service, and he was a past master at it, was cleverer than to use as a spy an editor who incessantly ridiculed and reviled him.

He wrote to Congress:

"Nothing but a good face & false appearances, have enabled us hitherto to deceive the enemy." [13]

The time was approaching, however, when false faces would lose their value and fighting must begin somewhere.

Desertion and delay in replacement had actually diminished his own Body Guard so that he mustered it out in February, 1777. [14] In April he began to form a new one, sending circular letters to the Virginia colonels at Morristown, asking each to furnish him with four men "nearly of a size" either five feet nine or ten, of good character, "sober, young, active, and well made":

"In doing this I wish to be extremely cautious, because it is more than probable, that, in the course of the campaign, my baggage, papers, and other matters of great public import, may be committed to the sole care of these men. . . . I am satisfied, there can be no absolute security for the fidelity of this class of people, but yet I think it most likely to be found in those, who have family connexions in the country. You will therefore send me none but natives, and men of some property, if you have them. I must insist, that, in making this choice, you give no intimation of my preference of natives, as I do not want to create any invidious distinction between them and the foreigners." [15]

"Send me none but natives," seems to have been the origin of another of his famous sayings that he never said:

"Put only Americans on guard tonight."

His caution in this case was due to his remembrance of the foreigner in his guard who had been hanged for plotting to assassinate him in New York. He put his new guard under command of Captain Caleb Gibbs and it was ready May 1st, 1777. He added at the same time a troop called the Cavalry of the Commander-in-Chief's Guard. Some of these were from "Lady Washington's Dragoons" of Baylor's regiment. [16]

Various organizations had begun to adopt fanciful titles such as "Congress's Own Regiment" and "General Washington's Life Guards," and on April 15th Congress passed a resolution that such terms were improper. Washington replied that they were not authorized by him and had, in fact, been forbidden "in terms of severe reprehension." [17]

Among the organizations styling themselves by his name was a German group recruited later by Captain Von Hee, who had served under Frederick the Great. From this no doubt rose the legend, said to be taught in some German schoolbooks, that Washington had a Life Guard made up solely of Germans and that he gave his commands to them in German. [18] If he ever knew a word of that language, he kept it a secret.

He had entered Morristown on January 6th, 1777, announcing that he would remain there only a few days. It was nearly six months before he could write to Congress on May 28th, 1777, that he was moving to Bound Brook. [19]

He marched only twenty miles due south, taking with him about 8,000 men, whom he had somehow assembled. He was now only seven miles from the British post at Brunswick and his position was almost unapproachably strong.

He was bewildered by Howe's behavior, as everybody has always been. Howe had had his troubles, too. He had waited for great reinforcements that he realized were necessary to hold any post he might conquer. He waited also for tents and for grass to appear on the hills to feed his horses. The grass came and the tents came at last but the reinforcements were refused, save for a few draft troops. The bulk of England's men were being entrusted to Burgoyne for his great plan of conquest from the north. So Howe moved out glumly with what men he could afford, about 10,000, and pushed into New Jersey far enough to separate Washington from Princeton. He gave out word that he would be in Philadelphia in six days.

Washington told Morgan's riflemen to scout and annoy the enemy. He promised them spears to use against horsemen and, remembering old times, gave this advice:

"It occurs to me, that, if you were to dress a company or two of true woodsmen in the Indian style, and let them make the attack with screaming and yelling, as the Indians do, it would have very good consequences, especially if as little as possible were said or known of the matter beforehand." [20]

A Lieutenant Martin fell in with a party of Howe's light horse and was "unnecessarily murdered with the most aggravated circumstances of barbarity" according to Washington, who was so shocked by the sight of the butchery that he actually sent the corpse to Cornwallis with a letter:

"I wish not to wound your Lordship's feelings, by commenting on this event; but I think it my duty to send his mangled body, to your lines as an undeniable testimony of the fact should it be doubted, and as the best appeal to your humanity for the justice of our complaint." [21]

The body was refused at the outpost, but the letter was carried to Cornwallis, whose reply is not at hand. Graydon, then a prisoner, says that the body was brought to the post of Sir George Osborne "who with much admired *sang froid*, simply returned for answer, that 'he was no coroner.' This circumstance was a theme of considerable merriment, and the *bon mot* of sir George not a little applauded." [22]

Philadelphia was in such alarm that Congress begged its late scapegoat, Benedict Arnold, to take command in the city, called out militia, and sent Arnold to the Delaware to fortify it against a crossing. Washington wrote Arnold that he could hardly believe Howe capable of trying to cross a river with Arnold on the other side and Washington in the rear:

"Should they be imprudent enough to do it, I shall keep close upon their heels, and do every thing in my power to make the project fatal to them." [23]

Howe stretched his line out nine miles to Somerset, keeping the Raritan creek between him and Washington.

On June 22, the British fell back in haste. Still Washington would not be drawn down into the lowlands, but "kept the main army paraded upon the heights," while sending Greene and Morgan in pursuit.

In the early morning of June 26, 1777, Howe rushed out of Amboy with his whole army in several columns, and drove north through Metuchen to Westfield, as if to cut Washington off from the Hudson and seize a pass in the hills. Lord Stirling, who had pushed up too close, was surprised by Cornwallis and badly roughed, losing three brass cannon and two hundred men, at a cost of seventy killed and wounded for Cornwallis. What Howe had done to Lord Stirling was an evidence of what he would have done to Washington, if he could have coaxed him off his foothills.

Having struck at Washington's left flank, then at his right, without being able to draw him into an engagement, Howe gave up and abandoned New Jersey forever. That was the whole purpose of his feint toward Philadelphia and Washington had not failed to include it among his guesses.

It was the neatest bit of what he called "the Art Military" that he ever had a chance to display, and he managed it to perfection.

The British historian Stedman gave Washington high praise for the ease with which he "penetrated into the designs of the commander in chief, and eluded them by his cool, collected, and prudent conduct." [24]

The same emotions were felt by the frivolous Nicholas Creswell, who had escaped from Virginia in time to see part of one battle. He had known Washington slightly at Mount Vernon in 1775. In 1777 he has a different story of different times and a different man:

"Washington is certainly a most surprising man, one of Nature's geniuses, a Heaven-born General, if there is any of that sort. That a Negro-driver should, with a ragged Banditti of undisciplined people, the scum and refuse of all nations on earth, so long keep a British General at bay, nay, even, oblige him, with as fine an army of Veteran Soldiers as ever England had on the American Continent, to retreat—it is astonishing. It is too much. By Heavens, there must be double-dealing somewhere. General Howe, a man brought up to War from his youth, to be puzzled and plagued for two years together, with a Virginia Tobacco planter. O! Britain, how thy Laurels tarnish in the hands of such a Lubber! . . . Washington, my Enemy as he is, I should be sorry if he should be brought to an ignominious death." [25]

And now ensued for Washington another period of unwelcome peace, for all the battle clouds gathered and broke in the North. He was still commander-in-chief and responsible for every battle but it could not have pleased him to sit idle and write letters, while other soldiers fought desperately and won victories that never came his way in all his life.

According to tradition it was in that Northern fighting—at Fort Stanwix—that the Stars and Stripes were flown for the first time, anticipating Washington's alleged first appearance with the flag at Brandywine. Neither legend will bear close scrutiny and there is reason to believe that the Stars and Stripes were never carried by troops during the Revolution. It is certain that the fame of Betsy Ross is one of the most unwarranted renowns in all history.

It was not until mid-'77 that Congress agreed upon a new flag, as an improvement on the thirteen stripes and the Union Jack evolved outside Boston. On June 14, 1777, it was resolved that "the flag of the thirteen United States be thirteen stripes, alternate red and white; the union to be thirteen stars, white on a blue field, representing a new constellation, the stars to be arranged in a circle."

The name of Betsy Ross is attached perhaps imperishably to this emblem, and the story is told that three weeks before June 14th, Washington and Robert Morris and Colonel John Ross called on Elizabeth Gascom Ross, widow of an upholsterer, and asked her to make the flag whose design they offered her. She suggested changing the stars that Washington had drawn with six points to the familiar five points, and this was agreed on. She made the first flag, her shop is a shrine and her name immortal. So the story ran, and runs.

But, in the first place, Washington was not in Philadelphia during this period and could not have called on her. There is no record of his having taken any part in any such interview. In the second place, she seems not to have been the widow of the man she is said to have married. That she made flags there is little doubt, as that was her trade.[26] But that she made the first flag and altered its design in Washington's presence is sheer legend. By a coincidence, the coat of arms of the Washington family has three stars and two red bars on white ground, but this was a coincidence merely.

Francis Hopkinson put in a bill for designing the flag of the United States, the seal and other things, and spent years in a thwarted effort to collect from Congress. The credit has been claimed for him as he claimed it himself.[27] But Mr. Ballard Thruston's researches have riddled this attribution also.[28] He doubts that the flag flown at Fort Stanwix (said to have been made of an officer's blue coat and a camp woman's red petticoat) carried the design authorized by Congress.

Worse yet, he finds no real evidence that the official flag was used at all during the Revolution. The stars and stripes were meant for the navy only. There were no materials for the army flag in this country, and they were ordered from France. But they did not arrive until the winter of 1782-3, and there is no record that they were ever distributed. Thus the flag itself vanishes into legend with the designer.

XV

HOWE PLAYS HIDE-AND-SEEK

" ART for art's sake!" inspires and deludes artists and
artisans in war as in other human amusements. The
artistic phase of combat is an enchantment above the
bloody prose of battle, the poetry of heroism, triumph or
tragedy, the mathematics and the dull bookkeeping of paymaster, quartermaster and commissary, the stupidity and brutality of the drill ground, the subordination and slavery of rank,
the drudgery and fatigue of grinding marches and soul-weary-
ing camps.

Even here Washington was denied the usual privilege of
generalship. He had begun the war without that foundation
for all strategy, a National Objective.[1] There was no nation
and no common objective. Napoleon's Maxim V states that
"every war should have a definite object." Washington and
his men lacked that when he headed the stampede of Southern
and Western volunteers in a dash to the rescue of Boston.

Gradually a nation grew up about Washington. In spite
of itself, and with no more authority than derives from accre-
tion, a union coalesced and an objective appeared. The theory
of Independence was hardly so much developed as invented
suddenly.

The radicals discovered America in a far truer sense than
Columbus did when he stumbled on an island and assumed it
to be a part of India. Likewise, the America of the Revolutionists was not at all what they thought it was, and it grew
into what they never dreamed it would be.

England also, a mob of shopkeepers gradually consolidating
into a vast department store, crushing competition and at the
same time, resenting the renewal of outlawed royal pretensions,

was developing in unforeseen directions. When George III and his ministry pushed through the Habeas Corpus bill in February, 1777, England was more shocked than America. The nation was almost split with a civil war. There followed what Englishmen called the "partial secession" of the "Friends of America," [2] meaning liberals who feared that the oppression of America would soon be extended to themselves; they approved of many American ideals but abhorred the anarchy of independence.

As the war rolled on, the British ministry seemed to onlookers to have decided at last to take the one obvious inevitable strategical step toward military victory. It promised fatality for the American hopes and caused profound alarm. A prettier example of grand strategy and the art of map work was never submitted to opposing players in the war-game.

What drove Washington almost out of his mind was the fact that the British played only half of the game; he could not understand why they did not complete the inescapable maneuver. He was like the nervous insomniac in the old story, who heard the man next door fling down one shoe, but not hearing him regretfully put the second one down softly, lay awake all night moaning, "Why, in God's name, doesn't he drop the other shoe?"

All of Howe's movements were completely baffling to Washington because Howe would not drop the other shoe after Burgoyne had so dramatically hurled the first one.

Washington must often have stood in his tent with his "family" about him and studied his map, seeing the battle ground plain before him: the thirteen colonies divided by a huge gorge, running north and south. Down part of it the Hudson river spilled when it turned south into the ravine just above Albany. But the big ditch ran on north to the St. Lawrence river, and that struck off northeasterly at an angle of forty-five degrees until it met a gulf and an ocean—England's own Atlantic.

To the seafaring British, almost immobilized on land by their inability to find horses enough for transportation of munitions and supplies, the mouth of the St. Lawrence was a gift of nature. It was not only far closer to the base of supplies than Boston, but it led to further water-carriage, for just below Montreal was the northern tip of Lake Champlain, hardly more than a wide canal just south of whose southern tip lay another canal called Lake George. Near that the Hudson.

Thus, with the exception of a small amount of portage through harsh wilderness, there was a water-route all the way from England down through the center of the colonies.

Van Tyne says that Burgoyne's expedition was not based on the Hudson as a capital strategic point for splitting the colonies, though General Robertson had said that in 1775 he and Gage and Howe himself at first had thought "taking possession of the Hudson the best of all plans." [3]

The British had no sooner occupied Boston and stirred up the rebellion than they recognized that they were in the wrong place for a revolution. Burgoyne persuaded General Gage that the Hudson river was the base for a continental war and when Gage was called home he urged the abandonment of Boston and realignment on the Hudson. Howe himself in a letter dated October 9th, 1777, admitted the possession of the Hudson as "a primary object." [4] When he had abandoned Boston in 1776 he had his eyes on the Hudson, though he sailed to Halifax to refit. But when he returned with his brother, Lord Howe, captured New York with disgraceful ease in August, 1776, and hunted Washington across the Jerseys, he apparently forgot the Hudson and settled down for a comfortable winter in New York.

Burgoyne, however, who went home to resume his seat in parliament during his military recess, worked with Germain to forward a plan for a campaign from Canada downward, and devoted all his tact to converting the King to his project while they rode together in Hyde Park. [5]

General Carleton, the governor of Canada, was another who had long believed that the true way to America was by way of the Hudson. In October, 1776, he chased the last of the rebel invaders off Canadian soil. They took refuge in "The Gibraltar of America" at Ticonderoga, half way down Lake Champlain. If Carleton had shown a little more energy he could have driven the Americans out of Ticonderoga, and held it through the winter as the jump-off for a spring drive down the Hudson. But he returned to winter quarters.

Gates was in command at Ticonderoga and was ready to evacuate at the first show of British strength, but Benedict Arnold was also there and Carleton knew better than to attack him for he had a little fleet on Lake Champlain. According to Admiral Chadwick, "the mere existence of this force throughout the summer of 1776 was the chief cause of our success in the Revolution." [6] It was destroyed at last, but in the words of Captain Mahan:

"Never had any force, big or small, lived to better purpose or died more gloriously, for it had saved the Lake for that year." [7]

In saving the Lake, Arnold saved the river. In saving the river he saved the nation. He knew it, too, and his great genius was poisoned by lack of reward, his soul was perverted into that pitiful horrible dual rôle he played in American history as its despised savior and its thwarted betrayer.

That the strategic supremacy of the Hudson, or North, river was axiomatic to the Americans is shown in a letter Washington wrote to Putnam:

"The importance of the North River in the present contest, and the necessity of defending it, are subjects which have been so frequently and so fully discussed, and are so well understood, that it is unnecessary to enlarge upon them. These facts at once appear, when it is considered that it runs through a whole State; that it is the only passage by which the enemy from New York, or any part of our coast, can ever hope to cooperate with an army from Canada; that the possession of it is indispensably essential to preserve the communication between the east-ern, middle, and southern States; and, further, that upon its security, in a great measure, depend our chief supplies of flour for the subsistence of such forces, as we may have occasion for, in the course of the war, either in the eastern or northern departments, or in the country lying high up on the west side of it. These facts are familiar to all; they are familiar to you. I therefore request you, in the most urgent terms, to turn your most serious and active attention to this infinitely important object." [8]

Though Burgoyne's Plan is available for study in its original form, "Thoughts for Conducting the War from the Side of Canada (Germain Papers, February 28, 1777), there is a welter of disputes concerning its scope and its failure. The clearest and most cogent account is perhaps that of Miss Jane Clark,[9] who has had the advantage of going over the Clinton and Germain manuscripts as they have been recently brought out of their dusty oblivion by Mr. William L. Clements, who purchased and imported them.

According to her monograph, Burgoyne really offered three plans. Germain and the King selected one by which Burgoyne's army would either draw American troops to the north and relieve pressure on Howe, or carry to Howe enough reinforcements to enable him to crush the entire army of the enemy. Burgoyne was to report to Carleton, who was to order him to "proceed with all expedition to Albany and put himself under the command of Sir William Howe."

Howe stubbornly persisted in his plan to capture Philadelphia by water and Germain made no definite attempt to stop him. This was partly due to Germain's inability to realize the magnitude and wildness of the American scene. Even now only the travelled British grasp it. As Miss Clark says:

"Germain thought Howe would take a little week-end run down to Philadelphia, occupy it without a struggle, perhaps delay there a day or two for the mere routine of organizing the Tories into companies for the defence of the city, return to New York, and sail up the Hudson with all flags flying. There would be a cheery, 'Burgoyne!' 'Howe!'; the war would be ended, and Germain would be a viscount.

"That this is no exaggeration becomes apparent when we find that in a Germain letter which Howe received as late as August 16, 1777, the minister, approving of the Philadelphia plan, expressed the hope that Howe's Pennsylvania campaign would be completed in time to cooperate with Burgoyne, who was expected by the same cheerful optimism to reach Albany before September. To Germain, the war was to be won by Tories, the Army provisioned from the country; every successful foraging raid of Howe's was a victory, and the efforts of the Americans, 'Effects of Despair' and 'Symptoms of Weakness.' "

One thing is certain, Germain neither notified Burgoyne of Howe's Philadelphia scheme nor ordered Howe to aid Burgoyne. The neglect is so appalling from the aftermath that it has been accounted inconceivable, and various stories have been put forward to explain why Howe failed to receive what, in fact, Germain never sent.

According to Lord Shelburne, Germain's orders to Howe were written at the same time with Burgoyne's, but never forwarded. According to another legend, Germain being in haste to get to the country would not wait for a fair copy to be made and later forgot the matter; the orders were pigeonholed and found long afterwards. According to another, the orders were sent but not entered in the office letter book, and there was no way of contradicting Howe's denial that he ever received them.[10] Miss Clark goes on:

"There is one point, which seems never to have been considered. Even if Howe had received the instructions to act on the Hudson, it is doubtful whether he would have followed them. Although Germain has been justly blamed for trying to run the war from London instead of letting the generals on the spot run it, he gave Howe a freedom which was checked only by the paucity of troops he sent him.

"Howe, who was 'in fashion' at home did not hesitate to reply politely that the request could not be granted, as when he put off altogether the King's favorite project of a diversion to the coasts of Massachusetts and New Hampshire."

It is to be remembered that both the Howes were the illegitimate grandsons of George I and his mistress, the Baroness Kilmansegg, and George III regarded them as kinsmen.

The idea of an attack on the coast of New England as a

diversion has been often ridiculed as one of the King's mad quirks, but it had the approval of many strategists, and might well have been effective. It is to be remembered that Burgoyne was crushed by a belated rush of New England volunteers who might not have rushed if their own lands had been menaced. General Robertson said:

"Had a corps been sent by sea to alarm New England, it would have kept their militia at home. At that time I was going to America with 1700 men, if the winds had carried us to that coast, I thought that such an appearance, and burning a few barns, would have brought back the New England army. . . . I meant to alarm the coast, rather than distress it. . . . I never burnt a house in my life; I have often prevented it; but at that time it would have answered a great end." [11]

The King's idea of an attack on the coast was heard of by spies in England, transmitted to Paris, thence to Congress, thence to Washington. There was uncertainty as to whether Burgoyne or Howe or both would attack at Boston or elsewhere, for there was some belief that Burgoyne would not try for the Hudson. In his perplexity, Washington sent letters to all the governors of Eastern States to call out their militias and guard against a landing.[12]

But Howe was not even tempted either to detach a few men for the purpose of frightening the New Englanders, or to advance up the Hudson by land or water and greet Burgoyne. He went on with his plan and suffered nothing but wind and tide to vex him. For the direful results of his obstinacy, he and his brother the Admiral were subjected to almost unparalleled abuse in England, accused of mercenary treason and subjected to every contempt, though Admiral Howe, after the storm was over, accomplished magnificent things in sea-battles far from America. Even American historians have not spared the Howes their best reviling, though the independence of their country was unquestionably due to an expedition which an English critic called "one of the most frantic that could enter into the human mind." [13]

From the moment that his spies informed him of Burgoyne's arrival in Canada, Washington was sure that Howe and Clinton would try to force their way up the Hudson river, sink the iron chain that was strung across it, and pass the forts that aligned the heights. He wrote to Putnam to call on the neighboring militia for reinforcements:

"The importance of preventing Mr. Howe's getting possession of the Highlands by a *coup de main* is infinite to America." [14]

His situation was, as he said, "truly delicate and perplexing" since if he marched to Peekskill, Howe could push right on to Philadelphia. But Howe gave no signs of an interest in Philadelphia, for Washington learned from "deserters and others" that Howe was putting horses and "large supplies of provisions, water, and provender," on board the ships in the harbor. This indicated a longer journey than the Hudson. It might mean Boston, possibly Philadelphia, hardly Charleston in this "sickly weather."

Washington kept protesting how "embarrassing" Howe's conduct was. It is legitimate for an enemy to deceive and slaughter but to embarrass is unpardonable.

Howe was only one of Washington's acute embarrassments. Congress was also embarrassing, for while it had commissioned him commander-in-chief and had even made him a dictator in everything but name, it had kept the Northern army in its special care, "considered that as a separate department, appointed the officers in some instances to that command themselves." [15]

General Gates was increasingly embarrassing. He seemed to consider both the North and Congress his private and separate departments. He had got the command away from Schuyler once, but Schuyler got it back again. The persevering Gates continued to expend his stratagems on Congress in the increasing hope not only of recapturing Schuyler's command but of unseating Washington himself.

Now Burgoyne began to be embarrassing. On July tenth Washington received a thunderbolt letter from Schuyler. The Gibraltar of the North, Fort Ticonderoga, had been surrendered without a blow. St. Clair had not only evacuated the stronghold early on a Sunday morning, but had vanished.

This finished what little credit Schuyler had in Congress with any but the New Yorkers. As Samuel Adams wrote:

"It is indeed droll enough to see a General not knowing where to find the main Body of his Army." [16]

Congress accepted Washington's advice to hasten Benedict Arnold north, and Arnold hurried off with his usual speed. Washington poured out his wrath on St. Clair—or rather the public wrath tempered with his own mercy:

"I will not condemn or even pass a Censure upon any officer unheard; but I think it a duty, which General St. Clair owes to his own Character, to insist upon an opportunity of giving the Reasons for his sudden evacuation of a post, which, but a few days before, he by his own letters thought tenable at least for a while. People at a distance are apt to form wrong conjectures; and if General St. Clair has good reasons for the step he has taken, I think the sooner he justifies himself the better. . . . If he is reprehensible, the public have an undoubted right to call for that Justice, which is due from an officer, who betrays or gives up his post in an unwarrantable Manner." [17]

St. Clair wrote to Washington very sorrowfully:

"It gives me a very painful sensation to know myself, but for a moment, the subject of a doubt with you. I have, however, the strongest hopes, when your Excellency comes to be fully informed of our situation and force, you will not condemn me; and, although I am not solicitous about the opinion of the world (though very far from disregarding it), I wish to hold a character with your Excellency something more than merely negative." [18]

To St. Clair's grief over his defeat was added the dismay of a storm of abuse in the newspapers. The public refused to believe his protestations. They believed he had the great numbers he had pretended to have (for British consumption) and reviled him for cowardice, even accused him of treachery. He demanded a court-martial both from Washington and from Congress.[19]

Congress was in a state of rage at all its generals. The opposition to Schuyler was aligning New England against New York. Schuyler's friends blamed New England's non-support for his failure. New England retorted that the militia would not serve under Schuyler. Samuel Adams was so furious at Schuyler and St. Clair that he could not explain the evacuation of Ticonderoga "even upon the Principle of Cowardice. The whole Conduct seems to carry the evident Marks of Deliberation and Design." [20]

There was national ire among the citizens and among the soldiery. People were reminded of Admiral Byng, whom England had shot for merely avoiding a battle. The word now was:

"America must have a *Byng*." [21]

Even John Adams wrote to his wife, "I think we shall never defend a post until we shoot a General." [22] Yet he always denied that he had any animosity to Schuyler.

From such far-reaching feuds, Washington managed to keep himself aloof. Nobody ever proposed shooting him, though he lost many battles. He was always impersonal. When the battle in Congress over Schuyler came to the breaking point, the opponents of Gates made a last effort to keep him from Schuyler's post and forced through a resolution asking that Washington select a man to take command in the north.[23] But he sidestepped the inevitable embroilment and wrote a letter that is strange, coming from a commander-in-chief invited to choose his most important lieutenant at a most important post:

"At the same time that I express my thanks for the high mark of confidence which Congress have been pleased to repose in me by their Resolve, authorizing me to send an Officer to command the northern army, I should wish to be excused from making the appointment. For this many reasons might be mentioned, which, I am persuaded, will occur to Congress upon reflection. The northern department in a great measure has been considered as separate, and more peculiarly under their direction; and the officers commanding there always of their nomination. I have never interfered further than merely to advise, and to give such aids as were in my power, on the requisitions of those officers. The present situation of that department is delicate and critical, and the choice of an officer to the command may involve very interesting and important consequences." [24]

When he learned that Congress had ordered both Schuyler and St. Clair to come down from the north and report at his headquarters, he still maintained his determined attitude of subordination, and wrote to Congress for instructions:

"As these gent^n . . . will probably be down in the course of a few days, I shall be glad to be informed what I am to do with 'em when they arrive. I . . . should be at a loss what to say, or how to conduct myself respecting them, without receiving some directions." [25]

Washington, having tried to penetrate wildernesses as a young commander in 1754, with Braddock in 1755, and with Forbes in 1758, felt sure that Burgoyne would never succeed. He kept his head in all the panics, and wrote of Burgoyne with the vision of a prophet:

"The success he has had will precipitate his Ruin. From your accounts he appears to be pursuing that line of conduct, which of all others is most favorable to us; I mean acting in Detachment. This conduct will certainly give room for Enterprise on our part, and expose his parties to great hazard. Could we be so happy, as to cut one of them off, supposing it should not exceed four, five, or six hundred men, it would inspirit the people and do away much of their present anxiety."

His most immediate anxiety was still Howe, concerning whose wavering he added:

"His conduct is puzzling and embarassing beyond measure; so are the informations which I get. At one time the ships are standing up towards the North River; in a little while they are going up the Sound; and in an Hour after they are going out of the Hook." [26]

Cantankerous Congress refused to grant Arnold his true rank even while he was dashing to the fray. Yet he waived his rights. Old John Stark, hero of Bunker Hill and Trenton, had been so miffed when Congress in March '77 promoted junior officers over his head as well as Arnold's that he had resigned, but he came in again now, though strictly as an independent ally, not a Congress officer.

He represents one of the most picturesque and obscure phases of the Revolution, for, during it all, a civil war was waging between New York State and New Hampshire. New York claimed sovereignty over certain territory now known as Vermont, then known as the Hampshire Grants. The Grants would not secede from New England. When New York tried to compel them to, and endeavored to collect quit rents as from a Colony, the Grants fought. The result was often bloody, and always an embarrassment to Washington. It involved charges of treason against Ethan Allen as well as his more important brother Ira, and the whole region.

Even now, in the desperate fear of British invasion, Stark was financed by a patriotic individual, John Langdon, who backed him with $3,000 in cash and seventy hogsheads of rum. And Stark fought as a Hampshire Grants man, not a United States man. And he fought so splendidly that his courage and Arnold's combined stratagems and bravery threw Burgoyne into his first grave difficulties.

Washington sent many letters and his only available reinforcement. He added a kindling word about the Hessians and Indians in referring to an enemy: "Who, not content with hiring Mercenaries to lay waste your Country, have now brought Savages, with the avowed and express intent of adding murder to desolation." [27]

This horrified reference to the British employment of Indians was mere propaganda, for there were Indians also with the Americans. Burgoyne really abhorred the savages and had to be compelled to use them,[28] while Washington's devotion to the use of Indians was lifelong.

Restlessly Washington darted hither and yon. He moved eleven miles closer to the Hudson, back of Haverstraw, deep into a mountain pass through the Highlands, called the Clove, or Smith's Clove. Here he spent a night in an old log house with his family on the floor about his bed.[29]

Then next day he fell back again to the mouth of the Clove. He moved again as far as the boundary line of New York at Ramapo, south of the present Ramapo and Suffern. Tradition says that he climbed a peak called Torn Rock and studied the scene through a telescope. In the rock is a fissure through which a hidden stream runs, making a perpetual chuckling sound. Legend says that Washington lost his watch here and it has never ceased to tick—a pleasant instance of his progress toward deification.[30]

At last the great word came. On July 23, 1777, Howe and his great fleet of "170 sail of Topsail vessels, and about 50 or 60 smaller ones" finally stood out to sea.

There was still just a possibility that Howe might be aiming at Philadelphia, and Washington urged Congress to have a sufficient number of proper look-outs fixed at the Capes of Delaware to report the arrival of any fleet.[31]

When Howe confided to Clinton his plan of going to Philadelphia Clinton thought he was joking or using what they called finesse. He told Howe that it was "only a Feint intended to deceive us all . . . I should expect to see him return with the first Southerly Blast and run up the North River." [32]

Among the Clinton letters was found a little secret memorandum to Captain Drummond with instructions not to open it. It was a sort of private bet that Howe was incapable of abandoning Burgoyne. It said:

"By God these people can not mean what they give out they must intend to go up Hudson's river & deceive us all, if they do I for one forgive." [33]

Howe took with him 13,779 men and left to Clinton a force which Howe considered sufficient, though Clinton said he had really fit for duty not exceeding 7,200 men, barely "adequate to the Garrisoning the numerous and extensive Works and Posts, in Long, Staten, and York Islands, and Paulus Hooke."

He called it in his manuscript history a "Defensive too much starved." In a private letter he called it "a D——d starved deffencive." Clinton fully expected that the moment Howe "had decidedly gone to sea Mr. Washington would move with everything he could collect either against General Burgoyne or me, and crush the one or the other."

It is strange that this attack on New York seems never to have occurred to Washington. He could perhaps have taken the city and still have had abundant time to reach Philadelphia for the same defence he put up there. He lost Philadelphia as it was; he might have had New York in exchange. He did indeed send Sullivan to raid Staten Island, August 22nd, and had feints made at other points, but with such small forces that Sullivan, de Borré and Smallwood were put to rout with heavy loss and Sullivan subjected to the censure of Congress. Clinton wrote of Washington's neglected opportunity:

"How easily might he have landed under cover of Batteries rased there, on the Plains of Haerlem? and when there, and in Possession of Brooklyn and Staten Island . . . he could without much difficulty have rendered my Hold of New York very precarious, or at least have destroyed my Magazines & burnt the Town." [34]

Among the Clinton papers in the William L. Clements collection is one he calls "A Memorandum not to be shewn to any body but very particular friends." Referring to conversations with Howe he says:

"I represented What if W—— had not been a blockhead might have hap'ned, while the Comr. in Chief was at sea, an attempt to murder me or crush B[urgoyn]e"

In a memorandum on Howe's "Narrative" he wrote of Sullivan's attack on Long Island:

"With respect to my own Post, it was threatened & once attacked with 7000 22. augt—had it been with 14000, as would have been the

Case if Washington had not been a Blockhead, I should have lost Staten and Long Island—even as it was—the good Conduct alone of the officers commanding at those Stations saved them."

While Howe was encountering the most adverse and unusual opposition from the weather, adverse winds and fatal heat, and Burgoyne was unable to penetrate the forest for the trees, and Clinton was cowering in the little metropolis, Washington was trying to peer through the misty distances that shrouded his personal objective.

After waiting in vain to see Howe's ships on the Hudson, he decided that, after all, the strange man must have intentions against Philadelphia. It was still possible, of course, that Howe had merely run out to sea "with a view of returning when our Troops should be drawn of." But the danger of storm and dispersion of the fleet made it improbable that the whole voyage was an excursion to deceive. He called on Congress to get out the militia.[35] As he drove his men hotfoot across New Jersey, he was writing to Christopher Ludwick:

"I imagine you must by this time have a considerable parcel of hard Bread baked. I am moving towards Philadelphia with the Army, and should be glad to have it sent forward. . . . You will continue baking as fast as you can."[36]

He wrote to a colonel to have spies sent back to Staten Island to see what troops Howe had left there. He wrote to General Mifflin in Philadelphia to have the territory where a battle might be fought with Howe and all his probable places of landing reconnoitered. He wanted information as to "grounds convenient for incamping" for covering and securing the forts on both sides of the Delaware, "gaining an accurate knowledge of all the roads and bypaths." He wanted good guides, and above all he wanted to keep his troops out of Philadelphia for two reasons, one strategical, the other moral:

"I would not by any means have the troops enter Philadelphia, not only on account of its being pent up between two rivers but as it would serve to debauch them and introduce diseases, and would be detrimental to the city and disagreeable to the inhabitants." [37]

On July 31st, 1777, one element of suspense was ended. Washington announced:

"General Howe's object and operations no longer remain a secret. At half after nine o'clock this morning, I received an express from Congress, advising that the enemy's fleet, consisting of two hundred and twenty-eight sail, were at the Capes of Delaware yesterday in the forenoon. This being the case there can be no doubt but he will make a vigorous push to possess Philadelphia, and that we should collect all the force we can to oppose him." [38]

Leaving the troops to follow, Washington galloped to Philadelphia, arriving at ten o'clock in the night. He sat down to write letters north and south about the panic in front of Burgoyne and in front of Philadelphia and the need of troops, troops, troops. The next day, August 1st, 1777, he studied the defences of the Delaware and rode fifteen miles south to Chester to get earlier news from the mouth of the river. He spent the night there, and it must have been a sleepless one for at ten o'clock a messenger galloped in to say that Howe's fleet was "gone again, out of sight and out of all the bounds of reason again."

He wrote to his brother in weary disgust:

"The troops under my command have been more harrassed by marching & countermarching, than by any thing that has happened to them in the course of the campaign." [39]

He now decided that the inscrutable will-o'-the-wisp, Howe, was going up the Hudson after all. So Washington ordered Sullivan, who was pushing on from Morristown, to turn around and retrace his steps. [40]

Howe kept out of sight until Washington was in nearly as perfect a frenzy as Burgoyne, who had written July 30th, 1777, from the deeps of the oceanic forests to Lord Germain:

"I have spared no pains to open a correspondence with Sir William Howe. I have employed the most enterprizing characters and offered very promising rewards, but of ten messengers sent at different times and by different routes not one is returned to me, and I am in total ignorance of the situation or intentions of that general." [41]

But long before this reached Germain in London, Burgoyne had given his name as a new word in the language, to the intense amazement of Lord Germain, who proved himself more of a seer than he imagined, and justified Howe more than he would ever after confess, by his statement that: "If Burgoyne's army is not able to defeat any force that the Rebels can oppose to it, we must give up the contest." [42]

A further consideration of Howe's points of view is given in Appendix III. It proves that Howe was neither so purposeless nor so big a fool as everybody thought him. Perhaps nobody could have been.

XVI

LAFAYETTE APPEARS AND HOWE REAPPEARS

THE day before Washington reached Philadelphia Congress issued orders for the arrest of all the officials of the old régime and all disaffected persons.[1] Among the persons taken up were Governor Penn, grandson of the founder, James Tilghman, the father of Washington's devoted aide, Tench Tilghman, and Benjamin Chew, at whose house he had dined and whose house was soon to exert a profound influence on his military hopes.

The Congressmen agreed by a vote of eleven states to place Gates in command of the Northern army.[2] They also "directed" Washington to pass the news on to Gates; which he did, cautiously avoiding anything like a personal order:

"Sir, You will perceive by the enclosed copy of a letter from Congress, that they have destined you to the command of the army in the northern department, and have directed me to order you immediately to repair to that post. I have therefore to desire you will, in pursuance of their intention, proceed to the place of your destination, with all the expedition you can, and take upon you the command of the northern army accordingly. Wishing you success, and that you may speedily be able to restore the face of affairs in that quarter, I am, with great regard, Sir, yours, &c."[3]

In Philadelphia the foreign supplicants for glory and commissions continued to pester Washington. In spite of all he had said against commissioning the immigrants from all Europe, he learned that on July 31st, 1777, Congress had blandly given a major-general's commission to a nineteen-year-old French runaway from his father, his King, and his pregnant young wife. The only reason Congress gave for making this boy a major-general was "in consideration of his zeal, illus-

143

trious family and connections"—not a word about military experience or ability; yet, in the event, an infinitely wise deed.

This was, of course, the Marquis de la Fayette—or Lafayette. Along with him came various others furnished with contracts by Silas Deane in Paris, among them "Baron De" Kalb, whose chief errand in America was to persuade Congress to invite his patron, the Comte de Broglie, to take Washington's place as Generalissimo, and save the country.[4]

Lafayette, having wheedled his way inside the bars that Congress was trying to keep up, did not neglect his companions but expressed a longing to attach himself to Washington. In language that would have been mere rhetoric from the average adventurer, but was in his heart simple sincerity, he expressed his thanks for his commission, and his opinion of the American cause:

"I not only consider'd it as the cause of Honor, Virtue, and universal Happinness, but felt myself empressed with the warmest affection for a Nation who exhibited by their resistence so fine an exemple of Justice and Courage to the Universe.

"I schall neglect nothing on my part to justify the confidence which the Congress of the United States has been pleased to repose in me as my highest ambition has ever been to do every thing only for the best of the cause in which I am engaged. I wish to serve near the person of General Washington till such time as he may think proper to entrust me with a division of the Army." [5]

Lafayette was greatly beloved because he loved greatly. There is an overwhelming sweetness in his letters to the beautiful young wife whom he abandoned without daring even to bid her farewell, though she was soon to become a mother. She could not feel a jealousy of his frank and frantic eagerness for glory, or his idolatry of the very name America. As he wrote later to Henry Laurens:

"The moment I heard of America, I loved her; the moment I knew she was fighting for freedom, I burnt with a desire of bleeding for her; and the moment I shall be able to serve her at any time, or in any part of the world, will be the happiest one of my life." [6]

THE MARQUIS DE LA FAYETTE
(From the painting by Alonzo Chappell)

To Washington the word "America" meant what it meant to Lafayette, whose young soul could swing from the most amorous tenderness to the most sonorous eloquence and mean them both. He could write to his wife and "implore pardon with a caressing grace," says Doniol, who decorates his ponderous tomes with this lad's billets-doux to the forsaken girl to whom he appeals:

"I hope that as a favor to me you will become a good American: it is a sentiment made for virtuous souls. The welfare of America is intimately bound up with the welfare of all mankind: it is going to become the respectable and the sure haven for virtue, honesty, tolerance, equality and a tranquil freedom." [7]

He was not ashamed to confess that he risked all for Glory. He could write to Washington:

"I know well, my dear general, that you will do everything to procure me my one ambition, glory (*la seule chose que j'ambitionne, la gloire*)." [8]

Glory is a great word and as necessary to certain patriots as bread.

In France, monarchy though it was, there was a mystic tremor of a mighty travail to come, a sort of annunciation of a far-off birth. To men like Lafayette that birth was already prefigured in the new world. Delteil says in his biographic rhapsody:

"To the eyes of this Court of France, wearied somewhat of libertinage, Liberty appeared in the guise of a cool, fresh virgin, almost a savage, . . . bearing a heart in each breast. . . . Lafayette attempted and accomplished the finest escape from the world. Therein he proved great, prophetic and eternal. From birth every man should know by heart the great word he uttered: 'I will stand my chance.' Is that not America's motto? . . . All you who lament, away with you, be off! All you who dream, seize your dream by the throat and give it a fine child. Only the dead dream.

"This child of nineteen knew how to be off, how to clear out of it all. That is why I grovel in admiration before him. . . .

" 'What man has not his little America?' he reflects. Each man must some day discover America, under penalty of death. To discover America means to open one's eyes, to become oneself, to be." [9]

This is more than poetry and as much as poetry. One can imagine the effect of this fiery zealot on Washington, sick of the quarrels, cowardices, jealousies, resignations, desertions, nakedness, hunger, flight, defeat, confusion, when a youth from France walked into his sordid world with a touch that rekindled all the dead and stinking embers that had once blazed high.

Lafayette's first glimpse of his idol was at a public dinner given in Philadelphia about the first of August, 1777. He describes his sensations in his memoirs, which he wrote in the Cæsarian third person:

"M. de Lafayette beheld for the first time that great man. Although he was surrounded by officers and citizens, it was impossible to mistake for a moment his majestic figure and deportment; nor was he less distinguished by the noble affability of his manner." [10]

Learning that Lafayette was serving without pay, Washington was particularly gracious, and invited him to make headquarters his home, warning him that he would not find there the luxuries he was used to at court. Washington also apologized for his soldiers before a royal officer:

"I am here to learn, and not to teach," said Lafayette, adding in his *Memoirs*, "This tone had success because it was not common to the Europeans."

So Lafayette joined the other young men at Washington's table and was treated with the deference due his titles in both countries and his wisdom. Washington always had hospitality to spare but when he learned that this young man was taking seriously Congress' little joke about making him a major-general and was actually asking for a command, he wrote with some asperity to Congressman Benjamin Harrison:

"What the designs of Congress respecting this Gentleman were, and what line of conduct I am to pursue to comply with their design & his expectations, I know no more than the child unborn, and beg to be instructed. If Congress meant, that this rank should be unaccompanied by command, I wish it had been sufficiently explained to him. If, on the other hand, it was intended to vest him with all the powers of a major-general, why have I been led into a contrary belief, and left in the dark with respect to my own conduct towards him?" [11]

This did not promise well for that Lafayette who was gradually to win deeper into Washington's heart than any other man. Harrison wrote back:

"I remember well a conversation's passing betwixt you and I on the subject of the Marquis de la Fyatte's commission, and that I told you it was merely honorary. In this light I look'd on it, and so did every other member of Congress." [12]

So the matter rested, and Lafayette accompanied Washington as an officer without command, just as Washington had accompanied Braddock, who showed the same deference to Washington, in his bluff way, that Washington in his shy and gracious manner showed to Lafayette.

On August 16th, 1777, there was promising news from the north. Troops under Herkimer had tried to relieve Fort Stanwix—on the Mohawk river—and walked into a trap. Herkimer mortally wounded sat on a saddle propped against the tree and smoked a pipe while the woods resounded with battle cries and war whoops. Both sides lost heavily and both sides claimed a victory at this battle of Oriskany, but it was far enough from a defeat for the Americans to claim the honors. [13]

Another proof of the polyglot nature of the war was the fact that the senior officer of the Tories with Burgoyne was Lieutenant-Colonel Peters, graduate of Yale. An Indian girl fought with the Oneidas on the American side against Burgoyne's Indians and the patriots were headed by General Herkimer, who signed his own name Herchkeimer, and when he ordered "the battalions to march immediately to Fort Edward with four days' provisions and ammunition fit for a battle," worded it thus:

"ser yu will order your bodellgen do mercks immiedeetleh do ford eduard wid for das profiesen and amonieschen fied for an betell." [14]

Close on Oriskany came word of an indubitable success on August 16th. It was war by a third party to the war, the independent army of the outside state of the Hampshire Grants under command of General Stark.

Among the many claimants to the glory of saving America, the names of Stark and Ira Allen should stand high. It is plausibly argued that the battle of Bennington gave Burgoyne his first mortal check. Without it he could probably have reached Albany and all the supplies he needed, as well as union with Clinton, command of the Hudson, and such final discredit for the rebels that France would never have entered the war.

Therefore, Ira Allen, who proposed the independent regiment, John Stark, who commanded it, and the Hampshire Grants-men who filled it saved the day and changed the history of the world. The Grants, or Vermont, existed as a free and separate republic for thirteen years and overawed Washington himself. He evaded committing himself in the "serious dispute" between New York and Vermont, saying, "I do not chuse to give any Determination." [15]

The embarrassing thing was that the news of Stark's great contribution to freedom reached Congress in the midst of a storm of rage at his insubordination, and an effort to pass a vote of censure. It was dropped with a thud. [16]

On August 21, 1777, Washington and his officers decided that they might as well join the war against Burgoyne. The general agreement now was that Howe must be on his way to Charleston, whither it was useless for Washington to try to follow. Instead of remaining here "Idle & inactive on the remote probability of his returning this way," Washington asked Congress to permit him to go northeast and make it clear to the officers there that he should command. [17]

Congress approved Washington's "plan of marching towards Hudson's river" and ignored his request for clarification as to the northern command, telling him curtly "to act as circumstances may require." [18] But before Washington could get his army started eastward Congress was startled into another of its profound salutes, and hastily

"*Resolved,* That the president inform General Washington, that Congress never intended by any commission hitherto granted by them, or by the establishment of any department whatever, to supersede or circumscribe the power of General Washington as the commander in chief of all the continental land forces within the United States." [19]

The situation was suddenly much the same as when Howe was driving Washington across the Delaware and Congress was putting its little printing press into a wagon for departure.

Howe was here again! After everybody had ceased to expect him at the front door, he pounded on the back. He had sailed round into Chesapeake Bay and was two hundred miles up it when he was discovered.

Resolutions came popping now, ordering prisoners and stores removed from danger, the treasury at Baltimore protected, the militia called out in Pennsylvania, Maryland, Delaware, Virginia; boats, grain, cattle, wagons, carts and horses removed or destroyed.[20]

Washington sent orders flying to General Sullivan to leave off his bootless raids on Staten Island and come to him at once; to New England to turn out "and by following the great stroke struck by Genl Stark near Bennington, entirely crush Genl Burgoyne, who by his letter to Colonel Baum seems to be in want of almost every thing." [21]

Receiving the news of Howe's approach on August 22nd, he marched south early the next morning, down the Old York Road, and camped within five miles of Philadelphia. Though the morrow was a Sabbath, he determined to impress the Tories and Quakers and the faint hearts generally with the might of his army. He issued a pathetically minute description of what everybody should do to make the best effect with such sorry means:

"The whole Line is to march by Subdivisions at half distance—the Rank Six paces asunder which is to be exactly observ^d in passing through the City and great attention given by the Officers to see that the Men carry their Arms well and are made to appear as decent as circumstances will admit.—'T is expected that every Officer without exception will keep his Post in passing through the City, & under no pretence whatever leave it, and if any Sold^r shall dare to quit his ranks. He shall receive 39 Lashes at the first halting place afterwards. . . .

"Not a Woman belonging to the Army is to be seen with the troops on their march through the City. . . . The Drums & fifes of each Brigade are to be collected in the Centre of the Brigade and a tune for the quick step to be play^d, but with such moderation that the men may step to it with ease & without dancing along or totally disregarding the Musick which is too often the case—The men are to be excus^d from carrying their Camp Kettles tomorrow." [22]

Washington rode at the head with Lafayette at his side and his staff following. The troops wore sprigs of green in their hats to give a touch of festivity and the only touch of uniformity.

Having duly impressed Philadelphia, they crossed the Schuylkill river and part of the troops camped at Darby. Monday the 25th they passed through Chester to Naaman's creek, Washington and his staff riding on into Delaware where he took up his headquarters on Quaker hill, in the "pretty town" of Wilmington. At six o'clock that evening he learned that "the Enemy began to land this morning about Six miles below Head of Elk, opposite to Cecil Court-House." [23]

The next morning he rode sixteen or eighteen miles "with all the horse, save Sheldon's, to reconnoitre." This region was not only new to him, but untrue to him, filled chiefly with Quakers loyal to their King and hating all war. Washington complained that he moved "thro' a Country from which I could not derive the least intelligence (being to a man disaffected)." [24]

It was also largely without knowledge even of the English language. John Adams described the people as "in politics . . . a breed of mongrels or neutrals, and benumbed with a

general torpor." [25] Washington was issuing clarion calls like
this concerning the invader:.

"Their all is at stake—they will put the Contest on the event of a
single battle—If they are overthrown, they are utterly undone—The
War is at an end—Now then is the time for our most Strenuous endeavours,—One bold Stroke will free the Land from Rapine, Dev-
astations & burnings, & Female Innocence from brutal Lust & Violence." [26]

But at the same time his own orderly books reiterated such
ancient appeals as these:

"We complain of the cruelty & barbarity of our Enemies,—but does
it equal ours?—they sometimes spare the property of their friends, but
some amongst us, beyond expression barbarous, rob even them—Why
did we assemble in Arms, was it not to defend the property of our
Countrymen? Shall we then to our Eternal shame & Reproach be
the first to Pillage & Destroy it . . . the Commander in Chief most
solemnly assures all, that He will have no mercy on Offenders against
these orders—their Lives shall pay the forfeit of their crimes—Pity—
under such circumstances would be the height of Cruelty—" [27]

The weather at the time was so exceedingly hot that the
scant uniforms of the men were less of a burden than usual
and Washington took a tip from the British. Noting that
Howe's troops, in order "that their movements may be light
& easy" had "disencumbered themselves of all their baggage
even to their Tents, reserving only, their blankets & such part
of their clothing as is absolutely necessary," he called on his
own men to do the same immediately.[28]

A few days later he gave out the information that he also
had disencumbered himself:

"He wishes to share in every hardship to which his Army is expos'd
Divests himself & family of every Species of Baggage, save his
Blankets." [29]

He did not spare himself fatigue or risk. While he was
reconnoitring the British lines he was overtaken by a hurricane
of rain and lightning that tossed the British ships. Washing-

ton was driven to take cover for the night at a Tory farm house near Gray's Hill, only two miles from the Head of Elk. Lafayette, Greene, and Weedon shared his quarters and his danger.

Charles Francis Adams made a ferocious attack on George Washington for his rashness:

"What now ensued illustrated most strikingly the absence of cavalry on either side. To one trained practically in the methods of modern warfare it reads like a burlesque, exciting a sense of humor as well as a feeling of amazement. While Howe's army lay at Elkton, preparing in a leisurely way to take up its line of march to Philadelphia, Washington, it is said, accompanied by Greene and Lafayette, with a few aides, went forward to reconnoitre. In other words, the two generals, most prominent in the army and necessary to its preservation as well as effectiveness, accompanied by a distinguished foreign guest, actually went out in person on a scout. . . .

"They seem to have been utterly without escort and ran fully as great a risk of being gobbled up as did Lee, eight months before. That they did not now share Lee's fate was pure luck." [30]

Washington's old friend, Landon Carter, scolded him and received this reply a month later, written in Washington's own hand and spelling:

"Accept my sincere thanks for your sollicitude on my Acc^t—and for ye good advice contained in your little paper of the 27th Ult^o— at the same time that I assure you, that It is not my wish to avoid any danger which duty requires me to encounter. I can as confidently add, that it is not my intention to run unnecessary risques—In the Instance given by you, I was acting precisely in the line of my duty, but not in the dangerous situation you have been led to believe.—I was reconnoitring, but I had a strong party of Horse with me. I was, as (I afterwards found) in a disaffected House at the head of Elk, but I was equally guarded ag^t friend and Foe.—the information of danger then, came not from me. . . .

"P. S. I am persuaded you will excuse this scratch^d scrawl, when I assure you it is with difficulty I write at all." [31]

Washington took the liberty of putting Count Pulaski in command of the horse, hoping that Congress would confirm his action.[32] Benjamin Franklin had sent this famous Polish hero to America with a letter of praise for his great battles against Russia, Austria, and Prussia, and he speedily justified his reputation.

Washington's guess that Howe would be in distress for horses was more than justified. The voyage had been particularly severe, with heat at times so "horrid," says Montresor, that on one occasion they saw the "pitch melting off the seams" of the vessels.[33] There were also gales and lightning storms. The coast of Maryland was in places strewn with the carcasses of Howe's dead horses.[34]

Suddenly the fleet sailed away leaving the army ashore, and Washington was again bewildered. He imagined now that Howe's ships would go round into the Delaware and be met by the army, which could easily march across the narrow peninsula. He hoped that a tempest might disperse the fleet and leave Howe at his mercy, but his hope was not overheard, and his providence missed an excellent opportunity.

Greene warned Washington that he had selected a bad position at Red Clay Creek for a battle and on September 9th he fell back, a reconnaissance having convinced him that the enemy "only meant to amuse us in front, while their real intent was to march by our right, and by suddenly passing the Brandywine and gaining the Heights upon the north side of that River, get between us and Philadelphia, and cut us off from It." [35]

So he marched at two in the morning and seized those heights himself, while Howe came along slowly, his engineers surveying the roads.

There were about four thousand Germans with Howe. He had hoped to have some Russians, but the deal fell through. The rest were English, Scotch, Irish and Welsh, and a considerable number of American-born loyalists, especially a band called The Queen's Rangers.

Washington's army was even more cosmopolite. In his entourage were the West Indian Alexander Hamilton, of Scotch and Huguenot blood; the Pole, Pulaski; the Frenchmen, Lafayette, Baron de St. Ouary, Chevalier du Plessis, and Colonel de Fleury. Stephen Moylan was an Irish Catholic, as was Colonel John Fitzgerald, and Richard Meade was of Irish descent. Washington was fond of the Irish and liked to have them about him. His former adjutant-general Hand was of Irish birth.

Of his major-generals, Greene was a Rhode Island Quaker, Stephen, a Virginian; Sullivan, though violent anti-Catholic, the son of a scholarly Irish school teacher; [36] Lincoln was from Massachusetts, Lord Stirling was of New York birth but Scotch descent; Knox, a Boston bookseller whose father came from Ireland via the West Indies.

The brigadier-generals included Peter Muhlenberg, of Virginia, born in Pennsylvania of German parents and educated in Germany, a Lutheran clergyman turned Espiscopalian. During the battle he was recognized by fellow students on the other side who hailed him by his old nickname, Devil Pete— *"Hier kommt teufel Piet."* [37] Muhlenberg's own Virginia soldiers were largely Germans from the valley settlements. Another Virginia brigadier was Weedon, a captain in the army of Hanover before he came to America. The Chevalier Prud-homme de Borré, who had arrived from France in March, [38] was serving as brigadier and had under him a German battalion from Maryland. The Irish-born Frenchman, Thomas Conway, had a brigade. In view of the unusual turmoil and confusion of this battle, the cries must have resembled the scenes about Babel at the confusion of the tongues.

There is great dispute as to the numbers engaged. With the usual generosity of one nation for another on such occasions, each gives the other a majority. Before the battle Americans were all agreed that Howe was vastly outnumbered. After the battle the odds were reversed. An American roll captured by the British gave the strength at 12,900 rank and file. [39] This would make a total of about 15,000, which is the strength that Light Horse Harry Lee assigns. Major Tallmadge who was with him says, "We were about eighteen thousand strong." [40]

It is noteworthy, however, that two months after the battle of Brandywine Washington wrote to Patrick Henry:

"The army which I have had under my immediate command, has not, at any one time since General Howe's landing at the Head of Elk, been equal in point of numbers to his. In ascertaining this, I do not confine myself to Continental troops, but comprehend militia . . . I was left to fight two battles, in order if possible to save Philadelphia, with less numbers than composed the army of my antagonist, whilst the world has given us at least double. This impression, though mortifying in some points of view, I have been obliged to encourage, because, next to being strong, it is best to be thought so by the enemy; and to this cause principally I think is to be attributed the slow movements of General Howe." [41]

British accounts give Howe less than the Americans. Montresor says he embarked 17,000 men including artillerymen,[42] but Clinton says that Howe sailed with 13,000 rank and file, which excludes officers, sergeants and drummers. Kemble says that Howe had "upwards of 13,000." Howe's own report says that he had 13,799 privates, which, with an allowance for officers, sergeants and drummers, would make his total about 15,500.[43] This statement being official and made to his own government is probably reliable. He must have had some sick and he had lost some prisoners.

Howe had tried in vain to decoy Washington from the hills of New Jersey, only sixty miles' march from Philadelphia. Now he had taken a six weeks' voyage and landed seventy miles distant. He was better than half way there by now, however, and Washington was again in the hills before him, in a position that everybody admitted to be well selected.

XVII

THE BATTLE OF THE BRANDYWINE

WASHINGTON selected commanding ground north-east of Chads's Ford as the key of his defence, threw up redoubts and established his artillery. On the other side of this ford was another hill to which he ordered an advance guard under General Maxwell. About two miles to the right of Washington's position was a high ridge on which sat Birmingham Meeting House, a Quaker chapel, which he took over for a hospital, to the disgust of the Quakers.

Convinced that he had chosen the best ground there was in the landscape, which he had to take as he found it, Washington put what militia he had (General Armstrong's men) on his left in a rough place not likely to be menaced, for the stream there dashed between cliff-like banks. General Wayne commanded the center at Chads's Ford and General Greene was back of him with the reserves.

General Sullivan claimed the command of the right and he was very tetchy—especially as he had just come down from the attack on Staten Island and had succeeded so ill, through no fault of his own—no general ever fails through a conscious fault of his own—that Congress had called for a court of inquiry. Smarting with two insults from Congress he was determined not to repeat his misfortune at the Battle of Long Island, where he had been captured.

To make sure that his center should not be approached without notice, Washington before daybreak sent General William Maxwell of New Jersey and the light infantry across the creek to push toward Howe's camp, uncover and delay his approach. Maxwell's videttes went far down the road early in the morning, but stopped at Welsh's tavern for a little drink. The next they knew the British were in the tavern with them. The

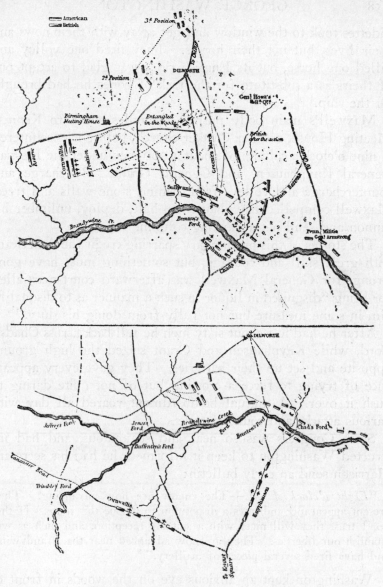

The Battle of the Brandywine.

The lower map shows the forenoon positions; the upper, the
afternoon.

(From Sparks' *Life of Washington*.)

videttes took to the window and got away with their news and their lives, but not their horses. They fired one volley and killed one horse, but its English rider was glad to accept one of theirs as a substitute for the rack of bones he had brought off the ship.[1]

Maxwell's main body pushed six miles south to Kennett Meeting House, another Quaker church, before it encountered at nine o'clock a column of about 4,000 men under the Hessian General Knyphausen, and General Grant. By charge and countercharge and volleys from behind stone walls and trees, Maxwell compelled Knyphausen to halt, deploy, unlimber his cannon and send out a flanking column.

The stories of this preliminary sparring credit the Americans with great skill and courage, but something must have gone wrong, for General Maxwell was afterward court-martialled for being "disguised in liquor in such a manner as to disqualify him in some measure but not fully from doing his duty." [2]

After he had lost about sixty men he fell back across Chads's Ford, while Knyphausen and Grant seized the high ground opposite and set up their batteries. They gave every appearance of trying to force a crossing but of not quite daring to push it over. A mutual bombardment roared all day with various attacks and counterattacks.

Since Congress was so near and so anxious, and had instructed Washington to keep it informed, he had his secretary Harrison send an early bulletin:

"*Eight o'clock A. M.*—The enemy are now advancing. Their present appearance indicates a disposition to pursue this route. If they do, I trust they will meet with a suitable reception, and such as will establish our liberties. They are now advanced near the Brandywine, and have fired several pieces of artillery." [3]

Washington kept an anxious eye on the woods in front of him to see where the other column of Howe's army would strike him, expecting at any moment to hear that it had hit Sullivan's line on the right.[4]

But his eyes were blinded by the thick haze that rose from

the creek and swathed the opposite woods in night-like gloom. He trusted to Sullivan's patrols to keep ransacking the fog, though he had not provided any light horse. Sullivan, however, had picked up a few mounted men and sent them to the outlying fords. Though they reported that there was nobody on the right of the army, Sullivan sent out a captain to reconnoiter, but he never returned.[5] Not until nearly noon did Washington have a hint of the whereabouts of Howe's main column in that mysterious haze. Then came a note received by Sullivan and passed along:

"Great Valley Road, Eleven o'clock, A. M.

"Dear General, A large body of the enemy, from every account five thousand, with sixteen or eighteen field-pieces, marched along this road just now. . . . We are close in their rear with about seventy men. Captain Simpson lay in ambush with twenty men, and gave them three rounds within a small distance, in which two of his men were wounded, one mortally. I believe General Howe is with this party, as Joseph Galloway is here known by the inhabitants, with whom he spoke, and told them that General Howe was with him. Yours,

James Ross, Lieutenant-Colonel." [6]

Washington and his staff seem to have been stunned to learn that Howe was wandering so far off in that direction, and dazed that he should have dared to split his army in two in the very presence of the enemy. They thought it a "terrible error" and were puzzled by "the very magnitude of the blunder." [7]

With a sudden exultation Washington resolved to rebuke Howe's solecism. He ordered Sullivan to push across the Brandywine at once and smash the wandering column. He himself would wedge in between it and Knyphausen and crush the Hessian left while Greene smote the center, and the militia on his far left would attack the Hessian right. This would have been magnificent if it had succeeded and insane if it had failed. Light Horse Harry Lee said it was "wisely determined." [8]

But during the complicated preparations for this advance

Washington began to doubt. What if Howe were after all not lost in the fog but on his way around that dangerous right flank? He determined to make assurance doubly sure before he moved. He had an order written to Colonel Theodoric Bland:

"Chad's Ford, 11th September, 1777,
20 minutes after —— o'clock.

"Sir,—I earnestly entreat a continuance of your vigilant attention to the movements of the enemy, and the earliest report not only of their movements, but of their numbers and the course they are pursuing. In a particular manner I wish you to gain satisfactory information of a body confidently reported to have gone up to a ford seven or eight miles above this. It is said the fact is certain. You will send up an intelligent, sensible officer immediately with a party to find out the truth, what number it consists of, and the road they are now on. Be particular in these matters. I am sir, your humble servant, G. W." [9]

Now came another message from Sullivan that contradicted the first and cancelled Colonel Ross' information that Howe's army was wandering off to the right:

"Brenton's Ford, 11 September.

"Dear General, Since I sent you the message by Major Moore, I saw Major Spear of the militia, who came this morning from a tavern called Martin's, at the fork of the Brandywine. He came from thence to Welch's Tavern, and heard nothing of the enemy about the fork of the Brandywine, and is confident they are not in that quarter; so that Colonel Hazen's information must be wrong. I have sent to that quarter, to know whether there is any foundation for the report, and shall give your Excellency the earliest information. I am, &c. John Sullivan." [10]

This meant that the whole space in front of Washington's position from the forks to Welsh's tavern had been scoured and no sign of the British had been discovered. One man said 5,000 were there; another said nobody was there. Where then was anybody? He dared not assume that Howe had divided his forces, after all, and passed beyond the space. If Washington carried out the plan he had just improvised, Sullivan would plunge through empty woods and find nobody and while he and Greene were crushing Knyphausen between them, Howe might roll in out of the fog and crush him against Knyphausen.

He hastily issued orders countermanding Sullivan's instructions and recalling Greene's men.

And now what was to be done? All this shilly-shally had taken precious hours punctuated only with the thud of Knyphausen's and Knox's irritating cannon and the bravado of each side daring the other to wade into the creek.

Suddenly there was a commotion. A farmer on a horse was insisting on seeing Washington, and his staff was trying to keep the interloper from interrupting the general's meditations. But he would not be denied. He was Squire Thomas Cheyney, one of the few Whigs in that region, and a mortal enemy of the pacifist or loyalist Friends, though his father was a Quaker. His mother was a Presbyterian and this was "the Presbyterian war."

He had left his bed early, saddled his horse and ridden out scouting in such haste that he had not stopped to put on coat or stockings. He caught sight of the British before they had reached the crossing and he knew of a narrow defile where two hundred men could stop them. The British saw him and fired on him, but he escaped and rode to Washington. The staff tried to keep the barelegged old man at a distance, but he pushed through to Washington, who regarded him with suspicion as a probable Tory, especially as Cheyney's information was contradicted by the reports of Washington's own scouts.

"If Anthony Wayne or Perse. Frazer were here you would know whether to believe me or not," Cheyney pleaded. "I have this day's work as much at heart as e'er a Blood of you."

But Washington shook his head; he had just had word from Major Speare, who had just come from there and seen nobody. Cheyney insisted that he also had just come from there, and had come fast. The British had not been imaginary, nor the bullets they fired at him. His good mare's fleet legs had saved him from the crow's-meat the British rode on. He had tried to tell Sullivan but had been rudely received and had pushed on to Washington.

He dropped to the ground and marked out in the dust the fords, the roads, the forks, the British approach behind Washington's right. Washington still refused to believe. Cheyney cried:

"You are mistaken, general; my life for it, you're mistaken, by hell it is so, put me under guard until you find my story true." [11]

In a fearful dubiety between the fierce certainty of this man and the calm assurance of the report in his hand, Washington could not know which to believe. His decision meant lives and deaths, the death perhaps of a cause, of a nation. While he wavered, two o'clock passed. At length a courier galloped up from Sullivan bringing a message and an enclosure. Probably Washington read the enclosure first, seeing that it was from his own investigator, Colonel Bland. It was a thunderbolt of confirmation for Squire Cheyney:

"A quarter past One o'clock.
"Sir, I have discovered a party of the enemy on the heights, just on the right of the two Widow Davis's, who live close together on the road called the Fork Road, about half a mile to the right of the Meeting-house (Birmingham). There is a higher hill in their front.
Theodoric Bland."

This was stupefying. An hour ago, "a party of the enemy" had already appeared behind Washington's right wing! How had they got there? They must have marched seventeen miles from Kennett Square to reach that spot. How many were there? What was Bland's idea of a "party"? Was it merely a small patrol?

Washington's huge hands must have turned wooden as he unfolded Sullivan's message. It showed that Bland had evidently delayed to estimate the number of the British and sent a verbal message to Sullivan, who wrote nearly an hour later:

"Two o'clock, P. M.

"Dear General, Colonel Bland has this moment sent me word, that the enemy are in the rear of my right about two miles, coming down. There are, he says, about two brigades of them.   He also says he saw a dust back in the country for above an hour.   I am, &c.

John Sullivan." [12]

This was sickening, no less.   Howe had done it again! Once more, as on Long Island, he had worked in round behind Sullivan unnoticed.   In front of Washington was Knyphausen, pretending to advance, pretending to retire, just as the Hessian De Heister had done at Long Island, waiting only for the signal guns from the rear.   And now they were bound to boom at any moment.

Major Ganoe has explained Howe's maneuver as "pinching."   Knyphausen was the thumb, Howe the long forefinger coming round.[13]   Washington was pinched out, and a few moments of delay might mean that he was pinched in, caught, strangled.

It was cruelly hot now and men were dropping here and there from the heat, but his sweat must have turned cold. Foreseeing the familiar panic, he ordered Greene to make all possible speed in a slanting line to the northwest, place himself across the probable line of fugitives and hold the road to Philadelphia so that Howe should not pen him in on this narrow peninsula between the British army and the British fleet.

While Greene called his brigadiers, Weedon and Muhlenberg, to put their brigades in motion Washington turned over the guarding of the ford to Anthony Wayne and Proctor's batteries, and ordered the rest of the artillery to follow him.

Knyphausen saw most of the American artillery wheeling off to the right as Greene got under way with magnificent energy and struck out through the woods with his men on a trot.   He broke many records, and one brigade of his infantry, as he says himself, marched and ran "between three and four miles in forty-five minutes." [14]

Washington determined, of course, to get into the thick of the stampede, but he did not know his way in this wilderness. Among the farmers standing about gaping at the Yankee rebels, was an old man named Joseph Brown. Washington asked him to lead the way to Sullivan's troops by the shortest road. Brown was aged and unwilling, Washington was insistent. Brown made many excuses. Finally one of the staff swung from the saddle, drew his sword and threatened to run it through the old man if he did not mount in his place and guide the general to the battleground. It was about three miles as the crow flies and Brown might have thought he was on one as his mount soared the fences, swerved around the trees, clattered over the rocks and leapt the gullies. Washington's big horse kept his nose at the flank of Brown's and Washington's voice kept up a constant:

"Push along, old man! Push along, old man!"

Behind him was the long tail of the staff. They came out on the road half a mile west of Dilworth town, which lay between Chads's Ford and Philadelphia. Here the battle was so close that Washington had no further need of Joseph Brown, who fell off, abandoning the horse and the field of glory.[15]

Washington found before him an unusually fine example of the art of jumbling troops. If Howe and Cornwallis had not stopped for dinner, Washington would have been captured probably. But a seventeen-mile march beginning at daybreak had wearied the men of whom Howe was always so careful, so he had called a halt for food and repose behind Osborne's hill.

There is a remarkably clear picture of this scene painted by Joseph Townsend, who saw it as a young man of twenty-one. The Quakers, evicted from the Birmingham Meeting House by Washington's surgeons when they took it over for a hospital, held their midweek meeting in a wheelwright's shop. As they dispersed the British came out of the woods.

"In a few minutes the fields were literally covered over with them, and they were hastening towards us. Their arms and bayonets being raised, shone as bright as silver. . . .

"They inquired what sort of a man Mr. Washington was. My brother had a knowledge of him by being with him at his quarters at Chadd's Ford, and replied that he was a stately, well proportioned, fine looking man, of great ability, active, firm and resolute, of a social disposition, and was considered to be a good man . . . to which one of them answered 'that he might be a good man, but he was most damnably misled to take up arms against his sovereign.' "

The boys also caught sight of General Howe:

"He was mounted on a large English horse much reduced in flesh, I suppose from their being so long confined on board the fleet. . . . The general was a large, portly man, of coarse features. He appeared to have lost his teeth, as his mouth had fallen in." [16]

When Sullivan learned that the enemy was in back of him, he was confronted with what General Carrington calls "one of the most difficult elements of Grand Tactics,—defined in the Preface as the 'Art of handling force on the battlefield,' . . . The best troops in the world would have found it slow of execution, while no less vital to success in the existing emergency." [17]

In the American army of that time the maneuver was more awkwardly managed than in Europe, and even Lafayette ridiculed the method. But at best it is not simple.

Unless such difficulties are realized, the supreme test of battles and the nature of their procedure cannot be grasped. Sullivan's problem was easy to state and almost impossible to perform without hopeless entanglements even on a parade ground. His men had been lying along a creek winding through a forest when he learned that the enemy were marching toward him in a line parallel to his and back of it. He must now pick up all those thousands of men spread out for miles from northwest to southeast, direct them and set them down on a high ridge running from southwest to northeast. He must break the line into its elements and set the elements to marching on separate slanting routes to a new alignment at right angles to their present position.

The simplest way to do this was to command them to fall in, change from line to column, march forward a mile or two, execute a simple column right, march a mile or two further, swing from column to line and halt.

But this was out of the question with the enemy coming forward all the while in battle formation, muskets popping and cannon belching. One of the most inevitable rules of warfare forbids marching in column along a hostile front; it simply means the presentation of a long slowly moving target to the foe.

What Sullivan had to do was to move his brigades, regiments and platoons (keeping their faces to the enemy) so that when they arrived their present right would still be on the right like separate chessmen from one side of the board to the cater-corner side. The thing is so involved and requires so much coolness, obedience and indifference to bullets that only long practice on the drill ground enables officers and men to manage it there, not to speak of the battlefield.

Because the general public knows nothing of military machinery it can never be brought to visualize these difficulties, and thinks them silly. Hence, army officers who understand the necessity for long drills and strict discipline are prevented from having their way in times of peace and brutally disgraced for their failures in time of war; majestic nations are destroyed and professional soldiers and mercenaries triumph over high-minded, dull-witted pacifists who prefer principles and platitudes to the "saber-rattling" of "militarists."

Because of what he saw on this day and on other days, Washington cried out again and again for preparedness and left the plea as his chief counsel to a nation that has since been as deaf as it was then. Because he could not persuade his own fellow-citizens to give him a regular army and let it be well drilled for such emergencies as this, he was compelled to see the cause he loved sink deeper and deeper under defeat after defeat until it had finally to look to a foreign monarchy to save it.

It was because of such scenes as Washington saw before him when he galloped through the woods above the Brandywine that he sympathized with such martyrs as Sullivan, a brave man, a devoted patriot, subjected to the most cancerous torment and the most withering humiliations because he sought the post of greatest danger and the heaviest responsibility. He was even now under the eye of a politician, Congressman Burke, who was sneering at him and preparing new degradations for him.

Sweating with heat and wrath at his incompetent scouts, Sullivan flung himself at the solution of his hopeless problem in the bitter knowledge that his men and officers had lost confidence in him and that his infernally bad luck had not yet ceased to make him play the pitiful clown in tragedy after tragedy. Just because he was so humiliated his pride was a frenzy, and his complex problem was insanely concerned with military etiquette, one of those miserable contests that are accounted contemptible among jealous actresses jostling for the center of the stage and the spotlight. They are just as common in other professions, and nowhere more than on battlefields for liberty. On the battlefield, the place of honor is not the center but the extreme right.

As Sullivan bravely dashed for this sacred post, the fussy old Chevalier de Borré, one of Congress's imported fops from France, who had arrived but the other day, set out for the right, and claimed it with voluble broken English. Sullivan sputtered his Maine dialect in vain. Brave old de Borré pushed in ahead of him.

A happy thought struck Sullivan. By taking a roundabout route on a great arc he would come in at the right of the Frenchman after all. He made a détour, of nearly two miles according to the watchful Congressman Burke, only to reach the ground too late to beat the Frenchman and too late to arrange his own troops, especially as he and Milord Stirling had had another contredanse as to their relative positions. They were friends and it was "After you, My Lord," and "After you, Mr. Sullivan," until the British were on them, before they had time to dig in or deploy properly. As a result of all this, Sullivan left a gap of half a mile in the line and the British caught him with his left flank exposed.[18]

Having dined comfortably the British came around Osborne's hill at half past three, in three columns with reserves a little aft. They had a steep rise to climb to reach the American position near the Birmingham Meeting House, in whose walls the bullets left many a mark and on whose floors the bloodstains of the wounded are still pointed out.

What the British saw is described by Captain Montresor who found the new line in a position, "remarkably strong, having a large body advanced, small bodies still further advanced and their Rear covered by a wood wherein their main body was posted with a natural glacis for ¾ of a mile." [19]

A New Jersey surgeon, Ebenezer Elmer, paints the American picture:

"A large Column Came on in front playing ye Granediers March & Now the Battle began w^h proved Excessive severe the Enemy Came on with fury our men stood firing upon them most amazingly, killing almost all before them for near an hour till they got within 6 rod of each other, when a Column of the Enemy came upon our right flank w^h Caused y^m to give w^h soon extended all along ye line." [20]

During this fierce work about the Birmingham Meeting House, the Sixth Pennsylvania Regiment had the help of a number of soldiers' wives and girls, devoted camp-followers who repeatedly took the empty canteens from their husbands and friends, ran with them to the creek, filled them and returned with them through the hottest fire in spite of all protests.[21]   These women at least gave a good answer to Washington's comment of August 4th, 1777: "The Multitude of women . . . are a clog on every movement," and his order "to get rid of all such as are not absolutely necessary." [22]

The Seventh Virginia was nearly cut to pieces, and reduced to two hundred men almost too exhausted to retreat. The twenty-one-year-old Major Cropper, a friend of Washington's, though bayoneted in the thigh, finding that his flag had been captured, tied his red bandana handkerchief to a ramrod and hoisted it for a standard, and limped away with his men. The Virginia general Woodford leapt from his horse to embrace him, crying, "The boy we thought lost is found!" and Washington publicly commended him.[28]

Sullivan had one grim consolation: de Borré's men (mostly from Maryland) broke first. The old Gaul was fearless and did his best, though wounded, but his men overran him and swept him away with such precipitance that afterward Congress invited him to stand court-martial. He answered, "The Americans won't fight!" resigned and went back to France to match a few ugly facts with the glowing fictions of the American propagandists in Paris.

Sullivan's men did not last much longer than de Borré's, and he also was soon offering to resign to escape Congressional punishment. He was not even spared the knowledge that even now in the busiest hour of his life, Congressman Burke, riding about and watching him with a jaundiced eye, was occasionally trying to rally some of Sullivan's fugitives for him.

Everybody questioned Sullivan's generalship but nobody doubted his courage and energy. While the shuttling fragments of his division were settling into what places they would under fire, many of them refused the test and fell away. He tells the story himself in his letter to Congress:

"No sooner did I form one party, but that which I had before formed ran off, and even at times when I, though on horseback and in front of them, apprehended no danger. I then left them to be rallied by their own officers and my aide-de-camps; I repaired to the hill where our artillery was, which by this time began to feel the effects of the enemy's fire. This hill commanded both the right and left of our line, and, if carried by the enemy, I knew would instantly bring on a total rout, and make a retreat very difficult. . . .

"Lord Stirling and General Conway, with their aide-de-camps, were with me on the hill, and exerted themselves beyond description to keep up the troops. Five times did the enemy drive our troops from the hill, and as often was it regained, . . . General Conway, who has seen much service, says he never saw so close and severe a fire. . . . When we found the right and left oppressed by numbers and giving way on all quarters, we were obliged to abandon the hill we had so long contended for, but not till we had almost covered the ground between that and Birmingham meeting-house, with the dead bodies of the enemy." [24]

With all he had to do, Washington, in the late afternoon, remembered that the ever-watchful and helpful Congress had ordered him to report twice a day at least.[25] He stopped fighting to write, but refrained from alarming his masters with a description of what was raging about him even then. With thoroughgoing guile he substituted hope for realism:

"*Five o'clock P. M.*—When I had the honor of addressing you this morning, I mentioned that the enemy were advancing, and had begun a cannonade. I would now beg leave to inform you, that they have kept up a brisk fire from their artillery ever since. Their advanced party was attacked by our light troops under General Maxwell, who crossed the Brandywine for that purpose. . . . What loss the enemy sustained cannot be ascertained with precision; but from our situation and briskness of the attack, it is the general opinion, particularly of those who were engaged, that they had at least three hundred men killed and wounded. Our damage is not exactly known; but, from the best accounts we have been able to obtain, it does not exceed fifty in the whole.

"After this affair, the enemy halted upon the heights, where they have remained ever since, except a detachment of them which filed off about eleven o'clock from their left, and which has since passed the Brandywine at Jones's Ford, between five and six miles above Chad's. The amount of it is not known, the accounts respecting it being various, some making it two or three thousand strong and others more. Generals Sullivan, Stirling, and Stephens with their divisions, are gone in pursuit, and to attack it if they can with any prospect of success. . . . At half after four o'clock, the enemy attacked General Sullivan at the ford next above this, and the action has been very violent ever since. It still continues. A very severe cannonade has begun here too; and I suppose we shall have a very hot evening. I hope it will be a happy one." [26]

This is one of the least pessimistic chronicles on record. In the midst of ruin, he was able to say that the morning skirmish at Chads's Ford damaged the British nearly as much as their total losses in the whole day's work, but did not explain how he could imagine that where his side lost fifty, the other lost three hundred. He referred mildly to the British main army as a "detachment" two or three thousand strong—or "more"; —and made the astounding statement that Sullivan, Stirling and Stephen, tactically surprised and almost incapable of defence, had "gone in pursuit."

He closed the fairy story with a dumbfounding allusion to the prospects of "a very hot evening" and the hope that it would be "a happy one." This was not a desperate fable for an hysterical wife, but an official message to Congress. Surely bad news was never more gently broken.

Knyphausen's fumbling with the somewhat tipsy Maxwell had been, of course, pure fooling. The moment he heard Cornwallis' cannon, he had thrown off the mask for a real attack. He had to conquer the ferocious battler, Anthony Wayne, but gradually the Americans were reduced to a frantic and largely unsuccessful effort to carry off their cannon. Wayne was able to get away only because Greene's left wing reached out to shelter him.

General Greene was a real general and did his work superbly. When fugitives rolled back upon him, he held his own men steady, opened his ranks to let the runaways through, then closed them and flung off the pursuers. When he had to fall back, he retired in good order, making approach dangerous. He thus maintained a fine retreating front for an hour and a quarter. He lost a hundred killed and wounded, and as he said himself, "saved hundreds of our people from falling into the enemy's hands," enabled most of the artillery to get off, and helped the left wing to escape. For his reward he had such silence that even he was bitter enough to complain:

"Both the General and the public were as much indebted to me for saving the army from ruin as they have ever been to any one officer in the course of the war; but I was never mentioned upon the occasion." [27]

Washington afterward explained verbally that too much was being said about his partiality to Greene and his complete dependence on him, and he was afraid of openly praising the Virginians who made up Greene's force lest he anger the other colonies. Muhlenberg, too, was hurt by the omission of all mention and Washington's old crony, Weedon, who is also credited with having checked the British and "saved the army from complete rout," [28] is said to have "expostulated warmly with Washington" over the public slight.[29]

Among the distinguished warriors in this whirlpool battle was Count Pulaski, who borrowed some of Washington's own Guard and led them in charges that drove back the British at dangerous crises. The legend is that he had recourse to German in his excitement and shouted:

"Vorwärts, Brüdern, vorwärts!"

The Frenchman, Comte Louis de Fleury, was presented with a horse by Congress for his bravery. The Baron de St. Ouary's gallantry led him too close to the enemy and he was captured. Lafayette had a narrow escape from the same bad luck.

Following Washington he had ridden straight into the press in such a state of battle-rapture that at one time he was within twenty yards of the British. He did not even notice a bullet wound in his left leg below the knee, until after he had dismounted while trying to organize a fleeing pack for resistance. Some officer informed him that he had a bootful of blood. Major de Gimat helped him back into the saddle.[30] Later he had to halt to have it bandaged, but continued riding hard through an indistinguishable cloud of ghosts. He described the scene in his Memoirs:

"The rout became complete . . . In the midst of this horrible confusion and the darkness of night, it was impossible to recognize one another; but at Chester, twelve miles from the battlefield, there was a bridge that had to be crossed. Lafayette busied himself with stopping the fugitives at this spot; order was a little reestablished, the Commander-in-Chief and the generals arrived, and Lafayette had time to have his wound dressed." [31]

He himself tells how Washington asked the surgeon to give him special care, saying:

"Treat him as if he were my son; for I love him as if he were."

He was helpless for six weeks, but wrote to his wife with his inextinguishable felicity: "Messieurs the English have gratified me with a bullet!" and again:

"Dear Heart: . . . Let me tell you about my wound; it is a mere flesh wound, and does not touch bone or nerve. The surgeons are amazed at its healing so quickly. They fall into an ecstasy at every dressing, and say that it is the loveliest thing in the world. For my part, I think that it is ugly, a nuisance, and painful enough; but it is all a matter of taste. . . . There, dear Heart, is the story of what I pompously call my wound in order to give myself airs and make myself interesting." [32]

Lafayette was a slim youth with a child for a wife, but the Falstaffian Knox wrote equal tenderness to his huge spouse:

"My dear girl will be happy to hear of her Harry's safety; for, my Lucy, Heaven, who is our guide, has protected him in the day of battle. You will hear with this letter of the most severe action that has been fought this war between our army and the enemy. Our people behaved well, but Heaven frowned on us in a degree. We were obliged to retire after very considerable slaughter of the enemy: they dared not pursue a single step." [33]

Washington probably wrote as sweetly to his "dear Patsy," but she burned his words. At midnight he was too exhausted to write to anybody. Even when he remembered Congress he asked his aide Harrison to write the report. Harrison was so "distressed" that he passed the responsibility on to the new Adjutant-General Pickering, who made a brief statement and

took it to Washington at the Pennsylvania Arms in Chester
before Washington rode further north to sleep in the old stone
house of John McIlwain in the present village of Leiperville.
Washington asked him "to add a consolatory hope that another
day would give a more fortunate result." Pickering drafted
a brief official account ending:

"Notwithstanding the misfortune of the day, I am happy to find the
troops in good spirits; and I hope another time we shall compensate
for the losses now sustained." [34]

Pickering also made a mental note which he wrote down
long afterward:
"Thus the day was closed. In the course of it, I had observed nothing which indicated commanding talents in the
General." [35]
In spite of the "consolatory hope" injected into Washington's report, Clinton wrote: "Washington's was the most *beaten
letter* ever read." [36]
He had been forced to abandon his wounded as well as the
field and the next morning came a polite note from the serene
Mr. Howe inviting him to send surgeons to care for his
men, "as I shall not be so situated as to give them the necessary relief." Washington replied with equal politeness and
sent Doctor Rush and three others. [37]
Howe gave his own loss as 8 officers, 7 sergeants and 74
privates killed; 48 officers, 40 sergeants, 5 drummers and 395
privates wounded, 6 missing. This includes the slight Hessian
losses and is official. [38] He claimed to have taken "near four
hundred prisoners" and to have inflicted a total loss of about
three hundred killed and six hundred wounded on the Americans.
Greene estimated the American loss at twelve hundred
killed, wounded and missing.
A general's estimate of an enemy's numbers and losses is
almost invariably false, but his official reports home have to
be fairly accurate because of the bookkeeping involved, the

payrolls, the ration returns, replacements, requisitions, and other considerations. Howe's statement should, therefore, be accepted, as also his claim to have taken eleven cannon from the Americans, including two of the six captured at Trenton.[39]

Washington had never yet made an official report of losses, and since he had to keep his propaganda cheerful or destroy the public confidence on which he relied, he was compelled to continue the policy he maintained throughout the war of magnifying his numbers and minimizing his losses.

Lieutenant John Marshall, afterwards the Chief Justice (who was present at the battle, retired only when his horse had been wounded twice and lived to write a life of his chief), admits that the American loss was greater than the British and says of the propaganda following this battle:

"The opinion was carefully cherished that the British had gained only the ground; and that their loss was still more considerable than had been sustained by the Americans."[40]

But there was great dejection since even the most highly colored reports after the battle differed so woefully from the big talk that preceded it. John Adams had written to his wife on August 29th:

"Howe will make but a pitiful figure. . . . The Continental army . . . is in my opinion more numerous by several thousands than Howe's whole force. I am afraid that he will be frightened, and run on board his ships, and go away plundering to some other place. I almost wish he had Philadelphia, for then he could not get away."[41]

Before the battle Alexander Hamilton had written a prophecy of victory in case Washington fought, and declared, "We shall, I hope, have twice the enemy's numbers."[42] Many had expected that the army would, as Alexander Graydon expressed it, "surround and make a breakfast of Mr. Howe and his mercenaries." Now the wonder was:

"Could not a population of two millions of souls have furnished fighting whigs enough for the purpose? Where were the multitudes which used to appear in arms, in the commons of Philadelphia? Where

the legions of New-England men that hemmed in Gage at Boston?
Where, in short, the hundred and fifty thousand men in arms throughout the continent, spoken of by gen. Lee and others, at the beginning
of the contest?" [43]

The contrasts between boasts and reality were nauseating,
for everybody realized that once more Washington owed his
salvation and the existence of his army to the temperance in
victory of General Howe, to whom no monuments have ever
been erected, though the Bostonians put a monument to his
eldest brother in Westminster Abbey because of his mere kindliness. Yet what did he ever do for Americans compared to
Sir William? Tom Paine was soon broadcasting that question
in a vitriolic pamphlet, in which he said that very thing:

"Sir William has undoubtedly merited a monument; but of what
kind, or with what inscription, where placed or how embellished, is
a question that would puzzle all the heralds of St. James's." [44]

The Americans were so irritated by Howe that they seemed
unable to forgive him for not destroying them. The British
naturally were ravenous for his blood.

Du Portail said, "If the English had followed their advantage that day, Washington's army would have been spoken of
no more." [45]

Howe wrote to Germain that his troops were worn out with
the twelve-mile march and the battle, but he added:

"The Enemy's Army escaped a total Overthrow, that must have
been the Consequence of an Hours more Day Light." [46]

While Washington escaped open censure, there was an increasing feeling that he was fatally unlucky and since few
quite dared to assail him his officers were attacked as whipping
boys in his stead.

This Congressman who had been "amang 'em takin' notes,"
Mr. Burke of North Carolina, had defended Schuyler in vain
and now attacked Sullivan as too "unfortunate," too wanting
in military genius and too much of a "marplot" to be left in

command longer. Sullivan wrote him a hot letter and received a cold reply detailing what Burke had heard and seen, and implying distrust of Washington:

"I heard officers in the field lamenting in the bitterest terms that they were cursed with such a commander; and I overheard numbers during the retreat complain of you as an officer whose evil conduct was forever productive of misfortunes to the army . . . you have not sufficient talents for your rank and office. . . . Nor do I think you the only officer in our army who is deficient in them. Nor were my endeavours to free the army from insufficient officers intended to be confined to you." [47]

Sullivan wrote to Washington and Washington not only wrote to him with friendship and justice, but went further and administered a most uncharacteristic rebuke to Congress for meddling with his officers in such a crisis:

"Tho. I would willingly pay every attention to the Resolutions of Congress, yet in the late instance, respecting the recall of Genl. Sullivan I must beg leave to defer giving any order about it, till I hear further from that Honble. Body. Our situation at this time is critical and delicate, and nothing should be done to add to its embarrassments. We are now most probably on the point of another action, and to derange the Army by withdrawing so many Genl. Officers from it, may and must be attended with many disagreeable, if not ruinous consequences. . . . And, I am obliged to observe, in justice to my own Character, that I can not be answerable for the consequences which may arise from a want of Officers to assist me." [48]

Washington had added another black wreath to his laurels without disturbing them. A few years later the Marquis de Chastellux visited the battlefield of the Brandywine with Lafayette and a number of Frenchmen, and went over the whole ground carefully. De Chastellux finds no fault with Washington's conduct of and in this battle, but makes this fine comment:

"When a general has foreseen every thing, when he has made the best possible dispositions, and his activity, his judgment, and his courage in the action correspond with the wisdom of his measures, has he not already triumphed in the eyes of every impartial judge? and if by any unforeseen accidents, the laurels he has merited drop from his hands, is it not the historian's duty carefully to collect, and replace them on his brow?" [49]

XVIII

HE TRIES TO SAVE PHILADELPHIA

IN spite of the disaster on the Brandywine, the watchword of the day was Washington's assurance that the troops were "in good spirits."

To keep them so, "The Honb!e Congress in Consideration of the Gallant behaviour of the Troops on Thursday last their fatigue since & from a full Conviction that on every future occasion they will manifest a bravery worthy the cause they have undertaken to defend," was "pleas'd to order 30 Hhds. of Rum to be distributed among them in such a manner as the Commander in Chief shall direct." [1]

The only good military news was from the North, where General Gates was arousing enormous enthusiasm and gleaning all the credit for dealing mortal blows at Burgoyne. Washington published these bulletins and made them festival:

"To Celebrate this Success, The Gen! orders that at 4 oCl. this Afternoon, All the troops be paraded & Serv'd with a Gill of Rum pr Man." [2]

It was at this time that John Adams paid Washington a quaint tribute for taking a further share in the hardships of his men, and the needed economy of the people:

"General Washington sets a fine example. He has banished wine from his table, and entertains his friends with rum and water. This is much to the honor of his wisdom, his policy, and his patriotism. And the example must be followed by banishing sugar and all imported articles from our families. If necessity should reduce us to a simplicity of dress and diet becoming republicans, it would be a happy and glorious necessity." [3]

Extreme simplicity of dress had certainly been reached by the soldiers, for Washington had persuaded them to discard all their baggage except their blankets and they had left most of those on the field at Brandywine. His troops were in such a state of nakedness that he had to send Hamilton on an expedition to Philadelphia carrying a begging letter for clothes with a menace of threat for help.[4]

His men were exactly in the condition described by General Jedediah Huntington, who had just made a similar appeal for the garrison at Peekskill:

"The Troops are bare footed, bare leg'd and almost bare a—d do procure all the Shoes, Stocking and breeches possible Linnen Overalls even for Winter, will be serviceable as they hide Rags."[5]

The hot weather turned bleak, and sharp rains not only lashed Washington's men but thwarted his plans, for he had not given up his determination to stop Howe. The day after Brandywine he left Chester, which was in a panic that spread like wildfire to Philadelphia, and set Congress to packing for another moving-day. By Saturday, the thirteenth, Washington was right back where he had started from on the joyous parade through Philadelphia—at Schuylkill Falls, five miles north of Philadelphia.

On Sunday he turned the army round, crossed the Schuylkill again through waist-deep water, and headed west "to get between the Enemy and the Swedes' Ford, and to prevent them from turning our right flank, which they seem to have a violent inclination to effect."[6]

Howe's men had hardly stirred on the day after the battle, and Montresor noted that "the peasants" were "employed in burying the dead Rebels . . . who have now become very offensive."[7]

Howe moved slowly northwest, trying to squeeze Washington west, cut him off from Philadelphia and perhaps crush him before taking over the city. In this strongly loyalist country, Howe was generally treated as the savior and Washington as the hated invader. The Tories were as a cloud of spies about every step Washington took, and he could gain no trustworthy information from them. But he was still eager for a battle on his own terms and pushed along the old Lancaster road approaching the Brandywine again at Warren Tavern, north of the hateful forks. He spent the night of September 15th, 1777, near there in the home of Joseph Malin.[8]

The next morning, he sent off his baggage in the expectation of battle and ordered Count Pulaski with the cavalry to uncover the British advance parties. Colonel Bentalou, who served with him, describes a clash he had with Alexander Hamilton who doubted his word when he brought news that the whole British army was near:

"Washington apologized for his aid, remarking that he was a young man, who had no intention to offend him; and then naturally said to Pulaski, 'Count, what would you advise?' or something to that effect.

"Pulaski replied, that he thought a detachment of about three hundred infantry, with the cavalry he had with him, could retard the enemy's approach sufficiently to give time to prepare for their reception. The detachment was instantly ordered out, under the command of Brigadier-General Scott, and, in great bustle and hurry, the whole army moved on to form the lines." [9]

This body of 300, according to Adjutant-General Pickering, "shamefully fled at the first fire." [10]

Howe with his usual ingenuity seized high ground near the White House tavern, and easily beat off an attack on his right by Anthony Wayne. Then it began to rain. It rained famously. Luckily it was driving into the faces of the advancing British, for whom the Americans had no other bullets. Their powder was soaked so promptly and thoroughly that not a flint would snap. The British arms were equally useless and the battle had to be called off—"fortunately for the American army," says Adjutant-General Pickering, who added another poor opinion of Washington to his impressions at Brandywine. He gives an unflattering portrait of his chief in a letter he wrote long afterward, describing what happened after the picket had fled:

"Having been in the army but just three months, and in that

time not having found it possible to accost the General with ease (altho' I could converse without difficulty with every other general officer); and being naturally diffident; you will imagine how urgent was the occasion when I could address him in this language;

" 'Sir, the advancing of the British is manifest by the reports of the musketry. The order of battle is not completed. If we are to fight the enemy on this ground, the troops ought to be immediately arranged. If we are to take the high grounds on the other side of the valley, we ought to march immediately, or the enemy may fall upon us in the midst of our movement. *Pray, Sir, decide.*'

" 'Let us move'—was the General's instant answer."

Of another occasion during a night march, Pickering says:

"General Greene and I fell together, in the rear of the army. In that situation I thus accosted him,

" 'General Greene, I had once conceived an exalted opinion of General Washington's military talents; but since I have been in the army I have seen nothing to enhance that opinion.' In fact, it was lowered, and so Greene must have understood me; for he answered promptly and precisely in these words—

" 'Why the General does want decision: for my part, I decide in a moment.' " [11]

On the 17th of September Congress had made another of its ghastly bestowals of dictatorship with the usual string to it. He was to be emperor for sixty days only.[12]

On the 18th the Dictator resumed his rain-march. Always hoping to deal a lucky blow, even while he dodged and side-stepped, Washington dreamed of cutting off Howe's baggage train and crippling his rear guard. He entrusted this ticklish business to Anthony Wayne, who heeled Howe's army, looking for his chance. Wayne wrote to Washington from near the tavern of Paoli on the Lancaster road:

"There never was, nor never will be a finer opportunity of giving the enemy a fatal blow than the present—for God's sake push on as fast as possible.

"We only want you in their rear to complete Mr. Howe's business. I believe he knows nothing of my situation, as I have taken every precaution to prevent any intelligence getting to him." [13]

But Howe knew all the while. The Tories gave him eyes everywhere. The next night Wayne's force was surprised by General Grey and so nearly wiped out that the affair has since been known as the "Paoli Massacre." To prevent his soldiers from using anything but the silent bayonet, Grey took their flints from them and was ever after known as "No-Flint" Grey. A shudder of horror went over the people as the story of the disaster grew. Wayne was promptly court-martialed for criminal negligence and replied hotly that, while he was beaten, he was not even surprised.

On the 18th Alexander Hamilton, sent with some horsemen to cross the Schuylkill and destroy a stock of flour near the Valley Forge before the British could capture it, ran into them and was forced to flee across the river. He wrote at once to Congress:

"If Congress have not left Philadelphia they ought to do it immediately without fail; for the enemy have the means of throwing a party this night into the city." [14]

At 9 o'clock, he wrote again and his letters reached Philadelphia about midnight. The Congressmen were routed out of their beds at two or three A.M. and went scurrying off to Lancaster by way of Trenton. John Adams confided to his diary the growing distrust:

"O, Heaven! grant us one great soul! One leading mind would extricate the best cause from that ruin which seems to await it for the want of it. We have as good a cause as ever was fought for; we have great resources; the people are well tempered; one active, masterly capacity, would bring order out of this confusion, and save this country." [15]

After collecting slowly at Lancaster, Congress decided that the town was too near the danger of interruption and moved on to York, Pennsylvania, in angry impatience with Washington, who did his best with what hungry, soggy men he had. They were not enough to cope with Howe's united army and on the 23rd he wrote from a camp near the present Pottstown to Putnam to send him reinforcements from the Hudson, amounting to "twenty-five hundred privates and non-commissioned fit for duty. . . .

"Send on this detachment without the least possible delay. No considerations are to prevent it. It is our first object to defeat, if possible, the army now opposed to us here." [16]

To replace these troops he ordered Putnam to "get what aid you can from the militia." He soon had reason to regret this stripping of the forts. On the 24th he wrote to Gates, a letter whose inditing could not have given him any pleasure:

"Sir, This army has not been able to oppose General Howe's with the success that was wished, and needs a reinforcement. I therefore request, if you have been so fortunate as to oblige General Burgoyne to retreat to Ticonderoga, or if you have not and circumstances will admit, that you will order Colonel Morgan to join me again with his corps. . . . You will perceive, I do not mention this by way of command, but leave you to determine upon it according to your situation." [17]

It took this letter twelve days to reach Gates, who described his deadlock with Burgoyne, and added that he could not spare Morgan.[18]

Howe passed through the Valley Forge on the 21st, set fire to it and destroyed it, then crossed the Schuylkill again. On the 25th he entered Germantown in a windy rain. On September 26th, 1777, he sent Cornwallis to take possession of Philadelphia. Cornwallis entered the city at 10 in the morning "amidst the acclamation of some thousands of the inhabitants mostly women and children." [19]

The rebels still had two strong forts, Fort Mercer, at Red Bank, New Jersey, and Fort Mifflin, on Mud Island nearly opposite, guarding the river, the bed of which was filled with obstructions, so that Howe was out of touch with the fleet and

the sea from whence must come his supplies.[20]   The necessity
he was under of clearing the Delaware compelled him to divide
his troops or perish.

Washington watched like a hawk for another chance to
swoop down on a detached garrison as at Trenton, but he also
had to scatter his own forces on the opposite side of the Delaware, all about Philadelphia, and as garrisons for the forts.
Having moved from Pottsgrove on September 26th to Pennypacker's Mills, where he made his headquarters in the stone
house of Samuel Pennypacker, he went to a council of war and
proposed an immediate attack on the British.   Seventeen officers
were gathered together, fifteen of them voting.   All but five
were in favor of waiting for more reinforcements.

On October 3, 1777, he had the luck to intercept two British
letters, indicating that Howe had drawn off a part of his forces
and sent them across the river into New Jersey to attack Bill-
ingsport.   Then in the words of the Marquis de Chastellux,
who went over the battlefield a few years later:

"General Washington thought it was time to remind the English,
that there still existed an American army. One is at a loss whether most
to extol the sage intrepidity of the chief, or the resolution displayed by
his army in making an attack on the same troops, whose shock they
were unable to sustain a month before." [21]

Chastellux discussed this battle with Washington and many
participants, and he assigns less than 4,000 British to the town,
though others give far more.[22]

The American force is also variously described.   On September 28th Washington informed the council of war that he had
8,000 Continental troops and 3,000 militia.   Knox says, "We
were more numerous after the battle of Brandywine than before." [23]

Washington's battle plan would seem to be final evidence
that he greatly outnumbered the British, for he laid out an
assault in four directions, and it would seem hardly sane to
attempt with inferior numbers to surround an enemy.   To

credit the British with equal or greater numbers implies in Washington an astounding audacity and an amazing confidence in the ability of his troops to divide into four parts and crush a superior enemy. Yet he definitely states in at least three letters that he had fewer men than Howe at Germantown. It is confusing at best.[24]

XIX

THE BATTLE OF GERMANTOWN

FOURTEEN miles is a long night-march with a battle instead of a breakfast waiting at the end of it. Before the business was over, the luckiest of Washington's men plodded "upwards of thirty miles without rest, besides being up all the preceding night without sleep." Lieutenant Mc-Michael wrote in his Diary that he "marched in twenty-four hours 45 miles, and in that time fought four hours, during which we advanced so furiously thru' buckwheat fields, that it was almost an unspeakable fatigue." [1]

The patriots were helped along at first by the dream that Germantown was to be another Trenton. At Trenton the garrison had been celebrating Christmas and the colonel was still drunk when the Americans arrived. At Germantown it was the Americans who had been drinking—many of them too much. Two lieutenants and one general were drunk enough to be cashiered by court-martial afterwards. Others escaped court-martial by being captured, for André says:

"The Rebels were each equipped with a piece of white paper in his hat, which made us imagine they meant a surprise by night . . . the power of strong liquors had been employed. Several, not only of their Soldiers but Officers, were intoxicated when they fell into our hands." [2]

Washington's plans for this battle were far the most elaborate he ever made. For that reason they have been criticized with a severity that has not often been exercised against his conduct. [3]

We have a drawing of this "disposition of the American Army for Battle." [4] The design is of the simplest. It resembles somewhat Hannibal's half-moon formation at Cannae nearly two thousand years before, except that Hannibal put his weakest force in the centre and achieved the miracle of surrounding a superior number with an inferior, then nearly annihilating it. Ten years later a Roman, Scipio Africanus, returned the insult. He also put his strongest troops in the wings, his weakest in the center, then with forty-eight thousand men practically annihilated seventy-four thousand Carthaginians at Ilipa in Spain.[5]

Washington put his strongest troops in the center. His plan shows a center of two wings; Sullivan commanded the right which was made up of four brigades; on account of the grave shortage of general officers, only one brigade had a general in command—Anthony Wayne. The left center wing was commanded by Nathanael Greene, whose four brigades were commanded from left to right by Generals Weedon, Muhlenberg, Scott, and Woodford.

To the right of the right wing three brigades of militia under General Armstrong extended in a slanting line. To the left of the left wing was another slanting line of militia. In the rear of the center marched Lord Stirling commanding the reserves, composed of the brigades of Nash and Maxwell.

With this formation Washington proposed to rush down on Germantown at daybreak. His army might be compared to a huge crab advancing with claws outstretched to reach round the enemy and close him in. The only trouble was that this crab was to go into battle in four different parts down four different roads and assemble during the battle. This would have been asking a good deal even of the lengendary glass snake, which collected itself only after the battle was over. It was important, too, that the claws of Washington's army should be strong and should work around well ahead of the body. This task, being entrusted to the militia, and on very bad roads, could hardly have been expected to succeed.

The plan might have worked at that as a surprise, but for the refusal of the British to sit still while it developed. Then there was the fog also and an exceedingly solid house that stood at a strategical point near the head of the road into Ger-

mantown, a mile from the camp of the British army.   This
house was stout as a fort, though it had been built as the residence of Benjamin Chew, chief justice of Pennsylvania and
Washington's friend for years.   Both had long agreed that
independency was unthinkable, but Chew had not been elastic
enough to change his mind, and, just before Washington
reached Philadelphia, Chew had been arrested and shipped to
Fredericksburg, Virginia, with many wagonloads of Quakers.
Washington was soon wishing that Chew had taken his house
with him.

His plan proposed to employ all four of the roads leading
towards Germantown, though the outside roads were seven
miles apart.   He assigned one of these highways to each of his
four columns and set down the most elaborate and exact directions as to their actions and destinations—thus for the militia:

"General Armstrong to pass down the Ridge Road by Levering's
Tavern and take guides to cross Wissahiccon Creek about the head of
John Vandeerings mill dam so as to fall in about Jos[h] Warners new
house.

"Smalwood and Foreman to pass down by a Mill, formerly Daniel
Morriss's and Jacob Edjes Mill into the White marsh Road, at the
Sandy Run—thence to white Marsh Church—there take the left hand
road which leads to Jenkins's Tavern on the old York Road, then keep
down the old York Road below Armitages beyond the Seven mile
Stone; half a mile from which, a Road turns off short to the Right
hand fenc'd on both sides, which leads through Enemy's Encampment
at Germantown Market House." [6]

A pretty plan and it would have won a prize in a sham
battle.   Washington had even arranged to have two distant
bodies of troops make a noisy pretence of attack on Philadelphia so that Lord Cornwallis would not hurry out to reinforce
Germantown.[7]   Washington had thought of a hundred things
and provided for and against them.

But the Providence that watched over him took a day off,
and the Providence that watched over the British thought of
a hundred things that Washington had not foreseen.   It even
plagiarized the idea of a protective fog from the legends of

Long Island. This fog, as Light Horse Harry Lee points out, "withheld from us the important advantage resulting to assailing troops from a clear view of the enemy's incipient measures to repel the assault."[8]

Washington's army did not even reach the field on time or in order. This was not surprising in view of the length of the night march. What general would not wear himself out keeping himself and his sleepy soldiers awake and in column all night; trying to find Vandeering's mill dam in the dark so as to fall in about Josh Warner's new house, or the road that turned off short to the right half a mile from the Seven Mile Stone?

There was such befuddlement before, during and afterward that various generals differed over an hour in their estimates of the time spent in an unusually brief battle, and differed by miles in their statements as to the unusually small ground covered.[9]

Howe made a speech before the House of Commons defending all his actions and inactions and his failure to throw up even a breastwork:

"The Affair of German Town has been maliciously called a Surprize—Indeed I did not expect the Enemy to approach so soon after so recent a defeat, but we had early notice of their Intention. I made no Works because it argued an Inferiority, & was a great Fatigue to the Troops . . . the Army was not surprized."[10]

Against this was Howe's own statement that "the patroles discovered the enemy's approach and the army was immediately ordered under arms." It was also alleged that General Grant had to force his way to Howe's presence and it was claimed that, if it had not been for Musgrave, " 'Tis likely our active hero might have been surprised in bed," for "he was deeply engaged somewhere, or with somebody."[11] This somebody was, of course, Mrs. Loring, once more zealous for the rebel cause. It was charged that Howe had been gambling all night and had turned in only an hour before he was turned out.

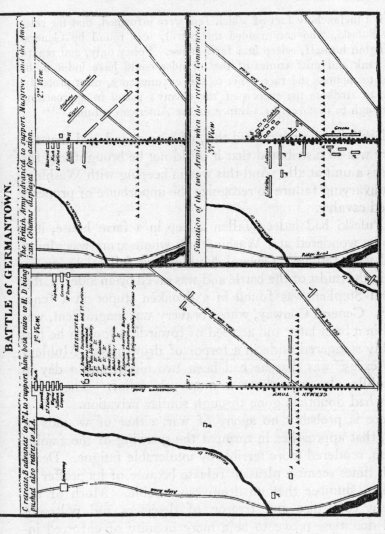

THE BATTLE OF GERMANTOWN.

This map shows vividly the three phases of the battle: 1st, the advance of the Americans; 2nd, the hold-up at the Chew House; 3rd, the jumble of Wayne's and Stephen's troops just before the general retreat.

(From Johnson's *Life of Greene*.)

Howe's claim that his patrols were the more alert is supported by the American testimony of Johnson in his "Life of Greene":

"It is a melancholy fact of which few were informed, that the celebrated Pulaski, who commanded the patrol, was found by General Washington himself, asleep in a farm house. Policy only, and regard to the rank and misfortunes of the offender could have induced the general to suppress the fact. Yet to this circumstance, most probably, we are to attribute the success of the enemy's patrol in approaching near enough to discover the advance of the American column." [12]

Pulaski's vindicator denied this, of course, and said that the cavalry was so distributed that it could not be brought into the action as a unit at all. And this was in keeping with Washington's unvarying failure to recognize the importance of properly handled cavalry.

If Pulaski had indeed fallen asleep in a farm house, it is not to be wondered at. Washington's whole army was almost ruined with fatigue. General Muhlenberg fell asleep on his horse in the midst of the battle and was saved by an aide. Later General Stephen was found in a drunken stupor in a fence corner. General Conway, whose bravery was magnificent, was found in a barn later and accused of cowardice, though he had probably staggered aside in a torpor of drowsiness. Muhlenberg's excuse was that he had been two nights and a day in the saddle almost without a moment's relief. The other officers had doubtless gone through similar privation.

There is probably no agony of war, either of wounds or terror, that approaches in torment the gnawing of the famine of sleep, rendered more terrible by intolerable fatigue. Death at such times seems a pleasant release because of its proffer of unbroken slumber that no drum can trouble. Much of the apparent cowardice and treason of deserters and poltroons would doubtless prove to be a mere insanity of enforced insomnia, if anybody cared to enquire. John C. Fitzpatrick says that "Washington could have obtained hardly more than three consecutive hours of sleep in any twenty-four during the eight years of the Revolutionary War." [13]   He was doubtless as haggard-eyed as the rest at Germantown, but responsibility and opportunity kept him going.

With cockcrow, vanished Washington's dream of an impetuous charge pouring in from all directions and repeating the Paoli surprise on a grand scale, for not one of his columns was on the ground and ready for the word.   Even Sullivan was not in time for the good long rest, the careful deployment and the advance in battle array called for by the plan.

Greene was over half an hour late.   His account of the battle has disappeared, but when he was criticized for "unnecessary delay," he branded the charge "as infamous a falsehood as ever was reported."   But he never recovered from the accusation of mismanaging his approach and years afterward wrote, "At Germantown I was evidently disgraced." [14]

His route was four miles longer than the rest, and a guide misled him along a wrong road in the night.   Once in the environs of the town he had a villainous time getting forward over marshes, through thickets and numerous fences.   Even then his brigades were wrong-end-to and Conway criticized him for taking further time for a long unnecessary countermarch to realign his units.   Lafayette said that he was "delayed by a ridiculous precedence of divisions."

As a result of these mishaps, Sullivan had to begin the quadruple battle alone, and the day had broken before he had crossed Chestnut Hill.   Yet the sun had hardly peeped through the dense mist before it vanished, and left a dreary twilight for the forenoon.   Conway in advance encountered the first British picket at Mount Airy.   Captain Allan McLane of the Philadelphia light horse charged and drove it in, but it had time to fire two cannon before retiring.   These cannon killed several soldiers and also woke the whole British Army.

The British 2d Light Infantry swarmed up to support the picket so viciously that Conway had to throw forward his entire brigade to hold the ground.   As this Irishman of French training wrote to Charles Carroll—and it should be remembered to his credit:

"At Germantown, with little better than four hundred men, I began the attack, and was fighting three quarters of an hour before any individual came to support me." [15]

Further reinforcement came to the British front: the 40th Regiment under Lieutenant-Colonel Musgrave, a singularly fine officer of vast experience and resource, and grim enough in appearance since he had been shot through the mouth and had a hole in his cheek. He surprised the American surprise, and completely wrecked it. He nailed Conway to the ground until Sullivan had to form and rescue him. Then Musgrave impertinently tried to flank Sullivan, who had to turn aside and protect himself at a time when he was supposed to be charging on the main body.

He found himself with both flanks in danger because Greene had not come up. Sullivan's plans were already upset completely but he improvised new ones with skill and intelligence. Calling Wayne's division to his left, he withdrew part of Conway's brigade from the road to work over to his right and protect that.[16]

One quaint proof of the strange risks of battle was given here. Colonel Hall of the Maryland troops advancing on foot ordered Major Howard to call in an advanced company. Major Howard advising against it, Colonel Hall demanded Major Howard's horse, saying that he would bring it in himself. "Riding one way, and looking another, the horse ran with him under a cider-press, and he was so hurt that he was taken from the field." [17] This was one way of getting promotion for Major Hall.

Sullivan, under charges for bad conduct at Staten Island, was supported by Anthony Wayne, who was awaiting court-martial for letting himself be surprised in the Paoli affair. Now was his chance to repay "massacre" with massacre. Wayne wrote to his wife of what followed:

"Our people Remembering the Action of the Night of the 20th of Sep'r near the Warren—pushed on with their Bayonets—and took Ample Vengeance for that Nights Work—Our Officers Exerted themselves to save many of the poor wretches who were Crying for Mercy —but to little purpose; the Rage and fury of the Soldiers were not to be Restrained for some time—at least not until great numbers of the Enemy fell by our Bayonets." [18]

When Sullivan had his little army in hand he ordered a general advance and drove Musgrave backward through his own advance camp. As Sullivan says:

"They made a stand at every fence, wall, and ditch they passed, which were numerous. We were compelled to remove every fence as we passed, which delayed us much in the pursuit."

Before Sullivan was anywhere near the main body, Howe was up with the advance. An old Germantown man alleged that he had heard Howe exclaim:

"My God, what shall we do? we are certainly surrounded." [19]

But the man was eighty-two when he told this reminiscence of far-off boyhood and there is more plausibility in the account of a British officer, General Hunter, who was with the troops that Sullivan and Wayne drove back so slowly. He gives a lively account of the British side:

"The pickets came in and said the enemy were advancing in force. They had barely joined the battalion when we heard a loud cry, 'Have at the bloodhounds, revenge Wayne's affair!' and they immediately fired a volley. We gave them one in return, cheered and charged. . . . We charged them twice till the battalion was so reduced by killed and wounded that the bugle was sounded to retreat. . . . But this was the first time we had ever retreated from the Americans, and it was with great difficulty we could get the men to obey our orders. . . .

"By this time General Howe had come up, and seeing the battalion retreating, all broken, he got into a passion, and exclaimed,

" 'For shame, Light Infantry, I never saw you retreat before, form! form! it is only a scouting party.'

"However he was quickly convinced that it was more than a scouting party as the heads of the enemy's columns soon appeared. One coming through Beggarstown with three pieces of cannon in their front immediately fired with grape at the crowd that was standing with General Howe under a large chestnut tree. I think I never saw people enjoy a discharge of grape before, but we really all felt pleased to see the enemy make such an appearance, and to hear the grape rattle about the Commander-in-Chief's ears, after he had accused the battalion of having run away from a scouting party." [20]

Howe was always cool in action, a big man, six feet tall and bearing a frequently noticed resemblance to Washington, whom he had always defeated before. For the present he must have fallen back, as was proper, to the main body when the advance was naturally withdrawn. But Colonel Musgrave did not fall back. Courage and genius inspired him to occupy the Chew House as a citadel.

In the fog Sullivan and Wayne passed on without even noting the disappearance of Musgrave and his six companies— about 120 men in all. Tom Paine, who was in the battle, paid Musgrave the compliment of saying that he had five hundred men there.[21] Indeed his six score did the work of thousands.

Musgrave turned the house into a Gibraltar on which the central wave of the American reserve split and spent itself. A maelstrom formed and eddied about the house, and its widening swirls changed the whole current, disorganizing the Americans and giving the British main body time to organize against what was evidently more of a surprise than Howe cared to admit; for General Clinton said that "Had Washington left a corps to observe this house, and proceeded, there is no saying what might have been the consequence." [22]

The Colonel's brother, Sir William Musgrave, wrote a letter, found among the papers of King George III, observing that the Colonel was "under the divine providence, one of the principal means to prevent a considerable part of the K's Army from being surprized at German-Town . . . the saving 4000 of his Majesty's force must be allowed to be a very useful service." [23]

While Sullivan and Wayne pressed on past, Musgrave was

posting his men at windows on the roof and in the cellar and barricading himself against a siege. Up to this time the British line had held nowhere for long and Washington told Paine at breakfast the next day that he had had every expectation of continuing the pursuit on into Philadelphia.[24] Feeling the need of saving some ammunition for this final clash, he called Adjutant-General Pickering to him and directed him to find Sullivan:

"Go ahead, and say that I am afraid he is throwing away his ammunition, and to try to reserve himself for a more general action."

Pickering says:

"I did go; falling in with him a little below Chew's house. On my returning, many shots were fired at me from the house; it was my first notice that an enemy was there. On rejoining the General, I found him listening to a discussion between General Knox and some other officers, on the question whether the troops then behind should advance, regardless of the enemy in Chew's house, or that the latter should be summoned to surrender.

"Knox urged the summons. He said it would be unmilitary to leave a castle in our rear. I answered:

" 'Doubtless that is a correct general maxim, but it does not apply in this case. We know the extent of this castle (Chew's house) and to guard against the enemy's sallying and falling on the rear of our troops, a small regiment may be posted here to watch them: and if they sally, such a regiment will take care of them. But (I added) to summon them to surrender will be useless. We are now in the midst of the battle; and its issue is unknown. In this state of uncertainty, and so well secured as the enemy find themselves, they will not regard a summons: *they will fire at your flag.*'

"However, a subaltern officer (Lieutenant Smith) of Virginia with a flag and drum was sent with a summons. When arrived in full view, a shot from a window of the house gave him a wound of which he died." [25]

Major Tallmadge confirms this: "Through the importunity of Gen. Knox (which I distinctly heard), Gen. Washington permitted him to bring his field artillery to bear upon it, but without effect. During this transaction time elapsed, the situation of our troops was uncomfortable, their ardor abated, and the enemy obtained time to rally." [26]

Failing to shatter it, efforts were made to set the house on fire, but Musgrave's men picked off the incendiaries. An old Germantown citizen afterward described the wreckage that remained when the battle passed, and the lucky boys of the town who had seen a war brought to their very doorsteps, and had watched it with reckless interest, could study the ruins with every room bloody and dead soldiers in the yard.[27]

After the failure of various attempts to burn the house out, if not down, two young men, John Laurens of South Carolina and the dazzling twenty-year-old Frenchman, Chevalier de Mauduit du Plessis, resolved to put an end to the nuisance. With a gaiety much needed in the chronicles of this miserable day, the Marquis de Chastellux describes what followed:

"M. de Mauduit making no doubt that they were following him with all the straw in the barn, went straight to a window on the ground floor, which he forced, and on which he mounted.

"He was received, in truth, like the lover who mounting a ladder to see his mistress found the husband waiting for him on the balcony:

"I do not know whether, like him too, on being asked what he was doing there, he answered, *I am only taking a walk;* but this I know, that whilst a gallant man, pistol in hand, desired him to surrender, another less polite entering briskly into the chamber, fired a musquet shot, which killed, not M. de Mauduit, but the officer who wished to take him. After these slight mistakes, and this little quarrel, the difficulty was for him to retire. . . . He returned safe and sound, and Mr. Laurens, who was in no greater haste than he, escaped with a slight wound in his shoulder." [28]

The delay meant a breakdown of the whole American machine. Washington soon saw this and decided to push on, leaving the too bookish Knox to try to demolish the house with his artillery and a supporting regiment. Even for the brief time he loitered here Washington was afterwards ridiculed and censured by his multiplying critics, who blamed him for being always under the thumb of either Greene or Knox. Even when Greene's belated wing came up, Woodford's brigade was arrested by a heavy fire on its right flank from the Chew house and halted to drum on the walls with useless fieldpieces. John Marshall, who was with this brigade, says that Musgrave also broke Greene's line and caused its elements to lose touch.[29]

The bedevilment of the troops held up at the Chew house was not the whole of its evil. There was the stupefaction it caused among the troops that had gone on past at the uproar of the cannonade breaking out behind them.

Though Wayne and Sullivan were on opposite sides of the main road fighting from house to house and field to field, they could not see each other. The impulsive Wayne, hearing the racket at the Chew house, imagined that Sullivan was being overwhelmed back there, and magnanimously resolved to wheel about and rescue him. The result of this was, of course, that he unwittingly abandoned Sullivan, exposed his left flank to the stiffening attack of the upcoming British and left him to shove on alone with the reinforcement of a few brave individuals who had come across the creek from where the bulk of the militia loafed and looked on as uselessly as the boys of Germantown. They were not encouraged to enter by the added clouds of smoke from several fields of hay and stubble set on fire by the British.[30]

According to his lights, Wayne did the brave and the wise thing when he turned back toward the Chew house to support Sullivan; yet never was a brave and wise deed more ironically punished, for Wayne not only ruined Sullivan but ran into Greene's right brigade under General Stephen, which had just arrived at the right spot at the wrong time—nearly an hour overdue.

The Germantown boys who scampered about the battlefield and the terrified women who packed into the cellars and peered through the windows of their bullet-spattered, window-shattered homes, afterward described the warriors as negroes of frightful mien, for the soldiers had to bite off the ends of their cartridges before ramming them home and the powder spread around their mouths and over their faces till they were masked in black. The wet of the smoky fog smeared their clothes with soot as well and it was soon almost impossible to tell friend from foe.

Greene's four brigades drove into the fight with fiendish eagerness to make up for lost time. They crushed such British advance parties as met them out on the Old Limekiln Road, sent them flying, artillery and all, and crowded in toward the main road where they had been told to engage the British right and surprise it.

Instead, General Stephen's blackfaces surprised Anthony Wayne's blackfaces scurrying back to support Sullivan and re-crossing the ground already mopped up during Greene's ab-sence. Stephen's men naturally supposed that the blurred wraiths troubling the fog were British, and fired into them. Wayne's men in the same delusion fired back. How many were killed nobody knows but Wayne's men, exhausted and run-ning low in ammunition, finally broke and fled from Stephen's men, just as Stephen's more timorous souls broke and fled from Wayne's.

This ludicrous yet tragic encounter in which two American divisions in the middle of a battlefield whipped each other, then fled from each other, caused the "flight from victory" to become a haunting phrase. General Stephen apparently used it first. In a letter he wrote to Washington when his head had cleared, he described an even more farcical flight than Wayne's, for after Wayne's men had fled from Virginians, the rest of Stephen's men fled from British who were trying to surren-der! [31] This was one of the most peculiar panics in all the peculiar history of battle stampedes.

The Reverend General Muhlenberg, another Virginian, was quite as drunk as Stephen, but from hard work and hard riding and lack of rest. He commanded one of the brigades of

Greene's division and when they pierced to the centre of the village, they came on with such vigor that the British gradually yielded ground. Muhlenberg led a bayonet charge, drove through the British tents and took many prisoners. One of his colonels, Mathews of the 9th Virginia, made a rich haul.

Thus the left wing though tardy had already accomplished its mission, turned the enemy's right flank and gained his rear. The advantage of surprise was lost, but they had part of the British main line clamped between them and Sullivan all ready for destruction according to the programme. If Wayne had not disappeared in the thick smoke and if Sullivan's ammunition had not abruptly given out, great things might have been done.

Suddenly the Maryland men began to waver. When their officers howled at them they held up empty ammunition boxes in eloquent pantomime. Bayonets were too few to rely on. All of Sullivan's men rapidly reached the same condition. Their arms were useless but they had God-given legs. Some of the militia, it seems, had been secretly spilling their precious cartridges on the ground so that when they came in they could point to their empty cartridge boxes with pardonable pride. With the exception of a regiment of impatient and intrepid North Carolinians, Armstrong's militia wing of several thousand had been held up and kept from their mission by 300 Hessian chasseurs who stopped them at a bridge across the Wissahickon.[32]

The commanders of the British left wing instead of chasing Sullivan through the fog wisely restrained their well-disciplined troops and brought them to the aid of the shattered British right wing. Now it was Greene who was caught in the vise, with Muhlenberg far off behind the enemy's line. But this magnificent preacher-soldier having cut through with the bayonet, cut back with the same weapon and rejoined Greene. He brought with him all of his regiments except the 9th Virginia under Colonel Mathews. That ill-starred officer, dragging along his covey of prisoners, was compelled to surrender not only his captives, but himself and his whole regiment—four hundred in a mass, practically the only prisoners the British kept.

Greene was confronted now by three British generals, Grey, Grant and Agnew. He had driven back the Guards, the 25th and the 27th. "No-Flint" Grey, having found that the militia on the American far right were merely spectators, left them to the Hessian chasseurs and dived into the fog with all his men. Grant had with him the 5th, the "Die hards," and the 55th.[33]

Greene by now was so exhausted and so depressed at the abrupt shift from victory for disaster that his officers said he did not want to survive the disgrace.[34] But he had to save his people and he exposed himself to death with mournful pertinacity.

As soon as Muhlenberg rejoined him they took up the backward fight. During the struggle through the village with its stout houses, its little yards and strong fences, Muhlenberg, who insisted on bringing up the rear of his men, narrowly escaped capture several times. He came to one fence that his exhausted horse refused. While Captain Hubley and others were pulling it down to let him through, Muhlenberg actually fell asleep.

He was wakened "by the whistling of a ball past his ear, and the cry running along the British ranks—'Pick off that officer on the white horse!' Turning round, he saw a young English officer who had taken a musket from one of his men, and fired at him personally. He was about renewing the experiment, when the General, drawing a pistol from his holster, although at some distance, shot him through the head. His fall stopped the firing, and the General rejoined his brigade." [35]

Washington as always was fearless. He kept a close watch on Sullivan, who says:

"I cannot help observing, that, with great concern, I saw our brave commander exposing himself to the hottest fire of the enemy, in such a manner, that regard to my country obliged me to ride to him, and beg him to retire. He, to gratify me and some others, withdrew a small distance; but his anxiety for the fate of the day soon brought him up again." [36]

He was especially active in the all too familiar business of trying to check fugitives. Major Tallmadge describes this futile work:

"In less than thirty minutes, our troops began to retire, and from the ardor of pursuit, were in full retreat. . . . Notwithstanding all our attempts to rally the retiring troops, it seemed impossible to effect it, even by the presence of the Commander-in-Chief. I threw my squadron of horse across the road, by order of Gen. Washington, repeatedly, to prevent the retreat of the infantry; but it was ineffectual." [37]

One dismal incident of the American retreat was the collapse of General Adam Stephen, whose men had deserted him on the field. On the way home Lieutenant Benjamin Grymes found him lying in a fence-corner, seized him by the collar, straightened him up and ordered him about his business.[38]

The Americans were perhaps lucky to have started their flight when they did, for fresh troops under Lord Cornwallis were just coming into the field from Philadelphia.

Howe says of Cornwallis in his report, that

"He followed the Enemy Eight Miles on the Skippach Road, but such was the Expedition with which they fled, he was not able to overtake them. The Grenadiers from Philadelphia, who, full of Ardor, had run most of the Way to German Town, could not arrive in time to join in the Action. The Country in general was so strongly enclosed and covered with Wood, that the Dragoons had not any Opening to charge, excepting a small Party on the Right, which behaved most gallantly." [39]

It was perhaps these dragoons who administered to Pulaski a parting humiliation when he left the field where he had had no chance to shine. As he hovered about the rear of the retreat, his horsemen were suddenly attacked and in their haste to escape, rode right into and through Greene's men, who needed only that exquisite touch of being run over by a drove of their own horses.

At first they supposed them, of course, to be British dragoons, and those who could get up and run, got up and ran. They scattered so fast and far that Greene was in danger of having to abandon his precious cannon. The story is told that Greene, unable to assemble enough men otherwise, was driven to the expedient of calling them in one by one and making them lay hold of one another's hands. He thus collected a chain strong enough to form a rear guard and even to fire a volley or two from the cannon.[40] Charles Francis Adams ridicules the story of clasped hands as impossible and asks what the men did with their muskets: "Did they then, firmly clasping each other's hands, chant a hymn; or did the Major-General commanding hearten his followers by singing a comic song?"

Wayne also did good rearguard action on his road and threw off his pursuers with "a few Cannon shot and some Musketry." Wounded twice, he wrote to his wife:

"Upon the Whole it was a Glorious day—Our men are in the highest Spirits—and I am Confident we shall give them a total Defeat the next Action; which is at no great Distance. My best love and wishes to all friends Adieu my Dear Girl Ant'y Wayne." [41]

That was just the sort of thing to write home to one's dear girl, and all the American reports kept up the same fictional style for the dear public. But there was no disguising the fact that the men had dragged themselves through a long night's march, had spent their last energies in a battle of strange confusions and chagrins and bafflements, and now were turning home with nothing to show for their toil but black faces, empty cartridge boxes, empty stomachs, and many empty places in their ranks.

It was doubtless the exhaustion that gave their flights the deliberation that won the praise of Tom Paine, who was on Nathanael Greene's staff: "The retreat was extraordinary. Nobody hurried themselves." [42] How could anybody hurry?

Some had marched twenty miles the night before. All would march more than twenty-five miles back. Pickering said that there was some resentment at Washington's carrying them so far needlessly, but he was in no mood to halt within easy reach of the British. To make sure of their safety he marched six miles farther on the retreat than on the advance, all the way to his old camp at Pennypacker's Mills. At eight o'clock that night he stopped at the house of a farmer for a moment:

"He would only take a dish of tea, and pulling out the half of a biscuit, assured the family the other half was all the food he had taken since the preceding day." [43]

The accounts of that forenoon's losses are inconsistent as usual. The British official return, probably reliable, states that Howe lost 4 officers and 66 men killed; 30 officers and 420 men wounded; 1 officer and 13 men missing; a total loss of 534.[44] This was a little less than his loss of 583 at the Brandywine.

The American loss as eventually given out by the Board of War was almost exactly the same as before: 400 prisoners, 152 killed and 521 wounded,[45] a total of a little over a thousand— twice as many killed as Howe had. Münchäusen, however, says "Of the enemy, we have buried over 300, and have captured 438, among whom are 47 officers." [46]

Washington either did not realize at first how heavily his men had suffered, or felt it necessary to release the truth gradually. On the day following the battle he issued an order of encouragement and congratulation to his troops, blaming the fog alone.[47]

The story spread that he blamed Greene, and though he afterwards denied this with his usual cordiality, the rumor ran wild and was propagated by those who disliked him but felt it safer to attack his favorite.

A letter of the time mentioning this gives also another reason for failure—the chaotic commissariat:

"Greene is much blamed. The general threatened the Commissary with the halter, he says their neglect prevented him from attacking the enemy on the west side of the Schuylkill." [48]

This last reference is doubtless to the belief that the British were in such panic that Howe was planning to abandon Philadelphia and retreat to Chester.

There is nothing in the British reports to indicate any such panic in Howe's mind, or in his army, though there was much excitement and anxiety over the surprise and the ferocity of the attack. It is unquestionably true that if Howe had lost 4,000 of his men at Germantown, his remaining force would have been in desperate straits.

Washington wrote to Congress of the fine spirit of his troops, but after stating that he had "sustained no material loss of men," he had to add a postscript to that very letter, "it is more considerable than I at first apprehended." Later he admits that "our loss will amount in killed and wounded, to upwards of three hundred." Ten days later he confesses it "in killed, wounded and missing, about one thousand." [49]

Still he solaced himself with rumors of British panic:

"The tumult, disorder, and even despair, which, it seems, had taken place in the British army, were scarcely to be paralleled; and it is said, so strongly did the ideas of a retreat prevail, that Chester was fixed on as their rendezvous." [50]

He and his men stood so much in want of a knowledge of having damaged the enemy dreadfully that they were ready to believe anything. Eleven days after the battle Washington was capable of writing:

"P. S. By sundry concurring accounts of persons out of Philadelphia and from Deserters, the Enemy's loss in the action of the 4th was very considerable. The lowest say it was 1500 killed and wounded, others 2000, and some as high as 2500. Perhaps the two last are exaggerated, but there are many reasons to believe that the first cannot much exceed the mark. For they were compleatly surprized and drove in great disorder for a long time and for a considerable distance at every point of attack." [51]

He magnified the British loss three times as its minimum and five times as a maximum, on the hearsay of deserters, who naturally found that their welcome varied with the welcome of their reports. Lafayette put the case clearly:

"Throughout this revolution the greatest difficulty was, that in order to conceal misfortunes from the enemy, it was necessary to conceal them from the nation also; that by awakening the one, information was likewise given to the other; and that fatal blows would have been struck upon the weakest points before democratic tardiness could have been roused to support them. It was from this cause that, during the whole war, the real force of the army was always kept a profound secret; even Congress was not apprised of it, and the generals were often themselves deceived." [52]

It is consequently practically impossible to give exact figures concerning the American strengths and losses, and they must be computed from various hints. The British were under no such necessity to use their returns for propaganda, and had to make fairly accurate statements to their royal master.

There was no disagreement about one fact: Washington had lost two battles, and two thousand men in them, and the capital of the United States. He had an army busy with accusations of cowardice and drunkenness. His visions of a further attack were not relinquished but he had to announce the loss of a brigade of Jersey militia, determined to go home, and "alarming desertions" among the men engaged in the "water defence on the Delaware." [53]

There was a crippling shortage of general officers and very bad news from the Hudson river where the men he had drawn off to support his own army left a force which might prove inadequate. If the British reduced the forts on the Hudson, he foresaw:

"This would open the navigation of the river, and enable the enemy with facility to throw their force into Albany, get into the rear of General Gates, and either oblige him to retreat, or put him between two fires. The success of the present attempt upon Peekskill may, in its consequences, entirely change the face of our northern affairs, and throw them into a very disagreeable and unfavorable train." [54]

The worst happened in two days. Forts Clinton and Montgomery were easily captured by Clinton, and Washington had the blame for that added to the blame for defeat in two battles and the humiliation and discomfort of Congress once more in exile from the capital.

But General Gates came out from between the two fires with such a radiance about him that he was hailed as the longawaited, the only genuine savior of the country. There were people so tired of Washington's two years' bad luck that Congressman Lovell, the partisan of Gates, was soon moved to rejoice even in the disaster that brought Washington low:

"I have reason to think the battle of Germantown was *the* day of salvation offered by Heaven to us." [55]

He was piously thanking heaven for offering the country salvation, not from Howe, but from Washington!

THE DOLDRUMS

"IT is in vain to look back to our disappointment on the 4th Instant at Germantown. We must endeavor to deserve better of Providence, and, I am persuaded, she will smile upon us." [1]

For once Washington thought of Providence as a "she."

Congress joined him in the sombre duty of propagating Germantown as something so near to victory as to have smitten the British with dismay and prepared them for complete ruin in the next battle, which, it was promised, would follow almost immediately. Congress thanked Washington for his "wise and well concerted attack"; thanked the army and ordered a medal struck for Washington. [2]

But this was all publicity. Everybody knew that, though the army had marched up the hill all night and down the hill all the next day, the flight had been a panic with the commander throwing cavalry across the road in vain. The men ran around the horses and later the horses ran over the men.

Everybody blamed everybody else and General St. Clair, who visited the camp, found a general agreement that "there was strange mismanagement and it has produced infinite Courts Martial." [3] St. Clair himself was waiting for Congress to make ready to try him, as was General Schuyler. Nearly every general in the Revolution was sooner or later brought before a court-martial or a Congressional committee on most serious charges.

General Sullivan was now tried for bungling the Staten Island attack: he was acquitted; Wayne for letting his men be surprised and massacred at Paoli: he was acquitted; Maxwell for being disabled with liquor at Brandywine: he was acquitted; Stephen for drunkenness at Germantown and afterward. He was found guilty and cashiered.

This was a heartbreaking finish for Stephen, who had begun his military life with the Virginia troops in 1754 and had come within an ace of being Washington's superior. He was with the troops that surrendered at Fort Necessity when Washington signed the capitulation confessing the "assassination" of Jumonville. Washington afterward vowed he did not know that the word was used.

In 1776, for some reason, Dr. Benjamin Rush asked General Stephen to write his biography. In it he states that he had refused to sign the capitulation because it contained the word "assassination." This was giving Washington the lie direct, but it was too far off to matter.[4]

Stephen was highly praised for his skill and bravery in frontier fighting and his revolutionary service was his twelfth campaign.[5]

Yet Washington seems never to have cared for him, perhaps because of his drinking and perhaps because of their bitter contest for the post of burgess from Frederick county. As far back as 1761, Washington had written on the eve of his own election:

"At the cock fight on Saturday last I promised to be at a Wedding at Mendenhalls Mill Yesterday, . . . I intend this day to pass along the North Mountain . . . and from thence to Winchester in order to wait my doom on Monday . . . Colo. Stephens proceedings is a matter of ye greatest amazement to me . . . His conduct throughout the whole is very obvious to all who will be convinced, but I find there are some that do not choose to have there Eyes opened. . . .

"You can be no Friend to a Person of Colo. Stephens Principals; I hope . . . you will contribute your aid towards shutting him out of the publick trust he is seeking . . . but as Sheriff I known you cannot appear in this, nor would I . . . have you do anything that can give so designing a Man as Colo. Stephens ye least handle." [6]

By very clever electioneering Washington beat Stephen 505 to 294.

And now he had shut his ancient rival out of another public trust, and he approved the sentence of dismissal without comment.[7] If he had any regret for the disgrace of his old companion at arms, he seems to have suppressed it. He was certainly more than consoled since the vacancy made an opening for Lafayette, who had for some time been a major-general with nobody to command. On October 14th, 1777, he wrote to Washington in a dialect so amusing that one can almost hear him plead:

"I do not do myself the honor of wisiting to you as many time as I would chuse because I fear to disturb your important occupations. Give me leave, dear general, to speak to you about my own affairs with all the confidence of a son, of a friend as you favourd me with those two so precious titles . . . Now that the honable Congress is settled quete and making promotions, that some changements are ready to happen in the divisions . . . I am not used to tell what I am, I wo'nt make no more any petition to Congress . . . Europe and particularly france is looking upon me—that I want to do some thing by myself, and justify that love of glory which I lett be known to the world . . . do you not think this want is right?"[8]

Washington wrote to Congress an unusually cordial letter insinuating the wisdom of assigning Lafayette to Stephen's division—he did not have the authority to do even that without permission.[9] No attention being paid to this letter, he wrote again three weeks later reminding Congress that Lafayette had distinguished himself in a skirmish in New Jersey.[10] To this Congress replied by complying with Washington's request. The boy was now a real major-general, proud of the fact that his troops were raggedest of all.

The day after Germantown Washington returned a prisoner without stopping to discuss the still unsettled cartel:

"General Washington's compliments to General Howe,—does himself the pleasure to return to him a dog, which accidentally fell into his hands, and, by the inscription on the collar, appears to belong to General Howe."[11]

Howe's dog did what his master never learned to do: he followed Washington until he overtook him. One can easily picture Washington bending over to bid the dog good-by, the

smiles that followed the animal as he passed the soldiers out
on his march to the point of contact between the lines; the flag
of truce put up by his American escort; the signal from the
British sentry line to advance; the conferring of the two parties
while the dog stood wagging his tail and refusing to be military; the mutual salute and about-face, with the dog looking
back at the rebels, then leaping against his leash and jerking
his new attendant out of stride; his final arrival at headquarters
and the fond rebukes he accepted from that tender-hearted
officer. It was an experience for a dog, to have taken so much
of the time and thought of two commanders-in-chief. But he
has left no reminiscences.

Washington was hot for another assault on Germantown,
but he did not have men enough and the usual "distress for
want of shoes" was "a powerful obstacle." Furthermore it
was necessary to establish new magazines and what he called
"a new elaboratory" for making new ammunition. A repulse
and pursuit would have exposed his army "to the most imminent danger of being ruined." [12]

He changed camps restlessly and the time was filled with
the dull routine of desertion and court-martial.

A captain of the 1st Virginia was found guilty of cowardice
and two lieutenants were found guilty of drunkenness at Germantown. Others were acquitted. A private was found guilty
of plundering and sentenced to run the gauntlet through fifty
men. Another private who drew a sword on two captains was
sentenced to run a gauntlet of two hundred men. A major was
tried for wounding a lieutenant with his sword, abetting a riot
and attempting the life of a captain. He was reprimanded. As
late as December 22nd a captain was found guilty of cowardice
at Germantown and association with him denounced as scandalous, and on January 3rd a captain was found guilty of
cowardice at Brandywine. [13] A French officer from his camp
said:

"Confusion and bad discipline prevailed too much to expect anything
good . . . Everybody cries against poor General Washington." [14]

He had stripped the Hudson forts of vital troops only to add them to his own defeats. He had lost the Hudson and endangered the North, and he was rapidly losing the Delaware river and with it the last chance of starving the British out of the capital, which he had also lost.

Any other general would have been replaced instantly and driven into a blacker oblivion than Adam Stephen's. Only the magic of Washington's personality sustained his retainers, and it was impossible that honest doubters should not have felt that he had been given chances enough. He had to admit that the loss of the forts "might have been attended with fatal consequences, had not there been a most providential intervention in favor of General Gates's arms on the 7th instant." [15]

Even providence was swinging round to Gates.

Soon Washington was breaking more bad news. Some of the most picturesque fighting of the Revolution distinguished the contest for the Delaware forts, but Washington was not present. Howe and his brother the Admiral had attacked from two opposite points and converged. The need of men compelled Howe to give up Germantown and as soon as he evacuated it, Washington moved his camp to Whitemarsh, thirteen miles from Philadelphia. He was able to ride to the Chew House, a monument to his fatal error, and to watch from the roof a tower of smoke. But it came from his own burning ships.[16]

On November 23rd Washington must write:

"I am sorry to inform Congress, that the enemy are now in possession of all the water defences . . . most if not all the armed vessels have been burned by our own people." [17]

The next day in fear of Howe he was calling Greene's troops in from the Jerseys, leaving them open to the enemy, and he was begging Greene for wisdom:

"Think, therefore, I beseech you, of all these things, and prepare yourself by reflection and observation (being on the spot) to give me your advice on these several matters." [18]

Washington's other officers were accusing him of letting Greene do his thinking, and Congress was wondering if the two of them could ever do any winning. The word "Fabius" was beginning to be a dreary joke. Now Congressman Lovell wrote:

"Our Affairs are Fabiused into a very disagreeable position." [19]

As if Washington had not enough torments, a number of sweetly pious pacifists assailed him, a delegation of Quakers and the first Chaplain of Congress Duché, who had turned Tory. Their meddling is discussed in the fourth Appendix.

While the news from Washington's army and fleet strung one disaster upon another, he was issuing rum and setting off fireworks to celebrate the joyous bulletins from the department of his rival.

XXI

HIS RIVAL TRIUMPHS

TOM PAINE gave Washington the credit for the success of the northern army because of the care he had taken of its interests.[1] But who else would have such a thought? When Congressman Dr. Benjamin Rush read Paine's words, he wrote to Gates about it:

"*Common Sense* I find has assigned your conquests entirely to the Southern army. . . . Nothing is now wanting to mix with the incense-burning but to lay the defeats of Brandywine and at Germantown upon you." [2]

Congressman Lovell objected even to Washington's calling his army the "Grand Army." He said it was "inconsiderate" and "very sickening to even a strong Stomach." [3] This in spite of the fact that Washington used the expression in a humble tribute to the Northern army when he announced that it had driven Burgoyne backward, and hoped it would be "a powerful stimulus" to the troops under his immediate command. There was a touch of envy in his dolorous confession: "we suffer ourselves in every instance to be outdone," though there was force "sufficient to crush our Foe." Two days later he must proclaim:

"The Gen¹ has his happiness Compleated . . . Gen¹ Burgoyne and his whole Army Surrenderd themselves prisoners of War, let every face brighten, and every heart expand with grateful Joy and Praise to the Supreme Disposer of all human Events, who has granted us this signal Success. The Chaplains of the Army are to prepare short discourses, suited to the Joyful Occasion." [4]

It was Washington's dubious privilege to transmit the news of Burgoyne's capture to Congress, and with a vague uncertainty that robbed the message of its conviction. Gates never reported the victory to Washington, and ignored him completely in the matter. For this Gates has been much abused. But he has enough to answer for without this gratuity, for the Northern department was not under Washington's command, and Washington himself had kept aloof from it so completely that he would not even suggest a commander for it, and when directed to notify Gates of his selection worded the message as if he were merely a channel of transmission.

Gates held back his own positive despatches until he had finished debating the terms with Burgoyne and had made sure of his captives on October 17th, 1777. Then he sent the news by his adjutant, James Wilkinson, who fell ill and "nearly expired under the anguish of a convulsive cholic." Unable to keep to a saddle, he rode in a wagon to Albany, where he halted for recovery.[5]

Governor Clinton, who was at Albany, rushed off a despatch to Congress, dated October 15th, telling of the signing of the capitulation. The messenger passed through Washington's camp on his way. According to C. W. Peale, the artist, when the despatch came, Washington was sitting on the side of a bed in an old farm house near Skippack creek, and Peale was seated in the only chair, painting a miniature of him for Martha. Peale says that Washington merely glanced at the despatch, and "remained apparently unconcerned until the sitting was finished."[6]

But this was probably the report of another of Gates' victories, for Adjutant-General Colonel Pickering gave a very different account. One afternoon, while Pickering and Paymaster-General Palfrey were with him in a house on the Skippack Road, Washington was discussing the rumor that he would be replaced by Gates if Gates whipped Burgoyne, when, through a window, an express-rider was seen coming down from the north. Palfrey went out to stop him and, finding that his despatch was from Albany and addressed to Congress, borrowed it to show the general. The rider told Palfrey of Bur-

goyne's surrender, and he told Pickering. They went into the
room together and handed the letter to Washington. Pickering's biographer, who often heard him tell the story, says:

"Not a word was spoken. Washington unfolded the document, and
proceeded to read it aloud, Pickering and Palfrey watching his expression. As he read, his voice began to falter, his articulation became slow,
and broke under the intensity of his feelings; as it became apparent
that the letter was announcing the surrender of Burgoyne and his entire
army, he could read no more, but passed it to Colonel Palfrey, signi-
fying that he wished him to finish it, which he did, aloud. As he concluded, Washington lifted his countenance and his hands towards
Heaven, and was lost in a rapture of adoring gratitude.

"He demonstrated a mind incapable of envy or selfishness; transported with joy at a victory the honor of which would be another's,
and its effect perhaps fatal to his own personal ascendancy and fame,
but which gave earnest of the success of the great cause. Colonel
Pickering used to say, in relating this scene, that the spectacle was truly
sublime. He beheld humanity in its noblest grandeur,—a man to
whom self was nothing, his country every thing. The image and per-
sonification of a Patriot was transfigured before him." [7]

Washington forwarded Clinton's despatch to Congress, but,
since it had come so indirectly instead of in a swift hosanna
from Gates, there was doubt of its authenticity. Days passed
with no confirmation and Congress had almost begun to despair
when Wilkinson finally turned up October 31st with Gates'
official report, a copy of the Convention, and a request for direction as to his future movements. Gates urged promotion for
his Adjutant, Wilkinson, saying "from the beginning of this
war, I have not met with a more promising Military Genius."
Congress voted that he be "continued in his present employment, with a brevet of brigadier general." [8]

Humiliations direct and indirect were now showered on
Washington. After Germantown Congress had ordered "a
medal to be struck." The resolution did not state what this
medal for defeat was to be made of, but it was ironic. To
Gates, Congress voted thanks for defeating "an army of the
enemy of 10,000 men" and the capture of "the main army

of six thousand men." Major-Generals Lincoln and Arnold were included in the thanks, but for General Gates it was ordered that "a medal of gold be struck . . . in commemoration of this great event."

He was told that he was to stay in command of his army. Next, he was requested to do all he could to recapture the Hudson forts, Clinton and Montgomery, and it was specifically voted that Washington could not recall from him a larger "detachment" than 2,500 men, including Colonel Morgan's corps. Later in the day someone proposed that Washington might ask for more men, "after consulting with General Gates." Even this little compliment was snowed under by a negative of 27 to 5.[9]

Congress resolved that Heaven had helped Gates, and December 18th was set apart for a day not only of thanksgiving and prayer, but of repentance as well: confession of "manifold sins, whereby they had forfeited every favour" and a supplication "that it may please God, through the merits of Jesus Christ, mercifully to forgive and blot them out of remembrance"; also "to take schools and seminaries of education, so necessary for cultivating the principles of true liberty, virtue and piety, under his nurturing hand." Inspiration was asked for the commanders of army and navy, also prosperity for the people.[10]

After Germantown the French treasurer, Vergennes, politely complimented the anxious American commissioners on possessing an army willing to attack again so soon after the defeat at the Brandywine. Since it only scored another defeat, however, the compliment was idle. But when Gates, the Englishman, captured Burgoyne's whole army, the French sat up and took notice, and began to make ready to do what Washington prophesied they never would do: join the war as allies.

The colonies were not the only ones who believed in bribing Providence by extra Lents. George III proclaimed a day of fast for England as soon as he heard of Burgoyne's disaster. The friendly Whigs, however, made verses:

"First General Gage commenced the war in vain,
Next General Howe continued the campaign,
Then General Burgoyne took the field, and last
Our forlorn hope depends on General Fast." [11]

Europe agreed that America had finally found both an army and a general. The general was Gates. Reverend Hezekiah Smith of Haverhill, Massachusetts, said that Saratoga was "the

WASHINGTON AND GATES.

(As presented to their admirers in *Bickerstaff's Boston Almanac* for 1778.)

grandest conquest ever gained since the creation of the world." [12] Sir Edward Creasy placed Saratoga among his *Fifteen Decisive Battles of the World.* And it was won by the idol of New England, Gates, the man whom New England had secured by going on a military strike!

In spite of the generous terms Gates had granted (largely because Clinton was sending cold chills up his back) the surrendered officers and men were shamefully treated. Burgoyne surrendered under a solemn "convention" that his officers and men should be shipped at once to England on parole not to fight again in America. Hence England called them the Convention Troops and resented the American habit of calling them the Convention Prisoners. General Phillips considered them "passengers."

When Congress realized that the return of those regiments would permit England to release their equivalent from garrison duty elsewhere, Congress blandly refused to keep the word pledged by its personal representative.[13] James Truslow Adams says: "In spite of the protests of Washington and other high-minded Americans, the supreme legislative body thus placed an indelible stain upon American honor." [14]

Washington's protests did not last long. In fact he suggested another way of nullifying the agreement without openly violating it. He wrote that England could by "the most scrupulous and virtuous observance of the convention" place the troops in garrison and send out others, so he apparently thought it would be perfectly scrupulous and virtuous to thwart the enemy by postponing the embarkation for months through the simple device of refusing to sell the British a morsel of salt or any provisions whatever for the voyage. He gave orders to that effect and repeatedly emphasized the importance of the subterfuge.[15]

Congress not only refused to surrender the prisoners but kept them in arctic quarters. Wood was too expensive to waste on captives. The snow was a foot deep in the rooms of some of the officers and they had to patch their breeches with their coattails. Their letters home were written with ink that froze on the pen, and letters from home were not forwarded to them, but passed around and read with laughter. The prisoners were ill fed as well, kept on prison ships and finally bundled off to Virginia where some of them were farmed out almost like slaves.[16] An effort was even made to encourage desertion among them and to enlist the deserters. This, as Washington protested, was a foolish trick, since many of them deserted and pretended to enlist, only to escape and return to the British army, absolved of any obligation.[17]

Finding that Congress would not keep the promise to allow

the embarkation of the Convention Troops, Burgoyne asked that he might go to England on parole to recover his broken health, to settle his accounts with the Treasury and to defend himself against accusations. At the same time he wrote to Washington begging his influence in the matter. Congress granted his plea, but Washington's letter is so beautiful that Burgoyne's descendants still cherish it:

"I was only two days since honored with your very obliging Letter of the 11th of February.—Your indulgent opinion of my character, and the polite terms in which you are pleased to express it, are peculiarly flattering; and I take pleasure in the oppertunity you have afforded me of assuring you, that far from suffering the views of national opposition to be imbittered and debased by personal animosity, I am ever ready to do justice to the merit of the Gent.n & soldier—and to esteem, where esteem is due, however the idea of a public enemy may interpose—You will not think it the language of unmeaning ceremony if I add, that sentiments of personal respect, in the present instance, are reciprocal.

"Viewing you in the light of an officer contending against what I conceive to be the rights of my Country, the reverses of fortune you experienced in the Field, cannot be unacceptable to me; but, abstracted from considerations of national advantage; I can sincerely sympathize with your feelings as a Soldier—the unavoidable difficulties of whose situation forbid his success, and as a man, whose lot combines the calamity of ill health, the anxieties of captivity, and the painful sensibility for a reputation, exposed where he most values it, to the assaults of malice & detraction. . . .

"Wishing you a safe and agreeable passage with a perfect restoration of your health, I have the honor to be very respectfully Sir
Yr most Obedt Sert " 18

To this Burgoyne wrote a grateful reply, saying:

"I find the character, which I before knew to be respectable, is also perfectly amiable; and I should have few greater private gratifications in seeing our melancholy contest at an end, than that of cultivating your friendship." 19

When he faced his enemies in England and placed the blame for his defeat on Germain's shoulders, he read Washington's letter to Parliament and said:

"I think the letter, though from an enemy, does honor to the human heart." [20]

The important thing to Washington and Gates now, was that Burgoyne's menace was annulled, and both generals were keen for the next move. Washington wanted the Northern army to send him enough men for an attack on Philadelphia, and he felt that the remainder would be enough to recapture and re-fortify the Hudson river, and even to storm New York.

It is almost incredible that so great a victory as Saratoga was followed, not by a sweep of enthusiasm but by a quarrel between generals while two armies loafed. Yet, perhaps Gates would hardly have been human if he had been content to turn his victorious troops over to another hero, a hero whom he did not love and quite sincerely did not trust. To expect that of him would be to ask more than even Washington might have done. Gates knew that Washington neither loved nor trusted him. Whether patriotism or timidity hampered Gates, he served his legitimate ambition ill.

He was not even clever. He took Colonel Daniel Morgan, of all men, to one side and mumbled that the main army was so dissatisfied with Washington that the best officers were ready to resign unless he were replaced, and—and—well— To this Morgan replied:

"I have one favor to ask of you, which is, never to mention that detestable subject to me again; for under no other man than Washington will I ever serve." [21]

For that reason, perhaps, Gates forgot to mention Morgan's superb fighting in his despatches. He reluctantly returned Morgan and his men to Washington, but the backing, even the order, of Congress justified him in refusing to part with the bulk of his idle force in order to lift Washington out of his ditch.

Congress had positively refused to permit Washington even to ask for more than 2,500 men, but he thought that an appeal to Gates might succeed, so he sent Alexander Hamilton to plead with him for "a very considerable part" of his men unless he had some other important project on hand. Hamilton was also to ask Putnam for troops. Though Gates had not yet written a line to him, Washington sent a letter congratulating him on the "signal success" of his army, and meekly regretting that Gates had not sent him word of such interesting news. He explained Hamilton's mission and expressed his assurances that Gates would do all in his power "to facilitate the objects I have in contemplation." [22]

That was the least of Gates' inclinations. On Nov. 2nd, 1777, he wrote a few lines telling Washington that he was returning Morgan's riflemen, and adding the curt statement:

"Congress having been requested immediately to transmit copies of all my despatches to them, I am confident your Excellency has long ago received all the good news from this quarter."

When two leaders of two armies exchange such grim courtesies, there is winter in the wind.

Hamilton set out on his mission and paused at Fishkill to leave instructions with Putnam to send Washington two Continental brigades and a brigade of militia. He met General Poor and instructed him to hurry to Washington. When he reached Albany he found Gates established there, and very stubborn.[23]

Gates alleged a fear that Clinton might come up the river and destroy the arsenal at Albany, or go on and recapture Ticonderoga. He objected to leaving New England open to the British. Hamilton was afraid of Gates' immense popularity and his ability to render Washington's actions "odious" by appealing to New England and describing the danger to which Washington would subject it. So Hamilton had to be satisfied with one extra brigade that he squeezed out of Gates.

When he passed through Fishkill on his way back, he was shocked to find that Putnam had ignored all his instructions. Poor's troops had had a mutiny, a captain killed a soldier and was killed by the soldier's friend. Furthermore:

"They were under an operation for the itch." [24]

Hamilton borrowed money enough to quell the mutiny with part of the eight months' back pay; then wrote to Putnam:

"Sir: I cannot forbear confessing that I am astonished and alarmed beyond measure to find that all his Excellency's views have been hitherto frustrated, . . . the cause of America is put to the utmost conceivable hazard . . . I now, sir, in the most explicit terms, by his Excellency's authority, give it as a positive order from him, that all the Continental troops under your command may be immediately marched." [25]

Putnam protested to Washington that Hamilton's orders would leave him with only three hundred Continentals and no militia, and that Hamilton's letter contained "unjust and injurious reflections" on him. He declared that he would not remain at his post and send all his troops away.[26] Washington answered, defending Hamilton's urgency and waxing mildly sarcastic:

"I could wish that in future my orders may be immediately complied with, without arguing upon the propriety of them. If any accident ensues from obeying them, the fault will lie upon me and not upon you." [27]

To keep Putnam out of mischief he ordered him to turn his "most serious and active attention to this infinitely important object," the erection of new fortifications and obstructions for the defence of the Hudson.[28] He was particularly eager to see a strong fortress at West Point, which thus first came into its fame.

Gates' delay in sending the Northern troops to Washington had prevented him from saving the Delaware river forts, but Washington reaped the blame. After reconnoitring the British lines Washington tried again to bring his officers to agree upon an attack on Philadelphia during the absence of Cornwallis out foraging with about two thousand men, but the council of officers on November 24th, 1777, voted against him, eleven to four. His plan of attack was another dawn assault in several

MAJOR-GENERAL HORATIO GATES

(From the painting by Gilbert Stuart)

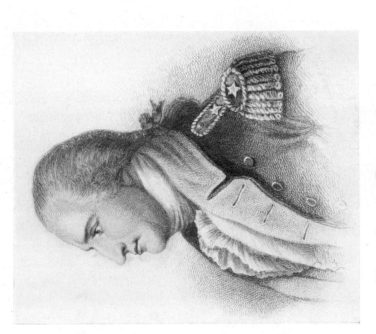

MAJOR-GENERAL BENEDICT ARNOLD

(From the etching by H. R. Hall)

directions as at Germantown; only now, instead of attacking a camp without even a breastwork or a trench, he would hurl his tatterdemalions against a chain of fourteen exceedingly strong redoubts. The officers thought it would be "madness." Again they undoubtedly saved Washington from as bad a disaster as he had sought in vain outside Boston.

Despite his sensational popularity and the lobbying of his partisans, Gates was not strong enough to take Washington's high office away, and he was left without a task. His party in Congress had power enough, however, to establish him as the head of a new Board of War, constituted November 27th, 1777.[29] The other members were Mifflin, Colonel Pickering, Joseph Trumbull, and Richard Peters. Of these, Peters was a confessed idolater of Washington's; while Pickering revered his virtues, but could not see his military qualifications. Mifflin and Gates, of course, had the minimum of affection for Washington.

The very appointment of Gates and Mifflin to a board that was theoretically superior to Washington and advisory direct to Congress, proved how close he stood to demotion.

Not all of Washington's thoughts were given, of course, to his ungrateful opponents, or to military matters. He mingled a startling naval project with his domestic interests. On November 14th, 1777, he was writing to Jacky Custis about renting a farm and advising him to follow the inclinations of "your mamma." Then he made this agreement to go in with Jackie, Lund, and Colonel Baylor on the purchase of a privateer.

"It is perfectly agreeable, too, that Colonel Baylor should share part of the privateer. I have spoken to him on the subject; he still continues in the same mind, and will write to you on the subject. I shall therefore consider myself as possessing one fourth of your full share, and that yourself, Baylor, L. Washington, and I are equally concerned in the share you at first held." [30]

Little is known of this piratic venture. According to one account the boat was never finished. Otherwise Washington might not have been so forgotten as a privateer.

Many of the officers had been speculating heavily in that field. Greene wrote, "Were I at liberty, I think that I could make a fortune for my family." But he had conscientious scruples against anything that hurt the army recruiting. Knox was not so restrained and frequently bought shares in privateers. But he was always a loser; all his ships were captured.[31]

Congress, in spite of its loss of giants like John Hancock, John Adams and others of its founders, was feeling an access of power from a new justification, new credentials and a new unity. A Congressman wrote:

"The child Congress has been big with, these two years past, is at last brought forth—(Confederation) . . . you will think it a Monster."[32]

The day after the committee was appointed to draft the Declaration of Independence, another had been appointed to draw up Articles of Confederation. The Declaration was ready in a month; the Articles two and a half years later.

They were destined to serve as a most unsatisfactory Constitution for the next ten years, before they were replaced by an equally unsatisfactory agreement known as the Constitution. The Articles were not ratified, however, by the thirteenth colony until 1781, when the fighting was practically over. The method of ratifying the Constitution itself was a violation of the Articles.[33]

The Confederation was only, says Max Farrand, "a gentleman's agreement."[34] Each state had one vote and a two-thirds vote was required for the exercise of Congress' powers and there was no power to force any state to obey. Any one state could block the will of the rest. There was no president, no executive at all. There was no judiciary. The colonies had as yet no idea of a permanent fusion. They were thirteen republics in a temporary league. The allies in the World War were of no less unity than the colonies—a partnership in an emergency. General Pershing was hardly more alien than Washington, who also was a foreign representative (from Virginia), temporarily in command of cooperating nations, like Foch.

To Washington, however, the nation was the thing. He was fighting, not for Virginia in a necessitous alliance, but for a country that he had discovered in the mists and must consolidate and bind together until adhesion became cohesion.

The news of Burgoyne's surrender reached Howe from the Americans. That was one bit of military information they transmitted without delay or disguise. Howe could not believe it at first, then he bowed his head to the inevitable avalanche of blame. He had written home "that the War was now on a different scale that they had many French officers & a large quantity of Artillery."

Being of peaceful mood he had lovingly chastised the Rebels in battle. Now he found himself confronted no longer with green farmers and inexperienced colonial officers. The best engineers of Europe were pouring in and lending the most expert aid, often at their own expense. Kosciuszko designed works that helped to break Burgoyne; du Coudray and de Portail built fortifications. Pulaski handled the cavalry, and laid out at least fifty thousand dollars of his own money on it. We have seen on the balcony of the Chew House the young Chevalier de Mauduit du Plessis. Washington praised "the gallant conduct of the young gentleman at Brandywine, Germantown, and his distinguished services at Fort Mercer." [35]

Few Americans have even heard the names of de la Radière buried with military honors in New Jersey; of the Marquis de la Rouerie, who fought under the simple sword-name of Colonel Armand; of the Marquis de Valory, or the Marquis de Vienne, or the fearless de Fleury, de Gimat, de Pontgibaud. Obscure bands of militia were often commanded by Frenchmen—to say nothing of the multitude that came over after the alliance. [36]

But Howe knew the difference and dared not risk what he would have ventured before. Outside Boston, Washington had bewailed the lack of engineers. Now he had some of the best in Europe, also the best drill masters in the world, men who knew how to maneuver troops, fiery young men, too, who looked upon a wound as a decoration.

Howe could get little food, less supplies, no reinforcements. He was in despair and legitimately convinced that neither he nor anybody else could do the job before him. On October 22nd, 1777, he sent home to Germain his resignation.

"From the little attention My Lord [has] given to my Recommendations since the commencement of my command I am led to hope I may be releived from this very painful Service. I have not the good fortune to enjoy the necessary confidence and Support of my Superiors." [37]

What Howe did from then on was *post mortem*. He hated the thought of slaughtering his own men or the enemy's. It was like fighting after an armistice had been declared. His mind had confessed that the war was lost. When his troops grew too restless he took them out for a parade and a challenge to Washington, who had moved up close as if he wanted a fight. On December 4th Howe decided to spar with Washington a little. He marched out during the night with nearly all his force to Chestnut Hill, about three miles from Washington's camp at Whitemarsh. Washington's useful spy, Major John H. Clark, Junior, sent him full details, and Captain Allen McLane of the Delaware Light Horse was ready for Howe as he came out and checked his advance with brilliant cavalry rushes.

Having been reinforced by about 4,000 men from the North, Washington was on equal terms with whatever Howe could bring against him. On the first day Washington sent out General Irvine to attack Howe's advance. The General was wounded, and abandoned by his runaway men. Howe did nothing but feint at Washington's right. The next day he moved up to within a mile of the left and stood still, repeating the shadow-boxing tactics he had used in New Jersey to tease Washington off the hill. He teased in vain.

Sunday, the 7th, he maneuvered still further to Washington's left and the American expected an encircling movement. Colonel Morgan and Colonel Mordecai Gist with the Maryland militia attacked the advance on the right. The Americans fought well, but Cornwallis threw them back.

The next day, to the surprise of everybody including his own disgusted officers, Howe marched about all day, lighted fires on the hills at night, left them burning and slipped back to Philadelphia, to be further denounced.

Washington acknowledged casualties of 43 or 44 men, before all returns were in. It was a small loss for a three days' encounter of 30,000 men. Light Horse Harry Lee quotes Washington as saying:

"Better would it have been for Sir William Howe to have fought without victory, than thus to declare his inability." [38]

December chill had led the American soldiers to burn the abatis meant to protect them and now gave warning that it was time to be thinking of winter quarters. Cadwalader strongly urged Wilmington, Delaware, especially as it would otherwise be seized by the British. Washington was favorably inclined, but consulted everybody concerned, and had a different opinion from each counsellor. In the meanwhile he set out to cross the Schuylkill on a bridge of "36 waggons, with a bridge of Rails between each," says Dr. Albigence Waldo, writing with numb fingers in his diary, and adding:

"It snows—I'm Sick—eat nothing—No Whiskey—No Forage—Lord—Lord—Lord . . . Cold & uncomfortable." [39]

When part of the men were over, Cornwallis was descried with several thousand men on a foraging expedition. Sullivan recalled the troops and broke down part of the bridge. Cornwallis fell on General Potter's men, who behaved well enough to win Washington's praise, but were scattered.

There was debate as to Cornwallis' strength and purpose. Washington was sure he was merely on a foray, and was inclined to attack, but was persuaded not to. Reed says that it was "somewhat mortifying" to sit and watch Cornwallis burning houses and plundering "in the face of our whole army," but "The General has suffered his own better judgment to be controlled by others." [40]

Young John Laurens wrote to his father:

"The want of provisions—I could weep tears of blood when I say it—the want of provisions rendered it impossible to march . . . Gen¹ Sullivan's retrograde movement was unspeakably unlucky. If we had persevered in crossing in the first instance, or if we had even crossed in the evening of the first day, the flower of the British army must have fallen a sacrifice to superior numbers." [41]

A committee of congressmen had been visiting Washington to discuss his plans for a winter campaign, and persuade him to attack Philadelphia. He answered that his army was in no condition to linger outdoors and ought to get under better cover than canvas; that an attack on Philadelphia could not hope for success, and that there was great indifference to the service among his officers and "universal aversion to continue in the Field during the Winter." [42]

His officers nearly all agreed with him when their opinion was asked. General Weedon wrote:

"This Army—it is Sir the Bullwork of America and should be nursed and cherished as the salvator of her Liberties. The Troops that compose it are not more than mortal, and cannot work Maricles." [43]

Washington himself favored hutting his men in Wilmington where mild weather could be expected and provisions and supplies secured by way of the Delaware river. This raised a great outcry against him.

The Pennsylvania Council and Assembly drew up a hot Remonstrance and presented it to Congress, declaring that if Washington went into winter quarters at Wilmington, "Pennsylvania and New Jersey will be abandoned to the ravages of the British, and the inhabitants would be obliged to fly to the neighboring States, or submit to such terms as the enemy may subscribe."

Congress forwarded this to Washington with a strong reminder of the danger of exposing New Jersey "to the particular resentment of a merciless enemy." [44] The Council threatened Congress with the loss of all the state's financial support, and called on Anthony Wayne for help. He proposed a compromise: winter quarters at Valley Forge where Philadelphia would be under constant menace. The compromise was a most unwise one, according to Walton, and the insistence on the acceptance of the paper money at par made Tories of many patriots:

"It is doubtful if any location could have been secured where supplies were more difficult to secure than at Valley Forge. If any thing had been left in Chester county after the raids of two armies, it had been carried away by the action of the Board of War before Washington came to Valley Forge." [45]

In a dismal endeavor to prepare his chilly troops for the worst, Washington tried to warm them, for lack of anything pleasanter or more accurate, with poetic oratory. He issued a long and fervid exhortation on December 17th, 1777, stating many things that he did not believe.[46]

On the next day, as a crowning insult of misfortune, he had to ask his half-starved, half-naked, altogether despondent army to pause for the day of Thanksgiving and Praise voted on November 1st in honor of the distant victory of his secret enemy, Gates. John Adams had written to his wife of this Thanksgiving:

"One cause of it ought to be that the glory of turning the tide of arms is not immediately due to the Commander-in-chief nor to southern troops. If it had been, idolatry and adulation would have been unbounded; so excessive as to endanger our liberties, for what I know. Now, we can allow a certain citizen to be wise, virtuous, and good, without thinking him a deity or a savior." [47]

He was now so far from being deified, that in spite of the exposure of the Conway Cabal, and his most insistent protests,

Congress just five days before, on December 13th, 1777, had made Conway a major-general and appointed him inspector-general.[48] This was Washington's particular occasion for gratitude. The army's reasons are given by General Dearborn:

"This is Thanksgiving Day through the whole continent of America, but God knows we have very little to keep it with this being the third day we have been without flour or bread—and are living on a high uncultivated hill, in huts and tents. Laying on the cold ground, upon the whole I think all we have to be thankful for is that we are alive and not in the grave with many of our friends." [49]

The next day the army moved to the slopes in front of the valley by way of the old Gulph Road, "and not an improper name neither," writes Dr. Albigence Waldo—"for this Gulph seems well adapted by its situation to keep us from the pleasures & enjoyments of this World." Thus he describes himself and his companions:

"Poor food — hard lodging — Cold Weather — fatigue — Nasty Cloaths—nasty Cookery—Vomit half my time—smoak'd out of my senses—the Devil's in't—I can't Endure it . . . smoke & Cold—hunger & filthyness—A pox on my bad luck. There comes a bowl of beef soup—full of burnt leaves and dirt, sickish enough to make a Hector spue—away with it Boys—I'll live like the Chameleon upon Air. Poh! Poh! crys Patience within me—you talk like a fool. . . .

"See the poor Soldier, when in health—with what cheerfulness he meets his foes and encounters every hardship—if barefoot, he labours thro' the Mud & Cold with a Song in his mouth extolling War & Washington. . . .

"There comes a Soldier, his bare feet are seen thro' 'his worn out Shoes, his legs nearly naked from the tatter'd remains of an only pair of stockings, his Breeches not sufficient to cover his nakedness, his Shirt hanging in Strings, his hair dishevell'd, his face meagre; his whole appearance pictures a person forsaken & discouraged. He comes, and crys with an air of wretchedness & despair, I am Sick, my feet lame, my legs are sore, my body cover'd with this tormenting Itch . . . and all the reward I shall get will be—'Poor Will is dead.' . . .

"Ye who Eat Pumkin Pie and Roast Turkies, and yet Curse fortune for using you ill, Curse her no more, least she reduce your Allowance of her favours to a bit of Fire Cake, & a draught of Cold Water, & in Cold Weather too." [50]

Washington's men were not alone in their misery. From the other garrisons he heard the same story. It was two years and a half now since Washington had taken command of the great uprising—and still he must protest to Congress in a famous letter—an infamous letter considering the prosperity of the country:

"Unless some great and capital change suddenly takes place in that line, this army must inevitably be reduced to one or other of these three things.—Starve—dissolve—or disperse, in order to obtain subsistence. . . .

"Yesterday afternoon . . . behold! to my great mortification, I was not only informed, but convinced, that the men were unable to stir on acc^t of Provision, & that a dangerous mutiny begun the Night before, & which with difficulty was suppressed by the spirited exertions of some officers was still much to be apprehended for want of this article.

"This brought forth the only Com[missar]y in the purchasing Line, in this Camp; and, with him, this melancholy & alarming truth—that he had not a single hoof of any kind to slaughter, & not more than 25 bar^{ls} of Flour!—From hence form an opinion of our Situation when I add, that, he could not tell when to expect any. . . . Three or four days of bad weather would prove our destruction. . . .

"Since the month of July we have had no assistance from the quartermaster-general. . . . The soap, vinegar, and other articles allowed by Congress, we see none of, nor have we seen them, I believe, since the battle of Brandywine. The first, indeed, we have now little occasion for; few men having more than one shirt, many only the moiety of one, and some none at all."

He struck back at the authors of the Remonstrance with devastating scorn:

"I can assure those gentlemen, that it is a much easier and less distressing thing to draw remonstrances in a comfortable room by a good fireside, than to occupy a cold, bleak hill, and sleep under frost and snow, without clothes or blankets. However, although they seem to have little feeling for the naked and distressed soldiers, I feel superabundantly for them, and, from my soul, I pity those miseries, which it is neither in my power to relieve or prevent." [51]

And that was his Christmas gift to the nation, as Valley Forge was the nation's gift to him and his men.

And so the year with the three sevens, of which so much was expected, guttered out like a candle. The gloomy prophecy of "three gallowses" had not been fulfilled, nor any of the eminent Scotch divine's bright promises: that the colonies should be independent; that there should be a war in Europe, and that a star should fall from the crown of Great Britain.

XXII

THE CONWAY CABAL

TO give the name of Conway to the activity of 1777-78 against Washington is even more unreasonable than to call America "America" after a man named Amerigo Vespucci. For Vespucci at least pretended to have discovered America, but Conway denied all share in any cabal against Washington, and protested that the real cabal was against himself. Yet to hope to change the name of the cabal would be as futile as trying to persuade people to call North and South America Columbia or Cabotia.

Even the traditionally volatile French were startled by the virulence of envy poisoning the sons of Liberty. Mauroy wrote to the Count de Broglie:

"This country is like ours, subject to the same passions, save that the passions are all naked and lack that art which renders ours endurable." [1]

Thomas Conway, an Irishman in the French service, came over with du Coudray in the first shipload sent by Beaumarchais. Du Coudray had hardly landed when he set the American generals to resigning in clusters. When he died he left a superior trouble maker in Conway, who soon had Washington and all the generals in convulsions of mutual accusation.

Conway was born in Ireland (just a year after Washington was born in Virginia) February 27th, 1733. He was taken to France at the age of six and raised there. The Vicomte de Noailles [2] says that he was major with the rank of colonel when he was engaged in Paris by Silas Deane and sent to Congress with a request for a high post in view of his great experience, ability and devotion. It is only fair in view of what followed and the general contempt for Conway to quote Deane's account

235

of him to the Secret Committee of Congress, November 29th,
1776:

"I have recommended several officers to your service, but none with
greater pleasure, scarce any one with so much confidence of his answering great and valuable purposes, as the bearer, Colonel Conway, a
native of Ireland, advanced in this service by his merit. His views are
of establishing himself and his growing family in America; consequently he becomes our countryman and engages on the most certain
principles. This gentleman has seen much service; his principal department has been that of training and disciplining troops, and preparing
for action; and, from his abilities as well as from his long experience,
he is considered as one of the most skilful disciplinarians in France." [3]

It is not quite clear why Washington took so immediate a
dislike to him, unless he suspected him of the authorship of
a number of caustic criticisms published under the pen name
"De Lisle." The authorship was never fastened on Conway,
but he must have done a vast amount of verbal castigation of
Washington and it doubtless reached Washington's ears. Conway fawned on Lafayette and called himself Lafayette's
soldier. After a period of admiration Lafayette wrote to
Washington:

"I found that he was an ambitious and dangerous man. He has
done all in his power, by cunning manœuvres, to take off my confidence
and affection for you." [4]

Conway apparently fell into the company of the Congressmen and the officers who lacked confidence in Washington. He
kept asking for a major-generalcy and Washington constantly
opposed him, going so far as to write to R. H. Lee a letter
seeming to imply that he would resign if Conway were promoted, though he afterwards denied any such intention. Of
the plan to appoint Conway a major-general, he said:

"It will be as unfortunate a measure as ever was adopted. I may
add, (and I think with truth,) that it will give a fatal blow to the
existence of the army. . . . It is a maxim with him, to leave no service
of his own untold, nor to want any thing, which is to be obtained by
importunity. . . .

"After allowing him every thing that his warmest friends will contend for, I would ask, why the youngest brigadier in the service (for I believe he is so) should be put over the heads of all the eldest, and thereby take rank and command gentlemen, who but yesterday were his seniors. . . . No day passes over my head without application for leave to resign. Within the last six days, I am certain, twenty commissions at least have been tendered to me. . . . I have been a slave to the service; I have undergone more than most men are aware of, to harmonize so many discordant parts; but it will be impossible for me to be of any further service, if such insuperable difficulties are thrown in my way." [5]

To this R. H. Lee answered that the appointment had not been made and probably would not be, though Congress had been told that it would be "very agreeable to the army, whose favorite Mr. Conway was asserted to be." [6]

Conway was convinced of his own right to promotion and gave good reasons enough for it, at least from his viewpoint, when he wrote to Charles Carroll of Carrollton of the Board of War, November 14th, 1777, a letter in which there seems to be no guile and much dignity:

"Of all the French officers who came to this continent, I am the most advanced in rank, and the only field officer bearing rank in actual service. . . . The French gentlemen told me, Sir, that you asked in a most despising manner what I had done. Indeed I must confess that I did not do all that I wish to have done, but I hope I have done as much as was left in my power. . . . At the Short Hills I was first ready, and first attacked, drew up in battle, stopped the enemy, and made my retreat without running, and without losing a single prisoner. . . . At Brandywine my brigade remained the last upon the ground, and though I had been abandoned pretty early by the brigades of the right and left, my brigade continued fighting until it was flanked on both sides by the enemy. That same brigade was the first or rather the only brigade that rallied to oppose the enemy's pursuit, when for want of ammunition it was ordered to be relieved at the close of the evening by a French brigade which had not yet been engaged. At Germantown, with little better than four hundred men, I began the attack, and was fighting three quarters of an hour before any individual came to support me. . . .

"You asked upon what grounds I could call for the rank of major general. Because I can be more useful at the head of a division than at the head of a small brigade. Because in my young days I had a larger command before the enemy than what I have had in your army. Because being twenty years constantly studying military operations, having travelled through Europe to take a view of the different armies, having been lately employed in making out a set of field manœuvres, having practiced and tried said manœuvres last year in the presence of several experienced generals, both German and French, I thought myself more qualified to command a division than such major generals who had never seen a line of battle as they confess themselves, before Brandywine, and as it too well appeared.

"It was for want of knowledge and practise in forming the lines that Brandywine was partly lost. I can assign many other reasons for the loss of that battle. It was for want of forming the line and of manœuvering that we miscarried at Germantown, our left wing composed of the largest part of our army, having lost near an hour in an useless countermarch, as it appears by the several testimonies given at a court martial now sitting, of which I am a member.

"I am far from thinking myself a general, but I believe that after having studied and practiced this trade steadily during almost all my life, I may venture to say that I know somewhat more of it than the brave, honest men who never made it their business. . . . I was much surprised at the reflections which you made upon the subject, as I am conscious that I have done nothing in my life that could make me contemptible in the eyes of any honest man." [7]

In another letter Conway objected to being under the command of the bibulous Major-General Lord Stirling:

"I commanded fifteen hundred men in France, and here I command five hundred under the orders of a major-general who is not able to command one hundred although a brave man . . . I cannot remain under the orders of a man who will not let people do good, who cannot do it himself because he knows nothing of the matter, and if he did cannot do anything reasonable after dinner." [8]

Some of the cautious Americans no doubt enjoyed the privilege of using a foreigner to pull their chestnuts out of the fire, and were perfectly willing to let him burn his paws instead of their own.

The result was the famous, complicated and odious scandal known as the Conway Cabal, a matter so bewildering and distasteful that one can understand why Edward Channing is content to dismiss it from his history with a footnote of references and a brief statement that it is "enshrouded in the mists," and "intimately connected with the story of James Wilkinson, whose life as he himself relates it was a mystery from beginning to end." [9]

But it presents Washington in so many phases of character and action and presents the world in which he had his being so variously that it deserves detailed consideration.

After the battle of Brandywine Conway apparently wrote to Gates a letter containing thirteen criticisms of the conduct of that engagement, and naturally of Washington. No effort was spared to bring this letter to light but it was kept dark. Its fame had apparently spread far and wide, before Gates sent his beloved adjutant, Wilkinson, to Congress with news of the capture of Burgoyne; for Wilkinson heard of it when he rested for a day at Easton, Pennsylvania, and fell in with Dr. William Shippen, the director-general of military hospitals.

Wilkinson moved on to Reading, where there were "two Eastern members of Congress." He took tea with them at the home of General Mifflin, who did not idolize Washington. They also knew of Conway's criticisms. The next day he was held up by a violent rain and Lord Stirling, who was confined in the village in consequence of a fall from his horse, earnestly requested him "to take a pot luck dinner with him." Other guests were his aides-de-camp, Majors McWilliams and Monroe (later President of the United States). Wilkinson admired Lord Stirling's character and "noble deportment," but "I speak of his foibles with reluctance . . . his addictions were notorious." [10]

Stirling was so famous for his potations that in 1776 the British had represented him in a farce as howling for liquor and being reminded by his valet: "You drank stinkabus enough last night to split the head of an Indian." [11]

The whole republic was shaken almost apart by what two drunken officers had babbled. If his own story is to be believed—and it is not disproved—Wilkinson was evidently so besotted that he could never to his dying day recall a word of the conversation with Lord Stirling, who was in his usual after-dinner state. But his aide, McWilliams, told his Lordship that Wilkinson had said that he had seen a letter from Conway to Gates containing this phrase:

"Heaven has been determined to save your country or a weak general and bad counsellors would have ruined it."

So in the cold gray morrow, Lord Stirling forwarded the story and the phrase to Washington with a statement: "Such wicked duplicity of conduct I shall always think it my duty to detect." [12]

When Washington learned from Lord Stirling what Stirling had learned from what McWilliams had learned from the drunken Wilkinson's memory of a letter Gates had shown him, Washington wrote to Conway one of the briefest of his countless letters:

"Sir, A letter, which I received last night, contained the following paragraph.

"'In a letter from General Conway to General Gates he says, *"Heaven has been determined to save your country, or a weak General and bad counsellors would have ruined it."*' I am, Sir, your humble servant." [13]

Simply that and nothing more.

It was a bombshell to Conway, but he went to Washington at once to defend himself, saying that he had never written those words. He also demanded the truth of Wilkinson, who denied that any such expressions were in the letter as he remembered it. Conway threw the lie at Stirling. Stirling demanded an explanation of Wilkinson, and the exact words of Conway's letter. Wilkinson replied:

"I can scarce credit my senses, when I read the paragraph in which you request an extract from a private letter, which had fallen under my observation. I may have been indiscreet, my Lord, but be assured I am not dishonourable." [14]

In the meanwhile Mifflin, ignorant of Wilkinson's share in the taradiddle, had written to Gates informing him that an extract from Conway's letter to him had been procured and sent to Washington and by him inclosed to Conway "without remarks." [15]

This threw Gates into wild confusion and alarm. He could not imagine who had betrayed him or how far. He wrote to Conway praising him for "the dignity of a virtuous soldier," but adding:

"I intreat you, dear General, to let me know which of the letters was copied off." [16]

Gates suspected Hamilton at first, and told the befuddled Wilkinson so. In his increased rage, he rashly hoped to disgrace Hamilton before Washington, and ventured, in his utter ignorance of the fact that Washington possessed only the indirect quotation of a single phrase, to write him a timorous bluffing letter:

"I shall not attempt to describe what, as a private Gentleman, I cannot help feeling, on representing to my Mind, the disagreeable Situation, which confidential Letters, when exposed to public Inspection, may place an unsuspecting Correspondent to; but, as a public Officer, I conjure your Excellency, to give me all the Assistance you can, in tracing out the Author of the Infidelity, which put Extracts from General Conway's Letters to me, into your Hands. Those Letters have been stealingly copied; but, which of them, when, or by whom is to me, as yet, an unfathomable Secret. . . .

"It being unknown to me, whether the Letter came to you from a Member of Congress, or from an Officer, I shall have the Honour of transmitting a Copy of this to the President, that the Congress may in Concert with your Excellency, obtain as soon as possible, a Discovery, which so deeply Affects the Safety of the States. Crimes of that Magnitude ought not to remain unpunished." [17]

Washington seems to have been genuinely amused by his command of the situation and to have relished the comic opera nature of the plot against him, for he answered Gates with letters of high comedy that are epic in their sarcasms. He had the laugh on Gates, who did not dream that it was his own pet Wilkinson who had exposed him; also on Conway for complaining of Washington's "bad counsellors,"—to which Washington added the gay comment:

"One of whom, by the bye, he was."

Since Gates had sent a copy of his letter to Congress, Washington returned his answer the same way with a note of apology for the trouble he gave. His letter is filled with a majestic scorn that cannot help smiling. It must have made Gates writhe as he read it. Washington told Gates frankly what has already been recounted; that Colonel Wilkinson told McWilliams "not in confidence, that I ever understood," what Conway had written to Gates, which phrase Lord Stirling had sent to him, and the exact note he had sent to Conway "without having any thing more in view than merely to shew that Gentl. that I was not unapprized of his intriguing disposition." He assured Gates that he had never mentioned the letter to anyone outside his family except Lafayette.

"I never knew that General Conway (who I viewed in the light of a stranger to you) was a correspondant of yours; much less did I suspect that I was the subject of your confidential Letters. . . . I considered the information as coming from yourself, and given with a friendly view to forewarn, and consequently forearm me, against a secret enemy, or in other words, a dangerous incendiary; in which character, sooner or later, this country will know Genl. Conway—But, in this, as in other matters of late, I have found myself mistaken." [18]

When Gates recovered from the shock of learning that his own protégé, Wilkinson, had let the matter escape, he wrote at once to say that Washington would be pleased to learn that

"The paragraph which your excellency has condescended to transcribe, is spurious. It was certainly fabricated to answer the most selfish and wicked purposes."

He went on to describe Conway's letter as containing "very judicious remarks upon that want of discipline, which has often alarmed your Excellency," and assured him that it contained nothing about a weak general or a bad counsellor. Since so much false rumor had exaggerated the letter he decided to return it to the writer, rather than risk the feelings of sensitive officers, who might feel hurt by Conway's remarks. Then he tore into Wilkinson, accused him of duplicity, of trying to lay the blame on another officer, of forgery and guile amounting to treason—all for the purpose of injuring Conway.[19]

In answer to this Washington wrote an even more crushing letter giving Gates the lie with most exquisite relentlessness, pointing out how irreconcilable Gates' own statements were with one another—playing with irony and ending with wrath.[20]

After this terrific lacing, Gates had just strength enough to implore a truce and express an earnest hope that "no more of that Time so precious to the Public, may be lost upon the Subject of General Conways Letter." [21]

Washington consented to drop the controversies and agreed with Gates' desire "of burying them hereafter in silence, and, as far as future events will permit, oblivion . . . it is particularly my wish to avoid any personal feuds or dissensions with those who are embarked in the same great national interest." [22]

But Gates was by no means finished with the affair. He refused to sanction Wilkinson's service as secretary to the Board of War, and denounced him as a betrayer. Wilkinson was aghast: "he, an old major general, who had borne a commission in Braddock's defeat, the conqueror of a whole British army . . . I, a boy of twenty, without experience, without patronage."

In fury he resigned his brevet as brigadier and wrote Gates demanding an explanation. Gates answered with a quotation from Washington's letter stating what Wilkinson had disclosed, and repeating his charge that Wilkinson tried to shift the blame. He also offered any other "satisfaction" Wilkinson might command.

Wilkinson hastened to York where Gates was stationed, and challenged him. A duel was arranged between the second best general in the army and his former adjutant!   But this was the encounter as Wilkinson tells it:

"I found General Gates unarmed and alone, and was received with tenderness, but manifest embarrassment; he asked me to walk, turned into a back street . . . he burst into tears, took me by the hand, and asked me, 'how I could think he wished to injure me? . . . I should as soon think of injuring my own child.'

"This language not only disarmed me but awakened all my confidence, and all my tenderness; I was silent, and he added, 'besides there was no cause for injuring you, as Conway acknowledged his letter, and has since said much harder things to Washington's face.'

"Such language left me nothing to require, it was satisfactory beyond expectation." [23]

Now Wilkinson wanted Stirling's life. He wrote to Gates, "My Lord shall bleed for this." [24] Stirling was at Valley Forge and Wilkinson set out thither. Colonel Moylan, Colonel Biddle and Doctor Shippen agreed that it would not be necessary to shoot Lord Stirling provided he would admit that the fateful conversation "passed in a private company, during a convivial hour." Stirling graciously gave him that admission in writing and added that Wilkinson's mention of the letter would never injure his honor.

Now Washington invited Wilkinson to dine at headquarters. Wilkinson says he declined, but was asked again, and again declined, saying that he had been charged with "betraying private confidence to curry favour with the General," and this would "countenance the calumny." He was asked a third time and accepted.

According to Wilkinson, Washington was very cordial, approved all he had done and "spoke freely of the cabal which had been formed against him, and mentioned the persons whom he suspected to be at the bottom of it." Then he showed Wilkinson the whole correspondence with Gates, on which Wilkinson exclaims:

"This exposition unfolded to me a scene of perfidy and duplicity, of which I had no suspicion. . . . Sad requital for all my services; a monstrous deed! the justice of Heaven soon precipitated him from the pinnacle of undeserved fame to the abyss of humiliation." [25]

Wilkinson was out of employ for more than a year, when Congress appointed him clothier-general.

Conway, however, had in the meanwhile received his major-generalcy in Washington's despite. Congress assigned him to the newly created post of inspector-general, for which he was eminently fitted, however unpopular.

Though thus humiliated and defeated, Washington showed the strictest regard for the commission Congress had given to Conway and the frankest distaste for the man himself. Conway wrote to Washington:

"If my appointment is productive of any inconvenience, or anywise disagreeable to your Excellency, as I neither applied nor solicited for this place, I am very ready to return to France, where I have pressing business; and this I will do with the more satisfaction, as I expect even there to be useful to the cause." [26]

Washington replied that his appointment as inspector-general gave nobody any uneasiness, but his "extraordinary promotion" to major-general would cause remonstrances. To this Conway answered on December 31st, 1777, not unworthily:

"There is nothing extraordinary in it, only that such a place was not thought of sooner. The general and universal merit, which you wish every promoted officer might be endowed with, is a rare gift. We see but few of merit so generally acknowledged. We know but the great Frederic in Europe, and the great Washington on this continent. I certainly never was so rash as to pretend to such a prodigious height. Neither do I pretend to any superiority in personal qualities over my brother brigadiers, for whom I have much regard. But you, Sir, and the great Frederic, know perfectly well, that this trade is not learnt in a few months. I have served steadily thirty years; that is, before some of my comrade brigadiers were born. Therefore I do not think that it will be found marvellous and incredible, if I command here a number of men, which falls much short of what I have commanded there many years in an old army." [27]

Again he offered to retire to France and wished the General "a happy new year and a glorious campaign."

Referring to Conway's comparisons of Washington with Frederick the Great, President Laurens said that "the taunts and sarcasm" were "unbecoming his Character and unpardonable." [28]

"If Gen. Conway pretends sincerity in his late Parallel between the great F—— and the great W—— he has, taking this Letter into view, been guilty of the blackest hypocrisy—if not, he is chargeable with the guilt of an unprovoked sarcasm, and is unpardonable."

Yet Conway had a certain justification for reference to Frederick, even for sarcasm in the matter. He had written to Gates in November of an experience in camp and the contemptuous treatment his wisdom had received from Washington's officers, when he recommended the text book used by Frederick the Great:

"General Varnum answer'd that there were some men in this continent who knew more about manouvres than the King of prussia this made me Dumb. however untill those men mentionn'd by general Varnum can be found out unless he be himself one of them I will send you when you are at Leisure a plan concerning the instruction of the army." [29]

It is to be noted that Baron Steuben is immortally praised for making exactly the criticisms and giving exactly the advice Conway offered.

At that time Frederick the Great was a world figure laughing at Washington's blunders, and even Laurens could not imagine a polite comparison of his friend Washington with such a giant. Posterity would make Frederick the lesser man, though perhaps the greater military genius.

Washington declined to assume responsibility for mistreatment of the inspector-general and he sent Conway's letters to Congress with a warm personal comment:

"If General Conway means, by cool receptions, . . . that I did not receive him in the language of a warm and cordial friend, I readily confess the charge. I did not, nor shall I ever, till I am capable of the arts of dissimulation. These I despise, and my feelings will not permit me to make professions of friendship to the man I deem my enemy, and whose system of conduct forbids it. At the same time, truth authorizes me to say, that he was received and treated with proper respect to his official character, and that he has had no cause to justify the assertion, that he could not expect any support for fulfilling the duties of his appointment." [30]

On January 10th, 1778, Conway wrote impatiently:

"Sir; I remain in a state of inaction until such time as your Excellency will think fit to employ me. I understand that your aversion to me is owing to the letter I wrote to General Gates. I have made you a candid answer upon that subject, and such an answer as must satisfy you and every man of a liberal disposition. There is not a subaltern in Europe but what will write to his friends and acquaintances, and mention freely his opinion of the Generals and of the army; but I never heard that the least notice was taken of these letters. Must such an odious and tyrannical inquisition begin in this country? Must it be introduced by the Commander-in-chief of this army raised for the defence of liberty? It cannot be, and I am satisfied you never had such thoughts. . . .

"I cannot believe, Sir, neither does any officer in your army believe, that the objection to my appointment originates from any body living but from you; . . . Since you will not accept of my services, since you cannot bear the sight of me in your camp, I am very ready to go wherever Congress thinks proper, and even to France; and I solemnly declare, that, far from resenting the undeserved rebuke I met with from you, I shall do every thing in my power to serve this cause." [31]

And now the famous letter reappears on the scene.

On January 27th, 1778, Conway writes to Washington that his letter has been returned to him from Gates. He had kept no copy of it and only now could say that he found "with great satisfaction, that the paragraph so much spoken of does not exist in said letter, nor any thing like it." He says the letter has been read by several members of Congress and he would have published it if President Laurens had not objected that it would inform the enemy of the dissension. He adds:

"I am a victim to calumny these two months past, and perhaps longer. I met with a reception from your Excellency such as I never met with before from any general during the course of thirty years in a very respectable army. Your mind has been embittered and prejudiced against me. Now that you are undeceived, I hope that your resentment will fall upon the authors of the forgery." [32]

His statements were confirmed by President Laurens, who advised against publication and confessed that the quotation was missing, though worse was included.

"I have seen the Letter . . . Genl. Washington was misinformed, the letter does not contain the words which had been reported to him, but ten times worse in every view." [33]

The "ten times worse" was probably this paragraph which he copied from the letter:

"What pity there is but one Gates! But the more I see of this army, the less I think it fit for general action under its actual chiefs and actual discipline. I speak to you sincerely and freely, and wish I could serve under you." [34]

The upshot of all the pother was that Conway never wrote the immortal words which young Wilkinson in his cups could never remember babbling to Stirling's aide, and which Stirling, getting them at second hand, sent to Washington and Washington to Conway.

Yet, if Wilkinson had not got drunk and made some reference to this letter, Washington would never have been able to dazzle his critics by the unexpected disclosure that they were being overheard. That brief letter of his was like the quick flash of a searchlight suddenly thrown on a group of burglars.

Conway's unpopularity with American officers in general is perhaps explained by his alleged habit of asking some of the curious creatures he met:

"Did Congress see you before they appointed you?" [35]

That was more Irish than French, but the wit came home too sharply to please its victims. Still, Washington said worse of them.

Conway has been damned forever for the Conway Cabal, in which he had done nothing creative or inspiring. In fact, Lovell, and some of the others most hostile to Washington, despised and resented Conway's pretensions and persistence. They dropped him and hugged their grievances.[36]

Poor Conway had his faults but he paid too high a price for them. Quite unintentionally he saved Washington's command from those who wanted to take it away, saved him both from those who disliked him or his cherished counsellors, and from those who feared him as too great.

XXIII

IDOLATERS AND ICONOCLASTS

THE sense of reverence for either men or gods has of late almost vanished from the average human soul. In the eighteenth century, however, it was still unusual to find anybody rash enough to deny the knee to one or more deities in heaven and to one or more direct agents on earth.

The humble private soldiers of the Revolution had no hope of anything better than a change of bosses and many of them must have accepted the watchword a German mercenary heard a rebel soldier cry out repeatedly during a night raid of Clinton's in September, 1777, when in the pitch dark he thought the Germans were comrades:

"Es befand sich nämlich einer von den Rebellen . . . und beständig schrie! God damn the King and God save the master Washington!" [1]

Surgeon Thacher tells of a crazy man who fell on his knees before General Gates and prayed God to forgive the general "for endeavoring to supersede that godlike man Washington." [2]

The American revolution was, however, pushed through largely by skeptics of royal sanctity, who were always mortally afraid that the result of their dangers and labors would be a mere substitution of one monarch for another.

There is picturesqueness in the utterances of those who thought they loved him wisely but not too well. Early in 1777, John Adams had protested in Congress:

"I have been distressed to see some members of this house disposed to idolise an image which their own hands have molten. I speak here of the superstitious veneration that is sometimes paid to Genl Washington." [3]

Canny John Adams thought that Washington should not
have been permitted to serve without pay. With marvellous
knowledge of human nature he declares that every public office
ought to yield an honest subsistence and independence, and
points out how often in history demagogues have pretended
to be disinterested patriots and have won the mob with gifts.
Of Washington's power he said:

"I answer, that, great as his talents and virtues are, they did not
altogether contribute so much to it as his serving without pay, which
never fails to turn the heads of the multitude. His ten thousand officers
under him, and all his other admirers, might have sounded his fame as
much as they would, and they might have justly sounded it very high,
and it would not all have produced such ecstasies among the people
as this single circumstance. Now, I say, this is all wrong. There
should have been no such distinction made between him and the other
generals. He should have been paid, as well as they, and the people
should have too high a sense of their own dignity ever to suffer
any man to serve them for nothing . . . it has been the people themselves who have always created their own despots." [4]

Adams always denied that he took part in any cabal against
Washington. He left Congress in weariness and disgust November 11th, 1777, hoping to be allowed to resume the practice
of law and earn a living. He reached home only to find that
he had been appointed commissioner to France. [5] In his later
years he wrote to a friend:

" 'The Father of his Country,' 'The Founder of the American Republic,' 'The Founder of the American Empire,' etc., etc., etc. These
Ascriptions belong to no Man; no! nor to any twenty Men; nor to
any hundred Men, nor to any thousand Men." [6]

Dr. Benjamin Rush was ardent for independence and insistent upon a republic of equality; he opposed every tendency
to one-man domination, upheld congressional supremacy, and
wanted that Roman ideal to prevail by which the senate called
generals from the plough and sent them back. Otherwise he
threatened to propose flatly putting the civil power in the hands
of the army.

He feared Washington as a potential king and, though, like Brutus, he may have loved him, he loved the republic more, and seemed to conspire against his friend.[7]

Henry Laurens in writing of the opposition to Washington connects the crowd of grafters (who have never yet been exposed) with his timorous and still anonymous detractors. He accuses both friends and enemies of Washington of being thieves and profiteers, and blames for the melancholy state men in Washington's "implicit confidence" for whom he "entertains the most favorable sentiments.

"These taken together form a Club whose demands upon the Treasury and the War Office never go away ungratified . . . in all such junctoes, there are prompters and Actors, accomodators, Candle snuffers, Shifters of scenes and Mutes." [8]

Nothing is healthier in a republic than a cantankerous faction of skeptics, as nothing is more unwholesome in a republic than an overwhelming spirit of veneration for one man. By such means nearly all republics have been changed to tyrannies.

John Adams had written that he favored an annual change of generals. Long afterward he remembered that the appointment of Washington to the command had been immediately regretted by nearly half of those who voted for it—"another instance of Apparent Unanimity and real regret in nearly one half." [9]

On December 18th, 1777, Benjamin Harrison wrote to Robert Morris from Williamsburg, Virginia, accusing R. H. Lee and the Adamses of plotting against Washington and planning "to divide the command." [10]

On January 6th, 1778, Dr. Craik wrote a letter of alarm to Washington. Craik was the old Scotch surgeon who had been with him on his first military expeditions in 1754, and was at his bedside when he died. Craik is mentioned in his will as "my compatriot in arms and old and intimate friend." Mr. Prussing says his "devoted friendship proved again the slander of coldness in Washington." [11] To Craik the mere questioning of Washington's ability was conspiracy, and he wrote:

"Base and Villainous men thro Chagrin, Envy, or Ambition are endeavouring to lessen you in the minds of the people and taking underhanded methods to traduce your Character—The morning I left Camp I was informed by a Gentleman, whom I believe to be a true Freind of yours, that a strong Faction was forming Against you with the New board of War and in the Congress. it alarmed me exceedingly."

He said that gossip put at the bottom of the plot "R. H. L., G-l M-n, and G-s." With almost passionate expressions of love and faith, he urged Washington to "have an Eye toward these Men." [12]

Next, Patrick Henry received an anonymous letter dated January 12th, 1778, praising him for being the first who "taught us to shake off our idolatrous attachment to royalty," and calling on him to act again in defence of the country against the ruination facing it, and the condition of the Southern army reduced to a "mob," though "A Gates, a Lee, or a Conway, would in a few weeks render them an irresistible body of men." [13]

The writer begged Henry if he recognized the handwriting not to mention it, but to burn the letter. Instead, Henry sent it to Washington at once, saying:

"I am sorry there should be one man who counts himself my friend who is not yours." [14]

Washington's fine letter of gratitude for Henry's letter contains this passage, confessing how it hurt to be stabbed in the back by a man who praised him to his face.[15]

Just as he was sealing the envelope he received Henry's second letter and enclosed a second letter of his own in which he stated his conclusion that Dr. Rush was the author of the anonymous letter "so far as I can judge from the similitude of hands.

"This man has been elaborate and studied in his professions of regard for me; and long since the letter to you. My caution to avoid any thing, which could injure the service, prevented me from communicating, but to a very few of my friends, the intrigues of a faction, which I know was formed against me, since it might serve to publish our internal dissensions; but their own restless zeal to advance their views has too clearly betrayed them, and made concealment on my part fruitless." [16]

From all sides Washington learned of the stealthy procedures against him. Somebody gave President Laurens an anonymous document, said to have been picked up on the stairs. He was requested to transmit it to Congress. But he sent it to Washington, though disclaiming that he was either "a party Man or an Informer." [17]

This paper was a fierce detailed criticism of Washington's generalship—just the sort of criticism for which Wayne, Sullivan, St. Clair, Schuyler and other generals had been called to account before courts-martial. It began as a Credo:

"I believe . . . that the proper method of attacking, beating, and conquering the enemy has never as yet been adopted by the Commander-in-chief; . . . that the many fruitless and unaccountable marches have had a great tendency to fill the hospitals with sick; . . . that the late success to the northward was owing to a change of commanders; that the southern army would have been alike successful, had a similar change taken place; . . . that it is a very great reproach to America to say there is only one general in it . . . that the people of America have been guilty of idolatry, by making a man their god; and the God of heaven and earth will convince them by woful experience, that he is only a man; that no good may be expected from the standing army, until Baal and his worshippers are banished from the camp." [18]

Washington's answer to this bill of indictments was a letter asking that the paper be submitted to Congress, welcoming any investigation and meekly admitting that he was not above error:

"Why should I expect to be exempt from censure, the unfailing lot of an elevated station? Merit and talents, with which I can have no pretensions of rivalship, have ever been subject to it. My heart tells me, that it has been my unremitted aim to do the best that circumstances would permit; yet I may have been very often mistaken in my judgment of the means, and may in many instances deserve the imputation of error." [19]

He makes a majestic figure standing in the rain of abuse with his hands tied by a love of country that would not permit him to close in battle with his accusers. Compared with the ego-maniacs who forbid criticism, crush freedom of speech, as-sassinate or execute possible rivals, and tread human liberties under foot, he becomes what is better than any of the gods, a man upholding mankind—not godlike, for the gods demand supremacy and claim supernal virtues, admit no flaws of heart or mind. Washington was pure Man, and at his greatest when he was most meek.

It was long believed that since R. H. Lee wrote much in cipher, his purpose was sinister and his letters, if decoded, would reveal his share in the Conway and other intrigues. But Dr. E. C. Burnett has recently deciphered all that can be found and published them in his invaluable and monumental work, *Letters of Members of the Continental Congress,* and he says that there are no revelations about the Cabal, though painful enough matter about the factions and faults of Congressmen.[20]

From Lund Washington came a letter dated Mount Vernon, February 18th, 1778, in which the incessant suspicion of R. H. Lee's loyalty seems to be thoroughly contradicted. Washington's eminent neighbor, George Mason, was profane in his praise. Lund writes:

"Lee declares no such thing or even a hint has ever been mentioned in Congress, and that he should look upon it as one of the greatest misfortunes that could befall this continent, should you by any means whatever give up the command of the army, for fully convinced he was in his own opinion no other man upon this continent was equal to the task; . . . the Supreme Being has been pleased to save and protect in the most miraculous degree the only man in whom every one could confide in.

"Mr. Mason is of opinion it is a Tory manœuver for he thinks no friend to America can be an enemy to you, for 'by God,' which was his expression, there is not nor ever was in the world a man who acted from a more laudable and disinterested motive than you do." [21]

General Varnum wrote to Greene at this time:

"Next to God Almighty and my country, I revere General Washington, and nothing fills me with so much indignation as the villainy of some who dare speak disrespectfully of him." [22]

John Jay is said to have told his son that the world would never know how strong the opposition to Washington was and the story runs that a day was definitely set for one of the congressmen in the Cabal to move for a committee to go to Valley Forge and put Washington under arrest. The Cabal had counted, according to this tradition, on a majority, but missed it by one vote. William Duer of New York, who was dangerously ill, resolved to appear himself at the risk of his life, but Gouverneur Morris arrived in time to save him from the necessity and the conspirators finding their majority gone, did not bring forward the motion.[23]

This legend is probably a distortion of certain well-known facts. There is a letter from William Duer to Robert Morris dated April 12th, begging Gouverneur Morris to hasten to Congress "for the sake of our Country . . . we cannot bring as many members absolutely essential to our Safety, without you, especially the Establishment for the Army." [24]

But this refers to the vital matter of granting half-pay to the officers for seven years, without which provision for their future Washington held that the officers would almost all resign and the army dissolve. There was intense opposition to this half-pay plan, and it is significant that Lovell, Rush and others who were connected with the Cabal were also opposed to the standing army and the half-pay guaranty.

Whatever the legends may be worth, and in spite of the vast and murky rumors that filled the nation, not an inkling of the Cabal or of any motion to unseat Washington appears in any of the records of Congress. Washington himself said afterward that no whisper of the kind was ever heard there.

One or two Congressmen might have been glad to bring about a recall, particularly James Lovell, always Washington's inveterate belittler and Gates' devoted partisan. His attacks are so full of venom that they are picturesque. He wrote to

Samuel Adams of "a Resolve which was meant to rap a Demi G—— over the Knuckles . . . one great Man whom no Citizen *shall* dare even to talk about." [25]

He sent Gates what he called an anecdote concerning the notorious affection of Washington for Greene and Knox:

"ANECDOTE.—Doctor Craig [Craik], the Clitus of this army, spoke very freely to a great man on the subject of favouritism and impenetrable reserve, and gave a free opinion on the probable consequences. It was taken kindly, and given out that a change would happen in conduct. Thus it took place. The two privy councillors, (supposed to be Greene and Knox), absented themselves three or four days from table. Reed and Cadwalader were caressed, and appeared as substitutes. But the great man's feelings were too much hurt by the apparent banishment of his dear, dear. They were restored, and, wonderful to tell, he has now two sets of favourites, friends, the one ostensible only, to blind the army, and the other real, and at the bottom of every movement. Again, Reed and Cadwalader, though good men, have no commissions in the army, yet their advice is taken on all occasions, and good authority says they sit in all councils of war. Do you recollect a similar adventure." [26]

Lovell wrote to Gates in November, 1777, that he was needed in many places, but,

"We want you most near Germantown. Good God! what a Situation are we in!" [27]

It must have been he that wrote the letter dated November 17th, 1777, in the Gates papers, though only a copy exists in a secretary's hand. This letter strongly insists that the resignations of which Washington complained so bitterly were really due to resentment of Washington's partiality and arrogance; and that the true cabal was Washington's, not Conway's:

"Repeated Slights & unjustifiable Arrogance combined with other Causes to drive from the Army those who would not worship the Image & pay an undeserved Tribute of praise & Flattery to the great & powerful.—The List of our disgusted patriots is long and formidable —their Resentments keen against the reigning Cabal and their powers of Opposition not despicable." [28]

A staunch opponent of Washington's was Jonathan D. Sergeant who wrote to Lovell on November 20th, 1777, denouncing Washington for "such blunders as might have disgraced a soldier of three months standing." [29]

Among those who resented Greene and Knox was Anthony Wayne, who blamed them both for the loss of the battle of Germantown. His impetuous spirit naturally chafed at the caution of "Fabius" and he wrote to Gates:

"I most Sincerely Congratulate you on the Unparrelled success of our Arms under your Conduct . . . which must eventually save this (Otherwise) Devoted Country . . . I don't yet despair . . . if our Worthy General will but follow his own good Judgment without listning too much to some Council." [30]

Mifflin was very close to Washington at first and highly respected by him. As a Pennsylvanian he had urged Washington to hasten to the rescue of his state as soon as Howe sailed from New York, but Washington under Greene's advice would not move until he was sure that Howe would not go to Boston or up the Hudson. To pacify Mifflin he called a council of war and Greene dominated it, whereupon Mifflin quit in a huff and left the camp, complaining that Washington was ruled by Greene and sacrificed all for New England.[31]

Graydon heard Mifflin complain that Greene alone possessed the ear of George Washington.[32] Yet Pickering wrote that Mifflin was "disgusted at the jealousies entertained of him, at camp and elsewhere, that he was or had been, aiming to remove General Washington a thing he absolutely disavows." [33]

Mifflin's own letters so furiously deny any disloyalty to Washington that he also may have been slandered or at least misunderstood by those who surrounded Washington with jealousy as well as devotion. He was either an arrant double-dealer or, what is quite possible, a cruelly misrepresented victim of faction.

Washington wonderfully managed his detractors as well as his worshippers. The middle men were, of course, abhorred by the fanatics on both sides. Of these was Pickering, who endured storms of abuse then and long after Washington's death for the temperance of his admiration. Some accused him of ingratitude, others, he said, deemed him "guilty almost of blasphemy."

One of those who rebuked Pickering was Judge Richard Peters, who had been accused of being involved with the Cabal, and wrote Robert Morris denying it: "As to the General I love him to a Degree of Adoration." He was so fervid that even Baron Steuben, according to Pickering, broke out with a good-natured protest:

"Damn you, Peters, you are an Idolater."

Pickering says that Washington's military deficiencies had become perfectly apparent at a very early period; but it was "important to maintain, during the revolution, the popular opinion in his favour," and his faithful officers did not disclose what they knew of his defects.[34]

Against the myth-making, god-building cult that grew up rapidly, such a man as Pickering lost a vain and painful battle. His political life was embittered because he was what his biographer calls "an abhorrer of man-worship." [35] He objected even to his sister's naming her baby "George."

Adams said that Pickering cherished a deep contempt for Washington while pretending to be his adorer. Pickering answered Adams with the same charge and retorted: "I never adored any man; I never flattered any man," but he equally denied contempt, saying that Washington's "pure and disinterested zeal, fortitude and magnanimity were never surpassed in any cause; and amidst difficulties and discouragements that perhaps were never equalled. Such a character no one could view with contempt." [36]

As for Washington, in spite of all his idolaters, he never asked anybody to bow down and worship him. He knew that he had critics as everybody has, but they were somewhat thwarted by the fact that Washington anticipated their criticisms and admitted them in advance. He never told anybody that he was a great general. He said he made mistakes and owed his escapes to the enemy's indolence. He never pretended that he knew how to save the country single-handed. He constantly proclaimed that he needed the help of everybody.

He was in a bewildering situation and he admitted that he was bewildered. Such adoration as reached him embarrassed him, but abuse and suspicion hurt him to the quick. He was, after all, a lonely farmer caught in an endless war.

Tench Tilghman wrote to Robert Morris of the Cabal and of Mifflin's Brutus-like wounds:

"What are his inducements God only knows, but I am sure no man stood higher in the General's good opinion. . . . I have never seen any stroke of ill fortune affect the General in the manner that this dirty underhand dealing has done." [37]

He expected criticism, but now and then he felt that he was persecuted. A flash of the feeling and the brave suppression of protest may be found in his copy of a letter he wrote to Governor Livingston from Valley Forge, concerning an intrigue the governor had complained of. He added these lines:

"Even the devices of private enemies whose ill will only arises from their common hatred to the cause we are engaged in, are to me tolerable; yet, I confess, I cannot help feeling the most painful sensations, whenever I have reason to believe I am the object of persecution to men, who are embarked in the same general interest, and whose friendship my heart does not reproach me with ever having done any thing to forfeit. But with many, it is a sufficient cause to hate and wish the ruin of a man, because he has been happy enough to be the object of *his country's* favor." [38]

On second thought he crossed this all out, preferring not to complain of his own wounded feelings, when his men were enduring such multitudinous torments at Valley Forge.

XXIV

VALLEY FORGE

A BARE-HEADED, half-naked sentinel stands in the snow with his bare, bleeding feet in his hat.

There have been innumerable descriptions of the miseries of Valley Forge. The name is a national synonym for the huddled wretchedness of martyred patriots. But the soldier standing in his hat to keep his feet from freezing sums them all up most poignantly.[1] Homely, pitiful, he shivers, blowing on his hands, staring with smoke-reddened eyes into the sleet to descry a British raider, his long musket slipping from his gaunt shoulder, his stomach empty, his heart sick, his thoughts on his home and his vague reasons for leaving it. When his tour of duty is over, there is no blanket for him, no straw, perhaps no meat, no bread.

The words "Valley Forge" are written across American history in the red footprints of its soldiers. Years afterward Washington told Dr. Gordon, "Through the want of shoes and stockings, and the hard frozen ground, you might have tracked the army from White Marsh to Valley-forge by the blood of their feet."[2]

Washington saw them first as he rode in the rear of his army on that nineteen-mile march, and he demanded of the first officer he met:

"How comes it, sir, that I have tracked the march of your troops by the blood-stains of their feet upon the frozen ground? Were there no shoes in the commissary's stores?"

The officer replied that the supply was exhausted before his regiment was reached.

Washington was so overcome that he could only groan, "Poor fellows!" and gallop on.[3]

261

They ceased to be a novelty as he passed along the line of march and settled down in the camp. Though the men hobbled about their tasks, blanketless, coatless and on naked feet, the unbearable cruelty of it was that all the while, "hogsheads of shoes, stockings and clothing, were at different places, upon the road and in the woods, lying and perishing, for want of teams, and proper management, and money to pay the teamsters." [4]

The bare feet of the soldiers had stained the ice on other fields and roads the previous winter. There would be bloody footprints on the snow the next winter, and the bitterer winter of 1779-80. It seems that there will always be bloody footprints where American soldiers march in snow. Robert E. Lee's men, of course, went barefoot and, in the words of the ex-slave who was his bodyguard, "left behind more blood than the Yankees ever drew." [5]

But the Union soldiers, too, were often shoeless, and worse. Sentinels in the city of Washington were seen "in freezing weather in their drawers, without trousers or overcoats." In the Army of the Potomac men mounted guard without trousers, and colonels were seen on horseback in dressing gowns and slippers. Soldiers meeting women often backed away, because "for very shame's sake they would not dare turn their faces." [6]

In the World War the 165th New York regiment plodding the Vosges mountains left bloody footprints in the snows of France—and was shod thereafter with French shoes. [7] The French were still supplying the Americans with shoes and weapons!

The privations of 1777 were not due to national poverty, but to disorganization, and inefficiency combined with ruthless greed and corruption.

There must have been reasons for such language as Congress uttered officially in the drastic resolution of December 20th, calling upon the states to "seize . . . all woollen cloths, blankets, linens, shoes, stockings, hats, . . . all stock, and every kind of provision," and give payment by draughts on the clothier-general or the purchasing commissaries. To this was added a Jeremiad:

"5. And whereas, great waste of cloathing has arisen from the want of fidelity or skill in the persons employed to make up the same: . . .

"7. And whereas, certain persons, devoid of, and in repugnance to every principle of public virtue and humanity, instigated by the lust of avarice, are, in each State, assiduously endeavouring, by every means of oppression, sharping, and extortion, to accumulate enormous gain to themselves, to the . . . great injury of the public service. . . . It is most seriously recommended to the several legislatures . . . to inflict such punishment upon all atrocious offenders before described, as shall brand them with indelible infamy."

In a circular letter, Congress gave further emphasis to its disgust:

"Unhappy the case of America! laws unworthy the character of Infant republics are become necessary to supply the defect of public virtue, and to correct the vices of some of her sons; and she is called upon by the grand principle of self preservation, to guard against the parricide of those whom she has fostered in her own bosom." [8]

On the last day of the year the president of Congress was ordered to write to the president of the council of "Massachusetts Bay":

"It is with inexpressible concern that Congress learn the extortionate views and demands of the proprietors of cloathing lately purchased or attempted to be purchased within your State by Mr. ——, deputy cloathier general, for the use of the continental troops, now exposed in the field to the severities of the season; and that those individuals should even add to the crime of extortion a greater, if possible, that of refusing to deliver the goods upon the credit of the thirteen United States, whereby they not only wound the public credit, but in all probability will be the means of many brave soldiers perishing in the field, merely for want of necessary cloaths.

"This irrefragable evidence of the depravity of morals, in so many of the citizens of these states, is a most alarming circumstance; and if the several governments do not speedily exert their authority to effectually suppress such unheard of extortion, it will unquestionably issue, and at no very distant period, too, in the destruction of the liberties of this Continent." [9]

Three British shiploads of clothes were captured and announced as on the way, never to appear. Speculators diverted the cargoes and hid them in swamps. Enough shoes were captured from British vessels for all the men.[10] Yet they wrapped their feet in rags and Lafayette tells how "their feet and legs froze till they grew black, and it was often necessary to amputate them."[11]

Allen McLane had uniforms made for his rough riders out of all his table and household linen, but it was not material one would choose for winter cavalry service without overcoats.

At times the men fit for duty were so few that naked men going on duty borrowed the clothes of men who had them.[12]

On the 23rd of December Washington reported 2,898 men unfit for duty because barefoot and otherwise naked. As late as the 5th of February the returns gave 3,989 men in camp unfit for duty for lack of clothes and shoes.[13]

Many soldiers died for want even of straw to lie in. For that reason inoculation was at first impracticable and small pox raged, along with dysentery and other diseases.

As soon as Washington had led his men to Valley Forge they were set to building the huts for which explicit orders had been given. There was timber enough in a forest that rapidly disappeared. From his own pocket he offered a prize of twelve dollars to the first squad in each regiment to complete its hut, and about twelve hundred were made.

The fortification of the camp was a matter to which much attention was given. Earthworks were thrown up at various strategic points and strong redoubts built.[14] The troops were encamped also in such order as to be in readiness to break and retard any surprise. Fortunately General Howe could not be goaded into an attack, though his critics in America and abroad made their usual denunciations. If he had made the attempt he would have probably captured with ease all of Washington's guns because he did not have the horses to carry them off or even to shift them.

Having promised to share the hardships of his men, Washington would not move from his cold tent into the house chosen for his headquarters until the huts were under way, and the tents washed and folded for storage against the next campaign.

Hunger meant not only feeble resistance to disease, but mutinous thought. A French officer described a half-naked soldier peering from his hut and muttering:

"No bread, no soldier." [15]

Though it cost the nation $3⅓ a month to feed each soldier, he did not get fed.[16] Salt beef and pork were rare, fresh meat still more infrequent. At one time the army had no meat at all for seven days.[17] Salted herring was the chief reliance, and that was usually so much decayed that the fish could not be separated but had to be dug out of the casks in a mass. Washington wrote on February 16th, 1778:

"It is a subject that occasions me more distress, than I have felt since the commencement of the war; . . . For some days past, there has been little less than a famine in camp. A part of the army has been a week without any kind of flesh, and the rest three or four days. Naked and starving as they are, we cannot enough admire the incomparable patience and fidelity of the soldiery, that they have not been ere this excited by their suffering to a general mutiny and dispersion. Strong symptoms, however, of discontent have appeared in particular instances; and nothing but the most active efforts everywhere can long avert so shocking a catastrophe. Our present sufferings are not all. There is no foundation laid for any adequate relief hereafter." [18]

Where the soldiers are gaunt with starvation the horses are bound to perish, and the hideous detail of helpless animals screaming with famine was not wanting.

"The horses are dying for want of forage," Varnum writes to Greene. Knox writes: "Hundreds of our horses have already starved to death." [19] On March 21st, 1778, Washington wrote of his men and beasts:

"They have been (two or three times) days together without provisions; and once, six days without any of the meat kind. Could the poor horses tell their tale, it would be in a strain still more lamentable, as numbers have actually died from pure want." [20]

The carcases of the dead horses lay about in such numbers that Washington feared for the health of his men.[21]

For lack of horses, soldiers yoked themselves with grape-vines to little wagons they made themselves.[22]

Impressment was tried in every field for clothes, for wagons, for grain and meat. Favoritism and oppression and graft embittered even the patriots, and the people resented, resisted, defended their property with weapons or hid it.

People took their wagons to pieces and sent their horses into other districts or even into other states. They broke the wheels, and sometimes were so enraged that they burned wagons rather than let the patriots seize them. Ordinarily, however, self-interest guided them. They preferred to sell to the British, and Washington wrote as late as March 27th, 1778:

"Although I have made a number of severe examples, I cannot put a stop to the intercourse . . . A lieutenant has been detected in Lancaster county purchasing horses, in conjunction with the inhabitants, one of whom and the lieutenant have been executed." [23]

The orderly books show several cases of Pennsylvanians given one hundred lashes or hanged for dealing with the British.

In the winter war for sustenance, the British had far the better of it since they could and did pay hard money for what they bought, and this was a final argument even with the waverers, to say nothing of the great loyalist majority in that region. It was almost impossible for Washington to persuade the farmer to sell to him because he paid in the worthless paper. On market days when the roads were full of country people on their way to Philadelphia the British sent bodies of troops, sometimes as large as two thousand, ten miles out on the roads to convoy the loaded wagons.

Washington abhorred the thought of living off the people in whose neighborhood he was. He had always done his utmost to curb the plundering of his soldiers. To set forth now as a wholesale marauder himself was most distasteful, but he was

convinced at last that the starvation of his army was entirely
due to the selfishness of his fellow-Americans or their loyalty
to the king.

Congress actually reprimanded him for his "delicacy in exerting military authority . . . a delicacy, which though highly
laudable in general, may, on critical exigencies, prove destructive to the army and prejudicial to the general liberties of
America." Thereupon his master gave him orders:

"It is the desire and expectation of Congress, that General Washington should, for the future, endeavour as much as possible to subsist
his army from such parts of the country as are in its vicinity." [24]

Having been taught his place, he bowed and proceeded to try
to scrape from already barren ground and inhabitants whose
feeble affection was completely alienated, sustenance for his
starvelings. He directed his light horsemen not only to try
to starve the British by cutting off their supplies, but to confiscate what they found.

Greene made the most elaborate forays and Light Horse
Harry Lee shone, but Allen McLane was the most dashing
of the raiders and his picturesque feats should be popular.
There was no trick that he did not try, frequently dressing his
men in British uniforms. He was out in all weathers even on
nights when it was so cold that he had to empty his canteen
of rum into his boots to keep his feet from freezing. This
was a double hardship, for there was a better place for rum.
He noted that his men attacking the enemy were "more eager
to cut off the canteens of the British soldiers than to seize their
persons." [25]

There were many brushes with the British, and the Americans did not always win. Among their bitterest foemen were
their fellow countrymen in the British ranks, the Queen's
Rangers and James' and Hovenden's loyalists. Among their
captures was a quantity of cloth for Washington's naked men.
Hovenden once wrested a drove of no less than one hundred
and thirty fat cattle from the soldiers taking them to hungry

Valley Forge. Other devastating raids were made by Sir William Erskine with eight thousand troops, and another by Colonel Mawhood of Princeton fame.[26]

The patriots were desperate enough to consider enlisting Indians. Even negro slaves were thought of. General Varnum favored their enlistment and John Laurens pleaded with his father to permit it, alleging Washington's approval. He encountered:

"That monstrous popular prejudice, open mouthed against me, of undertaking to transform beings almost irrational, into well-disciplined soldiers, of being obliged to combat the arguments, and perhaps the intrigues, of interested persons. . . . Those who fall in battle will not lose much; those who survive will obtain their reward . . . You ask, what is the General's opinion upon this subject? He is convinced that the numerous tribes of blacks in the southern parts of the continent, offer a resource to us that should not be neglected." [27]

Washington was farmer enough to realize that it was wasteful to seize grain and carry it to camp for threshing, so he ordered the farmers to thresh it themselves. When he had reason to suspect their enthusiasm for the cause he sent squads of sixteen men each to every farm to hunt out hidden supplies, thresh the grain themselves and bring it in, along with the clean straw, which was sorely needed.

Back of the torments of the healthy loomed the hell of the hospitals, so called. The number of sick was enormous. The Quaker and the Baptist meeting houses in the valley were taken over. Temporary hospitals were built for contagious diseases, barns and private houses were filled with the ailing. The Moravians several miles away in Bethlehem did what they could. Of this settlement Beveridge says:

"Valley Forge poured upon it a Niagara of starvation, disease, and death. One building, scarcely large enough for two hundred and fifty beds, was packed with nearly a thousand sick and dying men. Dysentery reduced burly strength to trembling weakness. A peculiar disease rotted blood and bones. Many died in the same foul pallet before it could be changed. The beds were 'heaps of polluted litter'. Of forty of John Marshall's comrades from a Virginia regiment

which was the 'pride of the Old Dominion', only three came out alive;
'A violent putrid fever,' testifies Marshall, 'swept off much greater
numbers than all the diseases of the camp.' " [28]

The scandalous graft, inefficiency and neglect that characterized most of the hospitals were not missing here, and the
sick, ill-nourished and bled at every opportunity, made little
resistance. The dead were thrust into unmarked graves so
shallow that they were "disinterred by hungry swine." Woodman says that he saw the decaying bones lying about above the
eroded soil fifty years later.[29]

When Congress could think of nothing else or agree upon
nothing else, it could always appoint a day of fasting and
prayer. It seems impossible that at such a time of famine anybody could solemnly propose a day of fasting; but on February
27th, 1778, a committee of three had been appointed to prepare one, and on March 7th it submitted a proclamation that
won approval.

April 22nd was set for confessing "iniquities and transgressions, for which the land mourneth." Congress recommended
that the inhabitants abstain on that day "from labour and recreations." [30]

On that same March 7th Washington wrote to Congress a
passionate letter about the cruelty of leaving the prisoners in
British hands, of "the unhappy violation of the flag of truce,"
and humbly begged the removal of all impediments to "preservation of the public faith and my personal honor." [31]

That was his prayer and Congress let him fast.

XXV

DID HE PRAY AT VALLEY FORGE?

THE three most popular pictures of Washington, infinitely multiplied, displayed and propagated, represent him, first, crossing the Delaware; next, collaborating with Betsy Ross in the designing and making of the new flag; and finally praying in the snow at Valley Forge outside the house of Isaac Potts. The fact that all three scenes are mythical undoubtedly aids in giving them preference over any merely authentic scenes.

There is a dazing perversity in a public that reveres its forefathers yet prefers to see them doing things that cannot be proved and give its chief favor to people who did not do the things they are famous for.

Isaac Potts' fame is one of the curiosities of history. There is no doubt that Washington crossed the Delaware in a boat amid floating ice. There is proof that Betsy Ross at least made flags. But that Washington ever prayed at Valley Forge there is not a shred more of evidence than exists for every fantastic ghost story, fairy story, legend, or other "I heard an old man say." The same spirit that speeds the Potts anecdote has no hesitancy in assuring the visitor at Valley Forge that a certain stone house there, called the Potts House, was the actual place of Washington's residence. Yet John C. Fitzpatrick says:

"Up to now the Valley Forge Headquarters has been known as the Isaac Potts House, but this is an undeserved honor. Despite the cheap sentimentality of the prayer story, proof is lacking that Isaac Potts was at Valley Forge that winter, and proof is lacking that he owned, in 1777-78, the house now pointed out as Headquarters. The accounts show that Deborah Hewes was paid by Washington for the use of her house and furniture at Valley Forge, and it is an injustice to Mistress Hewes that she, up to now, has been ignored. Isaac Potts only

270

came into possession of the house near the end of the war, and not until forty years afterwards was the place pointed out as Washington's Headquarters. By then Potts's long residence had fixed it in the minds of the country folk as the Potts House. Rightfully it should be known as the Hewes House, and Mistress Deborah's name should be recalled instead of the Quaker Isaac's." [1]

Before Washington reached Valley Forge the British had occupied the place on September 21st, 1777, and remained two days, gathering in the rebel supplies that had been stored there in great quantity. When they left, they carried off the supplies and, in the words of Captain John Montresor, the British engineer who was there, "set fire to the Valley Forge and destroyed it." [2]

There is good reason to believe that the house afterwards known as the Isaac Potts house and exhibited now as the headquarters was too badly burned to be habitable when Washington arrived three months later, and that it was restored long after he left. One argument for this is that the whole of Valley Forge had been owned since 1771, not by Isaac Potts, but by William Dewees. An authority for this is Washington himself, who issued this order April 29th, 1778:

"Complaint having been made by Mr Dewees, proprietor of the Valley Forge, that the Soldiers pull down the Houses, and break up the Fire Bays, at what is called the New Forge, upon Valley Creek; The Commander in Chief strictly forbids all Persons from further damaging the S^d Buildings & works which he hopes will be punctually attended to—especially when they consider the great loss, which Mr Dewees, has already Suffered by the Enemy, & by the great waste which our army has been under the necessity of Committing, upon his wood, & other Improvements—" [3]

Furthermore, in 1785, William Dewees petitioned Congress for reimbursement of his loss by the British destruction of his entire property, and mentioned as part of it, "Two large Stone Dwelling Houses," valued at £600. Getting no redress, he laid the claim before Congress in 1794 and kept it there until 1832. If either of the stone houses had been in a shape for occupancy by Christmas, Dewees could hardly have claimed total loss. Hence Mr. Fitzpatrick concludes:

"The belief in the Isaac Potts Headquarters is called seriously into question. There is no credible evidence . . . that Isaac Potts owned the stone house at that time, . . . or had anything to do with the iron works before the close of the war." [4]

Yet even this is no proof that Isaac Potts was a liar, because there is not a morsel of historical evidence that he ever told the story. There is not a line written by him or by anybody that talked to him. There has never been even a pretence of testimony closer than that of somebody who said he heard some very aged person say that old Isaac Potts had told the story. Such hearsay evidence at third hand would not be listened to in any jury trial, yet it is accepted as gospel proof that Washington had a habit of taking his woes to God aloud in the open air.

There is an odd quirk, too, to this famous legend. It is used as a final proof of Washington's extreme piety. Yet the Quaker in whose house he lived was astounded at finding him on his knees. Should he not rather have been surprised at not finding him on his knees?

For the first printed version of the tale we are indebted to Parson Weems, the author of the most interesting, most popular and most imaginative of all historical novels based on the life of Washington. The credibility of the Parson has been impeached beyond redemption. While he is romancing, he makes a whole-hearted job of it, beginning with his title page, on which he says that he formerly was what he never was, "Former Rector of Mount Vernon Parish." There was never even a Mount Vernon Parish. When his attention was called to the slip, he changed it to "Former Rector of General Washington's parish," which was another thing that never was.

His intimacy with Martha is shown by the fact that he referred to himself as "Your unknown friend." His first little edition contained eighty pages. His second claimed to be "Faithfully taken from authentic documents." In the fifth edition of 1806, enlarged to two hundred and fifty pages, this dull guaranty was changed to "with curious anecdotes, equally honorable to himself, and exemplary to his young countrymen." [5] The use made of his description of the prayer is not especially honorable to the users, or exemplary to anybody.

Having cast truth adrift on the title page, Weems sailed merrily on his sea of fancy to the end of Washington's life, of which he gives an entirely false account. He states without a qualm that the dying Washington said, "Thank God, I am not afraid to die"; that at his request everybody quit the room, "and, according to his wish, left him—with his God," that he prayed fervently; and that he "closes his eyes for the *last* time, with his own hands—folds his arms decently on his breast, then breathing out, *'Father of mercies, take me to thyself.'*—he fell asleep." [6]

All of this is absolutely disproved at every point by the detailed testimony of those who were at his bedside, and who show that Washington's last hours were as devoid of a religious thought as his last will and testament, in which there is not a gift to a religious purpose or a hint of concern with any phase of theology after the opening phrase, "In the name of God, Amen," which was the legal formula. As for his body, Washington simply wrote, "It is my express desire that my Corpse may be Interred in a private manner, without parade or funeral oration." [7] Yet Weems in a special chapter on this Will, has the audacity to give the impression that it is intensely pious.[8]

It is to the unscrupulous and often ridiculously evangelistic Weems that the Potts prayer fable owes its vast popularity. Even he does not claim to have had it from Potts himself. He was not even sure of the name.

Sharply contrasted both in spirit and in letter is the story of a Baptist minister quoted by Reverend E. C. M'Guire, who published in 1836 a book called "The Religious Opinions and

Character of Washington," largely as an answer to a public debate in New York City in which Robert Dale Owen had denied Washington's faith in Christianity. There is a third witness no more remote than the rest, though no closer than 1862—eighty-four years after the event. This is cited in Reverend T. W. J. Wylie's "Washington, a Christian."

Parson Weems' story is as follows:

"In the winter of '77, while Washington, with the American army, lay encamped at Valley Forge, a certain good old FRIEND, of the respectable family and name of Potts, if I mistake not, had occasion to pass through the woods near head quarters. Treading in his way along the venerable grove, suddenly he heard the sound of a human voice, which, as he advanced, increased on his ear; and at length became like the voice of one speaking much in earnest. As he approached the spot with a cautious step, whom should he behold, in a dark natural bower of ancient oaks, but the commander in chief of the American armies on his knees at prayer! Motionless with surprise, friend Potts continued on the place till the general, having ended his devotions, arose; and, with a countenance of angelic serenity, retired to head-quarters. Friend Potts then went home, and on entering his parlour called out to his wife, 'Sarah! my dear Sarah! all's well! all's well! George Washington will yet prevail!'

" 'What's the matter, Isaac?' replied she, 'thee seems moved.'

" 'Well, if I seem moved, 'tis no more than what I really am. I have this day seen what I never expected. Thee knows that I always thought that the sword and the gospel were utterly inconsistent; and that no man could be a soldier and a christian at the same time. But George Washington has this day convinced me of my mistake.'

"He then related what he had seen, and concluded with this prophetical remark—'If George Washington be not a man of God, I am greatly deceived—and still more shall I be deceived, if God do not, through him, work out a great salvation for America.' " [9]

Compare with this vivacity the best Mr. M'Guire can do:

"Extract of a letter from a Baptist minister to the Editor of the (Boston) Christian Watchman, dated Baltimore, January 13, 1832: . . .

" 'You will recollect that a most interesting incident, in relation to the life of the great American Commander-in-chief, has been related as follows:—That while stationed here with the army, he was frequently observed to visit a secluded grove. This excited the curiosity of a Mr. Potts, of the denomination of *"Friends,"* who watched his movements at one of these seasons of retirement, till he perceived that he was on his *knees* and engaged in *prayer.*

" 'Mr. Potts then returned, and said to his family, *"Our* cause is *lost,"* (he was with the tories,) assigning his reasons for this opinion. There is a man by the name of Devault Beaver, now living on this spot, (and is eighty years of age) who says he has had this statement from Mr. Potts and his family. I had before heard this interesting anecdote in the life of our venerated Washington, but had some misgivings about it, all of which are now most fully removed.' . . .

"That an adjacent wood should have been selected as his private oratory, while regularly encamped for the winter, may excite the inquiry of some. The cause may possibly be found in the fact that, in common with the officers and soldiers of the army, he lodged during that winter in a log hut, which, from the presence of Mrs. Washington, and perhaps other inmates, and the fewness of the apartments, did not admit of that privacy proper for such a duty." [10]

Compare them both with this letter from James Ross Snowden:

"The following note was written to the Rev. T. W. J. Wylie, D.D., pastor of the First Reformed Presbyterian Church, of Philadelphia, February 28, 1862:

"My Dear Sir—Referring to your request, I have to say that I cannot lay my hands at present upon my father's papers. I recollect that among his manuscript 'Reminiscences,' was a statement of his interview with Mr. Potts, a Friend, near Valley Forge, who pointed out to him the spot where he saw General Washington at prayer in the winter of 1777. This event induced Friend Potts to become a Whig; and he told his wife Betty, that the cause of America was a good cause, and would prevail, and that they must now support it. Mr. Weems, in his 'Life of Washington,' mentions this incident a little differently; but my father had it from Mr. Potts personally, and the statement herein made may therefore be relied on as accurate. . . .

"Dr. Wylie says, 'We have heard the incident just related from the lips of the late Dr. N. R. Snowden, who was informed of it by the person himself." [11]

Compare all three with Benson J. Lossing's version:

"Isaac Potts, at whose house Washington was quartered, relates that one day, while the Americans were encamped at Valley Forge, he strolled up the creek, when, not far from his dam, he heard a solemn voice. He walked quietly in the direction of it, and saw Washington's horse tied to a sapling. In a thicket near by was the beloved chief upon his knees in prayer, his cheeks suffused with tears. Like Moses at the Bush, Isaac felt that he was upon holy ground, and withdrew unobserved. He was much agitated, and, on entering the room where his wife was, he burst into tears. On her inquiring the cause, he informed her of what he had seen, and added, 'If there is any one on this earth whom the Lord will listen to, it is George Washington; and I feel a presentiment that under such a commander there can be no doubt of our eventually establishing our independence, and that God in his providence has willed it so.' " 12

Mr. Weems' Potts stumbled on Washington's genuflexion and cried to his wife, "Sarah! my dear Sarah! all's well! all's well!"

Mr. Beaver's Potts shadowed Washington, caught him at prayer, and sighed to his family, "*Our* cause is *lost!*"

Mr. Snowden's Potts, whose wife was Betty, not Sarah, simply told her that the cause of America was a good cause, and that they must now support it.

Lossing's Potts sees a horse tied to a sapling and finding Washington in a thicket with his cheeks suffused with tears, steals away and also bursts into tears. Weems' Washington was of an "angelic serenity." His Potts cheerfully gave up his Quaker disbelief in the consistency of sword and gospel. Beaver's Washington made no sound, and his Potts was disheartened, but not converted from Toryism. Lossing's Potts, like Weems', is already an ardent rebel and Washington's cause is "our cause."

It would be hard to present such a scene with more contradictions, yet with more assurance as to details and dialogue in each case. The mutual contradictions are no greater than their common contradiction of Washington's own character and customs.

That a Quaker should have contributed the one vivid account of Washington on his knees is odd, since, on March 20th,

1778, Washington wrote to General Lacey a quite dissimilar tribute to the Quakers:

"Sunday next being the time on which the Quakers hold one of their general meetings, a number of that society will probably be attempting to go into Philadelphia. This is an intercourse that we should by all means endeavor to interrupt, as the plans settled at these meetings are of the most pernicious tendency. I would therefore have you dispose of your parties in such a manner as will most probably fall in with these people." [13]

The final criticism of the prayer legend is the very quality that gave it wings: the dramatic power. A Quaker seeing the mighty Washington in prayer at once confesses that the manifest opposition of heaven is overcome. Once Washington is on his knees with a petition, God is helpless. This is magnificent theatre, but suspicious history.

It is as if a Philistine seeing Jacob wrestle with the Lord should run home at once crying, "Jacob wins!" All that Jacob brought away from his combat was a dislocated hip, a change of name to "Israel," and a blessing. "Therefore the children of Israel eat not of the sinew which shrank, which is upon the hollow of the thigh, unto this day." All that Washington brought away was a series of disappointments increasingly bitter for three years more, when he was permitted to share in the foreign battle of Yorktown.

Almost more dumbfounding than the enormous cultivation of the flimsy Potts legend is the utter neglect of a story that has affidavits to back it, and indicates a state of faith far greater than mere prayer. Why does no one describe Washington's conversion to the Baptist faith and his total immersion?

The writer of the present volume owes to a Baptist minister a copy of the bulletin of the William Jewell College, of Liberty, Missouri, in which it is maintained with a real effort at substantiation, that the well-known Revolutionary chaplain, the Reverend John Gano, immersed Washington at Valley Forge. He had been christened as an infant, but he was baptised again at the age of forty-six. The author of this bulletin, L. C. Barnes, points out the reasons for Washington's secrecy as to this conversion and also the chaplain's:

"The personal confidence of Gano and Washington was doubly sealed by their mutual Masonic vows. But Gano's children could not quite consent to let the remembrance utterly perish. . . . A careful examination of this 'perishable remembrance' has . . . reduced it to the form of legal evidence, . . . three strictly independent lines of the direct transmission of the 'remembrance' from John Gano to us. The testimony is of the same character in this respect, as much of the testimony in the New Testament concerning the life of Christ. It is more direct than some of that. In the present case it is as if we had explicit testimony concerning the Baptism of Jesus given by children of John the Baptist." [14]

Since the pamphlet is rare and seems to have escaped the attention of the biographers, a little space may be spared for citations. First is an affidavit by the Reverend John Gano's grandson, eighty-three years old at the time. He swears that he has heard his mother, Margaret Hubbell (née Gano) "say that her father baptized (immersed) General Washington." Next is an affidavit from Margaret Ewing:

"I have often heard my aunt . . . the eldest daughter of Rev. John Gano, say that . . . he baptized General George Washington, at Valley Forge, to the best of my recollection. She, Mrs. Hubbell, also said that General Washington, for prudent reasons did not desire that his baptism should be made public. Rev. John Gano . . . was an intimate personal friend of General Washington."

These affidavits were secured in 1889 for the author of the bulletin by a clergyman and a college president. Mr. Barnes says:

"This two-fold testimony seems to make it certain that Chaplain John Gano told his eldest daughter that he baptized General George Washington. There is no known reason for doubting the competence or the veracity of any of the links in this evidence. In fact, there is only one link between the witnesses and the man who performed the service. Such evidence is not to be whiffed away. It is either to be accepted or disproved. If disproved, it must be by something more substantial than conjectural hypotheses."

He supports it by the signed statement of a man whose mother received the story from David Benedict, author of "The History of the American Baptists," who received it direct from Stephen Gano, a surgeon in Washington's army, a Mason, and a believer in private baptism. R. M. Gano of Dallas, Texas, made affidavit that from many sources he learned that there were forty-two eye-witnesses of the immersion and that the reasons for secrecy were Washington's desire for it and the fact that he was not actually joining the Baptist church.

Mr. Barnes gives among many arguments one to the effect that Washington was drawn to the Baptist church because his own was so strongly Tory, as were the Methodists, while the Baptists, like the Presbyterians, were ardent rebels, having been cruelly persecuted in Virginia by Washington's original church. It is impossible to follow the argument further here. It is also unnecessary, since its ingenuity carries so little conviction that the Baptist clergyman who forwarded it said in his letter:

"To me, the whole thing seems impossible. As an Anglican Washington was probably tinged with the contempt commonly held for Baptists and was probably too preoccupied with matters pertaining to the conduct of the war to give much thought to the matter of whether he had been Scripturally baptized.

"It would be a matter of no little personal gratification to me if I could believe it. I too am a Baptist, and a minister, but I can't believe it." [15]

This is a dignified and honorable attitude, and characteristic of those intelligent and scrupulous clergymen who are capable of regretting an improbability but incapable of foisting it on the public as genuine.

Yet the Gano baptism is something that the Pottsites ought to dispose of or drop their legend, for theirs has not one written line of evidence, while the Gano story has affidavits of direct descendants and Gano was a prominent evangelist, and a famous chaplain of the 1st New York Brigade under General James Clinton. He visited Virginia in his youth and he was for a long time at Morristown with Washington.

Perhaps the reasons for the failure of the Gano legend to prosper are its definiteness, its affidavits and its confinement to one sect. The Potts story inspires all sorts of believers to eloquence. It is vague and pathetic and lends itself to fine writing and tremulous oratory. The Gano legend is a vivid proof of the valuelessness of affidavits. Anybody can get them for anything. They are like testimonials to patent nostrums, which guarantee miracles and make them commonplace. Testimonials can show at least one miracle per bottle.

If the more earnest reader grows impatient at the space given to these two legends, let him realize that the Valley Forge prayer has been and still is celebrated to such a degree that it has become perhaps the most famous and familiar anecdote of Washington's life. It has been fixed in bronze on the Sub-Treasury Building in New York, and in legends everywhere more lasting than bronze. The very ground has been treated as sacred; the Potts house has been established as a shrine; a million dollar chapel is in course of erection at Valley Forge to give further proof of Washington's orthodoxy. And in 1928 the United States Government issued two million two-cent stamps showing Washington praying at Valley Forge.

One may be permitted to italicize what the Reverend W. Herbert Burk, the leading spirit in this movement, says in the *American Magazine* for August, 1929: "I wanted to build a church commemorative of *what I regard as the most significant incident of the War for Independence—Washington upon his knees praying for his army.*"

Postage stamps are not evidence—at least not evidence of the scenes they depict; but it is striking that the only stamp ever issued by the Government showing an American at prayer should represent a man who in his innumerable letters seems never once to have mentioned the name of Christ, who never would kneel in church, and uniformly and conspicuously refused Communion. The testimony for these facts is positive and irrefragable.

Repetition creates belief, but it does not create truth. Visual representation creates conviction but proves nothing except the imaginative skill of the artist. The selective partiality of legend is one of its quaintest idiosyncrasies. Everybody knows of the Valley Forge Prayer. Only a few have heard of the prayer at Princeton. Why is it not equally "the most significant incident of the War for Independence"?

"The late Joseph Eastburn, who was a lay-minister in the Presbyterian church, in Philadelphia, related to his friend, Mr. Richard Loxley, that while he, Eastburn, was on camp duty near Princeton, he heard when entering a thicket, the audible utterance of some solemn voice, and seeking further for the cause, found Gen. Washington upon his knees in prayer. He retired hastily, fully satisfied in his own conviction, that he was a great man who feared God, and *trusted* in his worship. In after years, when Mr. Eastburn had become religious, and when Washington had become President of the United States, it became matter of concern to Mr. Eastburn, that the President should sanction the theatre by his presence . . . he could not forbear to open his mind to the President by a letter, offering him therein, his reasons for asking him as a Christian man, to avoid the drama. Mr. Eastburn believed that it had the effect, to cause him to go no more; for he never after heard of its occurrence." [16]

This is circumstantial enough. But Washington spoiled it all himself by including in his Diaries not only many references to his attendance on the theatre during his presidency, but this line on the last Saturday night of his second term, February 27th, 1797:

"Went to the Theatre in the Evening." [17]

Watson tells many similar stories, always with a certain remoteness of authority. Thus:

"The late Gen. Cobb, who was long a member of Gen. Washington's military family . . . has informed us . . . throughout the war it was understood in his military family that he gave a part of every day to private prayer and devotion.

"Jacob Ritter . . . told me that he had a neighbor, whose house Washington visited one day, while he was . . . at Whitemarsh, and . . . the father and son, as they told Mr. Ritter, heard Gen Washington in his chamber, at his prayers, praying extemporary, for himself, and the happiness and prosperity of the nation, &c.

"The Wampole family . . . in Montgomery county, told me, that they knew of his habitual retirement to his chamber to pray, and that they sometimes overheard him so engaged.

"The New York Mirror, of May 1834, gives an account of Washington being benighted and stopping at the house of a poor man, near the Highlands, and that the family related that they heard him pray at length, for himself, and his country." [18]

With no flippant intent, a further instance is given of the amazing powers of growth that legend has over historical information—as weeds flourish and strangle flowering plants. The compiler of this biography was once asked in sober earnestness by a visiting Englishman if there were any truth in the following story, which had been seriously told to him as true:

At Valley Forge Washington, being in a mood for long and earnest prayer, closed his tent and instructed his orderly to admit no one under any circumstances until further notice. After a time, during which the sentinel heard the low murmurs of appeal to heaven, an officer—General Greene, as the narrator remembered—approached with vitally important and urgent news. The sentinel forbade him to enter. The general brushed the man aside and knocked impatiently on the tent pole. Washington, without rising from his knees, drew his pistol, turned and fired through the tent, put the weapon back in its holster, and bent his head again in prayer. The narrator had not been told whether or not the general was wounded or killed.

There is something unconvincing about this story, but if all of Parson Weems' "curious anecdotes" are to be sanctified, why not the improvement upon one of them, an improvement which Weems would doubtless have adopted with joy if he had thought of it?

Besides the war-prayers, there are various statements that Washington took communion publicly during the Revolution. In the Presbyterian Hospital, Philadelphia, there is a large painting representing him accepting the cup at an outdoor service under apple trees of Morristown. It is claimed that he wrote to the Presbyterian clergymen asking permission to partake.

Mr. M'Guire says that this was in 1780. Rev. W. J. Johnson in his "George Washington, the Christian," revises this to 1777. Among the testimonies is the typical one of Mr. Asa C. Colton who, in 1836, wrote to Mr. M'Guire that no living witness to the fact could be found. He called on the son of Reverend Doctor Johnes.

"By reason of his great age, he can say nothing upon the subject, but Mrs. Johnes, who is much younger, gives it as an unquestioned family tradition. . . . It is thought by some, that the Rev. Dr. Richards, of Auburn Theological Seminary, New-York, is in possession of the very note, written by General Washington to Doctor Johnes, relative to his admission to the communion."

Doctor Richards, when appealed to, answered:

"I can only say in reply, that I never saw the note to which you allude,—but have no doubt that such a note was addressed by Washington to Doctor Johnes . . . The report . . . was universally current . . . and . . . never contradicted." [19]

It is a familiar fact that when a theory is dubious and we cannot prove it, we say "undoubtedly," "unquestionably," "without doubt," "everybody knows," and such things. Of course, to say that a report was "universally current" is the least respectable thing that can be said for it. Even to say that a venerable clergyman made a certain statement does not quite prove it. Many venerable clergymen repeated a report that was universally current concerning the flatness of the earth and its immobility. They made it very unpleasant for persons who asked for further evidence, as they still make it uncomfortable for persons who are not satisfied with their venerable repetitions.

Sparks in his essay on Washington's "Religious Opinions" cites the Morristown communion, but with the usual indirectness: from Dr. Hosack's "Life of De Witt Clinton," where it is given, as a story given to Dr. Hosack by the Reverend Samuel H. Cox, who said,

"I have the following anecdote from unquestionable authority . . . I received it from a venerable clergyman, who had it from the lips of the Reverend Dr. Jones himself. To all Christians, and to all Americans, it cannot fail to be acceptable." [20]

But America is a large country and among its numerous millions are many so narrow-minded as to be unable to reconcile such accounts with the inability of anybody to produce from Washington's writings one line announcing such a devotion as the anecdotes indicate. There are many passages indicating and inculcating a respect for the Christian religion, and he gave abundant evidence of his belief in the value of "religion," without defining it narrowly. If everybody were satisfied to let the matter rest there, a chapter on the riddle of his beliefs would be needless. But if he believed what it is claimed he believed, and if he were, as is so incessantly asserted, "a man of prayer," he went out of his way to interpolate problems that conflict with such easy assumption.

Dr. Jones tells a venerable clergyman, who tells Reverend S. H. Cox, who tells Dr. Hosack that Washington asked for a Presbyterian communion. Yet when Origen Bacheler held his debate with Robert Dale Owen in 1831, he tried on every hand to find someone who had seen Washington take communion. He appealed to Reverend William Jackson, rector of the church at Alexandria, which Washington attended, and he tried to secure a witness, but gave it up, and wrote, "Nor can I find any old person who ever communed with him." So Bacheler honestly owned his inability to prove the point.

Nelly Custis in 1833 wrote that she and the general always left the church before communion, "sending the carriage back for Mrs. Washington."

There are other memories of old people who remembered that Washington would not communicate.[21]

There is absolutely direct testimony. The Reverend Doctor James Abercrombie, who was rector of the church that Washington attended in Philadelphia, wrote the following account, not of what he had heard about, but of what he saw:

"As Pastor of the Episcopal Church, observing that, on Sacrament Sundays, General Washington, immediately after the desk and pulpit services, went out with the greater part of the congregation,—always leaving Mrs. Washington with the other communicants,—she *invariably* being one,—I considered it my duty, in a Sermon on Public Worship, to state the unhappy tendency of example, particularly of those in elevated stations, who uniformly turned their backs upon the celebration of the Lord's Supper.

"I acknowledge the remark was intended for the President; and as such he received it. A few days after, in conversation with, I believe, a Senator of the United States, he told me he had dined the day before with the President, who, in the course of conversation at the table, said that, on the preceding Sunday, he had received a very just reproof from the pulpit for always leaving the church before the administration of the Sacrament; that he honoured the preacher for his integrity and candour; that he had never sufficiently considered the influence of his example, and that he would not again give cause for the repetition of the reproof; and that, as he had never been a communicant, were he to become one then, it would be imputed to an ostentatious display of religious zeal, arising altogether from his elevated station. Accordingly, he never afterwards came on the morning of Sacrament Sunday, though, at other times, he was a constant attendant in the morning."[22]

Washington was courteous and just, yet the stark fact protrudes that he said he was never a communicant and that rather than be present at communion he left the church. When rebuked, he stayed away altogether!

Against this official document the numerous assertions that he was a communicant are confusing.

To Doctor Abercrombie the situation appealed as it does to many, for he said in concluding the letter from which the above excerpt is made:

"That Washington was a professing Christian is evident from his regular attendance in our church; but, Sir, I cannot consider any man as a real Christian who uniformly disregards an ordinance so solemnly enjoined by the divine Author of our holy religion, and considered as a channel of divine grace. This, Sir, is all that I think it proper to state on paper. In a conversation, more latitude being allowed, more light might, perhaps, be thrown upon it. I trust, however, Sir, you will not introduce my name in print."

There is an anecdote, as good as any other, that Dr. Abercrombie said of Washington, "Sir, he is a Deist." Deist was at that time, and still is in certain quarters, a term of even greater reproach than "atheist," for an atheist is only a foreigner, while a deist believes in the fatherhood and direction of an all-wise, all-powerful, though inscrutable and terrible, god, but not in the divinity of Christ or His blood atonement for the sins of man otherwise damned with Adam. Reverend Dr. Bird Wilson, to whom Dr. Abercrombie made this remark, was the biographer of Bishop White, and he preached a sermon published in the *Albany Advertiser* in 1831, in which he said:

"When the war was over and the victory over our enemies won, and the blessings and happiness of liberty and peace were secured, the Constitution was framed and God was neglected. He was not merely forgotten. He was absolutely voted out of the Constitution. The proceedings, as published by Thompson, the secretary, and the history of the day, show that the question was gravely debated whether God should be in the Constitution or not, and after a solemn debate he was deliberately voted out of it. . . . Washington was a man of valor and wisdom. He was esteemed by the whole world as a great and good man; but he was not a professing Christian." [23]

The numerous protestations that Washington was frequently on his knees are strangely confronted by the letters of the patriotic Bishop White, who succeeded Duché as chaplain of Congress. Bishop White wrote to Colonel Hugh Mercer:

"His behaviour was always serious and attentive; but as your letter seems to intend an inquiry on the point of kneeling during the service, I owe it to truth to declare, that I never saw him in the said attitude. During his Presidency, our vestry provided him with a pew, ten yards in front of the reading desk. It was habitually occupied by himself, by Mrs Washington, who was regularly a communicant, and by his secretaries.

"Although I was often in company of this great man, and had the honour of dining often at his table, I never heard any thing from him that could manifest his opinions on the subject of religion. . . .

"Within a few days of the leaving of the Presidential chair, our vestry waited on him with an address prepared and delivered by me. In his answer, he was pleased to express himself gratified by what he had heard from our pulpit; but there was nothing that committed him relatively to religious theory."

Bishop White wrote to the Reverend B. C. C. Parker:

"I do not believe that any degree of recollection will bring to my mind any fact which would prove General Washington to have been a believer in the Christian revelation; further than as may be hoped from his constant attendance on Christian worship, in connection with the natural reserve of his character."

He wrote again to Colonel Mercer, who was not satisfied with his first letter:

"In regard to the subject of your inquiry, truth requires me to say, that General Washington never received the communion, in the churches of which I am parochial minister. Mrs Washington was an habitual communicant." [24]

This irrefutable denial is ignored, but a million dollar chapel is built on the word of somebody who heard somebody say that Isaac Potts told various stories.

The recent publication of Washington's diaries and the constant appearance of submerged letters written by him, to him, and about him, have played havoc with the old descriptions of his character. For a century or so nobody could contradict the Reverend Lee Massey's statement, "I never knew so constant an attendant in church as Washington." [25] Yet Washington's own diaries prove such statements so false that one can only wonder how they could have been made.

Bishop Meade scornfully denied that Washington was interested in fox-hunting or anything so contemptible as plays or playing cards.[26] He went so far as to call Washington "the great high priest of the nation," as a later Virginia Bishop called him, "a soldier of the Cross."

The diaries prove that for years at a time he stayed away from church far oftener than he went, that he hunted foxes incessantly, gambled moderately but persistently, rarely missed a theatre, conducted business and pleasure on the Sabbath. It is recorded also that he was twice arrested for violation of the Sunday laws.[27]

It has been noted that while he recorded many visits to church, he never once mentioned the subject of the sermon or expressed a pious thought upon it. In his advice to his stepchildren and others whom he befriended, he gave no religious advice whatever.

Every clergyman knows that frequent attendance at church is no evidence of faith in the doctrine. The World's Work published some years ago an anonymous article, "Why I Go to Church," whose author confessed that, though he utterly disbelieved in every article of faith, even in life after death, yet he felt that it was well to keep the churches going and make the children attend them.

In 1929 The Christian Century published and on August 31st, 1929, The Literary Digest quoted, a questionnaire addressed to regular church-goers emphasizing the fact that doctrinal belief was not the guiding motive in the great majority of cases. Though only one man in nine went to church regularly, few of those who went felt more than "a sense of the presence of God."

That Washington often felt this may well be granted. But millions of heathen and savages have felt the same way. Washington frequently upheld the dignity of the churches, and he was a very frequent attendant, but no one has yet found in his works anything more than a vague and passing reference to Christian dogma.

In his will he left not a penny for a religious purpose. In his prolonged dying agonies, though he knew he was doomed, he made no request for a clergyman or a prayer, and uttered no word of religious significance.

This monumental negative was so disconcerting to those who are interested in proving his devoutness that Reverend Mr. M'Guire, searching Tobias Lear's lengthy description in vain for a religious thought, was driven to accusing Tobias Lear not only of omitting all such references, but of not encouraging the dying man to them! Mr. M'Guire says:

"It is indeed a matter of regret that the individuals who attended the Father of his Country in his last moments, were not such as would most readily encourage the expression of his religious feelings, or carefully record them when uttered. The author of the memoranda, it is known, had but little sympathy with the illustrious subject of his narrative in reference to religion; nor had his other attendants, it is believed, any more, at least at that time, though professionally eminent and distinguished men." [28]

This includes Dr. Craik, his lifelong and most intimate friend. One might make a point of such facts as that Washington's cherished friends, Craik, Lafayette, Paine, Lear, were irreligious men. And one might remark on the desperation of an advocate who would accuse them of suppression.

Other persons, discovering a little manuscript book of prayers in any hand but Washington's, declared that he composed them as a pious lad in his teens. We have documents in his boyish hand proving that he bought rum, lost money at cards, and got Indians drunk for the fun of it, but that hand is very different from this hand. Furthermore the little book, published in facsimile and widely distributed, plainly could not have been written by anybody before the eighteenth century was past, to say nothing of being written in the middle of it.

Yet this impossible document was held so precious that it was proposed to give each leaf to a separate church, as if it

were the divided skeleton of a saint. The collection is reproduced in Johnson's "George Washington, the Christian," as
the finest proof of Washington's prayerfulness and of what
Washington never apparently felt, "a deep consciousness of
sin." Many libraries cherish these facsimile booklets called
"Washington's Prayers," which cannot be called forgery because the person, a young woman probably, who copied or compiled them, probably after Washington's death, and from some
book of prayers, could never have dreamed of their ascription
to Washington.[29]

The same innocence cannot be granted to those who have
made the enormous distribution of a document called "Washington's Prayer," for this is lifted and twisted without the
honesty of an acknowledgment from a circular letter over four
thousand words long, issued over his name to the Governors
of the Thirteen States, June 8th, 1783.[30] This letter is not even
in his handwriting, though he did sign it as he signed all manner of documents drawn up by some of his many secretaries.
He may have dictated it and felt it at the time, but it was an
open letter to the governors of the states beseeching their help
and not heaven's; reciting the outrageous injustices heaped
upon the soldiers, pleading for justice, for a regular army, for
a union of the jealous colonies, for the payment of debts, for
submission to taxation.

In this supremely eloquent prayer to the politicians he urged
that the half-pay measures for which he begged so hard at
Valley Forge should not be forgotten, but remembered as a
debt of honor. He warned the country that there must be
preparedness for future war and uniformity of equipment and
discipline for the militia. At the end of a long, long catalogue
of the needs of the country, he added an exordium, beginning:

"I now make it my earnest prayer, that God would have you, and
the State over which you preside, in his holy protection . . . and
finally, that he would most graciously be pleased to dispose us all to do
Justice, to love Mercy, and to demean ourselves with that Charity,
humility and pacific temper of mind, which were the Charactaristicks

to be usefull to his Country, and who, even in the shade of retirement, will not fail to implore the Divine benediction upon it. —

I now make it my earnest prayer, that God would have you, and the State over which you preside, in his holy protection, — that he would incline the hearts of the Citizens to cultivate a spirit of subordination and obedience to Government, — to entertain a brotherly affection and love for one another, for their fellow Citizens of the United States at large, and particularly for their brethren who have served in the Field, and finally, that he would most graciously be pleased to dispose us all to do Justice, to love mercy, and to demean ourselves with that Charity, humility and pacific temper of mind, which were the Characteristicks of the Divine Author of our blessed Religion, and without an humble imitation of whose example in these things, we can never hope to be a happy Nation. —

I have the honor to be
with great regard and esteem
Sir
Your most Obedient Servant

G Washington

WASHINGTON'S CIRCULAR LETTER TO THE GOVERNORS
(From this "Washington's Prayer" was devised)

of the Divine Author of our blessed Religion, and without an humble imitation of whose example in these things, we can never hope to be a Happy Nation.—

"I have the honor to be with great regard and esteem Sir Your Most Obedient Servant, George Washington."

From this long, long document, this argumentative prayer to the unruly colonies and their congresses, the tail has actually been chopped off, dressed up, engrossed, illuminated, distributed and vastly displayed under the name, "Washington's Prayer."

As an opening the word "God" has been improved to "Almighty God." The give-away phrase, "the state over which you preside," has been changed into "The United States." The special appeal for the soldiers has been deleted and to finish it off neatly these words appended:

"Grant our supplication we beseech thee, through Jesus Christ, our Lord."

To change Washington's opening "Sir" (meaning a Governor) to "Almighty God," is an impudence that promises well, yet hardly prepares us for the superlative forgery of changing his "I have the honor to be with great regard and esteem Sir Your Most Obedient Servant," into "Grant our supplication we beseech thee, through Jesus Christ, our Lord."

The vandalism toward Washington is hardly so great as the sneaking blasphemy of offering these stolen phrases as a prayer to God. Washington was doing his utmost to mollify and reconcile thirteen political leaders and their mobs. The distortion of his purpose is astonishing, yet this unspeakable dishonesty has been cast in bronze, and nailed up in churches and elsewhere as a proof that Washington also prayed. It has even been included in a Prayer Book for Soldiers and Sailors.

The negative influence of that prayer on heaven was manifest in the chaos that followed, including a great mutiny of the soldiers. Even on the state legislatures it had no effect.

It brought forth nothing but polite and formal compliments to Washington while underneath, as Randolph wrote, "the murmur is free and general against what is called the unsolicited obtrusion of his advice." [31]

It is only common justice to Washington to protect his high integrity from those who lack it. This audacious, unscrupulous and sacrilegious "Prayer of Washington" with its appended, "through Jesus Christ," is really an emphasis of his peculiar avoidance of the name of Christ.

He seems to have made a tabu of the word. For example: In 1776, Congress decreed a day of fasting and prayer for May 17th, and included an admonition to "confess and bewail our manifold sins and transgressions . . . and, through the merits and mediation of Jesus Christ, obtain his pardon and forgiveness." [32]

Washington's orders for May 15th, 1776, omit that phrase and simply invite the soldiers "humbly to supplicate the mercy of Almighty God, that it would please him to pardon all our manifold sins and transgressions, and to prosper the arms of the United Colonies." [33]

The resolutions of Congress calling for a day of fasting and prayer on December 18th, 1777, speak again of prayer for forgiveness "through the merits of Jesus Christ." [34]

Washington's orders omit all reference to such a prayer and refer only to "publick Thanksgiving and praise & Duty calling us Devoutly to Express our grateful acknowledgments to God for the manyfold blessing he has granted us." [35]

It is perhaps not stretching a point to note another odd indication of his reticence: On May 21st, 1778, Gouverneur Morris, in the course of a letter to Washington, used these words:

"Had our Saviour addressed a Chapter to the Rulers of Mankind, . . . I am persuaded his good sense would have dictated this Text— Be not wise overmuch."

To this Washington answered with striking evasion of the sacred name, and a cynical reference to the feeble influence of divine admonitions:

"Had such a chapter as you speak of been written to the rulers of mankind it would I am persuaded, have been as unavailing as many others upon subjects of equal importance." [36]

Much has been made of his respect for chaplains. In his youthful dealings with the Royal Governor Dinwiddie, he demanded a chaplain.

His references to the importance of religious services were constant and satisfactory. They could hardly have been otherwise. The most irreligious general would hardly have dared to flout the autocracy of the church at a time when church-going was universally compulsory, and each colony had its church supported by taxation. In early Virginia staying away from church was, for a time, punishable by death.

He had so many difficulties to contend with that to have stirred up religious bigotry would have been insane. In that very dread he could and did protest against too many chaplains and the danger of arousing religious dissension. All his life he was trying to persuade the Christians not to quarrel among themselves. He could and did sacrifice religious scruples to military sensibilities. He never hesitated to march or fight on Sunday and in the confused state of October 7th, 1777, he issued an order telling the chaplains that Sundays were so inconvenient for religious services that they must make arrangements for the performance of divine service "at other times." [37]

Overmuch has been made of his endless allusions to Providence. It is evidence of a belief in a higher power, but it has no special Christian meaning. Otherwise every heathen who believed in a god was a Christian.

He called Providence "she" at least once, and once spoke of "Providence or some other unaccountable something." It was a word, a universal habit. Often he used it as John Joseph

Henry did when, in describing Arnold's campaign against
Quebec and the ripping open of a canoe, he said that the men
would have been drowned "but for that interference of Providence, which is atheistically called presence of mind." [38]

One who reads Washington's writings widely and spends
much time with his life-story is tempted to believe that with
him, as with vast numbers of men of all sorts, religion was a
matter of minor importance. But to permit such an idea to
prevail concerning Washington is intolerable to certain zealots
who cannot bear to think of him as playing cards, going to the
theatre, racing horses, swearing, drinking, distilling and selling
whiskey, or being anything but a man of resounding piety. It
is intolerable to them that the Father of his Country should
not be a haloed saint, incessantly on his knees.

A non-partisan might wonder why there is such deafening
silence about Benedict Arnold's great and unquestioned orthodoxy. His letters abound in pious phrases; he went to war
with a band of young men whose banner and drum bore a religious motto. After his great naval battle on Lake Champlain in 1776, which has been referred to as saving the nation,
he said in his despatch, "We have great reason to return our
humble and hearty thanks to Almighty God," and Gates in his
report stated, "It has pleased Providence to preserve General
Arnold." Nickerson calls Gates "unctuously pious."

Arnold actually joined the church anew in 1779, just before
he joined the British secret service. His proclamation to his
fellow soldiers explains eloquently that what they call his
"treason" was really an evangelic effort to restore

"Ye Consolations of that Religion for which your Fathers braved
the Ocean, ye Heathen, and ye Wilderness? Do you know that the
Eye which guides this pen lately saw your mean and profligate Congress at Mass for the soul of a Roman Catholic in purgatory, and
participating in the rights of a Church against whose Anti-christian
Corruptions your pious Ancestors would have witnessed with their
Blood."

His proclamation "To the Inhabitants of America" contains such phrases as "God Incline the Guilty to resign their Ambition," "The Protestant Faith," and "I pray God."

Three of his sons were distinguished officers and a grandson a prominent clergyman.[39]

Yet one never hears Arnold's name linked with Washington's as an ornament of the church; one never finds his pious utterances searched for nor his ecstasies illustrated on canvas.

A letter of Washington's is mangled and enlarged into a prayer and cast in bronze, but nobody puts alongside it in bronze or on illuminated vellum Burgoyne's proclamation declaring that he came to restore the Constitution and rescue the country from persecution, torture and "the profanation of religion." He promises this "by the blessing of God" and "in consciousness of Christianity," and trusts to "stand acquitted in the eyes of God" for any necessary harshness.[40]

In his mind and that of countless others, the British were crusaders against pagans and infidels. It is not to be expected that Americans should recognize any such ridiculous claim, but it is to be regretted that so many of them insist on the still more ridiculous claim that the Revolutionists were holy crusaders for the salvation of Christianity from the alliance of their Britannic and Satanic majesties.

To take the cross from the uniform of such a scoundrel as Richard Cœur de Lion and put it on so noble a man as Washington is clever propaganda but no more.

There is a curious similarity in the same posthumous missionary efforts to convert Lincoln into a gospeller. He is needed in the ranks and is constantly referred to as a man of prayer, whose strength and success lay in that habit. In a volume called "The Latest Light on Lincoln," the frontispiece represents Lincoln kneeling in prayer,—not in the outer snow but in the solitude of his office. The artist has, however, put in a bust of Washington to remind the beholder.[41]

Yet Rhodes says that Lincoln was "an infidel if not an

atheist." [42] Lincoln's law partner, Lamon, tells of the occasion on which he ran for Congress against a clergyman and was assailed as "the atheist Congressman." Later the piety of some of his public allusions was due, according to Lamon, to his anxiety to be popular. It is known that the religion in the Emancipation Proclamation was interpolated by Chase with Lincoln's permission.

Mrs. Lincoln, like Mrs. Washington, was a religious woman, but she said of Lincoln that "he had no hope and no faith." She must have wrangled with him as Martha (who was reported to be fond of curtain lectures) must have remonstrated with Washington about leaving her alone in church and fleeing from the sight of communion. Still, clergymen, having fought Lincoln as an infidel when he was obscure, find it useful when he is immortal, to claim him as the most pious of men, next to Washington.

It would have been both unwise and unjust for either Washington or Lincoln to insult the deep religious convictions of so many of the citizens. If Washington believed in prayer, he must have realized full well the baffling fact that dazed Lincoln so that he included it in his second inaugural address:

"Both read the same Bible, and pray to the same God; and each invokes his aid against the other. It may seem strange that any men should dare to ask a just God's assistance in wringing their bread from the sweat of other men's faces; but let us judge not, that we be not judged. The prayers of both could not be answered—that of neither has been answered fully. The Almighty has his own purposes. 'Woe unto the world because of offenses; for it must needs be that offenses come; but woe to that man by whom the offense cometh.'"

When Washington drove the British out of Boston, every clergyman of his church but one went with them. When the British evacuated Philadelphia, every Episcopalian clergyman went with them. Washington knew that the church he had been reared in abhorred him as a greedy tyrant, an impious rebel against his king and his God. He knew that he had nearly destroyed his own church in America. He knew that the British and the Tories implored God to defeat him as earnestly as patriotic clergymen made the counter-prayer. He may or he may not have added his petitions to the chaos. But if he ever made a written confession of his faith it has not survived. When such a document turns up, proper respect should be paid to it. Until then—

If verbal anecdotes cannot be discounted, if they are all to be believed, Washington was both a fervent Christian and a man of vile life. If people are to be believed who assert that they have seen letters but cannot quite produce them on demand, then Washington's damnation is as easy as his apotheosis, and we are at the mercy forever of that most irrepressible of human traits, the love of myths, and the joy of enhancing them as they are passed along. Artistic and dramatic ecstasy and their close kin, religious exaltation, provide a creative conscience that despises the clods and bogs of fact.

What the historian would call proof or "documentation" in the case of Washington is exemplified in the case of President McKinley. When the Spanish war left the Philippine Islands helpless to the first power willing to seize them, it was decided in the treaty with Spain that the United States should buy them from Spain for twenty million dollars.

This leap into imperialism across the Pacific Ocean startled and revolted the old-line thinkers and Senator Hoar among others declared that the acquisition of the Philippines would be a violation of "the Declaration of Independence, the Constitution, and the whole spirit of American institutions." [43]

But President McKinley took the problem to heaven to decide and, in an address to fellow Methodists, made this statement:

"I walked the floor of the White House night after night, and I am not ashamed to tell you, gentlemen, that I went down on my knees and prayed Almighty God for light and guidance more than one night. And one night late it came to me this way—I don't know how it was, but it came. . . . There was nothing left for us to do but to take them all, and to educate the Filipinos, and uplift and civilize and

Christianize them, and by God's grace do the very best we could by them as our fellow-men for whom Christ also died. And then I went to bed, and went to sleep and slept soundly." [44]

This is definite, distinct, and incontrovertible. When such a document appears in the case of Washington, no historian will question it. Until such a personal statement from Washington transpires, one can only say that, so far as the evidence reveals he never saw fit to make one, and it is therefore not quite honest for anyone to credit him with great enthusiasm for specific dogmas concerning which he himself kept silent.

Thomas Jefferson went to church as regularly as Washington did, read the Bible far more diligently, made a profound study of religions, compiled a book on the "Morals of Jesus," and spoke of him with reverence. He wrote, "I am a Christian," but insisted that Christ had "every human excellence," and "never claimed any other." He believed that Christ's reason had not reached its maximum when he was crucified, hence his doctrines were "defective." [45] The clergy united in denouncing Jefferson as an atheist and a menace to the nation.

Benjamin Franklin was not convinced of the divinity of Christ. Recently discovered letters show that he was a Pythagorean, believing in a great god surrounded by lesser gods, and that Christ was only one of the prophets. [46] Since it is not customary to call Jefferson and Franklin Christians, it is odd to see such wrestling for Washington, who took far less interest in religion than either of them. A close friend of Abraham Lincoln's said of him:

"I don't know anything about Lincoln's Religion—don't think anybody knew." [47]

That would probably represent the exact situation with respect to Washington's exact creed. If he knew himself, he never told. It is probable that he never found time to make up his mind as to the finer points. He left them to other people to fret over. He was too busy about other things.

XXVI

HOLDING THE ARMY TOGETHER

IN "the drear of that winter," [1] the place of blankets, clothes, shoes and foods was only partly supplied by alcohol. Albigence Waldo wrote:

"Were Soldiers to have plenty of Food & Rum, I believe they would Storm Tophet." [2]

On January 1st, 1778, General Greene complained to Washington of the dangerous lack of Tophet-mixture:

"It gives me the greatest pain to hear the murmurs and complaints among the officers for the want of spirits . . . nothing but bread and beef to eat morning, noon, and night, without vegetables, or anything to drink but cold water; . . . there are great quantities of whiskey sent into the Jerseys at Easton, and . . . a full supply might be had for the use of the army if some person was sent there to seize." [3]

Washington did his best for his soldiers and his heart went out to them when their rum was short. When rum could not be had even wine would help. Very often when a ship was captured with liquor aboard, the choicest of it was sent as a compliment to the commander. [4]

On January 3rd, 1778, Washington acknowledged such a gift, and added:

"I am obliged to you for your promise of the prize wine . . . if the quantity should be any thing considerable, you must not be forgetful of the poor fellows who are exposed to the severity of the weather . . . many of them are not yet under cover." [5]

With even liquor wanting to mitigate the harsh realities desertion became a mortal peril. Anonymous letters were circulated declaring that Congress was unfair and indifferent and unworthy of support. British agents went among the soldiers.

299

Women frequented the camp and enticed the men away until Washington issued an order forbidding soldiers "such Interviews" and ordering all such women immediately turned out of camp, suspicious women to be tried and punished.[6]

In spite of the most vigorous application of the whiplash and the hangman's noose desertion continued. The Tory, Galloway, who had charge of Howe's secret service, says that 2,300 Continentals deserted to Philadelphia and were registered, besides seven or eight hundred who never reported; most of them were "nearly naked, . . . some without shoes, very few with whole breeches and stockings."[7] The number is probably no exaggeration. Adding to the three thousand that went into the British lines, the great numbers that stole away elsewhere, it might be said that almost a quarter of the army deserted.

With these and the thousands of sick subtracted from his army it can be seen why Washington was alarmed. Galloway claims to have had it from officers of Washington's army that in February he "had not 4000 effective men." In other words, one man out of four was a soldier, and three out of four were sick, naked, or absent with or without leave.

The conduct of the soldiers that remained was bad and that of many officers who did not desert by way of resignation, was worse. "In February 1778 twelve separate Courts were set up to try officers for embezzlement, stealing dead men's effects, cowardice in the field, and such-like offences."[8] Washington had, of course, to go over the findings of all these courts and approve or disapprove the verdicts. He was not notably merciful.

The orderly books reveal the intensity of the irritation and restlessness of an army twice defeated, marched almost to death and then starved, frozen and bullied. Part of the resentment was due to the brutality, selfishness and indifference of certain officers. General Muhlenberg spoke with scorn of these swaggerers as "God-damn-me and damn-my-eyes fellows."[9]

Henry Woodman's mother wept as she told him of the re-membered brutalities General Weedon inflicted on his starving men, driving them from a great feast of buckwheat cakes. When he was asleep the family flung food from the windows to the ravenous guards freezing outside.[10]

In the grist of the court-martial mill cruel and dishonest officers are mingled with desperate and worthless soldiers. Take a few of them as they come in various Orderly Books transcribed from Washington's official orders: A commissary found guilty of theft, sentenced to be "mounted on a horse back foremost without a Saddle, his Coat turn'd wrong side out his hands tied behind him & be drum'd out of the Army (Never more to return)." An ensign for being drunk and threatening his colonel: "Cashiered with Infamy." A captain for "stealing a Hatt" from another: cashiered and fined "30 dollars for the hatt." A lieutenant for fatally wounding a soldier: acquitted.

A captain for "fraudulently detaining two months pay" from a soldier: cashiered. An ensign "for emblezzeling the Effects of a Dead Soldier and theft": acquitted. A lieutenant for "taking Jack Browns Allowance of Whiskey": cashiered. A lieutenant "for getting drunk and playing Cards and Beat-ing Capt[n] Laird on the Sabbath Day . . . the General thinks his Continuance in the Service would be disagreeable to it— And as one part of his Charge against him was gaming, that alone would exclude him from all Indulgence—the Vice is so pernicious a nature that it never will escape the severest punish-ments with his approbation." There are several trials for gambling, all severely punished. Yet on April 7th, 1778, a reminder is added that a few Continental lottery tickets are to be had.

A lieutenant "tryed first for Attempting to commit sodomy, . . . 2[d] for Perjury": found guilty and sentenced to dismissal with infamy.

"The Comm[r] in chief approves the Sentence & with abhorrence & Detestation of such infamous Crimes, orders L[t] ——— to be drumm'd out of Camp tomorrow M^g by all the Drums & Fifes in the Army never to return."

A lieutenant for striking another: acquitted. The Commander-in-Chief "wishes the Officers of his Army to consider themselves as a band of Brothers, cemented by the Justice of the Common Cause . . . and that they would settle all personal disputes among themselves, in an Amicable manner." A lieutenant for striking a lieutenant: cashiered. A captain for "scandalous and infamous behavior" and threatening the life of another: cashiered. A soldier for striking a lieutenant: 100 lashes.

A soldier for threatening a lieutenant with a loaded musket: guilty "but the extreme and unpardonable warmth with which the Officers conducted themselves, renders the action of the Prisoner excusable." This must have been extraordinary provocation, for ordinarily the private soldier had no rights against his officer. And his social status was kept low.

Washington had been revolted by the democratic level on which the New England officers stood with their soldiers. Now a Virginia lieutenant was tried for buying shoes from a soldier and "frequently Messing and sleeping with the Soldiers."

Even to accuse an officer of condescension was considered libellous, unless proved true, and a captain was tried for propagating the dreadful report that a colonel had been seen in a sergeant's tent "drinking either tea or coffee" with the sergeant's "lady, her mother, . . . and his family, to the prejudice of good order and military discipline." The captain proved his scandal true and was acquitted. The fate of the democratic colonel is not indicated.[11]

With a maximum of seventeen thousand men in camp, reorganization under way, no help from quartermaster or commissary departments, Washington had need of help from his officers. Yet now he began to lose generals and others by wholesale.

"Between two and three hundred officers have resigned their commissions, and many others with difficulty dissuaded from it."

"The Virginia line has sustained a violent shock. . . . Not less than ninety have already resigned to me. The same conduct has prevailed among the officers from the other States . . . it will shake the very existence of the army, unless a remedy is soon, very soon, applied." [12]

The shortage of generals was so acute that General Huntington wrote:

"By reason of Suspensions, being Prisoners, Illness and one thing or other there are only nine Brigadiers & five Maj. Generals for Duty in the Line, and two of them are Frenchmen. when there are not less than fifty or Sixty on the List." [13]

In these days an army of 17,000 with five major-generals and nine brigadiers would be in an embarrassed condition, since, by the Tables of Organization for the United States Army in 1925, one modern division calls for a war-strength aggregate of 19,993 officers and men, only one major-general and three brigadiers.[14]

Of the few good officers Washington found it hard to retain any. He now lost his right-hand man, General Nathanael Greene, who was with difficulty persuaded to take the post of quartermaster-general, abandoned long since by Mifflin. Greene was reluctant to give up the line, where he had "a fair prospect of honor and laurels," for a staff post of untold difficulties and neither honor nor laurels. But he wrote to Knox:

"His Excellency presses it upon me exceedingly. I hate the place, but hardly know what to do." [15]

At last, after much bickering over conditions, and insisting that he should command the right wing in any battle, he accepted and took over the office on March 23rd, 1778. Affairs in that quarter immediately improved, but trouble and scandal began for him owing to the speculative element in his task.

Colonel Jeremiah Wadsworth was made commissary-general and immediately food appeared. The famine was over—temporarily. A wreath for Colonel Wadsworth should never be forgotten.

Lafayette also was taken away from Washington's side; for Gates, as head of the Board of War, at once revived his dream of a Canadian invasion, and persuaded Congress to authorize it. Washington was opposed to the division of effort, but Congress was taking apparent pleasure in disregarding his opinions.

It occurred to someone that Lafayette would be a good man to head the expedition since he was French and Catholic and would stimulate rebellion among the French Canadians. It is said that a stronger motive was the desire to detach the wealthy young nobleman from Washington's influence and win him over to Gates, whom he much admired.[16]

Conway was made second in command of the Canadian expedition, and it was expected that he would also help to bring about a French Catholic uprising. Lafayette was eager for the chance, though he hated to leave Washington. He wrote to his wife who expected him home, and apologized for the "air of ridiculous importance," but explained that he was really "more necessary to the American cause at this moment than you may imagine. . . .

"General Washington would be really unhappy if I were to suggest my going away. . . . In the position that he occupies he is in danger of being surrounded by flatterers or by secret enemies; but he knows he has in me a loyal friend to whom he may open his heart and who will always tell him the truth. Not a day passes that he does not hold a long conversation with me or write me a long letter." [17]

When Lafayette was ordered by Congress to go to Canada, Washington's first word of it was a notice from the Board of War enclosing to him a commission for Lafayette. He handed it over with the word,

"I would rather they had selected you for this than any other man." [18]

With passionate loyalty Lafayette wrote to Congress that he would accept only on condition that he remained under the orders of Washington and reported to him. Congress could deny him nothing. He went to York to consult with the Board and was entertained at dinner in Gates' own home and seated at his right. Surrounded by the Cabalist officers, Lafayette was called on for a toast. Rising, he cried an omitted name: "The Commander-in-chief of the armies of the United States!"

This caused all the consternation he expected and he writes in his memoirs: "Some merely raised their glasses to their lips, while others cautiously put them down untasted." [19]

Benedict Arnold, who knew what it meant to attack Canada in winter and was still lying wounded in Albany, wrote in astonishment that strangers like "the Marquiss de Faillitte and General Conway" should be sent out with no knowledge of "the many difficultys enevitably attending the Expedition."

The garrison of five hundred at St. Johns could keep off ten thousand men. Even if the Canadians were won over, they would have to be furnished with arms and ammunition. If the troops could reach their destination, which they could not, how were they to live? how return? He ended his tirade with the wise strategy that characterized him:

"If it is alledged that the Troops sent on this Expedition, may be replaced by Malitia, would it not have been a more prudent Step to have reinforc'd General Washington with them, and enabled him to drive Mr. Howe & his Banditti from the Country, that, once done, Canada falls of course, probably without the Risk or Expence of an Expedition. I am fully persuaded Congress have been precipitated into this Measure by disigning or ignorent men without having the necessary Information on so important an Affair." [20]

It is no wonder that Washington admired him and tried to get him to his side. After his salvation of Gates, Congress restored him to the rank he claimed—"to a violated right," as Washington said. Sending him his commission, Washington wrote to him January 20th, 1778:

"May I venture to ask whether you are upon your legs again, and, if you are not, may I flatter myself that you will be soon? . . . as soon as your situation will permit, I request that you will repair to this army, it being my earnest wish to have your services the ensuing campaign." [21]

It is notable that John Paul Jones was treated as badly as Arnold in the matter of seeing far inferior officers preferred to him.

Lafayette arriving at the far end of his fool's errand, cried out to Washington:

"Why am I so far from you and what business had the board of War to hurry me through the ice and snow without knowing what I should do, neither what they were doing themselves? . . . to run myself through all the blunders of madness or treachery, (God knows what) . . . I have been deceived by the board of War."

In a long letter he detailed the miserable facts. He wrote to Gates, hardly masking his rage:

"We want monney, Sir, and monney will be spoken of by me till I will be enabled to pay our poor soldiers . . . I have seen a letter to Colonel Hay where you tell him that the very same 400,000 dollars you told me were for me, are destinated to him." [22]

Washington wrote to him with deep sympathy, and he stayed at Albany until Congress voted to abandon the expedition, with praise for Lafayette, but unspoken disgust for Gates and his faction, which suffered immensely from the outrageous folly of the failure. In April, Lafayette was back in Valley Forge, thrice welcome and more than ever convinced that Washington was the only reliable man in America.

Conway was perhaps unhappier than anyone else. He had been fooled with the rest and whatever his faults, he had reason enough for complaint. His letter deserves what is perhaps its first publication, especially as it serves to introduce Baron Steuben, who, during his absence, had slipped into the place that Conway had so laboriously arranged for himself. It is to be remembered that Conway is writing to his friend, Gates:

"Sir I was Determined to return to france Last fall, and was Detain'd in my way by Congress. I was sent to Camp Last December to the purpose of Beginning the functions of inspector General. I was prevented by General Washington from fulfilling these necessary functions, and in Consequence I left Camp with a view of pursuing my journey to france. I was Detain'd a second time by congress; the expedition to Canada was propos'd to me; I accepted; repair'd to Albany with the utmost Dispatch, and found Nothing readdy for an Expedition to Canada. I receiv'd orders Last month to remain in command at Albany; this month, I receiv'd orders from president Laurens to repair to Peekskill under the Command of General McDougall; now General McDoughall gives me orders to return to Albany, where it will be impossible for me to give any support to either the Western or Northern frontiers, as I have not in albany as many men as will guard the valuable stores in that place.

"This unaccountable way of Boxing me about is not the usage which I ought to expect as a Gentleman, and as an officer. I am the eldest officer you have in your army. I did not sollicit to Come over, I was frequently sollicited by your agent, and I can say that no foreign officer came over upon more liberal and generous terms.

"I hope I have served Like a man of honour During the Course of last Campaign. if I have committed any fault, let me be try'd. if I have not, what is the reason of this extraordinary usage I meet with? you have made me inspector last December. I went to Camp with a view of training your army, which is certainly the army in the world that Wants it most. my services were rejected, and I am told that Baron Steuben is now in possession of the same place to which I was appointed.

"I Do not pretend to be superior to Baron Steuben as to Genius or merit but having been peculiarly employ'd in training troops to all field manouvres, having much more practice than he has, speaking the Language, I can venture to say that I would have effected in one month or six weeks, what he will not be able to accomplish in six months. however if the army is train'd up properly it is not material who trains it up, and I am pretty well satisfy'd as to that point but the Campaign is opening; I am readdy to take the field if my services are Deem'd Necessary. if they are not, I Must represent to you that my honour, my principles, the regard I must pay to my rank in the french army will not permitt me to remain idle in a town, while troops are in the field.

"therefore, sir, if you have no occasion for my services I expect Congress will be so equitable as to accept of my resignation, and give me such a Certificate as will justify me in returning to france at the Beginning of a Campaign." [23]

With unfailing skill in saying the wrong thing, the luckless Conway worded his menace of resignation so that it could be seized upon. The faction that had used him was glad to drop him, and to his surprise his resignation was accepted. Denying that he had really resigned, Conway hastened to his friends in Congress and stirred up further trouble with deeper disaster for himself.

In the meanwhile Baron Steuben had gracefully established himself in the favor of Washington and the army. He had the tact to say that he did not demand any high commission. But he was soon as exacting as anybody else and gradually joined the pandemonium of ambition that roared about Washington.

Yet he contributed infinitely needed ideas of individual discipline, organization and marksmanship. He was permitted to do with the soldiers at Valley Forge as he liked. His criticisms were far more numerous than Conway's and his recommendations and methods the same.[24]

He was a real Baron, but he assumed the title of Lieutenant-General with as little excuse as Kalb called himself Baron.

At Valley Forge, he was received with all of Washington's grace. As he wrote:

"General Washington came several miles to meet me on the road, and accompanied me to my quarters, where I found an officer with twenty-five men as a guard of honor. When I declined this, saying that I wished to be considered merely as a volunteer, the general answered me in the politest words, that

" 'The whole army would be gratified to stand sentinel for such volunteers.' . . .

"On the same day my name was given as watchword. The following day the army was mustered, and General Washington accompanied me to review it. . . . I should be happy to die for a nation that has placed such confidence in me." [25]

He was not acquainted with the English language, though he speedily acquired a number of valuable curse-words. His first impressions were appalling considering that the army was now nearing its third year of service. They show what Washington had been unable to achieve for all his efforts. The English is not Steuben's, of course, but a translation:

"My determination must have been very firm that I did not abandon my design when I saw the troops . . . Where to commence was the great difficulty.

"The eternal ebb and flow of men engaged for three, six, and nine months, who went and came every day, rendered it impossible to have either a regiment or a company complete; and the words company, regiment, brigade, and division, were so vague that they did not convey any idea upon which to form a calculation, either of a particular corps or of the army in general. . . . Sometimes a regiment was stronger than a brigade. I have seen a regiment consisting of *thirty men*, and a company of *one corporal!* . . .

"The army was looked upon as a nursery for servants, and every one deemed it his right to have a valet; several thousand soldiers were employed in this way. We had more commissaries and quarter-masters at that time than all the armies of Europe together; the most modest had only one servant, but others had two and even three. If the captains and colonels could give no account of their men, they could give still less an account of their arms, accouterments, clothing, ammunition, camp equipage, etc. Nobody kept an account but the commissaries, who furnished all the articles. . . .

"The loss of bayonets was still greater. The American soldier, never having used this arm, had no faith in it, and never used it but to roast his beefsteak, and indeed often left it at home. . . .

"The arms at Valley Forge were in a horrible condition, covered with rust, half of them without bayonets, many from which a single shot could not be fired. . . .

"The men were literally naked, some of them in the fullest extent of the word. The officers who had coats, had them of every color and make. I saw officers, at a grand parade at Valley Forge, mounting guard in a sort of dressing-gown, made of an old blanket or woolen bed-cover. With regard to their military discipline, I may safely say no such thing existed. . . .

"Mr. De Conway had introduced platoons and many other things; but as he was not liked, they had allowed all his instructions to fall into disuse, so that I scarcely found a trace of them . . . The greater part of the captains had no roll of their companies, and had no idea how many men they had under their orders . . . The officers were not accustomed to remain with the troops when the army was in camp; they lived in houses, often several miles distant. . . .

"The internal administration of a regiment and a company was a thing completely unknown . . . It would be an endless task to enumerate the abuses which nearly ruined the army." [26]

Fortunately, French and other officers appeared who translated his remarks to the stupefied pupils in the school he opened at once. He was on the field at sunrise teaching the A. B. C.'s of drill. He irritated the officers and started still more feuds among them, and soon had Washington wishing he had never come over, especially as he also fell foul of Lafayette, whom he accused of "vanity and presumption" and who accused him of "methodic mediocrity." [27] But he pleased the soldiers by knowing how to do what was to be done and doing it. He took the rifle in his own hands and put it through its paces— a thing the American officers had thought beneath them. He was a true top sergeant with a delightful flow of that profanity which soldiers love to hear heaped upon their mates, at least when it comes from a man of ability and justice. Sometimes when he threatened to explode with exasperation he would call to his aides:

"My dear Walker, my dear Duponceau, come and swear for me in English."

He had that rarest and most lovable of traits in an officer, the readiness to admit his own errors and apologize for his own injustices. Few officers dare to acknowledge their mistakes. Even those who regret them fear that an apology will weaken discipline, though, as long as men are men, it will, of course, have the opposite effect.

What Robert E. Lee could do, Steuben could do. On one occasion he ordered a lieutenant arrested and ordered to the rear for throwing a line into confusion. Learning that he had arrested the wrong man, he called the lieutenant in front of the line, lifted his hat and kept it off in a driving rain while he acknowledged his own blunder and said:

"I ask your pardon.   Return to your command!" [28]

Under his invaluable teaching, the troops began to improve, to learn the manual, the marches and countermarches, and soon the simpler maneuvers. They began to dream of whipping the British at their own game.

Uniforms began to come in. Washington designed a coat to be made quicker and cheaper, but it seems not to have been adopted.[29] There was still no distinctive Continental uniform, and there would be none till the fourth year of the war. Consequently the British never knew just what to expect. Now and then they encountered organizations whose officers, out of their own pockets or from subscriptions by their communities, dressed their men in the smartest styles. To a great extent, however, the chief uniform of the Americans was their lack of uniform.

It is almost farcical that Anthony Wayne was still writing on July 12th, 1778, what he had written in January: "We have not Rec'd the least Article of Clothing . . . and are now— naked." [30]

Every fault that Conway and Steuben found with the army Washington had found and denounced from the beginning. He went on denouncing the same faults to the end. The people revered him as a god, and paid as much attention to his commandments and ideals as people usually pay to their gods.

XXVII

CLASHES WITH CONGRESS

WHILE the lot of these prisoners of winter in Valley Forge was being slowly bettered, nothing was done to diminish the ghastly condition of the prisoners of the British. Washington wrote:

"Our sick naked, and well naked, our unfortunate men in captivity naked!" [1]

Some of the ugliest phases of war were shown in the still unfinished business of settling a cartel for the exchange of prisoners. To the thousands already in British hands for more than a year, great numbers had been added by the captures at Brandywine, Germantown and elsewhere. These wretches were scandalously mistreated in the prisons at Philadelphia whither the unsurpassed fiend Conyngham had been brought to care for them. He almost surpassed himself in cruelty. Washington wrote to Howe and threatened retaliation. Howe denied the charges of cruelty and removed Conyngham, but merely to shift him back to New York. The prisoners went on freezing and dying of starvation.

Washington had just about completed arrangements for exchange when he learned from a newspaper that Congress had passed resolutions in December throwing all his plans as well as his pledges into the discard. Because Howe had made certain well-justified but unflattering remarks concerning American honor, Congress insisted on making his words good and refused to carry out Washington's agreements. [2] Furthermore, Congress demanded that Howe settle in advance in hard money or provisions for the expense Congress and the States had been put to in feeding his prisoners, and gave the States until June to file their claims against him, though every day and hour of delay meant untold agony, despair and death for the helpless prisoners.

Furthermore, it was stipulated that all loyalists or Americans in the British service when captured should not be exchanged but sent to their home states to be tried and punished as traitors. This, of course, Howe could never consent to under any circumstances, as he would be betraying the very people he was bound to support.

These and other conditions incensed Howe as gratuitous insults and further proofs of duplicity. Alexander Hamilton wrote to Governor Clinton a most savage attack on Congress, beginning with a reference to its "degeneracy":

"These men seem also to have embraced a system of infidelity. They have violated the convention of Saratoga, and I have reason to believe the ostensible motives for it were little better than pretences, that had no foundation . . . Still more lately, G. W.'s engagements with G. H. for an exchange of prisoners have been most shamefully violated, Congress have resolved that no exchange shall take place till all accounts are settled and the balance due the U. S. paid. The beauty of it is, on a fair settlement, we shall without doubt be in Mr. Howe's debt; and, in the meantime, we detain his officers and soldiers as a security for the payment—perhaps forever." [3]

It is interesting to compare Hamilton's fury in this private letter with Washington's handling of the same subject in his letter to Congress, where every charge is made but couched in the most courteous and appealing terms.

The spirit is the same he revealed long before Hamilton joined him, and the finest tact was never more gracefully employed in a matter where the temptation to wrath and scorn was more nearly irresistible. He wrote to Congress, and the delicacy of his phrasing is so ingenious that portions of it are here italicized.

"There are some circumstances attending this affair, which it may *possibly* be in the power of Congress *to throw light upon.* If they can, I *shall be obliged* by their *assistance.* . . .

"This resolution I *cannot consider as an intended infraction* of my engagements with General Howe; *yet* its operation is diametrically opposite both to the spirit and letter of the propositions *made on my part,* and acceded to on his. I *supposed myself* fully authorized 'by the *instructions* and intentions' of Congress to act as I did; and I now conceive, that the public as well as my own personal honor and faith are pledged for the performance. . . .

"But perhaps *it may be thought* contrary to our interest to go into an exchange, as the enemy would derive more immediate advantage from it than we should. *This I shall not deny;* but *it appeared to me,* that, on principles of genuine, extensive *policy,* independent of the considerations of compassion and justice, we were under an obligation not to elude it. . . .

"*Were an opinion once to be established* (and *the enemy* and their emissaries *know very well how to inculcate it,* if they are furnished with a *plausible pretext*), that we designedly avoided an exchange, it would be a cause of dissatisfaction and disgust to the country and to the army, of resentment and desperation to our captive officers and soldiers . . . it *may not* be a *little dangerous* to beget in the minds of our own countrymen *a suspicion,* that we do not pay the strictest observance to the maxims of honor and good faith. . . .

"This, added to the prospect of hopeless captivity, would be a great discouragement to the service . . . by dejecting the courage of the soldiery, from an apprehension of the horrors of captivity; and, finally, by reducing those, whose lot it is to drink the bitter cup, to a despair, which can only find relief by renouncing their attachments and engaging with their captors. . . .

"True *policy,* as well as good faith, *in my opinion,* binds us to *improve the occasion.*" [4]

But the heart of Congress was only scratched. He was told that he might proceed to the exchanges he had already arranged, but he was warned that his future cartel must conform to the conditions. [5]

The tone of this offended Washington so deeply that he remonstrated, but, as always, in the tone of meek subordination he invariably showed to his creator and lord.

"It gives me pain to observe they appear to contain several implications by which my sensibility is not a little wounded. I find myself extremely embarrassed by the steps I had taken . . . The views of

Congress . . . would at once overturn any cartel that could be formed. General Howe would never consent." [6]

Still Congress haggled and a committee drew up a long letter, beginning like a benignly spanking parent:

"Congress with great Concern perceive that your Sensibility is wounded by their Resolutions . . . You may rest assured that far from any Intention to give you Pain, their Resolutions have no other Motives or End, but the public Good; they, therefore hope that you will not in future be distrest by Apprehensions, as injurious to their Honor, as they are to your own Feelings." [7]

There follows a long rigmarole about the "Dignity, Safety and Independance of these States, The Duplicity of General Howe, and authentic Information that the Gentlemen appointed by you to negotiate the Cartel, held Opinions repugnant to the Sense of Congress."

Loftily the letter points out the flaws in Washington's plan, his mistakes, the needlessness of any "Embarrassment," and the reasons for persisting in the original resolutions. It was just such a manifestation of intractable confusion and stubbornness as has driven many a general in the field to turn on a many-headed senate and crush it, scatter it and take its power into one strong hand. Almost anybody but Washington would have done so, and this revolution would have gone the common way and ended in absolutism. Even with Washington's example two Napoleons and many less brilliant dictators destroyed the assemblies that created them. And they always found the weary populace glad to follow them.

The footling of Congress disgusted one of its own members so completely that he started a one-man revolution inside the chamber. And this was no other than Thomas Burke of North Carolina, who had harried General Sullivan and did not revere Washington. But he could not stand by and see him badgered and handcuffed while trying to rescue the captives from eternal doom.

The truth about this striking war in the chamber has only

recently come to light. Burke and others insisted on the deletion of offensive passages in the letter, and a hot dispute followed that lasted until ten o'clock at night. Seeing that a motion to adjourn was about to be lost, suddenly Burke rose and announced that "the states might vote as they pleased, he would upon his honor adjourn himself; and thereupon he immediately withdrew, by which means Congress could not proceed to business." [8] Congress sent a messenger to demand his return. Burke answered:

"Devil take him if he would come; it was too late and too unreasonable."

Congress proposed to use force. Burke answered that he was subject only to his own state. He went home to North Carolina, appealed to the legislature, was heartily approved and returned to Congress. The fury aroused by this affair is too complex to detail here, but it was one more instance of the general chaos.

Eventually, through Washington's prayers and diplomacy, a partial exchange was permitted, and among others General Charles Lee was at last released, not for Colonel Campbell and the six Hessians but for the British Major General Prescott, who having been once before captured and exchanged for General Sullivan, obligingly let himself be kidnapped to provide a swap for Lee. Throngs of others, officers and men, were left to starve in filth and send out useless petitions.

Washington's insistence upon the half-pay provision, without which he could hardly hope to retain officers or army, or enforce any discipline, provoked a hurricane. He pointed to the resignations and numbers of officers cashiered for misconduct as proofs of the crisis. He reminded Congress that though he himself was a proscribed traitor (and liable, therefore, to all the hideous penalties for treason) he would not profit a penny from the half-pay:

"I have declared, and I now repeat it, that I never will receive the smallest benefit from the half-pay establishment; but, as a man who fights under the weight of a proscription, and as a citizen, who wishes to see the liberty of his country established upon a permanent foundation, and whose property depends upon the success of our arms, I am deeply interested. But, all this apart, and justice out of the question, upon the single ground of economy and public saving, I will maintain the utility of it; . . .

"To . . . suppose that public virtue alone will enable men to forego the ease and comforts of life, to encounter the hardships and dangers of war for a bare subsistence, when their companions and friends are amassing large fortunes, is viewing human nature rather as it should be, than as it really is." [9]

It was now that he made one of his most tremendous utterances, another of those great classic wisdoms of his, a palinode to Patriotism by one who had seen it at its worst. Pointing out that a British officer's commission was an investment, saleable for from 1,500 to 4,000 guineas, while an American commission was so worthless that in the Virginia line alone ninety officers had recently thrown their commissions down, he wrote:

"Men may speculate as they will; they may talk of patriotism; they may draw a few examples from ancient story, of great achievements performed by its influence; but whoever builds upon them, as a sufficient basis for conducting a long and bloody war, will find themselves deceived in the end. We must take the passions of men as nature has given them, and those principles as a guide, which are generally the rule of action. I do not mean to exclude altogether the idea of patriotism. I know it exists, and I know it has done much in the present contest. . . . For a time it may, of itself, push men to action, to bear much, to encounter difficulties; but it will not endure unassisted by interest." [10]

The dread of militarism, of a standing army, of perpetual debt, of further impairment of the currency combined to alarm the majority. The Connecticut delegates called it "the most painfull and disagreeable question that hath ever been agitated in Congress." [11] After virulent wrangles a compromise was reached on May 15th, 1778, by which officers who served throughout the war should have half-pay for seven years and soldiers "the further reward of eighty dollars." [12]

Even this was good news to Washington and he wrote to

Gouverneur Morris a fine bit of pessimism that the compromise, "though not equal to my wishes, exceeded my expectations." Now he wanted the new regulations arranged at once and urged:

"For God's sake, my dear Morris . . . urge the absolute necessity of this with all your might." [13]

Into this boiling cauldron fell word that Lord North had prepared new conciliation measures and was sending commissioners to arrange peace with the surrender by the British of all the powers whose exercise had brought about the Revolution, and, of course, the surrender by the Americans of their Declaration of Independence, which, like the Emancipation Proclamation, had not been issued till after a year of war with no such thought in mind.

This threw everybody into a turmoil of indignation. Washington took the British plan as an evidence that war with France was feared and that France had probably at last recognized American independence. A committee was appointed to draw up a declaration of refusal to renounce independence or consider any terms of reconciliation until after England had recognized independence absolutely or had withdrawn her armies and fleets. This renewed defiance to the peace makers was unanimously adopted on April 22nd, 1778, which, curiously, was the day of official prayer and fasting decreed on March 7th.

The knowledge that a large part of the country was sick of the war and hopeless enough to be ready to give up independence stirred Washington so deeply that he began to write in defence of independence, now! nearly two years after the Declaration! He pleaded that such bitterness had been aroused by the war and English depredation that a reconciliation could never be permanent. It would only, "if I may be allowed the expression, be a peace of war."

He did think that it might be well to pretend to give up independence and make peace in order to scare France into going to war—never dreaming of the news now on the sea.

And he thought that it might be well to offer the Tories an amnesty to detach them from the British. At the same time he wrote another letter advising a more vigorous detachment of Tories—"shooting some of the most notorious offenders wherever they can be found *in flagrante delicto.*"

But to consider peace with England was as abominable as Congress' mistreatment of the troops, which was based on "the *jealousy,* which Congress unhappily entertain of the army, and which, if reports are right, some members labor to establish."

He pleaded against the fear of a standing army in this country, and wrote a sublime eulogy of that poor ragged band whose devotion is immortal:

"We should all be considered, Congress and army, as one people, embarked in one cause, in one interest; acting on the same principle, and to the same end. . . . Among individuals the most certain way to make a man your enemy is to tell him you esteem him such. So with public bodies; and the very jealousy, which the narrow politics of some may affect to entertain of the army, in order to a due subordination to the supreme civil authority, is a likely mean to produce a contrary effect; to incline it to the pursuit of those measures, which they may wish it to avoid.

"It is unjust, because no order of men in the Thirteen States has paid a more sanctimonious regard to their proceedings than the army; and indeed it may be questioned whether there has been that scrupulous adherence had to them by any other, for without arrogance or the smallest deviation from truth it may be said, that no history now extant can furnish an instance of an army's suffering such uncommon hardships as ours has done, and bearing them with the same patience and fortitude.

"To see men, without clothes to cover their nakedness, without blankets to lie on, without shoes, by which their marches might be traced by the blood from their feet, and almost as often without provisions as with them, marching through the frost and snow, and at Christmas taking up their winter-quarters within a day's march of the enemy, without a house or hut to cover them, till they could be built, and submitting to it without a murmur, is a proof of patience and obedience, which in my opinion can scarce be paralleled." [14]

On the solemn day of fasting and prayer and abstention "from labour and recreations" Washington wrote letters, including a bright and gay greeting to General Charles Lee, saying that the terms for his release had been finally arranged and he was sending for him.

Usually the day of fasting and prayer coincided with the loss of a battle or other great disaster. If Washington had been consulted later he would have said probably that sending for Charles Lee was the worst of disasters.

It is dramatic to read Boudinot's account of the two characters at this time, remembering that Boudinot came to believe Lee at least half-mad:

"When I was setting off from Camp, Genl Washington called me into his Room, and in the most earnest manner intreated of me, if I wished to gratify him. that I would obtain the Exchange of Genl Lee, for he never was more wanted by him. than at the present moment, and desired that I would not suffer trifles to prevent it." Finding that "quite new propositions were made for the Exchange of Genl Lee," he returned to submit them to Washington. "When he interrupted me with much Eagerness and asked me if I had exchanged Genl Lee, I informed him of what had been done; he replied sit down at this Table, and write a letter informing of my Confirmation of the Exchange & send one of my Horse Guards immediately to the Enemies lines with it, I assured him that next day would be time enough. but he insisted on its being immediately done. and I sent him accordingly, fixing the next day but one for Genl Lee's coming out to us.

"When the day arrived the greatest preparations were made for his reception all the principal Officers of the Army were drawn up in two lines, advanced of the Camp about 2 miles towards the Enemy.—Then the troops with the inferior Officers formed a line quite to head Quarters. All the Music of the Army attended. The General with a great number of principal Officers. and their Suites, rode about four miles on the road towards Philadelphia and waited till Genl Lee appeared.

"Gen Washington dismounted & recd Gen Lee as if he had

been his brother.—He passed thro' the lines of Officers & the Army. who all paid him the highest military Honors to Head Quarters, where Mrs Washington was. and there he was entertained with an Elegant Dinner, and the Music Playing the whole time.—A Room was assigned him. Back of Mrs Washington's Sitting Room, and all his Baggage was stowed in it.

"The next morning he lay very late. and Breakfast was detained for him. When he came out. he looked as dirty as if he had been in the Street all night. soon after I discovered that he had brought a miserable dirty hussy with him from Philadelphia (a British Sergeants Wife) and had actually taken her into his Room by a Back Door and she had slept with him that night.

"Genl Washington gave him the command of the Right Wing of the Army. but before he took charge of it, he requested leave to go to Congress at York Town; which was readily granted. Before he went I had an interview with him. . . . He said . . . That he found the Army in a worse situation than he expected and that General Washington was not fit to command a Sergeant's Guard.

"This mortified me greatly. after all the kindness shown him by Genl Washington. . . .

"He went to Congress, and as I was afterwards informed. he applied to Congress for a committee to meet and confer with him. The President Mr Laurence was directed to this Service, to whom Genl Lee communicated his Plan, which disgusted Mr Laurence so greatly that he would not even report it to Congress.—This lessened the General so greatly in the Eyes of Congress. that they never paid much respect to him afterwards—He returned to the army and took command of the right wing—

"He immediately began to rebel ag^t Genl Washington & to quarrel with the Marquise La Fayette. He assured himself that Genl Washington was ruining the whole cause." [15]

Washington continued to treat Lee with affectionate admiration until their historic and much-misstated clash on Monmouth field. Even thereafter it was Lee who did most of the fighting, and all of the mismanagement.

One of the two recorded laughs Washington enjoyed at Valley Forge was given him by Lee, who seems always to have fascinated him:

Congress having decided that a fresh proof of allegiance was advisable, required every officer to subscribe to a new oath, abjuring all allegiance to "King George the third and his heirs and successors, and his and their abettors, assistants and adherents." [16]

When Lee was called upon belatedly to swear to it on June 9th with other officers recently returned, he put his hand on the Bible, then withdrew it. Washington asked why. Lee with his inveterate impishness answered:

"As to King George, I am ready enough to absolve myself from all allegiance; but I have some scruples about the Prince of Wales."

Washington saw the nonsense and roared with laughter, as did the others about him. Whereupon Lee, having had his joke, put back his hand and gave his oath. [17]

At least one historian, Stryker, laboring under the *idée fixe* of Lee's treason, has found in this something sinister. His hesitation was "a faint expression of the treason in his heart." He took the oath "with no doubt a wicked mental reservation." [18]

John Fiske in his essay on "Charles Lee, the Soldier of Fortune," was also convinced of his definitely treasonable intent; and he comments:

"What a frightful situation for the Americans: to have, for the second officer in their army, the man whom the chances of war might at any moment invest with the chief command, such a man as this who had so lately been plotting their destruction! What would Washington, what would Congress, have thought, had the truth in its blackness been so much as dreamed of? But why, we may ask, did the intriguer come back? Why did he think it worth his while to pose once more in the attitude of an American? Could it have been with the intention of playing into the hands of the enemy? and could the British commander, knowing this purpose, have thus gladly acquiesced in his return?   It is hard to say, but probably this explanation is too simple to cover the case." [19]

Washington, having enough to be glum about, was fortunately permitted to laugh at Lee's little quip about the Prince of Wales. He needed the laugh.

THE BRIGHTER SIDE OF VALLEY FORGE

THE encampment, despite its sorrows and horrors, was not all misery. Gradually the men grew used to their arctic life, and privations became familiar. The weak and sick were eliminated by death or desertion. Then, as prisoners do in dungeons, they began to say, "This is not so bad. It might be worse."

Probably the oldest inhabitants in hell take a positive pride in the extent and duration of their damnation, become arrant snobs in wretchedness and lord it over the parvenu. The freezing soldier had the Irish comfort: "I'm alive. That's much— these days." He could write, as one did:

"I am very Happy in having my Health at this present time. And More so A Stedfast Resolution to Remain a Strong Libertine As long As my Much Ronged Country May Call for Soldiers Sword and Ball." [1]

By and by Washington felt it safe to thank the stout-hearted and rebuke the murmurers at the "trifling strokes of adversity." Somehow his fine rhetoric looks less pedantic in the bad spelling of the sergeant who copied it into Weedon's Orderly Book. It makes strange reading after the epic of miseries:

"Men worthy of the Envyable priviledge, Contending for the Rights of human nature, . . . The few Refractory Individuals who disgraced themselves by murmering it is to be hoped have repented such unmanly behaviour. . . . Occasional distress for want of provision and other necessaries is a spectacle that occurs in every Army and perhaps there never was one which has been in General so plentiful supply'd in respect to the former as ours. . . . Soldiers American Soldiers will dispise the meanness of Repining at such trifling strockes of Adversity, Triffling Indeed when compared with the Transcendent prize which will undoubtedly crown their patience and perseverance, Glory and freedom, peace & plenty to themselves and Comunity—The Admiration of the World, the love of their Country and the gratitude of posterity. Your General unceasingly employs his thoughts on the means of releaving your distresses; suply your wants and bringing your labours to a speedy and prosperous Issue—" [2]

Already Washington had forgotten his own thunderous murmurs; yesterday's hunger no longer gnawed, and the March rains were melting away the red flecks and the flinching toemarks of naked feet.

For nearly two months the wives of officers had been brightening the huts and sharing the hardships of the army women, who washed the clothes, filled the canteens in battle, and occasionally served as nurses. Some of them were quite respectable.[3]

On February 1st, 1778, Washington wrote to Jacky Custis:

"Your mamma is not yet arrived, but if she left Mount Vernon on the twenty sixth ultimo, as intended, may, I think, be expected every hour. Meade set off yesterday (as soon as I got notion of her intention) to meet her." [4]

She wrote of what she found:

"The general is in camp in what is called the great valley on the Banks of the Schuylkill. Officers and men are chiefly in Hutts, which they say is tolerable comfortable; the army are as healthy as can well be expected in general. The General's apartment is very small; he has had a log cabin built to dine in, which has made our quarter much more tolerable than they were at first." [5]

In partial exchange for the lost prayer legend the expense book reveals an otherwise unrecorded fact, that the first public celebration of Washington's birthday took place on February 22nd, 1778, at Valley Forge. In Pennsylvania the new calendar had been accepted. In Virginia it was ignored until after Washington's final birthday, which he celebrated at Alexandria in 1799 on February 11th. While he lived, then, he was a man with two birthdays a year.

We learn of the Valley Forge festivity from his expense accounts which show that he distributed a gratuity of 15 shillings to Procter's Fourth Continental Artillery band which apparently serenaded him on the twenty-second.[6] Having refused to accept any wages from the government, he charged this gift to the government as a legitimate necessity, as he charged the tips he always gave to servants for "extra trouble" in houses that he used as headquarters.

The fact that Washington tipped freely and liberally and recognized the tip as an essential part of a travelling man's charge against his employers, is of significance, both to those who maintain that tipping is unworthy of republicans, and those who maintain that it is not a proper deduction on an income tax return.

He also charged the government for Martha's visits to his various camps, excusing himself on the ground that he never once took the leave of absence allowed to all other officers.

Immediately upon Martha's arrival she began to entertain with dinners twice or thrice a week and Duponceau wrote that the officers called of evenings. He says:

"We were in a manner domesticated in the family . . . The evening was spent in conversation over a cup of tea or coffee. There were no levees or formal soirées, no dancing and playing, or amusements of any kind, except singing. Every gentleman or lady who could sing was called 'upon in turn for a song.' "[7]

General Greene's wife had been in camp since early January, and Duponceau praised her for speaking French, and being "well versed in French literature."[8]

A reminiscence of Martha in camp given to Lossing by an eighty-four-year-old woman pictures her as busy and kind and cheerful:

"I never in my life knew a woman so busy from early morning until late at night as was Lady Washington, providing comforts for the sick soldiers. Every day, excepting Sundays, the wives of officers in camp, and sometimes other women, were invited to Mr. Potts's to assist her in knitting socks, patching garments, and making shirts for the poor soldiers when materials could be procured. Every fair day she might be seen, with basket in hand, and with a single attendant, going among the huts seeking the keenest and most needy sufferers, and giving all the comfort to them in her power. I sometimes went with her, for I was a stout girl, sixteen years old.

"On one occasion she went to the hut of a dying sergeant, whose young wife was with him. His case seemed to particularly touch the heart of the good lady, and after she had given him some wholesome food she had prepared with her own hands, she knelt down by his straw pallet and prayed earnestly for him and his wife with her sweet and solemn voice. I shall never forget the scene." [9]

That Martha should have prayed with a dying sergeant was not improbable for she was a very religious woman.

Only two stories of Washington's laughter at Valley Forge have come down to us. They are unimportant but show a readiness for amusement. Nothing is harder to do than describe a scene that once provoked laughter in such a way as to make it provoke laughter again, and forever.

General Cobb of Washington's family is said to have said that "in his long intercourse with him, he had only met with one officer—Col. Scammel, who had the power of affecting the risibilities of the general. Scammel was full of ludicrous anecdotes and when dining at the general's table, was allowed to take the command, and to excite, beyond any other man, the general himself."

One of his laughs was at an impudent soldier. It seems that in felling the trees for the huts, innumerable stumps were left. Washington ordered that every time an officer or a private got drunk he must cut a stump. Thanks to the habits of the army, room for a large parade ground was speedily cleared. As the very final timber was vanishing under the hacks of a lugubrious toper, Washington happened to pass with his staff and he paused to comment:

"Well, my good fellow, you have found the last stump."

"Yes," the man growled, "and now when an officer gets drunk there'll be no stump to cut."

According to the undertaker who embalmed this remark, it struck Washington as very funny and he "laughed heartily, and some of the officers felt a sensation of great relief." [10] This last probably meant to reassure the graver reader that the officers probably expected Washington to freeze the half-frozen wretch altogether for his irreverence.

John Marshall was one of the camp humorists always making fun of the grumpier soldiers and displaying his athletic abilities.[11] Washington also was a famous athlete, and a giant of physical strength and agility. Barbé-Marbois says that Washington "sometimes throws and catches a ball for whole hours with his aides-de-camp." [12]

Ensign Ewing speaks of the officers playing "base" at Valley Forge.[13] This was the same as "rounders," and it is probable that Washington might have been seen there batting, running, catching and hurling with all the famed might of the arm that put a dollar across the Rappahannock, and could now throw a whole tent into a wagon unaided.

Why has no painter given us the Father of his Country triumphing in the father of the national game? To show him shrieking with laughter would be a much-needed antidote to the poisonous grandiosity in which the artists have so long imprisoned and falsified him. It would be a blessing if some genius were inspired to represent him as he was that day at the siege of Boston when he and his officers were suddenly alarmed by the warning of a British sally, and General Greene, who could not go to battle without his wig, was dancing about and bawling frantically for it and had it all the while on the top of his head. General Charles Lee said to him, "Your wig is behind the looking-glass, sir." When Greene caught sight of himself with his wig where it belonged, Washington fell over on a sofa in a fit of laughter.[14]

It is only an anecdote, but as authentic as the sadder ones.

We are told that once when Washington ordered an officer to cross a frozen river on a scouting expedition, and the officer returned to declare the ice unsafe, Washington in a swoop of rage at the coward threw an inkstand at him.[15] That would make an endearing portrait of him, and the artist could rely on it that he hit his mark. A few such pictures would rescue Washington from the morgue forever.

One of the sparse stories of this time concerns the order he issued against the dangerous females of Philadelphia. When he directed that all suspicious women should be hustled out of the camp, Mrs. Biddle is said to have stuffed him with a good dinner before she asked if the order applied to her. He is said to have said:

"Certainly not to Mrs. Biddle." [16]

That sounds like the gallant he always was.

On the sacred seventeenth of March Washington appears in a typical rôle between religious extremists. He never failed to show his affection for the Irish. In 1781 he was initiated into the Friendly Sons of St. Patrick, and inscribed his name on the membership roll.[17] On March 17th, 1776, he set "St. Patrick" as the countersign when he drove the British out of Boston. It is still apparently the local countersign.

On Patrick's Day at Valley Forge he was called upon to repress a riot occasioned by some Pennsylvania Germans who saw fit to make an effigy called a "stuffed paddy," which they displayed about the camp for their own amusement, and peril. Allen McLane himself describes the behavior of the Irish:

"They assembled in large bodies under arms and swearing vengeance against the New England troops, saying they got up the insult. The affair threatened a very serious issue. None of the officers could appease them. At that moment, Washington rode up to the Irish and kindly and feelingly argued with them and requested the Irish to point out the offenders and he would see that they would be punished. They could not designate anyone.

" 'Well,' said Washington with great promptness, 'I too, am a lover of St. Patrick's Day, and must settle the affair by making all the army keep the day.'

"He therefore ordered extra drink to every man in his command and thus all made merry and were good friends." [18]

The soldiers could be trusted to divert themselves with every occasion for battle, and fights were plentiful. There were also touches of sturdy humor such as the joke played on an unpopular brigade quartermaster whose mysterious nicknames were "Leg and a Piece" or "Five Pounds Ten." Young Ensign Ewing tells with unpunctuated breeziness of Mr. Anderson's anger:

"Some Rogueish chaps tied a sheaf of straw to the tail of Joseph Andersons B Quartermaster commonly called leg and a piece or five Pound tens horse tail and set it on fire and let him run which very much offended him and he set out to the Genl to enter a complaint."

He evidently lacked a sense of humor; but otherwise he would probably never have tried to be a quartermaster. How Washington received his complaint is not known. Washington did not like quartermasters.

He was indisposed on May Day when the camp was in carnival. Ewing says:

"May poles were Erected in everry Regt in the Camp and at the Revelle I was awoke by three cheers in honor of King Tamany The day was spent in mirth and Jollity the soldiers parading marching with fife & Drum and Huzzaing as they passd the poles their hats adornd with white blossoms." [19]

Tammany was the chief who sold lands to William Penn, and various societies took his name and held May festivals in his honor before he was monopolized by the New York society in 1789.[20] On this day in Valley Forge he was represented by a sergeant dressed in an Indian habit, and was attended by thirteen sergeants dressed in white, each with a bow and thirteen arrows. Thirteen drums and fifes made music and the privates marched in "thirteen Plattoons thirteen men each."

Some of them marched to headquarters "to do Honor to his Excellency" but an aide "informed them that the Genl was Indisposd and desird them to retire which they did with the greatest decency and regularity." They had a drink of whiskey each, provided by their generous officers. After "a song and dance in honour of King Tamany" they retired to rest.

The next day Washington was in better health and spirits for the diary says that after a dinner with General Knox, he joined the junior officers in a game:

"This day His Excellency dined with G Nox and after dinner did us the honor to play at Wicket with us." [21]

This was a kind of cricket played with a broad low wicket, a large soft ball, and a bat with a flat head.

When the officers gave plays in the Bakehouse the women's rôles were filled by men, of course. Congress had in 1774 forbidden "Horse Racing, and all Kinds of Gaming, Cock Fighting, Exhibitions of Shews, Plays, and other expensive Diversions and Entertainments," and would issue another embargo against plays later in 1778. Yet Martha and George attended the theatre at Valley Forge on May 11th, 1778, according to William Bradford, Junior, who describes the performance as brilliant and the death scene impressive:

"Cato was performed before a very numerous & splendid audience. His Excellency & Lady; Lord Stirling, the Countess & Lady Kitty, & Mr. Greene were part of the Assembly. The scenery was in Taste & the performance admirable—Col. George did his part to admiration—he made an excellent *die* (as they say)—Pray heaven, he don't *die* in earnest—for yesterday he was seized with the pleurisy & lies extremely ill." [22]

It was from Addison's *Cato* that Washington took the thought that he expressed more than once, and that has been sometimes credited to him as original:

> " 'Tis not in mortals to command success,
> But we'll do more, Sempronius, we'll deserve it."

He omitted the "Sempronius," of course, but the idea came to be a sort of motto and apology for his life. *Cato* was the play that Washington wrote about to Sally Fairfax in 1758, from depths of despondence, telling her how he longed to play *Juba* to her *Marcia*.[23]

Sally and her husband had gone to England before the war

broke out leaving Washington to look out for their interests, particularly their home, Belvoir, where he had spent so many hours. In 1775 Washington had written that he would be unable to supervise the estate on account of his military activities. He wrote to George William Fairfax from Valley Forge on March 11th, 1778, giving him news of his father, Lord Fairfax, his sister, Mrs. Warner Washington, and others. Washington was always a good homely gossip; and this letter shows him as a cosy tattler:

"What use you may have made of the information, I know not, having heard nothing from you these four years, nor been in Virginia these last three. I have heard, and fear it is true, that your seat (Belvoir) is verging fast to destruction. . . . Lord Fairfax, as I have been told, after having bowed down to the grave, and in a manner shaken hands with Death, is perfectly restored, and enjoys his usual good health, and as much vigor as falls to the lot of ninety. Your sister Washington goes on teeming but cannot produce a boy. Miss Fairfax was upon the point of marriage in December last with a relation of mine, a Mr. Whiting; but her ill health delayed it at that time, and what has happened since I know not. Your nieces in Alexandria are both married; the elder to Mr. Herbert, the younger to Mr. Harry Whiting, son of Frank in Berkeley. Mrs. Cary, her son Colonel Cary, Mr. Nicholas, Mrs. Ambler, and their respective families were all well about two months ago. Miss Cary is married to Tom Nelson, second son to the Secretary. Mrs. Washington, who is now in quarters with me, joins in most affectionate compliments to Mrs. Fairfax and yourself with, dear Sir, &c." [24]

This was just the sort of letter a sojourner abroad wants to receive from home. The Fairfaxes were loyalists, of course, and Tories were lucky who had Washington for an old friend. George Fairfax's eccentric brother, Bryan, visited Valley Forge on a delicate errand that would have brought many another loyalist a ride on a rail in the Tory uniform of tar and feathers. The troubled Bryan wanted to go to England and remain there during the war. He secured a pass through the lines from Washington but, before granting a passport, the British demanded from him an oath that might, he feared, part him forever from his family. So he turned back and visited Washington on his way home. In his gratitude for Washington's kindliness he sent back this tribute:

"That, at a time your popularity was at the highest and mine at the lowest, and when it is so common for men's resentments to run high against those, who differ from them in opinion, you should act with your wonted kindness towards me, has affected me more than any favor I have received; and could not be believed by some in New York, it being above the run of common minds." [25]

In his answer Washington wrote with personal warmth but bitterness toward England and the new peace feelers that were disturbing the country:

"The friendship, which I ever professed and felt for you, met with no diminution from the difference in our political sentiments. I know the rectitude of my own intentions, and, believing in the sincerity of yours, lamented, though I did not condemn, your renunciation of the creed I had adopted . . . our actions, depending upon ourselves, may be controlled, while the powers of thinking, originating in higher causes, cannot always be moulded to our wishes. . . .

"If you had been permitted to have gone to England, . . . your hope of being instrumental in restoring peace would prove as unsubstantial, as mist before the noon-day's sun, and would as soon dispel; for, believe me, Sir, Great Britain understood herself perfectly well in this dispute, but did not comprehend America. She meant, as Lord Camden, in his late speech in Parliament, clearly and explicitly declared, to drive America into rebellion, that her own purposes might be more fully answered by it; . . .

"And what punishment is there in store for the men, who have distressed millions, involved thousands in ruin, and plunged numberless families in inextricable woe? . . . having less dependence now in their arms than their arts, they are practising such low and dirty tricks, that men of sentiment and honor must blush at their villainy. Among other manœuvres in this way, they are counterfeiting letters, and publishing them as intercepted ones of mine, to prove that I am an enemy to the present measures, and have been led into them step by step, still hoping that Congress would recede from their present claims." [26]

The spurious letters he refers to are discussed in Appendix V. Washington took them rather lightly at first though they caused him much anger afterward. When asked for a copy of them at this time he answered that he had sent the only one he had "to Mrs. Washington, to let her see what obliging folks there were in the world." [27]

From Valley Forge he conducted a little real estate business, finding appalling hindrances in the uncertain value of the national money. He could be witty at times and now and then he gave a perfect character study, none more vivid than his psychoanalysis of a Mr. Alexander, from whom Jacky wanted to buy a home. Washington wrote that he thought Jacky had offered too high a price—

"But as you want it to live at—as it answers your's & Nelly's views —and is a pleasant seat & capable of improvement I do not think the price ought to be a capital object with you, but I am pretty sure that you and Alexander will never agree; for he is so much afraid of cheating himself that if you were to offer him five thousand pounds more than he ever expected to get for his Land the dread of injuring himself or hope of getting more, would cause him first to hesitate & then refuse." [28]

Suddenly all the fretting over the wavering American mind, the hopeless military situation, the despair of securing men and equipment enough for the next campaign went up with the smoke of the bonfires lighted in every patriot heart. Washington had always distrusted the talk that France would enter the war, though wild talk of such a possibility had dribbled over from France, but it was lost in the mass of disgusting details of personal wrangles among the American commissioners. They seemed to spend most of their time entertaining the French with their savage feuds, tomahawking one another with accusations of lying, thieving, stealing, cheating, adultery, and treason. The Lees and Silas Deane fought till Deane was charged not only with financial corruption but downright treason. Old Benjamin Franklin fascinated the French. Certain of them chose him as one of the greatest four men in human history. [29]

It is hard for us to realize what it meant to the world to learn that the lightning (the dreadful weapon of indignant gods to all religions until then) was after all only an exaggerated spark of electricity, and could be tapped with a kite

string, then run into a jar for preservation and the quaint jarring of people's knuckles. To the French, Washington was a
third rate farmer-soldier, of lofty virtues, and it was Franklin who managed the Revolution. It was the French who put
him, still living, into Latin as the man who "ripped the lightning from the skies and the scepter from the tyrants." But
to John Adams, Franklin was only a dirty-minded woman-
hunter with bastards scattered all over both hemispheres.
R. H. Lee called him "that wicked old man," accused him of
"malicious cunning," and wanted him recalled. There was a
cabal against Franklin, too, and it is said that if he had not been
pushed aside, Ontario would have been added to the United
States.

There would be ugly things to say and do, and the French
would soon be justified in accusing the Americans of leaning
back and letting them do all the work and pay the wages of
both.

Sufficient for the day was the rapture thereof. On May 5th,
1778, Washington's camp orders had been issued. They concerned the appointment of a man "to deliver out Boards, Plank,
&c," and the sentence of two deserters, each "to be hung by
his neck, till he be dead. Approv^d by the Commander in
Chief"; also a request, "If there be any Comb-Makers in the
Army, the Brigadiers . . . are desired to make a return of
them."

Suddenly the news came that a messenger, Simeon Deane,
had arrived from France and delivered to Congress on May
2nd a treaty signed by C. A. Gérard for the king and by
Benjamin Franklin, Silas Deane, and Arthur Lee for the
thirteen states.[30] Lafayette, weeping, seized Washington in
his arms and kissed him on both cheeks. When Washington
recovered, he issued "Genl After Orders. 6 o'clock P.M.
May 5th, 1778."

"It having pleased the Almighty Ruler of the Universe propitiously
to defend the cause of the United American States, and finally, by
raising us up a powerful friend among the Princes of the Earth, to

establish our Liberty and Independence upon a lasting foundation; it becomes us to set apart a day for gratefully acknowledging the Divine Goodness, and celebrating the event, which we owe to His benign interposition. The several Brigades are to be assembled at 9 o'clock tomorrow morning, when their Chaplains will communicate the intelligence contained in the Postscript of the Gazette of 2nd inst., and offer up a thanksgiving, and deliver a discourse suitable to the occasion."

Elaborate directions followed for the assembly of the troops, "a discharge of 13 cannons . . . a running fire of the Infantry," and evolutions on "the Grand Parade." The grandeur ends in two homely touches:

"Each man is to have a gill of rum . . . Each officer and soldier is to have a nosegay in his hat." [31]

On May the 6th when, says Mrs. Wharton, "May breezes had begun to blow through the lovely groves in which the army was encamped," [32] the ceremonies began early, with prayer and thanksgiving sermon, and the high-stepping maneuvers of Steuben's triumph. Washington rode round the line in splendor. Cannon and musketry and wild cheers startled the valley of groaning despair. Though not called for in the orders, there were throat-splitting cheers for Washington and Lady Washington. Finally there was banqueting with women and wine in the amphitheatre where the tables were "shaded by elegant markees." While the ladies waited beaming, the officers marched to the tables in lines of thirteen abreast, "and closely linked together in each other's arms."

"The General himself wore a countenance of uncommon delight and complacence." He lifted and drained his glass again and again in toasts to the King of France, and to the friendly powers, also to Congress, and to the States. At 6 o'clock Washington was permitted to retire. The throng rose to applaud and cheer. He mounted to the saddle amid tumult. A quarter of a mile away he turned his horse, and among his staff, swung his hat and cried a faint huzza! [33]

The common soldiers made a grand day of it, too, and Elijah Fisher of the Commander-in-Chief's Guard wrote in his diary:

"May 6th. We had Rejoicing on the account of the French declaring for us Independent and the howle of the Continental army was ordered to three larm posts in the senter and the army was all around us at there several stations (and there was a grand harber bilt and all the Commissioners were Envited to dine with His Exelency) our guard gave the first fire then thirteen Cannon then the fire began at the rite of the army and went through the howl line and fired three rouns apeace the Artillery Discharged forty-four Cannon and it was followed with three Chears for the King of France and three for the Friendly Powers of Europe and three Chears for the Thirteen United States of Amarica and His Exelency gave orders that every Prisoner should have his Freedom that belonged to the Continental army that they might taste the Pleasur of the Day." [34]

It was a shabby rural festival compared to the unheard-of pomp and glitter of the "Meschianza" held in Philadelphia five days later as a farewell to General Howe, whose resignation had been accepted at last. He had whipped Washington in every battle, yet he was going home in disgrace, while Washington in the valley was just climbing the hills of morning.

It was one of the greater ironies of history that Washington should have owed the ecstasy of this day and all his consequent glories and his elevation over perhaps all other men to the French, who had been his first inveterate enemies; whom, with the exception of one marquis, he never liked; whose language he would never learn; whom he would once more oppose and abhor, bringing on himself unimaginable abuse; against whom he would take the field, in his final year on earth, as their open enemy again, thus completing the round.

XXIX

THE RECOVERY OF PHILADELPHIA

WHILE Howe awaited the acceptance of his resignation impatiently, the loyalists had tried in vain to goad him into taking his big army out in the cold where Washington's almost helpless troops seemed to be positively begging to be gathered in. The Tories even tried the power of song, chanting of Mrs. Loring:

> "Awake, arouse, Sir Billy,
>   There's forage in the plain,
> Ah! leave your little Filly,
>   And open the campaign.
> Heed not a woman's prattle,
>   Which tickles in the ear,
> But give the word for battle,
>   And grasp the warlike spear." [1]

It took a little over six months for Howe to receive the acceptance of his resignation. The king appointed Sir Henry Clinton to succeed him, but Clinton was in New York and did not reach Philadelphia until May 8th. There was much to do before he could take over the command. Howe, for all his faults, was accounted just and very kind and was generally beloved by men and officers, and by the women. So they gave him a stupendous farewell festival. Galloway might gnash his teeth at the "vanity and presumption unparalleled in history," and a "triumph more magnificent than would have become the conqueror of America," but nobody cared and the "Meschianza" brought back medieval pomp for a day. In costumes designed by Captain André and the Tory Captain Delancey, the Ladies of the Blended Rose and the Burning Mountain greeted the White Knights and the Black Knights at a magnificent tournament and regatta. [2]

During the grand ball that night Captain Allen McLane, who had not been invited, visited the suburbs with a hundred infantry and some dragoons and flung a few camp kettles filled with explosives, then swam his horse across the Schuylkill and got away, while the Knights assured the ladies that the general alarm in the fleet and ashore was part of the celebration.[3]

The next day, when Philadelphia was planning to sleep it off, a spy brought word that Lafayette was advancing to attack the city. He was really supposed to be making a very secret reconnaissance in force to find out if the British had begun to evacuate as yet, for Washington suspected they must be moving soon lest the oncoming French fleet bottle up the Delaware. He warned Lafayette that the errand was difficult and dangerous, and he must guard against surprise, yet gave him no appropriate cavalry. One of the first to protest against his neglect of horse was Conway, whose contemptuous remarks may have reached Washington's ears. In any case, Conway had written to Robert Morris nine months before, urging that Colonel Armand's plea for cavalry be granted:

"What Light horsemen we have in this army are of no use in Military operations, they are merely employed as Messengers or Waiters to general Officers, which is absolutely ridiculous. I am confident that since the Beginning of this campaign not one Light horseman gave or got a trust or a cutt of a sword." [4]

Brevet-Brigadier General Charles Francis Adams, who served as a cavalry officer through the Civil War, found military "ineptitude" in Washington's long ignoring of the value of mounted patrols in a country rich in horses and horsemen and made for cavalry. Repeated misfortunes that cavalry could have prevented, showed that Washington lacked "military alertness," and "the cavalry flair so conspicuous in Cromwell and Frederick." At Brandywine, a year after Long Island, though Washington had several regiments of light horse, he made no use of them, and permitted Sullivan to be defeated once more by such a march around his flank as horsemen would easily have discovered in time. The "massacre" of Wayne's men at Paoli was a "foot-surprise," impossible with even a few videttes. It remained for a foreigner, Pulaski, to awaken Washington to the value of cavalry, but, as Adams indicates, Pulaski knew neither the language nor the country and was soon in trouble with his American officers. "Thus the first attempt at a Continental cavalry organization failed."

During the winter at Valley Forge Washington had begun to ask for a "superiority of horse," but even then his chief argument was that the British were "taking all the pains in their power to acquire an ascendancy in this respect." The British were stirred by a young man, Banister Tarleton, of evil repute in America because of his ferocity, but a genuine innovator. Washington, however, never gained a real sense of the need or the opportunity for cavalry, and Colonel Adams, after scathing references to the historians both for their "adulatory and indiscriminating hero-worship wherever Washington is concerned" and for their utter absence of any strategic instinct or military experience, goes on to say:

"The third year of active warfare was now drawing to its end, and . . . both Morgan and Arnold were in command of men who ought to have been on horseback with rifles on their saddle-bows, but who still marched and fought on foot with musket and bayonet. . . . The explanation seems obvious. Washington began his military career as a backwoods Indian fighter, and never forgot the lessons then learned, nor outgrew the experience. . . . Virginian though he was, there is from the beginning to the end of his military life, so far as I can discover, no indication of any adequate conception of the value and importance of the mounted man in military operations."

After this it is not surprising to find the dauntless infidel, Adams, going on to say of Lafayette's mission:

"It was, in fact, a reconnoissance in force; and, as such, should have been composed in the main of cavalry, with a strong infantry support and artillery contingent. The patriot army, however, had no cavalry to speak of, so Lafayette marched off with a command composed almost exclusively of foot." [5]

When Howe learned of his approach, it is said that he invited all his friends to dinner and promised to bring in "the Boy" as guest of honor. Even Admiral Howe went along to see the fun. Howe's plans were as clever as ever and just missed fire as usual. He sent General Grant one way with 8,000 men and fifteen guns to get round Lafayette's right and cut him off from retreat across the river. He sent "No-Flint" Grey to worry the left flank, while he and Clinton amused Lafayette and themselves in front.

Lafayette was just making arrangements with a young woman to go into Philadelphia and find out if the British were on their way to the transports, when a man came running up to him saying that another man had told him that Lafayette was all but surrounded, the militia having failed to keep watch. Only by the cleverest management did Lafayette make the river. Then he had to wade it with his men holding hands to brace them against the current, while his Indians swallowed their own war whoops and swam.

At the sound of the attack, Washington had been acutely alarmed and, mustering in haste all the force he could raise, reached the opposite shore and began to fire his cannon at the British. He could be seen through the smoke waving his hat at Lafayette.[6] The British had their long march for their sauce to the feast they planned, and it was reported that General Grant had a narrow escape from being cashiered. But Washington did not reproach Lafayette. Instead he boasted of him with fatherly pride:

"The Marquis by depending on the militia to patroll the roads on his left, had very near been caught in a snare—in fact he was in it—but by his *own dexterity* or the enemy's *want of it*, he disengaged himself in a very soldier-like manner. . . . Upon the whole the Marquis came handsomely off." [7]

A strange man, Howe,—so sleepy, so lazy, so neglectful that anybody could ridicule or abuse him; yet when he struck, Providence had to intervene to save his adversary. His last gesture in America was a snatch at Lafayette, which but to have escaped was accounted a matter for boasting. And now he was gone beyond the reach of Washington's revenge. His brother, the Admiral, also resigned but was not relieved until the end of the year. On the 24th of May Howe turned over his command to Clinton and embarked for home, leaving Mrs. Loring to the care of her husband, the Commissary of Prisoners. André wrote:

"I do not believe there is upon record an instance of a Commander-in-Chief having so universally endeared himself to those under his command; or of one who received such signal and flattering proofs of their love . . . The most gallant of our officers, and those whom I least suspected of giving such instances of their affection, shed tears while they bid him farewel." [8]

Howe had every reason to believe that the rebels with the aid of France would speedily assure Washington's triumph. It is puzzling that they did not, for Clinton's instructions were such as are sent to a beaten general, to extricate himself from a hopeless situation. Only the still more hopeless inanition of the Americans combined with Washington's inveterate bad luck to prolong the war for five more years.

Never was a soldier less delighted to find himself Commander-in-Chief than Clinton. His was the exact situation of the peasant to whom his dread monarch presented a white elephant that he dared not decline, and could neither feed nor manage. If he felt ruined by his success, imagine his emotions when he read his instructions. Of his force, which was not sufficient to conquer the northern colonies, he was to ship 5,000 to the West Indies and 3,000 to Florida, also to give up Philadelphia and get to New York, where he was to "wait the Issue of a Treaty to be proposed to the American Congress by Commissioners." If the treaty failed and he found himself in danger of being overpowered at New York, he was to sail to Rhode Island; if ousted from there, to go to Halifax, fortify that port, and send his spare troops to Quebec. He was also informed that he would receive only three more regiments of reinforcements and he must draft troops to fill his weakest

FOREIGN VOLUNTEERS IN THE AMERICAN SERVICE
(From B. J. Lossing's Life of Washington)

corps! He was "to endeavour without delay to bring Mr. Washington to a General Action. And if that could not be soon accomplished to give up every Idea of offensive operation within land, and employ the Troops . . . only in desultory Expeditions in Conjunction with the King's Ships of War."

Knowing that he could not secure enough convoy to assure the safety of his troops to New York over waters swarming with rebel privateers and soon to be invaded by French warships, he had nothing to do but retreat overland, and do his best to carry with him all the provisions he could and all of those unfortunate loyalists, who must now realize that they had guessed wrong again. Clinton says:

"I was not altogether without Hope that Mr. Washington might be tempted by his superior Number & many other advantages to measure his Strength with me in the Field; for his Army then at Valley Forge amounted to at least 14,000 Regulars, besides the 4,000 that were under Gates in the Jersies . . . and he could further swell his Numbers to any Magnitude he chose, by calling out the Militia of the neighboring populous Provinces, who were little inferior in Perseverance and Courage to their best Soldiers. . . . I must however confess that Mr. Washington had just now much stronger motives of Policy for declining a general Action than he ever had with Sir William Howe." [9]

By this last Clinton meant, of course, that the promise of French troops would save Washington from the necessity of risk. This was also the feeling of General Charles Lee and most of the other rebel officers. But, as Stryker emphasizes, Washington felt a strong personal necessity to fight and win a battle as an answer to the dissatisfaction with his Fabian tactics, his many defeats, and the feeling that he was inferior to Gates.[10]

Clinton's impatience to give Washington a lesson in tactics was restrained by visiting peace commissioners who replaced the Howes and had no more success.

Washington felt no friendship for the commissioners of peace. He believed that it was too late for reconciliation. A peace would "be the source of perpetual feuds and animosity." [11]

The thing had to be fought out. He rebuffed all advances.[12] He did not even answer the appeal of the Reverend Andrew Burnaby, who offered him the chance to achieve the "divine purpose" and acquire more glory and do mankind more service than "ever yet happened to the lot of any one man." [13]

Washington wanted to fight. He wanted cavalry, too. Lee's Legion, modelled on Pulaski's "ill conceived idea" was only half mounted.[14] Pulaski, unhappy and causing unhappiness among the jealous native officers, pleaded in vain to have the horse used for something besides orderly work.[15] Finally he resigned and asked permission to raise an independent corps of sixty-eight horse and two hundred foot. Washington accepted his resignation and asked Congress to grant the permission but disapproved his desire to enlist prisoners and deserters.[16]

He asked Congress to make Steuben a major-general since "his finances, he ingenuously confesses, will not admit of his serving without the incident emoluments." [17] Congress cheerfully acceded and thus the modest Steuben slipped into the rank that Conway gained with such friction. Steuben was welcomed by the regular clamor that greeted all promotions and when Washington, being short of generals, gave him temporary command of a division, "this was a source of offence to many," says Hamilton.[18]

Gates was relieved from the Board of War in April and assigned to a large command on "Hudson's River" with Mifflin. As Gouverneur Morris wrote rather gloatingly to Washington:

"As these Gentlemen ought not to receive Orders *immediately* from Congress they are as you will see permitted to leave the Board of War upon *your* Order . . . A propos of your Council of War. Should you determine on any Thing which considering the Course of human Affairs is I confess rather improbable Let Congress know Nothing about it. A Secret should never be trusted to many Bosoms." [19]

Once more Washington was hung in suspense waiting for the enemy to do something. He was worried about what ought to be done with the stores Clinton would leave and whom to put in charge of the city when it was evacuated. He wrote to Gouverneur Morris, underlining the words:

"*Between you & I*, I have no idea of marching more than a small detachment to the city, to prevent plundering and disorder till some kind of civil government can be established." [20]

Among his other perplexities was General Charles Lee, who was back in camp "with his usual train of dogs." [21] Also with his usual train of disturbances. Lee wanted the army reorganized on his plan. Washington was most polite in welcoming advice proceeding from "the fountain of candor" and not from "an itch for criticism," [22] and patiently recounted the reasons why he could make few or none of the improvements.

Lee put forth a fantastic idea that the British would not go to New York overland at all, but would march down the river and turn west to draw Washington out of Valley Forge and make him fight at a disadvantage; or they would take in the Susquehanna and support the Indians, who were now warring on the Western Border, and requiring serious attention as well as needed officers and troops. Lee was remembering, perhaps, the treasonable "scheme" he had written out for Howe, claiming that the Chesapeake was the vital spot to strike at; and he may have felt that his conscience, if he had one, compelled him to warn Washington of danger in that direction. Some historians have no hesitation in announcing that Lee tried to get Washington to go south in order "to open a free course for the escape of Sir Henry Clinton." [23] The attempt to prove both that Lee's plan was used by the British and that it was ignored by them amounts to cancellation, and the probability is that Howe was not influenced by it and Clinton was ignorant of it. In any case, Lee wrote to Washington and proposed that engineers at least be sent to survey the country and determine the best fords and positions. Washington thanked him and begged him to communicate his ideas freely, but paid no further heed to his advice.

Whatever Lee or others might think wise for him, Clinton

had orders to crawl into New York. He was afraid to take ship even if he could have been sure of safety, since contrary winds might detain him and "General Washington might have seized the opportunity of making a decisive push at New York." [24]

On the 8th of June, 1778, Martha left for Mount Vernon. When that gray dove flew home, the war was on. On the night of June 17th, Washington called a council of war. Nobody believed in bringing on a real battle, but Lee opposed doing anything even to risk one. He preferred building a "golden bridge" to expedite Clinton's dash for New York, since, he maintained, the French fleet would lock him up there, and with a French army coming over, it would be criminal to subject America's only important body of troops to the danger of a catastrophe. He did not believe that they were ready yet to meet British regulars in the open, and they had certainly given no indications of a reform. Though Steuben, du Portail and practically all of the officers agreed with him, his motives have since been impugned as a traitorous effort to make things easy for Clinton. [25]

Anthony Wayne alone strongly urged an attack. If it succeeded, the result would be "productive of the most happy Consequences." If it failed, the enemy could not pursue far without endangering his baggage and provisions. "On the Enemy's part it will have the Appearance of a Retreat—on ours, that of Pursuit—we may Inculcate the Idea of Besieging Clinton." [26] Hitherto Washington had always accepted the verdict of his council, but he was desperately set on giving battle and he called for opinions in writing. Before he could consider these arguments spies and scouts came galloping in on the forenoon of June 18th with great news: Clinton had left Philadelphia at night so silently that most of the inhabitants did not know he was gone; but as he stole out, Captain McLane stole in swiftly enough to overtake a few stragglers. [27] A bonny scout, that Scot! It was cleverer still of Clinton to get his army across the Delaware without being caught astraddle the river.

Washington was not yet sure whether Clinton would sail away or march. Later in the day he notified Congress:

"I have appointed General Arnold to command in Philadelphia, as the state of his wound will not permit his services in a more active line." [28]

Thus he dropped his most admired soldier into the hotbed of luxury and loyalism still warm from the British occupation. Arnold's physical wound grew better but the wound in his pride festered and his long agony and immobility seem to have changed him. Furthermore, he was settled close to that Congress which returned in haste, and was near enough to resume its feud with him. Worse yet, Arnold's lonely heart was subjected to the witchery of that exquisite siren, Peggy Shippen, to whom André had been so devoted. They made a fatal triangle and the wealth of the Shippens stirred Arnold to extravagances of perilous nature. In his order to Arnold, Washington included directions to "give security to individuals of every class and description, restraining as far as possible, till the restoration of civil government, every species of persecution, insult, or abuse, either from the soldiery to the inhabitants, or among each other." [29] Arnold carried out the spirit of this so well that he was soon accused of favoring the Tories suspiciously.

On June 21st, 1778, at noon, Washington was at Coryell's Ferry on the Delaware. Early morning rain was followed by such heat that he could do no more than cross. He sent Lee to halt on the first strong ground in New Jersey. In his perplexity as to the whereabouts of the British, according to Hamilton:

"The General unluckily called a council of war, the result of which would have done honor to the most honorable society of midwives, and to them only. The purport was, that we should keep at a comfortable distance from the enemy, and keep up a vain parade of annoying them by detachment. . . . General Lee was *primum mobile* of this sage plan. . . . The General, on mature reconsideration of what had been resolved on, determined to pursue a different line of conduct at all hazards." [30]

Another council was held at Hopewell at 9 A.M., June 24th, 1778, during an eclipse of the sun. The vote was again against a downright battle, though Greene and Lafayette were opposed to too much caution. Wayne wrote:

"I would not Advise Risking a Gen'l Action—unless Circumstances should Render success Certain, or such as not to leave you in a Worse situation, if Unfortunate, than if you had not Attacked. . . . a select Corps of field & other officers—with 2500 or 3000 Effective Rank & file Commanded by a Major—and two Brig'r Generals . . . should Immediately be Drafted, and March to gain the Rear of the left flank of the Enemy when they should take the first favorable Opportunity of Attempting an Impression in force . . . I would also wish the main body of your Army to be in a position on the left of their Rear so as to be Ready to Act effectively." [31]

Despite the council's adverse advice, Washington adopted this measure and pressed forward, though the troops were exhausted from the heat, which was broken only by heavy rains that impeded the march and spoiled the arms and the tempers. There was almost complete failure of food supply, the roads were mud or sand and the men suffered intensely from hunger and sun. As Elijah Fisher wrote, they "Mett with a good eal of Dificulty in giting along." [32]

Washington asked Lee to take a detachment and feel for the left flank and rear of the British, while Morgan gained the right flank and other officers drew close. Lee was miffed at the task and said that it was "a more proper business of a young, volunteering general, than of the second in command in the army." Meekly Washington acquiesced, gave Lafayette the post, and sent him ahead. When Lee thought it over and talked it over, he decided that the job was a bigger one than he thought. So he asked Washington for it back again.

As Hamilton wrote, Lee's conduct was "truly childish." [33] It was excruciatingly embarrassing to Washington, who must now either offend the cantankerous Lee or hurt the feelings of Lafayette by juggling him back and forth. Fortunately, Lafayette was as superior to little prides as Washington was. He even asked that he should not be considered, but sent anywhere. Washington thanked him for his "politeness in wishing to ease" General Lee of his "uneasiness." [34]

All this management of other people's girlish sensitivenesses must have tested the breaking strain in Washington, with his own patriotism and his own good name involved in the fierce effort to find just where in the hills the British were. The weather was that intolerable mixture of summer shower and blaze that makes existence a torment. The sandy soil seemed to prolong the distances and keep all the roads uphill. Both armies were in full marching order and the Hessians were almost suffocated in their heavy equipment. At one time nearly a third of them fell by the wayside.[35] For once the nakedness of the Americans was welcome, but they fainted like women, and the famous Jersey mosquitoes were doubtless impartial, though the Hessians, having less immunity, were so poisoned that the faces of some were swollen beyond recognition.

The writer took part in such a march at the Mexican border in 1916 when, of two New York regiments totalling about eighteen hundred men, half of one regiment and two thirds of the other were knocked down by the heat. First, individuals dropped at intervals, then in increasing numbers. Sometimes one could see a whole squad reel drunkenly to the side of the road and sprawl gasping, blazing with sunstroke or shivering with heat prostration. Many recovered quickly when dragged into the shade and helped, but others were disabled for long periods. That was simply a practice march, but the wholesale agony of an army in merciless heat is almost more ghastly than in the bitterest cold. The torments of the British were the worse because the rebel militia swarmed ahead of them breaking down bridges and causeways, and filled the wells with dirt.[36]

At the village of Kingston, Washington was met by a superb white war-horse, a gift from Governor Livingston of New Jersey. He rode the beauty to the battlefield.[37]

A most endearing picture of Washington in these anxious days and one that is to be remembered in the clash he had with Lee, is given in Custis' recollections of an account he had from Colonel Daniel Morgan himself. It explains why Morgan was so passionate a devotee of his chief. He could not tell the story himself without tears and a choke in his throat: Washington sent for Morgan at night and told him to take a detail of twenty-two and make the most careful survey he could of the positions, without attracting attention. Under no circumstances whatever was he to fire a single shot or put up any resistance. Having enforced this point and "filling two glasses of wine, the general continued,

" 'And now, Colonel Morgan, we will drink a good night, and success to your enterprise.' "

Morgan and his men did their work well, creeping so close that they could smell the Hessian pipes. Just as a farmer's rooster warned them to flit, a body of English horse passed so close that Morgan simply could not resist the target. He gave the order to fire and destroyed or scattered the whole detachment. Realizing the depth of his guilt, Morgan ordered his men to follow as he slunk toward camp, feeling that he deserved his certain fate, saying to himself:

"You are broke, sir, and there is an end of Colonel Morgan."

Colonel Alexander Hamilton came galloping toward him. Washington had heard the volley and sent to make sure who fired it. Morgan confessed and was ordered to wait for the commander, who was making the rounds. Washington greeted him with sternness and amazement. "Morgan was brave, but it has been often and justly, too, observed," says Washington's adopted son, "that that man never was born of woman, who could approach the great Washington, and not feel a degree of awe and veneration from his presence."

Morgan quailed, and admitted that the temptation was too great for him, "flesh and blood could not refrain." Washington said:

"Colonel Morgan, you will retire to your quarters, there to await further orders."

Morgan went to his tent to grieve his heart out. The next day Hamilton came to him and Morgan dolefully offered his sword. Hamilton tried to speak, but Morgan broke in on him with bitter regrets, till at last Hamilton managed to say that he was invited to dinner at headquarters at three o'clock. Then the little Hamilton had to fight for his hand to save it from being crushed. The other officers greeted Morgan with warmth, and, after dinner, as Custis tells it:

"The cloth removed, Washington bid his guests fill their glasses, and gave his only, his unvarying toast, the toast of the days of trial, the toast of the evening of his 'time-honored' life amid the shades of Mount Vernon—'*All our Friends.*' Then, with his usual old-fashioned politeness, he drank to each guest by name. When he came to 'Colonel Morgan, your good health, sir,' a thrill ran through the manly frame of the gratified and again favorite soldier, while every eye in the pavilion was turned upon him. . . .

"And often in his after life did Morgan reason upon the events which we have transmitted to the Americans and their posterity, and he would say: 'What could the unusual clemency of the commander-in-chief toward so insubordinate a soldier as I was, mean? Was it that my attacking my enemy wherever I could find him, and the attack being crowned with success, should plead in bar of the disobedience of a positive order? Certainly not. Was it that Washington well knew I loved, nay adored, him above all human beings? That knowledge would not have weighed a feather in the scale of his military justice. In short, the whole affair is explained in five words; *it was my first offence.*" [38]

There is another story of Washington at this time. Major Richard Howell, late Governor of New Jersey, had a twin-brother, a surgeon also with the army. The major fought at Brandywine, and Germantown and was at Valley Forge. On the day before the battle word came that his twin-brother was dying, not far away at a tavern, and he must come at once if he would see him alive. He obtained permission to go but overheard the junior officer who replaced him saying:

"Howell was very willing to get leave of absence, for he well knew there would be hot work."

Whereupon the major threw himself into the ranks as a private, fought bravely and never saw his much-loved brother again. The story reached Washington's ears and he sent for Howell, who confirmed it, whereupon Washington rebuked him gently:

"Howell, I admire your bravery, but it was your duty to go to your brother." [39]

In the mass of anecdotes concerning the patriotic contempt for human ties, it is an agreeable disappointment to find that Washington did not try to console the heartbroken young man with some bombastic platitude, and it encourages one to feel even more certain that some of his magniloquences have been set on stilts by those who like that sort of thing. It is almost unique among anecdotes of heroes in its realization of the great truth that in a time of grief and pain, the human heart longs, not for proverbs or minimizing of its woe, but for more sorrow and more self-reproach. That is the literal and spiritual meaning of the word "sympathy."

Clinton had only one road to march on and his progress was snail-like with a train of fifteen hundred wagons, carriages and carts, twelve to fourteen miles long. He had met at his second halt a rain of fourteen hours without cessation, drenching baggage, and soldiers and making bogs of the highway. His caravan must have made a sorry spectacle for Von Eelking, who says that Clinton "had scarcely 13,000 men," describes the train as made up of masses of baggage dragged along by the affluent British officers, carriages, draft and saddle-horses, "mistresses and every kind of other useless stuff." He wonders what some of "Washington's primitive or puritan regiments from the back settlements" would have thought if they had captured this material.[40]

Anburey says that Clinton one day "sat upon a stone for near an hour viewing the baggage as it passed along, and debating in his own mind, whether he should not give instant orders to destroy it." He decided not to give the Americans the exultation or the British the disgrace. If he had sacrificed the loot and fought it out with his whole army, he might have accomplished one of the most influential might-have-beens in human history.

The leisureliness of Clinton's progress whether enforced or intentional was such that the first forty miles took him a whole week. He had put his cavalry on the transports knowing perhaps the impotence of Washington's mounted forces. C. F. Adams is amazed that "to a wagon train, eleven miles in length, the American cavalry offered no obstacle.

"To have stopped that train's forward movement, and, in so doing, to have thrown the whole column into confusion, would in our day have been a simple matter . . . A Fabian policy, combined with economy in horse-keep, came somewhat high at that juncture." [41]

Clinton feared the marshes and the creeks and was afraid of being surrounded, shoved into a trap, and "Burgoyned." He says he expected a clash at "Mount Holy" and planned "to play over the same Game with him as on Long Island in 76 by turning his left and cutting off his Retreat." He only pretended that he was going to cross the Raritan and ordered his troops to follow the road through Freehold (or Monmouth Court House) to the Navesink. He says:

"I hoped to draw the Enemy down from the Hilly Country in the Hope that an Opportunity might offer of getting a fair stroke at him before I finally took my leave. And as he would be thus thrown behind me, I should by placing the Elite of my army between him & my Baggage have it more effectually in my Power to defend it from Insult & to seize all advantages as they offered. For tho the Principle of my March was unquestionably Retreat, I wished to avoid every appearance of a precipitate one." [42]

He halted at Freehold on Friday, June 26th, as if to invite Washington to a try at arms and did not move until early Sunday morning. He was just one day's march from high ground at Middletown, where he would be unapproachable. Lafayette, Wayne and Greene talked to Washington and encouraged his resentment at being nothing more than an escort to General Clinton. He had at last, too, a big superiority in numbers for he knew that Clinton would be compelled to keep nearly half of his army immobilized about his wagon train while Washington's men could move with freedom. Early in the afternoon of June 27th, 1778, he called several officers to Headquarters and told Lee that he intended to have the enemy attacked the next day, and by Lee's troops, and he desired Lee to call his officers together to concert a mode of attack. There was afterwards contradiction as to whether he indicated a willingness to bring on a general action. Lafayette went to Lee, asked to go with him, and was welcomed cordially. Lafayette was zealous for glory and a chance to atone for letting Howe surprise him and chase him into the river.

Late at night Washington had Hamilton draft a letter to Lee urging an attack before the British could get out of reach, and instructing him to notify Morgan to attack also. This letter reached Lee after 1 A.M. and he says he asked Hamilton if he thought that Washington meant that Lee must attack "at all events," and that Hamilton replied:

"I can't conceive that General Washington could mean to give orders so extremely positive . . . but . . . the circumstances must be very extraordinary and unforeseen, which . . . could justify the not doing it." [43]

Washington doubtless slept little or none that night. The heat was stifling. Then there was another great thunderstorm. His soul was stormy and stifled, too, and he resolved to deal the British a stroke that should show them, and the French, and certain Americans how well the "grand army" deserved its name, and how much it had learned during the winter term at Steuben's school. He may have dreamed that since the country was hilly and wooded and marshy, he might pile the British in upon themselves and smash them. At least he might wrest from them part of that twelve-mile train of loot and precious stores, uniforms for his naked, equipment for the badly armed,

and provisions for his muddy, sweaty, herring-gutted starvelings.

The most remarkable evidence of Steuben's training is the
fact that we have, for the first time, actual figures showing the
number of his men. The Prussian had managed to extract
exact returns from those woeful bookkeepers. On June 22nd,
1778, at Coryell's Ferry the Field Return showed that Washington had 6 major-generals, 15 or 16 brigadier-generals, 28
colonels, 39 lieutenant-colonels, 35 majors, 258 captains, 583
subalterns, 1,173 sergeants, 691 drummers and fifers, and
10,697 rank and file fit for duty—an aggregate of 13,525.
Lee estimated his advance body at 4,100 men, though he was
charged with 5,000 men and Stryker figures it out that he had
6,000.[44]

A word as to the terrain. Inland from Navesink Highlands
and about eighteen miles southwest of the base of Sandy Hook
lay the village of Freehold, consisting of some forty houses, an
old English church, and the courthouse of Monmouth County.
Five miles northwest of Freehold lay Englishtown, to which
the county road led across three wet ravines, wide morasses,
with a brook running down the western ravine. Light Horse
Harry Lee said of it:

"This country abounds with defiles of a sort: the valleys are cut by
small rivulets with marshy grounds, difficult to man and horse, and
impracticable to artillery, except in particular spots." [45]

It had not been reconnoitred and the reports of the various
officers afterward are so conflicting that it seems impossible
to reconcile them with the actual landscape. Washington's
tension is shown in the countersign he gave, "Sharp and Keen."

It is said that Dr. David Griffiths, surgeon and chaplain with
the Virginia troops, called on Washington that night and
warned him that Lee would misconduct himself on the field.
Afterward Dr. Griffiths testified that he met Lee on the battlefield and that Lee spoke of his opposition to a battle and the

hopelessness of the Americans without sufficient cavalry and no skill in maneuvers.[46]　If the night visit of the chaplain took place, it had no discoverable effect on Washington, for he did not remove Lee from command or even accuse him of insubordinate intentions.　Though he was aware of Lee's opposition to a general action, he also knew that all his generals were against committing the army to a death grapple.　He had no one else to send.　Greene was a quartermaster now, Lafayette a young foreigner, Dickinson a New Jersey militiaman.　He had only Stirling left.　He was driven to do what Jomini describes as a violation of the art of war:

"To commit the execution of a purpose to one who disapproves of the plan of it, is to employ but one-third of the man; his heart and his head are against you; you have command only of his hands." [47]

There never was a battle, perhaps, in which the reader had a wider choice of selections or a more curious figure to judge. Lee's conduct has been described by those who knew him and by historians who have studied him as the proof of insanity, genius, treason, heroism, inspiration, confusion.　The result of his morning's work has been described by high authorities as the salvation of the army from Washington's rashness and as the planned destruction of the army thwarted by Washington's brilliance.

XXX

THE BATTLE OF MONMOUTH

THE dawn of June 28th, 1778, found Washington confident that when he arrived at Monmouth Courthouse in the village of Freehold his advance body under Lee would be holding the British fast. Into the thick of this battle he would throw his main army at the most effective points, and overwhelm the enemy, or at least drive him away from his fifteen hundred wagons. But if that gorged serpent were permitted to glide unscotched one day longer into the high ground at Middletown, it would be safe and he ridiculous.

He had kept reminding Lee that the attack must be made the moment the British moved. It was important that Lee should be on the ground betimes. But Lee was for once imperturbable. He was one of those men who are always in a hurry except when hurried.

General Dickinson, pushing through the woods with his Jersey militia, saw the head of the British python stir and move off at the crack of dawn. He sent a messenger to Washington at 5 A.M. with a word for Lee as he passed. The messenger found Washington waiting with his men, whom he had ordered to "disencumber themselves of packs and blankets." He "instantly put the army in motion and sent orders by one of my aides to General Lee" that he was "marching to support him." The aide he sent was Richard Meade and he instructed Meade to tell Lee to have his men also leave off their packs. To make sure of his exact instructions Meade ventured to suggest that there might be circumstances to make an attack improper. Washington answered that while there might be "very powerful reasons," he was exceedingly anxious for Lee to attack.[1]

Meade spurred away and found Lee a mile beyond Englishtown, still waiting for the British to move, and very angry at the contradictory information. He was ordered to attack as soon as the British moved. Had they moved? Lee sent Wayne forward to take command of the advance. When he rode forward, he met General Dickinson, whom he addressed with his usual heat, blaming him for the mixed information. General Dickinson answered in the same spirit and according to Lee, said to him:

"General Lee, you may believe it or not, but if you march your party beyond that ravine now in your rear, which had only one passage over it, you are in a perilous situation." [2]

Steuben says that he went back from the van and told Washington in Englishtown that he doubted if the British could be overtaken. Washington put this doubt into his first report, but he urged his army forward, while Steuben went to a house in Englishtown and took an hour and a half of rest. [3] He had been reconnoitring all night.

While the main army was swinging forward toward Monmouth, Washington took a late breakfast at the home of Doctor James English in Englishtown. He is said to have stated that "he did not like fighting on the Sabbath, but he must yield for the good of his country." [4] At half-past eleven he sat down to write a brief report to Congress according to his regular instructions. Perhaps remembering Steuben's report he confessed a doubt that Lee would be able to reach the British in time; but mentioned that Morgan and some militia were on their flank. [5]

Washington's army had gone on ahead before he was ready to leave Dr. English's home. The doctor rode with him as he galloped past his troops and went to the front. On the way, he met Dr. James McHenry riding back. McHenry was his new secretary, a young Irishman who had come to America in 1771, studied surgery, joined the rebels, been captured at Fort Washington and kept in captivity for two months and on parole for over a year. He served at Valley Forge as surgeon and Washington became unusually friendly toward him. [6] Mc-

Henry says he told Washington that he had just left General Lee advancing to the left of Monmouth and had asked Lee if he had any information to send back:

"He desired me to inform His Excellency that . . . the rear of the enemy was composed of fifteen hundred or two thousand—that he expected to fall in with them, and had great certainty of cutting them off. . . . he spoke it with a fix'd and firm tone of voice and countenance, which suggested to me the certainty of succeeding, and I made the report accordingly to General Washington." [7]

About this time Major John Clark, formerly confidential secret agent to Washington, paused on his way to the front to ask Washington if he "had any commands to General Lee." Washington made this significant answer, which Clark wrote out afterward with some reluctance when Lee appealed to him "on honor to relate the facts":

"You will inform General Lee that 'tis my Orders he annoy the Enemy as much as in his power, but at the same time proceed with caution and take care the Enemy don't draw him into a scrape: that I have information the Enemy's rear have left Monmouth, have ordered the troops with me to throw off their Packs, and will march on to reinforce him."

Clark goes on:

"I then put my Horse to near full speed and soon arrived at the high Ground on the left of Monmouth Village where I found General Lee: I called him aside, and delivered the above Orders to him, which I did and still do conceive *to be discretionary* and *as such he received them*, as he replied.

"'I give you my word, I shall not advance a foot further, my men are fatigued excessively and it would be sacrificing them to pursue.' " [8]

In the meanwhile Washington rode on, his hopes mounting as he drew nearer to the field. What happened next is told in varied sequence by various eye-witnesses and nobody can be sure of the details. But something like the following is perhaps a justifiable account.

As Washington approached the Meeting House, outside Monmouth where the road forked, Colonel Alexander Hamilton rode back from the front and told him the van and the enemy's rear would soon engage. "He advised General Washington to throw the right wing of the army round by the right, and to follow with the left wing directly in General Lee's rear to support him." Lieutenant-Colonel Fitzgerald confirms this and says that Knox proposed this movement "in very strong terms," implying some confusion among Lee's troops. Hamilton did not like Lee's dilatory tactics or his lack of a definite purpose.[9] He had found everything in confusion and had foreseen trouble.

Washington halted the army for a few minutes and gave the orders advised by Hamilton. He directed Greene to turn off to the right and march to a point south of Monmouth Courthouse. While he was marching away Washington was approached by "a countryman," really Lieutenant-Colonel Thomas Henderson, a physician whose house had been burned by the British the day before. He was not in uniform and was taken for a farmer by the others.[10] To Washington's amazement, on being asked where he came from, he said (according to Tilghman):

"'From towards the Court-house.'

"'What news?' he was asked. He said he heard our people were retreating."

He heard it from a fifer, he said, and down the road came "a fifer, who appeared to be a good deal frighted.

"The General asked him whether he was a soldier belonging to the army, and the cause of his returning that way; he answered, that he was a soldier, and that the Continental troops that had been advanced were retreating. On this answer the General seemed to be exceedingly surprized, and rather more exasperated appearing to discredit the account, and threatened the man, if he mentioned a thing of the sort, he would have him whipped." [11]

Tilghman says that Washington "not believing the thing to be true, ordered the fifer under the care of a light-horseman, to prevent his spreading a report and damping the troops who were advancing." [12] Two of the aides, Harrison and Fitzgerald, asked and gained Washington's permission to ride ahead and see what was going on.[13] Washington pushed forward himself and met two regiments coming back. He asked a captain where these troops were going. The officer must have been more afraid of Washington than of the enemy, for he answered, first, that they were very much fatigued, and had been ordered off to refresh themselves, and next, that they had been sent to find two cannon that had been left in danger on the field somewhere! Washington must have seen that the man was out of his head with the heat or panic, for instead of scarifying him for two such improbable tales, and denouncing his men for cowards, Washington simply "desired him to take his men into a wood near at hand, as they were exceedingly heated and fatigued." He added:

"And draw some rum for them, and keep them from straggling!"

Now Washington saw the heads of several columns beginning to appear. The first officer he met belonged to Shreve's regiment. Tilghman describes this:

"The General was exceedingly alarmed, finding the advance corps falling back upon the main body, without the least notice given to him, and asked Colonel Shreve the meaning of the retreat; Colonel Shreve answered in a very significant manner, smiling, that he did not know, but that he had retreated by order, he did not say by whose order. . . . General Washington desired Colonel Shreve to march his men over the morass, halt them on the hill, and refresh them." [14]

He was himself a bewildered stranger in this twisted country and he was dazed by the abrupt reversal of his high hopes. His own secretary, McHenry, afterwards wrote that he called to him Colonel Stewart and Colonel Ramsay, and took the latter by the hand:

" 'Gentlemen,' said he to them, 'I shall depend on your immediate exertions to check with your two regiments the progress of the enemy till I can form the main army.'

" 'We shall check them,' said Colonel Ramsay." [15]

While the two colonels were hurrying forward to the superb work they did that day, Lee appeared.

Now came the immortal scene that everybody knows. Every patriotic heart cherishes the vision of how Washington rode that day, in such enormous wrath that he—even he!—"swore like an angel." Some of the historians write of the oath with a ladylike awe as "strongly expletive," or "a terrific eloquence of unprintable scorn." [16] General Scott, who was a very profane man, is quoted by Custis as saying when asked if Washington ever swore:

"Once. It was at Monmouth, and on a day that would have made any man swear . . . he swore till the leaves shook on the trees, charming, delightful. Never have I enjoyed such swearing before, or since . . . he swore like an angel from Heaven." [17]

Unfortunately for conviction, General Scott's own testimony after the battle shows that at this time he was still at a distance trying to extricate himself from being surrounded by the British. When he finally joined the main army he fell in with Lord Stirling's left wing.[18] There is some curiosity among the irreverent as to the exact oath Washington used, and the curse ranges from "damned poltroon" upward. Lafayette is quoted as saying on the porch of Justice Hornblower in Newark in 1825 that the only time he ever heard Washington swear was when he rebuked Lee at Monmouth and called him "a damned poltroon." But that was forty-seven years later and General Carrington says that Justice Hornblower's son-in-law wrote him that Lafayette never was on that porch and that he did not mention Monmouth in Newark.[19] Furthermore, Lafayette was not on that part of the battlefield when Washington and Lee met. It is highly improbable that Lafayette ever made such a statement. In his testimony after the battle he did not even give a hint of being present. In his *Mémoires* he writes only this: " 'You know,' said Lee, 'all this was against my advice.' " [20] We have, however, the description of that meeting as given under oath shortly after the battle by eye-witnesses whose words were taken down by the court. It is sheer butchery of high art to repeat the shabby truth, but Dr. McHenry says that instead of Washington charging on Lee, Lee rode up to Washington! And while he was busy!

"General Washington, upon his approaching, desired of General Lee the cause of the retreat of the troops? General Lee hesitatingly replied, Sir, Sir. General Washington then repeated, I think, the question a second time; I did not clearly understand General Lee's reply to him, but can just remember the words confusion, contradictory information, and some other words of the same import. The manner, however, in which they were delivered, I remember pretty well; it was confused, and General Lee seemed under an embarrassment in giving the answer." [21]

Colonel Tench Tilghman does say that Washington rode up to Lee, yet he adds the even more debasing note that Lee, instead of being crushed with shame, did not quite hear what Washington said! and asked him to repeat it! This is as anticlimactic as the stupidity of the very deaf man in the poem by James Whitcomb Riley who "had to request it to thunder again."

"When General Washington rode up to him, with some degree of astonishment, and asked him what was the meaning of this? General Lee answered . . . Sir, Sir. I took it that General Lee did not hear the question distinctly.

"Upon General Washington's repeating the question, General Lee answered, that from a variety of contradictory intelligence, and that from his orders not being obeyed, matters were thrown into confusion, and that he did not chuse to beard the British army with troops in such a situation. He said that besides, the thing was against his own opinion. General Washington answered, whatever his opinion might have been, he expected his orders would have been obeyed, and then rode on towards the rear of the retreating troops." [22]

Colonel Meade, when asked if he had heard any conversation between Washington and Lee, could only reply:

"I heard General Lee remind General Washington that he was averse to an attack or a general engagement, or words to that purport; and I think I heard General Lee also tell General Washington that he was against it in Council, and that while the enemy were so superior in cavalry we could not oppose them." [23]

Another witness was Captain Mercer, Lee's aide-de-camp:

"General Washington first accosted General Lee, by asking him: What is all this? General Lee not well hearing him, the question was repeated. General Washington in the second question asked: What all that confusion was for, and retreat? General Lee said he saw no confusion but what had arose from his orders not being properly obeyed. General Washington mentioned that he had certain information that it was but a strong covering party of the enemy. General Lee replied that it might be so, but they were rather stronger than he was, and that he did not think it was proper to risque so much, or words to that purport; General Washington replied, then he should not have undertaken it, and passed by him. . . .

"General Lee then said that he had nothing further to do, and rode after General Washington in front; by the time we got up the enemy appeared immediately in front, and their artillery began to play. General Washington seeing General Lee, asked him if he would take the command there, or he would; if General Lee would take the command there he would return to the main army to arrange it; General Lee replied that His Excellency had before given him the command there; General Washington told him he expected he would take proper measures for checking the enemy there; General Lee replied that his orders should be obeyed, and that he would not be the first to leave the field, and General Washington then rode to the main army. General Lee immediately ordered that the artillery should be brought to the height he was on, and begged of General Knox, who was by, to try to halt them, as he had a greater influence over them than he had." [24]

Lieutenant-Colonel Brooks testified to the same effect,[25] so did General Knox [26] and Brigade-Major Shaw.[27]

Those are all the witnesses to the scene who were called on to testify. Washington wrote afterward that he was "not conscious of having made use of any very singular expressions," and he would certainly have admitted that to curse a major-general before his troops would be "very singular." [28] There remains only Lee's own account. After telling of his appalling difficulties with an unknown country and unknown officers, men without uniform, organizations without colors, and the confusion of finding orders given everywhere in conflict with his own, he described how the retreat started in spite of him. Believing it a good idea, however, in view of the increasing numbers of the British and the danger of disaster, he fell back, withdrawing the elements of his command from position to position, seeking in vain for a good one and finding only posts where the British could find better, until a Mr. Wikoff told him that he owned a farm, on ground behind the long defile and the big morass, and that it would be an ideal spot for defence. Lee determined to form there and put up a real resistance. He was proud of what he had done and in this spirit he met Washington:

"When I arrived first in his presence, conscious of having done nothing that could draw on the least censure, but rather flattering myself with his congratulation and applause, I confess I was disconcerted, astonished and confounded by the words and manner in which His Excellency accosted me; it was so novel and unexpected from a man, whose discretion, humanity and decorum I had from the first of our acquaintance stood in admiration of, that I was for some time incapable of making any coherent answer to questions so abrupt and in a great measure to me unintelligible.

"The terms, I think, were these—'I desire to know, sir, what is the reason—whence arises this disorder and confusion?' (the manner in which he expressed them was much stronger and more severe than the expressions themselves.) When I had recover'd myself sufficiently, I answered, That I saw or knew of no confusion but what naturally arose from disobedience of orders—contradictory intelligence—and the impertinence and presumption of individuals, who were vested with no authority, in intruding themselves in matters above them and out of their sphere: That the retreat, in the first instance, was contrary to my intentions, contrary to my orders, and contrary to my wishes. . . . To which he replied:

" 'All this may be very true, Sir, but you ought not to have undertaken it unless you intended to go through with it.'

"Now, what His Excellency meant by saying that I should not have undertaken what I had no intention of going through with, I confess I did not then, nor do I at this day, understand. . . .

"There were some expressions (I cannot precisely recollect them) let fall by the General, which, at the instant, convey'd to me an idea that he had adopted new sentiments, and that it was his wish to bring on a general engagement. This idea drew from me some sentences, such as related in Colonel Tilghman's evidence. It remain'd with me for some moments, but was entirely banish'd by what subsequently passed: . . . I was more confirm'd than ever in the original idea I had set out with, viz.: that it never was his intention to court or hazard a general engagement." [29]

Officers who did not like Lee—and they always had reasons enough for disliking him—showed their prejudice in the tone of their testimony against him, but even the testimonies of those more friendly to him give not a sign of any battle ardor on his part, nor any inspired seizure of opportunity, or magnetic control of men. His retreat lacked, indeed, the panic that disgraced the Brandywine. The troops were not entangled as at Germantown nor surrounded as at Long Island. There was no sudden stampede. He did not lose a gun or a battalion. He did not lose anything but an opportunity.

About 3 A.M. he had ordered forward Colonel Grayson with the Virginia Continentals and some other troops, in all about 600 men, also a few cannon under Lieutenant-Colonel Oswald, an Englishman who had come to America shortly before the Revolution. Lee and Wayne rode far to the front till they saw a small party of British. Lee began to distribute his troops here and there with high hopes of cutting off the British rear guard. He sent word of this back to Washington, the only message he sent, and a misleading one, for it encouraged Washington to expect success. Anthony Wayne and Colonel Butler, after a skirmish with Simcoe's Rangers, pushed forward, Wayne sending back a request for more troops to take advantage of the British retreat.

By ten o'clock Oswald's cannon were playing on the responding British, and Wayne was confident of victory if he could get reinforcements, but Lee restrained his impetuous advance, since he planned to push in between the rear guard and the main body. Lee was full of enthusiasm and told Lafayette, who was restlessly waiting for a task:

"My dear Marquis, I think these people are ours."

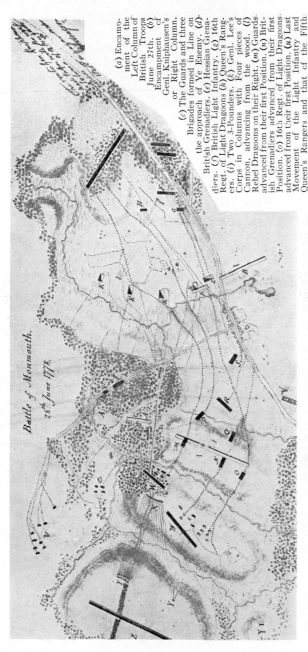

Battle of Monmouth.
28th June 1778.

(a) Encampment of the Left Column of British Troops June 27th. (b) Encampment of Genl. Kniphausen's or Right Column. (c) The Guards and three Brigades formed in Line on the approach of Ye Enemy. (d) British Grenadiers. (e) Hessian Grenadiers. (f) British Light Infantry. (g) 16th Regt. of Light Dragoons (h) Queen's Rangers. (i) Two 3-Pounders. (k) Genl. Lee's Corps in Columns with Four pieces of Cannon, advancing from the wood. (l) Rebel Dragoons on their Right. (m) Guards advanced from their first Position. (n) British Grenadiers advanced from their first Position. (o) 16th Regt. of Light Dragoons advanced from their first Position. (u) Last Movement of the Light Infantry and Queen's Rangers and that of the Fifth Brigade to connect them with the Line. (w) Position to which Genl. Lee retreated through the Woods on the right, and occupied it till the Light Corps and sustaining Fifth Brigade had repassed the Morass when the whole fell back to the Position A (in which the Hessian Grenadiers had remained) and from thence in the Cool of the Evening continued their March to join the Column beyond the River. (x) British Artillery. (y) Rebel main Artillery arriving from English Town. (z) Washington's army.

The Battle of Monmouth

(Clinton's own map, by permission of William L. Clements)

(Lee advanced to the upper right, and retreated to the left where the main battle was fought. In the lower left corner at "Y" is Cobb's Hill, above it Wenrock brook, behind which was Washington's line.)

He rode to Colonel Grayson and said:

"By God, I will take them all."

Yet when Wayne again pleaded for reinforcements and sent word that the British were on the run, Lee sputtered:

"Pho, pho, it is impossible." [30]

The British rear guard was at this time only about 2,000 strong, but Clinton soon reinforced it and prepared a definite counter-attack under Cornwallis. When Lafayette asked permission to meet this with vigor, Lee said that Lafayette did not know British soldiers and the Americans could not stand against them. The Frenchman answered:

"British soldiers have been beaten and they may be again."

Later Lee changed his mind and ordered Lafayette to take troops and attack. The heat may have touched Lee. He could still swear, call out, "Where is that damned blue regiment going?" ride up to an officer who was puzzled by conflicting orders and shout:

"By God, sir, I will let you know that I am your General, and you had no business to leave the field without my orders." [31]

Some officers testified that they had no orders at all. Some testified that Lee took splendid care of the troops, looking to their ammunition, ordering them taken to the woods to escape the sun, telling the fainting men where water was, seeing that the artillery had infantry to protect it, sending officers like du Portail and others to verify reports and select new positions, ordering retreating regiments back to their posts and demanding that others stand their ground. Lee seems to have been chiefly alarmed by the knowledge of the deep morass back of him, and the ravine with only one crossing. Wayne was in front of it, too, and Lee thought he might be cut off. When Lee was reminded that the visible enemy troops were few, he retorted that they naturally kept their main force under cover of the woods. Clinton's story of the battle shows that this was true.

"I could not entertain so bad an opinion of Mr. Washington's military Abilities as to suppose he would risk his avant Guard over those difficult passes without the Support of his Gros [i.e., his main army], or that he would venture to support thro such a Country. . . .

"His whole Corps would probably have fallen into the Power of the Kings army if he had made a Stand in front of the first Defile and not retreated with the Precipitancy he did . . . especially as the affair must have been finished long before Mʳ Washington's main Army could possibly be near enough to support him." [32]

Lee exposed himself to fire without fear and everybody except Hamilton found him calm. Hamilton himself was greatly excited, also very brave, though badly hurt when his horse was shot and fell with him. While the retreat was made with little loss, it was made with no honor. As Laurens says:

"All this disgraceful retreating, passed without the firing of a musket, over ground which might have been disputed inch by inch." [33]

When Meade rode straight from Washington, Lee mumbled, "They are all in confusion." When Meade asked for particulars, Lee repeated, "They are all in confusion." [34] When Laurens asked him for some word to take to Washington, "he answered that he really did not know what to say." [35]

Harrison asked various officers why they retreated. None of the generals knew. One colonel said, "He could not tell, that they had lost but one man." Another: "By God! they are flying from a shadow." Harrison said that he asked Lee's aide, Mercer:

" 'For God's sake, what is the cause of this retreat?' Mercer answered,

" 'If you will proceed, you will see the cause; you will see several columns of foot and horse.'

" 'I replied,' says Harrison, 'that we came to that field to meet columns of foot and horse.' " [36]

On reading the testimony of some of the officers, one can only believe that Lee behaved like a drunken idiot. Other officers of equal merit and rank picture him as calm, resourceful, brilliant. The reader's character will probably control his choice of whom to believe, though it is hard to see on what ground so many historians base a charge of treason. If Lee had wanted to betray his troops he would surely have led them into a trap, not have extricated them so carefully. If he had wanted to betray his troops he would hardly have put up so excellent a resistance when Washington first rebuked him, then turned the troops over to him, and left him in command of the forward elements. For, after the first sharp cross-examina-tion of Lee, Washington gave him back his men and instructed Lee to organize the resistance while he went to hasten forward the main body. At this time young Hamilton grew impassioned and the old Lee was over-placid.

The story is told that during the morning Lee asked two or three officers to tell him if he looked calm and collected or how. Boudinot takes the odd question as sufficient evidence of "a partial Lunacy." [37] Hamilton testified to Lee's intrepidity but noted "a certain hurry of spirits." [38] He did not tell it all, if Lee's testimony is to be accepted:

"When General Washington asked me whether I would remain in front and retain the command, or he should take it, and I had answered that I undoubtedly would, and that he should see that I myself should be one of the last to leave the field, Colonel Hamilton flourishing his sword, immediately exclaimed, that's right, my dear General, and I will stay, and we will all die here on this spot. . . .

"Observing him much flustered and in a sort of frenzy of valour, I calmly requested him to observe me well and to tell me if I did not appear tranquil and master of my faculties; his answer was, that he must own that I was entirely possessed of myself; well, then (said I), you must allow me to be a proper judge of what I ought to do. Sir (I added) if you will take pains to examine that hill in our front, you will perceive that it so eminently commands this we are on, that it would be unpardonable to risk anything more on it than what necessity will oblige us; as to myself, I am as ready to die as what you possibly can be, but I am responsible for something more than my own person, I am respon-sible to the General and to the continent for the troops I have been entrusted with. When I have taken proper measures to get the main body of them in a good position, I will die with you on this spot, if you please." [39]

This story was confirmed in full by Mercer and somewhat by Harrison, who heard part of it. [40] G. W. P. Custis tells it long afterward but manages as usual to give a few false turns, ascribing the scene to Washington:

"Lieutenant-Colonel Hamilton, aid to the general-in-chief, leaped from his horse, and, drawing his sword, addressed the general with— 'We are betrayed; your excellency and the army are betrayed, and the moment has arrived when every true friend of America and her cause must be ready to die in their defence.' Washington, charmed with the generous enthusiasm of his favorite aid, yet deemed the same ill-timed, and pointing to the colonel's horse that was cropping the herbage, unconscious of the great scene enacting around him, calmly observed, 'Colonel Hamilton, you will take your horse.' " [41]

Custis thought that Lee was a "brave and skilful commander," but "he expected, by throwing things into confusion, to lessen the merits of Washington in the public estimation, for he aspired to be the commander of the army." This astonishing interpretation can only mean that Lee let himself be driven from the field in order to prove that he should be commander-in-chief! This is even quainter than the theory of treason, according to which Lee retreated in order to destroy the army.

But whether Lee were traitor, coward, supreme strategist, bungler, or whatsoever he was in his heart, Washington's problem was the same: nearly half of his army was rolling back on the main body at a moment when he had expected to roll forward with it. Also, a great body of British grenadiers and dragoons was rolling down on top of the avalanche of disorganized regiments.

The Monmouth battle field has been pretty well erased under the wear and tear of years, the smoothing down of agriculture and civilization, and the building of a railway. The old road along which Lee retreated has been replaced by a later highway. The bogs and morasses have been turned to meadows. At that time the ground was chiefly distinguished by three ravines. The battle proper was fought across the Western Ravine, through which runs Wenrock Brook, over which was a bridge. The higher ground was on the western side and the ravine was a morass. Three quarters of a mile to the east was the Middle Ravine with a long causeway across it. A mile or so further to the east was the East Ravine, beyond which some of Lee's men had penetrated to Briar Hill, when he started to call them in. Their total retreat was about two and a half miles before they ran into Washington at a point a little to the east of the West Ravine. The main army of the Americans was some distance west of the West Ravine. The British line was stumbling through the heat and crossing the Middle Ravine along the causeway and spreading out over the high ground.

Washington's aide, Harrison, startled him with this news and announced that the full weight of the British would be on him in fifteen minutes.[42] Everybody agrees that Washington was never more glorious, more resourceful. He did not argue long with Lee, but his habitual justice throttled his wrath and he offered Lee the chance to retrieve himself by taking command on the spot while he brought up the main body. He instructed certain elements to form on a hill behind a hedge. He shouted for some artillery to go forward as he rode to the rear.[43]

In Washington's absence Lee busied himself posting the artillery to hold the British, and asked Knox to help rally the men since Knox had more influence than he. Knox testified that Lee's disposition of the guns was excellent. He says that Lee "in very forcible terms, pressed me to hasten them," and approved Knox's choice of ground.[44] British horse drove them back, however, and again Lee helped Knox find a knoll which he said "was formed by nature for the purpose." By this time Stirling's men came up and held the position. Knox praised Lee's conduct and never agreed with the denunciation of him.

The British dragoons began to threaten Oswald's position and his men were dropping at the side of the guns, stricken with the sun, the others hardly able to load and fire. Voices cried to him, "Retreat! retreat!" He started to fall back, but Lee rode up to him and ordered him to keep firing until he himself gave the order to retire. Lafayette's aides rode to

Oswald and ordered him back but he refused to obey anybody but Lee. Lafayette himself then said that he brought Lee's orders and pointed out the next position for the guns. Oswald's testimony gave Lee great credit for conduct on that day, and Oswald's own work was distinguished.[45]

By now Washington was back with the main army and he apparently decided that Lee and his corps were exhausted by their long march out and their two miles and a half retreat in the merciless sun, so he ordered them to fall to the rear and assemble in Englishtown. Washington also broke Lafayette's heart by sending him to the rear of the reserve. He took complete charge himself now and rode his great white gift-horse so hard that suddenly the charger sank under the burden of his great weight, his ferocious demands, and the blazing sun. He keeled over and died.[46]

Washington, dripping with sweat doubtless and reeling a little from the inner and outer furnaces, waited impatiently until his mulatto servant, Billy Lee, brought up Washington's own "chestnut blood mare with long mane and tail." Washington vaulted to her back and she did not fail him in the terrible hours that followed. As he dashed here and there among the shifting regiments he cried encouragement to his troops, and they cheered him. Lafayette said afterward, "I never beheld so superb a man."

The two colonels whom Washington had first flung out to sacrifice themselves in front of the British made a noble holding-fight of it. Stewart was soon wounded and carried off. Ramsay maintained the ground till he was without troops, and his horse dead. He was afoot but when a British dragoon rode at him he fought back with his sword. When the dragoon fired his pistol, Ramsay closed with him, wounded and dragged him from his horse and was trying to ride off on it when other dragoons came up. He fought them sword to sword—*cominus ense*, says McHenry, until surrounded and badly wounded, when he was taken prisoner. "Gen¹. Clinton paid a proper attention to such uncommon prowess, and generously liberated the Colonel the following day on parole." [47]

Steuben rejoined at this time and was sufficiently refreshed to be entrusted with bringing order out of chaos on the left wing. The men knew him so well that when he called for the fugitives to turn and face the advancing enemy they "wheeled into line with as much precision as on an ordinary parade," and Alexander Hamilton said that he had never conceived until that moment the value of military discipline.[48] Steuben helped Stirling post the batteries and seems to have taken the initiative away from his lordship, for Steuben wrote afterward with some poetic license:

"I commanded on the left wing of the first line, and was fortunate enough to decide the day to our advantage." [49]

Later Washington sent Steuben back to gather up the still retreating troops of Lee, form them, and bring them up as reinforcements. Steuben saw Lee twice in Englishtown and described him as sitting on a horse before a house; he was dazed and incredulous of the story of English repulse.[50]

When General Greene, on his way to the point south of Monmouth Courthouse, heard the battle raging, he left the road and turned aside to Washington's support, selecting a strong position behind the morass of the West Ravine. His biographer, Judge Johnson, makes this striking comment, after praising Lee's retreat as drawing the enemy further from his baggage, and involving him amidst morasses and being "perhaps . . . the real cause of the partial success which ensued. . . .

"Had not Greene risked his reputation by deviating from his commander's orders, the event might have been truly disastrous. . . . Such are the vicissitudes of human fame! Lee in the morning had ventured on the same thing, perhaps with equal judgment and effect, and was ultimately ruined. Greene, not deterred by the offence, which Lee had given on the occasion, on the same day ventured on disobedience, and perhaps saved the army, certainly much increased his own reputation." [51]

One of the best inspirations of the day was Knox's selection of Comb's Hill, a sort of headland jutting out into the West Ravine at a distance from the right wing but at a point where the artillery he placed on it flanked the British and the enfilade was so complete that one round shot is said to have passed along the front of an advancing British platoon and shattered every musket in the line.[52] This artillery was under the immediate command of Knox's brigade-major, the Chevalier de Mauduit du Plessis, who served it with supreme skill.

And now the real battle of Monmouth began. Whether wise or unwise, the retreat of Lee had been in effect the falling back of a strong advance party to the main position, which had been selected in haste, but could hardly have been improved. It was a duel between George Washington and Sir Henry Clinton, both fearless and skilful. Captain Kemble indeed says, "Sir Henry Clinton showed himself the Soldier, but not the wise General, on this occasion, exposing himself and charging at the head of a few Dragoons." [53]

Washington had thrown Colonels Stewart and Ramsay to the eastern or British side of the morass where he had first met Lee. They formed the advance of the left and the first British blow fell on them. On a line with them and to their right, Wayne had Varnum's brigade and Livingston's regiment formed behind a hedgerow behind an orchard, with some men in an old barn. Back of Wayne there was the bridge across Wenrock brook to the high ground of the main position. Over the heads of this front line went on an artillery duel, the heaviest ever known in America till then, and splendidly conducted on both sides.[54] The British had to conquer Wayne and the others on the eastern side of the brook before they could hope to reach the main body with bayonet or effective musketry.

The heat was in itself a bombardment under which men fell dead without a wound from human weapons. Thirst swelled the tongues of many survivors till they could not speak. The mosquitoes were an Egyptian plague. On both sides desperately thirsty men risked and lost their lives at the building called the Parsonage, where a line waited at the well. In the distant graveyard villagers stood on monuments to see the game and some were hurt or killed by shell and flying fragments of tombstones. The church was soon reeking with the blood of wounded and dying soldiers.

Anthony Wayne won most of the glory of that battle. His men stood up to the British steel bayonets and did not run. They rolled up their sleeves and met the grenadiers and the guards and beat them off. Of this great fighting, Wayne's biographer says:

"The repulse of the bayonet-charge of the British guards and grenadiers, forming the *élite* of their infantry, and regarded by their countrymen ever since the days of Crécy and Agincourt as the most formidable warriors in the world when armed with such a weapon, by a body of American yeomen, most of whom were Pennsylvanians, under a Pennsylvanian general, men who were inferior in numbers and imperfect in discipline, who had just been rallied after an ignominious retreat, and were engaged in battle for the first time on that day, must be considered in the progress of the Revolution as a prodigious historical event. . . . Hesitation in meeting our enemies in the open field had had, as the history of the Revolution clearly shows, up to this time, a controlling influence in the councils of war called together by Washington. He was taught by the results of this battle that the oftener he 'acted the general,' as Wayne called it, the more likely would permanent success follow." [55]

In front of Wayne's line occurred one of those strange displays of battle etiquette that occasionally adorn the horror of carnage with a touch of delicate grace, such a moment as the legendary pause at Fontenoy when the English officers are said to have cried, "Fire first, gentlemen of the French guards," and the French replied, "Nay, fire you first, messieurs."

At Monmouth, when Lieutenant-Colonel Henry Monckton, brother of Lord Galway, had been twice repulsed by Wayne, he turned his back on the Americans, thirty yards away, and made a little British speech to his men, telling them whatever was the then equivalent of the late "Cheerio! Carry on!"

Wayne's men could hear this brief oration in the apple orchard, and Wayne kept them quiet with a reminder to kill off the officers first:

"Steady, steady, wait for the word then pick out the King birds."

When Monckton finished he called on his men to follow, whirled and charged. The rebel line blazed. Among the dead was Monckton. He fell so close to the hedge that the rebels pushed through and seized his body and the flag of the wounded color bearer. There is a legend that the British soldiers regained Monckton's body and while some fought off the Americans, others dug a grave with their bayonets and buried him as they wept.[56] But the legend is implausible as well as untrue. Wayne's men captured the body and Washington paid it full military honors later, for which Clinton formally thanked him. The grave is still in the churchyard under a monument.[57]

This was the high moment of Anthony Wayne's Bunker Hill for he was soon after overwhelmed and outflanked by the next wave of British and he and his men retreated to the opposite side of the ravine under the guns of the main line. Now the British rolled in waves against Stirling's left wing but were not able to get across the morass under the fine artillery work, especially as guns were placed to enfilade them from the left. Cornwallis then tried to storm the right wing, but Greene held fast and Mauduit du Plessis riddled his line with solid shot. The invincibles of England were stopped and held fast by Americans, who at last had learned how to give and take in the open, to maneuver under fire and display the intelligent heroism that only discipline can develop. It was largely to Steuben's drill-ground practice that the army owed such examples as McHenry describes:

"A small party of infantry were ordered to re-occupy a piece of ground, from which we had forced the enemy, and to which they were again advancing. In rising the hill our infantry received an unexpected charge from the grenadiers, which threw them into confusion. But recovering themselves, suddenly they formed under the enemy's fire, advanced, and very gallantly made themselves masters of the post. This was in face of our front line—of the front line of both armies, and had a most beautiful appearance. The rallying and charge were admirably executed." [58]

By late afternoon the troops were in such a state of exhaustion that Clinton could get nothing more out of his men. He yielded the battlefield to Washington, and fell back, taking up a strong position with flanks braced by woods and morasses and a narrow defile in front. Washington accepted this as a confession of British defeat and prepared to perfect the success he had wrested from disorder and built up with the finest generalship. He ordered General Poor and the Carolina brigade to attack the British right and Woodford their left and posted his artillery to shatter their center. But, by the time the troops were maneuvered into position for the advance, night had fallen. Lee having recovered his wits, came back to the field with his aides mounted on fresh horses, their own having been killed. He reported to Washington for duty, but the battle was over. [59]

The soldiers camped where they fell and Washington flung himself on the ground under a tree by the side of Lafayette, who says in his memoirs:

"The general and he passed the night lying on the same mantle, talking over the conduct of Lee." [60]

In view of the way Lee had sniffed at the command offered him until it was handed to Lafayette, then had demanded it back, taken the leadership away from Lafayette and not only kept him idle on the field but refused to fight it out, Lee's interests could hardly have been in the hands of a less devoted attorney.

Almost as great a mystery as Lee's behavior is the non-appearance of Daniel Morgan. It had been an essential part of Washington's plan to have Morgan attack the right flank the moment the British moved, while Lee attacked the left. Lee sent him orders and he acknowledged them:

"Mannsquare [Manasquan] Brook, June 29, 1778.
"Sir, General Lee wrote me yesterday, at one o'clock in the evening, he intended to attack the enemy's rear this morning, and ordered me to attack them at the same time on their right flank." [61]

It was alleged that he lost his way, but he had excellent guides and the firing was audible. He could have marched to the guns. His action is inexplicable, but no complaint was ever made of it.

There was so much on this afternoon to exalt the heart of Washington, that he was able even to laugh at one ludicrous happening. His pompous mulatto, Billy Lee, with a pack of other body servants rode out to a high point under a sycamore. Washington saw the dusky spectators and pointed them out, prophesying that the enemy would take a shot at them. Whereupon a six-pound shell knocked off a limb over their heads and the black cloud scattered with such gusto that even Washington smiled. [62]

To this day belongs the legend of the woman who carried water and hence was called "Molly Pitcher." Many women performed such services and were seen on battlefields. But this Molly, according to tradition, was the wife of a cannoneer who was shot down, whereupon she took his place at the gun, loading and firing with such vengeful fury that, on the next day, General Greene led her, still covered with blood and dirt, before Washington, who gave her the rank of lieutenant, and half-pay for life. Some say that he made her only a sergeant but gave her a gold piece. Custis says that Washington made her a washerwoman at headquarters and often joked with her.

She was a young Irish wife; she was a mere camp trull; she was an infantryman's woman; she was a cannoneer's girl. Her name was Molly Maban, Hanna, Hayes, or McCauley. Lossing said that she died of "licentiousness." She was so many and so various that some have said she was nobody at all. General Stryker states that "a most diligent search of the pension records" shows no pension or half-pay to any woman for service at Monmouth. Yet he finds some evidence that a German girl, Molly Ludwig, married a barber named Hayes, who was at Monmouth. After the war she married a good-for-naught named McCauley, and in 1822 was granted an annuity for life by the Pennsylvania legislature. She lived at Carlisle as a rough, common woman who swore like a trooper and smoked and chewed tobacco. She was buried there in 1832 and her monument is still visible. Van Tyne says of her: "As all historians know, that good woman's reputation was so tarnished that a society of patriotic women in Philadelphia gave up the idea of a monument to her, and thanked their lucky stars when certain contemporary testimony was brought to their attention." [63]

The most remarkable features of this battle were that it was the longest of the Revolution, that the heat played mortal havoc on both sides, and that it was also the last important clash in the north.

Parson Weems, meaning perhaps to draw a moral as usual, and remembering Paul's first Epistle to Timothy, v. 23, "Drink no longer water," states that "numbers, on both sides, died of the extreme *heat,* and by drinking *cold water.*" He underlines the words as a warning.[64] Surgeon Thacher says that "the intense heat of the weather, great fatigue, and drinking cold water, proved fatal to about sixty or eighty men of each party." Water was in ill repute in those days.[65]

The losses of the Americans, according to an incomplete return of Washington's, were 8 officers and 61 enlisted men killed, 19 officers and 142 men wounded, 132 men missing, a total of 362 casualties. He reported also 6 horses killed, 2 wounded; but so many horses were abandoned to die that the air of the field was unbearable for weeks.

The British returns are puzzling and there seems good reason to accuse Clinton of understating them. He admitted almost exactly the same as the Americans: 4 officers and 61 men killed, 15 officers and 155 men wounded, 64 missing, and 59

men dead of fatigue, a total of 358 casualties.[66]   But Colonel
Van Dyck, who had charge of the American burial parties,
stated that he buried 217 British and 29 Americans.[67]   Washington, evidently taking Van Dyck's burials to be all British,
puts the number of British dead at 245, not including 4 officers, and speaks also of "several fresh graves and burying
holes found near the field, in which the enemy put their dead
before they quitted it." [68]   At Germantown, where the British kept the field, they claimed to have buried twice as many
dead as the Americans admitted.   It seems to make a difference who does the burying.

There is also great discrepancy as to the numbers of deserters.   Knyphausen wrote to his Landgrave that 236 of his
men deserted.[69]   Montresor says that 350 Germans deserted.
Arnold says that 136 British and 440 Hessians, 576 in all,
turned up in Philadelphia.[70]   Many of them had wives and
sweethearts there and became citizens.

Clinton stole away at ten o'clock, leaving to Washington's
care such of his wounded as he dared not move.   He sent in
under a flag a word of gratitude to Washington for his generous and humane treatment of the wounded and for the
honors paid to General Monckton's body.

Clinton naturally put the best face he could on the battle.
He had expressed a wish to draw Washington into a general
engagement.   He got his wish and drew out of it at night,
retired many miles to high ground by the sea and, as he says,
waited for two days to be attacked.

"It would be sufficient honor to the troops, barely to say, that they
had forced a corps, as I am informed of near 12,000 men, from two
strong positions; . . . under such disadvantages of heat and fatigue,
that a great part of those we lost fell dead as they advanced, without
a wound." [71]

In his unpublished history he ridicules Washington's pretensions to a victory.   As a retreat Clinton could claim that his
march was a triumph.   He had carried 1,500 wagons dripping
with spoil and "lost not a cart."   The Americans laughed at

Clinton for saying that he took advantage of the moon. He seems to have taken advantage rather of the almanac for the moon was new and set at ten. On the other hand the British historian, Stedman, mocks the American claim that the British got away in silence. He says that there was heavy firing for five minutes at some stray cattle or horses just as the British began to move.

He gives Lee credit for conduct "worthy of applause and admiration," "unjustly punished," but he blames Washington for not flanking Clinton with his fresh troops.[72]

Clinton ridiculed Stedman's suggestion that his flanks might have been successfully turned. Some of the British partisans compared Clinton's retreat to that of Xenophon and his ten thousand Greeks through the Persian Empire.[73] Such wreaths beautify a tomb but also advertise the burial. The Americans had often used the same flowers to enhance their own retirements and had congratulated themselves on their skill in flight. If Washington had made Clinton's retreat it would have been hailed as a masterpiece of cool bravery.

But no one could deny the brutal facts that, after more than three years of war the British had abandoned the rebel capital, and two states, and had stolen away from a battlefield at night after a hand-to-hand engagement with the rebel general.

And he was a general, an American general. Coming on a field where the British-bred soldier, Lee, was retreating in disorder, he checked his men, drew them into array, beat off repeated assaults by the best troops England had, buried their dead and cared for their wounded on the field of combat.

It was a thousand pities that this one clean triumph had to be sullied by a prolonged dispute with his second in command.

XXXI

THE ELIMINATION OF LEE AND OTHERS

WHILE he sent a very brief despatch to Congress the day after the battle, saying, "We forced the enemy from the field and encamped on their ground," and making no mention of Lee, Washington did not write a detailed report until July 1st, 1778. He explained his failure to pursue:

"The extreme heat of the weather, the fatigue of the men from their march through a deep sandy country almost entirely destitute of water, and the distance the enemy had gained by marching in the night, made a pursuit impracticable and fruitless. It would have answered no valuable purpose, and would have been fatal to numbers of our men, several of whom died the preceding day with heat . . .

"The catalogue of those, who distinguished themselves, is too long to admit of particularizing individuals. I cannot, however, forbear mentioning Brigadier-General Wayne, whose good conduct and bravery thro' the whole action deserves particular commendation. The behavior of the troops in general, after they recovered from the first surprise occasioned by the retreat of the advanced corps, was such as could not be surpassed." [1]

Before he wrote to Congress, he wrote to his army an order of congratulations and thanks to men and officers for their gallantry, good order and coolness. He had the unusual pleasure of thanking the militia. He praised Knox's artillery especially and gave the enemy as authority for the acknowledgement that "no artillery could be better served than ours."

Having fought a battle on Sunday, he called for thanksgiving on Tuesday, and incidentally mentioned a few familiar things for which he gave no thanks: •

"The men are to wash themselves this afternoon and appear as clean and decent as possible. Seven o'clock this evening is appointed that we may publickly unite in thanksgiving to the Supreme Disposer of human events for the victory which was obtained on Sunday over the Flower of the British Troops. . . . Complaint having been made to the Commander-in-Chief that certain persons belonging to the army have seized the property of inhabitants which had been concealed in order to escape the ravages of the enemy, he calls upon the commanding officers of corps to order a strict search of the soldiers' packs at parade time, that the offender may be discovered and brought to condign punishment . . . "The General further gives notice that the detestable crime of marauding will henceforth be punished with instant death." [2]

He released the New Jersey militia, whose time was up; ordered Morgan and other light parties to hover about the enemy, "countenance desertion" and prevent depredation. Then he moved toward the Hudson river. On July 3rd, at Brunswick, New Jersey, he wrote a friendly letter to Gates (who must have enjoyed this victory with proper moderation), describing the horrible progress thither:

"The march from Englishtown was inconceivably distressing to the troops and horses. The distance is about twenty miles through a deep sand without a drop of water, except at South River, which is half way. This, added to the intense heat, killed a few and knocked up many of our men, and killed a number of our horses. To recruit the former upon the airy, open grounds near this place, and to give the quartermaster-general an opportunity of providing the latter, will occasion a short halt, but you may depend that we will be with you as soon as possible." [3]

There was but one thorn in his flesh, Charles Lee, who was apparently driven into an increasing frenzy as he meditated the pitiable fall of his high pride. Lee had in an unusual degree the exceedingly human trait of believing that whatever is is wrong, whoever rules is a fool or a tyrant, and whatever is advised is the opposite of wisdom. Finding the miscalled "Fabian" Washington impatient for battle, the impetuous Lee automatically inclined toward avoidance of battle. Driven out to the van by jealousy of Lafayette and ordered to attack, he hesitated and was lost.

It is not necessary either to defend or to condemn Lee. It is enough to describe him. He was his own hell, and paid in full for the temperament he did not select. Had not the Indians called him "Boiling Water" in his early days? If Lee had been content to stomach criticisms as patiently as Washington had had to do for years, his retreat would have been added, no doubt, to the multitude of retreats and forgotten or even praised since it was not disastrous and preceded victory.

Washington did not order him in temporary arrest as he had done with Morgan recently, or call on him for an explanation. He did not, indeed, praise him for his agility in extricating his men as he had praised Lafayette for far worse blundering and panic at Barren Hill, but he said nothing of him in his preliminary report. Two days after the battle he appointed Lee to be major-general of the day as if nothing had happened: "Maj'r General tomorrow Lee," says the Orderly Book.

But the more Lee thought of it the more beautiful his retreat became, and the more unbearable Washington's subsequent success. Finally he reached for his pen and began to dig his grave with it.

Though he was so excited that he mixed his dates, he did not at first attack his chief. He simply told Washington that he had been misinformed by a pack of conspirators. Forty hours after the battle Lee wrote this first letter, a mélange of deference, insolence, courtesy, contempt, modesty and braggadocio. The reader can easily picture Washington as he read this appalling indictment by an inferior:

"From the knowledge I have of your Excellency's character, I must conclude, that nothing but the misinformation of some very stupid, or misrepresentation of some very wicked person, could have occasioned your making use of such very singular expressions as you did, on my coming up to the ground where you had taken post: they imply'd, that I was guilty either of disobedience of orders, of want of conduct, or want of courage. Your Excellency will therefore infinitely oblige me, by letting me know, on which of these three articles you ground your charge, that I may prepare for my justification; which I have the happiness to be confident I can do, to the Army, to the Congress, to America, and to the World in general.

"Your Excellency must give me leave to observe, that neither your-self, nor those about your person, cou'd, from your situation, be in the least judges of the merits or demerits of our manœuvres; and, to speak with a becoming pride, I can assert, that to these manœuvres the success of the day was entirely owing. I can boldly say, that had we remained on the first ground, or had we advanc'd, or had the retreat been con-ducted in a manner different from what it was, this whole army, and the interest of America, would have risk'd being sacrificed.

"I ever had (and I hope ever shall have,) the greatest respect and veneration for General Washington; I think him endow'd with many great and good qualities; but in this instance, I must pronounce, that he has been guilty of an act of cruel injustice towards a man who certainly has some pretensions to the regard of ev'ry servant of this country; and, I think, Sir, I have a right to demand some reparation for the injury committed; and unless I can obtain it, I must, in justice to my-self, when this campaign is closed, (which I believe will close the war,) retire from a service, at the head of which is placed a man capable of offering such injuries:—but, at this same time, in justice to you, I must repeat that I from my soul believe, that it was not a motion of your own breast, but instigated by some of those dirty earwigs who will for ever insinuate themselves near persons in high office; for I really am convinced, that when General Washington acts from himself, no man in his army will have reason to complain of injustice or indecorum.

"I am, Sir, and hope I ever shall have reason to continue, your most sincerely devoted humble Servant." [4]

Could any maniac have been more fantastically tactless and confused? Could any commander-in-chief have endured it? Common self-respect, to say nothing of that respect for his high command which Washington always scrupulously upheld; and common loyalty to his devoted fellow officers compelled this reply:

"I received your letter, (dated, through mistake, the 1st of July) expressed, as I conceive, in terms highly improper. I am not conscious of having made use of any very singular expressions at the time of my meeting you, as you intimate. What I recollect to have said, was dic-tated by duty, and warranted by the occasion. As soon as circumstances will permit, you shall have an opportunity either of justifying yourself to the army, to Congress, to America, and to the world in general; or of convincing them that you were guilty of a breach of orders, and of misbehaviour before the enemy, on the 28th inst., in not attacking them as you had been directed, and in making an unnecessary, disorderly, and shameful retreat." [5]

Instead of subsiding or apologizing, Lee retorted with a still higher tone of vicious personal insult:

"I beg your Excellency's pardon for the inaccuracy of mis-dating my letter. You cannot afford me greater pleasure than in giving me the opportunity of shewing to America, the sufficiency of her respective servants. I trust, that the temporary power of office, and the tinsel dignity attending it, will not be able, by all the mists they can raise, to offiscate the bright rays of truth. In the meantime, your Excellency can have no objection to my retiring from the army." [6]

He sent another letter saying that he would prefer a court-martial to a court of enquiry, a statement of the charge and, on the first halt, a trial. He wrote as if he were the commander-in-chief and Washington a meddlesome politician. On the same day Wayne and Scott made a formal statement to Washington describing the battle and stating that they never received either a plan of attack, or a notice of retreat, and adding that a most pleasing prospect of victory was lost by Lee's failure to support them. Washington immediately issued an order:

"A General Court Martial, whereof Lord Stirling is appointed President, will set in Brunswick tomorrow . . . for the trial of Major-General Lee."

He designated four brigadiers and eight colonels as members. Then he put Lee under formal arrest. The court did not get under way until July 4th, when the following charges were exhibited against Lee, to which he pleaded not guilty:

"First: For disobedience of orders, in not attacking the enemy on the 28th of June, agreeable to repeated instructions.

"Secondly: For misbehaviour before the enemy on the same day, by making an *unnecessary, disorderly,* and *shameful retreat.*

"Thirdly: For disrespect to the Commander-in-Chief, in two letters dated the 1st of July and the 28th of June." [7]

The testimony was so elaborate that the court adjourned, convened, and adjourned from day to day while following the

army in its marches. Lee's cross-examinations of witnesses and
his own long statement show keenness and calm; but outside
the court his behavior was the very opposite of sane. At such
a time, particularly in a military situation, there is a great necessity for decorum. But when the New Jersey *Gazette* published
what would seem to be a very laudatory account of the battle,
Lee wrote for publication a letter beginning:

"Not satisfied with robbing me and the brave men under my command of the credit due to us with respect to the affair of the 28th, such
an atrocious attack has been made on my conduct, and so gross are the
injuries I have received that I have demanded a Court-Martial."

In a postscript he added:

"To call the affair a complete victory would be a dishonorable gas-
conade—It was indeed a very handsome check, which did the Americans honor." [8]

Anthony Wayne wrote to Harry Lee of this note that it
"Savours of Insanity or flows from a Worse Cause." [9] Lee
wrote to Robert Morris, July 3rd, calling Washington the
Prince on the Throne:

"Not content with robbing me and the brave men under my command of the honor due to us—a most hellish plan has been formed
(and I may say at least not discourag'd by Head Quarters) to destroy
for ever my honour and reputation— . . . if I had been let alone, I
should with patience have suffered 'em to pick up the laurels which I
had shaken down and lay'd at their feet; . . . Washington had
scarcely any more to do in it than to strip the dead."

He told how he had been ordered to attack a covering party
and found himself in the presence of "the whole flower of the
British Army. . . . Seven thousand men—

"By the temerity, folly, and contempt of orders of General Wain
we found ourselves engaged in the most extensive plain in America—
separated from our main body the distance of eight miles—The force
we could bring to action not more than three thousand men . . .
Upon my Soul I feel I know the whole Army saw and must acknowledge that I did exhibit great presence of mind and not less address—
altho' my orders were perpetually counteracted."

He told how without loss he led the British till they were exhausted to the ground where Washington was posted and repeats that Washington had "nothing to do but strip their dead.

"The General has the madness to charge me with making a shameful retreat—I never retreated in fact . . . but by his positive order who invidiously sent me out of the field when the victory was assur'd—Such is my recompense for having sacrificed my Friends, my connexions, and perhaps my fortune for having twice extricated this man and his whole army out of perdition, and now having given him the only victory he ever tasted." [10]

This is surely the language of a maniac or of a drunken braggart. While under arrest and appearing before a court-martial, he scattered abuse everywhere. The public was hailing Monmouth as a great victory and Washington and Wayne as heroes, so Lee announces that the battle was not much of a battle anyway, but such as it was, Wayne was mad and Washington was mad, and the only sane hero was himself. No writer of wildest farce would dare indite such statements for such an occasion.

In answer to young Laurens' letter describing Lee's shameful retreat, President Laurens (who had been disgusted with Lee's plans when he visited Congress at York before rejoining Washington) wrote a letter whose torn remnants seem to convey the first suspicion of treason, a "Snare":

"A conversation at Yorktown, téte a téte, which, if the Gentleman had ever been sincere, discovered [a cha]nge,
some ungracious hints applied to an
love, had alarmed me.—You
were grounds for my suspicions
his pretences to leave Philadelphia, at
the justness of my observation that the whole
conduct in this City carried the face of Stratagem
not subsisted, a concerted Plan by which our Army was to have been
  disgraced
perhaps ruined: he would not have
    himself to the fatigue & hazards of loss by various

nd March, or if necessity had obliged him
Army would have been far enough
urs—whatever is is best—I now
indebted to the Man I suspected as
Judas whose example in all cases ought to be
fo[llo]wed by Men of his disposition." [11].

Lee could not even spare his own old friends. He accused Joseph Reed of writing the newspaper account. Reed answered:

"I cannot discover the Prudence' or Wisdom of diminishing the Number of your Friends at such a time,—& especially those who have Seats in Congress where alone you can expect to have those 'enormous Injuries' redress'd of which you complain." [12]

To this wise counsel Lee wrote frantically:

"If you mean Friends to support my cause on the present occasion—I despise the thought—I ask only for common justice—I know, I am conscious that nothing but cabal artifice, power, and iniquity can tarnish my name for a moment—but if They are to prevail, woe on the community as to myself—*impavidum ferient ruinae.* No attack it seems can be made on Gen. Washington, but it must recoil on the assailant—I never entertained the most distant wish or intention of attacking Gen. Washington, I have ever honour'd and respected him as a Man and as a Citizen—but if the Circle which surrounds him chuse to erect him into an infallible Divinity, I shall certainly prove a Heretick, and if great as He is, he can be perswaded to attempt wounding every thing I ought to hold dear, He must thank his Priests, if his Deityship gets scratch'd in the scuffle . . . My particular Friends have suffered their minds to be carried away in the general torrent of delusion, raised by all the wicked arts that Hell can prompt to its ministers." [13]

Here we have an exquisitely perfect exhibition of the mania of persecution added to the mania of grandeur—pure paranoia.

The only hellish arts, and the sole suppressing of free speech that Washington employed were the hellish arts of enduring Lee's abuse without a word of reply, and the utter suppression of his own right to speak. There is indeed something almost hellish in such nobility for it is ruinous to an opponent who lacks the same magic. Six months later, with Lee still assailing him in the public prints, Washington could write:

"It became a part of General Lee's plan, from the moment of his arrest, though it was an event solicited by himself, to have the world believe that he was a persecuted man, and that party was at the bottom of it. But however convenient it may have been for his purpose to establish this doctrine, I defy him, or his most zealous partisans, to adduce a single instance in proof of it, unless bringing him to tryal at his own request, is considered in this light. . . .

"His temper and plans were too versatile and violent to attract my admiration; and that I have escaped the venom of his tongue and pen so long, is more to be wondered at than applauded; as it is a favor, that no officer, under whose immediate command he ever served, has the happiness, (if happiness can be thus denominated,) of boasting." [14]

More than a year after the battle Lee was still publishing attacks and Washington still could say, with a touching modesty and a perfect self-portrait:

"The motives, which actuate this gentleman, are better understood by himself than me. If he can produce a single instance, in which I have mentioned his name, after his tryal commenced, where it was in my power to avoid it, and, when it was not, where I have done it with the smallest degree of acrimony or disrespect, I will consent that the world shall view my character in as disreputable a light, as he wishes to place it. . . .

"If I had ever assumed the character of a military genius and the officer of experience; if, under these false colors, I had solicited the command I was honored with; or if, after my appointment, I had presumptuously driven on, under the sole guidance of my own judgment and self-will, and misfortunes, the result of obstinacy and misconduct, not of necessity, had followed, I should have thought myself a proper object for the lash, not only of his, but of the pen of every other writer, and a fit subject for public resentment. But when it is well known that the command was in a manner forced upon me, that I accepted it with the utmost diffidence, from a consciousness that it required greater abilities and more experience than I possessed, to conduct a great military machine, embarrassed as I knew ours must be by a variety of complex circumstances, and as it were but little better than a mere chaos; and when nothing more was promised on my part, than has been most inviolably performed; it is rather grating to pass over in silence charges, which may impress the uninformed, the others know, that these charges have neither reason nor truth to support them, and that a simple narrative of facts would defeat all his assertions, notwithstanding they are made with an effrontery, which few men do, and, for the honor of human nature, none ought to possess.

"If this gentleman is envious of my station, and conceives I stand in his way to preferment, I can assure him, in most solemn terms, that the first wish of my soul is to return to that peaceful retirement, and domestick ease and happiness, from whence I came. To this end all my labors have been directed, and for this purpose have I been more than four years a perfect slave, endeavoring, under as many embarrassing circumstances as ever fell to one man's lot to encounter, and as pure motives as ever man was influenced by, to promote the cause and service I had embarked in." [15]

In such utterances and such attitudes, Washington attains a majesty of meek sublimity, a snowy patriotism that would almost justify his deification by his people, if that deification did not consist in forgetting how much he suffered and how little statuesque he was.

Against such a figure, Lee chose to hurl himself and break himself to pieces with an insanity that should earn him pity rather than damnation. Above all things, historians should abstain from trying to outrave the devils in him, and from slandering him more recklessly than he slandered Washington.

Lee's defence had one strong point, though it was a technical one. He was accused of disobedience of orders, yet there was abundant evidence that all his orders to attack included a qualification concerning strong reasons against attacking. He put the situation pithily in footnotes to one of his published articles:

"It must appear somewhat extraordinary, that when the principal and heaviest charge brought against me, was the disobedience of orders, these orders that it seems I disobeyed, should never have been attempted to be ascertained to the Court by the proper authority, but were left to the conjecture and wild constructions of those who might take the trouble to guess, and to the hardiness of those who might chuse to invent."

"It must be remarked, that disobedience to discretionary orders is, *prima facie*, a glaring absurdity; it is an impossibility; and yet it has been endeavoured to prove me guilty of this impossibility." [16]

But cases are rarely adjudged in reality on the strict evidence. There is a feeling in the air that decides for guilt or innocence, and the formal verdicts are often only awkward efforts to interpret it. The court-martial on August 12th found Lee guilty on all three counts, except that the second charge: "For misbehavior before the enemy by making an unnecessary, disorderly, and shameful retreat" was modified to read, "an unnecessary, and in some few instances, a disorderly retreat." He was sentenced "to be suspended from any command in the armies of the United States of North America, for the term of twelve months." [17]

This verdict was something like that against Captain Dreyfus, who was found guilty of "treason with extenuating circumstances." The severest critics of Lee denounced the verdict absurd, since if he were guilty he should have been executed or cashiered with infamy. Here was the Byng that Americans were waiting for. But he coincided with a victory.

General B. T. Johnson says that Lee's escape from death was due to "provincialism," reverence for England that made it impossible for the court-martial to send an ex-British officer out to be shot.[18] It is more probably true that the court-martial felt him guiltless of any real direct disobedience of orders. His disrespect to the commander-in-chief was what they punished. Most of all they punished him for being so difficult that he was really impossible.

The verdict was not submitted to Washington for his approval, but sent to Congress, where a decision was held up for nearly four months longer. Seeing how Lee had comforted himself while his career hung in the balance, it may be imagined that he made noise enough when he was voted guilty. Dr. Benjamin Rush feeling sympathy for him and yet a little sympathy for himself sent him another of those anonymous letters of his. Lee mocked him:

"Dear Rush, Your letter of no date, and sign'd with no name, ought, certainly either to make me laugh or make me cry. If it is from the excess of personal prudence, it ought to make me laugh— . . . Who the devil is, what the devil is it you are so all damnably afraid of? . . . be assur'd of this—that G. Washington saw, knew, and was almost as little concern'd in the affair of the 28th as he was in the battle of Philippi." [19]

The public was against him and it was dangerous to say a word in his defence. Major Evan Edwards wrote from Philadelphia:

"Matters have been so cursedly represented against you in this place that I have been almost mob'd in defending you—ten thousand infamous lies have been spread that I never heard before to byass the minds of the People against you. In the name of God, what are we come to?—So much for our republicanism." [20]

Lee took one intelligent step. He wrote to Major John Clark and asked him on his honor if his orders were not discretionary. Major Clark replied with the strongly confirmatory statement already cited in the previous account of the battle. Clark said in his letter:

"As you have requested it, I conceive it would be cruel in me to deny you. Much has been said with respect to the *letters* and *conversation* that passed between His Excellency and you. I suspend my judgment till better informed, and assure you that if I knew you had used him ill, I should declare myself your Enemy." [21]

Lee submitted Clark's statement to Congress with a request for its consideration, but Congress voted that it should be returned unread. This was not justice, but who expects justice in time of war—or peace? In the meanwhile Lee put his acquittal beyond the pale of all probability. He multiplied his attacks on Washington, who replied with silence. To Dr. Rush, Lee wrote with fanatic obstinacy:

"Your letter implies that I did blunder—now if I did I am incorrigible—for I declare solemnly if the transactions of that day were to be done over again—I wou'd do just the same—and I aver that my conduct was in every respect irreproachable—I aver that his Excellencies letter was from beginning to the end a most abominable damn'd lie — . . . I aver that my Court Martial was a Court of inquisition . . . if They cou'd have prov'd that I had only in the course of the day utter'd the word, retreat, They wou'd have sentenc'd me to an ignominious death, or at least cashier'd me with infamy—but this retreat tho' necessary was fortunately brought about contrary to my orders, contrary to my intention, by an accident, and if anything can deduct from my credit it is that I did not order this retreat which was so necessary."

Dr. Rush, always suspicious of Washington, wrote to John Adams, who was in France:

"Characters appear in One age, and are only to be known in another. General Conway, who was the *nerves;* Mifflin, who was the *Spirit;* & Lee, who was the *Soul* of our army, have all been banished from Head-Quarters. The last has been most unjustly condemned by a Court Martial for saving our army at Monmouth on the 28th of last June. Genl. Washington was his accuser. The Congress I believe disapprove of the Sentence, but are so much afraid of the workmanship of their own hands, that they are afraid to reverse it. I blush for my Country when I tell you that several Members of Congress leave the house when the affair is bro't on the carpet. Adieu, my dear friend. Cease not to love, and serve our dear country." [22]

To R. H. Lee, Charles Lee wrote:

"Great God grant me patience! for what sort of people have I sacrificed every consideration—what a composition of falsehood wickedness and folly! to be ruined for giving a victory to a man whose head was never intended for a sprig of laurels! but as Lear said, no more of this that way madness lies." [23]

To Aaron Burr he wrote:

"It is my intent, whether the sentence is reversed or not reversed, to resign my Commission, retire to Virginia, and learn to hoe tobacco, which I find is the best school to form a consummate *general.*" [24]

He wrote repeatedly to the President of Congress telling how great he was. He alienated what interest Reed took in him and Reed accused him of slandering Washington's morals:

"I only added one Piece of Advise to him to forbear any Reflections upon the Commander in-Chief, of whom for the first time I have heard Slander on his private Character, viz, great cruelty to his Slaves in Virginia & Immorality of Life, tho' they acknowledge so very secret that it is difficult to detect. To me who have had so good opportunities to know the Purity of the latter & equally believing the Falsehood of the former from the known excellence of his disposition, it appears so nearly bordering upon frenzy, that I can pity the wretches rather than despise them." [25]

Hard words were not all Lee had. Challenges to duels began to shower on him. Baron Steuben took umbrage at Lee's reference to him as one of the "very distant spectators" and he wrote in French saying that if Lee would name time, place and weapons, he would find that the Baron was neither a distant spectator nor tardy:

"Vous choisirez le lieus le temps et les Armes mais comme je n'aime à être Spectateur ni éloigné ni tardif; je demande de vous voir aussi près et aussi tôt que possible." [26]

In a moment of temporary sanity, Lee wrote a polite answer saying that he had not meant to insinuate any cowardice by his phrase, "distant spectators." Steuben accepted this, but Alexander Hamilton chuckled over Lee's letter as a proof of Lee's cowardice.[27] Imputations against Lee's courage are libellous. He was not afraid of anybody or of everybody. Hamilton himself was soon acting as second to young Colonel John Laurens, who challenged Lee for slandering Washington's morality. Lee accepted, but with the quaintness that characterizes most of his writings:

"I will do myself the Honour of meeting you attended by a Friend with a brace of pistols to-morrow ½ past 3. p.m. I would willingly bring a small sword at the same time, but from the effects of my fall and the quantity of Physick I have taken to baffle a fit of the Gout which I apprehended I do not think myself sufficiently strong on my legs." [28]

The devoted Major Edwards was Lee's second. As Hamilton describes the duel, Lee was wounded in the right side at the first fire but called for a second discharge. The seconds opposed but he insisted. During a long parley between the seconds Lee and Laurens chatted amiably as duelists do. Laurens said he had no personal enmity but that he resented Lee's abuse of Washington. Lee admitted that he had criticized Washington's military character "and might perhaps do it again," but that he had never spoken in terms of personal abuse of Washington, because he had always esteemed Washington as a man and such abuse would be incompatible with his own character as a gentleman.   Thus the cause of the duel having been denied after the duel, honor was considered satisfied and the second fire dispensed with.   Hamilton and Edwards signed a statement praising the "politeness, generosity, coolness and firmness" of both gentlemen.[29]   Afterwards, with that lovable streak that darts through his evil actions incessantly, Lee said of Laurens:

"The young fellow behaved splendidly.   I could have hugged him." [30]

Next in line came Anthony Wayne, who demanded satisfaction for Lee's strictures against him.   Lee wrote him that he made his comments in self-defence and that he had praised Wayne's courage.   Still, he would give him satisfaction as soon as he got through his business with Congress.[31]   Wayne answered amiably that he sincerely lamented "the illiberality of some persons (who may be truly called Persecutors)" and hoped to hear from Lee as soon as he had recovered his leisure and his health.   "Interim—I wish you every Comfort." [32] These two never fought and afterwards exchanged most friendly letters.

On the 5th of December, 1778, Congress approved the sentence of the court-martial and suspended Lee from military service for a year.   The vote was very close, six states voting to approve the court-martial, three paired, two voting for Lee, two not voting at all.[33]

About the same time Generals Schuyler and St. Clair were finally acquitted of the charges of misconduct in the campaign against Burgoyne fourteen months before.   The insinuation of treason had been made against them both, as against Lee.   It was a popular charge against anybody under suspicion, and a not altogether unnatural one in view of the way that thousands of natives swung back and forth from Toryism to rebeldom according to the success of the moment.

The most determined enemy of Lee in Congress was W. H. Drayton of South Carolina, who had accused him of treason in 1776 for his failure to join Washington in the New Jersey retreat before his capture.   Lee now challenged Drayton to a duel but, though Drayton was a rival of Lee's in pen-ferocity, he declined to fight, alleging immunity as a member of Congress.

To add to Lee's confusion he wrote a very spicy letter to the Jewish belle of Philadelphia, Miss Rebecca Franks, an exceedingly vivacious Philadelphia Tory, and she resented it as an outrageous indecency.   He grovelled in apology.[34]

The crowning malice of ill fortune was that he lost his dog. He advertised for him:

"Lost or stolen, on the seventh instant, a small English Spaniel D O G, the grounds of his colour is a very shining white, his ears mark'd with yellow; as likewise two or three yellow broad spots on his side and rump, his tail extremely bushy; had on a brass collar with General Lee's name.   Whoever will bring him to Capt. Clunn's, at Trenton; to Mr Clarkson's, at Brunswick; Mr. Stockton's, at Princeton; to Mr De Hart's at Elizabethtown; to General Knox, at Pluck'emin, shall receive Twenty Dollars reward." [35]

He retired to his estate in Virginia, emitting sparks and the most interminable accusations against Washington.   The brave Colonal Oswald resigned in disgust after Monmouth, became a printer and issued some of Lee's utterances.   When publishers were disinclined or afraid to publish his diatribes Lee assailed the country for suppressing the freedom of the press, in which England far excelled the land of alleged liberty.

When his year of suspension was nearly ended, he heard that Congress was not enthusiastic about paying his wages and he fired off a letter that made his dismissal from the service inevitable.   He was by now so unpopular that Dunlap openly published an open charge of treason.   Lee demanded a full investigation of the "hellish malignant libel" and appealed to the President of Congress:

"For Gods sake, Sir, if there is the least ground for suspecting my integrity let me be regularly called before Congress to clear up my character . . . if I have . . . been guilty of any treason it has been against myself alone." [36]

The appeal was ignored.

His grudge against Washington went on mounting until, a year and a half after Monmouth, he was able to write to Gates that Washington planned to kill him:

"I am confident as I am of my own existence, that it is the determin'd purpose of that dark designing sordid ambitious vain proud arrogant and vindictive knave W: to remove me from the face of the earth by assassination direct or indirect, and to ruin your fame and fortunes forever." [37]

He died still owing Washington a little money he had borrowed when they set out to Boston together in 1775 as first and second generals. The money was paid by the estate and Washington wrote to his sister, "Permit me to offer you compliments of condolence on the loss of so near a relation who possess'd many great qualities." [38]

Lee's flippancy and profanity naturally brought on him much extra abuse and his wickedness is often charged to atheism. No scruple is made of ignoring his frequent statements of his belief in religion as essential to the state and his high respect for Christ, though he doubted his divinity. His will is also unfairly quoted, only the first of these two paragraphs being cited:

"I desire most earnestly, that I may not be buried in any church, or church-yard, or within a mile of any Presbyterian or Anabaptist meeting-house; for since I have resided in this country, I have kept so much bad company when living, that I do not chuse to continue it when dead.

"I recommend my soul to the Creator of all worlds and of all creatures; who must, from his visible attributes, be indifferent to their modes of worship or creeds, whether Christians, Mahometans, or Jews; whether instilled by education, or taken up by reflection; whether more or less absurd; as a weak mortal can no more be answerable for his persuasions, notions, or even scepticism in religion, than for the colour of his skin." [39]

He died in Philadelphia, October 2nd, 1782, at the age of fifty-one, and the relenting Congress and citizens gave him a noble funeral. He is a fascinating figure from whatever angle observed, and added much drama and suspense to Washington's career. By an odd coincidence the greatest contrast in their characters was recognized in two contemporary observers. Major John Eustace wrote to Lee:

"I've ever thought and said Sir, that had you, your passions under a perfect command, as they have you, there wou'd not be your equal on earth." [40]

Gouverneur Morris on reading John Marshall's "Life of Washington" wrote to the author:

"Few men of such steady, persevering industry ever existed, and perhaps no one who so completely commanded himself. Thousands have learned to restrain their passions, though few among them had to contend with passions so violent . . . He could, at the dictate of reason, control his will and command himself to act." [41]

During his lifetime Lee held many friends and among them many of Washington's most devoted admirers, Knox, for instance. Lee thanked Greene for "the generous indignation you have express'd at the unworthy and scoundrel treatment I have receiv'd." [42] John Marshall believed that Lee would have been restored to the esteem of the army but for his haughty temper and the court-martial would never have been held "could his proud spirit have stooped to offer explanations instead of outrage, to the Commander-in-Chief." [43] Light Horse Harry Lee, who certainly revered Washington, wrote of Charles Lee:

"He possessed a sublime genius, highly improved by books and travel; but was eccentric from freedom of thought, which he uttered without reserve; sarcastic without malignity of heart, but with asperity of tongue; and imprudent, from an indisposition to guard himself by cramping mental independence."

"The records of the court-martial manifest on their face the error of the sentence; and it is wonderful how men of honor and of sense could thus commit themselves to the censures of the independent and impartial. If General Lee had been guilty of all the charges as affirmed by their decision, his life was forfeited; and its sacrifice only could have atoned for his criminality. He ought to have been cashiered and shot: . . .

"The truth is, the unfortunate general was only guilty of neglect in not making timely communication of his departure from orders, subject to his discretion, to the commander-in-chief, which constituted no part of the charges against him. This was certainly a very culpable omission; to which was afterward added personal disrespect, where the utmost respect was not only due, but enjoined by martial law, and enforced by the state of things; . . . But this offence was different, far different from 'disobedience to orders,' or 'a shameful retreat;' neither of which charges were supported by testimony; and both of which were contradicted by fact." [44]

This seems a fine and a fair statement of Lee's conduct on the battlefield. Of his later behavior enough has been said. Many of the historians, writing after the discovery of the notorious "Scheme" he submitted to Howe, have gone medieval, dug up his corpse and subjected it to the dishonors it escaped before burial. They insist that Lee was a vile traitor on the field of Monmouth, and go far beyond the fiercest abuse of his personal enemies. One biographer of Washington actually states that Lee had been paid in advance by Clinton to wreck the army and deliver Washington a prisoner. As a further reward for thus bringing about peace he would have secured a dukedom and Washington's Mount Vernon for his estate! [45]

Dawson says that his retreat was for the protection of Clinton's wagon train. General Carrington says that Lee was a coward and an incompetent, and retreated because, having thus defeated the very invasion he proposed in his Plan, if he had been captured he would have been put to death twice—at least the historian speaks of his "double penalty for treason." [46]

Small straws show which way the wind blows and there is conclusive importance to the question of Lee's treason in a frivolous piece of writing by Major André, who was very close to Clinton, and would have been grateful to Lee if he had been regarded as a traitor to the Americans. Instead, he wrote a dream—a fantasy in January, 1779, in which he refers to Lee with detestation as a traitor to the British:

"The celebrated Gen. Lee, whose ingratitude to his parent country was regarded with the utmost detestation, assumed (by direction of the court) the figure of an adder; a reptile that is big with venom, and ready to wound the hand that protects, or the bosom that cherishes it, but whose poison frequently turns to its own destruction." [47]

Strangely, it is to Jared Sparks that Lee is indebted for the fairest treatment. His biography is just and merciful, and he says that Lee's only indefensible fault at Monmouth lay in not sending word to Washington that he was retreating.[48]

Sydney G. Fisher is very judicious in his treatment of Lee:

"His retreat seems to have been both fortunate and necessary . . . He had brought the troops out of a bad strip of country about two and a half miles in length, in which all the positions were favorable to the British, and he had just reached a good position to make a stand." [49]

In general, however, Lee's treason is taken for granted as an easy insult to a despised character. No effort is made to explain just how the villain planned to manage his villainy or profit by it. Supposing Lee to have determined to save Clinton by ruining his own reputation, and to have succeeded in protecting Clinton by a misuse of the American army, why did the man who was capable of such complex underground conspiracy, come forth at once and proceed to stand out like Ajax and invite all the lightnings of Heaven? He attacked Washington, his officers, Congress and all the colonies in a defiance that was foolish and ruinous but certainly not sneaking.

Both Washington and Lee ordered Morgan to attack the opposite flank, and if Lee were a traitor for attacking, retreating, and reattacking, what was Daniel Morgan, who never attacked at all?

Henry B. Dawson, who was so sure of Lee's treason, was equally certain that General Israel Putnam was the very last of the Revolutionary heroes who should be chosen as a " 'household word,' which was synonymous with desperate courage, undeviating patriotism, and unquestioned integrity." He gave evidence in support of a charge that Putnam never left the plow to rush to Bunker Hill, that he was so far from being a hero there that Colonel Prescott publicly said he should have been shot, that he disobeyed Washington's orders on Long Island, and was to blame for letting the British turn the left flank and crush the army; that Washington thereafter always kept him out of important posts; that he had been accused of "a too great intercourse with the enemy"; that the loss of Forts Clinton and Montgomery was due to his mismanagement; that his officers were disgusted with him.[50]

The court-martial acquitted him of blame for the loss of the forts, but he was considered a handicap rather than a help. Against all this there is voluminous testimony in Putnam's favor. But so there is in the case of Lee. Putnam's disobedience of Washington's demand for troops and Hamilton's conflict with him have been described. On March 16th, 1778, Washington had written to Putnam very bluntly that "the people of the state of New York will not render the necessary support and assistance, while you remain at the head of the department." General MacDougall replaced him and he was sent to the humiliating task of hurrying up the new troops. Later Washington wrote:

"What am I to do with Putnam? If Congress mean to lay him aside *decently*, I wish they would devise the mode." [51]

Putnam rejoined Washington as commander of the right wing, but a stroke of paralysis disabled him in December, 1779.

The British engineer, Captain Montresor, who had served with Putnam in 1764, wrote in his Journal for 1777:

"Israel Putnam, of Connecticut, might have been bought to my certain knowledge, for one dollar per day, or 8 shillings New York Currency." [52]

There is no real evidence, however, of the least infidelity. But he was the sort of rough and burly, slovenly, democratic officer that Washington especially abominated, and his retirement was a relief. Strangely enough, the old bear lisped, and once cried out: "God, cuth it, gentlemen, . . . Here'th Wathington'th health in a brimmer."

The pet abomination of Washington was suddenly and dramatically disposed of on the very day, July 4th, 1778, when Lee's court-martial began. Washington did not learn of it till later, but it was Independence Day indeed for him, for it took Conway off his hands.

While in Albany, Conway had won the cautious praise of John Jay:

"Conway manages the Vermont troops properly; but of this say nothing." [53]

It was no longer fashionable to be caught praising Conway, who met nothing but rebuffs. Unable to secure the reconsideration of his resignation, he tried to secure a certificate of his services to take back to France. Even this honest acknowledgment was denied though he had taken a brave part in three battles. Gouverneur Morris was a leader in the movement to refuse him justice and wrote joyously to Washington of his opposition. Despondently Conway appealed to Gates:

"I must Begg Leave to Serve with you as a Volunteer." [54]

Washington, hearing that Conway was trying to get back, wrote to Gouverneur Morris saying he had heard that Conway was *"demanding* the command of a division of the Continental army . . . Can this be? And if so will it be granted?" [55]

On the same day Conway wrote to Congress:

"I am willing to apologize for the orthographical and grammatical faults; I am an Irishman, and learnt my English in France, but I do not conceive that any of these letters could be construed into a request to resign. I had no thoughts of resigning, while there was a prospect of firing a single shot, and especially at the beginning of this campaign, which in my opinion will be a very hot one." [56]

He followed his letter to York and tried to regain his commission but encountered such obstacles that he wrote again to Gates:

"I never had a sufficient idea of Cabals untill I reached this place my reception, you may imagine, was not a warm one I must except Mr. Sam Adams   Coll. Richard Henry Lee and a few others who are attached to you but who can not oppose the torrent . . . one Mr. Carroll from Maryland upon whose friendship I Depended is one of the hottest of the Cabal. he told me a few days agoe almost Litterally, that any Body that Displeas'd or did not admire the Commander in chief ought not to be kept in the army. Mr. Carroll might be a good papist, but I am sure the sentiments he expresses are neither roman nor catholick." [57]

Having nothing else to do Conway apparently resumed his inveterate habit of talking too much, and General Cadwalader answered his criticisms of Washington by reviving the story that he and General Reed had found Conway skulking in a farmhouse at the battle of Germantown, alleging as his excuse that his horse was wounded in the neck; and when they urged him to get another horse cravenly repeating that his horse was wounded in the neck.[58]

The implication of cowardice seems inconsistent with Conway's usual bravery and he promptly answered the charge by challenging Cadwalader to a duel. They met on July 4th, outside Philadelphia. As Major Garden tells it, Conway fired deliberately at the word but missed.

"General Cadwallader was about to do so, when a sudden gust of wind occurring, he kept his pistol down and remained tranquil. 'Why do you not fire, General Cadwallader?' exclaimed Conway. 'Because,' replied General Cadawallader, 'we came not here to trifle. Let the gale pass, and I shall act my part.' 'You shall have a fair chance of performing it well,' rejoined Conway, and immediately presented a full front. General Cadwallader fired, and his ball entered the mouth of his antagonist, he fell directly forward on his face. Colonel Morgan, running to his assistance, found the blood spouting from behind his neck, and lifting up the club of his hair, saw the ball drop from it. It had passed through his head, greatly to the derangement of his tongue and teeth, but did not inflict a mortal wound. As soon as the blood was sufficiently washed away to allow him to speak, General Conway, turning to his opponent, said good humoredly, 'You fire, general, with much deliberation, and certainly with a great deal of effect.' The calls of honor being satisfied, all animosity subsided, and they parted free from all resentment." [59]

But according to a letter of General Patterson:

"When the American shot, the ball went through his (Conway's) head, about ½ an inch above the upper side his lip and on the right edge of his mouth, and came out behind. He fell, and has never spoke since. I saw Doctor Shippen, who first dressed him, and says he thinks he may live yet. The challenge was by Conway; the Germantown the cause, when in the battle he left his division." [60]

Cadwalader is said to have exclaimed when he saw Conway bleeding at the mouth:

"I've stopped the damned rascal's lying tongue anyway."

Conway lived and being compelled to a long and painful silence apparently had time to come to his senses. While he was still uncertain of his recovery he wrote to Washington:

"Philadelphia, 23 July, 1778.
"Sir, I find myself just able to hold the pen during a few minutes, and take this opportunity of expressing my sincere grief for having done, written, or said any thing disagreeable to your Excellency. My career will soon be over; therefore justice and truth prompt me to declare my last sentiments. You are in my eyes the great and good man. May you long enjoy the love, veneration, and esteem of these States, whose liberties you have asserted by your virtues. I am with the greatest respect, &c.

"Thomas Conway." [61]

This was handsome enough and doubtless sincere. It ends in pathos the American career of a soldier of misfortune. Since he was punished sufficiently for his errors it is permissible to remember that he came to the colonies with his family to become a citizen, that his plans for the improvement of the army were wise, that he fought bravely in several battles and sought to fight more.

If Washington ever answered his letter, the text remains

concealed. Conway left Philadelphia on November 23rd, 1778, but apparently did not sail until January, 1779. He won some distinction in France, becoming a governor-general and winning decorations, according to Vicomte de Noailles who calls him *"Ennemi secret et archarné de Washington"* during the camp at *"Walley-Forge"* and says that *"général Cad Wallades* sent him a ball in the head." [62]

There was no one to say a good word of Conway except Charles Lee, who wrote an anonymous defence of him and of freedom of speech, pointing out how monstrous it was that in a republic a man should be hounded out of the country for criticizing a general. Lee's advocacy naturally did Conway no good and Sparks thought that it hurt Lee's chances with Congress, which shortly after confirmed the court-martial sentence. [63]

Cadwalader having tasted blood tried in vain to get a shot at General Mifflin, whom he suspected of instigating Conway to fight him. [64] Mifflin suffered great loss of prestige at this time. The cabal was a purely American affair and Conway a weak foreigner who was wrecked by cleverer men.

The cabal against Washington continued long after he was gone. In the course of time Cadwalader accused Joseph Reed of cowardice and treason before the battle of Trenton. Reed denied the charge furiously and the feud raged for decades. [65]

Having pursued thus far the processes of the removal of Lee and Conway from the throng of Washington's tormentors, it is time to return to his personal activities and follow him from Monmouth field onward through a brief period of unwonted cheer.

XXXII

ON THE CREST OF THE WAVE

"WE Selebrated the Independence of Amarica the howl
army parraded . . . the artilery Discharged thirteen
Cannon we gave three Chears &c. At Night his Exelency and the gentlemen and Ladys had a Bawl at Head
Quarters with grate Pompe." [1]

So Elijah Fisher of the Commander-in-Chief's Guard describes the festivities on the second Fourth of July. Washington doubtless danced at the "Bawl" as he always did when he
had the opportunity. Now he had the right.

Three days later Congress unanimously voted him its thanks,
no longer consolation praise for a Brandywine or a Germantown, but praise for "his great good conduct in leading on the
attack and gaining the important victory of Monmouth over
the British grand army, under the command of Lieutenant-
General Sir Henry Clinton." [2]

From New Brunswick he moved on to Paramus where he
spent a few days of such idyllic ease that it might have been
Paradise. On his way he even took time for a glance at scenery
for its beauty with no thought of its fitness for bloodshed. His
visit to the cascades of the Passaic and the gay days that followed are warmly painted by his Irish secretary, McHenry:

"After viewing these falls we seated ourselves round the General
under a large spreading oak within view of the spray and in hearing of
the noise. A fine cool spring bubled out most charmingly from the
bottom of the tree. The travelling canteens were immediately emptied
and a modest repast spread before us, of cold ham, tongue and some
biscuit. With the assistance of a little spirit we composed some excellent grog. Then we chatted away a very cheerful half hour—and
then took our leave of the friendly oak—its refreshing spring—and the

meek falls of Pasaic—less noisy and boisterous than those of Niagara, or the more gentle Cohoes or the waters of the Mohawk.

"From hence we passed thro a fertile country to a place called Paramus. We stopped at a Mrs. Watkins whose house was marked for head Quarters. But the General receiving a note of invitation from a Mrs. Provost to make her Hermitage, as it was called, the seat of his stay while at Paramus, we only dined with Mrs. Watkins and her two charming daughters, who sang us several pretty songs in a very agreeable manner.

"At Mrs. Provost we found some fair refugees from New York who were on a visit to the lady of the Hermitage; with them we talked —and walked—and laughed—and danced and gallanted away the leisure hours of four days and four nights and would have gallanted— and danced and laughed and talked and walked with them till now had not the General given orders for our departure. We left them however in the spirit of modern soldiership without much sighing in pursuit of the dangers of war and pleasures of variety.

"It was about 6 o'clock in the (15 July) morning when we bade adieu to the Hermitage—coasting it thro' narrow & stony roads to a place called Haverstraw in Orange County the state of New York." [3]

Mrs. Theodosia Prevost was the widow of a British colonel serving in the West Indies. He had recently died and she had fallen in love with Colonel Aaron Burr, whom Washington had sent direct from Monmouth on secret intelligence work near New York, observing the British shipping and movements. In 1782 Burr married Mrs. Prevost, a woman of extraordinary learning and intelligence. Their daughter, Theodosia Burr, was even more brilliant. [4]

Under Mrs. Prevost's roof Washington had the handsome privilege of writing a letter of welcome to Count d'Estaing, commander of the fleet of twelve ships of the line and four frigates that France had sent forth April 12th, 1778, to make good her treaty of alliance. The fleet reached the mouth of the Delaware July 8th and, finding that Clinton had evacuated the capital, moved up to Sandy Hook, arriving there July 11th to the great alarm of the British.

Washington's spies in New York gave him the first news of the French armada. [5] A British fleet from Cork under Byron was anxiously awaited and was expected to elude the French by coming down Long Island Sound. So Washington wrote to the Governor of Connecticut urging him to collect frigates and armed vessels and try to stop it. This "would be a fatal blow for the British army, which it is supposed at this time has but a very small stock of provisions on hand." [6] He sent John Laurens with a letter to d'Estaing promising every cooperation, describing how he would cross the Hudson to the east bank, and "then move down before the enemy's lines, with a view of giving them every jealousy in my power." [7] He must have held his high head a little higher when he received from d'Estaing a personal letter in these terms:

"I have the honor to inform your Excellency of the arrival of the King's fleet, charged by his Majesty with the glorious task of giving his allies, the United States of America, the most striking proofs of his affection. . . . The talents and the great actions of General Washington have secured to him, in the eyes of all Europe, the truly sublime title of the liberator of America." [3]

Pleasant reading, this, to the late victim of the ridicule of the cabal and the attacks of Lee, whose court-martial was sitting at Paramus and at many a subsequent camp. To make sure of d'Estaing's cooperation, Washington sent another aide to d'Estaing, Alexander Hamilton, "to satisfy any inquiries." With him went young Lieutenant-Colonel Fleury, "a gentleman of your nation, who has distinguished himself by his zeal and gallantry . . . He has also with him four captains of Vessels, whom I hope you will find very useful, from their knowledge of the coasts and harbors." [9] He sent two pilots, besides.

Foreseeing the possibility that something might thwart the attack on New York, he wrote to Sullivan to make ready for a possible descent of the French fleet on the British garrison at Newport, and advising him to engage pilots to go aboard on signal.[10] He left Paramus July 15th, and while his army was crossing the Hudson, inspected the new works which Kosciuszko was constructing at West Point. Then he moved over to White Plains, above New York City, and settled in camp ready for the combined sea and land assault on New York. He did not share the opinion of Pontgibaud, "We should have needed a hundred fifty thousand if we had wanted to attack the place, and we had but fifteen thousand." [11] But on finding himself again at White Plains whence he had been jostled out by Howe in 1776, he was moved to this reflection:

"It is not a little pleasing, nor less wonderful to contemplate, that after two years' manœuvring and undergoing the strangest vicissitudes, that perhaps ever attended any one contest since the creation, both armies are brought back to the very point they set out from, and that which was the offending party in the beginning is now reduced to the use of the spade and pickaxe for defence. The hand of Providence has been so conspicuous in all this, that he must be worse than an infidel that lacks faith, and more than wicked, that has not gratitude enough to acknowledge his obligations. But it will be time enough for me to turn preacher, when my present appointment ceases; and therefore I shall add no more on the doctrine of Providence." [12]

He had with him, too, "the largest body of regular troops ever assembled under the American banner." It was reported at nearly seventeen thousand rank and file fit for duty.[13] But lack of military opportunity and a willingness to let the French do all the fighting started the familiar forces of dissolution to work and the army ran away like sand in an hour glass. His restless Providence began to tease him, too, as of old and soon woke him from his dreams of storming down upon New York while the French ships crashed through the harbor. He wrote to Jacky Custis another might-have-been:

"If it had not been for the long passage of the French fleet, which prevented their arrival till after the evacuation of Philadelphia—or the shallowness of the water at the entrance of the harbor at New York, which prevented their getting in there—one of the greatest strokes might have been aimed that ever was; and, if successful, which I think would have been reduced to a moral certainty, the ruin of Great Britain must have followed, as both army and fleet must, undoubtedly, have fallen." [14]

This was from no lack of eagerness on the part of d'Estaing. The French built their warships with a much deeper draught than the British and could not cross the bar that the British ignored. D'Estaing made personal investigations during which an officer and several sailors were drowned, and Colonel Laurens was almost lost while taking Washington's letter to him. D'Estaing wrote to Congress of his zeal:

"Both officers and crews were kept in spirits, notwithstanding their wants and the fatigues of service, by the desire of delivering America from the English colors, which we saw waving, on the other side of a simple barrier of sand, upon so great a crowd of masts. The pilots procured by Colonels Laurens and Hamilton destroyed all illusion. These experienced persons unanimously declared, that it was impossible to carry us in. I offered in vain a reward of fifty thousand crowns to any one, who would promise success. All refused, and the particular soundings, which I caused to be taken myself, too well demonstrated, that they were right." [15]

Convinced that there was no way of reaching the British fleet in New York harbor, the French decided to attack Newport and sailed away on July 22nd. Surely Providence never played a more wanton joke on a faithful worshipper, for on the very day when d'Estaing turned his back on New York just the wind he needed blew into the harbor and a spring tide gave thirty feet on the bar—a flood on which he could have rolled in with ease and crushed the British who waited the end. Besides, the great Cork fleet had been scattered by the gales. [16]

With a sigh Washington relinquished the proud day he had planned and began sending troops off to General Sullivan, entrusting them to Lafayette, who cherished another hope of glory. But Washington must have known pretty well by now to expect the unexpected, or at least the undesired, from the luckless Sullivan. He was not disappointed. Thanks to Sullivan in part and to the state of the world he began to realize that so far as he was concerned, the French allies were just so many new difficulties.

XXXIII

THE FRENCH COME AND GO

STRANGELY, the same Washington who had started the Seven Years' War in Europe by slaying young Jumonville back in 1754, was now again instrumental in sending France and England to each other's throats. But from the moment of the sailing of the French fleet out of Toulon, the American Revolution sank back into comparative insignificance as a minor detail in a European conflict.

It is hard for Americans to realize their place in European perspectives, since they read only American histories of Europe, if any. One who explores European histories of America is startled to find how small a part the Revolution and the War of 1812 play in their pages. The international viewpoint, however, is of value and the American public at that time accepted it in effect if not in intention.

Washington had complained so bitterly of the national languor and indifference up to now that he had no new phrases for the regret and disgust awakened in him as he saw the almost total disappearance of what little interest his fellow citizens had taken in their troops. Instead of seizing the opportunity with a rush, the people relaxed. The annual decrease increased so precipitately that he was left as little more than the spectator of foreign battles and the domestic scramble for wealth. Another indirect result was an aggravated difficulty in securing supplies of money, equipment, and uniforms, for France now had need of all her own resources. She was no longer secretly aiding the enemy of her enemy, but was openly at war with a tremendous power, before whose reawakened energies she exerted a desperate and diminishing struggle for her own life.

Washington was mercifully spared—or unmercifully denied

—the knowledge of what was to come. He would never again fight a real battle for his country. Furthermore, from 1778 on, the war in which he would play so small a rôle was fundamentally a naval war. Fortunately for America the French alliance came about at one of those unusual times when the British navy was inferior to the French in sea-spirit and in skill. As soon as Spain joined France, though half-heartedly, in 1779, their combined fleets were greater and better than the British. Also the French commanders at sea were better than ever before or after. Oddly, too, the best of France's navies had been built up and was conducted by "two men, who had no knowledge of sea warfare." [1] But the all-powerful British navy had been let slip into a woeful condition.[2]

Captain James points out ironically the fact that the declaration of war between France and England followed just fifteen years after the declaration in 1763 of "a Christian, universal and perpetual peace, as well by sea as by land, and a sincere and constant friendship . . . between their Brittanic, Most Christian Catholic and Most Faithful Majesties." That War to End War had ended war for a perpetuity of fifteen years. Which is a fair average for perpetual peaces.

Lecky says of May, 1778:

"The moment was one of the most terrible in English history. England had not an ally in the world. One army was a prisoner in America; . . . The growing hostility of the German Powers had made it impossible to raise or subsidize additional German soldiers; and in these circumstances, England, already exhausted by a war which its distance made peculiarly terrible, had to confront the whole force of France, and was certain in a few months to have to encounter the whole force of Spain . . . Her ministers and her generals were utterly discredited." [3]

It seemed to need the challenge of France to wake the empire. The European flesh-markets had been drained, but suddenly there were volunteers from everywhere at home. The war ardor flamed and enraged even Pitt, "the friend of America," now the Earl of Chatham, who had opposed the persecution of the colonies and proposed the withdrawal of every British or German soldier, and the renunciation of every disputed claim; the Pitt who had shaken the stick on which his gouty figure leaned, and cried: "You cannot conquer the Americans! . . . I might as well talk of driving them before me with this crutch!" Now, on hearing that it was proposed to grant the colonies independence, he had himself carried into the House of Commons and stood with a friend at either side to hold him up while he made his last speech:

"My lords, I rejoice that the grave has not closed on me, that I am still alive to lift up my voice against the dismemberment of this ancient and noble monarchy." [4]

He fell in a convulsive fit and was carried home to his death-bed. The vote to grant America independence was defeated by only 50 votes to 33; but the same revulsion against France turned all the Friends of America into foemen. As G. M. Trevelyan says, "In the hour of need, to which her fools had brought her, Britain was saved by her heroes." [5] Lord North, detested by Americans, fought unwillingly and urged the grant of independence while Pitt. an American idol, killed himself denouncing it.

The warfare that followed concerned itself especially with the West Indies, which both France and England deemed more precious than the turbulent colonies. Conflict encircled the globe in battles for India, Gibraltar, the seven seas. Consequently the appearances of French fleets in American waters were only incidental to larger plans and French admirals bore orders that compelled them often to leave the American ports just as something great was about to happen.

To the Americans their comings and goings seemed mere whimsicality, stupidity or cowardice, and they turned upon the French a wrath they never quite felt for the mother country. Some of Washington's deepest tragedies were undergone as he found his high hopes nullified by compulsory abandonments that seemed to him outrageous desertions. His self-control was never so strained as by the incessant compulsion to present always the smiling face and the gracious word to his mercurial allies, who were, like his abominable militia, "here today and gone tomorrow." He rarely failed to do the right thing courteously, but some of his lieutenants and some of the people were blundersome, tactless or truculent.

While waiting for the remarkable series of misfortunes about Newport, he seems to have had a clash with his devotee, Nathanael Greene. The exact cause of it can only be gathered from Greene's letter of pained protest against some sharp rebuke. As his grandson, George Washington Greene, writes:

"It is well known, though not generally acknowledged, that Washington had a very quick temper, and was often led to sudden and violent manifestations of it. Few of those who lived on an intimate footing with him were with him long without witnessing, even when they did not draw it upon themselves, some hasty expression of his irritation." [6]

After the battle of Monmouth, Greene had returned to the mountain-moving drudgery of quartermaster-general, trying to replace the many horses lost in the heat of the battle and on the marches, and preparing proper camps for the advancing army. Apparently he had found it necessary to be at a distance on some occasion when Washington expected him to be at hand, and Washington had flared up at the disrespect or the inconvenience. Whereupon Greene made this gentle self-defence with evidences of deep, fresh wounds, old wounds from lack of appreciation, and a very definite resignation:

"Your Excellency has made me very unhappy. I can submit very patiently to deserved censure, but it wounds my feelings exceedingly to meet with a rebuke for doing what I conceived to be a proper part of my duty, and in the order of things. . . . I wrote you the reasons for my not waiting upon you in person were I had my letters to answer and many matters to regulate in my department, which prevented me from returning. Besides which it was almost half a day's ride, the weather exceeding hot, and myself not a little fatigued. . . .

"If I had neglected my duty in pursuit of pleasure, or if I had been wanting in respect to your Excellency, I would have put my hand upon my mouth and been silent upon the occasion; but as I am not conscious of being chargeable with either the one or the other, I cannot help thinking I have been treated with a degree of severity I am in no respect deserving of. . . . I have been more attentive to the public interest, and more engaged in the support of your Excellency's character than ever I was to my own ease, interest, or reputation. I have never so-licited you for a furlough to go home to indulge in pleasure or to im-prove my interest, which, by the by, I have neglected going on four years. . . . I have never been troublesome to your Excellency to pub-lish anything to my advantage, although I think myself as justly entitled as some others who have been much more fortunate, particularly in the action of the Brandywine. . . . As I came into the Quartermaster's department with reluctance, so I shall leave it with pleasure. Your influence brought me in, and the want of your approbation will induce me to go out." [7]

Washington's answer is not known, but he must have done something to close the breach, for the friendship was renewed and Greene continued to suffer at his task.

More obscure officers kept up an endless war over precedence till Washington groaned:

"We can scarcely form a Court Martial or parade a detachment in any instance, without a warm discussion on the subject of precedence." [8]

Benedict Arnold also posed a problem for he suddenly set his eyes on the command of the American navy. He was a superb ship-fighter, an amphibian genius and he probably thought both of glory and of prizes. He appealed to Wash-ington, who wrote to him a graceful evasion:

"You will rest assured, that I wish to see you in a situation where you can be of the greatest advantage, and where abilities like yours may not be lost to the public; but I confess myself no competent judge in marine matters to offer advice on a subject so far out of my line; believe me tho' that it is my desire, that you may determine, in this case, in a manner most conducive to your health, honor, and Interest." [9]

A fascinating If is offered for speculation on what would have happened if Arnold had been sent to sea. He might have rivalled Paul Jones and fastened his name among the revered heroes. He would at least have been removed from the temp-tations of high life in Philadelphia.

Washington finally yielded to Greene's homesickness and sent him to serve under Sullivan and take half of Lafayette's troops. This meant another blow to Lafayette's hopes, but he bore the disappointment with the meekness of a saint:

"I willingly part with half my detachment, since you find it for the good of the service, though I had great dependence on them. Any thing, my dear General, which you shall order or can wish, will always be infinitely agreeable to me." [10]

Naturally Washington thanked him. [11]

Now things began to go wrong with their familiar speed. Washington wrote Sullivan that he had stripped himself of troops and was inferior to the British in New York. He begged Sullivan to be careful but did not hamper him with orders from a distance. [12] D'Estaing reached Rhode Island before the promised American troops had arrived—they were "still at home" as d'Estaing wrote home. [13] Their delay of nine days wrecked the schedule, but when d'Estaing landed 4,000 soldiers and the British retired from their outer works, Sullivan rushed in to seize them without pausing to consult his allies. D'Estaing took this as a gross breach of military courtesy, as well as of a pledge, but he showed a patience that is more often encountered among the French than is admitted by other nations. [14]

The French found Sullivan a difficult and jealous man, as did many other officers. Had not Washington had to spank him into submission? Had he not fought at Brandywine for the right of the line as frantically as for the defeat of the British?

The unavoidable delay in the appearance of the American militia gave a British fleet under Lord Howe time to appear outside the harbor. Though inferior to the French, Howe did magnificent work in luring them from their prey to the stormy sea outside. Fearing to be caught between two fires, d'Estaing declined the American advice to attack the land forces, took his troops on board and sailed out to fight. That form of sparring known as gaining the weather gage occupied Lord Howe and d'Estaing for two days, when a hurricane that wrecked even the camps ashore did both fleets more damage than a battle.[15] To keep his pledge, d'Estaing returned to Newport and Greene and Lafayette went out to plead with him to renew the attack on the garrison. But d'Estaing insisted that his first duty to France and to America was to go to Boston and refit his damaged fleet. He could not be dissuaded.

Sullivan now declared war on France. He drew up a long and scathing denunciation of d'Estaing's action in carrying off his ships and his troops.[16]

Though the American force was only ten thousand, the protest was signed by three major-generals, including John Hancock, and by sixteen other generals. Counting Lafayette this meant a general for every five hundred men. Lafayette was furious and described his response to d'Estaing:

"I told these gentlemen that my native land is dearer to me than America, that whatever France does is right, that M. le Cte d'Estaing is my friend, and that I am ready to support these opinions by my sword, which has never been put to a better use. . . . They all apologized and said that they were far from requiring me to give my vote. In the mean time, M. le Comte, fancy my situation; for from this time forward I shall be in fear that I may have to resent every word I hear spoken." [17]

Undeterred by Lafayette's rage, Sullivan sent Laurens with the Protest to meet the fleet at the entrance to Boston Harbor. D'Estaing read it and replied with diplomatic grimness:

"This paper imposes on the Commander of the King's squadron the painful but necessary law of profound silence." [18]

Next Sullivan published an order to his troops indicating that America would prove herself "able to procure that by her own arms, which her allies refused to assist in obtaining." This incensed Lafayette so that he called on Sullivan, quarreled with him and all but challenged him. Sullivan published an order that amounted to an apology. Of course, all this came down on Washington's head. Lafayette sent him a long letter describing the outrageous treatment of his countrymen:

"Forgive me for it; it is not to the commander-in-chief, it is to my most dearest friend, General Washington, that I am speaking. I want to lament with him the ungenerous sentiments I have been forced to see in many American breasts. . . . Frenchmen of the highest character have been exposed to the most disagreeable circumstances, and yet, myself, the friend of America—the friend of General Washington, I am more upon a warlike footing in the American lines, than when I come near the British lines at Newport. . . . Whenever I quit you, I meet with some disappointment and misfortune. I did not need it to desire seeing you as much as possible." [19]

Of course, Washington wrote to his troubled son the exactly correct and gracious words:

"I feel every thing that hurts the sensibility of a gentleman, and consequently upon the present occasion I feel for you and for our good and great allies the French . . . In a free and republican government, you cannot restrain the voice of the multitude. Every man will speak as he thinks, or, more properly, without attending to the causes. The censures, which have been levelled at the officers of the French fleet, would more than probable have fallen in a much higher degree upon a fleet of our own, (if we had one) in the same situation. . . . Let me beseech you therefore, my good Sir, to afford a healing hand to the wound, that unintentionally has been made." [20]

He wrote also to Sullivan very tactfully:

"The success or misfortune of your army will have great influence in directing the movement and fortune of this. . . . First impressions you know are generally longest remembered, and will serve to fix in a great degree our national character among the french. In our conduct towards them we should remember, that they are a people old in war, very strict in military etiquette, and apt to take fire, where others scarcely seem warmed. . . . It is of the greatest importance also, that the minds of the soldiers and the people should know nothing of the misunderstanding, or, if it has reached them, that ways may be used to stop its progress and prevent its effects." [21]

Congress had heard of the wrangle from Sullivan and was gravely alarmed, ordering that it be kept secret at all costs. Washington tried to put forth some soothing propaganda and urged General Heath to do his utmost to spread the statement that the storm alone was to blame for driving the fleet to Boston. He even wrote to Governor Trumbull:

"I consider storms and victory under the direction of a wise providence who no doubt directs them for the best of purposes, and to bring round the greatest degree of happiness to the greatest number of his people." [22]

Sullivan answered Washington that "the first struggles of passion" had subsided and that all were friends again; but Greene wrote to Washington of Sullivan's indiscretion and the result of the fleet's departure: "Such a panic among the militia and volunteers that they began to desert by shoals. . . . Our strength is now reduced from nine thousand to between four and five thousand." [23]

Lafayette rode to Boston at Sullivan's request, seventy miles in seven hours. He persuaded d'Estaing to march overland with his troops while the ships were being repaired and to put himself under Sullivan's command. Though his rank was superior, d'Estaing consented to this humble step and wrote a charming letter to Sullivan. Lafayette, fearing to miss a battle, galloped back in six-and-a-half hours, arriving just too late.

Sullivan's force of 10,000 had been cut in two by desertion, and only fifteen hundred of the remainder had seen action, so he decided to retreat rather than face the British 6,000 shortly to be reinforced. The British and Hessians followed close and with the aid of warships routed Sullivan's troops, which had been without rest or food for thirty-six hours. A newly recruited regiment of negroes "distinguished itself by desperate valor." The American loss was 211. Amory set the British loss at 1,023. Fortescue gives it as 260. [24]

The next day Lord Howe with a hundred ships and many troops arrived and proved the wisdom of Sullivan's retirement. The Bostonians blamed the French for this disappointment, riots broke out between the citizens and the sailors and there was another Boston "massacre," this time of the allies. The Chevalier de Saint Sauveur was killed while trying to act as

peacemaker and another French officer badly wounded.   For
the sake of appearances it was agreed to lay the blame on some
British prisoners in town who were accused of fighting for
bread! [25]   Seething ancient race-hatreds also broke out at
Charleston, South Carolina, where the French sailors, being
driven from the town, fired on it from the ships.

Washington and d'Estaing exchanged beautiful letters but
the grand alliance had failed to capture either New York or
Newport.   Time and lives had been spent and affairs were no
forwarder.   Congress passed a resolution that "count d'Estaing
hath behaved as a brave and wise officer." [26]   Yet as Charlemagne Tower says:

"The failure of the expedition of the Comte d'Estaing at this critical
period of the history of the United States was, in every sense, an extraordinary example of ill luck.   Fate itself seemed to have entered into the
contest against the French admiral, and, with unremitting spite, to have
met him step by step, as if to deprive him of his success and cheat him
of his glory. . . . We owe it to the mature wisdom and the soothing
influence of General Washington in this time of impending trouble, as
well as to the generous personal conduct of the Comte d'Estaing himself, that the crisis was passed without lasting injury." [27]

Every effort was made, of course, to keep a cheerful front
for the benefit of the public and the enemy.   In November,
d'Estaing gave a banquet on one of his ships to "a large company of gentlemen and ladies" and "the entertainment was
highly elegant."   Absent in flesh, Washington was present in
a full-length portrait presented to d'Estaing by John Hancock.   The frame was covered with laurels.[28]   Lafayette was
at once determined to have a portrait of his own and he wrote
to Washington:

"Give me joy, my dear general, I intend to have your picture, and
Mr. Hancock has promised me a copy of that he has in Boston.   He
gave one to Count d'Estaing, and I never saw a man so glad at possessing his sweetheart's picture, as the admiral was to receive yours." [29]

This stirred Washington to unusual warmth:

"Your love of liberty, the just sense you entertain of this valuable blessing, and your noble and disinterested exertions in the cause of it, added to the innate goodness of your heart, conspire to render you dear to me; and I think myself happy in being linked with you in bonds of the strictest friendship. . . . Could I have conceived, that my picture had been an object of your wishes, or in the smallest degree worthy of your attention, I should, while Mr. Peale was in camp at Valley Forge, have got him to have taken the best portrait of me he could, and presented it to you; but I really had not so good an opinion of my own worth, as to suppose that such a compliment would not have been considered as a greater instance of my vanity, than a mean of your gratification; and, therefore, when you requested me to sit to Monsieur Lanfang, I thought it was only to obtain the outlines and a few shades of my features, to have some prints struck from." [30]

He ended the letter with a request that Lafayette try to find out something from his wife—"your fair lady, to whom I should be happy in an opportunity of paying my homage in Virginia, when the war is ended, if she could be prevailed upon to quit, for a few months, the gayeties and splendor of a court, for the rural amusements of an humble cottage." He had heard that a French ship had been captured by the British and among its treasures sold at auction in New York was "an elegant present" from the Queen of France to Martha. Nothing more seems to have been heard of it.

He had to write in a different tone when Lafayette asked his permission to challenge the Earl of Carlisle to a duel. The British peace commissioners had put forth some comments on the perfidy of France. Lafayette, without waiting to hear Washington's answer, wrote to the Earl and expressed his desire to "punish" him and thus add "to the glorious privilege of being a Frenchman."

D'Estaing was so anxious to prevent the duel that he wrote twice to Washington to intervene. Washington strangely managed to keep free of duels all his life, though they raged in his army, and he tried to dissuade Lafayette by gentle ridicule and refusal of permission, though he flattered his own countrymen in the process:

"The generous spirit of Chivalry, exploded by the rest of the world, finds a refuge, my dear friend, in the sensibility of your nation *only*. But it is in vain to cherish it, unless you can find antagonists to support it; and however well adapted it might have been to the times in which it existed, in our days it is to be feared, that your opponent, sheltering himself behind modern opinions, and under his present public character of Commissioner, would turn a virtue of such ancient date into ridicule. Besides, supposing his Lordship accepted your terms, experience has proved, that chance is often as much concerned in deciding these matters as bravery; and always more, than the justice of the cause. I would not therefore have your life by the remotest possibility exposed, when it may be reserved for so many greater occasions."

To d'Estaing he wrote in a tone of the most tender affection for his impulsive son-at-arms, describing his letter:

"I omitted neither serious reasoning nor pleasantry to divert him from a Scheme in which he could be so easily foiled, without having any credit given to him by his antagonist for his generosity and sensibility . . . The charms of vindicating the honor of his country were irresistible; but, besides, he had in a manner committed himself, and could not decently retract. I however continued to lay my friendly commands upon him to renounce his project; but I was well assured, that, if he determined to persevere in it, neither authority nor vigilance would be of any avail to prevent his message to Lord Carlisle. And tho' his ardor was an overmatch for my advice and influence, I console myself with the reflection, that his Lordship will not accept the challenge; and that while our friend gains all the applause, which is due to him for wishing to become the Champion of his Country, he will be secure from the possibility of such dangers as my fears w^d otherwise create for him." [31]

The peril was ended by the receipt of Carlisle's reply. He answered that he was on a public mission, responsible only to his country and his king, and that "all these national disputes will best be decided when Admiral Byron and the Comte d'Estaing meet each other." [32]

For the first and only time Washington seems to have entertained a suspicion of Lafayette's devotion to America. Suddenly Lafayette conceived a great plan: he would go to France to see his wife but also persuade the king to lend him 5,000 soldiers. With these and American troops he would conquer Canada and present it to America.

When France lost Canada, wise Frenchmen had predicted that the removal of the French menace would relieve the colonies of their dependence on England and bring about a revolution. Now there were wise Frenchmen who wanted Canada to stay English so that the colonies would still need the French and favor them in commerce. But Lafayette hurried to Philadelphia, laid the scheme before Congress, and won approval for it as a great surprise for Washington. Washington returned the surprise by declaring the whole thing impossible.

He wrote to Congress a long statement of the objections to such a diversion at such a time, but in a private letter to Henry Laurens he expressed a doubt as to whether Lafayette had really originated the scheme or was the tool of the French cabinet. In this private letter he reveals the statesmanship for which he was afterward so renowned, the never-swerving policy of America first, last and all the way:

"The question of the Canadian expedition, in the form it now stands, appears to me one of the most interesting that has hitherto agitated our national deliberations. I have one objection to it, untouched in my public letter, which is, in my estimation, insurmountable, and alarms all my feelings for the true and permanent interests of my country. This is the introduction of a large body of French troops into Canada, and putting them in possession of the capital of that Province, attached to them by all the ties of blood, habits, manners, religion, and former connexion of government. I fear this would be too great a temptation to be resisted by any power actuated by the common maxims of national policy. . . .

"France, acknowledged for some time past the most powerful monarchy in Europe by land, able now to dispute the empire of the sea with Britain, and if joined with Spain, I may say, certainly superior, possessed of New Orleans on our right, Canada on our left, and seconded by the numerous tribes of indians in our rear from one extremity to the other, a people so generally friendly to her, and whom she knows so well to conciliate, would, it is much to be apprehended, have it in her power to give law to these States. . . .

"England, without men, without money, and inferior on her favorite element, could give no effectual aid to oppose them. Resentment, re-proaches, and submission seem to be all that would be left to us. Men are very apt to run into extremes. Hatred to England may carry some into an excess of Confidence in France, especially when motives of gratitude are thrown into the scale. Men of this description would be unwilling to suppose France capable of acting so ungenerous a part. I am heartily disposed to entertain the most favorable sentiments of our new ally, and to cherish them in others to a reasonable degree. But it is a maxim, founded on the universal experience of mankind, that no nation is to be trusted farther than it is bound by its interest; . . . We have not yet attained sufficient vigor and maturity to recover from the shock of any false step, into which we may unwarily fall. . . . I would wish, as much as possible, to avoid giving a foreign power new claims of merit for services performed to the United States, and would ask no assistance that is not indispensable." [33]

Thus he was already establishing his policy of avoiding en-tangling alliances. He was warm of heart but wise and canny. Machiavelli was also warm of heart, and no more suspicious than Washington.

Congress, nevertheless, was unwilling to give up the project at which it had leapt, and proposed modifications. The French court, however, would have none of it, not caring to drive Eng-land to complete desperation and prolong the war. Further-more, France was as wise as Washington and unwilling to trust to American gratitude in case the colonies grew too strong.

Vergennes assured England through the French ambassador to Spain that he would guarantee England her Canadian pos-sessions, and he wanted Spain to have Florida so that the young republic would be hemmed in. He wished, indeed, to see America finally organized not in one but in three republics.

Even that would have been ten less than the number of re-publics Washington had to hold together.

Lafayette still felt that he must return to France, though he hated to sever his bonds with America lest they might not be easily re-knit. He visited Washington on October 6th, 1778, and secured his consent to a leave of absence, with the consent of Congress, to which he addressed a letter written as if to a bosom friend:

"As long as I thought I could dispose of myself I made it my pride and pleasure to fight under American colours, in defence of a cause which I dare more particularly call ours, because I had the good luck of bleeding for it. . . . I dare flatter myself that I schall be look'd on as a soldier on furlough, who most heartily wants to join again his colours, and his most esteemed and belov'd fellow-soldiers." [34]

Congress gave him permission and "an elegant sword" and he set out for Boston, but a long ride in the rain brought him down with a fever at Fishkill, where he lay in all the anguish of expected death far from his wife and child and his beloved land.

In his case, as in the case of his step-children, Washington displayed all the passionate thwarted father-love that glowed in his heart. He ordered the surgeon-general of the army to take charge of the sick youth, and, with all his multitudinous tasks upon him, found time and strength to ride every day eight miles from his camp to Fishkill and back to enquire how Lafayette fared, but he never entered the sick room for fear of exciting the patient. Dr. Cochran finally restored him to health and during his convalescence he saw Washington often. [35]

The frigate that was to carry him to France could not fill its crew except by employing a number of British deserters and they planned to seize the ship and take it into a British port as a prize. The plot was discovered in time and the ship reached France with thirty-three men in irons. Lafayette went home rather as an envoy from America than as a repentant prodigal. The king and his own people forgave him for his escapade and covered him with praise, but he left a great void in Washington's heart.

There was such a shortage of provisions in Boston that d'Estaing's fleet could not leave the harbor until the privateers brought in some well-laden British vessels. On November 4th, 1778, he set out for Martinique, on the very day that Major-General Grant and five ships of the line left New York with 5,000 of Clinton's troops in transports—just the number of soldiers that Grant had said was all he needed to cross the

American continent.   He was now on his way to the West
Indies, where he distinguished himself.   Three weeks later
Admiral Byron left Rhode Island for the same ports.   In the
meanwhile a squadron of frigates and one big ship escorted the
transports in which Lieutenant-Colonel Campbell and eight
battalions prepared an invasion of Georgia.

This was the same Colonel Campbell who had been so un-
handsomely treated as a prisoner in Boston and for whom
Washington had interceded so forcibly.   He captured Savannah brilliantly on December 29th, 1778, and was notably
kind to his prisoners.

D'Estaing and Byron fought with varying success but their
battles were far from Washington's ken.   The French allies
were again invisible and he was once more alone with his even
more troublesome fellow-countrymen.

XXXIV

THE COLLAPSE OF 1778

ASIDE from the fiasco of Rhode Island there was no large military activity. Washington was too weak to attack New York, and Clinton, having sent away so many men, had only strength enough to plead with Germain to let him resign.

There were raids here and there. In August, Lieutenant-Colonels Simcoe and Tarleton and their Tory followers gave a lesson in bush-fighting to the Indians friendly to Washington. Simcoe climbed a tree, sent a drummer boy on up to the top, and seeing the Indians advancing, ambushed and killed forty of them, which discouraged the enthusiasm of the rest for the rebel cause.[1]

"Mrs. Washington's Guards" were nearly annihilated in September. Washington's former aide, Colonel Baylor, commanded that regiment of light horse. While they were stationed at Tappan, New Jersey, "No-Flint" Grey, who had inflicted the Paoli "Massacre" on Wayne, once more took the flints away from his men, leaving them only their bayonets, and, as Anthony Wayne reported it, surprised Baylor's "detachment consisting of upwards of one hundred men, in their beds, refused any quarter, and in cold blood most barbarously and mercilessly put to the bayonet, men naked and unarmed, begging for compassion, being incapable of resistance."[2] Out of 104 men, 15 were killed, 17 wounded, including Colonel Baylor, were left behind and 39 prisoners carried off. The British had one man killed. Washington wrote of this "massacre":

"This affair seems to have been attended with every circumstance of cruelty. It is a small compensation for this accident that Colonel

Butler . . . surprised about an hundred Yagers below Tarrytown, killed ten on the spot, and took a lieutenant and eighteen men prisoners." [3]

In October, Count Pulaski's Legion was surprised near Trenton and two French officers and forty-eight men "butchered." [4] There was bloody civil war between rebels and Tories in Wyoming Valley, Pennsylvania, and the Indians there and elsewhere enjoyed the privilege of tomahawking and scalping. Marauders on both sides inflicted horrid cruelties on lonely farmers. Colonel Israel Angell records "A garrison Court Martial Set for this day for the trial of two villains for attempting to Commit a Rape upon a ould woman near four score." One was "ordered to Receave 100 Strips," the other 37.[5] In Washington's own Guard three men were sentenced to be hanged for robbing an old Tory. Two of them escaped.[6] The number of soldiers put to death for robbery of their fellow-citizens during the war would, if compiled, probably surpass that in some of the major battles. So would the total number of citizens slaughtered by the patriot marauders.

On September 16th, 1778, Washington's army left White Plains for a new camp at Fredericksburg, New York, within easy reach of West Point, of which he was jealous lest Clinton attack the unfinished works. He now had a little over 13,000 officers and men fit for duty.[7] In October there was a great festival in camp with skyrockets and salvos. Sergeant Fisher of the Commander's Guard describes it in his own way:

"The 17th. In Rememberance of Gen. Burgoin's Defeet the Day was selebrated with the firing of Canon and in throing of skilokets in the are thirteen Canon was fired then they begun to through the skilokets and a merry Day they had too at the Park of artilery." [8]

About this time Burgoyne's surrendered men were marched under guard from Massachusetts, where they had been viciously mistreated, all the way to Virginia. Clinton wrote:

"I was tempted by the Chances that presented themselves of recovering at least Part of those troops and attempting Mr. Washington's Rear. But the news had come too late to be of use." [9]

On November 27th, Washington disposed his army in winter quarters at various points on either side of the Hudson. He chose Middlebrook, New Jersey, for his own headquarters. While visiting Elizabethtown he enjoyed "a festive entertainment" in his honor on December fourth.[10] Learning that Clinton had moved up the Hudson river, he set out at four o'clock in the morning to meet the invader. He wrote to Joseph Reed in his lighter vein:

"Sir Harry's late extra manœuvre up the North-River kept me upon the march and countermarch from the 5th till yesterday . . . What did or could prompt the knight to this expedition, is beyond the reach of my conception, considering the unseasonableness of it . . . the enemy had landed . . . set fire to two small log'd houses, destroyed nine barrels of spoiled herrings, and had set sail for New York. Thus ended this notable expedition, which was conducted (in the preparation) with so much secrecy, that all the flag-boats to and from the city were stopped, and not a mouse permitted to creep within their lines." [11]

In more solemn tone, he had written to Gouverneur Morris that the officers were growing mutinous with despair:

"Can *we* carry on the war much longer? Certainly NO, unless some measures can be devised & speedily executed to restore the credit of our currency, restrain extortion, & punish forestallers. Without these can be effected, what funds can stand the present expenses of the army? And what officer can bear the weight of prices, that every necessary article is now got to?

"A Rat in the shape of a horse, is not to be bought at this time for less than £200; A Saddle under Thirty or Forty;—Boots twenty,—and shoes and other articles in the like proportion.—How is it possible, therefore, for officers to stand this without an increase of pay? And how is it possible to advance their Pay, when Flour is selling (at different places) from five to fifteen pounds pr cwt.,—Hay from ten to thirty pounds pr Tunn, and Beef & other essentials in this proportion?

"The true point of light, then, to place & consider this matter in is, not simply whether Gt. Britain can carry on the war, but whose Finances, (theirs or ours,) is most likely to fail." [12]

He was so despondent concerning the result of the French alliance that he already gave up hope unless Spain also came to the rescue:

Lancaster: Gedruckt bey Francis Bailey.

Des Landes Vater

Waschington

1779

WASCHINGTON DES LANDES VATER.

In the upper left-hand corner appears what is perhaps the first ascription of the title "Father of his Country" to Washington.

(From a German Almanac, Lancaster, Pa., 1779.)

"If the Spaniards would but join their Fleets to those of France, & commence hostilities, my doubts would all subside. Without it, I fear the British Navy has it too much in its power to counteract the Schemes of France." [13]

In a German almanac printed at Lancaster, Pennsylvania, in the latter part of this year he was for perhaps the first time called "the Father of his Country." [14] If he knew of the ascription he must have felt little flattered by the paternity. The phrase was applied by the Germans to almost any monarch, the Landgrave of Hesse, for instance. But he could pick up his subjects, export them for foreign service, and pocket the rent. Washington could not persuade his people to come forth and oust the invader even with bounties everlastingly increased. On September 8th, Congress had authorized him to give an additional bounty of ten dollars, "keeping this matter secret as long as he shall deem it necessary." [15] The draft had failed. Negroes were being enlisted—and worse yet, deserters—and by whole communities. He wrote to Massachusetts:

"It gives me inexpressible concern to have repeated information from the best authority, that the committees of the different towns and districts of your State hire deserters from General Burgoyne's army, and employ them as substitutes, to excuse the personal service of the inhabitants. . . . Indeed, Mr. Burgoyne could hardly, if he were consulted, suggest a more effectual plan for plundering us of so much money, reinforcing General Howe with so many men, and preventing us from recruiting a certain number of regiments; to say nothing of the additional losses, which may be dreaded, in desertions among the native soldiers, from the contagion of ill example and the arts of seduction, which it is more than probable will be put in practice." [16]

One could hardly believe this even from Washington, were there not so many other evidences that the public was hiring British hirelings to do its fighting. Yet in spite of all efforts, the end of 1778 showed an army with 2,000 fewer Continentals and 15,000 fewer militia than in 1777, which had turned out 20,000 fewer than 1776. [17] The aggregate enrollment for 1778, counting all the militia that had served as long as two months, was 51,046. The number of men capable of bearing arms was 250,000.[18]

Washington seems to have turned once more to his old friend Providence, to which he was far more faithful than it was to him:

"Providence has heretofore taken me up when all other means and hope seemed to be departing from me. In this I will confide." [19]

Or, as he put it in a letter to Thomas Nelson: "The rest is with the Gods." [20]

While he was crying out for help, the Virginia House of Delegates voted him a handsome gift of four geldings. In his acknowledgment to the Speaker, Benjamin Harrison, he implied that the Continental Congress was being gelded by the selfishness of the states and their practice of keeping their best men at home. His pessimism seemed never to find bottom. In every deep a lower deep. So now he wrote to Harrison of bad money, bad habits:

"What may be the effect of such large and frequent emissions, of the dissensions,—parties,—extravagance, and a general lax of public virtue, Heaven alone can tell! I am afraid even to think of It . . . if it is not a sufficient cause for gen[l] lamentation, my misconception of the matter impresses it too strongly upon me, that the States, separately, are too much engaged in their local concerns, and have too many of their ablest men withdrawn from the general council, for the good of the common weal. . . . It is much to be feared, my dear Sir, that the States, in their separate capacities, have very inadequate ideas of the present danger." [21]

He wrote this letter on December 18th at Middlebrook, but delayed sending it until the 30th when he added a prolonged postscript at Philadelphia. At his own suggestion he had been directed to report to Congress for conference on "the emancipation of Canada." He slipped into Philadelphia quietly on the 22nd. The Pennsylvania *Evening Post* said of his arrival:

"Too great for pomp, and as if fond of the plain and respectable rank of a free and independent citizen, his excellency came in so late in the day as to prevent the Philadelphia troop of militia lighthorse,

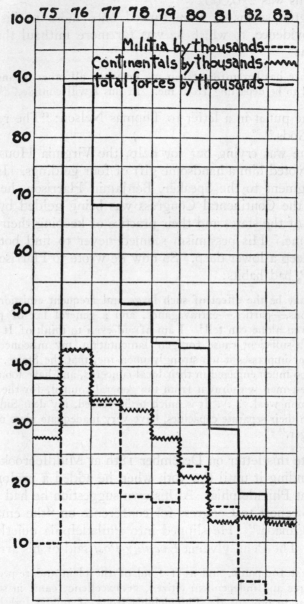

CHART SHOWING THE STEADY DECLINE OF THE AMERICAN FORCES.
(The numbers at the top indicate the years 1775-1783; the numbers at the side, thousands of men.)

Militia by thousands ------
Continentals by thousands ~~~~~~
total forces by thousands ———

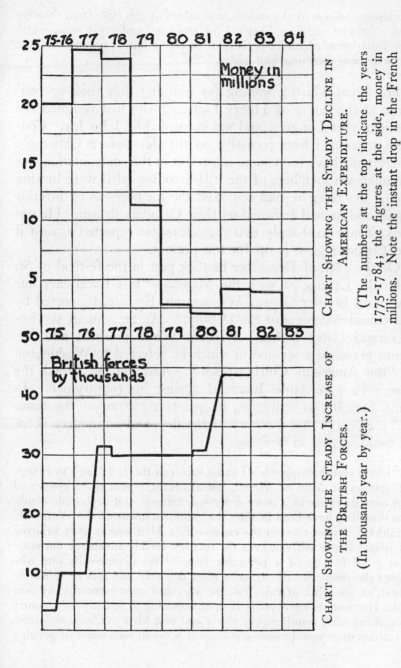

25 75-76 77 78 79 80 81 82 83 84

20

Money in
millions

15

10

5

50 75 76 77 78 79 80 81 82 83

British forces
by thousands

40

30

20

10

CHART SHOWING THE STEADY DECLINE IN
AMERICAN EXPENDITURE.

(The numbers at the top indicate the years
1775-1784; the figures at the side, money in
millions. Note the instant drop in the French
alliance in 1778-9.)

CHART SHOWING THE STEADY INCREASE OF
THE BRITISH FORCES.

(In thousands year by year.)

gentlemen, officers of the militia, and others of this city, from shewing those marks of unfeigned regard for this good and great man, which they fully intended, and especially of receiving him at his entrance into the State, and escorting him hither." [22]

He found Martha waiting for him and they took up residence at the home of Henry Laurens, who had resigned the Presidency of Congress and was succeeded by John Jay. Congress welcomed him formally on the day before Christmas. There must have been some constraint in the confrontation, for the unknown members of the still-brooding cabal were lurking among the rest; he had criticized the members as of inferior grade, and he had frowned on their Canadian dream. He opposed it now so sharply that the committee reported against it and Congress gave it up for the present.

On the 28th of December he took part in the festival of St. John the Evangelist with the Masons—"His Excellency our illustrious brother George Washington, Esquire, supported by the Grand Master and his Deputy." At the church services Reverend (later Bishop) William White presided and Dr. Smith preached a sermon in which he referred to Washington as "the American Cincinnatus." [23] And yet he ended the year with a veritable Jeremiad against his countrymen. In long, tumultuous sentences, he paints a picture of the times and the people that no Tory of the day, and no modern skeptic could surpass in cynicism:

"I have seen nothing since I came here (on the 22d Inst.) to change my opinion of Men or Meas^{rs}, but abundant reason to be convinced that our affairs are in a more distressed, ruinous, and deplorable condition than they have been in since the commencement of the War.—By a faithful laborer then in the cause—By a Man who is daily injuring his private Estate without even the smallest earthly advantage not common to all in case of a favorable Issue to the dispute—By one who wishes the prosperity of America most devoutly and sees or thinks he sees it, on the brink of ruin, you are beseeched most earnestly, my dear Colo. Harrison, to exert yourself in endeavoring to rescue your Country by (let me add) sending your ablest and best Men to Congress—these characters must not slumber nor sleep at home in such times of pressing danger—they must not content themselves in the enjoyment of places of honor or profit in their own Country while the common interests of America are mouldering and sinking into irretrievable (if a remedy is not soon applied) ruin in which theirs also must ultimately be involved.

"If I was to be called upon to draw a picture of the times and of Men, from what I have seen, and heard, and in part know, I should in one word say that idleness, dissipation & extravagance seems to have laid fast hold of most of them.—That speculation—peculation—and an insatiable thirst for riches seems to have got the better of every other consideration and almost of every order of Men.—That party disputes and personal quarrels are the great business of the day whilst the momentous concerns of an empire—a great and accumulated debt—ruined finances—depreciated money—and want of credit (which in their consequences is the want of everything) are but secondary considerations and postponed from day to day—from week to week as if our affairs wear the most promising aspect—after drawing this picture, which from my Soul I believe to be a true one, I need not repeat to you that I am alarmed and wish to see my Countrymen roused.—I have no resentments, nor do I mean to point at any particular characters,—this I can declare upon my honor for I have every attention paid me by Congress that I can possibly expect and have reason to think that I stand well in their estimation, but in the present situation of things I cannot help asking—Where is Mason—Wythe—Jefferson—Nicholas—Pendleton—Nelson—and another I could name—and why, if you are sufficiently impressed with your danger do you not (as New Yk. has done in the case of Mr. Jay) send an extra member or two for at least a certain limited time till the great business of the Nation is put upon a more respectable and happy establishment.—Your Money is now sinking 5 pr. ct. a day in this city; and I shall not be surprized if in the course of a few months a total stop is put to the currency of it.— And yet an Assembly—a concert—a Dinner—or supper (that will cost three or four hundred pounds) will not only take Men off from acting in but even from thinking of this business while a great part of the Officers of ye Army from absolute necessity are quitting the service and ye more virtuous few rather than do this are sinking by sure degrees into beggary and want.—I again repeat to you that this is not an exaggerated acc^t; that it is an alarming one I do not deny, and confess to you that I feel more real distress on acc^t of the pres^t appearances of things than I have done at any one time since the commencement of the dispute." [24]

The British were not unaware of these sordid phases of the conflict. As General Pattison wrote home:

"By some intercepted Letters from Silas Deane and others . . . it appears that Gen[l] Washington is highly disgusted, and that the Members of Congress and other Principal Leaders of Rebellion are quarrelling amongst themselves which it may be hoped, will be increased by the Check their New Allies have met with in the West Indies, and by our late Successes in Georgia." [25]

Those who nowadays uphold the tradition that the forefathers were of almost superhuman virtue must either ignore such a picture of the times or call Washington a slanderer.

XXXV

THE WAR WITH MONEY

IT must have pleased the French allies to learn that the Americans had frankly adopted a do-nothing plan for the campaign of 1779. In 1780 the French would be further dazed by the financial bankruptcy of their allies. Only two military schemes were considered for 1779: an attack on the British in New York and Newport, and an assault on the post at Niagara as a threat against Canada. But the people were tired, with the exhaustion of the lazy; and it seemed best to conserve their energies. That is the prose translation of the way Sparks put it:

"Washington recommended the defensive system, preferring what he deemed the greatest public good to the glory that might be acquired by large military enterprises." [1]

His own elaborate series of questions for Congress does not sound so hypocritical as all that. Of course he would have preferred glory acquired by large military enterprises since glory would have meant victory, but he knew the hopelessness of the situation, the peril of further debt and the emission of more bad money to annul what was already afloat.[2] In January, 1779, sailors in Philadelphia were so incensed at being paid in paper money that they terrorized the streets with clubs and threats.[3] The soldiers were restive everywhere. To keep men enough to hold the British where they were, meant an immense outlay for much-needed clothes, an increase in the ever-increasing bounties, and some provision for the officers; they simply could not live on the pay they were getting in the almost useless currency. At this time Greene, acknowledging a sum of money, wrote:

439

"It is no more equal to our wants than a sprat in a whale's belly . . . I suppose the treasury Board thinks we can live upon estimates and support the army upon calculations." [4]

Money had to be conquered before the British. It was now a matter of life or death. As Washington put it a little later:

"I never was, much less reason have I now, to be afraid of the enemy's *arms*; but . . . I have never yet seen the time in which our affairs (in my opinion) were at so low an ebb." [5]

He was trying to keep his own head as well as the nation's above the quicksands of the unstable currency. There was grave danger of complete bankruptcy for himself, his wife, and her son Jacky, to whom he acted as a remote financial adviser. At first he had declared that the man who refused to accept the paper money of Congress at its face value was a traitor, but nothing could save its face and there were limits even to his self-sacrifice, especially as he saw so many people battening on the miseries of the nation and ignoring the cause of liberty. His hottest rage was devoted to the "forestallers" and "engrossers"—a forestaller being one who found out what the army or the government was going to purchase in the future, and made haste to buy up the available supply at a low price in order to sell it to the nation at a heavy advance; an engrosser one who, as we say now, cornered the market, and made the government pay the ultimate exorbitance. The country was full of such people and they were piling up fortunes. For these men, whose names are lost in merciful oblivion, Washington had an abysmal hatred. He called them "those murderers of our cause, the monopolizers and engrossers." He exclaimed:

"I would to God, that one of the most atrocious in each State was hung in gibbets upon a gallows five times as high as the one prepared by Haman. No punishment, in my opinion, is too great for the man, who can build his greatness upon his country's ruin." [6]

He felt that ruin could be escaped solely by avoiding the use of money as far as possible, reverting to barter and making land deals by trade only, for he had implicit confidence in the future value of the soil, especially as lands were rising in price —as everything else was. He wrote to Jacky:

"A moment's reflection must convince you . . . that Lands are of permanent value; that there is scarce a possibility of their falling in price, but almost a moral certainty of their rising exceedingly in value. . . . A pound may not, in the space of two years more, be worth a shilling, the difference of which becomes a clear loss to the possessor and evinces, in a clear point of view the force and efficacy of my advice to you to pay debts, and vest it in something that will retain its primitive value; or rather, in your case, not to part with that thing for money, unless it be with a view to the Investing it in something of equal value; and it accounts at the same time, for the principal upon which I act with respect to my own Interest in the Dower Lands; for I should be wanting to myself, and guilty of an inexcusable act of remission and crimin¹ injustice to your mother not to secure an equivalent for her releasement of Dower; . . . two years hence, one hundred pounds in specie, may be worth, and will fetch, one thousand pounds of paper."

The prophecy was wildly flattering. In 1781 a hundred pounds in specie was worth 7,500 pounds in paper, and before the year was out it was worth infinity, for the paper was worth nothing. He tried to justify his shift from his former wrath at the villains who doubted the Congress money:

"It may possibly be said that this is setting up a distinction between Specie and Paper, and will contribute to its depreciation. I ask if there is a man in the United States that does not make a distinction when four to one is the difference, and whether it is in the power of an individual to check this when Congress, and the several assemblies, are found unequal to the task?" ⁷

This was a bit subtle, but he was driven to it. He often grows a little inarticulate in his letters home, but they are vivid:

"A Barr¹ of Corn which used to sell for 10/, will now fetch 40— . . . a Bar¹ of Porke that formerly could be had for £3, sells for £15, & so with respect to other articles which serves to enable the man who has been fortunate enough to succeed in raising these things to pay accordingly; but, unfortunately for me, this is not my case, as my

Estate in Virginia is scarce able to support itself whilst it is not possible for it to derive any benefit from my labors here."

He was extremely eager to increase his land-holdings but he could not raise money; also, he was grown exceedingly weary of slavery, not as cruelty but as business:

"If it could be accomplished by any means in my power, in ye way of Barter for other Land—for Negroes (of whom I every day long more & more to get clear of,) or in short—for any thing else (except Breeding Mares and Stock of other kinds) which I have in my possession; but for money I cannot, I want the means."

His character as a shrewd and ruthlessly keen trader led him not only to deceive according to the rules of the game but to abhor being deceived. Of John Marshall's father he writes:

"Marshall is not a necessitous man, is only induced to offer his Land for sale, in expectation of a high price—& . . . will practice every deception in his power to work me (or you in my behalf) up to his price, . . . Respecting Barry's Land . . . I had rather give Negroes—if Negroes would do, for to be plain I wish to get quit of Negroes. . . . In your Letter of the 29th you say you do not suppose I would choose to cut down my best Land, & build Tob° Houses, but what am I to do—or how am I to live.—I cannot support myself if I make nothing —& it is evident from y^r acc^t that I cannot raise wheat." [8]

He had bewailed the poor quality of the present Congress, but the unfortunate members had inherited insoluble problems left them by greater men. As McHenry said:

"Constitutional money . . . would have corrupted a community of angels." [9]

Immediately after Bunker Hill, in 1775, Congress had issued two million dollars in bills of credit to be redeemed proportionately by the states between 1779 and 1782. Here it was 1779 with affairs in worse condition than ever. The first Continental money had fared so well in the early raptures of patriotism that the emissions of paper totalled by November, 1779, more than $240,000,000, with perhaps other surreptitious issues. The states had published money of their own to the extent of over $200,000,000, more than half of this being uttered by Washington's own state. Besides these bills of credit there were vast obligations in the form of "loan-office certificates, the lottery tickets, . . . the quartermasters' certificates, the commissary certificates, . . . and many other sorts of paper acknowledgments of debt." [10]

When Washington was made Dictator in 1776, following his flight across the Jerseys, Congress voted five millions of money and pledged the faith of the nation for its redemption. When a hundred millions had been issued and people began to doubt the pledge, Congress renewed it on December 29th, 1778, and rebuked the rumor as "false and derogatory to the honor of Congress." [11] Still the gossip would not be hushed and when Congress was asked in September, 1779, if it meant to do anything besides print money and if there were really any hope of its redemption, a tremendous address to the public was drawn up, beginning, "Friends and Fellow Citizens!" describing the necessity for money to break the British chains, calling attention to England as "a kingdom crumbling to pieces; a nation without public virtue; . . . courting the vengeance of Heaven and revolting from the protection of Providence," praising the young republic and its "veteran" army and ridiculing as "impossible that America should think without horror of such an execrable deed" as repudiation:

"A bankrupt faithless republic would be a novelty in the political world, and appear among reputable nations like a common prostitute among chaste and respectable matrons." [12]

The more eloquent the expression of horror at a deed, the more ready the cleansed soul often is for its commission—as if one got rid of remorse in advance. Six months later Congress voted the nation a "novelty in the political world," and a common prostitute—i.e., it moved to redeem its money at 1/40th of its face value. It repudiated 39/40ths of the debt, thus becoming 1/40th pure, or only 39/40ths prostitute.

John Witherspoon called this "the first and great deliberate breach of public faith." The Reverend Ashbel Green quotes the bitter remark of a friend: "Congress first told a lie, then swore to it and by believing them, I have been reduced to poverty." [13] He had to pay $1,000 for a misfit coat, for example.

There was no definite promise on the money itself that it would be redeemed. It simply stated, "This Bill entitles the Bearer to receive" so many "Spanish Milled Dollars, or the Values thereof in Gold or Silver." [14] "Entitles" was not a synonym for "Guarantees." There was not even a date of payment.

Congress claimed that in printing money it was only the agent of the states and apportioned the obligations among them, asking them to compel its acceptance. Laws were passed branding a person who refused to honor the money at its face value as one "lost to all virtue and regard for his country." He was called a traitor, disciplined by tar and feathers, persecution, confiscation, all the luxuries of a loyalist. Efforts to fix prices followed with their unfailing result. Pelatiah Webster, a contemporary merchant and writer on finance, recognized the fact:

"It is no more absurd to attempt to *impel faith* into the heart of an unbeliever by *fire* and *faggot,* or to *whip* love into your mistress with a *cowskin,* than to force value or credit into your money by *penal laws.*" [15]

Nevertheless the effort was made and price fixing was attempted. Riots raged and many were fatally hurt. Consequently Webster could soon say that paper money had killed more men "and done more injustice than even the arms and artifices of the enemy." [16] Money changers multiplied and grew rich. Counterfeiting was easy and, since the Americans provided many counterfeiters of their own, it was not to be supposed that the British would neglect this form of bombardment. Their presses poured it forth. Travellers were furnished with bundles of it for distribution. Thomas Paine denounced this.[17] But the younger Pitt later distributed counterfeit French money to undermine the republic and Napoleon scattered forged Austrian bank notes.

The woes of the poor soldiers were appalling. They waited months, sometimes years, for their pay and got it in paper that had gone down and down in value while they waited. Officers with families to support sent home little bundles of paper, when they got it, but it could buy almost nothing. This, however, was a limited grievance, for the soldiers and officers made up only a small part of the populace. The blight struck the civilians, too. Worst of all, it attacked even the rich, the great creditors, and their heirs. Widows disposed of their handsome estates for a good price, only to find that they were paupers, since the money was almost worthless. Men who owed large sums went out and bought a mass of bills for a song, then offered it in full payment. A debtor could pay off an old thousand-dollar loan by investing a hundred in new money, or even less than that as time went on. Consequently the creditors tried to escape from the debtors. Hoping that things would improve, creditors actually went into hiding for fear their debtors should find them. The debtors often took soldiers with them, hunted down their creditors and made them sign a receipt at the point of the bayonet with the threat of a prosecution for treason behind it. Old John Witherspoon told how the debtors pursued the creditors "in triumph, paying them without mercy." [18]

Washington despised this method of burglary, especially as he was a heavy loser by it. He is said to have snubbed one devoted friend on learning that this was his practice. He explained his coldness by saying, "I tried hard to be civil . . . but that Continental money stopped my mouth." [19] How it came home to him is seen in two fierce letters he wrote to Lund concerning a "Mr. M." and his effort to settle a land-deal with depreciated currency to Washington's heavy loss:

"It is not harder then upon him to suffer a part than for me the whole—Such local disadvantages as these are to be placed to the misfortunes of the times—some men indeed are benefitted by them while others are ruined—I do not it is true come in under the latter class (so far as it extends to ruin) but I believe you know, that by the comparative worth of money, six or seven thousand pounds which I had in Bonds upon Interest is now reduced to as many hundreds because I can get no more for a thousand at this day than a hundred would have fetched when I left Virginia—Bonds, Debts, Rents (in Cash) and annuities undergoing no change while the currency is depreciating every day in value and for ought I know may in a little time be totally sunk. . . . If therefore I am to pay M. for his whole land at the price now agreed at by the acre, and to receive no Interest from Alexander I shall be very prettily handled between the two . . . You will do the best you can to have justice done me—their impositions afterw^ds I must submit to as a tax to dishonorable men.

"If Mr. M. possessed so little honor—I may say honesty—as to attempt paying me two shillings in the pound for a debt he was greatly indulged in (—the depreciation at the time he made the offer not exceeding this)—I must be content; for knowing nothing of your Laws, and being unwilling that any act of mine should injure the currency, I chose to make no difficulties in the case if the loss of the whole debt should be the consequence of it.—but why he should withhold payment from that time to this when less than a shilling in the pound will pay it, he can acc^t better than I.—Might he not with the same parity of reason—if the depreciation is still going on—wait six months longer and pay me with sixpence or even a penny in the pound?—Surely yes; and the palpable and obvious injustice of it needs no comment."

While struggling so hard for his rights he was ever eager to see that other men collected theirs from him, and he wrote to Lund, his manager, a voluntary offer of protection from loss:

"The depreciation of money and the sudden rise in the price of produce in the course of this year and other things principally to this cause owing render your present wages especially under short crops totally inadequate to your trouble and services—I am therefore willing that you sh^d receive a certain part of the last crop, to be disposed of by you for your own benefit—and so in future—this will give you the reward of y^r industry without subjecting you to the peculiar hardship resulting from depreciation as it is presumable that the price of produce will rise in proportion to the fall of the other—I do not at this time ascertain what the part shall be, because I wish you to say what you think is just and right—that it is my full wish to give, and more I do not think you would ask, therefore we cannot disagree." [20]

The Tory historian, Judge Jones, accused Lord Stirling of being a notorious bankrupt and paying debts of £80,000 with Continental money that cost him £1,000 in gold and silver. But Stirling's biographer says that Stirling was bilked of his estates and left with his debts, so that he died penniless.[21] Washington was beginning to fear the same fate.

Nathanael Greene was accused of growing rich through the depreciation. A quartermaster's salary came to him in the form of a percentage on his disbursements. This invitation to corruption was almost irresistible. Even by making no direct theft from the government, it was possible to speculate in money with enormous profit. Charges against Greene's honesty were soon made, and the clamors increased. They were perhaps unmerited, but it came to light a century afterward that he and Jeremiah Wadsworth, the commissary, went into a business partnership together and with the highest of motives followed St. Paul's advice to avoid even the appearance of evil.

Silas Deane was accused of unlimited robbery and treason, but more than fifty years after his death Congress paid his heirs money due him since 1778.[22] It was with Deane's brother Barnabas that Greene and Wadsworth became very silent partners, supplying the capital from their profits as quartermaster and commissary. Knowing how vicious criticism could be, they covered their interest well. In January, 1779, Greene and Wadsworth were in Philadelphia—with Washington—and made their deal with Deane then. In April, Greene wrote that it "should be kept a secret . . .

"The nearest friend I have in the world shall not know it from me, and it is my wish that no mortal should be acquainted with the persons forming the Company except us three. I would not wish Mr. Dean even to let his brother know it . . . he may inadvertently let it out into the broad World; . . . however just and upright our conduct may be, the world will have suspicions to our disadvantage." [23]

The next step toward secrecy was that the firm should carry a fictitious name; the next, that the members should not use their own names in their friendly correspondence. The next, that they should use a cipher code, since one of Silas Deane's letters had been intercepted and used as a proof that he "has a plan of Land jobbing." Furthermore Greene had found in Philadelphia "that certain Members of Congress are endeavoring to spread among the people that the avarice and extravagance of the Staff are the principal causes of all the depreciation of the money . . . I thought it most prudent to write them . . . I have received no answer to it yet." Two weeks later he writes to Wadsworth:

"The midnight politician which we have often talked about for his duplicity, who used to lodge with you in the same house in Philadelphia, thinks and says we are a set of rascals; that we are folding our arms and swimming with the tide, secure in our emoluments and regardless of the ruin and fate of our Country. . . . He further adds, if the people won't save themselves they may all go to h— and be damn'd. . . . You must be patient, and stand still and see the Salvation of the Lord! If I could be convinced in the least degree that my services gratis would lay the foundation for such a general reformation as they predict, I should not hesitate a moment to engage upon that footing, but I have no idea of any greater public benefit resulting from it than the saving of my commissions or salary." [24]

Though he offered to serve for a year without pay, to prove his patriotism, the suspicion of Greene went so far and his difficulties were so great that before the year was over he offered his resignation. Congress answered with a commission of investigation and reform. After spending a fortnight before the committee, Greene wrote to Wadsworth in this manner:

"Dear Sir: I returned last night from 2010. The 332 are as great a set of 1012 as ever got together. The 166 of 1292 are 1404 than the former. One of them I am sure is nothing less than a 1286; he . . . is from N 2013 . . . Take care what you 1411, . . . send the information in one letter, and what you say upon it in another.
Yours, you know who,

N 713." [25]

This letter from the quartermaster-general becomes eloquent when decoded, with the knowledge that 2010 means

Philadelphia; 332, Congress; 1012 rascals; 166 of 1,292, Board of the Treasury; 1,404, worse; 1,286, traitor; 2,013, Carolina; 1,411, write; 713, Greene.

The letter contained other statements:

"It is the intention of 1292 [*the Treasury*] not to let any 232 [*cash*] go through your hands, with a view of saving the 292 [*commission*]. . . . You may depend upon it that great pains is taking to 240 [*censure*] you and me. The plan is not to attack us personally; this they know will not answer; but to accuse the 1232 [*system*] of each, . . . Truth and righteousness is of no account with these 931 [*people*]. Any claim of merit for past services is not only laughed [at] but the person who should be foolish enough to make it would be severely *ridiculed*. Be upon the 1367 [*watch*] and be upon your 718 [*guard*], for depend upon it the hand of Joab is in all these things."

Soon after this, Congress changed the pernicious commission system, whereupon Greene refused to serve longer and resigned with such tartness that Congress was tempted to dismiss him, but finally accepted his resignation. As late as July 18th, 1781, Greene wrote to Wadsworth:

"How goes on our Commerce? Please to give me an account by the Table as letters are frequently intercepted." [26]

His name never appeared in the books of the firm, whose dealings were chiefly in the very supplies furnished to the army, including rum and gin, which the firm distilled. The discoverer of all this writes that "the integrity and honor" of the partners was "without stain; nor is there a vestige of evidence that its founders took undue advantage of their official positions to extend the business or increase the profits of the firm." [27] One may well agree with this, yet be dazed at finding Nathanael Greene dealing in government supplies under every possible mask. What would have been thought of him if the secret had come out at the time?

Greene, indeed, was later involved in an open scandal with a clothier, Banks, also a speculator. In order to cover his naked troops, Greene bought uniforms from Banks and guaranteed his paper. Banks went bankrupt and absconded, leaving Greene to pay more than £30,000. Learning this, Greene rode four hundred miles with loaded pistols only to find Banks dying. While waiting for Congressional relief, Greene also died, suffering from the accusation that he had been a silent partner with Banks. One biographer says that the insinuation was "a blow tenfold heavier than the loss of fortune." [28] Yet Greene had not been incapable of a silent partnership.

Washington wrote of him, "I spurned those reports which tended to calumniate his conduct." [29] Strangely, he wrote this letter to Wadsworth, never dreaming of the partnership. It is because Greene was so fine a patriot, warrior, military genius, that this digression is made as an example of how complicated financial matters were at that time. If Nathanael Greene could be a silent partner in a silent business dealing in the supplies he purchased as a government officer, and taking such advantage of the depreciation in currency as to pile up a great fortune by the end of the war, only to lose it through another speculator, what could be expected of the less devoted patriots?

Mixed up with Greene's financial troubles was Robert Morris, who made it possible for Washington to cross the Delaware and would make it possible for him to march to Yorktown. In 1779, Morris was formally accused of speculation in flour, of "engrossing" it. He absolved himself by saying he was acting as agent of the King of France. But there was ill feeling. He was mobbed in 1779. Tom Paine had attacked Silas Deane furiously; he attacked Robert Morris, insisting that delegates and agents of the United States had no right to engage in commerce and speculation. Paine had many quaint notions. He was on the committee that acquitted Morris of fraud,—with a verdict of "not guilty but don't do it again." Morris had done nothing wrong except to buy a ship's cargo before Congress could, to commit a monopoly and make large profits as a speculator while honored by the public confidence. The committee thought he should have been more patriotic.[30]

The germs of patriotic idealism were just sprouting. Thomas

Paine and George Washington set too high a standard. In 1781, Congress tried to make Morris end his commercial connections. He refused and Congress yielded.[31] Sumner says of Morris: "He never gave anything to the public, nor lost anything by the public service."[32]

Where a Nathanael Greene and a Robert Morris were growing rich by the war, it could hardly be expected that Benedict Arnold would lose the opportunity. Always under financial suspicion, he was soon covered with the most scandalous charges of profiteering as well as of friendship for the Tories. Though his salary was small he lived like a grand vizier, and yet the money he acquired by hook and by crook sufficed so ill that he began to long for the hard money of the British. The recent purchase of the Clinton Papers by Mr. William L. Clements and their thorough examination have established the fact that Arnold approached Clinton, offered himself for sale and began transmitting information to him in 1779, long before he was transferred to West Point.

With all these temptations for the powerful, the unscrupulous or the luckily placed to enrich themselves by selling the country short, the poor, the honest, and the unfortunate paid the taxes, since depreciation in money amounts to a tax. Furthermore, as W. G. Sumner says, "An excessive inflation of the currency is the same as having no currency at all."[33] The tragedy grew so bitter that people began to laugh about it sardonically. Barber shops were papered with money. In April, 1779, Washington wrote, "A wagon-load of money will scarcely purchase a wagon-load of provisions."[34] The money was called "cartload," indeed, because it took a cartload of it to buy real money or anything that real money could buy. A witty old gentleman said of the depreciation that a fast trotting horse could not quite keep up with it. People used money as cockades in their hats. They had mock funerals with money for the corpse. Some humorists "tarred and feathered" a dog by plastering him with sticky substance and then covering him with money and parading him through the streets.[35]

Money sank rapidly to the nadir where it cost more to print a bill than it was worth.[36]

Whether one should say that prices rose or money fell, there began that burlesque revaluation which every war brings about. By May, 1779, butter was $2 or $3 a pound in Philadelphia; shoes $25 a pair. Soon a hat cost $400, a pair of shoes $125, a suit of clothes $1,600, fishhooks 50 cents apiece; handkerchiefs $100.[37] In 1780 General Gates built a 100-yard fence to restrain prisoners and it cost him $500,-000.[38] In 1781, Tom Paine paid $300 for a pair of stockings. Jefferson got equal warmth out of 3 quarts of brandy for $355.50. A quartermaster paid £60 for shoeing two horses, £500 for four quires of writing paper, £15,000 for a thousand weight of bar iron.[39] A Bostonian paid $1,500 for getting his coat patched.[40] Captain Allen McLane exhibited a receipt in 1781:

"CAPTAIN A. M'LANE,   Bo't of W. NICHOLLS,
    January 5th, 1781.

1 pair boots	$600
6¾ yds. calico, at 85 ds.	752
6 yds. chintz, at 150 ds.	900
4½ yds. moreen, at 100 ds.	450
4 hdkfs., at 100 ds.	400
8 yds. quality binding, 4 ds.	32
1 skein of silk	10

$3,144

If paid in specie .... £18 10s."

The following scale of depreciation is also preserved:

"VALUE OF $100 IN SPECIE IN CONTINENTAL MONEY

	1777.	1778.	1779.	1780.	1781.
January	$105	$325	$742	$2934	$7400
February	107	350	868	3322	7500
March	109	370	1000	3736	0000" [41]

Perhaps we find it too easy to blame Congress for the bad money as for everything else. Mr. Charles J. Bullock estimates that there must have been at times as much as $300,000,-000 of paper money circulating among 3,000,000 people having no trade or commerce on a large scale, and he gives the money a total specie value of only $37,870,000,—"a tax of the most unjust and objectionable sort." Yet he adds:

"But whatever the loss, and whatever the injustice caused in this way, the fact remains that the issue of the paper money made possible the successful termination of the struggle undertaken against Great Britain. . . . 'How else could the war have been carried on?' Those writers who condemn *in toto* the issue of bills of credit, have generally fallen into the error of blaming Congress for not doing something that lay wholly beyond its powers. Thus Mr. Bronson, in asserting that taxation should have been instituted from the start, and that independence was won, not by paper money, but rather in spite of it, says, 'A firmer will, with a greater readiness to make sacrifices, would have opened a way.' But the 'greater readiness to make sacrifices' did not exist, and Mr. Bronson's criticism falls to the ground. Had 'a firmer will' been shown, had Congress attempted to levy taxes in 1775, the way would have been effectually closed, and not opened. Such a course would have occasioned a popular outcry that would have destroyed the authority of Congress, and rendered impossible the continuance of the war. But the experience of the country with the Continental bills of credit was sufficiently bitter to serve as an effectual lesson of the evils attending an irredeemable paper currency." [42]

Upon nobody else did the evils of bad money pray so heavily and so variously as on George Washington. He was a farmer, a landlord, a speculator in lands, a money-lender, a capitalist, a statesman, a recruiting-officer, and a general. Serving without pay or even the willingness to accept a reward, and for years without a sight of his home, he must keep up an army, decoy soldiers with false hopes of compensation, draw officers and men away from the temptations to speculate, persuade them to let their families suffer, and endeavor to provide them with breeches for their backsides, bread for their bellies, rum for their courage, and bullets for their guns. He wrote of public affairs that many people were actually doing what they could to delay peace:

"Speculation, Peculation, Engrossing, forestalling, with all their concomitants, afford too many melancholy proofs of the decay of public virtue, and too glaring instances of its being the interest and desire of too many, who would wish to be thought friends, to continue the war. Nothing, I am convinced, but the depreciation of our currency, proceeding in a great measure from the foregoing causes, aided by stockjobbing and party dissensions, has fed the hopes of the Enemy and kept the B. arms in America to this day. They do not scruple to declare this themselves, and add, that we shall be our own conquerors. Cannot our common country, Am^a, possess virtue enough to disappoint them? Is the paltry consideration of a little dirty pelf to individuals to be placed in competition with the essential rights and liberties of the present generation, and of millions yet unborn? Shall a few designing men, for their own aggrandizement, & to gratify their own avarice, overset the goodly fabric we have been rearing at the expense of so much time, blood, & treasure? And shall we at last become the victims of our own abominable lust of gain? Forbid it Heaven!" [43]

Of his own business and the bad behavior of one Davenport, with whose management of his tobacco he was discontent, he wrote:

"He & Hill has, I believe, divided the profits of my Estate on the York River, tolerably well betw^n them for the devil of any thing do I get; but why need I dwell upon or trouble myself much about trifles, when to speak within bounds, ten thousand pounds will not compensate the losses I might have avoided by being at home, & attending a little to my own concerns. . . . Alas! what is virtue come to—what a miserable change has four years produced in the temper & dispositions of the Sons of America! It really shocks me to think of it!" [44]

Again and again he denounces his countrymen's willingness to do almost anything "for the sake of a little dirty pelf." [45]

He writes of "the extinction of public spirit, the increasing rapacity of the times, . . . the declining zeal of the people, . . . the prevailing security and insensibility to danger, . . .

"If the enemy have it in their power to press us hard this campaign, I know not what may be the consequence. Our army, as it now stands, is but little more than the skeleton of an army; and I hear of no steps that are taking to give it strength and substance." [46]

And again:

"The cries of the distressed, of the fatherless and widows, come to me from all quarters. The States are not behind hand in making application for assistance, notwithstanding scarce any one of them, that I can find, is taking effectual measures to complete its quota of continental troops, or has even power, or energy enough to draw forth its militia. Each complains of neglect, because it gets not what it asks, and conceives that none others suffers like itself, because it is ignorant of what others experience, receiving the complaints of its own people *only*. I have a hard time of it, and a disagreeable task. To please everybody is impossible; were I to undertake it, I should probably please nobody . . . We now stand upon the brink of a precipice, from whence the smallest help casts us headlong. At this moment *our money does not pass.*" [47]

And again he writes that children are being recruited as substitutes for men and at an astounding premium:

"You may form a pretty good judgment of my prospect of a brilliant campaign, and of the figure I shall cut in it, when I inform you, that, excepting about 400 recruits from the State of Massachusetts (a portion of which I am told are children, hired at about 1500 dollars each for 9 months' service), I have had no reinforcement to this army since last campaign, while our numbers have been, and now are, diminishing daily by the expiring terms of men's services, to say nothing of the natural waste by sickness, death, and desertion." [48]

Such despondent notes are multiplied in his writings until one wonders what those historians could have read who dare assert that Washington's chief trait was his calmness under hardship and his immunity to despair. The chief of all his despairs would seem to be his despair of making the English language express his despair.

W. G. Sumner says of this particular season:

"In many respects the year 1779 marked the lowest ebb in politics and morals, as well as in finance, which was reached during the war. Congress was split up by factions and cabals. It seemed to have adopted, in respect to the currency, the recklessness of a hopeless bankrupt." [49]

But the sanest, though most cold-blooded, summing up of the situation is perhaps that of R. V. Harlow:

"It was a case of paper or nothing . . . To be sure, depreciated paper would inflict irreparable damage on some individuals, but what of it? . . . There is no more valid reason certainly for mourning over financial losses than over casualty lists . . . The rhapsodies of the Revolutionary leaders were morally no better than their financial experiments; perhaps they were just as inevitable . . . Enormous drafts on faith and hope—the bills were hardly more than that." [50]

XXXVI

DISSIPATION AND IDLENESS

"**T**HE pore Geneeral is not likely to come to see us,"
wrote Martha from Mount Vernon as the fourth winter of her husband's absence came on. Cold weather
always meant a long journey for Martha. Her bones were
better and better cushioned, but the roads were execrable and
she might well write to her brother with dread in November,
1778:

"I am very uneasy at this time—I have some reason to expect that I
shall take another trip to the northward—the pore Geneeral is not
likely to come to see us from what I can see hear—I expect to hear
seertainly by the next post . . . I cannot tell you more news than I
can I have had no letter since he came from the camp—by some neglect
of the post master my letters does not come regularly to hand. I am
with my Duty to my mamma my Love to my sister Aylett—my sister
and family and my dear Brother Your Eaver affectionate

M Washington" [1]

She reached Philadelphia before George, and on the 17th she
was honored with a grand ball at the City Tavern, the French
minister being one of the guests.[2] She must have recalled the
atrocious snub she had received when she passed through the
city in November, 1775, on her way to Boston. On that occasion the rebels planned a great ball in her honor, but it had to
be called off, not only because the better element would not
recognize her, but because the Puritans threatened to destroy
the building rather than permit an immoral dance to be held
there.[3] Now her husband was the friend and ally of the King
of France, and Lady Washington was the Queen of America.

On January 6th, 1779, George and Martha attended a ball

457

in honor of Benjamin Franklin's seventy-third birthday. Franklin's daughter, Mrs. Bache, wrote to her father:

"I have lately been several times invited abroad with the General and Mrs. Washington. He always inquires after you in the most affectionate manner, and speaks of you highly. We danced at Mrs. Powell's your birthday or night I should say, in company together, and he told me it was the anniversary of his marriage; it was just twenty years that night." [4]

Philadelphia was so extravagant at this time that when Mrs. Bache wrote to her father for a little extra money, he rebuked her—from Paris! On January 18th, Congress gave a banquet to the French minister. Washington was present, of course, and thirteen toasts were drunk with a roar of artillery after each. The number thirteen was being so much sanctified that the Tories ridiculed it:

"Thirteen is a number peculiarly belonging to the rebels. A party of naval prisoners lately returned from Jersey, say, that the rations among the rebels are thirteen dried clams per day; that the titular Lord Stirling takes thirteen glasses of grog every morning, has thirteen enormous rum-bunches on his nose, and that (when duly impregnated) he always makes thirteen attempts before he can walk; that Mr. Washington has thirteen toes on his feet, (the extra ones having grown since the Declaration of Independence,) and the same number of teeth in each jaw; . . . that Old Putnam had thirteen pounds of his posteriors bit off in an encounter with a Connecticut bear, ('twas then he lost the *balance* of his mind;) that it takes thirteen Congress paper dollars to equal one penny *sterling;* that Mrs. Washington has a mottled tom-cat, (which she calls, in a complimentary way, 'Hamilton,') with thirteen yellow rings around his tail, and that his flaunting it suggested to the Congress the adoption of the same number of stripes for the rebel flag." [5]

The Council of Pennsylvania with profound homage begged Washington to sit for his portrait while he was in town "that the contemplation of it may excite others to tread in the same glorious and disinterested steps." Washington modestly consented, "however conscious I am that your generous sensibility attributes infinitely too much to me." Charles Willson Peale painted the portrait and represented his subject at the battle of Princeton with the college buildings in the background. A Spanish agent, Don Juan Miralles, asked for five copies of it. He was in the country as a sort of glorified spy for his king, preparing for the entrance of Spain into the conflict. Two years later, for some mysterious reason, the portrait was assailed in lieu of the original, and the *Freeman's Journal* exclaimed:

"On Sunday the 9th. instant, *at night*, a fit time for the Sons of Lucifer to perpetrate the deeds of darkness, one or more volunteers in the service of hell, broke into the State House in Philadelphia, and totally defaced the picture of His Excellency General Washington, and a curious engraving of the monument of the patriotic General Montgomery, done in France in the most elegant manner. Every generous bosom must swell with indignation at such atrocious proceedings." [6]

Peale was able, however, to back the canvas with another and obliterate the obliterations. On his last day in Philadelphia, Washington yielded to John Jay's persuasion and called at the house of the French painter, Du Simitière, "& condescended with great good nature to Sit about ¾ of an hour." [7] From now on an increasingly large part of his life was devoted to the martyrdom of posing.

Philadelphia was trying to keep up its reputation for gaiety, vice and extravagance. The flight of the British and the return of the rebels had been followed by the compiling of a "Black List" of 490 persons charged with treason. Among those who did not flee were two prominent Quakers, Roberts and Carlisle, whose devotion to the British resulted in a sentence to death. Roberts' wife and children went literally on their knees to Congress, but leniency was refused. The two men died like Romans and were accounted martyrs. Mob-rule was so whimsical that even such strong whigs as Robert Morris, Mifflin and others narrowly escaped lynching for conduct that offended the rabble. In the Wyoming Valley about Wilkes-Barré there was ferocious civil war, with the loyalists in control and the

Indians adding grewsome touches. Still Philadelphia revelled. The gallants had planned to ostracize the ladies who had taken part in Howe's Meschianza but since this would have meant a shortage of dancing partners their disloyalty was over-looked.

The Pennsylvania Council had not been able to furnish shoes and clothes for the soldiers at Valley Forge and the army was still half-naked, but on December 1st, 1778, Joseph Reed's election as President of the Council was celebrated by a ban-quet costing over two thousand pounds and including "116 large bowls of punch, and 2 tubs of grog for artillery sol-diers. . . . 96 wine glasses and 5 decanters were broke." [8] The vice, extravagance and greed, the gambling in cards and in supplies while the army suffered and hungered and the officers endured every privation are vividly described in a letter writ-ten to Dr. McHenry at this time:

"My half years pay was spent on my Journey home. I was laughed at for my parsimony. I was mistaken it cost me 50 Dr. more . . . what think you of J. M'Lure betting 200 D. on the throw of a Die. one thousand Dolls. to lose or win in a Night is peddling.—The con-sequence of this will be very soon felt by the Army . . . Congress feels not for us, our Countrymen will soon avoid us, . . . lest we should want to borrow their Money from them. I cannot bear to resign & yet what Can I do. my Fathers opulent fortune is reduced to Nothing, it was chiefly in cash. exclusive of my Love for my Country & the Service, my attachment to his Excell^y makes me wish to remain & nothing but dire necessity Shall make me resign." [9]

Tench Tilghman wrote to "Dear Mac" from Philadelphia in January:

"A morning visit, a dinner at 5 o'clock—Tea at 8 or 9—supper and up all night is the round *die in diem*. Does not the Republic go on charmingly? By the Body of my father as honest Sancho used to swear, we have advanced as far in luxury in the third year of our In-depen^y as the old musty Republics of Greece and Rome did in twice as many hundreds." [10]

Greene had this to say of the capital:

"I dined at one table where there were an hundred and sixty dishes; and at several others not far behind. The growing avarice and a declining currency are poor materials to build an independence upon." [11]

In the camps, too, there was merriment, and all-night dancing. At Middlebrook the Reverend General Muhlenberg gave a banquet and ball attended by a great number of ladies. "And not one of the company was permitted to retire till three o'clock in the morning. Thus have the gallant Virginians commenced the new year." [12]

On February 2nd, 1778, Washington and Martha set out for Middlebrook. Washington's birthday was celebrated at camp, but still more vigorously in Virginia at the college of William and Mary where the students prepared a subscription paper for the festivities on February 22nd. The civil war that ensued is picturesquely described in the diary of a student. Governor Henry refused permission, saying that he "could not think of any kind of rejoicing at a time when our country was engaged in war, with such gloomy prospects." A grand ball was given, nevertheless, at the Raleigh tavern. To add to the éclat two cannon left unguarded were dragged to the Raleigh. A lieutenant with a platoon demanded them back. He was carried in and accepted some punch, but repeated that he had orders to take the pieces by force if necessary. When Colonel Innis and others declined to give them up, he reported to his Captain Digges, who appealed to Patrick Henry, who told him to use his own judgment. Thereupon

"In the pride of his power, with sixty men, he drew up in form; and demanded the cannon at the point of his bayonet! Innis stept up to Captain Digges, and shaking his cane at him, swore that he would *cane him*, if he did not depart instantly with his men! This enraging Digges—he said that if the pieces were not surrendered he *would fire upon the party. Innis repeating* his *threat*, ordered Finnie to charge the cannon with *brick bats:* the mob in the street, and the gentlemen of the ball, re-echoing the order. The pieces were soon charged with brick bats: Innis all the while firmly standing by the Captain at the head of his men, *daring him to fire!* After some delay, the Captain retreated with his men; and the evening closed with great joy."

The next day Colonel Innis was arraigned before the Hustings Court for riot and confronted by the valiant Captain Digges. Again the Colonel threatened to cane the captain, but he was released and walked out triumphantly with the "friends, who had shared the honors of the preceding night." [13]

The chief glory of February, however, was a celebration at Pluckemin of the anniversary of the French alliance, postponed to the 18th on account of Washington's absence. General Knox and his artillery were the hosts. There was the usual cannonade, also a banquet, fireworks and a grand ball. The fireworks were displayed in a temple one hundred feet long with thirteen arches, paintings, "allegoric of the progress of our empire." The banquet hall with tables removed "left a range for about thirty couple to foot it to no indifferent measure," according to a correspondent of the Philadelphia *Packet*, who goes on:

"The ball was opened by his excellency the general. When this man unbends from his station, and its weighty functions, he is even then like a philosopher, who mixes with the amusements of the world, that he may teach it what is right, or turn its trifles into instruction." [14]

General Knox wrote of this affair with pride:

"A most genteel entertainment given by self and officers. Everybody allowed it to be the first of the kind ever exhibited in this State at least. We had about seventy ladies, all of the first *ton* in the State, and between three and four hundred gentlemen. We danced all night,—an elegant room. The illuminating, fireworks, &c., were more than pretty. It was to celebrate the alliance between France and America." [15]

He does not mention, but Dr. Thacher does, that Washington had "for his partner the lady of General Knox." [16] The contrast the tall Washington must have made with Mrs. Knox as his partner is revealed in a letter Greene wrote to his wife. As a girl Lucy Flucker had been a belle, but she and her husband grew as rotund as their own mortars. Greene wrote to his wife of Mrs. Knox:

"She is fatter than ever, which is a great mortification to her. The General is equally fat, and therefore one cannot laugh at the other.

They appear to be extravagantly fond of each other; and, I think, are perfectly happy." [17]

Perhaps this harping on Mrs. Knox's figure was to atone for a letter Greene had written to his wife in 1777 when he instructed her to write to Mrs. Knox about buying her some clothes for which Greene was to pay Knox at camp. Greene cautioned her:

"Remember when you write to Mrs. Knox you write to a good scholar, therefore mind and spell well; you are defective in this matter, my love; a little attention will soon correct it. Bad writing is nothing, if the spelling is but good. People are often laughed at for not spelling well, but never for not writing well. It is said it is ungenteel for gentlemen to make observations upon ladies' writing. I hope you won't think it unkind in me. Nothing but the affection and regard I feel for you makes me wish to have you appear an accomplished lady in every point of view." [18]

In this same letter he had suggested naming the new baby "Martha Washington," as their first had been named George Washington. Mrs. Greene was with him in camp at Morristown and the mother of George and Martha Greene did her share magnificently in making General Washington forget his troubles for a while.

With her help, Washington performed a feat of endurance perhaps never equalled until of late when the dance-Marathons have shown what human strength can attain. To have danced for three hours and more without rest was an achievement even for a Washington. General Greene is himself the authority for the athletic feat:

"His Excellency and Mrs. Greene danced upwards of three hours without once sitting down. Upon the whole we had a pretty little frisk." [19]

Martha apparently had grown too fat to dance and Greene had the asthma all his life, so they probably sat it out. Surgeon Thacher describes Washington at this time, having "had the honor of being numbered among the guests at the table of his

Excellency, with his lady, two young ladies from Virginia, the gentlemen who compose his family, and several other officers. . . .

"He is feared even when silent, and beloved even while we are unconscious of the motive. . . . In conversation, his Excellency's expressive countenance is peculiarly interesting and pleasing; a placid smile is frequently observed on his lips, but a loud laugh, it is said, seldom if ever escapes him. . . . Mrs. Washington combines in an uncommon degree, great dignity of manner with the most pleasing affability, but possesses no striking marks of beauty. I learn from the Virginia officers, that Mrs. Washington has ever been honored as a lady of distinguished goodness, possessing all the virtues which adorn her sex, amiable in her temper and deportment, full of benignity, benevolence and charity, seeking for objects of affliction and poverty, that she may extend to the sufferers the hand of kindness and relief." [20]

The mildness of the season was such that after January 10th there was no severe weather, and at the beginning of April "the fruit trees were budded on the 1st, and in full blossom on the 10th." The spring indolence and gaiety made a sharp contrast with the winter before at Valley Forge. There would hardly have been a hint that war still raged if it had not been for the typical hangings of deserters. Thacher sandwiches a morose scene between festivals. One day the crowd gathers to see five men in a cart, and sitting on their coffins with halters about their necks. At the last moment, Washington pardons three of them. The other two are hanged, the brother of one of them clinging to him in wild grief, embracing and kissing till torn asunder. A few days later thirteen cannon greet the French minister and the Spaniard whom Thacher calls "Mirilliars." There is a gorgeous review with ladies on a stage to watch. Washington "on his noble bay charger" was "incomparably more majestic" than the foreigners. Later Washington gives equal hospitality to a number of Indian chiefs.[21]

Martha wrote of this:

"Yesterday I saw the funniest, at the same time the most ridiculous review of the troops I ever heard of. Nearly all the troops were drawn up in order, and Mrs. Knox, Mrs. Greene, and myself saw the whole performance from a carriage. The General and Billy, followed by a lot of mounted savages, rode along the line. Some of the Indians were fairly fine-looking, but most of them appeared worse than Falstaff's gang. And such horses and trappings! The General says it was done to keep the Indians friendly towards us. They appeared like cutthroats, all." [22]

There was a new Indian war on—or, rather, the eternal Indian war was flaring higher. Incidentally, the private soldiers were muttering, and the first of those mutinies began that were to grow and grow until they threatened to wreck the republic and make Congress a victim of its own soldiers. Washington was not sympathetic with the money troubles of the privates:

"The depreciation of our Currency and the advance of necessaries are made the ostensible reasons for these disturbances. These are evils which are felt by all, but by none less than the common soldier who is intirely fed and chiefly cloathed by the public." [23]

He was indignant when the New Jersey legislature yielded to the demands of their troops and granted £200 to each officer and $40 to each soldier to enable them to pay their debts before beginning a campaign:

"All that the common soldiery of any country can expect is food and cloathing. . . . The idea of maintaining the families of the soldiers at the public expense is peculiar to us, and is incompatible with the finances of any government. Our troops have been uniformly better fed than any others. They are at this time very well clad, and probably will continue to be so." [24]

His advice for the treatment of a mutiny was given in a letter to Putnam, whom he had the unusual privilege of praising:

"To use every means for discovering the Authors of the mischief —to inflict instant punishment on them and reclaim the rest by Clemency. The impression made on the minds of the multitude by the terror of the example—and their inability to take any resolution when deprived of their Ring leaders—are a sufficient security against farther attempts." [25]

He wrote to Sullivan questioning the wisdom of General Varnum who "quelled the Rioters by fair words." He doubted their value in a serious case. He was to acquire more and more acquaintance with mutinies. He had one to deal with now—a mutinous major-general. Edward Rutledge had written to Washington from Charleston, South Carolina, on December 18th, 1778:

"If report, and loud report too, is to be credited, that spirit of cabal and destructive ambition, which has elevated the factious demagogue in every republic of antiquity, is making great head in the centre of these States; and, if not soon extinguished, will do more essential injury to the cause of America than the swords of Sir Harry and his whole army." [26]

A week later Rutledge wrote to John Jay:

"It is Christmas-day, and . . . I have time to tell you . . . that a damned infamous cabal is forming against our commander-in-chief, and that whenever they shall find themselves strong enough they will strike an important blow . . . Conway, the * * * *, and * * * * * * * are said to be at the bottom of this, besides an abundance of snakes that are concealed in the grass." [27]

In March, 1779, William Tudor made a speech in Boston that was supposed to be an effort to revive the opposition to Washington, for whom he had no military respect.[28] In March, Dr. Benjamin Rush wrote to Gates mentioning the retirement of Charles Lee and Mifflin and advising him to retire also to save himself from persecution.[29] Early in April, John Jay sent to Washington an extract from Gates' letter to Congress in which he spoke slightingly of Washington's alleged plan of attacking Canada and said that one letter of February 14th, 1779, was the only letter Washington had sent him since December.[30]

This shook Washington out of his policy of silence and he sent his entire correspondence with Gates to Jay as an example of "the artifices employed by some men to prejudice me in the public esteem." He told how he and Gates disagreed over the preparation for the Canadian expedition, how he had always said that it was impracticable while the British had armies in New York and Rhode Island; and how Gates pretended that Washington favored the expedition:

"From the beginning of last campaign to the middle of December, about seven months, I have copies of near fifty letters to him, and about forty originals from him. I think it will be acknowledged, that the correspondence was frequent enough during that period; . . . I have no great temptation to court his correspondence, when the transacting of public business does not require it. An air of design, a want of candor in many instances, and even of politeness, give no very inviting complexion to the correspondence on his part. As a specimen of this, I send you a few letters and extracts, which, at your leisure, I should be glad that you would cast your eye upon."

He told how politely he offered Gates the command of the important posts on the Hudson River, and what "evasive" and "extraordinary" replies he had. He reviewed the "direct breach" of the Conway cabal:

"After this affair subsided, I made a point of treating Gen. Gates with all the attention and cordiality in my power, as well from a sincere desire of harmony, as from an unwillingness to give any cause of triumph to our enemies, from an appearance of dissension among ourselves. I can appeal to the world, and to the whole army, whether I have not cautiously avoided every word or hint, that could tend to disparage Gen. Gates in any way. I am sorry his conduct to me has not been equally generous, and that he is continually giving me fresh proofs of malevolence and opposition. It will not be doing him injustice to say, that, besides the little, underhand intrigues which he is frequently practising, there has hardly been any great military question, in which his advice has been asked, that it has not been given in an equivocal and designing manner, apparently calculated to afford him an opportunity of censuring me, on the failure of whatever measures might be adopted. . . . I shall still be as passive as a regard to my own character will permit. I am, however, uneasy, as General G. has endeavored to impress Congress with an unfavorable idea of me; and, as I only know this in a private, confidential way, that I cannot take any step to remove the impression, if it should be made." [31]

To this Jay answered that Congress paid no heed to Gates' criticisms, and added:

"I have perused the several papers with which you favoured me. The delicacy, candour, and temper diffused through your letters form a strong contrast to the evasions and design observable in some others. Gratitude ought to have attached a certain gentleman to the friend who raised him; a spurious ambition, however, has, it seems, made him your enemy." [32]

In the words, "I shall still be as passive as a regard to my own character will permit," Washington shows one secret of his great strength. He let his detractors wear themselves out on his unresisting fame until the cabal began to disintegrate and on June 9th, 1779, Congressman Lovell wrote to Gates that R. H. Lee was leaving Congress, after a storm of unpopularity, and that Samuel Adams was about to resign. Feeling evidently lonesome, Lovell sighs:

"I wish you was Governor of Nova Scotia, and I a farmer." [33]

Late in May Martha left camp, or as Washington put it:

"Mrs. Washington, according to custom, marched home when the campaign was about to open." [34]

But she might as well have remained, for all the fighting her husband saw. There was no campaign. He had nothing to open one with. Martha's place was taken by occasional visitors. When he invited the surgeon-general and his wife to dinner at West Point, he wrote the following amiable warning:

"Dr. Doct!, I have asked Mrs. Cochran & Livingston to dine with me to-morrow; but am I not in honor bound to apprize them of their fare? As I hate deception, even where the imagination only is concerned; I will. It is needless to premise, that my table is large enough to hold the ladies. Of this they had ocular proof yesterday. To say how it is usually covered, is rather more essential; and this shall be the purport of my Letter.

"Since our arrival at this happy spot, we have had a ham, (sometimes a shoulder) of Bacon, to grace the head of the Table; a piece of roast Beef adorns the foot; and a dish of beans, or greens, (almost imperceptible,) decorates the center. When the cook has a mind to cut a figure, (which I presume will be the case to-morrow,) we have two

Beef-steak pyes, or dishes of crabs, in addition, one on each side the center dish, dividing the space & reducing the distance between dish & dish to about 6 feet, which without them would be near 12 feet apart. Of late he has had the surprising sagacity to discover, that apples will make pyes; and its a question, if, in the violence of his efforts, we do not get one of apples, instead of having both of Beef-steaks. If the ladies can put up with such entertainment, and will submit to partake of it on plates, once Tin but now Iron—(not become so by the labor of scouring), I shall be happy to see them." [35]

Another intimate touch is found in a note to Quartermaster Greene:

"Dear sir, I have lost—and cannot tell how—an old and favorite pen-knife, and am much distressed for want of one—if you have any in your stores, please send me one—if you have not, be so good as to get one immediately. Perhaps Mr. Bailey could furnish me. One with two blades I should prefer, when choice can be had." [36]

XXXVII

INEFFECTIVE GESTURES

"OUR cause is just, our counsels are firm and decided, and we trust that the zealous and able exertions of our officers will, under the Divine favour, be crowned with success." [1]

This was not Congress proclaiming piously. It was Lord George Germain haranguing Sir Henry Clinton. But the only divine favor Clinton pleaded for was this:

"For God's sake, my Lord, if you wish me to do anything, leave me to myself, and let me adapt my efforts to the hourly change of Circumstances." [2]

Lord George and King George had contrived a great Plan for 1779. It centered in the destruction of General George, whom Clinton was urged to bring to a "decisive action" or drive into the highlands so as to leave the inhabitants to follow "their inclinations and renounce the authority of the Congress, and return to their allegiance to His Majesty." [3]

To this Clinton wearily replied:

"To force Washington to an action upon Terms tolerably equal has been the object of every Campaign during the War, the difficulty of attaining that object in so strong a Country even with the Force Sir William Howe had by this time needs no illustration. Washington has at this Instant 8,000 Continental Troops in Jersey besides Militia."

Clinton could not agree with Germain's opinion that he could drive Washington to the mountains with what troops he had. He rather hoped to draw him forward "by indirect Manouvres" and to "strike at him whilst he is in motion." [4] Henry P. Johnston thought that Washington never understood Clinton's real plan and that "what he thought to be Clinton's chief aim was never seriously contemplated by the British gen-

470

eral." [5] In the spring Clinton sent General Matthews with ships and men to Virginia where they did much burning and looting and ship-destroying to encourage the lovers of His Majesty. On June 1st, 1779, Clinton captured King's Ferry on the Hudson river between Stony Point and Verplanck's Point, thirteen miles below West Point, hoping that Washington would leave Middlebrook, whereupon Clinton would seize his camp there and fight him as he tried to recover it. Washington regretted the loss of King's Ferry deeply since it robbed him of his easiest route of supplies. But he felt unequal to the task of regaining it. And Clinton felt unequal to the task of attacking Middlebrook, since the men he counted on did not come. He wrote:

"July, and no reinforcements arrived; . . . Good God! what could prevent the troops sailing in March or even April!" [6]

The explanation was a French fleet in the English Channel, reducing Clinton to Washingtonian immobility:

"Not a word from Europe these three months, not a farthing of money, no information, no *army*, nothing but good spirits and a presentiment that all will go well, a determination at least that nothing shall be wanting on my part; and I sincerely hope this will be the last campaign of the war—it must be mine." [7]

July 4th was a busy day. In honor of it, Washington pardoned all prisoners under sentence of death. In Philadelphia the 4th being a Sunday, Congress and the Pennsylvania Council and a great number of men and women attended Mass at the Roman Chapel in response to an invitation by the French minister to hear a Te Deum in celebration of the Declaration of Independence. This caused a shudder of horror to run through the Protestant element, to whom the British leniency toward Catholics in the Quebec Act had been one of the chief causes for the Revolution. And now the rebels and the Catholics were allies! And England was removing Catholic disabilities in order to recruit Irish soldiers against the rebels.

On July 3rd, Clinton sent out an expedition under Governor Tryon. On July 5th he sacked New Haven and, meeting with some resistance from militia, Yale students, and others, did more damage than he had planned.

But Clinton's purpose had been solely the decoying of Washington into Connecticut. He groaned:

"Nothing, however, could withdraw him from New Windsor." [8]

Washington began to feel in the air a general discontent with his indolence. Yet he dared not risk his little army. He would never get another, and could hardly keep this. Accident and a keen scout's observation brought him what he longed for. It chanced that on July 2nd, 1779, he sent Allen McLane to escort a Mrs. Smith through the lines with a flag to see her sons; and McLane kept his eyes open. He saw that the British had not finished their fortification of Stony Point and he got word at once to Washington.[9] On the night of July 6th, Washington reconnoitred the works himself through his spy glass. It occurred to him that he might give the dismal public another electrifying shock such as they had from the capture of the Hessians at Trenton. On July 9th he wrote to Anthony Wayne:

"While the enemy are making excursions to distress the country, it has a very disagreeable aspect to remain in a state of inactivity on our part. The reputation of the army, and the good of the service, seem to exact some attempt from it. The importance of Stony Point to the enemy makes it infinitely desirable, that this post could be the object. The works are formidable, but perhaps on a fuller examination they may be found accessible. A deserter yesterday informed me, that there was a sandy beach on the south side, running along the flank of the works, and only obstructed by a slight *abatis*, which might afford an easy and safe approach to a body of troops.

"I wish you to take every step in your power to ascertain this, and to gain a more accurate knowledge of the position in general, and particularly on the flanks and in the rear. Would it answer to send in a trusty, intelligent fellow from you in the character of a deserter, on some plan that might enable him to return with expedition? I beg you to inform yourself all you can, and to give me your opinion of the practicability of an attempt upon this post. If it is undertaken, I should conceive it ought to be done by way of surprise in the night." [10]

Wayne was always enthusiastic for action and Washington drew up for him most minute instructions of admirable imagination and skill:

"My ideas of the Enterprise in contemplation are these: that it should be attempted by the Light Infantry only, which should march under cover of night and with the utmost secrecy to the Enemy's lines, securing every person they find, to prevent discovery. Between one and two hundred chosen men and officers I conceive fully sufficient for the surprize; and apprehend the approach should be along the Water on the South side, crossing the Beach and entering at the *abatis*. This party is to be preceded by a Vanguard of prudent and determined men, well commanded, who are to remove obstructions, secure the sentries, and drive in the guards. They are to advance the whole of them with fixed Bayonets and muskets unloaded. The officers commanding them are to know precisely what Batteries, or particular parts of the line, they are respectively to possess, that confusion and the consequences of indecision may be avoided . . . A white feather, or cockade, or some other visible badge of distinction for the night, should be worn by our Troops, and a Watchword agreed on to distinguish friends from Foes . . .

"Secrecy is so much more essential to these kind of enterprises, than numbers, that I should not think it advisable to employ any other than the light troops. If a surprize takes place, they are fully competent to the business; if it does not, numbers will avail little . . . A knowledge of your intention, ten minutes previously obtained, will blast all your hopes; . . . These are my general ideas of the plan for a surprize; but you are at liberty to depart from them in every instance, where you may think they may be improved, or changed for the better. A Dark night, and even a rainy one, (if you can find the way,) will contribute to your success." [11]

He planned also to capture Verplanck's Point opposite in a simultaneous attack.

During the anxious days of preparation he learned of Tryon's raid. Impatiently he gave Wayne the word to attack and on the night of July 15th, 1779, Wayne carried out his orders with brilliant enhancements. His attack deserves all its fame. The British lost 63 killed and 543 prisoners, the fort, the artillery and the stores. Washington in writing to Congress praised Wayne handsomely, saying: "He improved upon the plan recommended by me, and executed it in a manner that does signal honor to his judgment and to his bravery." [12]

Owing to a complex confusion the attack on Verplanck's Point was not carried out. As at Trenton, only part of Washington's troops got into the action. Yet the capture, like the Trenton raid, was just what America needed as a pick-me-up to its pride. That was all it was, however, since, on the hasty approach of Clinton, Washington had to abandon his prize. For the comfort of the public he pretended that he had not expected to hold it, yet he wrote to ask Wayne if he thought it would be worth while to try to repeat the performance:

"I shall certainly not undertake anything (capital) without your knowledge—I wish for your opinion as a friend—not as a commanding officer of the light Troops—whether another attempt upon Stoney point, by way of surprize, is eligible—(In any other manner under present appearances, and information, no good, I am sure, can result from it)." [13]

Somehow Washington managed as a rule to draw glory from defeat and even the English king was as much puzzled by his avoidance of a battle as by his success in the raid.[14] But Clinton despaired and sent in his resignation, recommending Cornwallis as his successor. He did not like Cornwallis. The King refused.

Encouraged perhaps by the public rejoicing over the brief exploit against Stony Point, Washington cast about for another dramatic blow. His eyes fell on the peninsula across the river from New York where Jersey City now stands. It was then known as Paulus Hook—which Washington spelled "Powles Hook" or "Paules hook (within cannon-shott of the City of New York.)" [15] It had a garrison of two hundred men and he felt that a dash against it would be dramatic.

He talked to Major Henry Lee and asked him to look into the matter, warning him that "a few minutes delay" might expose him to capture. Lee had been with Wayne at Stony Point but only as a spectator in the reserve. He leapt at this opportunity, worked out his plan, submitted it and was told to go ahead. Everything went wrong as usual; half of the Virginians assigned to Lee refused to go with him because their officer was his superior in rank; a guide misled and lost part of the others, and the attack scheduled for midnight was begun at four in the morning of August 19th, 1779.

But Harry Lee was one of the geniuses who conquer the obstacles within as well as without, and he pressed forward over a marsh to the attack. Instead of taking away the flints of the muskets, he had them carried "with pans open, cocks fallen." Without a musket fired, though under heavy fire, he captured all the garrison except forty-odd Hessians who reached a stronghold, which he dared not delay to besiege. The alarm guns were booming in New York and dawn was breaking when he escaped with a hundred and fifty-cight prisoners, leaving fifty bayoneted to death. His own loss was two killed and three wounded. He could not bring off the artillery. The escape, indeed, was almost more brilliant than the surprise. In his report to Washington, he mentions that "self-preservation strongly dictated, on the retreat, the putting the prisoners to death, and British cruelty fully justified it; notwithstanding which, not a man was wantonly hurt." He did not set the barracks on fire as he planned, since they contained sick soldiers, women and children. He sent to Washington the flag of the fort.[16]

The Virginia officers who had refused to share the danger had Lee put under arrest and court-martialed. When he appealed to Washington to put in writing the minute verbal instructions he had given, it was proved to be Washington's own plan. So Lee was acquitted with honor and Congress awarded him a gold medal.[17]

Only disgrace and defeat were the rewards of an independent naval expedition that Massachusetts sent out against an unfinished fort at Penobscot. An English fleet arrived in the midst of the assault and ten Boston ships were captured or sunk. The fugitives wandered through a pathless wilderness for a hundred miles, many perishing of privation. The soldiers and sailors fell to quarreling and then to battle and fifty or sixty were killed in the mutual slaughter.[18]

The French fleet returned to raise more high hopes and crush them. D'Estaing appeared suddenly on the Southern coast and concerted an attack on the British in Savannah. His 3,500 troops joined 600 Continentals (including Pulaski's Legion) and 250 militia, in an assault on October 9th, 1779. The British, forewarned by a traitor, repulsed the attack, and Pulaski was mortally wounded. D'Estaing then sailed away, fearing both the British fleets and the approaching storms.

Washington had been led by Gérard to expect a cooperation with d'Estaing that would make possible his old dream of an attack on New York. He made his plans, wrote to the states to call out every man, sent to d'Estaing a number of suggestions for concerted assault.[19]

Clinton learned of this secret at once and prepared himself for a great battle by calling to himself all the troops in Rhode Island, abandoning ground that had been in British hands for nearly three years. He evacuated Stony Point as well. But d'Estaing did not appear and Washington had to cancel all his plans, all his hopes of honoring the year with something effective.

XXXVIII

THE WARS WITHIN THE WAR

DISGUSTING as the military inanition was to Washington, the people had grown used to it and to his complaints. They decided that England could never win in any case, and began to make such grandiose plans for what they would do after the war was over, that they could not be bothered to finish it.

The states were already imperialists before they were yet confederated. Washington frequently used the word "empire" and never took his eyes off the great West. During 1778 and 1779 he found time to write to Virginia and make inquiry as to those lands that had been granted to him and his brother officers in 1763. He had bought up the claims of other officers and he was impatient for a perfect title.[1]

The French minister Gérard found himself regarded less and less as a visiting angel and more and more as a dangerous rival, because he wanted to know what terms the states would accept in case England sued for peace. There was no modesty in the demands of the bankrupt states; they wanted room for unlimited expansion. They were even insisting on the right to fish on the coasts of Newfoundland. Independence was first, of course. As to the northern boundary, Congress still hoped to conquer Canada, but France was set against it and Washington had given up his feeling that it was either essential or possible. Europe wanted the young republic to end at the Alleghany mountains. The smaller and less ambitious states, Rhode Island, New Jersey and Delaware, were willing, but the other states would listen to no boundary east of the Mississippi river, and that free to navigation, with a free port below. Gérard, eager to hasten peace, pleaded with Congress

477

to give up the fishery rights and the Mississippi navigation. Congress yielded Newfoundland, but sent John Jay to Spain to bring that country round. He had a woeful time and suffered deep humiliation.

In the meanwhile Patrick Henry had written to Washington that if he acted at once, the two British posts on the lower Mississippi could be conquered by a mere four hundred men, and a claim made good to Western Florida; but Washington had no men and Congress paid no heed.[2] Consequently the way was left open for Spain, when she declared war on England, to seize those two posts herself, and claim all of Florida for her own. Furthermore, her king would not even recognize the independence of the colonies. A fine ally! Yet Congress consented to let Spain have Florida in return for free navigation of the Mississippi. To a most grandiose resolution addressed to "his Catholick Majesty" of Spain, who was allying himself to "his Most Christian Majesty" of France, the United States of America added the pathetic words:

"The distressed State of our Finances, and the great depreciation of our paper Money incline Congress to hope that his Catholic Majesty, if he shall conclude a Treaty with these States, will be induced to lend them money."[3]

Virginia all the while was acting like a separate nation whose western boundary was the Pacific Ocean. When Washington had written "Where is Mason—Wythe—Jefferson?" and complained that they were not in Congress, he did not know that they had been secretly managing a tremendous thing for the country's future without asking his aid or even letting him into the great conspiracy.

It is not often that such majestic results flow from deeds so crookedly managed. A militia major named George Rogers Clark had come back from Kentucky to Governor Henry and reported that spies he had sent out brought news of the withdrawal of all British troops from the Kaskaskia region below St. Louis on the Mississippi river. Clark urged that if he could get a few men and some money he could capture the

Illinois country and probably work his way round even to Detroit, in the meanwhile winning over the French settlers, cowing the Indians and accomplishing other strategical miracles toward removing the menaces against the western frontier.

Far-sighted Patrick Henry was so thrilled that he called Jefferson, Mason and Wythe into conference and won them over. They were afraid to let the legislature know of the plan, though its authority was necessary. So they drew up a blind bill authorizing the governor to use the militia "to act with any troops on an expedition that may be undertaken against any of our western enemies." The legislature, innocently supposing that this meant some vague foray against the Indians, passed the bill, and enlistments were begun under the personal pledge of the conspirators that a bounty of three hundred acres of land would be secured for each soldier.[4]

The expedition was Clark's idea, but Patrick Henry's acceptance of it and embellishment of it revealed high statesmanship as an empire-builder for Virginia. Secret authority of the widest scope was given to Clark along with twelve hundred pounds in depreciated currency, and he gathered an army of 175 men ostensibly for the relief of Kentucky. Not till he was well on his way did he let his soldiers know whither they were bound. Nothing could be more picturesque than his stealthy approach to Kaskaskia, his diplomacy with the French settlers and his subsequent expedition against Vincennes, the days of amphibious life in ice water and marshlands, and the manner in which he bluffed into surrender a garrison far outnumbering his little band. An extra prize was the person of Henry Hamilton, the British governor of Detroit, who happened to be at Vincennes. Clark wanted to push on to Detroit but the task was beyond his resources. He sent Hamilton to Virginia, where he was badly treated because his enthusiasm for collecting white scalps had won him the grim name, "Hamilton the Hair Buyer." He had surrendered under a capitulation, but treaties were poor protection for American captives and one of Burgoyne's officers, General Phillips, now in Virginia despite the terms of Burgoyne's Convention, appealed to Jefferson against barbarity. Jefferson, who had succeeded Henry as governor of Virginia, appealed to Washington for advice.

Washington answered evasively. He felt that Hamilton deserved rough handling as a "just retaliation," but also felt that the practice of war might not justify all the measures taken against him. Still, he said: "I should not hesitate to withhold from him a thousand privileges I might allow to common prisoners." In case it was thought expedient "to satisfy our people" by rigorous treatment, he advised the publication of Hamilton's cruelties "that the World, holding his conduct in abhorrence, may feel and approve the justice of his fate." [5] Later he besought milder treatment for Hamilton in view of the greater leniency of the British under Clinton toward American prisoners, whose exchange was still a matter of quarrel and delay.[6]

Clark's expedition was one of the most influential deeds in American history and geography. It cast into humiliating shade the futile efforts made by the officers Washington had sent to Pittsburg: General Hand and his successor, General MacIntosh, both of whom were unable to accomplish anything to the westward.

Washington seems to have known nothing of Clark's adventure until after the news of his capture of Kaskaskia reached Virginia in November, 1778. He saw the importance of it at once and planned new work for Clark. Virginia promptly established the county of Illinois as a colony of her own. An election was held for judges, and one of the first cases was that of a slave who was condemned for witchcraft and burned alive in June, 1779.[7] Land jobbery, feuds over titles, desertions, difficulties with depreciated money, drunkenness, Indian massacres, high prices and all the other evidences of assimilation with the United States were soon as characteristic of Illinois as of the rest of the nation.

Virginia's pretensions to all this land as well as to other territory excited the wrath of other states and delayed the ratifying of the Articles of Confederation. It was not until 1780 that Virginia relinquished Pittsburgh to Pennsylvania; the boundary lines were not agreed on until 1785. Maryland held out against the Western claims of Virginia until they were surrendered.

Washington was still embarrassed by the civil war in the northeast and the persistent declarations of independence and defiance issued by the New Hampshire Grants, whose complex position was described in a Resolution of Congress offering arbitration:

"Whereas disputes at present subsist between the states of New Hampshire, Massachusetts Bay, and New York, on the one part, and the people of a district called New Hampshire Grants, on the other, which people deny the jurisdiction of each of the said states over the said district, and each of the said states claim the said district against each other as well as against the said people." [8]

Ethan Allen and his Green Mountain Boys have retained a position of reverence in American schoolbook history, but they were a menace to the union throughout the war.[9] Washington had no desire to lead an expedition against them, especially not against such indomitable fighters as Stark had led against Burgoyne but New York state was eager and willing to war upon them.

How gravely the Green Mountain Boys compromised Washington's plans is shown in a letter from Governor Clinton, written on June 7th, 1779, complaining that Congress would do nothing against Ethan Allen and the other "revolted citizens" of New York, who had "seized & imprisoned the principal civil & military officers" of New York in that territory, driving New York to "the cruel dilemma" of "opposing force to force" on "the great principle of self preservation." Quaint and petty as it seems now to read of New York dropping out of the Revolution to crush Vermont and denouncing the rebellious colony in the very terms of England denouncing ungrateful Massachusetts, it was serious for Washington;

since Clinton's letter meant that New York could not keep up her quota of troops, might have to confiscate much-needed flour and might not contribute men for the Western expedition. In addition to all this, he reminded Washington of an old loan:

"I have therefore to request that your Excellency will be pleased to give the necessary Directions for returning within the State the six brass six Pounders together with their apparatus which the State lent for the use of the Army in 1776 or that in case of loss, you will order them to be replaced as soon as possible." [10]

On Washington these appalling feuds, wars within wars, and plots having the effect if not the purpose of treason, were all concentrated, for he stood forth alone as the man who must somehow keep all these wildcats from mutual destruction and divert a little of their ferocity towards inflicting harm on the common enemy.

Yet another interstate wrangle showed its baleful effects. An old war between Connecticut and Pennsylvania had brought about a condition that enabled the Tories and Indians to set up a reign of terror along frontiers no farther west than Wilkes-Barré, Pennsylvania, and central New York. About Wilkes-Barré was the Wyoming Valley where a Connecticut land company had established a colony of her citizens and defied a rival colony of Pennsylvanians. In 1769 the two colonies had begun the "Pennamite-Yankee War" and kept it up until the victory of the Connecticut men under Colonel Zebulon Butler in December, 1775.

During the Revolution, Connecticut, like a mother country, had called all her able-bodied colonists home from Wyoming Valley to fill her own quotas, leaving only old men, women and children to hold her territory. Pennsylvania was the most Tory of all the states and the loyalist elements in Wyoming combined with the Indians and British to oust the rebel Yankees. Colonel Zebulon Butler appealed to Washington in vain for troops and on July 3rd, 1778, marched out a small body of men to meet a large force under the Tory, Colonel

John Butler. The result was a crushing defeat for the patriots and the usual Indian atrocities toward the captives, the usual desolation.

The most frightful stories were told and enhanced by propagandists into such fiendishness that the name of Colonel John Butler has been a synonym for demon, a "Christian cannibal," ever since. The Indian chief Brant was joined in detestation, though he was not present.[11] But even in John Marshall's time, the exaggeration of these tales of horror was recognized in the revision of his biography of Washington.[12] Colonel John Butler's own reports show that he was horrified by such Indian cruelty as he witnessed in the battle and withdrew his forces as soon as possible to prevent further excesses. Nevertheless, the people were homeless and calling for protection and revenge.[13] In November, 1778, the village of Cherry Valley in New York was also destroyed by Tories and Indians. But it was not until the mid-season of 1779 that Washington could find time for counter attack. Now he planned to deal the Indians such a blow that they would never lift their heads again. He wanted to give them a lesson in what devastation could mean when conducted by civilized men. The command of the expedition having been declined by Gates was turned over to Sullivan. Washington's letters show the most careful preparation in every respect. He sent out questionnaires for trappers and traders to answer concerning rivers, fords, forage, everything that could have military importance in an unknown region.[14]

He was especially eager to whip the Six Nation Indians into submission, for the "admirable effect upon all the Western tribes, who tho' perhaps full as powerful in fact, yet pay the utmost respect to them, and would not willingly offend a people who had chastised the most warlike Nations." [15]

He did everything in his power to please the friendly Oneidas and Onondagas.[16]

But while this crusade boded ill for the Indians of the Six Nations (whose ability to form and maintain a federation

Franklin had envied in 1754), there was more in it than a mere clearing out of wild beasts. It was a wholesale venture in real estate, and its magnificent results were not appreciated until 1829 when a celebration was held in the rich and populous realms wrested from the Indians and turned over to the whites. The later celebrations of 1879 and 1929 emphasized the value of the conquest. But at the time its significance was not understood, nor the wisdom and scope of Washington's elaborate plans and precautions. His primary design was to destroy the menace of Indian and royalist raiders from which even Albany and Kingston feared attack, and release troops for use along the Hudson. A second purpose was to drive the Indians and Tories inside the British lines where they would be a burden on the enemy. According to Mr. A. C. Flick:

"One aspect of this problem has been almost entirely overlooked, namely, that the country of the Six Nations was an important source of food supplies for the British army as well as the Loyalists. Tens of thousands of bushels of nourishing corn usually left a surplus that could be sold at Niagara, Oswego, Montreal and Quebec and thus be made available for both the British Army and Navy for mush, griddle cakes, corn bread and pudding. In addition to corn the Indians sold to the British dried vegetables, dried fruits, and dried meats. These facts were known to patriot leaders like Schuyler, Hand and Washington. . . .

"Another factor had to do with Canada. At the outbreak of the Revolution strenuous efforts had been made to induce the Canadians, particularly those of French blood, to make common cause with the Revolutionists. . . . To threaten, and perhaps to take Oswego and Niagara, would not only encourage the American friends in Canada but also prevent the sending of troops and warships from the St. Lawrence to wage war to the southward. It also compelled the British government to send men, ships and supplies directly to Canada instead of to New York City. This important phase of the Sullivan-Clinton Campaign has been generally ignored by the historians of the Revolution. . . .

"Of far greater consequence in American history than any of the causes and objectives already mentioned was another that helped to shape the future of the American Republic. By 1779 Washington saw that the war was pretty much deadlocked . . . He saw that when

the terms of settlement were drawn up, if the young nation got nothing but a strip of land along the Atlantic with no opportunity for expansion westward, the struggle would scarcely be worth its cost.   Hence
the Sullivan-Clinton Campaign and the expedition under George Rogers
Clark farther westward were intended to stake down claims which
would assure to the United States western New York and Pennsylvania
and likewise the rich territory south of the Great Lakes farther west.
Not many leaders of 1779 saw the great prize, but Washington, the
seer, did.

"When these causes and purposes are clearly understood, the full
significance of the Sullivan-Clinton Campaign in the history of New
York State and America, will receive greater attention.   Those persons
who denounce it as a useless and abortive punishment of the misguided
Iroquois either do not or will not view it in all its relations . . .

"In the earlier accounts of the campaign the name of Philip Schuyler
scarcely appears.   It is now known that he, as Superintendent of Indian
Affairs, was continually consulted by Washington and his advice probably was the basis for Washington's decision.   The unprinted letters
exchanged between them make it quite certain that Schuyler largely
determined the character of the campaign.   Indeed Washington would
have been highly pleased had Schuyler accepted command of the army
led by General James Clinton.   Schuyler's contribution to the campaign might be regarded as a comparatively recent discovery." [17]

Washington showed his right to the name Old Fox in the
instructions he sent to Gates in case he should accept the command.   The first step was false propaganda:

"This will be best effected by hanging out false appearances to deceive the enemy there, and beget jealousies for their own security.
Among other expedients conducive to this end, one may be, to make
inquiry with an air of mystery, and yet in such a way as will spread
the idea, what force of militia could be derived from the State of
Massachusetts towards an invasion of Canada, by the way of Coos,
[Cohoes] in case of the appearance of a French fleet and army in the
river St. Lawrence.   You may employ this and any other artifices that
may occur to you for the purpose." [18]

To Sullivan he wrote:

.   "Nothing will contribute more to our success in the quarter where
we really intend to strike than alarming the enemy in a contrary one,
and drawing their attention that way.   To do this, you may drop hints

of an expedition to Canada by way of Coos. . . . You may also speak
of the probability of a French fleet's making its appearance in the spring
in the river St. Lawrence to co-operate with us. It will be a great point
gained if we can, by false alarms, keep the force at present in Canada
from affording any timely assistance to the savages, refugees, and those
people against whom the blow is levelled. I would wish you to keep
the motives of your joining to head-quarters a secret, because if it is
known that an officer of your rank is to take a command to the westward, it will be immediately concluded that the object must be considerable." [19]

There were the usual delays, broken promises, and failures
of men and supplies, but Sullivan finally marched with a force
which, as he did not omit to remark to Congress, was much
smaller than the British force and hence invited ruin.[20] This
complaint insulted Washington and he criticized it sharply
to Congress.[21]

It is a melancholy fact that one never encounters among the
Revolutionary commanders a feeling that any inferiority in
numbers is negligible and would be made up by patriotic fire.
They knew their men!

Eventually Sullivan's army moved west from Easton, Pennsylvania, and ascended the Susquehanna, while General Clinton's army went up the Mohawk to the headwaters of the Susquehanna and then down stream to Tioga, where the two
armies united and pushed through a garden land in which the
Indians had developed agriculture and built themselves substantial habitations and peaceful villages. The combined force
of about 4,000 men had to subsist on half rations while destroying immense crops not yet ripe enough to sustain them. Washington's instructions were drastic:

"The immediate objects are the total destruction and devastation of
their settlements, and the capture of as many prisoners of every age and
sex as possible. It will be essential to ruin their crops now in the ground
& prevent their planting more." [22]

There was only one battle, at Newton, which Sullivan easily
won; but to Washington's great regret it was found imprac-

ticable to attack Niagara. The army returned after a march of six or seven hundred miles with almost no losses except to the enemy's homesteads. Sullivan reported:

"The number of towns destroyed by this army amounted to 40 besides scattering houses. The quantity of corn destroyed, at a moderate computation, must amount to 160,000 bushels, with a vast quantity of vegetables of every kind. Every creek and river has been traced, and the whole country explored in search of Indian settlements, and I am well persuaded that, except one town situated near the Allegana, about 50 miles from Chinesee, there is not a single town left in the country of the Five Nations. It is with pleasure I inform Congress that this army has not suffered the loss of forty men in action or otherwise since my taking the command; though perhaps few troops have experienced a more fatiguing campaign." [23]

Some of the officers were ashamed of the work they had to do and not all the soldiers enjoyed the Vandalism of tearing green ears of corn from the stalks and throwing them in the river, girdling the apple trees, tearing up beans and other plants from the ground, piling them high and burning them with the houses.[24] To the protests of the officers against the degradation of their task, Sullivan replied:

"The Indians shall see that there is malice enough in our hearts to destroy everything that contributes to their support." [25]

It is not to be wondered at that the Indians transmitted to their descendants a suspicion that the sweetness and light so much advertised by the missionaries was not entirely confirmed by the soldiers. The expedition was more destructive than anything in American history. Nothing in the history of Hundom, indeed, shows more severity than this strange war on the very vegetables of the original inhabitants of that region. The patriots did not neglect to bring home a few scalps. That the number was small was due entirely to the nimbleness of the enemy. The ruthlessness of the procedure would be a less painful memory if the patriots had been as calm about their own sufferings as about those they inflicted, and if, on the very day that Washington transmitted the news of Sullivan's triumph, Congress had not appointed a committee to draw up a thanksgiving proclamation, which, when promulgated, read:

"Whereas it becomes us humbly to approach the throne of Almighty God, with gratitude and praise . . . that he hath gone with those who went out into the wilderness against the savage tribes; that he hath stayed the hand of the spoiler, and turned back his meditated destruction; . . . and above all, that he hath diffused the glorious light of the gospel, whereby, through the merits of our gracious Redeemer, we may become the heirs of his eternal glory: therefore,

"*Resolved,* That it be recommended to the several states, to appoint Thursday, the 9th of December next, to be a day of public and solemn thanksgiving to Almighty God for his mercies, and of prayer for the continuance of his favor and protection to these United States; to beseech him that he would be graciously pleased to influence our public councils, and bless them with wisdom from on high, with unanimity, firmness, and success; that he would go forth with our hosts and crown our arms with victory; that he would grant to his church the plentiful effusions of divine grace, and pour out his holy spirit on all ministers of the gospel; that he would bless and prosper the means of education, and spread the light of christian knowledge through the remotest corners of the earth." [26]

Since it was always a question whether Congress would appoint a day of fast and prayer for a defeat or a thanksgiving for a victory, it is interesting to know the difference the selection made in the conduct of the people. Judge Jones, Yale 1750, says:

"A Thanksgiving—a good breakfast, a superfluous dinner, tea in the afternoon, and a hot supper. A Fast—as much tea and toast as you can drink and eat of a morning, cold ham and punch at twelve, a hot dinner at five, tea and bread and butter at six, and a good supper at eight. Can any man find out the difference between a New England Thanksgiving, and a Fast, unless there is more eaten upon a Fast than at Thanksgiving." [27]

Judge Jones also makes the natural comment on the loud horror at the comparatively mild British raids on coast towns and the hosannas over the Indian extirpation:

"What the New England rebels termed barbarity in the British, was deemed a righteous, godly, and Christian-like act when perpetrated by themselves." [28]

At the same time Colonel Broadhead went out from Pittsburgh and marched four hundred miles in thirty-four days, having burned many towns and cut down the crops on many hundreds of acres, returning "with the scalps we had taken, and three thousand dollars' worth of plunder." [29] He also won the thanks of Congress and the right to thank heaven. The general result of the raid was to persuade many Indians that agriculture was a waste of time, but that scalping and the mutilation of the dead were good procedure. It was on one of these raids that a Lieutenant Barton wrote in his diary how he found two dead Indians "and skinned two of them from their hips down, for bootlegs: one pair for the major, the other for myself." [30] The massacre of the peaceful Moravian Indians in 1782 was a "black and inexcusable atrocity," which, says the biographer of the Indian chief, Brant, "transcends any and every Indian massacre which marked that protracted and unnatural contest. . . . The white men—not the Indians—are to be branded as the savages." [31] In spite of Sullivan's expedition, the Indians continued to line the borders with horror. And long after the war continued to harry the soul of Washington who harried them so unwearyingly.

During the early stages of the World War the American people learned to discredit the widespread propaganda that the Germans were in the habit of cutting off babies' hands and women's breasts. But when photographs were shown of their destruction of orchards, a shudder ran through the nation. There is something so beautiful about apple trees and peach trees that killing them seemed a kind of wanton assassination. No one reminded the Americans that Washington had ordered the same thing in a country where the Americans were as foreign as the Germans in Belgium. How many Indian apple and peach trees Sullivan destroyed is not known, but among many orchards, he mentions one that contained fifteen hundred trees.

Washington was delighted with the achievement and it gave him a certain prestige among the Indians, for in 1790 he was visited by three chiefs, who addressed him as "the great counselor in whose heart the wise men of all the *thirteen fires* have placed their wisdom," and added:

"When your army entered the country of the Six Nations, we called you the *town destroyer;* to this day, when your name is heard, our women look behind them and turn pale, and our children cling close to the necks of their mothers." [32]

Sullivan's expedition had the usual aftermath of disputes, scandals in the commissary and quartermaster departments, and recrimination.[33] Sullivan sent in his resignation from the army on the ground of ill health, and Congress accepted it on November 30th, 1779. He wrote to Washington asserting his friendship and warning Washington that the cabal was not yet dead, but waiting to collect new strength:

"Their plan is to take every method of proving the danger arising from a commander, who enjoys the full and unlimited confidence of his army, and alarm the people with the prospects of imaginary evils; nay, they will endeavor to convert your virtue into arrows, with which they will seek to wound you. The next stage is to persuade Congress, that the military power of America should be placed in three or four different hands, each having a separate quarter of the continent assigned to him, and each commander to answer to Congress only for his conduct. This, they say, will prevent an aspiring commander from enslaving his country. . . . I persuade myself, that your steady and prudent conduct will baffle every attempt." [34]

Greene confirmed this in March, 1780,[35] and accused Mifflin of reviving the cabal.[36] Washington acknowledged Sullivan's letter with warm friendship and admiration, and made this reference to the cabal:

"The most liberal professions of good will are very far from being the surest marks of it. . . . Against intrigues of this kind, incident to every man in a public station, his best support will be a faithful discharge of his duty, and he must rely on the justice of his country for the event." [37]

One unending war within the war was the jealousy of state for state and section for section. In a long confidential "Memoir on the Condition of America" sent home November 16th, 1779, by the heroic Chevalier de Fleury, who at Stony Point had "struck the British flag with his own hands," [38] there are many striking glimpses through a foreigner's eyes. He says of Boston:

"They are English toward the French, but Americans toward the English. Four years of war have somewhat worn the springs of patriotism." He tells how their chief men, Baudouin [Bowdoin], Adams and Hancock, "the King of the Rabble" (roi des halles), hate one another. In Pennsylvania, "the state most infested with royalists, the Quakers, Methodists, Anglicans, and other sects, which have a sort of affinity with monarchy, are intestine but paralytic enemies. Patriotism is nil at Philadelphia; it has become almost ridiculous. All the wealthy people are cankered at the heart, and hungry for peace at any price." In Maryland, not yet joined to the Confederation on account of land disputes, "the merchants are royalists." In Virginia, "the English are more feared than hated. Up to 1779 it was divided into two parties—that of Washington, and that of Lee and Gates, who wanted, as they said, to unmask the idol (demasquer l'idole).

"Congress is divided. Private animosities subdivided to infinity may be considered as forming two parties: that of the East, the four states of New England, Pennsylvania, Jersey, South Carolina; that of the South: Virginia, Maryland, New York, North Carolina, Delaware. The Eastern party, under the pretext that in a republic a man who has so much personal authority should not dispose of all the forces of the State, which would thus be at his mercy, upholds Gates almost in spite of himself, and supports him as a rival . . . His wife persuaded him to mix in politics. . . . As for Congress, in spite of the names of France and England, Country and Liberty, with which they hide their mutual animosities, the secret motive of their intrigues, their cabals, their everlasting barking (*aboyemens eternels*) is individual hatred, or that between state and state . . .

"General Washington is the Atlas of America, and the god of the army: his authority is gentle and paternal. He is perhaps the only man who could have effected a revolution. This great man has only one fault—a very creditable one—too much virtue for the chief of a party (in the quaint accents of the author: *le grand-homme n'a qu'un defaut Bien Respèctable, trop de vèrtu pour un chèf de party*)." [39]

Washington needed all of his virtue to uphold him. His army had learned to try mutiny as well as desertion, which continued its doleful popularity in spite of an amnesty and in spite of such extraordinary ferocity as that described in a letter from General Irvine who saw in camp:

"The head of a Corporal of the 1st Regt. . . . stuck up on the Gallows He was taken two nights ago by a party of Major Lees—who it seems were at first determined to kill all but on consultation or debate agreed to kill only one out of three—it fell to the Corporals lott— whose Head was Immediately carried to Camp on a pole by the two who escaped instant Death—these two Villains were of the same Regiment and have been tryed here this day—presume they will meet the same fate,—I hope in future Death will be the punishment for all such —I planly see less will not do—poor Magonigle behaved well at his Death— Tho he said no more than that he forgave all the World." [40]

While nothing could stop desertion, nothing could encourage recruiting. Washington, having long opposed bounties, was now driven to offer them. The $200 authorized at the beginning of the year to Continentals had accomplished nothing except to raise the bidding of the states. New Jersey bid $250. Virginia offered every recruit for the war $750, a suit of clothes every year, and a hundred acres of land. During the following year $1,000 was offered, and eventually $5,000 bounty per man, in Continental money.

This was in eloquent contrast with the $4 per man reluctantly offered by Congress in January, 1776. The only result of the bounties, according to Washington, was "a thousand evils" and more desertions. [41] He advised Congress to give a gratuity of a hundred dollars to the veterans and Congress voted that amount to all who had enlisted for the war prior to January 23rd, 1779.[42] But what was a hundred dollars of Congress money?

Despite the hardships of the soldiers there were not wanting then, as now, fierce pacifists whose suspicion of every soldierly instinct led them to accuse the officers of trying to encourage and prolong war for their own profit and glory! Washington always defended his men from such slanders, ridiculously vicious slanders considering the fact that the officers were all going broke and they found fewer and fewer chances for glory. So now he wrote to the Reverend William Gordon a justification of those superb few who endured everything:

"So far from the generality of officers wishing to have the war prolonged, it is my firm belief that there will not be enough left to continue it, however urgent the necessity, unless they are enabled to live, such is the present distress of the generality of them, and the spirit of resignation. The idle and foolish expressions of an individual does not by any means speak the sense of the body, and so far am I from believing that any number of them have views repugnant to the rights of citizens, that I firmly believe the contrary; but if I am mistaken, I can only say that the most distant lisp of it never reached my ears, and would meet with the severest checks if it did." [43]

The army had been reorganized into eighty battalions in March, and Steuben's drill method was published for general use, but what good did it do? Washington wrote another of his dismal letters on the gradual wasting away of his troops, and the end of the year showed that the states had furnished, all told, 10,000 less men than in 1778, which year had furnished 17,000 less men than 1777, which had furnished 21,000 less than 1776.[44]

Clinton, freed of fear of d'Estaing and contemptuous of anything Washington could or would attempt, sailed away to Charleston with an expedition bent on Southern conquest. Washington foresaw the attack and sent a few troops south; but he could do little. So 1779 ended in far greater depths than 1778, and the winter that came on with unforeseen haste was the coldest ever known. France had come in, Spain had come in, yet Washington, after a year and a half without one appearance on a battlefield, must write:

"I find our prospects are infinitely worse than they have been at any period of the War, and that unless some expedient can be instantly adopted a dissolution of the Army for want of Subsistence is unavoidable." [45]

XXXIX

STARVATION AND STAGNATION AT MORRISTOWN

"WITHOUT shoes and stockings, and working half leg deep in snow. Poor fellows, my heart bleeds for them, while I Damn my country as void of gratitude."

So wrote Colonel Ebenezer Huntington, Yale '75, on the day before Christmas, 1779, at Morristown. On February 6th, 1780, Captain Joseph Walker, Yale '74, wrote:

"We began & completed our Hutts which destroyed our cloathing still more, & to my certain knowledge we had not more than Fifty Men in the Reg^t return^d fit for duty, . . . many a good Lad with nothing to cover him from his hips to his Toes save his Blancket." [1]

Though it has never supplanted Valley Forge in popular memory, Morristown was the scene of far more cruel hardships for the army. Washington's famous phrase from Valley Forge, "This army must inevitably . . . starve, dissolve, or disperse, in order to obtain subsistence," was echoed two years later by his warning, "Unless some extraordinary and immediate exertions are made . . . the army will infallibly disband in a fortnight." [2] His desperation can be seen in one fact: At Valley Forge he had been rebuked for his reluctance to seize what his army needed, and he had punished plunderers with death and contumely. At Morristown he excused his men for marauding rather than meekly starving to death. When he found to his amazement that the inhabitants were "unwilling to give shelter to men, who have made and are still making every sacrifice in the service of their country," and that the magistrates were refusing aid, he told Greene to go ahead anyway:

"Necessity decides that you must proceed in quartering the officers yourself in such houses, as the good of the service may require." [3]

495

The Bostonians before the Revolution had bitterly resented the British quartering of troops among the citizens. Now Washington was quartering his in New Jersey. But "necessity decides." He wrote a circular letter to the magistrates:

"The present situation of the army, with respect to provisions, is the most distressing of any we have experienced since the beginning of the war. For a fortnight past the troops, both officers and men, have been almost perishing for want . . . they are now reduced to an extremity no longer to be supported. Their distress has in some instances prompted the men to commit depredations on the property of the inhabitants, which at any other period would be punished with exemplary severity, but which can now be only lamented, as the effect of an unfortunate necessity." [4]

He instructed his officers to go "delicately" but to seize what was withheld. He wrote another circular letter to the executives of the five states nearest:

"The situation of the army with respect to supplies is beyond description alarming. . . . We have never experienced a like extremity at any period of the war." [5]

Even before he moved to Morristown and began hutting his men, they were terrorizing the people. According to a Virginian version of his orders:

"Several Roberry of a very alarming Nature have been Commited in this neighbourhood by the Soldiers, accompanied by the most abhored Abuse to the Inhabitants . . . The Officers are desired to have their Rolls Called at Different times of the night a Greeable to a former order . . . the order heretofore Isued to prevent the Soldiers from Stragling in the night has proved unefectual Scarce a farmer in the Neighbourhood who has not been Robed & Insulted." [6]

Surgeon Thacher who was with the troops describes their forlorn estates: the officers lay down in huddles of five or six with their feet to a fire, which their "waiters" kept up all night. There was no shelter or forage for the horses:

"The poor animals were tied to trees in the woods for twenty-four hours without food, except the bark which they peeled from the trees." [7]

The country was rich in provision but "the people in the country are unwilling to sell the produce of their farms for the depreciated currency." The commissaries were helpless. As Washington wrote:

"At one time the Soldiers eat every kind of horse food but Hay." [8]

The officers were as bitter as the winds. Colonel Ebenezer Huntington, who could say, "my Washing Bill is beyond the Limits of my Wages," wrote his opinion of his fellow citizens:

"If the depreciation was Caused by the Rascallity of an Individual instead of many Rascalls, I should think any thing short of Eternal Damnation would be a light Punishment for the Crime . . . to Sacrafice the Army to Aggrandize a few D—d dirty Rascals, is below the Character of those who Pretend that they hath the Blood of a Freeman flowing in their Veins . . . a more Infernal Set of Villains never infested a Country. If the Laws of the Country will not admit of their distruction, point them out the Originals, & I will Imbrue my hands in their blood. . . . Empty belly's will push a Man to What, at other times he would avoid." [9]

The famine in food was partly due to the surplus of worthless money, partly to the sudden and unheard-of rigor of the winter. The commissaries looked on food and could not buy it; what they impressed could hardly be moved on the roads buried deep in snow. Boston and other cities were in grave danger of famine. The British suffered from cold and hunger in New York, and Knyphausen, who was in command there during Clinton's absence with the expedition against Charleston, saw the ships frozen fast in the harbor and called the sailors ashore lest they be captured by cavalrymen riding out on the ice. Thacher tells a story of Washington and "Mrs. Thomson, a very worthy Irish woman and housekeeper to General Washington." She said to him:

" 'We have nothing but the rations to cook, Sir.'

" 'Well, Mrs. Thomson, you must then cook the rations, for I have not a farthing to give you.' " [10]

On January 3rd, 1780, there was a blizzard. "No man could endure its violence many minutes without danger of his

life." Tents were torn away and officers and men buried like
sheep. The snow was from four to six feet deep, obstructing
the roads and shutting out provision so that the enfeebled
soldiers were "almost unable to perform their military duty, or
labor in constructing their huts." [11]

These were not completed till the middle of February. At
that time sleighs were "driven to New York over the ice from
Staten Island, an enterprise never yet attempted since the first
settlement of this country." [12] A soldier wrote:

"We have had a fast lately in camp, by general constraint, of the
whole army, in which we fasted more sincerely and truly for three days
than ever we did from all the resolutions of Congress put together . . .
the officers were obliged to release the soldiers from command, and
permit them to go in great numbers together into the country to get
provision where they could find it." [13]

On February 29th, 1780, Greene wrote of dire straits indeed. For two weeks the army could not forward military
despatches for lack of cash to pay the riders! There was not
a ton of hay in camp. The farmers would not feed the horses
and he said, "We shall be obliged to sell the poor cattle to keep
them from starving." [14]

Washington's headquarters after December 1st, 1779, were in
the home of the widow of Colonel Jacob Ford. It was a large
and beautiful home for a family but dreadful for a "Family."
Mrs. Ford kept two rooms for herself and her children, and
Washington had two log cabins built alongside, one for his
office and one for his kitchen. Across the way his guardsmen
were hutted. They were increased from 180 to 250 men and
were instructed when an alarm was given to rush to the General's house, station five men in every room, throw up the
windows and stand ready for assault. Alarms were frequent
—sometimes, says Lossing, "the attempts of some young
suitor, who had been *sparking* until a late hour, and attempted
to pass a sentinel without giving the countersign, caused the
discharge of a musket, and the commotion in the camp." On
these occasions Martha had to cower under the covers for hours

with five soldiers at each of the open windows of her room, the icy gale blowing in laden with snow.[15]

Washington was not content with the quarters selected for him and wrote with some asperity to Greene, who as quartermaster was responsible for his lodging:

"Appear[s] and facts must speak for themselves. To these I appeal. I have been at my pres[t] quarters since the 1st day of Dec[r], and have not a Kitchen to cook a Dinner in, altho' the Logs have been put together some considerable time by my own Guard. Nor is there a place at this moment in which a servant can lodge, with the smallest degree of comfort. Eighteen belonging to my family, and all Mrs. Ford's, are crowded together in her Kitchen, and scarce one of them able to speak for the colds they have caught.

"I have repeatedly taken notice of this inconveniency to Maj[r] Gibbs, and have as often been told, that boards were not to be had. I acqueesced, and believe you will do me the justice to acknowledge, y[t] it never has been my practice to involve the public in any expense I could possibly avoid, or derive benefits which would be inconvenient or prejudicial to others. . . . From what you have said, I am fully satisfied that the persons to whom you entrusted the execution of the business are alone to blame; for certain I am, they might by attention have obtained, (equally with others,) as many boards as would have answered my purposes long ere this." [16]

Greene was evidently growing a little afraid of Washington, who was ceasing to treat him with his original deference and breaking out at him occasionally. In a letter Greene wrote to Joseph Reed there is the timorous manner of the frequently rebuked:

"Much fault is found by a Southern gentleman, with your State, for want of proper exertions to save the army. . . . The great man is confounded at his situation, but appears to be reserved and silent. I write to you in the fullest confidence that you will not let the least hint drop from you of the information I give, as it may prove ruinous to me. I have difficulties enough, God knows, without adding to them." [17]

There was much dancing this winter to keep warm. Dancing was not expensive and "the most brilliant social season of the army of the Revolution" followed:

"Yesterday a Christmas dinner in compliment to the Washingtons at the Chevaliers. Next Thursday he gives a ball to thirty ladies; tomorrow another at Mrs Holkers. His Excellency intends having concerts once a week at his house, he entertaining generally with elegance. I have seen him wear cloathes of the Countess de Lauzun work, which does that lady great honor. Last Thursday the Assemblies commenced & there are private dances one a week; Tomorrow there is one at the City Tavern." [18]

There was infinite love making. Hamilton renewed his suit for the hand of the daughter of General Schuyler, who was in camp as a congressman with a committee of inspection. It is said that Steuben's aide, Captain Ben Walker, was telling Washington the sad story of his own love, only to evoke from him the cynicism:

"Women dont die of such trifles. Write to her and add another chapter to her book of sufferings." [19]

But the ability to dance and to make love are immemorial privileges of paupers, and the army of the republic was the pauper army of a pauper government. Indeed, Bancroft called them "A People without a Government," pointing out how "the habit of separatism grew with every year.

"In July, 1776, the United States declared themselves to have called a 'people' into being; at the end of 1778, congress knew no 'people of the United States,' but only 'inhabitants.' The name of 'the United States' began to give place to that of 'the confederated States' even before the phrase could pretend to historic validity. The attempt to form regiments directly by the United States completely failed; and each state maintained its separate line. There were thirteen distinct sovereignties and thirteen armies, with scarcely a symbol of national unity except in the highest offices. From the height of his position, Washington was the first keenly to feel and clearly to declare, that efficient power must be infused into the general government." [20]

This centrifugal tendency grew more marked in 1780 when Congress, for lack of passable money, had to ask the states to undertake the proportionate contribution of actual provisions to the army in terms of so much flour, so much meat, per state. Congress soon stopped the money-press and surrendered its power to the states from which it had more or less lawlessly usurped it. Madison wrote to Jefferson in May, 1780:

"The situation of Congress has undergone a total change from what it originally was. . . . They can neither enlist, pay nor feed a single soldier, nor execute any other purpose, but as the means are first put into their hands." [21]

While the army starved, the Congressmen trying to live on their salaries had resolved, on December 3rd, 1779, that Philadelphia was so expensive as to compel a removal in April to a cheaper town.[22] Yet there was such luxury among the profiteers that at one entertainment the pastry alone cost £800.[23]

With such floods of paper money poured out the taxes had brought in only $3,027,560. On January 10th, 1780, the Board of War reported that no clothing could be bought, for lack of money. As late as March 10th, there was only bread enough for ten days, and no money to buy more.[24]

People were taking lessons in finance; but Washington, who knew well what money really is, tried in vain to teach his stepson Jacky.

"A dollar is but a dollar, whether it passed in silver at 6s., or paper at £6, or sixty pounds. The nominal value, or the name, is but an empty sound, and you might as well attempt to pay me in oak leaves, with which I can purchase nothing, as to give me paper money that has not a relative value to the rent agreed on."

The money-lenders were in distress. Washington was a money-lender by trade, and as he put it in this same letter:

"Had you paid me the money at that time, I should have lent it to the public, if there had been no other use for it, as, it is not a custom with me to keep money to look at." [25]

It is odd to think of the commander-in-chief of the army being asked by the New York Congress to lend it money. This happened to Washington at a time when he had to refuse it, though he had previously made a loan to the Committee of Safety in that state.[26]

He must have hated many of his fellow countrymen more than he hated the British; for, while his affairs languished, most of the stay-at-homes cleaned up their debts and made merry. Many classes profited hugely by the condition of the currency, as is shown in a letter of the time:

"None have suffered on this account but salary men, those who depended on the value and interest of their money for a subsistence, and the poor among us. As to the rest, whether merchants, farmers, manufacturors, tradesmen, and day-laborers, the rise of their demands has all along been in proportion to the depreciation of the currency and the rise of the necessaries of life thereupon.

"It may seem strange, but 'tis a certain fact, that the American States, notwithstanding the vast depreciation of their paper currency, and the excessive high price of provisions of all kinds, are *richer* now in *reality*, and not in *name only*, than they ever were in any former period of time, and they are much better able to carry on the war than when they began it. . . . Our freeholders and farmers, by means of the plenty of paper money have cleared themselves of debts, and got their farms enlarged and stocked beyond what they could otherwise have done, and rather than give up their independency, or lose their liberties, would go forth to a man in defence of their country, and would do it like so many lyons." [27]

But the "lyons" did not stalk forth. In spite of all its dismal experience, Congress was actually capable of informing France on January 31st, 1780, that it was confident "of bringing into the field an army of 25,000 effective men, exclusive of commissioned officers" in addition to militia. Not a man had appeared by the middle of June, 1780.[28]

The quartermaster and commissary, clothiers, and medical departments of the army were undergoing reformation, but when Washington appealed to Congress to do something for the Continental regiments which were independent of the states, the situation of their officers having become "absolutely insupportable," and pointed out other crying needs for reorganization, there was hot debate on the subject, and the Chevalier de la Luzerne wrote:

"It was said, that this would be putting too much power in a few hands, and especially in those of the Commander-in-chief; that his

influence was already too great; that even his virtues afforded motives
for alarm; that the enthusiasm of the army, joined to the kind of dictatorship already confided to him, put Congress and the United States
at his mercy; that it was not expedient to expose a man of the highest
virtues to such temptations." [29]

Washington had written in March that affairs seemed to be
"verging . . . fast to a stagnation in every branch." [30] Stagnation was the word for the military activity. The heavy snow
and the ice in all the waterways left little room for anything
but raids. These were often carried out on sleighs. The taxi-
cab army of Paris in 1914 was foreshadowed in Lord Stirling's
fleet of five hundred sleighs in which he carried twenty-five
hundred men against Staten Island on January 17th, 1780.
He crossed on the thick ice through four feet of snow and
while only six were killed, five hundred men were "slightly
frozen." The raid was not a success. [31]

The British retorted with similar forays. Lieutenant-
Colonel Simcoe of the Queen's Rangers planned an attempt to
kidnap Washington:

"To arrive near Gen. Washington's quarters by day-break, to tie up
his horses in a swamp, and to storm the quarters, and attack his guard
on foot: . . . his only apprehension being in case Mr. Washington
should personally resist, by what means he could bring him off, and
preserve his life; . . . The same negligence in Gen. Washington's
quartering in front of his army, had attracted the notice of Capt. Beck-
with, Gen. Kniphausen's Aid-du-camp, and he had formed a plan to
carry off that general; for which purpose, cavalry were collected at
New-York." [32]

On April 19th the Chevalier de la Luzerne, minister of
France in place of Gérard, visited camp with young Don Juan
de Miralles of Spain, and every effort was made to impress
them with the splendor of a review under Steuben's management and a grand ball and fire works. The Spaniard could
not attend, having caught "pulmonic fever." Martha nursed
him herself. In a few days he was dead. The corpse, buried
with many diamond rings, diamond shoe and knee buckles, a

diamond studded gold watch, was guarded "lest our soldiers should be tempted to dig for hidden treasure." [33]

Washington walked on foot in the mile-long procession to the Roman Catholic funeral. He might have felt that he was also walking slowly behind the richly bedecked corpse of "Liberty," for there was nothing that was not funereal in the air. He was helpless to attack New York though Clinton had been able to detach an army and carry the war into the South. Nothing could be done to save the important city of Charleston from its impending doom under the relentless assaults of Clinton, and with it went far more than the town. Its surrender on May 12th, 1780, was obligingly communicated to Morristown through hand-bills secretly scattered by British sympathizers. In his unpublished history, Clinton wrote:

"By this very important Acquisition there fell into our Hands seven Generals & a Multitude of other Officers . . . about 6000 Men in Arms. The Rebel Lieut. Governor, the Council, and other civil Officers became also our Prisoners, and four Frigates . . . 5000 Stand of Small Arms, and a vast Quantity of Gunpowder." [34]

Not only was the capitulation of Charleston in many respects more costly to the American army than Burgoyne's to the British, but with it the American navy lost nearly half its fleet. By the end of the year, of thirteen frigates provided for in 1775 only one remained. This, three others, and one sloop made up the entire navy.[35] Such a disaster would have meant utter desolation to Washington, if it had not been for Lafayette, who suddenly and unexpectedly re-appeared with rhapsodic news.

XL

LAFAYETTE AS AMBASSADOR

NOT to know much of Washington's relations with Lafayette is to know little of Washington's real character. Those who have called him cold can never have read their letters. Love is the only word for their mutual devotion, which was as warm as affection could be between two busy and manly men devoted to their wives. The attachment is worthy of a place among the historic friendships. It did not even lack the expression of embraces, kisses and tears. After the battle of Monmouth they slept under one cloak among the dead.

Masculine kisses and tears are usually spoken of contemptuously as un-American, foreign, medieval and unmanly, yet if one reads far he will find that American heroes have wept as easily as others. At Washington's farewell to his officers he kissed all of them good-bye on their tear-drenched cheeks, and they, him. He wept frequently and creditably. In his letters to Lafayette one feels that his somewhat stilted language and even his somewhat stilted playfulness struggle to express an intense emotion.

Misfortune attended his correspondence of 1779 and 1780 in that not one of his letters ever reached Lafayette. Even his farewell—what would be called today a steamer-letter— arrived in Boston after Lafayette had sailed without knowing that Washington had not only disapproved but demolished his project for an expedition against Canada. He would have known it if he had received Washington's letter, which enclosed a long and cordial statement from Congress explaining that the exhaustion of resources and the derangement of finances made the expedition impossible, however desirable.

Washington expressed his regret for the delay the indecision had occasioned, and went on:

"I am persuaded, my dear Marquis, that there is no need of fresh proofs to convince you, either of my affection for you personally, or of the high opinion I entertain of your military talents and merit . . . Adieu, my dear Marquis. My best wishes will ever attend you. May you have a safe and agreeable passage, and a happy meeting with your lady and friends." [1]

With this letter he sent an introduction to Benjamin Franklin chanting the praises of Lafayette's services, "such proofs of his zeal, military ardor, and talents, as have endeared him to America, and must greatly recommend him to his Prince." [2] These letters were delayed by floods and ice, but Lafayette, while waiting for the ship to find a crew, had time to write three letters:

"Boston, 5 January, 1779.

"To hear from you, my most respected friend, will be the greatest happiness I can feel. The longer the letters you write, the more blessed with satisfaction I shall think myself. . . . My health is now in the best condition, and I would not remember I ever was sick, were it not for the marks of friendship you gave me on that occasion. . . .

"I hope you will quietly enjoy the pleasure of being with Mrs. Washington, without any disturbance from the enemy, till I join you again; . . . Farewell, my most beloved General; it is not without emotion I bid you this last adieu, before so long a separation. Don't forget an absent friend, and believe me, for ever and ever, with the highest respect and tenderest affection."

"On board the Alliance, 10 January, 1779.

"I open again my letter, my dear General, to let you know that I am not yet gone, but, if the wind proves fair, I shall sail to-morrow. . . . Adieu, my dear and forever beloved friend,—adieu."

"On Board the Alliance, Off Boston, 11 January, 1779.

"The sails are just going to be hoisted, my dear general, and I have but time to take my last leave of you. . . . Farewell, my dear general; I hope your French friend will ever be dear to you; I hope I shall soon see you again, and tell you myself with what emotion I now leave the coast you inhabit, and with what affection and respect I am for ever, my dear general, your respectful and sincere friend." [3]

Brand Whitlock thinks that Washington was "willing, or somewhat more than willing, just then, for the Marquis to absent himself for a little while, for so much ebullience and enthusiasm were trying at times to his reticence, and his own affection for the Marquis made his other officers jealous." [4] Whether this reading of Washington's mind is correct or not, he was soon lonely for his young friend, and Lafayette did not forget Washington even in the dazzling triumphs of every sort that surrounded him in Paris. His young wife met him with a two-year-old daughter that he had never seen, and they proceeded at once to collaborate in a son to bear the name, Georges Washington Lafayette. He was born before the year was out and the time would come when that child would be an exile like his father, going through like appalling tragedies. Through them all, as through his early glories, Lafayette's wife gave him a passionate devotion that he rivalled, both pouring out love in letters and proving it in deeds of unsurpassed fervor.

The beautiful ladies in France smothered Lafayette with kisses. In the theatre lines referring to him were flung at him from the stage. Franklin's grandson presented him with a magnificent sword voted to him by Congress. Even the scandal-mongers did not fail to do their best by him and provided him with a few spicy love-affairs.[5] The king, after keeping him for a period in formal arrest as a runaway, forgave him his disobedience and began to obey him to such an extent that, when Lafayette demanded great loans of money, troops, arms, clothes, for America, Prime Minister de Maurepas said, "It is lucky for the King that Lafayette has not taken it into his head to ship all the palace furniture to his dear Americans; the King can refuse him nothing." [6]

Hardly anybody could resist such sincerity. Doniol says: "It is plain that Vergennes yielded as Washington had done to the allure of La Fayette. That sagacity, that accuracy of vision (*justesse de vue*), in one so young, that immediateness so high-spirited as to veil what was hazardous, conquered Ver-

sailles as it had the army of the United States and Congress." [7]
Of Lafayette's miraculous ability to be a dual patriot, he says:

"With a rare measure of equal devotion, he filled the double rôle, doubly delicate, of an American general on a foreign mission and a French officer to whom his country is supreme." [8]

He had not only to satisfy a monarchy and a republic but to walk warily among the American representatives, for John Adams, Arthur Lee and Benjamin Franklin waged such ferocious war on one another that Lafayette dared not let the others know when he took counsel of the wise and witty Franklin. The French gazed on these feuds with natural disgust and anxiety and learned from Gérard that Congress was not only another scene of war, but that "in Congress there are evil heads and hearts of little honesty." [9] The spectacle was exhibited to the world of Frenchmen imploring the grave and reverend senators of America to soften their jangling voices. As Lafayette wrote to Washington:

"For God's sake prevent the Congress from disputing loudly together."

This appeal was included in his letter of June 12th, 1779:

"I had acquired such a habit of being inseparable from you, that I am more and more afflicted at the distance, which keeps me so far from my dearest friend, and especially at this particular time, as I think the campaign is opened, and that you are in the field. I ardently wish I might be near you, know every interesting event, and if possible contribute to your success and glory. . . . Serving America is to my heart an inexpressible happiness . . .

"I have a wife, my dear General, who is in love with you, and affection for you seems to me so well justified, that I cannot oppose that sentiment in her. She begs you will receive her compliments, and make them acceptable to Mrs. Washington. I hope you will come to see us in Europe; . . . Write to me how you do, and how things are going on. The minutest details will be interesting to me. Do not forget any thing concerning yourself." [10]

To Congress, however, he wrote in another strain. He actually wrote love letters to the president of Congress:

"Sir,—How happy I shall think myself whenever a safe opportunity of writing to congress is offered, I cannot in any way better express than in reminding them of that unbounded affection and gratitude which I shall ever feel for them. So deeply are those sentiments engraven on my heart, that I every day lament the distance which separates me from them, and that nothing was ever so warmly and passionately wished for, as to return again to that country of which I shall ever consider myself as a citizen; . . . To the letter congress was pleased to write on my account, I owe the many favours the king has conferred upon me; there was no time lost in appointing me to the command of his own regiment of dragoons, and everything he could have done, everything I could have wished, I have received on account of your recommendation." [11]

He thought for a time that he might lead an invasion of England, but the fleet did not arrive in time to convoy the transports across the channel. He drew up a plan for a French expeditionary force to America, of which Charlemagne Tower says: "It had a far-reaching influence upon the destinies of the United States . . . It represents, beyond doubt, his greatest service to America." [12] He arranged to have troops sent to America but took care that there should not be too many of them, for he had been warned of the American jealousy. While Washington was unable to raise enough men to move against the British, the French were advised to cut down the number they could easily have shipped. Lafayette counted on returning to America at their head, but the older and more experienced Lieutenant-General Rochambeau was selected. Another of Lafayette's beautiful pictures was erased from his hopes and he returned alone to America as a courier. In the meanwhile he had sent ahead of him the Count de Luzerne and the Marquis de Barbé-Marbois.

Not hearing from him, Washington had written in March how he regretted the failure of his letter to reach the ship and how grateful he was for Lafayette's adieu:

"Nor is there any thing more wished for by me, than opportunities of giving substantial proofs of the sincerity of my attachment to and affection for you."

He gave what news there was, regretted his inability to give commissions to two men recommended by Lafayette, slipped up on his who's and whom's in a tribute to "our great and good ally, whom we hope and trust, ere this, may be congratulated on the birth of a Prince," spoke of the King of Spain and the Empress of Russia and the threats of the British King, and the problem of war or peace. If war continued he counted on "sharing fresh toils and dangers" in "the Plains of America." If peace came, he would lose Lafayette since "the rural amuse-m^{ts} of an infant world, or the contracted stage of an American theatre," could not "withdraw your attention and services from the gayeties of a court, and the active part which you will more than probably be called upon to share in ye adm^n of y^r government." [13]

He wrote again on July 4th, 1779, of various British raids and ended his letter:

"When, my dear Marquis, shall I embrace you again? Shall I ever do it?—or has the charms of the amiable and lovely Marchioness—or the smiles and favors of your Prince, withdrawn you from us entirely? At all times and under all circumstances, I have the honor to be, with the greatest personal regard, attachment and affection—" [14]

One could not expect many letters from oversea in that day, but by September 12th he was puzzled and pained, imagining, of course, that his letters must have reached France. So he wrote:

"Often since you left this Country I have written to *you*, but have not been favored with a single line from *you* since you lay in Boston harbor. This I shall ascribe to any cause, rather than a decline of friendship. I feel my own regard for you so sensibly, that I shall never suspect a want of it in your breast."

He sent a hasty "scribble" telling of Stony Point, Paulus Hook, Sullivan's "chastisement" of the Indians, the Penobscot misfortune, and the Connecticut raid:

"The conflagration of Fairfield, Norwalk, and New Haven, by the intrepid and magnanimous Tryon, who, in defiance of all the opposition that could be given by the women and Children, Inhabitants of these Towns, performed this notable exploit with 2000 brave and generous Britons, adding thereby fresh lustre to their arms and dignity to their King." [15]

The depths of his tenderness for Lafayette are revealed in the account of the Marquis de Barbé-Marbois, who came to visit him in company with Luzerne in September. Here we catch a glimpse of Washington as a skilful yachtsman and a tireless player of ball:

"I have never seen anyone who was more naturally and spontaneously polite. . . . He asks few questions, listens attentively, and answers in a low tone and with few words. He is serious in business. Outside of that, he permits himself a restricted gaiety . . . he sometimes throws and catches a ball for whole hours with his aides-de-camp. He is reverent without bigotry, and abhors swearing, which he punishes with the greatest severity. As to his public conduct, ask his compatriots, and the universe. . . .

"We embarked with the General on the North River, or the Hudson, and sailed down it with the tide to West Point where the headquarters are, surrounded by the chief posts of the American army. The general held the tiller, and during a little squall which required skill and practice, proved to us that this work was no less known to him than are other bits of useful knowledge."

Of the shore dinner together he says:

"The river was being driven back by the tide, and the waves came right up to the tent-pins, where they broke with a solemn roar. A few steps away from us musicians played military and tuneful French airs. The banks and the forests of the mountain answered long to the cannon shots fired to the health of the King and Queen, and the opposite bank shone with the fires which the soldiers had lighted. Before my eyes was one of the most admirable spectacles in the world—the valiant and generous leader of a brave nation fighting for liberty. I was moved, and felt my eyes grow moist. . . .

"The general told me that he was drinking the health of the Marquis de Lafayette, and asked me if I had seen him before my departure. I answered that I had, and added that he spoke of him with the tenderest veneration. I said that the conduct of M. de Lafayette in America had made him generally esteemed, and had caused him to deserve the distinctions and favor granted him by the King. Washington blushed like a fond father whose child is being praised. Tears fell from his eyes, he clasped my hand, and could hardly utter the words: 'I do not know a nobler, finer soul, and I love him as my own son.'

"I asked him if he would not come to France some day, and enjoy the plaudits of a responsive nation which idolizes glory. He told me that he was only waiting for the end of the war to retire to his estates and to finish out his days there in the bosom of his family, after having paid the debt which every citizen owes to his country in times of trouble and misfortune." [16]

On September 30th, 1779, Washington wrote a very long letter, acknowledging Lafayette's letter of June 12th brought by Luzerne, and expressing his surprise that none of his own had arrived:

"Your forward zeal in the cause of liberty; Your singular attachment to this infant world; your ardent and persevering efforts, not only in America, but since your return to France, to serve the United States; your polite attention to Americans, and your strict and uniform friendship for *me*, has ripened the first impressions of esteem and attachment, which I imbibed for you, into such perfect love and gratitude, that neither time nor absence can impair . . . after our Swords and spears have given place to the ploughshare and pruning-Hook, I see you as a private gentleman, a friend and companion, I shall welcome you in all the warmth of friendship to Columbia's shores; and . . . to my rural cottage, where homely fare and a cordial reception shall be substituted for delicacies and costly living. This, from past experience, I know *you* can submit to; and if the lovely partner of your happiness will consent to participate with *us* in such rural entertainment and amusem^{ts}, I can undertake, in behalf of Mrs. Washington, that she will do every thing in her power to make Virginia agreeable to the Marchioness. My inclination and endeavors to do this cannot be doubted, when I assure you, that I love every body that is dear to you, consequently participate in the pleasure you feel in ye prosp^t of again becoming a parent, and do most sincerely congratulate you and your Lady on this fresh pledge she is about to give you of her love."

He gave his reasons for not promising to visit France after the war:

"Remember, my good friend, that I am unacquainted with your language, that I am too far advanced in years to acquire a knowledge of it, and that, to converse through the medium of an interpreter upon common occasions, especially with the Ladies, must appear so extremely awkward, insipid, and uncouth, that I can scarce bear it in idea."

After gay sarcasms on the English he answered Lafayette's line: "I have a wife who is in love with you," by indulging in some rather burly yet gallant flirtatiousness:

"But to conclude you requested from me a long letter—I have given you one—but methinks my dear Marquis I hear you say there is reason in all things—that this is too long—I am clearly in sentiment with you and will have mercy on you in my next—But at present must pray your patience a while longer, till I can make a tender of my most respectful compliments to the Marchioness.—Tell her, (if you have not made a mistake and offered your own love instead of *hers,* to me) that I have a heart susceptable of the tenderest passion, and that it is already so strongly impressed with the most favorable ideas of her, that she must be cautious of putting loves torch to it, as you must be in fanning the flame.—But here again methinks I hear you say, I am not apprehensive of danger—My wife is young—you are growing old and the Atlantic is between you—All this is true, but know my good friend that no distance can keep *anxious* lovers long asunder, and that the wonders of former ages may be revived in this—But alas! will you not remark that amidst all the wonders recorded in holy writ no instance can be produced where a young Woman from *real inclination* has preferred an old man—This is so much against me that I shall not be able *I fear* to contest the prize with you—yet, under the encouragement you have given me I shall enter the list for so inestimable a jewell."

He then "reversed the scene," sent Mrs. Washington's greetings, and ended:

"When I look back to the length of this letter, I am so much astonished and frightened at it myself that, I have not the courage to give it a careful reading for the purpose of correction. You must, therefore, receive it with all its imperfections, accompanied with this assurance, that, though there may be inaccuracies in the letter, there is not a single defect in the friendship of, my dear Marquis, yours, &c." [17]

Three weeks later he wrote again:

"On the 30th of last month, I wrote you a letter, which in point of length would almost extend from hence to Paris."

He told how Sullivan had "compleated the entire destruction of the country of the Six Nations; . . . These unexpected and severe strokes has disconcerted, humbled, and distressed the Indians exceedingly." He ended his news:

"It only remains for me now to beg the favor of you to present my respectful compliment to *your* (but have I not a right, as you say she has made a tender of her love to *me*, to call her *my*?) amiable & lovely Marchioness."

On March 18th, 1780, he acknowledged Lafayette's letter of October 10th, which had been received two weeks before:

"It filled me with a pleasure intermixed with pain. To hear that you were well, to find you breathing the same affectionate sentiments that ever have most conspicuously marked your conduct towards me, and that you continued to deliver them with unabated attachm^t, contributes greatly to my happiness. On the other hand, to hear that not one of the many letters, which I have written to you since you left this continent, had arrived safe, was not only surprizing but mortifying, notwithstanding you have the goodness to acc^t for it on its true principles."

By a persistent ill fortune even this letter never reached the Marquis, though Washington took pains to repeat much of the history previously recounted, telling of the removal of the war to the South and "the extreme cold, the deep snows, and other impediments." [18]

Suddenly with no warning whatever he received on May 7th, 1780, this letter:

"At the entrance of Boston Harbour, 27 April, 1780.
"Here I am, my dear General, and, in the midst of the joy I feel in finding myself again one of your loving soldiers, I take but the time to tell you that I came from France on board a frigate, which the King gave me for my passage. I have affairs of the utmost importance, which I should at first communicate to you alone. In case my letter finds you anywhere this side of Philadelphia, I beg you will wait for me, and do assure you a great public good may be derived from it. To-morrow we go up to the town, and the day after I shall set off in my usual way to join my beloved and respected friend and General.

"Adieu, my dear General; you will easily know the hand of your young soldier. My compliments to the family." [19]

When this letter fell into his hands Washington was caught off his guard, and he wept.[20] He answered in haste:

"Your welcome favor of the 27th of April came to my hands yesterday. I received it with all the joy that the sincerest friendship could dictate, and with that impatience which an ardent desire to see you could not fail to inspire. I am sorry I do not know your route through the State of New York, that I might with certainty send a small party of horse (all I have at this place) to meet and escort you safely through the Tory settlements between this place and the North River. At all events, Major Gibbs will go as far as Pompton, where the roads unite, to meet you, and will proceed from thence as circumstances may direct, either towards King's Ferry or New Windsor. I most sincerely congratulate you on your safe arrival in America, and shall embrace you with all the warmth of an affectionate friend, when you come to headquarters, where a bed is prepared for you. Adieu, till we meet. Yours." [21]

On May 10th, 1780, Lafayette reached Morristown and, doubtless, as usual, seized Washington in his arms and kissed him on both cheeks. They shut themselves up in headquarters while Lafayette told the great news he had brought. It was enough that he had brought himself. It was graceful that he should have remembered to bring a quantity of beautiful swords for the officers of his division. But he brought also a dazzling gift for the United States. He was the Prince lifting Cinderella Columbia from the ashes. He murmured to Washington in their secret conference that the King of France was sending a great fleet under Admiral the Chevalier de Ternay and an army of six thousand well-equipped and disciplined troops under Lieutenant-General the Comte de Rochambeau, who would place himself under Washington's orders.

Almost any other general would have lifted his head at this, and assumed a domineering tone, at least under the pretence, and the reality, of seeking the country's good. But the Virginia farmer did not forget the divine meekness of subordination. As Luzerne wrote to France:

"General Washington, whose circumspection increases in proportion to the confidence reposed in him by Congress, would not take upon himself the responsibility of arranging a plan of combined operations. After having assured the Marquis de Lafayette, that he would apply himself with all possible activity to hasten forward recruits and to collect provisions, he desired him to proceed immediately to Philadelphia, and concert further measures with the French minister, and particularly as to the expediency of acquainting Congress with the secret of the expected arrival of the French troops." [22]

Lest the British learn of it, Congress must not be told for Congress was leaky of secrets. So Washington sent Lafayette to Philadelphia with a request for a small committee to confer with him concerning an important project. The secret was kept from America to perfection until a New York paper published almost all the details, the British military intelligence having learned nearly everything long before Washington did. But the news was no less good for being public property. And now the key of Washington's letters was changed and he wrote to Governor Jefferson of Virginia to prepare signals in case the fleet were sighted there; to General Heath at Boston to send spies to Halifax for information useful to the French, and to provide pilots in case they should attack there.

The more he thought of it the more he wanted to capture New York. He wrote to Lafayette in Philadelphia urging him to "write to the Count de Rochambeau and Mon^r de Ternay in the following spirit, urging them in the strongest terms to proceed, both fleet and army, with all possible expedition to Sandy Hook." [23] He was eager that they should not linger at Newport and permit Clinton to return to New York Harbor. He remembered d'Estaing's failure to get into the Bay and promised better pilots. If the other fleet under Comte de Guichen could also be brought to the American waters, "we should have reason to flatter ourselves with every thing; without it, we have a great deal to apprehend." He wrote again in such enthusiasm that he threw all scruples aside:

"I impatiently wait, my Dear Marquis, to know the result of the arrangements you were to make with Congress. The time slides away so fast, and we have so little before us, that every moment is infinitely precious, and ought to be improved. We talked of a Proclamation to the Canadians. If it is not already done, I think it ought not to be delayed. It should be in your own name, and have as much as possible an air of probability. Perhaps it will be more plausible to have two different kinds struck; one intimating to them the arrival of a french fleet and army in the River St. Lawrence, to cooperate with these States, to be expected, by the way of Rhode Island, where they are to touch, for to answer some import^t purposes, and dwelling on the happy opportunity it will afford them to renew their ancient friendship with France, by joining the allied arms and assisting to make Canada a part of the American confederation, with all the privileges and advantages enjoyed by the other members; cautioning them by no means to aid the enemy in their preparations for defending the Province. The other proclamation should be drawn, on the supposition of the fleet and army being already arrived, and should contain an animating invitation to arrange themselves under the allied banners. In both proclamations you should hold yourself up as a French and American officer, charged both by King of France and by Congress with a commission to address them upon the occasion. It may indeed be well to throw out an idea, that you are to command the corps of American troops destined to cooperate with the French armament. The more mystery in this business the better. It will get out, and it ought to seem to be against our intention." [24]

He was so infatuated with high anticipation that he thought up a brilliant plan for fooling the British. He would have proclamations printed in French and English announcing that the French army and navy were bound for Canada. One or two of these would be allowed to fall into British hands as if by accident.

To make sure that this neat trick should not be discovered, he entrusted the printing of it to General Benedict Arnold, who had been for just about a year in the pay of Sir Henry Clinton! He did not tell Arnold the purpose of the secrecy, so Arnold turned the proclamation over to Clinton, believing it sincere. [25]

Washington never dreamed of suspecting Arnold. His only anxiety was for the American people.

XLI

THE FRENCH STALEMATE

PERHAPS the pleasantest way to describe what followed this glorious coming of French ships and soldiers to the rescue of the exhausted Americans would be to say that the people relied on Washington, Washington relied on Providence, and Providence, having brought the French to America, relied on them. And they failed to rise to the opportunity. It is always safe to blame the French.

Certain it is that the American people did the nearest thing possible to nothing. Which left Washington able to do little but write letters. The French held conferences.

The French farce-writer, Beaumarchais, was originally to blame. He was mainly responsible for sending over the first secret supplies that made possible Washington's victories at Trenton and Princeton. Ninety percent of the guns and ammunition that conquered Burgoyne came from the French.[1] Lafayette had now topped Beaumarchais by bringing over French money, men and ships in open alliance. The Americans politely relinquished the field to the visitors.

The distance to which the patriots carried this self-restraint is vividly shown by the expenditure in specie value.

In 1775 and 1776 the Americans spent on the war. . . . $20,064,666
In 1777 24,986,646
In 1778 24,289,438
In 1779 10,794,620
In 1780 3,000,000
In 1781 1,942,465
In 1782 3,632,745
In 1783 3,226,583
In 1784 548,525

$92,485,693

This is to say, that the moment the French came in the Americans cut their expenditures to less than a third; from over ten millions to an even three!

"This table," says Sumner, "shows how the country lapsed into dependence on France. . . . The round number opposite 1780 is very eloquent. It means anarchy and guesswork." [2] France spent in and for America about $12,000,000 a year for five years. In response to Washington's prayers the Americans raised in 1780 just 1,000 fewer men than in 1779; 8,000 less than in 1778. [3]

The total effective was further reduced by the surrender of 5,000 or more at Charleston, including two major-generals, the loss of nearly 2,000 men at Camden, and of many others in various minor engagements. The troops enlisted barely came up to half the quotas, in spite of the augmented bounties. While awaiting the French argosy, Washington described the miserable state of his army and its prospects in an unusually sombre letter announcing the mutiny of two regiments of the Connecticut line on account of hunger and five months' delay of pay. He added: "This matter, I confess, tho' I have heard of no further uneasiness among the men, has given me infinitely more concern, than any thing that has ever happened." [4] To President Reed he was even more despondent:

"This is a decisive moment; one of the most, (I will go further and say, *the most*) important America has seen. The court of France has made a glorious effort for our deliverance, and if we disappoint its intentions by our supineness, we must become contemptible in the eyes of all mankind; . . . The combined fleets of France and Spain last year were greatly superior to those of the enemy.—The enemy nevertheless sustained no material damage, and at the close of the campaign have given a very important blow to our allies. . . . What are we to expect will be the case, if there should be another campaign? In all probability the advantage will be on the side of the English. And then what would become of America? . . . In modern wars, the longest purse must chiefly determine the event. I fear that of the enemy will be found to be so." [5]

Washington had two words for the British activities: they "insulted" him or they "amused" him. And he had to accept both. In Westchester county they ravaged. In June, 1780, Knyphausen entered New Jersey with five thousand men, pushed through to Elizabethtown, burned Connecticut Farms, killed a minister's wife and many soldiers. Later in the month the British advanced to Springfield and in spite of the great bravery of Colonel Israel Angell, the adroitness of Major Henry Lee, and others, drove General Nathanael Greene off to a distance, burned the town and retired.

The Americans spoke of this retreat as one of fright, but Washington's true feelings came out in his letter to his brother-in-law, Fielding Lewis. It is striking that it was written just a little over five years after he took the command, and four years after the Declaration of Independence:

"I may lament in the bitterness of my soul, that the fatal policy which has pervaded all our measures from the beginning of the war, and which no experience however dear bought can change, should have reduced our army to . . . removing our stores from place to place to keep them out of the way of the enemy instead of driving that enemy from our country— . . .

"It may be asked how these things have come to pass? the answer is plain—and may be ascribed to . . . a fatal jealousy (under our circumstances) of a standing army—by which means we neglected to obtain soldiers for the war when zeal and patriotism run high, and men were eager to engage for a trifle or for nothing; the consequence of which has been that we have protracted the war—expended millions and tens of millions of pounds which might have been saved, and have a new army to raise and discipline once or twice a year, and with which we can undertake nothing because we have nothing to build upon, as the men are slipping from us every day by means of their expiring enlistments. To these fundamental errors, may be added another which I expect will prove our ruin, and that is the relinquishment of Congressional powers to the States individually—all the business is now *attempted*, for it is not done, by a timid kind of recommendation from Congress to the States; . . .

"We are attempting an impossibility, and very soon shall become (if it is not already the case) a many-headed monster—a heterogenious mass—that never will or can steer to the same point. The contest among the different States *now* is not which shall do most for the common cause—but which shall do least." [6]

Clinton, when he returned, would have a total of 17,500 men in New York. Washington figured that he would need at least twice this number for a siege. With the French only five thousand, the Americans must raise for various purposes at least forty thousand rank and file besides officers.[7] When the French fleet and troops arrived off Newport July 10th, 1780, he had to write, "Not a thousand men that I have heard of have yet joined the army." [8] He was ashamed of the impression the French would gain. He dared not leave his troops to go in person and receive Rochambeau, since the British were astir. So he sent Lafayette with most polite greetings and a detailed account of his "sentiments" to be communicated to Rochambeau for his consideration. First he stated his belief that "a decisive naval superiority" was absolutely essential, and he hoped that the French would make haste to combine with him in the capture of New York while they had it. He did not know that the very day before he wrote, the British Admiral Graves reached New York with enough reinforcements for Admiral Arbuthnot to take the superiority away from the French. Thus his plans were already cancelled in advance. Furthermore, he had few men and no provisions, and once more had to disgrace his hospitality by asking his guests for a loan:

"Another thing that gives me concern is the non-arrival of our arms and powder . . . we shall fall short at least four or five thousand arms, and two hundred tons of powder. We must of necessity, my Dear Marquis, however painful it is to abuse the generosity of our friends, know of them whether they can assist us with a loan of that quantity of arms and ammunition." [9]

The reason the arms and powder had not arrived was that after the French had provided and collected them, the Americans in Paris would not take the trouble to pick them up and carry them oversea. Vergennes wrote of this to Lafayette, and added:

"If we judge the firmness of the nation in general by the little zeal we note in her agents we shall have a very poor opinion. No cooperation, no agreement among them. Each is occupied with his passions or his paltry interests. . . . These people have a terrible name for business. The reproach cannot apply to Mr. Franklin. I believe his hands and his heart equally clean." [10]

Lafayette had also lost many of his illusions. Before he left for Europe he had written confidentially:

"I begin to realize that, seduced by a false enthusiasm for glory, I did a foolish thing in going over to the Americans. But I feel also that it would be a more foolish thing to come back. The wine is poured, it must be drunk to the dregs, but the dregs can already be tasted." [11]

Washington had long since lost his illusions, but not his doggedness. Suddenly his allies were shut up in Newport harbor by the British fleet and, instead of storming New York with the French, he had to write Rochambeau that since he could not reach Newport in time to reinforce the French, he would pretend to attack New York in order to keep Clinton from overwhelming Rochambeau. Clinton set forth for Newport. Washington moved toward New York. Clinton returned. And the battle season was already nearly gone. Washington's prophecy of May 25th, 1780, seemed to have come true:

"The succor designed for our benefit . . . will, in all probability, precipitate our ruin . . . the Country exhausted, the People dispirited, the consequence and reputation of these States in Europe sunk, our friends chagrined and discouraged, our Enemies deriving new credit, new confidence, new resources." [12]

The French had walked into trouble enough. While de Ternay's fleet was blockaded in Newport, the reinforcing fleet was blockaded at home in Brest harbor. When he learned of this, Washington was at Teaneck, New Jersey, and he signified his surrender to fate by ordering what militia had turned out, sent home. [13] Comte de Guichen had a fleet in the West Indies, but Washington watched for him in vain, and having feinted at attacking New York alone, crossed back to New Jersey and took up a camp at Tappan, or Orangetown, which his army did not leave all summer. He was practically in the position of having no allies at all. He did not know where to turn for help since Congress had relinquished the pretence of keeping up a national army and had turned the matter over to the thirteen allied sovereignties. As Washington wrote to Congressman Joseph Jones:

"I see one head gradually changing into thirteen. I see one army branching into thirteen, which, instead of looking up to Congress as the supreme controlling power of the United States, are considering themselves as dependent on their respective States." [14]

Now the women of America suddenly emerged from their obscurity and organized to contribute not only cash but toil. Washington had confessed that his army had no shirts, which would be "more peculiarly mortifying" when they joined the French.[15]

Joseph Reed had written to him in June that the women were subscribing cash for an army relief fund, and that Mrs. Reed expected to gather no less than "one hundred thousand pounds to be laid out according to your Excellency's direction, in such a way as may be thought most honorable and gratifying to the brave old soldiers, who have borne so great a share of the burden of this war." [16]

Martha joined the Philadelphia campaign and Mrs. Reed wrote on July 4th:

"The subscription set on foot by the ladies of this city for the use of the soldiers is so far completed, as to induce me to transmit to your Excellency an account of the money I have received, which, although it has answered our expectations, does not equal our wishes. But I am persuaded it will be received as a proof of our zeal for the great cause of America, and of our esteem and gratitude for those, who so bravely defend it. The amount of the subscription is 200,580 dollars, and £625, 6s. 8d. in specie, which make in the whole in paper money 300,-634 dollars." [17]

Unfortunately this dazzling $300,634 amounted in specie to no more than $7,500. The New Jersey women sent to

Washington $15,488, which was worth one-fortieth of that, or $387 in good money. Still, the spirit was beautiful and every penny had a place. Mrs. Bache and other ladies made up and sent 2500 shirts for the soldiers. Washington, of course, was grateful and gracious in his acknowledgments according to the spirit of the time:

"The contributions of the association you represent have exceeded what could have been expected, and the spirit that animated the members of it entitles them to an equal place with any, who have preceded them in the walk of female patriotism. It embellishes the American character with a new trait, by proving that the love of country is blended with those softer domestic virtues, which have always been allowed to be more peculiarly *your own*." [18]

Help of another sort was devised by the restlessly ingenious Thomas Paine, who on June 4th, 1780, proposed a subscription for funding the purchase of recruits and supplies and headed the list with £500. This was the first real step toward the formation of a bank in the United States. Subscribers executed bonds for their subscriptions. The idea was seized upon by the eager patriots, who thus partially redeemed Philadelphia from its indifference or hostility.

It is not usually realized that there was not a single gold or silver mine in the United States at that time to furnish hard money without importation, and up to 1780 there had never been anything resembling a bank in all the colonies. Tom Paine initiated the first one.[19] The bank promised to furnish the army three million rations and three hundred hogsheads of rum without profit, but with repayment of the cost by the United States. Congress agreed to guarantee £150,000 sterling within six months. This first bank provoked the hostility that afterward greeted all such experiments; it was soon misused for political purposes and lasted only until 1784. But Washington welcomed anything and hoped to see more banks elsewhere.[20]

Greene and Congress were still at war. He was only a little less of a favorite than Arnold. He was also accused of dishonesty or the permission of gigantic squanderings and embezzlements. Serious insinuations that he was enriching himself coincided with the basis for a reformation of the purchasing methods. He refused to serve under the new system and showed such high spirit that Congress planned to vacate his commission, publish him as a public defaulter, and prevent his returning to the line. Washington wrote beseeching that no such step be taken. With his usual mingling of evasive courtesy and subordination, he said that, in the absence of the documents, he would "neither condemn nor acquit General Greene's conduct for the act of resignation," but he pleaded that dismissal of Greene would show all the officers "the uncertain tenure by which they hold their commissions. . . . Such an act in the most despotic government would be attended at least with loud complaints. . . .

"If Congress by its mere fiat, without inquiry and without trial, will suspend an officer to-day, and an officer of such high rank, may it not be my turn to-morrow, and ought I to put it in the power of any man or body of men to sport with my commission and character, and lay me under the necessity of tamely acquiescing, or, by an appeal to the public, exposing matters, which must be injurious to its interests?" [21]

Congress hearkened to his advice and let Greene out quietly, appointing Pickering quartermaster-general in his place. Thus Washington received back a valued officer. He sent Greene out on a foraging expedition to Bergen, in August, but the soldiers exceeded their instructions to such an extent that Greene reported:

"There has been committed some of the most horrid acts of plunder by some of the Pennsylvania line that has disgraced the American arms during the war. The instances of plunder and violence is equal to anything committed by the Hessians. Two soldiers were taken that were out upon the business, both of which fired upon the inhabitants to prevent their giving intelligence. I think it would have a good effect to hang one of these fellows in the face of the troops, without the form of a trial. It is absolutely necessary to give a check to the licentious spirit which increases amazingly. The impudence of the soldiers is intolerable. A party plundered a house yesterday in sight of a number

of officers, and even threatened the officers if they offered to interfere." [22]

Washington answered:

"I entirely approve . . . You will, therefore, please to order one
of the soldiers detected in plundering, and also the deserters you mention, to be immediately executed." [23]

On this General Upton comments:

"The summary execution of American soldiers without trial, by
order of the 'Father of his Country,' the plundering of our citizens,
and the seizure of their property without payment were only a few of
the evils springing from unwise legislation." [24]

This was a most uncharacteristic act on Washington's part
and it might have given color to the widespread rumor that
the leading officers were urging him to seize the dictatorship
and save the country. Reed wrote to Greene about it and said
that Washington, "it is said, treated the proposition in a suitable manner." [25] The extent of the rumor is shown in a letter
from Lafayette first published, among others, in 1915:

"Some people say that Gᵃˡ Washington is to be made dictator. I do
not know that as his friend I ought to desire it for him, but I know
very certainly that I ought not to speak of or give the air of suspecting
that step, which yet seems to me infinitely important. After what the
French ministers have testified to me, I am very sure that they would
be charmed to deal with the General in their operations. . . . My
principles, republican and indeed entirely democratic, ought to make me
oppose such a measure and I should not approve it if I did not know the
man, and if I did not feel a dictatorship necessary for the public welfare." [26]

The need of some strong hand to replace the thirteen weak
fumblers was verified by the latest attempt of Congress to
do something helpful. Remembering what wonders it had
achieved at Saratoga by keeping its own Northern army independent of Washington, Congress decided to give its favorite,
Gates, a chance to save the South and achieve a "Burgoynade"
against Cornwallis, whom Clinton had left to mop up the dis-

integrating remnants of the rebellion. Without consulting Washington, a motion by Congressman Burke was put through assigning to Gates the command of all the Southern forces with authority to call upon all the Southern governors for the militia. Thirty thousand dollars was voted "to defray his expences on his way" and warrants drawn on Virginia and North Carolina for two hundred thousand dollars for his military chest.[27]

One of Gates' first steps was to offer a brigadier generalship to Colonel Daniel Morgan, whom he had offended at Saratoga. Since then, Morgan had played the prima donna by resigning from Washington's army because another officer had been given the command of the light infantry. Now he urged the appointment of Gates and welcomed him South.[28] Congressman Jones wrote to Washington to ask his opinion of the matter, but as always in the case of Gates, he kept his distance:

"Considering the delicate situation in which I stand with respect to General Gates, I feel an unwillingness to give any opinion (even in a confidential way) in a matter in which he is concerned, lest my sentiments (being known) should have unfavorable interpretations ascribed to them by illiberal Minds." [29]

No writer of fiction, no writer of fairy stories, could have contrived for a hero's vindication or a villain's downfall a more incredible revenge than fate inflicted on Gates. He took over the command from General Kalb, whom Washington had sent South, rejected the plan of operations Kalb and his officers had carefully prepared in their knowledge of the situation, and ordered the troops to march at once against the enemy. He would not wait for supplies. He intended to Burgoyne Cornwallis. Nothing dismayed him. When he learned on the day before the battle that he had only 3,052 men instead of the 7,000 he supposed he had, he answered with a bravado rare in that war:

"These are enough for our purposes."

The 3,000, it is true, included thirteen generals, but the militia had mostly no training at all and were making their début on a battlefield. They had with them a multitude of women. To crown all, he unwittingly administered to his whole army the day before the battle, what the bravest soldier never needs on such a day, a vigorous cathartic. Having no rum he distributed a gill of molasses per man. His own adjutant-general tells of it with becoming modesty:

"Nothing ought to be considered as trivial, in an army, which in any degree affects the health, or spirits of the troops; upon which often, more than upon numbers, the fate of battles depends. The troops of General Gates' army, had frequently felt the bad consequences of eating bad provision; but, at this time, a hasty meal of quick baked bread and fresh beef, with a desert of molasses, mixed with mush, or dumplings, operated so cathartically, as to disorder very many of the men, who were breaking the ranks all night, and were certainly much debilitated before the action commenced in the morning." [30]

The Revolutionary militia needed no help to make it run, but that medicament may have had some part in the record-breaking exodus from the battlefield of Camden, on the morning of August 16th, 1780, the third anniversary of the battle of Bennington. Though Gates' 7,000 were only 3,000, Cornwallis had no more than 2,000.[31] Furthermore, Sumter was near enough to have expected to be in the battle. Accounts vary as to whether Cornwallis struck Gates' militia while it was being maneuvered into position, or Gates blindly ordered his militia to charge the British regulars. Whatever happened, they broke at once and scattered in all directions. There were heroes and clever officers there, but they were flanked, surrounded, swept away or slain or captured. It was said that Gates had rebuked the cautious Kalb for timidity. In any case, Kalb kept the field and lost his life there, riddled with a dozen wounds, while Gates—!

Cornwallis claimed to have killed and wounded a thousand and taken a thousand prisoners with all the cannon and baggage. Eckenrode expresses a Virginian disgust for the Virginia militia by saying:

"The militia exhibited such agility in getting off the field that few of them, unfortunately, were killed." [32] John Marshall wrote that only three of them were even wounded, and added: "Never was a victory more complete." [33]

The British pursued the screaming women and the galloping men for twenty miles. At forty miles fugitives were still cutting horses adrift from wagons. But General Gates rode on for the almost unbelievable distance of a hundred and eighty miles! Of course, even the dismayed Americans howled with ridicule. Hamilton wrote to Duane:

"Did ever any one hear of such a disposition or such a fight? . . . Was there ever an instance of a general running away, as Gates has done, from his whole army? And was there ever so precipitate a flight? One hundred and eighty miles in three days and a half . . . what will be done by Congress? Will he be changed or not? If he is changed, for God's sake overcome prejudice, and send Greene."

And again:

"He showed that age and the long labors and fatigues of a military life had not in the least impaired his activity, for in three days and a half he reached Hillsborough, one hundred and eighty miles from the scene of action, leaving all his troops to take care of themselves, and get out of the scrape as well as they could. He has confirmed, in this instance, the opinion I always had of him." [34]

He wrote this to his betrothed, the daughter of that very General Schuyler whom Congress had laughed at when he could not find St. Clair's Army in the wilderness about Ticonderoga.

Wilkinson, Gates' old adjutant and the victim of the Conway Cabal, found a divine purpose in Gates' disgrace, a heaven-meant punishment for Gates' mistreatment of Wilkinson:

"The justice of Heaven precipitated him from the pinnacle of undeserved fame to the abyss of humiliation—an object of compassion." [35]

If anyone in the world could have been excused for exulting in the downfall of one so peculiarly his enemy, Washington was the man. But there seems to be nowhere a hint of a syllable uttered or written betraying any gratification or even mild censure of Gates. To Congress Washington wrote that the defeat was "the fatal consequences of depending on militia. . . . No *Militia* will ever acquire the habits necessary to resist a regular force. . . . I have never yet been witness to a single instance, that can justify a different opinion." [36]

To Gates' three letters to him he was too busy to reply until October 8th, 1780, when he explained his delay and said of the defeat:

"The behavior of the Continental troops does them infinite honor. The accounts, which the enemy give of the action, show that their victory was dearly bought. Under present circumstances, the System, which you are pursuing, seems extremely proper." [37]

Gates tried to re-create an army and he wrote to Washington with pitiful meekness of his efforts to stop the enemy and recover the lost ground:

"But if being unfortunate is solely a Reason sufficient for removing me from Command I shall most cheerfully submit to the Orders of Congress; and resign an office few Generals would be anxious to possess. . . . That your Excellency may meet with no such Difficulties— that your Road to Fame and Fortune may be smooth and easy is the Sincere wish of your most obedient servant."

"Some men may think they please my superiors by blaming me, and thus recommend themselves to favor. But you, Sir, will be too generous to lend an ear to such men, if such there be, and will show your greatness of soul rather by protecting than slighting the unfortunate. If, on the contrary, I am not supported, and countenance is given to every one who will speak disrespectfully of me, it will be better of Congress to remove me at once from command, where I shall be unable to render them any good service." [38]

When Congress voted after long delay that Washington should appoint a court of inquiry into Gates' conduct he selected Greene to be the head of it.[39] Both Greene and Henry Lee wrote in strong defence of Gates from blame or ridicule and some later historians have exposed the mistreatment of earlier chroniclers, the inevitable injustice done to one who suffers such a monumental disaster.[40] His burlesque flight seems to have actually consisted of several gallant but vain attempts to rally the panic-stricken men, then a realization that, since all the stores and munitions were lost, he should proceed at once to Hillsborough and begin rebuilding a new army. Washington had had this same thing to do so often that he was incapable of despising Gates.

Later he instructed the court of inquiry that "this affair be conducted with the greatest impartiality. . . . Should General Gates have any objection to the mode of inquiry . . . you will suspend proceeding in the affair, till he transmits his objection, and you receive further orders." [41] He informed Gates of this and of his aim to "execute the orders of Congress in the manner most consistent with justice to the public and to you." [42] There was too much war business at the time, however, and the court was deferred indefinitely. Gates had nothing to do but retire to his farm in Virginia, where he remained in deep bitterness of soul and the direst poverty for two years, waiting for the court that never met.

Few men have been plunged from greater heights to greater depths. The hero of one of the fifteen most decisive battles in history was now the clown in one of the most complete collapses in history. To the dismay of his disgrace was added the news that his only son had died and the news had been withheld. He was a tender-hearted man, capable of deep suffering and of sympathy with others. It is pleasant to learn that on his triumphant way South, expecting an Austerlitz, not a Waterloo, Gates had brought Morgan back to the army, and had written to General Lincoln, who had recently surrendered Charleston:

"Dear Genl Lincoln The series of Misfortunes you have experienced, since you were doom'd to the Command of the Southern Department, has affected me exceedingly. I feel for you most sensibly.— I feel for myself who am to succeed, to what? To the command of an Army without Strength—a Military Chest without Money. A Department apparently deficient in public Spirit, and a Climate that encreases Despondency instead of animating the Soldiers Arm. I wish to save the Southern States. I wish to recover the Territories we have lost. I wish to restore you to your Command and to reinstate you to that Dignity, to which your Virtues, and your Perseverance, have so justly entitled you:—with me you have experienced that the Battle is not to the strong. Poor Burgoyne in the pride of Victory was overthrown. Could the Enemy's Triumph over you, meet with the like Disgrace, I should be content to die in Peace, so might America be free and Independent; and its future Happiness under God rest solely upon Itself. You will oblige me very much by communicating any Hints or Information, which you think will be useful to me in my Situation. You know I am not above Advice, especially where it comes from a good Head and a sincere Heart. Such I have allways found yours to be; and as such, shall always venerate and esteem both. I mean not by this to urge you to divulge Matters the obligation of your Parole of Honor, commands you to conceal." [43]

The author of this letter was not the Gates of historical caricature. The more we learn of our favorite villains and fools the better we realize that there are reasons for giving them more sympathy than contempt. After his debacle Gates very humbly threw himself on Washington's mercy and on May 22nd, 1781, wrote that Washington had done all he could to protect him. [44] Having seen Lee and Conway eliminated from the opposition, it is beautiful to see how Washington eliminated Gates from the little company of his enemies. On March 18th, 1782, Washington wrote him a letter that seems to be missing, expressing deep sympathy for his distresses and asking him if he would accept a command in the army! [45] This was perhaps the letter of which the following story was told by Dr. William Read:

"Having occasion to call on General Gates, relative to the business of the department under my immediate charge, I found him traversing the apartment which he occupied, under the influence of high excitement; his agitation was excessive—every feature of his countenance, every gesture betrayed it. . . . An open letter which he held in his hand, was often raised to his lips, and kissed with devotion; while the exclamation repeatedly escaped them—'Great man! Noble, generous procedure!' When the tumult of his mind had subsided, and his thoughts found utterance, he, with strong expression of feeling, exclaimed—'I have received this day a communication from the Commander in Chief, which has conveyed more consolation to my bosom, more ineffable delight to my heart, than I had believed it possible for it ever to have felt again. With affectionate tenderness he sympathizes with me in my domestic misfortunes, and condoles with me on the loss I have sustained by the recent death of an only son; and then with peculiar delicacy, lamenting my misfortune in battle, assures me, that his confidence in my zeal and capacity is so little impaired, that the command of the right wing of the army will be bestowed on me so soon as I can make it convenient to join him.' " [46]

Congress repealed, at Washington's suggestion, the order for the court and Gates, released from exile, wrote to him:

"I beg your Excellency to believe, that I am always ready to obey your commands, and shall be most happy when I can execute them to your satisfaction. I have but to entreat, that no attention to me or my rank may interfere or break in upon any part of your arrangements." [47]

He rejoined the army immediately and Washington gave him the command of the right wing—the most graceful form imaginable of heaping coals of fire on a heavy head. In after years, in riding over the battlefield on his southern tour in 1791, Washington expressed his belief that if Gates had "been ½ a mile further advanced, an impenetrable Swamp would have prevented the attack which was made on him by the British Army, and afforded him time to have formed his own plans." [48] This was typical of his unwillingness to pursue a beaten enemy or waste his soul on a revenge or a contempt.

Gates' fellow-victim in the disasters of 1780, General Lincoln, while on parole, had busied himself with securing not only his own exchange but that of all the other soldiers who were still ignored and hopeless. He collaborated with General Phillips of Burgoyne's betrayed convention troops.

Strangely, Washington was now the obstacle. The year before he had accused Congress of cruelty for reluctance to advantage the British by an exchange. He had now veered round to the Congressional opinion. He did not object to the release of captive officers, but he was willing to let the private soldiers wait, especially as the British would receive permanent regulars in return for men a majority of whose enlistments had already expired.[49] Congress agreed with Washington.[50] It was the British who protested at the heartlessness of this as well as at the expense and inconvenience of caring for the hungry mob. Their Commissary of Prisoners, Joshua Loring, protested:

"If your superiors are cruel enough not to suffer the men who fight their battles, to be exchanged, we shall be under the necessity of sending them to some other parts." [51]

General Lincoln wrote to Washington, pleading the sufferings of the captives, their bitter feelings because of neglect, and the evil effect on recruiting.[52] He expressed the very sentiments that Washington had emphasized to Congress, and at length Washington and Congress relented. Washington wrote Lincoln to proceed with the exchange of privates as well. It was only now, after more than five years, that an understanding was reached. One hundred and fifty officers and 476 privates in New York were set free first and Lincoln and other officers released from parole.[53]

The return to service of General Lincoln still left Washington with a grave shortage of officers according to the standards of that era. Of the twenty-three major-generals commissioned up to this time, resignations, disabilities, deaths, and courts-martial had done for all but eight: Greene, Heath, Stirling, Lincoln, Arnold, Lafayette, Robert Howe and Steuben.

Lee, Gates, and Conway had ceased to be rivals. Greene was mentioned as his successor in case anything happened to him, though Washington evaded the effort to make him commit himself to the nomination of a contingent heir to his difficulties.[54]

He was now about to lose the only officer whose fiery valor and whose tactical brilliance in action had been more dazzling though less steadfast than his own—the only other officer who has been credited with actually saving the republic from destruction—Benedict Arnold. Strangely, there was a distinct religious element in the affair, and the French were to blame for this as well as for the sarcasm of coming to save America only to get themselves locked up in Newport.

XLII

EXIT ARNOLD

THE French alliance had not only provoked the ridicule and hostility of the Tories, but caused uneasiness among the patriots because of the recognition of Catholics as friends.

The French soldiers were not religious missionaries and many of them had succumbed to the influence of Voltaire, who had kissed and embraced Franklin and visited the wife of Lafayette to pay homage to her husband as a sword of freedom. Many had gone far beyond Voltaire, of whom the French lady cried: "Voltaire! But he is a bigot. He believes in a God!" [1]

Lafayette himself was irreligious according to his own account for he says that when his very pious wife was on her deathbed in one of her deliriums she was "mistaken about me for a moment or two, persuading herself that I had become a fervent Christian." She could not persuade him to call himself one even in her last pitiful hours. Later he did a work like Voltaire's in trying to remove the oppressions under which Protestants labored in France. [2]

It has a significance in the riddle of Washington's own religious opinions that his most beloved friend was a skeptic.

But whatever their convictions individually, the French were formally and legally Catholic and the amenities compelled a courtesy toward ceremonies which had been to most of the colonies not only infamous but illegal since the colonies had been founded. When congressmen attended the funerals of distinguished Frenchmen buried with Catholic rites, people felt that a Revolution indeed was going on. Some shuddered, some laughed. William Palfrey wrote to Gates in 1779 that he had hopes of seeing him one day "with a Cardinal's hat, as some

536

of our most rigid dissenting Members of Congress assisted last Sunday in singing Te Deum at the Chapel."[3]

To the Anglican clergy, the alliance was the final proof of sacrilegious treason and Washington came in for his share of abuse as an apostate. A Presbyterian clergyman might put him in poetry as the instrument of Jehovah, but he was the chief of the damned according to the Reverend Jonathan Odell, born in New Jersey, descended from one of the founders of Massachusetts, and a graduate of Princeton. Benjamin Franklin's Tory son as Governor of New Jersey had inducted him into his Anglican rectorship. Owing to his loyalism he suffered arrest and persecution and finally fled to the British lines where he served as a chaplain and with much literary skill wrote satires in Drydenian couplets.

In that ambitious work, "The American Times," published in 1780, under the pen name "Camillo Querno," Congress is Pandemonium, and the American heroes are brought forward one after another in a grand review of devils. Washington is the head devil and his excoriation begins with a sneering reference to the defeats of his early years. There is not room for the whole passage but enough must be quoted to show how he looked to a large part of the most respectable and reverend element of the native-born population:

> Strike up, hell's music! roar, infernal drums!
> Discharge the cannon—Lo! the warrior comes!
> He comes, not tame as on Ohio's banks,
> But rampant at the head of ragged ranks.
> Hunger and itch are with him—Gates and Wayne—
> And all the lice of Egypt in his train. . . .
>
> Hear thy indictment, Washington, at large;
> Attend and listen to the solemn charge:
> Thou hast supported an atrocious cause
> Against thy King, thy Country, and the laws;
> Committed perjury, encourag'd lies,
> Forced conscience, broken the most sacred ties;
> Myriads of wives and fathers at thy hand
> Their slaughter'd husbands, slaughter'd sons demand;

That pastures hear no more the lowing kine,—
That towns are desolate, all—all is thine;
The frequent sacrilege that pain'd my sight:
The blasphemies my pen abhors to write;
Innumerable crimes on thee must fall—
For thou maintainest, thou defendest all. . . .
What could, when half-way up the hill to fame,
Induce thee to go back, and link with shame?
Was it ambition, vanity, or spite,
That prompted thee with Congress to unite;
Or did all three within thy bosom roll,
"Thou heart of hero with a traitor's soul?"
Go, wretched author of thy country's grief,
Patron of villainy, of villains chief. . . .
I swear by Him, who rules the earth and sky,
The dread event shall equally apply;
That Clinton's warfare is the war of God,
And Washington shall feel the vengeful rod.[4]

One looks in vain for the name of Benedict Arnold among the Reverend Jonathan's devils. The omission is explained by the fact that Odell was actually serving as the go-between for Arnold's secret dealings with Major André. In his first approaches to the British Arnold used the names "John Moore," and "Gustavus." His wife's old friend, John André, in his answers called himself "John Anderson." And we find a letter from Arnold to André addressed:

"Mr. John Anderson, merchant, to the care of James Osborne, to be left at the Reverend Mr. Odell's." [5]

In his satire, "The Word of Congress," Odell has the couplet:

"Imagination must it not surpass,
That Congress should proceed in pomp to Mass?" [6]

This very horror plays a prominent part in Arnold's attempts to justify his treason. According to Randolph G. Adams, the religious motive was important among his four reasons: anger at Congress: resentment at the Pennsylvania authorities; need of money to keep up his position and reimburse him for his sacrifices and expenses; finally, "a real and sincere indignation at the French alliance, which, as a New England Protestant, and as an inheritor of the traditions of the colonial wars, he could not abide." [7] Furthermore Arnold was now a member of the Anglican church.

Mr. Adams thinks that Tory influence had little weight with Arnold, and doubts the Tory sentiments of the Shippen family into which he married, though it is now certain that his wife took a valuable enough part in his treason to earn from Clinton a handsome sum of money. Among Clinton's memoranda is this in his own autograph:

"His wife obtained for her services, which was very meritorious, 350 pounds." [8]

The king gave her a pension.[9] Part of the correspondence with Major André, who had been a devoted swain of hers in Philadelphia, concerned millinery and vanities for the decoration of her pretty body as a further disguise of the real purpose.

Washington had spies upon spies and a most elaborate intelligence system, yet he never turned up Arnold. At this time it was Ethan Allen who enjoyed his profound suspicions. His under-cover men in New York told him that Allen was in communication with Clinton. In July, 1780, Washington instructed Schuyler to investigate the rumor, and, if it could be confirmed, arrest Ethan Allen at once.[10] Allen was too clever for the investigators, and was not molested, though he and Ira Allen were in constant dealings with Frederick Haldimand, governor-general of Canada since 1778, negotiating a separate exchange of prisoners, and trying to guarantee the integrity of the New Hampshire Grants whichever way the war ended. The negotiations went on for years, though Allen said he would accept "no damd Arnold plan to sell his country and his own honour." [11]

Uneasy about Allen, but never dreaming that his most admired warrior, Arnold, was long since a hireling of the enemy, Washington kept trying to make use of his superb military abilities. But Arnold was difficult. The wound he received on October 7th, 1777, was still painful, yet he managed to conduct himself at Philadelphia in a manner to excite wrath and suspicion of his financial honesty.

Anthony Wayne, after Arnold's treason was known, wrote of him that he was not only a poor soldier, and a coward, but a low thief as well:

"What think you of his employing Sutlers to retail the publick Liquors for his private Emolument, & furnishing his Quarters with beds & other furniture by paying for them with Pork, Salt, Flour, &c drawn from the Magazines—he has not stopped here—he has descended much lower—& defrauded the old Veteran Soldiers who have bled for their Country in many a well fought field, for more than five Campaigns, among others an old Serg't of mine has felt his rapacity . . . The dirty—dirty acts which he has been capable of Committing beggar all description." [12]

Congress paid no attention to his bill for four years' back pay.[13] From the first he was always accused of graft, though Wayne was almost alone in doubting his valor. When the gossip grew too hot in Philadelphia, he demanded a court-martial, but important witnesses to his alleged misconduct were out of the state and stayed out, so that when he was finally tried without them, he was acquitted except on a minor charge of using public wagons for private transportation and sentenced to be reprimanded by Washington. One of the most beautiful bits of English ever uttered has been published as Washington's response to the compulsion put upon him:

"Our profession is the chastest of all. Even the shadow of a fault tarnishes the lustre of our finest achievements. The least inadvertence may rob us of the public favor so hard to be acquired. I reprimand you for having forgotten, that, in proportion as you had rendered yourself formidable to our enemies, you should have been guarded and temperate in your deportment towards your fellow-citizens. Exhibit anew those noble qualities which have placed you on the list of our most valued commanders. I will, myself, furnish you, as far as it may be in my power, with opportunities of regaining the esteem of your Country." [14]

But Barbé-Marbois seems to have been the author of this exquisite rebuke. Like the ancient historians and some popular modern biographers he did not hesitate to enliven his work with his own dialogue and letters where he thought he could improve upon history or supply its gaps. Washington's actual words, which were good enough, are given in the Orderly Book of April 6th, 1780:

"The Commander-in-Chief would have been much happier in an occasion of bestowing commendations on an officer who has rendered such distinguished services to his Country as Major Genl. Arnold. But in the present case a sense of duty and a regard to candour oblige him to declare that he considers his Conduct in the instance of the permitt as peculiarly reprehensible both in civil and military view, and in the affair of the waggons as imprudent and improper." [15]

A little thing like a court-martial could not damn a general in Washington's eyes, else he would have had few officers. Unproved accusations of dishonesty could not disqualify, else he would have lost Greene. He continued to tempt Arnold to the field. But Arnold, already sold to England, knew that he would be of little use to Clinton in camp or in battle, and the mere transmission of such information as reached him in Philadelphia gave him small value. Dozens of spies were doing as much. He had his eyes on West Point. If he could get that, he could present the English with the whole Hudson river, the whole war. He had saved the river once from Carleton, and once from Burgoyne; he had earned it and thought he had a right to sell it. He appealed to Washington for West Point, but Washington declined. His wife apparently shared his eagerness, for Robert Morris afterward recalled a significant happening:

"On a particular occasion Mrs. Arnold was dining at the house of Colonel Morris. After dinner, a friend of the family came in, and congratulated Mrs. Arnold on a report that her husband was appointed to a different, but more honourable command. The information affected her so much as to produce hysteric fits. Efforts were made to convince her that the general had been selected for a preferable station. These explanations, however, to the astonishment of all present, produced no effect." [16]

We have Washington's own account of his unwitting torment of Arnold. One evening in 1786 after dinner at Mount Vernon, he told the whole story and Tobias Lear set it down in his diary at once:

"I confess I had a good opinion of Arnold before his treachery was brought to light; had that not been the case, I should have had some reason to suspect him sooner, for when he commanded in Philadelphia, the Marquis la Fayette brought accounts from France of the armament which was to be sent to co-operate with us in the ensuing campaign. Soon after this was known, Arnold pretended to have some private business to transact in Connecticut, and on his way there he called at my quarters; and in the course of conversation expressed a desire of quitting Philadelphia and joining the army the ensuing campaign. I told him that it was probable we should have a very active one, and that if his wound and state of health would permit, I should be extremely glad of his services with the army.

"He replied that he did not think his wound would permit him to take a very active part; . . . and intimated a desire to have the command at West Point. I told him I did not think that would suit him, as I should have none in my garrison but invalids. . . .

"While the army was crossing at King's ferry, I was going to see the last detachment over, and met Arnold, who asked me if I had thought of anything for him. I told him that he was to have the command of the light troops, which was a post of honor, and which his rank indeed entitled him to.

"Upon this information his countenance changed, and he appeared to be quite fallen; and instead of thanking me, or expressing any pleasure at the appointment, never opened his mouth." [17]

Eventually Washington granted him the post. With greedy haste Arnold prepared a cipher letter to André and included in it certain reminiscent disclosures to identify himself as the true "John Moore." This very letter is in the William L. Clements collection. It is written all in numerals but with it was found the following decipher:

"I wrote to Captⁿ B— on the 7th of June, that a F— fleet and army were expected to act in conjunction with the A— army. At the same time I gave M^r S— a manifesto intended to be published in C—a, and have from time to time communicated to him such intelligence as I thought interesting, which he assures me he has transmitted to you . . . I have accepted the command at W. P. as a Post in which I can render the most essential Services, and which will be in my Disposal. The Mass of the People are heartily tired of the war, and wish to be on their former footing . . .

"As Life and fortune are risked by serving His Majesty, it is necessary that the latter shall be secured as well as the emoluments I give up, and a compensation for Services agreed on, and a Sum advanced for that purpose—which I have mentioned in a letter which accompanies this, which Sir Henry will not, I believe, think unreasonable. I am, Sir,

July 12th 1780   your hble Servt
Mr Jno ANDERSON   J MOORE

"P.S.—I have great confidence in the Bearer, but beg Sir Henry will threaten him with his resentment in case he abuses the confidence placed in him, which will bring certain ruin on me. The Bearer will bring me 200 guineas, and pay the remainder to Captⁿ. A— who is requested to receive the deposit for Mr Moore." [18]

He wanted cash in advance. Later he stipulated for a guarantee of £10,000 if the plan failed; £20,000 if he delivered the fort. Clinton naturally welcomed the offer of such a stronghold, as any general would have done; but he had lacked a guarantee that he was not being duped by a clever letter-writer. He tells his own story in his unpublished history:

"An Overture of that Sort, coming from an Officer of Mr Arnolds Ability and Fame could not but attract my Attention; and as I thought it possible that like another General Monk he might have repented of the Part he had taken and wish to make Attonement for the Injuries he had done his Country by rendering her some signal & adequate Benefit. I was of course liberal in making him such offers & Promises as I judged most likely to encourage him in his present Temper. A Correspondence was after this opened between us under feigned Names; in the course of which he from time to time transmitted to me most material Intelligence; . . .

"In the Mean time, wishing to reduce to an absolute Certainty whether the Person I had so long corresponded with was actually Major General Arnold commanding at West Point, I acceded to a Proposal he made me to permit some Officer in my Confidence to have a personal Conference with him, when every thing might be more explicitly settled between us than it was possible to do by letter—and as he required that my Adjutant General, Major Andre (who had chiefly conducted the Correspondence with him under the Signature of John Anderson should meet him for this purpose on neutral Ground, I was induced to consent to his doing so from my great Confidence in that Officers Prudence & address . . . I could have no reason to suspect that any bad Consequence could possibly result to Major Andre from such a Mode, as I had given in it Charge to him *not to change his Dress or name on any Account,* or possess himself of writings by which the nature of his Embassy might be traced." [19]

Arnold occupied as headquarters the country mansion of Colonel Beverly Robinson, son of an eminent Virginian at whose house in New York Washington had met Mary Philipse on his first Northern visit in 1756. Robinson had remained a loyalist and he tried now to get in touch with Arnold from the war sloop *Vulture,* using a pretended interest in his confiscated property as a disguise. This house, though headquarters for West Point, was on the opposite side of the Hudson and two miles down river.

On one occasion when Arnold tried to meet Robinson, British gunboats fired on his barge and almost ended Arnold's treason in advance. Later in September, André sent a man ashore to meet Arnold under a flag of truce but some concealed Americans lay in ambush and drove the boat off. Of this lucky outrage Winthrop Sargent says:

"It is occasion of shame to an American to be compelled to relate how treason was thus blindly fought by treason: since it was through this unjustifiable affair that the interview between André and Arnold was induced, and their consequent detection occasioned." [20]

Neither second-sight nor Providence suggested to Washington the subterrene burrowings of Arnold and Clinton beneath the Gibraltar of his strategy. His one thought was the capture of New York before snow flew. He was almost alone in his frenzy. He held a Council of War and found his officers cold.[21]

Harry Lee, recognizing the helplessness of the army, wrote a private letter criticizing Washington's strategy in the starved condition of the force:

"It was originally idle to build the operations of this campaign on the expectation of taking the town of N. York. It was too much to expect. Had our views been more proportionate to our ability, our Southern prospects might have been better. . . . To operate seriously or effectually against New York required a very great supply of ammunition & ordnance of every sort; more I venture to declare, than ever was in possession of the United States. Thus it is blundering policy every where; repeated mistakes must in the end produce ruin." [22]

The French were as polite as they could be, but their clear, cold eyes saw that the republic had been over-advertised in France. Lafayette wasted his eloquence on his fellow-countrymen. They treated him as the American he was officially, and refused to serve under him:

"They are not pleased with me . . . my particular friends assure me that they like neither my conversations in writing nor my politics, and that they suspect me . . . of depreciating in this country the aid and friendship of France. You will see by my replies, that, without having done wrong, I crave pardon. I would fall on my knees, if they wish, and I believe that I would let them beat me. . . . You will laugh at this, and I, though now in a rage, will also laugh eventually." [23]

Lafayette returned from Newport without accomplishing much. Rochambeau and de Ternay insisted on conferring with Washington himself. They dared not leave Newport; he dared not leave his army. Lafayette wrote from camp a long letter embodying Washington's ideas for the New York assault.[24] But Rochambeau saw that Washington's desire was the last flicker of a forlorn hope.[25] He felt that France must send more men, money and ships, and he was old enough soldier to refuse to be hurried into a disaster. He drove Lafayette frantic by seeming to treat him as an importunate infant, but he wrote in his memoirs:

"I ought to say in justification of La Fayette that he actually voiced the sentiments of General Washington, and that the latter made use of his youth and his ardor to express them with more energy." [26]

To the passionate youth he wrote a letter that Lafayette kept all his life. Doniol speaks of the fatherly tenderness of it: "serenity and a wisdom simple and sweet give it eloquence." [27] He called himself "old papa Rochambeau," but he insisted on meeting Washington in person in spite of Lafayette's insistence that it would "embarrass" that general to confer so long before the arrival of the second French fleet now blockaded at Brest, and that there would be time enough when that fleet arrived. [28]

There was nothing for Washington to do but go meet this man. He asked Rochambeau to come as far as Hartford, Connecticut, on September 20th, 1780, and advised him to keep the time secret. [29] In the meanwhile he took advantage of an act of Congress empowering him to act beyond the confines of the United States and wrote to the Comte de Guichen a shamelessly frank picture of the desperate situation of the country, describing the collapse of the South and the North, "the savages desolating the frontiers." [30]

He appealed to de Guichen to come to the rescue, had his letter translated into Luzerne's cipher and sent it forth. De Ternay also sent out a cry to de Guichen. But he had sailed for France and never received the letters.

Washington wrote to Arnold on September 14th, 1780, to expect him on his way to Hartford, provide him with a guard and boats, adding:

"Keep this to yourself, as I want to make my journey a secret!" [31]

Arnold did not tell anybody but Clinton. He carried Washington over the river in his own barge, and it was afterwards recalled that he seemed uneasy because Washington kept his spyglass fastened on the British sloop, the *Vulture*, and commented on it in low tones to another officer. Arnold jumped, too, when Lafayette suddenly exclaimed: "You are in correspondence with the British,—perhaps you can find out what has become of de Guichen." [32]

Washington dined with Arnold at Joshua Hett Smith's house, near Haverstraw. Arnold stayed the night, discussing affairs with Washington and his companions, Knox, Lafayette, the French engineer, de Gouvion, and six aides-de-camp. To silence any possible rumors Arnold showed a letter he had had from Beverly Robinson asking an interview concerning his estate. Washington embarrassed him by saying that it was a civil matter and he ought not to meet Robinson, thus frightening Arnold out of holding an open conference with him.

That same night in New York Clinton and André were at a military banquet and Clinton was announcing that André, whom he had made adjutant-general on August 31st, was departing on a secret errand. He added: "Plain John André will come back Sir John André." [33]

Tuesday morning, Arnold turned back to his new duties with the British, who had bought him, and Washington rode on to meet the French, who were supporting him and his country. He had twenty-two dragoons for escort, and they made a brave showing as they galloped through the countryside and the villages. But they were paupers bluffing their way on a begging errand. They were actually worried about their ability to pay for their meals on the road. As Dr. Gordon says:

"The general, with the rest of the company, mustered up and borrowed all the money they could, in order to pay their expences. They could procure no more than 8000 paper dollars. Such was the scarcity even of that depreciated commodity at camp. . . . They put on a good countenance when in Connecticut, called for what they wanted, and were well supplied; but the thought of reckoning with their host damped their pleasure. However, to their great joy, when the bills were called for, they were informed, that the governor of Connecticut had given orders that they should pay nothing in that state, but should be at free cost." [34]

After two days of riding he reached Hartford, and met Rochambeau's party. They were saluted with thirteen guns and Connecticut's best imitation of the Field of the Cloth of Gold. The French had been impatient to have a look at this figure who was stirring Europe so deeply and were greatly impressed by his majestic form in its "buff vest, buff breeches, buckles at the knee, long spurred boots, white neck cloth and blue buff-lined coat, that shone with a pair of rich massive epaulets." [35]

One of Rochambeau's aides was a handsome young Swede, Count de Fersen, the lover of Marie Antoinette, and destined to be at her side in enormous drama. Lafayette also would be there. How many of these swarming Counts and Dukes were on their way to gorgeous tragedy! Fersen wrote to his stormy old father that he feared for America lest it meet the fate of Poland, whose citizens were similarly divided. He said that the Tories were of the higher class, the Whigs "people of the lowest birth and no property." Of Washington he wrote:

"He looks the hero; he is very cold; speaks little, but is courteous and frank. A shade of sadness overshadows his countenance, which is not unbecoming. . . . The two Generals and the Admiral were closeted together the whole of the day we passed at Hartford. The Marquis de Lafayette was called in as an interpreter, as Washington does not either speak French or understand it. They separated mutually pleased with each other; at least they say so." [36]

Washington was soon converted to the French view that nothing could be done as things were. They drew up a document in two columns to be sent to the King of France. In one column the French expressed their opinions; in the other, Washington his. This double-barrelled appeal included a statement signed by Rochambeau and de Ternay that it was "an indispensable necessity to reinforce the fleet and the army in ships, in men, and in money" (*en vaisseaux, en hommes et en argent*). Opposite was Washington's signed statement that it was absolutely necessary for the king to furnish "yet more ships, and men and money" (*des vaisseaux, des hommes et de l'argent*).[37]

Rochambeau decided to send his son with the appeal. De Ternay sent an officer and gave them a ship. Washington resolved to send an emissary of his own, selecting later young John Laurens, whose father, Henry, was an emissary to Holland. Friday, September 22nd, 1780, the French set out for Newport with thirteen cannon for a farewell salute. The next day Washington left Hartford and Governor Jonathan Trumbull—"Brother Jonathan."

In the meanwhile bewildering accidents had taken place, such a concatenation of narrow escapes ending in new entanglements as would be beyond the impudence of fiction.

André had come North in uniform with Clinton's specific orders not to quit it, not to enter the American lines, and not to carry on his person any incriminating documents. Arnold's emissary, Joshua Hett Smith, rowed out to the *Vulture* and brought him ashore. Before he knew it he was led inside the lines. He and Arnold had a long conference at the home of Smith, which was on the west side of the river, and arranged for a British attack on West Point, which would be captured with ease, owing to Arnold's carefully planned dispersal of the troops and Clinton's possession of complete information. Before André could return to the *Vulture*, the sloop was attacked by a meddlesome officer. Colonel Livingston had been annoyed by the sight of her, had asked Arnold for cannon and, being put off, had with difficulty borrowed a small gun and some powder from Colonel Lamb, who wrote to him:

"Firing at a ship with a four pounder, is in my opinion, a waste of powder; as the damage she will sustain, is not equal to the expense." [38]

But Colonel Livingston's bombardment made the *Vulture* shift her moorings and drop down the river further, with a result that saved the United States the three years' work and the three million dollars spent on West Point, to say nothing of the hundred odd millions and the thousands of lives spent on the war. But for Livingston's target practice and some lazy oarsmen and a hundred other petty details, André would have got away with his plans, Clinton would have made his dash with the ships and men in waiting, captured the fortress, the garrison, and perhaps Washington, too. With Clinton in possession of the whole Hudson, Washington's small starved army cut off from New England and the French, the war would soon have been over in all probability. That was constructive cannon-firing. But innumerable other things had to back it up.

When the dismayed Arnold and André saw from Smith's windows the retirement of the *Vulture*, there was nothing left but to send André south by land on a horse. This meant that he must not wear his uniform. Arnold so ordered and forced on André documents minutely describing everything that Clinton might want to know. Smith heard of a handsome American uniform left in the care of Mrs. Cornelia Beekman. He asked for it. Mrs. Beekman refused to give it up. Thus she joined the long procession of those who unwittingly saved the republic. Smith had to furnish André with plain clothes. He got the doomed man across the river to the east side, but an inquisitive militia officer, though he accepted Arnold's pass, was so puzzled by their desire to ride south at night that they stopped with him to quiet him. He saved the republic.

On September 23rd, Smith and André set out on the road to White Plains. They passed Colonel Samuel B. Webb, who knew André well, stared at him and was not quite sure of him, so did not detain him and lost a chance to save the nation with a great deal of economy.

Fifteen miles from White Plains, Smith decided that he had had enough, broke his promise to Arnold and sent André on alone into what might as well have been an African jungle. He described a grand circle, in which miles and miles were retraced, and trotted into and out of ambush after ambush before he blundered into his three immortal captors near Tarrytown and entered schoolbook fame with them.

Opinion at the time varied as to whether these three men were incorruptible patriots or mercenary blackguards. They were probably the latter, but being unable to figure out how to sell André to the British safely, turned him over to Colonel Jameson at Armonk. He decided that André's possession of a pass from Arnold made it necessary to send him back to Arnold under guard with a letter explaining his capture. This put the game in Arnold's hands again. The idea may or may not have been André's, but it warned Arnold, and gave him the chance of escape that André had lost.

Jameson also sent a messenger to find Washington and give him the papers found on André. This messenger hunted for Washington on the road he had taken to Hartford, but he had taken another one back. The messenger missed him altogether. Providence was apparently determined to rescue Arnold.

After André had been sent north, Major Benjamin Tallmadge, who had done much secret service work for Washington, learned of Colonel Jameson's action, and criticized it as "a glaring inconsistency." After a prolonged wrangle, he persuaded his Colonel to recall "John Anderson." Jameson consented to this but, says Tallmadge, "*would persist* in his purpose of letting his letter go on to Gen. Arnold." He afterwards wrote to Washington expressing his profound regrets. If Providence had inspired him to listen to Tallmadge, Washington would have learned of André's capture and the unwitting Arnold would have been apprehended with ease.

The weary André, having been in the saddle since dawn, was overtaken near Peekskill and dragged back, reappearing at Armonk Sunday morning. Major Tallmadge recognized him as a soldier by the way he faced about as he paced the room. Suddenly André called for pen and ink and wrote a letter to Washington disclosing that the prisoner in a servant's shabby garb was really the adjutant-general of the British Army, and that he was within the lines against his stipulation and intention.[39]

The facts will forever divide the opinions of mankind as to the justice of his fate. He was dragged within the American lines in uniform; hence did not enter them as a spy. He had a prisoner's right to escape in any disguise. Besides, he was detained, ordered by the commandant to change his clothes, and thus sent out of the lines on a pass from the commandant and with a guide intrusted to restore him to his own lines. He was captured in neutral territory.

These technical defences will always lead the British to say that he was no spy. The loathsomeness of Arnold's conduct and André's share in it will always lead Americans to say that, whatever he was, his release or exchange was unthinkable.

Tallmadge yielded, as everybody did, to the overwhelming charm of André. On learning who he was, and his plight, he says, "My Agitation was extreme, & my Emotions wholly indescribable." [40] With a strong escort of cavalry he set out for West Point with André. When Sparks was writing his history he wrote to Tallmadge, then an old man, and asked him a number of questions. In answering them Tallmadge said of André:

"It often drew tears from my Eyes to find him so pleasant & agreeable in Conversation on different Subjects, when I reflected on his future fate, & that, too, as I believed, so near at hand. . . . So deeply were my feelings interested in the fate of this unfortunate young Man, that I believe I have never narrated the story, nor perused the account of his merited, but ignominious Death without shedding tears of sorrow over such blighted prospects. I hope & trust this will be the last trial of my feelings in this way." [41]

Tallmadge told André that he "had a much-loved Class mate in Yale College by the name of Nathan Hale," and André was much "troubled."

Saturday night Washington slept at Litchfield, Connecticut. Sunday morning he dined in Fishkill—dined with Joshua Hett Smith, who had abandoned André, and whose ambiguous sympathies swung from rebel to Tory, managing to betray both. Now Washington takes up the story again in Lear's diary and tells how Luzerne kept him from capturing Arnold:

"I met the Chevalier Luzerne towards evening, within about 15 miles of West Point (on his way to join the Count at Rhode Island), which I intended to reach that night, but he insisted upon turning back with me to the next public house; where, in politeness to him, I could not but stay all night, determining, however, to get to West Point to breakfast very early. I sent off my baggage, and desired Colonel Hamilton to go forward, and inform General Arnold that I would breakfast with him. Soon after he arrived at Arnold's quarters, a letter was delivered to Arnold which threw him into the greatest confusion. He told Colonel Hamilton that something required his immediate attendance at the garrison, which was on the opposite side of the river to his quarters; and immediately ordered a horse, to take him to the river; and the barge, which he kept to cross, to be ready; and desired Major Franks, his Aid, to inform me when I should arrive, that he was gone over the river and would return immediately.

"When I got to his quarters and did not find him there, I desired Major Franks to order me some breakfast; and as I intended to visit the fortifications I would see General Arnold there. After I had breakfasted, I went over the river, and inquiring for Arnold, the commanding officer told me that he had not been there. I likewise inquired at the several redoubts, but no one could give me any information where he was. The impropriety of his conduct when he knew I was to be there, struck me very forcibly, and my mind misgave me; but I had not the least idea of the real cause. When I returned to Arnold's quarters about two hours after, and told Colonel Hamilton that I had not seen him, he gave me a packet which had just arrived for me from Col. Jemmison, which immediately brought the matter to light." [42]

The package from Colonel Jameson was a thunderbolt from the blue. Washington had come from the French in a mood of despair or, at best, indefinite deferment of hope. Now he learned that the man to whom he had entrusted the citadel of the union had been dealing with the British for its surrender.

An awful sorrow was Washington's first mood. Tears were in his eyes suddenly and he could only hand the papers to Lafayette and mumble:

"Arnold is a traitor and has fled to the British."

Then came the panic of universal suspicion. He gasped:

"Whom can we trust now?" [43]

The sentinel at Arnold's headquarters said that when Washington came to the house, he carried a small riding-switch broken off from some tree and during the first onset of his emotions chewed the entire switch to pieces. [44] Recovering from his first daze, Washington began to act with resolution. He ordered Hamilton to ride with all speed to a post on the river eight miles below where he might fire on Arnold's barge if it had not already passed. He hastily organized every defence he could against the assault he expected at any moment from Clinton.

Hamilton was far too late to overtake Arnold, who had indeed found time to write a letter to Washington and send it ashore under a flag. Hamilton forwarded it to Washington. Arnold began with a phrase that he was forever using, a veritable trade mark of his: "The heart which is conscious of its own rectitude." It was doubtless perfectly sincere. There was probably never a villain, a thief, martyr, murderer, tyrant, saint, bigot, reformer, zealot, whose heart was not "conscious of its own rectitude," and utterly assured that the world's opposition to its activity was an evil to be overcome or undermined. Without the consciousness of one's own rectitude one can neither save a country nor betray it. Arnold declared that his step was due to "a principle of love" to his country, but he did not expect to be understood. He asked protection from a "mistaken vengeance," upon his wife, who was "as good and as innocent as an angel," and her return to him or her friends in Philadelphia. He also asked for his clothes and offered to pay for them if required! [45]

In the midst of the appalling avalanche of revelations and menaces of peril, Washington and his staff found, as men have so often found in a great crisis, that some hysterical woman must first be taken care of and quieted. Before proceeding with the saving of the nation, Washington and his friends had to deal with the poor little, pretty little traitress, Mrs. Arnold. According to Hamilton:

"At a lucid interval she inquired of the doctor if General Washington was in the house, desiring to see him. Believing that she intended to say something which would explain the secret of Arnold's unaccountable absence, he hastened below, and conducted the general to her chamber, who remained no longer than to hear her deny that he was General Washington, and to witness the return of her dis-traction." [46]

Hamilton wrote to his betrothed, Miss Schuyler:

"It was the most affecting scene I ever was witness to. She, for a considerable time, entirely lost herself. The General went up to see her, and she upbraided him with being in a plot to murder her child. One moment she raved, another she melted into tears. Sometimes she pressed her infant to her bosom, and lamented its fate, occasioned by the imprudence of its father, in a manner that would have pierced insensibility itself. All the sweetness of beauty, all the loveliness of innocence, all the tenderness of a wife, and all the fondness of a mother showed themselves in her appearance and conduct. We have every reason to believe that she was entirely unacquainted with the plan, and that the first knowledge of it was when Arnold went to tell her he must banish himself from his country and from her forever. She instantly fell into a convulsion, and he left her in that situation." [47]

Hamilton found a rival in Lafayette, who wrote of her to Luzerne:

"She has recovered her reason this morning, and as, you know, I am upon very good terms with her, she sent for me to go up to her chamber. General Washington and every one else here sympathize warmly with this estimable woman, whose face and whose youthfulness make her so interesting. She is going to Philadelphia; and I implore you, when you return, to use your influence in her favor. It would be exceedingly painful to General Washington if she were not treated with the greatest kindness. . . . As for myself, you know that I have always been fond of her, and at this moment she interests me intensely. We are certain that she knew nothing of the plot." [48]

It is curious, in view of later history, how Aaron Burr and Hamilton kept taking opposite sides of the same questions even at remote distances. Washington, who could never be outdone in chivalry, treated Mrs. Arnold with the tenderest consideration and sent her to her parents in Philadelphia with a guard to protect her from insult or worse by the frantic inhabitants. She rested for one night at the home of Burr's fiancée, Mrs. Prevost, with whom Washington and his staff had spent such pleasant days at Paramus. There, according to Burr's *Memoir*:

"The frantic scenes of West Point were renewed, and continued so long as strangers were present. Mrs. Prevost was known as the wife of a British officer, and connected with the royalists. In her, therefore, Mrs. Arnold could confide. As soon as they were left alone Mrs. Arnold became tranquillized, and assured Mrs. Prevost that she was heartily sick of the theatrics she was exhibiting. She stated that she had corresponded with the British commander—that she was disgusted with the American cause and those who had the management of public affairs —and that, through great persuasion and unceasing perseverance, she had ultimately brought the general into an arrangement to surrender West Point to the British." [49]

For this anecdote Burr has been repeatedly reviled as the foul slanderer of an innocent woman. Even Trevelyan denounces his "guile" and "malice." His "base calumny" has even been explained by the story that he was present, escorted Mrs. Arnold part way and in the carriage "basely made love to this afflicted lady . . . being indignantly repelled, he treasured up his revenge, and left a story behind him worthy of his false and malignant heart, to blast this amiable lady's fame, when there might be no one to disprove or deny it." [50]

Burr was elected by acclamation to be the roué of his time, though Hamilton was by his own public confession no Galahad. But Burr's profligacy did not include the slander of women and the recent disclosures of the Clinton papers prove that Burr was disgustingly accurate, as he so often was. In Philadelphia, Mrs. Arnold was suspiciously received and the Pennsylvania Council finally banished her from the state, on the ground that her residence was "dangerous to the public safety." [51] She was permitted to go to her husband, and spent her later years in England.

Her devotion to Arnold and to their children seems to have been quite perfect and her letters reveal a singularly noble character. Arnold's devotion to her seems to have been equally ardent and, if one can tolerate a trace of virtue in villains, theirs is one of the most touching love stories in history. [52] The public in England as well as in America made sure that Arnold should have his hell on earth and his wife went through it with him. But he played hell with America first, and nothing is more puzzling than to find the good Americans of that time declaring that Providence had indubitably intervened to save America and thwart Arnold. What kind of Providence could it have been that wanted to save America, yet intervened at every step to save Arnold from such simple and economical opportunities to be rid of him, left him to burn, slay, and harry the land for a year and get away scot-free, while poor André, the helpless victim of his bungling, was left to die in shame, breaking his own warm heart and the hearts of his enemies and winning immortal fame as one of the most lovable and pathetic figures in human chronicle? Providence either bungled or did not care—or was indeed then and still "inscrutable."

XLIII

EXIT ANDRÉ

WITH Washington the pen had to do the work of the sword. Finding West Point all prepared for easy capture by the British and expecting them to appear at any moment, he began to call in the scattered garrison and all other forces within reach.

He wrote to Colonel Lamb to leave West Point and go to Stoney and Verplanck Points where the British must first be checked.[1] He asked who was next in command and Colonel Nathaniel Wade was named. "He is a true man," he said. "I am satisfied."[2]

He wrote to Colonel Wade to take Lamb's command.[3]

The next day he wrote again advising that provisions and water be supplied to the works. Wade answered that all the food they had was pickled fish, but there was water enough.[4] Washington wrote to an officer whom Arnold had sent out on a distant wood-cutting expedition, to return; to Colonel Livingston to come to see him at once; to Colonel Ebenezer Gray to march his men to him at once; to Major Low, commander of the Massachusetts levies of militia, to march to him at once. His main reliance was, of course, on his army at Tappan. He wrote to Greene:

"I request, that you will put the division on the left in motion as soon as possible, with orders to proceed to King's Ferry, when, or before they arrive there, they will be met with further orders. The division will come on light, leaving their heavy baggage to follow. You will also hold all the troops in readiness to move on the shortest notice. Transactions of a most interesting nature, and such as will astonish you, have been just discovered."[5]

He wrote to Colonel Jameson to be exceedingly careful that André should not escape:

"I would not wish Mr. André to be treated with insult; but . . . he is not entitled to the usual indulgences . . . and is to be most closely and narrowly watched."

He repeated in a postscript, "André must not escape." [6] He cast about him for confederates of Arnold. Being short handed, he sent the French engineer, Gouvion, with a platoon to arrest his late dinner companion, Joshua Hett Smith. Gouvion broke down his door, dragged him out of bed from the side of his wife, refused to wait for a horse, and marched him on foot eighteen miles to the Beverly Robinson house, where he was confronted by the fierce Washington who threatened to hang him on the same tree with André.[7]

After a night of frantic activity, the dawn brought troops. Greene's camp had been wakened by the alarm. Hamilton, always forethoughtful, had sent a messenger from Verplanck's Point to Greene without waiting to consult Washington:

"There has just been unfolded at this place a scene of the blackest treason . . . I came here in pursuit of Arnold, but was too late. I advise your putting the army under marching orders and detaching a brigade immediately this way." [8]

This reached Greene before eleven o'clock at night. Drums rolled, fifes shrieked, lights darted here and there, as the men were dragged from their slumber and hurried into line. Washington's order did not come till after three in the morning, by which time Greene had already sent the left division on its way.[9] Anthony Wayne describes his all-night march and his reception by Washington. His tone is very grandiloquent, but it ends up with a flirtatious note:

"Our army was out of protecting distance—the troops in the possession of the Works a spiritless *Miserabile Vulgus*—in whose hands the fate of America seemed suspended—in this Situation His Excellency—(in Imitation of Cæsar & his tenth Legion)—called for his *Veterans*—the Summons arrived at One OClock in the morning—&

we took up our Line of March at 2—& by sun rise arrived at this place distant from our former Camp 16 miles—the whole performed in four hours in a dark night—without a single halt or a man left behind— When our approach was announced to the General he thought it fabulous—but when convinced of the reality—he received us like a God— & retiring to take a short repose—exclaimed—'All is safe, & I again am happy'—May he long—very long Continue so—

"The protection of that Important place is committed to my Conduct until a proper Garrison arrives—I shall not throw myself into the Works—but will dispute the Approaches *inch* by *inch* and at the point of the bayonet, decide the fate of the day in the Gorge of the Defiles— at every expense of blood, until death or Victory cries—'*hold*'—'*hold*' — . . . my Conduct will never require the palliation of a friend, or memory cause a blush to shade the cheek of any *tender* acquaintance. Apropo' there is one to whom you'l be so Oblig^g as to present my kindest wishes." [10]

General Irvine also made the night march and speaks of the condition Arnold had arranged:

"I made a rapid march and found the place on my arrival in a most miserable condition in every respect. About 1800 militia had been at the Post, but were chiefly detached on various pretences. Those who remained had not a single place assigned them, nor had a single order what to do. I have not heard from Head Quarters to-day, but I have reason to believe that Major André and Smith must be hung." [11]

But the British did not appear. Clinton was thrown into a panic of his own by Arnold's unexpected appearance on the *Vulture*—what a name for a ship devoted to such errands! All of Clinton's pretences toward Chesapeake Bay were unmasked and he knew that Washington would be waiting for him. But his chief dismay concerned the fate of his beloved André.

Daybreak of Tuesday, September 26th, brought to Washington not only Wayne's troops, and the prisoner Smith, but also the prisoner André. After the two days of riding from suspense to suspense, André had ridden thirty miles during a night of rain, in such shabby dress that Tallmadge lent him his own dragoon cloak in spite of André's reluctance to accept it. Tallmadge says that when he reported to Washington and answered many inquiries, he asked if Washington would see the prisoner. Washington shook his head and it seems that he never laid his eyes on André.[12] André and Joshua Smith were taken across the river to West Point, but, fearing the danger of a rescue, Washington sent them to Greene at Tappan with a letter enjoining the greatest vigilance, their confinement in separate houses, under "strong, trusty guards trebly officered, that a part may be constantly in the room with them . . . I would wish the room for Mr. André to be a decent one, and that he may be treated with civility . . . Smith must also be as carefully secured, and not treated with asperity."[13] Washington had André's breakfast sent from his own table every day.[14] He put McDougall in command at West Point until General St. Clair could replace him. On the 26th Washington had time to write to Governor Clinton; to General Heath asking him to join the army; to Congress, of course, telling the whole story and recommending André's captors "to the thanks of their country," and other rewards.[15] He wrote also to Rochambeau:

"By lucky accident, a conspiracy of the most dangerous nature . . . has been detected."[16]

That would do for French infidels, but to President Reed he wrote his usual acknowledgment to Providence:

"That overruling Providence, which has so often and so remarkably interposed in our favor, never manifested itself more conspicuously."[17]

To John Laurens he wrote:

"In no instance since the commencement of the war has the interposition of Providence appeared more conspicuous than in the rescue of the Post & Garrison of West Point from Arnold's villainous perfidy. How far he meant to involve me in the catastrope of this place does not appear by any indubitable evidence and I am rather inclined to think he did not wish to hazard the more important object of his treachery by attempting to combine two events the lesser of which might have marred the greater . . . but for the egregious folly—or the bewildered conception of Lieut Col° Jameson who seemed lost in astonishment and not to have known what he was doing I should as certainly have got Arnold." [18]

He added a comment on Laurens' statement to him that Arnold's punishment would be "the permanent, increasing torment of a mental hell": [19]

"I am mistaken if at *this time*, Arnold is undergoing the torments of a mental Hell. He wants feeling!—From some traits of his character which have lately come to my knowledge he seems to have been so hackneyed in villainy—& so lost to all sense of honor and shame that while his faculties will enable him to continue his sordid pursuits there will be no time for remorse."

Lafayette thought of Arnold's remorse as Laurens did, and wrote to Luzerne of the "miraculous chain of accidents and circumstances . . . a combination of accidents" that saved West Point, and his regret that one who had "shared our labors with us" and "shed his blood for the American cause" should "sell his country to the tyrants whom he had fought against with glory." He added:

"My knowledge of his personal courage led me to expect that he would decide to blow his brains out (this was my first hope); at all events, it is probable that he will do so when he reaches New York." [20]

But Arnold's heart was "conscious of its own rectitude" and he lived to invade Virginia, capture and burn Richmond and mock the efforts of Lafayette and the whole French fleet and army rushed thither to trap him. He burned and harried and slew in New England, too, and Providence protected him from a single wound under his new employers.

Washington was in a frenzy to have him and hang him in the flesh as he was being hanged in effigy in every American town. To take him alive became the fascinating endeavor of no end of efforts. Light Horse Harry Lee in his Memoirs tells how Washington said to him:

"I have sent for you, in the expectation that you have in your corps individuals capable and willing to undertake an indispensable, delicate, and hazardous project. Whoever comes forward upon this occasion, will lay me under great obligations personally, and in behalf of the United States I will reward him amply." [21]

Lee concocted a scheme by which Sergeant-Major John Champe would pretend to desert, get to Arnold and kidnap him. It delighted Washington, who wrote to Lee:

"The plan proposed for taking A—, the outlines of which are communicated in your letter which was this moment put into my hands without a date, has every mark of a good one. I therefore agree to the promised rewards, and have such entire confidence in your management of this business as to give it my fullest approbation; and leave the whole to the guidance of your own judgment, with this express stipulation, and pointed injunction, that he, A—d, is brought to me alive. No circumstance whatever shall obtain my consent to his being put to death. The idea which would accompany such an event would be that Ruffians had been hired to assassinate him. My aim is to make a public example of him—and this should be strongly impressed upon those who are employed to bring him off. The sergeant must be very circumspect— too much zeal may create suspicion—and too much precipitancy may defeat the project. The most inviolable secrecy must be observed on all hands. I send you five guineas; but I am not satisfied of the propriety of the sergeant's appearing with much specie—this circumstance may also lead to suspicion as it is but too well known to the enemy that we do not deal much in this article. The Interviews between the party in and out of the city, should be managed with much caution and seeming indifference, or else the frequency of their meetings &c., may betray the design and involve bad consequences; but I am persuaded you will place every matter in a proper point of view to the conductors of this interesting business." [22]

What followed reads more like Dumas than dull history. When Champe fled he was so hotly pursued by his own men that only by great luck did he escape death at their hands. He swam to a British ship under the most convincing fire from Americans, reached New York, wormed himself into Arnold's environment, bribed confederates, learned Arnold's habits, which included "his custom to return home about twelve every night, and that previous to going to bed he always visited the garden. During this visit the conspirators were to seize him, and being prepared with a gag, intended to have applied the same instantly."

Washington was highly gratified with the progress of the plot and ordered Lee to be waiting with troops at Hoboken when Champe crossed the dark river with his prisoner. They waited in vain. Champe did not come. Arnold put his men, including Champe, on a transport that very day and carried them off to Virginia, where Champe could not even desert until the campaign was nearly over. Congress decreed a day of Thanksgiving and prayer on December 7th because of "the late remarkable interposition of his watchful providence, in rescuing the person of our Commander in Chief and the army from imminent dangers, at the moment when treason was ripened for execution." [23] If Providence deserved a national holiday for allowing treason to ripen before plucking it, how can one deny the equally remarkable interpositions to protect Arnold from harm?

It is usual to describe his horrible remorse, his bitter humiliations in England, and his wretched death caressing his old uniform and repenting his evil life. He had his miseries, gigantic disappointments, and his insults, and he lost heavily in speculation; but so did Washington have his miseries and far worse insults. Arnold ended in far better estate than innumerable patriots who stuck to the army and starved. He was sixty when he died in his bed, having outlived Washington a year and a half; and he died in far less physical agony.

Joshua Hett Smith, his helper in the betrayal of André, laid all the blame for his action on Arnold's deceitful assurances that his purpose was to obtain useful intelligence from New York. He was acquitted, arrested by a civil group, escaped, lived on a pension from the king, and died in New York in 1818.[24] All of the country's revenge and all the vindictiveness of circumstance were concentrated on André, of whom Jared Sparks says:

"It was his singular fortune to die, not more beloved by his friends, than lamented by his enemies, whose cause he had sought to ruin, and by whose hands his life was justly taken." [25]

There is much disagreement as to that word "justly," and the execution of André is the one deed of Washington's life from which the British have withheld the profound admiration they have almost unanimously heaped upon the man who dealt the empire the greatest blow it ever suffered. The well-nigh unbearable regret for André's sacrifice is due to his own behavior. A secret service man against America on earlier occasions, he was notable chiefly as a frivolous gallant, a pet of the ladies, an intolerably handsome fellow, a painter, a draughtsman, a writer of farces and ribald poems, a singer of gay songs, and an insatiably zealous actor of plays. Yet, like so many other actors, when he left the theatre he was impatient of masquerade, and said, "I pretend not to play the hero, or to be indifferent about life." [26] When he found himself a prisoner, he threw off disguise and conducted himself with a gracious sweetness and altruism, strangely combined with dauntless valor. His own frank admissions made it impossible for the court-martial to acquit him, once it disregarded his claim that he was lured against his will into the American lines and his uniform taken from him by the orders of the commander on whose pass he left the lines. These facts were emphasized by the British, who did their utmost to save him. Colonel Beverly Robinson, as soon as he learned from Arnold of André's capture, wrote to his old friend, Washington, from the *Vulture*, off "Sinsink," September 25th, 1780:

"Major André cannot be detained by you without the greatest violation of flags, and contrary to the custom and usage of all nations; and as I imagine you will see this matter in the same point of view that I do, I must desire you will order him to be set at liberty and allowed to return immediately. Every step Major André took was by the advice and direction of General Arnold, even that of taking a feigned name, and of course not liable to censure for it. I am, Sir, not forgetting our former acquaintance." [27]

As soon as Arnold reached New York, Clinton wrote a polite demand for the return of "the King's Adjutant General":

"I have the honor to inform you, Sir, that I permitted Major André to go to Major General Arnold at the particular request of that general officer. You will perceive, Sir, by the enclosed paper, that a flag of truce was sent to receive Major André, and passports granted for his return. I therefore can have no doubt but your Excellency will immediately direct that this officer has permission to return to my orders at New York." [28]

With this was a copy of Arnold's report to Clinton claiming that André was under the protection of a flag of truce:

"I apprehend a few hours must return Major André to your Excellency's orders . . . I commanded at the time at West Point, had an undoubted right to send my flag of truce for Major André." [29]

The tone of both letters was perhaps unhappy. The assurance of André's immediate release was rhetorical, of course. It was unlikely that Washington would recognize Arnold's right to betray his country. The intention automatically cancelled his commission and annulled his oath of allegiance. Though Arnold sent Smith for André with a flag of truce, they came ashore without one since it was dark. In any case, its purpose would have robbed it of sanctity. This was made very plain in Washington's reply to Clinton:

"Major André was employed in the execution of measures very foreign to the objects of flags of truce, and such as they were never meant to authorize or countenance in the most distant degree; and this gentleman confessed, with the greatest candor, in the course of his examination, 'that it was impossible for him to suppose, that he came on shore under the sanction of a flag.' " [30]

He did not reply to Beverly Robinson's letter. In order to give the case the fullest possible sifting, he organized a court consisting of nearly every general within reach, six major-generals and eight brigadiers. Sparks asked Tallmadge why Wayne was omitted and Tallmadge answered:

"The Commr in Chief selected the Board . . . & no one took upon him the liberty to enquire why A. was Appointed . . . & B. omitted." [81]

It was perhaps remembered that André had recently written a long and hilarious parody on the "Ballad of Chevy Chace," ridiculing a defeated foraging expedition led by Wayne and Irvine. It was called the "Cow-Chace," and presented Wayne as stopping in the midst of battle to dally with a siren. It may have been thought that Wayne and Irvine would be suspected of too great prejudice to be eligible.[82]

The verdict of the court-martial was inevitable. It was made intensely distressful by André's prompt verbal denial that he was under a flag of truce, and a frank statement that he wrote out for the court.[33] Steuben said: "It is not possible to save him. He put us to no proof, but in an open, manly manner, confessed every thing but a premeditated design to deceive. Would to God the wretch who drew him to death could have suffered in his place!" [34]

The court found him "a spy from the enemy" and agreed "it is their opinion he ought to suffer death." André's irresistible magnetism enthralled them so that it is said that "the whole court shed tears on signing the report" and that the pen shook in the hand of Greene and he bent his head in vain to hide his tears.[35] This was only the beginning. History does not show any victim more deeply pitied or bewept by his executioners. On September 30th, 1780, Washington approved the opinion and ordered the execution the next day,— "a duty from which his soul revolted; and it is asserted that his hand could scarcely command his pen." [36] But he was resolved to see it through and urged Captain Ebenezer Smith to take particular care that the food of the guards should not be drugged to aid André's escape. He said to Smith:

"Treachery is all around me, and I hardly know whom to trust, but I know I can trust you." [37]

Captain Smith said that the certainty of his execution overwhelmed André at first. "The agony of his mind as he walked the room was most distressing, and it seemed to me that his very flesh crawled upon his bones." Smith was overjoyed by the reprieve that came during the afternoon. For Washington was so eager to be just that he granted an appeal from Clinton, begging him to see Lieutenant-General Robertson and two others, Lieutenant-Governor Elliott and Chief Justice Smith.[38] Washington postponed the execution for a day and sent Greene to meet the visitors. Greene refused to discuss the matter with the eminent civilians and allowed only General Robertson to land, freezing him with the words:

"I do not meet you as an officer, but as a private gentleman. It is in this quality alone that General Washington allows me to meet you. The case of an acknowledged spy does not admit of discussion." . . .

"But Arnold also asserts that he was under a flag."

"We believe André rather than Arnold." [39]

Robertson's suggestion that Rochambeau and Knyphausen be asked to decide the matter was rejected. Baffled, Robertson handed Greene a long letter from Arnold, thanking Washington for his "polite attention" to Mrs. Arnold, taking on himself the blame for all of André's and Smith's actions, and making a desperate threat:

"If that gentleman should suffer the severity of their sentence, I shall think myself bound by every tie of duty and honor to retaliate on such unhappy persons of your army as may fall within my power, that the respect due to flags, and to the law of nations, may be better understood and observed. . . . Forty of the principal inhabitants of South Carolina have justly forfeited their lives, which have hitherto been spared by the clemency of His Excellency Sir Henry Clinton, who cannot in justice extend his mercy to them any longer, if Major André suffers; which, in all probability, will open a scene of blood at which humanity will revolt.

"Suffer me to entreat your Excellency, for your own and the honor of humanity, and the love you have of justice, that you suffer not an unjust sentence to touch the life of Major André. But if this warning should be disregarded, and he suffer, I call Heaven and earth to witness, that your Excellency will be justly answerable for the torrent of blood that may be spilt in consequence." [40]

Greene is said to have tossed this letter to the ground, but it must have been picked up again. He showed to Robertson André's letter to Washington and then, according to Robertson:

"Green said one thing would satisfy them—they expected if André was set free, Arnold should be given up. This I answered with a look only which threw Green into confusion. I am persuaded André will not be hurt." [41]

Others seem to have made the same suggestion. Colonel Simcoe of the Queen's Rangers says:

"Amongst some letters which passed on this unfortunate event, a paper was slid in without signature, but in the hand writing of Hamilton, Washington's secretary, saying, 'that the only way to save André was to give up Arnold.'" [42]

There is little question that Washington would have exchanged anybody, almost his right eye, for Arnold; but that Clinton should give up such a detestable failure even for André, was inconceivable in any of the curiously twisted codes of human honor. One can only say the conclusive word, "It simply isn't done."

Yet some of the Americans were apparently excited enough to believe that it might be done, for Harry Lee wrote to Simcoe, with whom he was on those peculiarly exquisite terms possible to two cavalry leaders whose hope to cut each other to pieces on the field does not interfere with every other courtesy:

"I am happy in telling you, that there is a probability of Major Andre's being restored to his country, and the customs of war being fully satisfied."

But before the letter went, the word came that Clinton would not exchange Arnold for André and Lee added the postscript:

"Since writing the foregoing, I find that Sir Henry Clinton's offers have not come up to what was expected, and that this hour is fixed for the execution of the sentence. How cold the friendship of those high in power!"

To this Simcoe replied:

"I am at a loss to express myself on the latter paragraphs of your letter; I have long accustomed myself to be silent, or to speak the language of the heart. The useless murder of Major Andre would almost, was it possible, annihilate that wish which, consentaneous to the ideas of our sovereign, and the government of Great Britain, has ever operated on the officers of the British army, the wish of a reconciliation and speedy re-union with their revolted fellow subjects in America. Sir Henry Clinton has the warmest feelings for those under his command, and was ready to have granted for Major Andre's exchange, whatever ought to have been asked."

Simcoe laid his plans to make a desperate sortie for the recapture of André, believing that Washington would refer him to Congress for final decision as usual. But for once Washington did not ask the consent of Congress. He simply forwarded the papers, and ordered the execution for the next day. To Simcoe and the other British officers there was something intolerable in the thought that André must die. Simcoe wrote:

"Major Andre was murdered upon private not public considerations. It bore not with it the stamp of justice; for there was not an officer in the British army whose duty it would not have been, had any of the American Generals offered to quit the service of Congress, to have negotiated to receive them; so that this execution could not, by example, have prevented the repetition of the same offence . . . no European general would on this pretext have had his blood upon his head. He fell a sacrifice to that which was expedient, not to that which was just: what was supposed to be useful superceded what would have been generous." [43]

That stout old Tory, Judge Jones, who hated Clinton as fervidly as he hated Howe, blamed Clinton for abstaining from reprisal. Incidentally he states the amusing cynicism that the entire patriotic force had its price:

"If Great Britain, instead of expending £1,000,000 in pursuing the American war to no kind of purpose, had applied, at the first, only £200,000 to the same uses as the money given to Arnold was, the whole rebel army, the Congress, and all the conventions, and committees, within the revolted Colonies, might have been purchased."

But his chief venom was for Clinton, whom he blamed for not assuming a threatening tone and for sending Robertson "a superannuated, worn out, timid, irresolute, forgetful, old gentleman." He tells what he would have done:

"By all the powers above, had I been Commander-in-Chief, and André my first friend, my best adviser, and my bosom confidant, I would have sacrificed among the treacherous Carolina conspirators, but what his manes should have been appeased, and the murder of the great, the good, and virtuous youth, fully, amply, and completely revenged! In order to save André's life, and obtain his discharge, General Clinton had taken up and confined in the prevost, about 20 inhabitants of the city of New York and Long Island. He had the fullest evidence, the clearest testimony, that these people had carried on a treasonable correspondence with the rebels for many years, had acted as spies within the British lines, and given rebellion every information in their power. These fellows had, upon the reduction of Long Island and the city of New York, renewed their oaths of allegiance to the King, lived upon, and enjoyed their estates, protected by the Crown. A correspondence carried on by people thus circumstanced, giving every necessary intelligence to the rebels of the proceedings and designs of the Royal army, was, by the laws of Great Britain, under whose protection they lived, to all intents and purposes, treason. Governor Robertson was directed to acquaint Washington with this circumstance, and to assure him in the most peremptory manner, that in case André was executed as a spy, every one of these men should share the same fate. Robertson accordingly assured the rebel chief, that this was Clinton's fixed and unalterable resolution. Washington knew the man, despised his threats, and hanged André. But, though strange to relate, yet actually true, within ten days after the execution of André, he, Clinton, discharged all these fellows from the prevost, suffered them to live upon their own estates, and that, without ever exacting a parole, or taking the least security for their future good behaviour. What could be expected from a Commander-in-Chief sent to America to quell a serious rebellion possessed of so little resolution, such indecision, and such rank timidity? No wonder the war ended as it did!" [44]

It was fortunate for history that Clinton did not slay these captives of his, for Washington would probably have slain an equal number. He was ruthless and immovable on the subject of reprisal as later events will show. That he had many spies in New York his correspondence proves. But he assumed that their risk was what he paid them for—in hard money, too. Fortescue, the modern historian of the British Army, puts the case of André coldly:

"Beyond all doubt this sentence was perfectly justified by the rules of war, but equally beyond all doubt it was pronounced in the hope that Clinton, in order to save André, would surrender Arnold. . . . Moreover, the Americans at large had not shown themselves particularly scrupulous in the observance of the rules of war, and Washington himself little more scrupulous than others. He had indeed discountenanced the use of split bullets by his men, as well as wholesale breach of parole by his officers; and he had strongly reprobated the sale of British medicines, which had been supplied for the benefit of American prisoners, by American doctors for their own profit. Yet we find him suggesting of his own motion that a party of an American regiment, which happened, unlike other corps, to be dressed in scarlet, should be furnished with the buttons of some English regiment, in order that they might pass for English soldiers and kidnap General Clinton. Now, had these American soldiers, thus attired, been caught in the act, Clinton would have been perfectly justified in hanging every one of them; and their blood would have been upon Washington's head. It seems to me, therefore, unquestionable that the rigorous execution of André's sentence was employed chiefly as a means of putting pressure of a peculiarly cruel kind upon Clinton; and it was for this reason and for no other that it was so much resented by the British Army and the British nation. Meanwhile, the fact remains unshaken that Washington acted within his right in confirming the sentence. Any charges of ungenerosity against him are entirely beside the mark; for it is not the business of a general to show generosity to his enemies, rather it is his duty to withhold it if he think generosity impolitic." [45]

Many of the Americans did wear British uniforms for secret purposes. Allen McLane often put his men in them. Tallmadge shortly after the execution described how he and his men "being in the uniform of some of the Enemies Corps" were taken for British by a Tory who offered to help them kidnap Governor Clinton and seize West Point.[46] To return to André's story: After his interview with General Greene, General Robertson waited all night on his boat hoping for good news. Greene sent him a brief note saying that he had reported the conversation to Washington but "it made no alteration in his opinion or determination." [47]

General Robertson then wrote a long and intensely earnest appeal to Washington, pointing out that Clinton "had never put to death any person for a breach of the rules of war, though he had, and now has, many in his power," that André was dear to him and he would be "infinitely obliged by his liberation," and would "have any person you would be pleased to name set at liberty." [48]

Nothing could move Washington from his grim resolve to get on with the hanging. Expecting to die on October 1st, André had written an ultimate petition asking that he might be shot,—granted a "professional death."

"Buoyed above the terror of death, by the consciousness of a life devoted to honorable pursuits, and stained with no action that can give me remorse, I trust that the request I make to your Excellency at this serious period, and which is to soften my last moments, will not be rejected.

"Sympathy towards a soldier will surely induce your Excellency and a military tribunal to adapt the mode of my death to the feelings of a man of honor. Let me hope, Sir, that if aught in my character impresses you with esteem towards me, if aught in my misfortunes marks me as the victim of policy and not of resentment, I shall experience the operation of these feelings in your breast, by being informed that I am not to die on a gibbet. I have the honor to be your Excellency's most obedient and most humble servant,

"John André,
"*Adj. Gen. to the British Army.*" [49]

Strange it was to see that title, "Adj. Gen. to the British Army" at the end of a pitiful prayer to the rebel chief. But Washington would not grant the prayer. Hamilton, who was chilling toward Washington, wrote to Miss Schuyler:

"Poor André suffers to-day. Every thing that is amiable in virtue, in fortitude, in delicate sentiment, and accomplished manners, pleads for him; but hard-hearted policy calls for a sacrifice. He must die— . . . I urged a compliance with André's request to be shot; and I do not think it would have had an ill effect; but some people are only sensible to motives of policy, and sometimes, from a narrow disposition, mistake it. When André's tale comes to be told, and present resentment is over, the refusing him the privilege of choosing the manner of his death will be branded with too much obstinacy." [50]

In his letter to John Laurens, Hamilton was more careful; he wrote that when Washington did not even answer André's plea, his motive was "to evade an answer, to spare him the sensations which a certain knowledge of the intended mode would inflict." [51] But when André on his death march caught sight of the gallows and the wagon below it with an empty coffin for him to stand on, he flinched as if the bullet he implored had struck his heart. According to Ensign Bowman, one of the two officers with whom he linked arms, he said:

"I have borne everything with fortitude, but this is too degrading! As respects myself it is a matter of no consequence, but I have a mother and sisters who will be very much mortified by the intelligence." [52]

Then he marched on to his destination. Captain Van Dyk, who was one of his four escorts, described what followed his first glimpse of the gibbet:

"He put his hands upon his hips, looked up to the gallows, then bowed his head a little down, vewed his feet, and so up, untill his head rose to its natural position, biting his underlip and Shakeing his head . . . the hangman let the waggon under the gallows, and the Commanding Officer then said, Major Andre, you will please to get on the waggon, Major Andre advanced to the hinder part of the waggon, puting his hands upon It, made a motion as tho intending to Jump on, but faltering, he put his right knee on, and then raised himselfe up into the waggon, turned himselfe to the guard, placing his hands on his hips

"The Commanding Officer, who was on horseback then Said, Majr Andre, If you have anything to say, you can now Speek, for you have but a short time to live, Major Andre with his hands on his hips, Said, I have nothing more to say Gentlemen, but this, you all bare me witness, that I meet my fate as a brave man. . . . Major Andre . . . took the halter out of the hangmans hand, . . . put It over his head & drew the knot close on the right side of his neck—he then tied a white hankerchief over his eyes, with much apparent composure of mind——the hangman haveing secured the end of the halter to the top of the gallows, descended from the waggon——the Commanding officer directed the hangman to tie his armes Slack behind him——Major Andre then takeing a white hankerchief out of his right hand coat pocket, gave It to the hangman, who tied his armes as directed (this was don that he shuld not rais his armes while hanging) the Commanding Officer then gave a Signal, by the falling of his Sword, for the hangman to drive off——the hangman then led the horses from under the gallows, and Major Andre Swingd off he had not hung more than half a minute, neither had he as yet, made any Struggle, when the Commanding Officer, ordered a Soldier to bare down on his Shoulders, that he might not be long in agony, and he immediately died." [53]

A thousand people watched him die and from the little child who slipped a peach into his hand to his three captors who watched, all mourned him with tears.[54] To all of them from the child, whose gift he kept till he was out of her sight, to the fifers playing "The Blue Bird," whom he complimented on their excellent music, he showed a courtesy that was like the benediction of a saint. Only to the executioner (who was a Tory promised his freedom and who had covered his face and hands with pitch) did he show a trace of the awful impatience he felt with his fate. To him he cried:

"Take off your black hands!" [55]

Where was there ever such grief at an execution? Colonel Tallmadge wrote: "I can remember no instance where my affections were so fully absorbed in any man. When I saw him swinging under the gibbet, it seemed for a time as if I could not support it." [56]

André's alert thoughtfulness was such that he wrote to Clinton reminding him, "I have a Mother and Three Sisters, to whom the value of my Commission would be an object. . . . It is needless to be more explicit on this Subject." He added words of appreciation for the courtesy he received from Washington and everyone; but most of all he tried to remove from Clinton's soul the burden of any feeling of responsibility or self-reproach for André's death, and to leave with him a message of gratitude:

"With all the Warmth of my heart I give you thanks for your Excellencys profuse Kindness to me, and I send you the most earnest wishes for your Welfare which a faithfull affectionate and respectful Attendant can frame." [57]

This letter is in the Clements collection and to one who holds it in his hand and reads it there comes a feeling of strange resentment at the destruction of so gentle a youth. Hamilton wrote:

"Never, perhaps, did a man suffer death with more justice, or deserve it less . . . he died universally esteemed and universally regretted." [58]

Washington wrote of him: "He was more unfortunate than criminal." [59] It might seem that something better could be done for such a man than to add to his misfortunes. Numerous men had been released from a death sentence because of the French alliance, or because it was the Fourth of July or for some personal reason. A good excuse could have been found for reprieving André. Still, since all must die, perhaps he was fortunate. Kept in jail, exchanged or paroled, he would simply have been a ridiculous failure. His death swung him into eternal glory.

Yet what good did it do to kill him? It gave England a more beautiful martyr than Nathan Hale and robbed America of the right to denounce the executioner of Hale. It could not prevent any other Englishman from doing the same thing. It enabled historians to accuse Washington of vindictive cruelty. Lord Mahon called it "by far the greatest, and perhaps the only blot in his most noble career." [60] Clinton, of course, was overcome. He shut himself up in solitude for three days and would allow no publication of the fact that hanging had been André's fate. He wrote of Washington:

"The cruel & unfortunate Catastrophe convinced me, that I was much mistaken in my Opinion of both his Policy & Humanity. For delivering himself up (as it should seem) to the Rancour excited by the near Accomplishment of a Plan which might have effectually restored the Kings authority & tumbled him from his present exalted

Situation he burnt with a Desire of wreaking his Vengeance on the principal Actors in it; and consequently regardless of the acknowledged Worth & Abilities of the amiable young Man, who had thus fallen into his Hands, and in opposition to every Principle of Policy & Call of Humanity he without remorse put him to a most ignominious Death; and this at a Moment when one of his Generals was by his own appointment in actual Conference with Commissioners whom I had sent to treat with him for Major Andres Release . . .

"Mr Washington ought also to have remembered that I had never in any one Instance punished the disaffected Colonists (within my power) with Death, but on the Contrary had in several shewn the most humane attention to his Intercession even in favor of avowed Spies. His acting therefore in so cruel a Manner in opposition to my earnest Solicitations could not but excite in me the greatest Surprise; especially as no Advantage whatsoever could be possibly expected to his Cause from putting the Object of them to Death. Nor could he be insensible (had he the smallest Spark of Honor in his own Breast) that the Example (tho ever so horrible and ignominious) would never deter a British Officer from treading in the same Steps, whenever the Service of his Country should require his exposing himself to the like Danger in such a war. But the Subject affects me too deeply to proceed;—Nor can my Heart cease to bleed whenever I reflect on the very unworthy Fate of this most amiable & valuable young Man, who was adorned with the rarest Endowments of Education, and Nature, and (had he lived) could not but have attained to the highest Honors of his Profession!!!" [61]

To his sisters Clinton wrote:

"The horrid deed is done. W. has committed premeditated Murder." [62]

In England the news provoked a fury of rage. A writer in a London paper argued that there was a vast distinction in spies, that execution of André was not requisite, and that the French must have instigated Washington to the crime. He reminded them that their ally, Washington, had once before not only murdered a Frenchman, but "expressly signed his confession of having assassinated (*assassiné*, that was the term) Mons. Jumonville," that a Frenchman had built an epic poem on the theme, and that England should never have let him serve again. [63] This was republished in Rivington's *Gazette* and probably met Washington's eyes. A poetess in England, Miss Anna Seward, a friend of André's, wrote a long elegy:

"Oh Washington! I thought thee great and good,
Nor knew thy Nero-thirst of guiltless blood.
Severe to use the power that fortune gave;
Thou cool, determined, murderer of the brave!

.   .   .   .   .

Remorseless Washington! the day shall come
Of Deep repentance for this barbarous doom;
When injured André's memory shall inspire
A kindling army with resistless fire,
And when thy heart appalled, and vanquished pride,
Shall vainly ask the mercy they denied.
With sorrow shalt thou meet the fate you gave,
Nor pity gild the darkness of thy grave."

This so grieved Washington that after the war, according to Trevelyan, he sent one of his aides-de-camp who was in England to visit the poetess, to show her André's letters and his own, and "to assure her that no circumstance in his life had ever given him so much pain as the necessary sacrifice of André, 'and, (next to that deplorable event,) the censure passed upon himself in a poem which he admired, and for which he loved the author.' Miss Seward was touched by the compliment, and quite ready to be convinced by the evidence. 'From the hour,' (she wrote,) 'that I conversed with General Washington's officer, and perused the papers, I have regretted the injustice of which I had been guilty.' " [64]

Altogether, the André episode is the least gratifying deed in all Washington's life. There were abundant reasons for justifying the execution as the usual and proper thing, but there was never a time when a gesture of reckless mercy would have been less harmful, more potent for the confusion of the enemy. It is not good war to give one's enemies the opportunity to add to their dead a perfect martyr, an irresistibly beautiful saint.

André was buried near the gallows, but a monument was set up in Westminster Abbey in his honor. The king pensioned his mother and sisters and ordered the army into mourning.

In 1821, the first British warship to ascend the Hudson river since the Revolution sailed by permission up to Dobb's Ferry and anchored while a party went to Tappan and lifted from their humble resting place the bones of André and took them home. A peach tree planted by the grave had woven a perfect network of fine roots about his skull.[65] Even in the dank mold of his coffin there was something strangely, exquisitely beautiful.

A story is told with some authority that long before André's death two prominent Philadelphia ladies on their way to dine with Washington and other officers, believed they saw in a grove of cedars the corpse of a British officer hanging from a limb. As they drew near, it "swung around as though by a natural torsion of the rope," and disclosed the face of Captain André. They were so shocked that they told Washington they had seen a ghost. He politely ridiculed their credulity and finally laughed aloud at it; it was the first time one of them had ever seen him laugh.

Years afterward this lady dined with him again, and reminded him of the story and his mirth. "He was much disturbed, . . . and bade her never to refer the subject to him more; that it was a matter he would not recur to, since it had already greatly troubled and perplexed him." [66]

XLIV

THE DEMISE OF 1780

"**A** CRIME so atrocious was too enormous to be thought of as finding many imitators. It is less the example that I dread than the motives on which the treason was based, for, they can flourish in *a country where jealousy is somehow the essence of government.*" [1]

So wrote Vergennes concerning Arnold's treason, which did not add to American prestige in Europe, where the loss of Charleston and the stampede at Camden had aroused cynicism, especially as Gates had been routed by a very small army. [2]

Washington invited André's three captors to dinner, gave them the silver medals voted by Congress and on his own account a sword and a brace of pistols apiece with the warning that they "might expect to be hunted like partridges." [3] But they all outlived him a score of years and are cherished as heroes though Tallmadge later opposed an increase in their pensions on the ground that they were merely robbers and would have let André go if he had had more money. It was the bitterness of Tallmadge's whole life that Colonel Jameson refused to listen to his prayer, which was to hold André back and let Tallmadge go to West Point to make Arnold prisoner before he learned of André's capture. [4] That would have been a might-have-been indeed, but all that Tallmadge got for denouncing André's captors was the abuse of the public. They are still schoolbook demigods with a monument and Tallmadge unknown.

The cloud of Arnold's shame overspread for a time all who knew him. His secretary and aide, Colonel Richard Varick, was so horrified by his position that he could not write a coherent letter for days. [5] He demanded a court of inquiry which Washington granted while assuring him that his character was "unimpeached." The court eventually absolved both him and Major Franks with unsullied honor.[6]

Washington put McDougall, then St. Clair, in command at West Point, but Greene set his heart on the post and got it away from St. Clair—by flattery, according to St. Clair's biographer.[7] Washington consented with a warning that he would have to camp there himself probably, because the army would be so small.[8] He was soon shipping Greene south to replace Gates, but with the warning:

"I think I am giving you a general, but what can a general do, without men, without arms, without clothing, without stores, without provisions?"[9]

Congress yielded to his persuasions and authorized another reorganization of the army for the war. In order to hold the officers, Congress granted at last half pay for life, the measure that Washington had urged for three years.[10]

He sent a circular letter to the states reminding them "how few men you will have left after the first of January next," reviewing the war, the disasters and the narrow escapes from ruin, which he credited entirely to the enemy's "torpid inactivity . . . permitting us to hover about their quarters when we had scarcely troops sufficient to mount the ordinary guards." He berated the spendthrift economy that would sink any government:

"America has been almost amused out of her liberties. We have frequently heard the behavior of the militia extolled upon one and another occasion, by men who judge only from the surface, by men who had particular views in misrepresenting, by visionary men whose credulity easily swallowed every vague story in support of a favorite hypothesis. I solemnly declare, I never was witness to a single instance that can countenance an opinion of militia or raw troops being fit for the real business of fighting."[11]

While he was trying to conquer the enemy and the disintegration of his own nation by the flying quill, he was active as host and dinner-giver to French visitors, who looked upon this prodigy of the wilderness with awe, and painted portraits of extreme vivacity. The Marquis de Chastellux called upon him in November, 1780, and his description shows the idle camp in a state of almost luxurious ease:

"He conducted me to his house, where I found the company still at table, although the dinner had been long over. . . . A fresh dinner was prepared for me, and mine; and the present was prolonged to keep me company. A few glasses of claret and Madeira accelerated the acquaintances I had to make, and I soon felt myself at my ease near the greatest and the best of men. The goodness and benevolence which characterize him, are evident from every thing about him; but the confidence he gives birth to, never occasions improper familiarity." [12]

The dinner lasted till nine at night, then Washington conducted the Marquis to the room prepared for him and his aides, apologizing for its smallness, "always with a noble politeness, which was neither complimentary nor troublesome." Breakfast was at nine the next morning. At Lafayette's quarters, they found "a large bowl of grog, which is stationary on his table, and is presented to every officer who enters." At dinner that afternoon there were twenty guests. Starvation was not conspicuous and Washington's diet is described:

"The repast was in the English fashion, consisting of eight or ten large dishes of butcher's meat, and poultry, with vegetables of several sorts, followed by a second course of pastry, comprised under the two denominations of pies and puddings. After this the cloth was taken off, and apples and a great quantity of nuts were served, which General Washington usually continues eating for two hours, *toasting* and conversing all the time. These nuts are small and dry, and have so hard a shell, (hickory nuts) that they can only be broken by the hammer; they are served half open, and the company are never done picking and eating them."

At seven-thirty the dinner was over, but an hour later there was supper:

"I returned to the dining-room, protesting against this supper; but the general told me he was accustomed to take something in the evening. . . . The supper was composed of three or four light dishes, some fruit, and above all, a great abundance of nuts, which were as well received in the evening as at dinner. The cloth being soon removed, a few bottles of good claret and Madeira were placed on the table. . . . After supper the guests are generally desired to give a *sentiment;* that is to say, a lady to whom they are attached by some sentiment, either of love or friendship, or perhaps from preference only. This supper, or conversation, commonly lasted from nine to eleven, always free, and always agreeable."

Two days later the Marquis rode in fair weather on one of Washington's best horses:

"It is the General himself who breaks all his own horses; and he is a very excellent and bold horseman, leaping the highest fences, and going extremely quick, without standing upon his stirrups, bearing on the bridle, or letting his horse run wild; circumstances which our young men look upon as so essential a part of English horsemanship, that they would rather break a leg or an arm than renounce them."

During this ride he saw a strange freak, "a very curious *lusus naturæ,* but as hideous as possible." Surgeon Thacher describes a visit Washington paid to this same pathetic figure and his rather sad joke:

"This is a monster in the human form. He is twenty-seven years of age, his face from the upper part of his forehead to the end of his chin, measures twenty inches, and round the upper part of his head is twenty-one inches, his eyes and nose are remarkably large and prominent, chin long and pointed. His features are coarse, irregular and disgusting, and his voice is rough and sonorous. His body is only twenty-seven inches in length, his limbs are small, and much deformed, and he has the use of one hand only. . . . General Washington made him a visit, and asked, 'whether he was a whig or tory?' He replied, that 'he had never taken an *active* part on either side.' " [13]

Of Washington the Marquis de Chastellux retained an impression almost idolatrous:

"The continent of North America, from Boston to Charles Town, is a great volume, every page of which presents his eulogium. . . . This is the seventh year that he has commanded the army, and that he has obeyed the Congress; more need not be said, especially in America, where they know how to appreciate all the merit contained in this simple fact. . . . It will be said of him, At the end of a long civil war, he had nothing with which he could reproach himself. If any thing can be more marvellous than such a character, it is the unanimity of the public suffrages in his favour. Soldier, magistrate, people, all love and admire him; all speak of him in terms of tenderness and veneration . . .

"On asking the General which of our professional books he read with the most pleasure; he told me, the King of Prussia's Instructions to his Generals, and the Tactics of M. de Guibert; from whence I concluded that he knew as well how to select his authors as to profit by them." [14]

Lafayette, having been thwarted in a surprise attack on Staten Island from the failure of his boats to arrive, wrote a long letter imploring Washington to take some action; even defeat would be better than the stagnation:

"The French court have often complained to me of the inactivity of the American army, who, before the alliance, had distinguished themselves by their spirit of enterprise. They have often told me, your friends leave us now to fight their battles, and do no more risk themselves." [15]

To this Washington replied gloomily enough:

"It is impossible, my dear Marquis, to desire more ardently than I do to terminate the campaign by some happy stroke; but we must consult our means rather than our wishes, and not endeavor to better our affairs by attempting things, which for want of success may make them worse." [16]

He resolved, however, to attack New York City at all costs, and issued elaborately minute orders for a surprise assault on the night of November 24th while ostensibly moving to winter quarters. He even had boats on wheels ready for quick embarkation. But some British ships accidentally got in the way and he gave it up in disgust.[17] He moved on to winter quarters at New Windsor, a few miles north of West Point. The quarters here were "little better than those at Valley Forge." [18] There was a paralyzing lack of soldiers, the state quotas were "never half complete in men, but perfectly so in every species of want." The poverty of the army was almost inconceivable:

"We have neither money nor credit adequate to the purchase of a few boards for doors to our log huts. . . . We cannot despatch an officer or common express upon the most urgent occasion."

He was not only permitted to pay his own salary but to feed himself:

"But this is a matter of trivial concern . . . that I have not been able to obtain a farthing of public money for the support of my table for near two months. . . . It would be well for the troops if, like chameleons, they could live upon air, or, like the bear, suck their paws for sustenance during the rigor of the approaching winter." [19]

As for the ancient nakedness, he wrote:

"By collecting all our remnants, and those of a thousand colors & kinds, we shall scarcely make them comfortable. Uniformity, one of the essentials of discipline, & every thing in the appearance of a Soldier, must be dispensed with;—and what makes the matter more mortifying is, that we have, I am positively assured Ten thousand compleat suits ready in France & laying there because our public agents cannot agree whose business it is to ship them—a quantity has also lain in the West Indies for more than Eighteen months, owing probably to some such cause. You tell me there is cloathing enough lately arrived in private bottoms to supply the army.—This my dear Sir is only tantalizing the Naked—such is the miserable state of Continental credit that we cannot command a yard of it." [20]

"We have enumerable objects of distressing want." [21]

He was not able even to bring off a little attempt to kidnap General Knyphausen or Clinton, on Christmas night. The careful plan he agreed on with Colonel Humphreys was disclosed by a spy in camp. Clinton knew all about it, and responded with plots to kidnap Washington, which were likewise carried to him by spies in Clinton's camp.[22]

At this time the far-off hand of Catharine of Russia was felt in the Revolution. England had begun to deal with neutrals on her private oceans in the heavy-handed manner that brought on the War of 1812. The neutrals had made the usual grand rush to the Golconda of supplying belligerents, and England not only published a list of forbidden wares but proceeded to search all suspicious foreign vessels, and hold those caught with contraband. She had a treaty of alliance with Holland obliging the Dutch to join her if France declared war, but the Dutch had been doing so well with secret supplies to the American colonies that when France went to war with England, Holland added France to her contraband market, and began negotiations for a treaty of alliance with America. Henry Laurens, on the way to Europe to close the deal, was captured with his documents. He was thrown into the Tower as a traitor and Holland brought to book. The British fired on and stopped a Dutch admiral with a fleet convoying merchant vessels, but Holland swallowed the indignity as humbly as the United States, in 1807, digested the degradation of seeing her warship, the *Chesapeake*, fired on, halted and searched by the British *Leopard*.

When, however, the Russians were hampered in their commerce by Spain, Catharine announced her determination to protect her ships, and put twenty men-of-war into commission. Spain apologized, but England was at bay. Catharine called on the other nations for assistance and formed a Baltic league with Sweden and Denmark. This so-called "Armed Neutrality" was joined by Prussia, the Holy Roman Empire, Holland, Austria, Portugal, and the two Sicilies, all agreeing to act together against British search and seizure, all maintaining that a neutral could carry any goods of any belligerent except munitions. "Free ships make free goods," was the motto.[23]

It was now England against the world. But once more her heart enlarged with the opposition and she paid little heed to what Catharine was soon calling her "Armed Nullity." There was rejoicing, however, among the Americans when the Armed Neutrality was announced. Franklin was delighted, but Washington showed his usual foresight in European politics, a foresight that was uncanny in view of the fact that he had never been abroad. He wrote to Jefferson:

"The Accession of Holland and Portugal to the Northern League of neutrality will be undoubtedly very embarassing to Great Britain— But this I think may be relied upon, that the more she is insulted and oppressed by the European Powers, the more she will endeavour to revenge herself upon us—She can make no Impression upon them, and she will therefore bend her whole force against us, in hopes of Possessing herself of such an Extent of Territory in America, as will enable her to insist upon Terms, should a negotiation take place; which may be highly derogatory to these States." [24]

The Armed Neutrality faded rapidly as a hindrance to England, though its principles were subject to frequent resurrection. It came to light again when England and Germany were making neutrality impossible in the World War. Its more immediate effect on the Revolution was to lead England to call Holland out into the open, and declare war against her, December 20th, 1780. Promptly Admiral Rodney descended on the island of St. Eustatius and took it February 3rd, 1781, along with nearly two hundred merchant ships. This was the vast trading post for munitions and all supplies; Dutch, French and Americans, and English too, traded there. Its loss was thought to be a deathblow to the American cause.[25]

The amount of American speculation going on may be seen from the fact that the fall of St. Eustatius hit the magnates of the 25,000-town of Philadelphia for $2,500,000—"half a million pounds Hard cash"—in paper money a sum almost incalculable.[26] English merchants trading under cover were also heavy losers, and more than 2,000 American merchants and seamen were taken prisoner by Admiral Rodney.[27] Strange to say, the conquest helped England little. Rodney sent home thirty-four Dutch vessels laden with spoils: twenty-two were captured in the English channel by a French squadron and the remaining twelve were taken by French and American privateers. The island itself was retaken soon but was no longer useful as a dépôt. Yet at first the entrance of Holland into the war seemed so futile that the colonists might have parodied the old saying, and exclaimed, "One more ally and we are ruined." The end of 1780 found Washington still sinking deeper in the deeps. He wrote to Cadwalader:

"We are now drawing an inactive Campaign to a close.—The beginning of which appeared pregnant with events of a favourable complexion.—I hoped, but hoped in vain—that a pro[s]pect was displaying which would enable me to fix a period to my Military pursuits, and restore me to domestic life.—The favourable disposition of Spain— The promised succour from France—The combined force in the West Indies—The declaration of Russia (acceded to by other powers of Europe—humiliating to the naval pride & power of Great Britain)— The superiority of France & Spain by Sea in Europe—The Irish claims —and British disturbances, formed in the agregate an opinion in my breast—which is not very susceptable of peaceful dreams—that the hour of deliverance was not far distant. . . . But alas! these prospects, flattering as they were, have proved delusory, and I see nothing before us but accumulating distress.—We have been half our time without provision & are like to continue so.—We have no Magazines, nor Money to form them.—And in a little time we shall have no Men, if we had Money to pay them.—We have lived upon expedients till we can live no longer—In a word, the history of the War is a history of false hopes and temporary devices, instead of system & ecconomy." [28]

The worst of the situation in Washington's eyes was that he had been utterly defeated in his war-long struggle to unify the colonies and develop an America. Now he must write to Congressman Sullivan:

"If in all cases ours was *one* army, or *thirteen* armies allied for the common defence, there would be no difficulty in solving your question; but we are occasionally both, and I should not be much out if I were to say, that we are sometimes *neither*, but a compound of *both*. . . . It is well known, that in the early stages of this war I used every means in my power to destroy all kinds of State distinctions, and labored to have every part and parcel of the army considered as Continental. The steps, which have led to a different sentim:, and to our present system of politics, you are not to be informed of. We must take things as they are." [29]

The colonies were now once more an unlucky thirteen. Congress would cease the printing of national money in March,

1781, and leave the troops to the individual states to feed and equip. The Continental Congress seemed to have given up the struggle to gain control. So Washington ended the year in unusual despair:

"If individual States conceive themselves at liberty to reject, or alter any act of Congress, which in a full representation of them has been solemnly debated, and decided on; it will be madness in us, to think of prosecuting the war." [30]

The French were still shut up in Rhode Island and the Admiral de Ternay died, it was said, "of chagrin." [31] Washington's last letters of the year concerned the ambitious activities of Virginia and her Colonel George Rogers Clark, who wanted to attack Detroit. Of him Washington wrote, begging that every aid be given him:

"The inability of the Continent to undertake the reduction of Detroit, which, while it continues in possession of the enemy, will be a constant source of trouble to the whole Western frontier, has of necessity imposed the task upon the State of Virginia, and of consequence makes it expedient to confer the command upon an officer of the State. This being the case, I do not think the charge of the enterprise could have been committed to better hands than Colo. Clark's. I have not the pleasure of knowing the Gentleman." [32]

XLV

MUTINY

THE new year opened with a paralyzing crash—"the event I have long apprehended would be the consequence of the complicated distresses of the Army. . . . At what point this defection will stop, or how extensive it may prove, God only knows." [1]

The nation was faced with exactly the situation that greeted Russia in 1917, when the soldiers attacked and slew their officers, defied and denounced the government, elected their own committees and representatives, and marched against their own Duma instead of the enemy. The Bolshevik mutiny was far vaster, as the Russian army was, but in the little host of the thirteen colonies the outbreak was terrifying. The whole Pennsylvania Line, of about 2,400 men, in the early night of January 1st, 1781, turned a New Year's celebration into the open revolt of about a quarter of the entire army. [2] For Washington's force was reduced at that time to a winter skeleton, and its spirit was so uncertain that he dared not command any element of it to oppose the mutineers. He could only stand by and watch the officers being humiliated and Congress intimidated, while he wondered if the mutiny would spread like wildfire. Wayne had seen it coming and had written on December 16th, 1780:

"I sincerely wish the Ides of Jany was come & past." [3]

The Pennsylvania officers had previously threatened the mutiny of unanimous resignation rather than accept Washington's recommendation of Major McPherson, who had seen no service. [4] The example they set was soon followed by the men. It is a commonplace error to describe the Pennsylvania Line as

strongly Irish, and blame their Keltic blood for their turbu-
lence, but the men were largely of Scotch-Irish descent, at
least a third of German origin. Their grievance was a peculiarly overt breach of contract by the nation, which had already
broken its contracts to furnish food, clothing, and pay, and had
furnished instead starvation, nakedness, and paper as worthless as it was late. These men were not come-and-go militia.
They had enlisted for "three years or the war." They believed that this meant a maximum of three years as nobody
had expected the war to last so long. When a number of
men who had served their three years called for their discharge,
they were not only refused but roughly handled, and kept for
a year longer.[5] In January the three years would be up for
the bulk of them. Worse yet, recruiting agents came into
camp and paid hard money to six months' troops who reenlisted
—no less than $25 apiece and in coin! The old soldiers could
not even collect back pay in paper and they could not secure
release when their time was up. This was slavery, no less.
As Wayne wrote, their tempers were "much soured by neglect
& every extreme of wretchedness."[6]

About nine o'clock in the night of January 1st, 1781, they
issued in a body from their huts and began to howl, fire guns,
skyrockets. They fell into line with their arms, seized food,
ammunition, six cannon, and Wayne's horses to draw them.
The officers, who had been holding a New Year's revel, were
appalled by this sudden ghostlike mustering in the gloom,
and ordered the men back to their huts. When they would
not go the officers mounted their horses and charged them with
swords slashing, while unmounted officers attacked them with
the spear-like espontoons that some of the officers carried. The
horses trampled many, the swords and espontoons marked
many for life. But the men fired, killed one captain, and
wounded other officers with "strokes from muskets, bayonets,
& stones," says Wayne.[7]

When he and his staff rode up and threatened the men with
pistols, they ringed him with bayonets. He tried oratory, and

promised to right their wrongs. They said he had no such power; their business was with Congress and the Pennsylvania Council. They fired a volley over his head. He anticipated Napoleon by opening his coat and crying:

"If you mean to kill me, here's my breast." [8]

They told him they would not harm him. The officers brought up another regiment to recapture the cannon, but this regiment dispersed instead and joined the mutiny, or held aloof. Wayne begged his men not to go to the British. They told him they would hang any man who tried it. Wayne said:

"I'll not leave you, and if you won't allow me to march in your front, I'll follow in your rear." [9]

On January 3rd the Line set out for Philadelphia and got as far as Princeton under command of Sergeant Williams, a British deserter fond of liquor. A sergeant was at the head of each regiment, and a Board of Sergeants as war council. They marched in fine order. Lafayette and St. Clair hastened to try their powers. Lafayette wrote that they told him "they would die to the last man at my command, but that I did not know all they had suffered." He was afraid of the prospect. "I vow it is frightful to pass the winter killing one another without the enemy enduring any loss . . . these brave people have suffered with us for four years, have been wounded with us." They "had received not a penny of pay for fifteen months . . . nor clothes, nor food," and had been "kept for a year beyond their enlistment."

He confessed:

"It is very inconvenient to draw the sword against these mutineers when the certainty of crushing them is not great enough to encourage an attack."

He and St. Clair were politely ordered to move on, and he wrote to Luzerne:

"Gal Washington is much embarrassed as to what he ought to do." [10]

A mutiny is a ticklish business. The Pennsylvania men had shown their willingness to shoot down officers, stab them with bayonets, chase them out of camp. What would they do to Washington? Of all ways for a hero to perish for his country, the least glorious is to be spitted on the bayonets of his own men. If St. Clair, Lafayette, Laurens, Wayne could do nothing, what could Washington do? His first impulse was to rush to the scene and he gathered "a small Escort of Horse." [11] But he did not go. This cannot be imputed to timidity, for he never showed any caution as to his own safety. What he was afraid of was that in his absence his own surly, hungry troops might mutiny, leaving West Point to be seized easily by the enemy. Furthermore, the demands of the mutineers were directed toward Congress and he assumed that Congress would be dealing with them before he could reach the place. [12] Besides, as he wrote later:

"I was convinced that the unhappy precedent they had set, and the shock which discipline had received by the revolt, would only be increased by my appearance among them, without the means of enforcing obedience; the necessity of doing which, for the support of Military authority, was so essential as to be attempted at almost every hazard. But to choose for the best, in such perplexing circumstances I was driven to, was not very easy." [13]

He could not tell where the next outbreak would come. He imagined the whole army "only waiting to see the effects of the Pennsylvania insurrection." [14] One thing was certain: it was "vain to think an army can be kept together much longer, under such a variety of sufferings as ours has experienced." [15] He sent Knox to the four governors of New England with a letter begging for clothing and money instantly. [16] He wrote to Wayne to advise Congress not to flee from Philadelphia as some advised. He wrote to General Heath to try the temper of the New England troops. Heath sent a woman among them to listen. She heard them say they would not help put down the Pennsylvania Line. With his own men Washington was afraid "even to express a doubt of their obedience." [17] He dreaded especially that the British should seduce the men and was afraid to have them harshly treated lest they

turn to New York. Clinton's secret notes show that he learned
of the mutiny as soon as Washington did. He moved 5,000
troops to Staten Island to be near. He sent two or three
emissaries offering the mutineers welcome and protection.
They were in no mood to "turn Arnolds." They refused to
slay the unfortunate emissaries as their officers requested, but
turned them over to the officers, who hanged them promptly,
which seems somewhat barbarous since they had to obey their
master. Clinton's only comment was, "I thought the Experiment was worth the Trial." [18] He let the opportunity slide
to deal a fatal blow. He was turning as indolent as Howe,
whom he had scarified for the same vice.

Congress and the Pennsylvania Council cooperated in a decision to appease the men at all costs. Joseph Reed was sent
to Princeton and with some uneasiness went into the soldiers'
camp, prepared, as he said, "on some principle, or perhaps
no principle, to dismiss them." [19] The final agreement was
that no soldier should be detained for a longer time than his
enlistment called for; that "three years or the war" meant not
more than three years; that back pay should be settled, with
adjustment for depreciation; that clothes should be furnished
for the journey home, and that a soldier's oath should be accepted as to the date of his enlistment. When it was found
later that many of the soldiers had perjured themselves liberally, the state was still glad to be rid of them so cheaply.
The Pennsylvania Line was disbanded for future reorganization and Wayne was temporarily without men.

Reed had conceded only what should have been granted
long since without a mutiny. The soldiers majestically refused
even to accept the reward of fifty guineas offered for the capture of the British spies. Altogether they behaved like gentlemen and Americans of a later date. But at that time common soldiers had no real rights—especially none to gentle-
manly behavior. Even the simple justice done to them by
Congress seems to have been far more than Washington wished
to grant. He did not believe in dealing with private soldiers

across a bayonet, and regretted the leniency, or the necessity for it, as one usually repents fair dealing after a quarrel, during which one was glad enough to get it.[20]

He soon had a chance to show how to handle a mutiny in his own way, for, on the night of January 21st, 1781, he learned that the New Jersey Line had revolted. The New Jersey legislature promptly appointed commissioners to discuss their grievances, which were the same as those of the Pennsylvanians. The men insulted their officers but lacked resolution and were soon overawed. Washington did not lack resolution. As he wrote to the states:

"Persuaded that without some decisive effort, at all hazards to suppress this dangerous spirit, it would speedily infect the whole army, I have ordered as large a Detachment as we could spare from these posts, to march under Major General Howe, with orders to compel the mutineers to unconditional submission—to listen to no terms while they were in a state of resistance, and on their reduction, to execute instantly a few of the most active, and most incendiary leaders. I am not certain what part the troops detached for this purpose will act, but I flatter myself they will do their duty. I prefer any extremity to which the Jersey troops may be driven to a compromise." [21]

In an unpublished letter to Colonel Barber of the Jersey Line, he wrote:

"This affair, if possible, must be brought to an issue favourable to subordination, or the army is ruined . . . if you have force enough to do it, I wish you to compel the mutineers to unconditional submission. The more decisively you are able to act the better." [22]

Howe's soldiers made a hard march through deep snow and surrounded the mutineers, who made no resistance; three ringleaders were tried by field court-martial and sentenced to death. One of them was spared and the soldiers were permitted to express their contrition and pledge perfect obedience. Washington was glad of the chance to strike a resounding blow for always flouted discipline.

He delivered a sermon in the form of General Orders:

"*Head-Quarters*, 30 *January*, 1781.—The General returns his thanks to Major-General Howe for the judicious measures he pursued, and to the officers and men under his command . . . It gave him inexpressible pain to be obliged to employ their arms upon such an occasion, and he is convinced that they themselves felt all the reluctance, which former affection to fellow-soldiers could inspire. . . .

"The General is deeply sensible of the sufferings of the army. He leaves no expedient unessayed to relieve them, and he is persuaded Congress and the several States are doing every thing in their power for the same purpose. But, while we look to the public for the fulfilment of its engagements, we should do it with proper allowance for the embarrassments of public affairs. We began a contest for liberty and independence, ill provided with the means for war, relying on our own patriotism to supply the deficiency. We expected to encounter many wants and distresses, and we should neither shrink from them when they happen, nor fly in the face of law and government to procure redress." [23]

It was now that he called on Congress for permission to increase the number of lashes permissible in flogging a soldier. The original thirty-nine had been raised to a maximum of a hundred, which he found "entirely inadequate." He spoke in General Orders of "the puny punishment of a hundred lashes." He recommended five hundred, but Congress would not oblige him. It was during the anxious days of the Jersey mutiny that Washington found his way through other perils that threatened to drown him literally.

One thinks of Washington always as a landsman, though he was a good sailor, according to Barbé-Marbois's previously quoted evidence of his skill. There is a dramatic anecdote by another Frenchman. Comte Mathieu Dumas, aide to Rochambeau, describes Washington in a rôle superior to that of Julius Cæsar, so often represented as reassuring a terrified pilot by the egomaniacal word: "Be calm, you carry Cæsar." Washington relied on Providence to save the nation he was trying to construct, but we have from his lips none of those self-glorifications that Napoleon and other generals uttered, or are said to have uttered, concerning their being Men of

Destiny. Washington never relied on fate. He lent a hand, and a big hand, wherever there was room for one.

So the Comte Dumas tells how he and a number of French gentlemen visited West Point with Washington and made an unexpected voyage on the stormy night of January 22nd, 1781. They had expected to return by horse, but Washington saw that Lafayette's old wound, the one he gained at Brandywine, was troubling him and he proposed to return by boat to the camp at New Windsor, five miles or more upstream. He counted on an ascending tide, but the current turned and great cakes of ice rushed down upon the boat as on the Delaware. The cold was bitter and heavy snow filled the black air. The waves rose high on the broad Hudson and the boat shipped much water. Landing among the rocks in the heavy surf was so perilous that the master of the oarsmen lost his nerve. Whereupon Washington took the helm, saying:

"Courage, my friends; I will steer. My place is at the helm."

And he landed them safely, though there were still miles to walk before they reached headquarters.[24]

One might draw a pretty moral from this, but the facts are enough.

XLVI

HAMILTON, AND HIS MOTHER HUMILIATE HIM

INTO his forty-ninth birth-month intimate rancors crowded. The French honored him on February 12th, 1781, with a holiday, a parade and the firing of a salute. As Rochambeau wrote to him:

"We have put off celebrating that holiday till to-day, by reason of the Lord's day and we will celebrate it with the sole regret that your Excellency be not a Witness of the effusion and gladness of our hearts." [1]

Washington acknowledged this graciously twelve days later.[2] But at heart he was not friends with the French. He could not resist the nausea of the feast of hopes with the after-taste of indigestible and immovable facts. Rochambeau was sullen, too. As his companion, the Duc de Lauzun, says:

"We had been ten months away from France and we had not yet received a single letter nor one penny in money." [3]

If Washington had known that the royal troops were paupers also, it might not have been so odious to have to explain that one reason for not keeping up the chain of correspondence was "the absolute want of money." Also, his Family was so much reduced by various contingencies "that I had for some days but a single Aide." [4] He was now to lose his most important one.

Ambition and a growing impatience with Washington had determined Alexander Hamilton to escape his environment. He was apparently willing to go anywhere provided it was away, and do anything provided it was at a distance from Washington. He asked Lafayette to ask Washington to give him command of a battalion in Lafayette's raid on Staten Island. Lafayette told him that Washington refused: first, because of the dissatisfaction likely to be caused among the other officers; second, because Hamilton was needed in the Family. On November 22nd, 1780, he had written to Washington direct that he wanted "to act a conspicuous part in some enterprise that might perhaps raise my character as a soldier above mediocrity." He asked for light infantry and permission to attack Bayard Hill. He put it in writing "to avoid the embarrassment of a personal explanation." [5] This in itself was proof of a lack of cordiality in their relationship. The prayer was not granted.

His next try was for the post of adjutant-general, to succeed Scammel, who resigned because he was bankrupt beyond further service. Both Lafayette and Greene urged his appointment.[6] But Washington had already proposed Edward Hand to Congress. When he learned too late, he wrote to Greene that there would have been trouble if Hamilton had been promoted above the full colonels on the staff.[7] Next Hamilton tried to go to France. Lafayette pleaded with Congressmen to grant him the wish, but John Laurens received the appointment.

Hamilton cast his eyes everywhere. The Board of Treasury was now consolidated into one man called "The Financier." Hamilton had already thought much on money and had written in October, 1780:

"We must have a government with more power. We must have a tax in kind. We must have a foreign loan. We must have a bank —on the true principles of a bank. We must have an administration distinct from Congress, and in the hands of single men under their orders." [8]

Sullivan asked Washington what he thought of Hamilton, and Washington replied that they had never discussed finance, but,

"There are few men to be found, of his age, who has a more general knowledge than he possesses; and none, whose soul is more firmly engaged in the cause, or who exceeds him in probity and sterling virtue." [9]

Congress made Robert Morris The Financier.

On February 16th, 1781, Hamilton broke with Washington in a scene of much formality but little real dignity. Major Wilkinson had from General St. Clair a very circumstantial story:

"The General was just mounting his horse, to visit his advanced post, when he recollected a letter he had recently received from the British commander, which it occurred to him he might have occasion for whilst at the lines; he called Colonel Hamilton, and requested him 'to hand the letter to him.' The Colonel returned to the office, but not being able to place his hand on it, reported, that 'it was mislaid.' The General replied:

" 'I must have it.'

"Search was again made without effect, and Colonel Hamilton returning, repeated that the letter had been mislaid, and expressed his sorrow at not being *able to find it.* The General rejoined with warmth,

" 'Sir you shall find it.' Hamilton was astonished, but replied promptly,

" 'I shall find it, Sir, but must let you know, that in addressing me, you do not speak to a menial.' " [10]

Some such scene may well have taken place and Henry Lee tells a somewhat similar story of Washington's fierce rebuke for a delay that Hamilton could not help.[11] But Hamilton wrote to his father-in-law a precise account of what really ended his career as aide:

"An unexpected change has taken place in my situation. I am no longer a member of the General's family. This information will surprise you, and the manner of the change will surprise you more. Two days ago, the General and I passed each other on the stairs. He told me he wanted to speak to me. I answered that I would wait upon him immediately. I went below, and delivered Mr. Tilghman a letter to be sent to the commissary, containing an order of a pressing and interesting nature.

"Returning to the General, I was stopped on the way by the Marquis de La Fayette, and we conversed together about a minute on a matter of business. He can testify how impatient I was to get back, and that I left him in a manner which, but for our intimacy, would have been more than abrupt. Instead of finding the General, as is usual, in his room, I met him at the head of the stairs, where, accosting me in an angry tone:

" 'Colonel Hamilton,' said he, 'you have kept me waiting at the head of the stairs these ten minutes. I must tell you, sir, you treat me with disrespect.' I replied, without petulancy, but with decision:

" 'I am not conscious of it, sir; but since you have thought it necessary to tell me so, we part.'

" 'Very well, sir,' said he, 'if it be your choice,' or something to this effect, and we separated. I sincerely believe my absence, which gave so much umbrage, did not last two minutes."

What follows shows Washington's swiftness in recapturing self-control and his willingness to apologize even to a subordinate who had kept him standing on a stairway for ten long minutes while he chatted. Hamilton goes on, showing how ruthlessly he rejected his chief's proffer of reconciliation and subjected him to a further and final humiliation. And a King, a general, or an employer can be most agonizingly humiliated by a truculent subordinate:

"In less than an hour after, Tilghman came to me in the General's name, assuring me of his great confidence in my abilities, integrity, usefulness, etc., and of his desire, in a candid conversation, to heal a difference which could not have happened but in a moment of passion. I requested Mr. Tilghman to tell him—1st. That I had taken my resolution in a manner not to be revoked. 2d. That, as a conversation could serve no other purpose than to produce explanations, mutually disagreeable, though I certainly would not refuse an interview if he desired it, yet I would be happy if he would permit me to decline it. 3d. That, though determined to leave the family, the same principles which had kept me so long in it would continue to direct my conduct towards him when out of it. 4th. That, however, I did not wish to distress him, or the public business, by quitting him before he could derive other assistance by the return of some of the gentlemen who were absent. 5th. And that, in the mean time, it depended on him to let our behavior to each other be the same as if nothing had happened. He consented to decline the conversation, and thanked me for my offer of continuing my aid in the manner I had mentioned. Thus we stand. I wait Mr. Humphrey's return from the eastward, and may be induced to wait the return of Mr. Harrison from Virginia."

The letter goes on to explain how he had always disliked the office of aide and how he had come to dislike Washington increasingly for his bad temper and indelicacy and need for "incense." A part of this has already been quoted in chapter XIII. He tells next how he rebuffed all of Washington's advances toward a warm friendship:

"I was always determined, if there should ever happen a breach between us, never to consent to an accommodation. . . . I resolved, whenever it should happen, not to be in the wrong. I was convinced the concessions the General might make would be dictated by his interest, and that his self-love would never forgive me for what it would regard as a humiliation. . . . For three years past I have felt no friendship for him and have professed none. . . . At the end of the war I may say many things to you concerning which I shall impose upon myself till then an inviolable silence.

"The General is a very honest man. His competitors have slender abilities, and less integrity. His popularity has often been essential to the safety of America, and is still of great importance to it. These considerations have influenced my past conduct respecting him, and will influence my future. I think it is necessary he should be supported . . . a public knowledge of the breach would, in many ways, have an ill effect. It will probably be the policy of both sides to conceal it, and cover the separation with some plausible pretext. I am importuned by such of my friends as are privy to the affair, to listen to a reconciliation; but my resolution is unalterable." [12]

To General Greene, who had also felt Washington's brief ferocities, Hamilton wrote:

"Harrison has left the General to be a chief-justice of Maryland. I am about leaving him to be any thing that fortune may cast up—I mean in the military line. This, my dear General, is not an affair of calculation, but of feeling. You may divine the rest, and I am sure you will keep your divinations to yourself." [13]

To Doctor McHenry he spoke with the freedom of one aide to another:

"The Great man and I have come to an open rupture. Proposals of accommodation have been made on his part, but rejected. I pledge my honor to you that he will find me inflexible. He shall for once at least repent his ill-humour. Without a shadow of reason and on the slightest grounds—he charged me in the most affrontive manner with treating him with disrespect. I answered very decisively 'Sir, I am not conscious of it, but since you have thought it necessary to tell me so, we part!' . . .

"We have often spoken freely our sentiments to each other. Except to a very few friends our difference will be a secret, therefore be silent. I shall continue to support a popularity that has been essential—is still useful. Adieu, my friend. May the time come when characters may be Known in their true light.   A. H." [14]

General Schuyler wrote to Hamilton with a combined loyalty to his son-in-law, to Washington and the cause, that he was "afflicted" by the news; he found no impropriety in Hamilton's conduct, yet "it may be attended with consequences prejudicial to my country, which I love, which I affectionately love. . . .

"It is evident, my dear sir, that the General conceived himself the aggressor, and that he quickly repented of the insult. . . . It falls to the lot of few men to pass through life without one of those unguarded moments which wound the feelings of a friend. Let us then impute them to the frailties of human nature, and with Sterne's recording angel, drop a tear, and blot it out of the page of life. . . . Make the sacrifice. The greater it is, the more glorious to you. Your services are wanted. They are wanted in that particular station which you have already filled so beneficially to the public, and with such extensive reputation." [15]

Lafayette was pained by the quarrel between two men for whom he had such warm friendship and hoped that Hamilton would not leave Washington's side. From Virginia he wrote: "If you quit him . . . come and share my exile." [16] He did not mention the matter to Washington until there was no chance of reconciliation, then Lafayette wrote to him:

"Considering the footing I am upon with your Excellency, it would perhaps appear to you strange, that I never mentioned a circumstance, which lately happened in your family. I was the first who knew of it, and from that moment exerted every means in my power to prevent a separation, which I knew was not agreeable to your Excellency. To this measure I was prompted by affection for you; but I thought it was improper to mention any thing about it, until you were pleased to impart it to me." [17]

To this Washington answered in some bewilderment at Hamilton's imposing silence on him while spreading the news himself:

"The event, which you seem to speak of with regret, my friendship for you would most assuredly have induced me to impart to you in the moment it happened, had it not been for the request of H—, who desired that no mention might be made of it. Why this injunction on me, while he was communicating it himself, is a little extraordinary. But I complied, and religiously fulfilled it." [18]

The miracle, of course, is that Washington should have so rarely lost his temper in such incessant torments. Hamilton, in April, asked him for an assignment to a command and Washington answered that his unpleasant experience in rousing opposition to the appointment of Major McPherson prevented such a step. He added with a veiled allusion to their one-sided quarrel:

"I am convinced, that no officer can with justice dispute your merit and abilities. . . . My principal concern arises from an apprehension, that you will impute my refusal of your request to other motives, than those I have expressed; but I beg you to be assured I am only influenced by the reasons which I have mentioned." [19]

Washington as usual was above revenge. He did what he could to advance Hamilton in the war and throughout his life. Late in the year he wrote to Greene of the "perfect good understanding between you, the Marquis, and myself.

"I hope it will never be interrupted, and I am sure it never can while we are all influenced by the same pure motive, that of love to our country and interest in the cause in which we are embarked. I have happily had but few differences with those, with whom I have the honor of being connected in the service. With whom, and of what nature these have been, you know. I bore much for the sake of peace and the public good. My conscience tells me, I acted rightly in these transactions; and, should they ever come to the knowledge of the world, I trust I shall stand acquitted by it." [20]

Shortly after Hamilton left him he interceded with Congress to grant a belated lieutenant-colonelcy to another aide, Tench Tilghman, whose unbroken devotion to Washington proved that it was not impossible to love him and endure his moods. Tilghman's failure to push himself forward was in further contrast with Hamilton's insatiate ambition. Of Tilghman, Washington wrote:

"This gent[n] came out a capt[n] of one of the light Inf[y] Companies of Phil[a], and served in the flying Camp in 1776. In August of the same year he joined my family, and has been in every action in which the main army was concerned. He has been a zealous servant and slave to the public, and a faithful assistant to me for near five years, great part of which time he refused to receive pay. Honor and gratitude interest me in his favor, and make me sollicitous to obtain his Commission. His modesty and love of concord placed the date of his expected com[n] at the 1st of April, 1777, because he would not take rank of Hamilton and Meade, who were declared aides in orders, (which he did not choose to be) before that period, altho' he had joined my family, and done all the duties of one, from the 1st of Sept[r] preceding." [21]

In July, Hamilton, impatient of idleness, coldly returned his commission to Washington, who, instead of letting the insolent young man rot in desuetude, sent Tilghman to him with an urgent request that he retain his commission and a promise to find a command for him soon. Hamilton wrote to his wife:

"Though I know you would be happy to hear had I rejected this proposal, it is a pleasure my reputation would not permit me to afford you. I consented to retain my commission, and accept the command." [22]

In August he wrote to his wife, "I am unhappy; I am unhappy beyond expression. I am unhappy, because I am to be so remote from you." [23]   Through Washington's courtesy, he was on his way to Virginia where he would reveal his characteristic ability and valor and such characteristic appetite for glory that he was ready to shove others aside. He was a brilliant man who never forgot the rights of Alexander Hamilton. Washington was a greater man who generally overlooked the rights of George Washington.

Washington must have wondered why men like Joseph Reed and Hamilton denied his appeals to stay with him and help him. But their refusals of his outstretched hands could never have filled his heart with such ashes and his mind with such bewilderment as came from his own mother. He could denounce Arnold and offer rewards for his capture, but what could he do to his mother? The old lady had gone about her work as quietly as Arnold did. Without even dropping a hint of her plans to her son, the Commander-in-Chief of the armies and reputedly the richest man in the colonies, she simply informed the Assembly of Virginia that she was ignored and starving to death and needed help!

With Virginian courtesy, the Assembly prepared to vote her a pension, and not annoy Washington about it. But Benjamin Harrison decided that he ought to warn his friend, and sent him a letter that Washington remembered and described with a shudder two years later. His mother had gifts for tormenting her son as badly as he tormented her. When he was deep in the wilderness with Braddock in 1755 had she not asked him to get her a Dutch servant and some good butter? [24] He had explained his inability with reverent patience then, but now he cried out against her to his brother, John Augustine; for at a time when he was desperate with his own financial anxieties and the nation's problems, she invaded his camp in New York with a demand that he find her a good overseer who could make some money for her. He expostulated to his brother:

"It is too much, while I am suffering in every other way (and hardly able to keep my own estate from sale) to be saddled with all the expence of hers, and not to be able to derive the smallest return from it. . . . While I am talking of my mother and her concerns, I am impelled to mention some things which have given, and still continue to give me pain. About two years ago, a gentleman of my acquaintance informed me, that it was in contemplation, to move for a pension for her in the Virginia Assembly; that he did not suppose I knew of the measure proposed; and that he did not believe it would be very agreeable to me to have it done; but wished, however, to know my sentiments thereon. I instantly wrote him, that it was new and astonishing to me, and begged that he would prevent the motion if possible; or oppose it, if made; for I was sure she had not a child that would not be hurt at the idea of her becoming a pensioner—or in other words, receiving *charity* from the public.

"Since then I have heard nothing of *that* matter; but learn from very good authority, that she is, upon all occasions and in all companies, complaining of the hardness of the times, of her wants and difficulties; and if not in direct terms, at least by strong innuendoes, endeavors to excite a belief that times are much altered, &c., &c., which not only makes *her* appear in an unfavorable point of view, but *those also* who are connected with her. That she can have no *real* wants, that may not easily be supplied, I am sure of. *Imaginary* wants are indefinite; and oftentimes insatiable; because they sometimes are boundless, and always changing.

"The reason of my mentioning these matters, is that you may enquire into her real wants, and see what is necessary to make her comfortable. If the rent is insufficient to do this, while I have anything, I will part with it to make her so; and wish you to take measures in my behalf accordingly. At the same time, I wish you to represent to her in delicate terms, the impropriety of her complaints, and *acceptance* of favors, even where they are voluntarily offered, from any but relations. It will not do to touch upon this subject in a letter to her, and therefore I have avoided it." [25]

To Benjamin Harrison, who had informed him of her appeal to the Assembly in February, 1781, he had written promptly:

"I do not delay a moment to thank you for the interesting matter contained in it, and to express surprize at that part which respects a pension for my mother. True it is, I am but little acquainted with her *present* situation or distresses, if she is under any. As true it is, a year or two before I left Virginia (to make her latter days comfortable and free from care) I did, at her request, but at my own expence, purchase a commodious house, garden and Lotts (of her own choosing) in Fredericksburg, that she might be near my sister Lewis, her only daughter,—and did moreover agree to take her land and negroes at a certain yearly rent, to be fixed by Colo. Lewis and others (of her own nomination) which has been an annual expence to me ever since, as the estate never raised one half the rent I was to pay. Before I left Virginia I answered all her calls for money; and since that period have directed my steward to do the same.

"Whence her distresses can arise, therefore, I know not, never having received any complaint of his inattention or neglect on that head; tho' his inability to pay my own taxes, is such I know, as to oblige me to sell negroes for this purpose—the taxes being the most unequal (I am told) in the world—some persons paying for things of equal value, four times, nay ten times, the rate that others do.—But putting these things aside, which I could not avoid mentioning in exculpation of a presumptive want of duty on my part; confident I am that she has not a child that would not divide the last sixpence to relieve her from *real* distress. This she has been repeatedly assured of by me; and all of us I am certain, would feel much hurt, at having our mother a pensioner, while we had the means of supporting her; but in fact she has an ample income of her own.

"I lament accordingly that your letter, which conveyed the first hint of this matter, did not come to my hands sooner; but I request, in pointed terms, if the matter is now in agitation in your Assembly, that all proceedings on it may be stopped, or in case of a decision in her favor, that it may be done away and repealed at my request." [26]

Her distress is pictured in an undated letter she wrote to her son, John Augustine. This was formerly assigned to the year 1774, but Conway later believed that it was written in 1781:

"Dear Johnne,—I am glad to hear you and all the family is well, and should be glad if I could write you the same. I am a going fast, and it, the time, is hard. I am borrowing a little Cornn—no Cornn in the Cornn house. I never lived soe poore in my life. Was it not for Mr. French and your sister Lewis I should be almost starved, but I am like an old almanack quite out of date. Give my love to Mrs. Washington—all the family. I am dear Johnne your loving and affectionate Mother.

"P.S. I should be glad to see you as I dont expect to hold out long." [27]

She had been left in care of her daughter. But Betty's husband, Fielding Lewis, had bankrupted himself for his country. A wealthy man in 1775, he maintained and equipped three regiments, lent $35,000 to the state, and built and conducted a factory of small arms at Fredericksburg. Finally, depreciated currency did for him.[28] He could not pay his taxes and was at this time so wrecked in health that he had only a few months more to live. In the words of Mrs. Fleming, "He died the day the Battle of Yorktown was fought with his guns." [29] Washington's sister was left so poor that she had to open a girl's school. During the war she made cartridges and led in charity. Conway published one of her letters to Washington:

"Oh! when will that day arrive when we will meet again. I trust in the Lord it will be soon,—'till when, you have the prayers and kind wishes for your health and happiness of your loving and
"Sincerely affectionate sister, Betty Lewis." [30]

It may well be true that Washington's mother endured many privations since his once-wealthy sister was so driven; but it was unendurable that she should be supported by the state. A few days before Washington wrote Harrison to stop her pension he wrote a letter of high political ethic to his stepson Jacky Custis, who had become an assemblyman, and was absenting himself from sessions in disgust at the procedures of the majority. Washington's counsel is typical of his own lofty patience:

"I do not suppose, that so young a senator as you are, little versed in political disquisitions, can yet have much influence in a populous assembly, composed of Gentl^n of various talents and of different views. But it is in your power to be punctual in your attendance (and duty to the trust reposed in you exacts it of you), to hear dispassionately and determine coolly all great questions. To be disgusted at the decision of questions, because they are not consonant to our own ideas, and to withdraw ourselves from public assemblies, or to neglect our attendance at them, upon suspicion that there is a party formed, who are inimical to our cause and to the true interest of our country, is wrong, because these things may originate in a difference of opinion; but, supposing the fact is otherwise, and that our suspicions are well founded, it is the indispensable duty of every patriot to counteract them by the most steady and uniform opposition." [31]

That was Washington's piety to the nation yet unborn. He would not imitate other men's sins of omission or commission. He would not use their derelictions as excuses for derelictions of his own. Rather he did their duties for them and repaired their neglects by superhuman exertions. While other men put their own interests first, then their state's and the nation's last, if anywhere, Washington forgot Virginia for the nation. Evil times were settling there.

The Tory element had been comparatively slight in the Old Dominion, but, in 1781, the state began to waver dangerously in its enthusiasm for the cause and the presence of British troops encouraged loyalist outbreaks, which were roughly suppressed. Among the leading patriots was Colonel Charles Lynch, whose violence "is said to have given origin to that famous euphemism, 'lynch law.'" There was a growing state of anarchy everywhere in Virginia, taxation was resisted, the jails were packed.[32] The hardships of the planters were augmented and persecution and confiscation were wreaked upon the loyalists. Washington interceded for his absent friend, George William Fairfax, and pleaded that his property should not be subjected to confiscation. It was his repayment for old Fairfax kindnesses to him, and for the kindnesses the Fairfaxes had shown to American prisoners in England.[33]

The perfectness of his devotion to the cause of the nation is seen in the rebuke he administered to Lund Washington. Lafayette wrote to him of a British naval raid on the coast of Virginia:

"When the enemy came to your house, many negroes were ready to join him; this news did not much afflict me, for those kinds of interest touch me little; but you cannot conceive how unhappy I was to learn that M. Lund Washington went on board the enemy battleships and consented to give them provisions. This conduct of the person who represents you on your property must certainly produce a bad effect and it contrasts with the courageous answers of some neighbors, whose houses were burned in consequence. You will do what you think best, but friendship imposes on me the duty of revealing the facts confidentially." [34]

Washington thanked Lafayette for the bad news and took it as a proof of "the bond, which unites us in friendship." He excused Lund for having "a false idea" that he was "more the trustee and guardian of my property than the representative of my honor." [35] To Lund he wrote:

"I am very sorry to hear of your loss. I am a little sorry to hear of my own; but that which gives me most concern is, that you should go on board the enemy's vessels, and furnish them with refreshments. It would have been a less painful circumstance to me to have heard, that in consequence of your non-compliance with their request, they had burnt my House and laid the Plantation in ruins. . . . I am thoroughly persuaded, that you acted from your best judgment, and believe, that your desire to preserve my property, and rescue the buildings from impending danger, were your governing motives, but to go on board their vessels, carry them refreshments, commune with a parcel of plundering scoundrels, and request a favor by asking a surrender of my negroes, was exceedingly ill judged, and 'tis to be feared, will be unhappy in its consequences, as it will be a precedent for others, and may become a subject of animadversion. . . . I have as little doubt of its ending in the loss of all my negroes, and in the destruction of my Houses; but I am prepared for the event; . . . I do not know what negroes they may have left you, and as I have observed before I do not know what number they will have left me by the time they have done—but this much I am sure of, that you shall never want assistance when it is in my power to afford it." [36]

The pendulum of Washington's soul was capable of amazing swings. At times he seems like a miser or a Shylock or a petty swindler, with his petty cash excitements, his penny-paring, his careful records of every cent given to his mother, his step-children, his wife; his shrewd and tricky deals in land. Yet, when he gave he gave. "Business is Business" was the rule in one cell of his compartmented mind, but in another the rule was "Charity is Charity"; in another, "Patriotism is Patriotism." He could have said that the only way a poor young man can rise to the majesty of squandering great gifts is by watching shillings carefully. Benjamin Franklin of *Poor Richard* canniness was in France fighting the war where it was very largely won—in the courts of Europe with the weapons of diplomacy. Washington was in the bleak fields of America serving seven years without wage, watching his beloved estates go to ruin, and denouncing his steward because he did not let the enemy burn Mount Vernon rather than pay them a little tribute. Petty economies alone make possible such spendthrift munificences.

In the meanwhile, other Virginia gentlemen, and gentlemen in all the other states, were busy in other ways. Captain X, a Commissary, "refused Corn at forty Dollars pr: bushel," and let Captain Y buy it and sell it to him for "60 Dollars pr: Bushel." "These Gentlemen refused to purchase whiskey . . . at £45 pr: Gall: and gave Capt: Y. £60 for the same whiskey which he bought at the price." Officers who were buying horses for Baron Steuben's troops assessed them at "at least three times their value. . . . One guelding worth £10,000 was valued at £35,000." [37]

Against such patriots Washington could hardly war. These secret thieves denounced the loyalists, who fought in the open. And there were more than 6,000 loyalist soldiers with Cornwallis in the South.[38] Against these and the British regulars, Greene and Steuben and later Lafayette had to fight like terriers resisting a tiger, while Washington waited in the North for the French to make it possible for him to move.

HE OFFENDS THE FRENCH

HAVING lost Burgoyne's army in the try for the Hudson, having been forced to evacuate Philadelphia in order to hold New York, and despairing of forcing Washington into a trap where he could be destroyed and the Northern colonies conquered, the British began to make ready for a grand effort in the south.

Clinton left Cornwallis to work upward from Charleston while he prepared to drive in a wedge at Chesapeake Bay and work up through the friendly settlements in Pennsylvania. This was the plan that had been agreed upon in England in the autumn of 1776, the Scheme that Charles Lee had vainly recommended in 1777. Cornwallis and Clinton agreed on something for once—that the Chesapeake should be the seat of the war, even at the cost of abandoning New York.[1] But Cornwallis wanted to conquer Virginia. Clinton wanted desperately to get back into Philadelphia. Thanks to the feud between them, everything went wrong.[2] Cornwallis complained that Clinton hampered him with far-off orders just as Clinton complained of Germain.

At the very outset of his advance, after annihilating Gates at Camden, Cornwallis had lost, through no fault of his own, his invaluable left wing. The brilliant Scotch officer, Major Ferguson, inventor of "the first breech-loading rifle ever used by regular troops in actual battle," had organized a large body of loyalists and armed them with his rifles. In the course of his raids he found himself on King's Mountain in South Carolina, where he was suddenly surrounded by a band of over-the-mountain men led by a group of "Associated Colonels." On October 7th, 1780, they killed or captured every single man

and officer of Ferguson's. It was "not a battle, it was a battue."
Excepting a few foreign officers only Americans were present.
Whigs slaughtered Tories with the frightful atrocity that char-
acterized both sides in the Southern campaigns.[3]

The blow crippled Cornwallis and destroyed his confidence
in the loyalists on whom he relied. In January, 1781, he was
further crippled by the crushing defeat of his cavalry leader,
Tarleton, whom Daniel Morgan whipped with an inferior
force at the Cowpens—largely by a canny use of the militia.
Knowing their habits he instructed them to fire two volleys and
run. That was the one thing they could be relied on to do.
But when they ran they found a river in front of them and had
to obey his second order, which was to fall in behind his few
regulars. When the militia ran, the British came on pell-mell,
crashed into the regulars and were destroyed. Then Morgan,
whom tradition cherishes as a rugged hero, but who was also
a supersensitive prima donna, quarreled with Greene, and alleging "sciatic pains" left the war in disgust.[4] He had resigned
from Gates, resigned from Washington, and now resigned
from Greene. Yet he was a man of astonishing ability and
by his victories at Bennington and at Cowpens delivered mortal blows at both Burgoyne and Cornwallis.

The smashing of Tarleton robbed Cornwallis of further
initiative and resource and he now faced Nathanael Greene,
who won undying fame by such dazzling shiftiness about the
strategical chessboard that nearly every one of his defeats and
retreats left his clever enemy in a worse position than before.
But Greene had little joy of his triumphs and was chiefly
aware of his distresses, the hostility of Congress, the failure
of his militia to stand fast at critical movements, and of the
rains and flooded rivers that saved him from annihilation in
exhausting flights.

At the battle of Guildford Court House, March 15th, 1781,
he dealt Cornwallis another deadly blow in the guise of a defeat. He fainted with fatigue, having seen his men scatter in
panic though they outnumbered Cornwallis two or three to one.

The steadier Continentals inflicted such loss on Cornwallis that he had to withdraw, and Fox said in the House of Commons, "Another such victory would destroy the British army." [5]

Cornwallis issued a proclamation of amnesty: "Whereas by the blessing of Almighty God, his Majesty's arms have been crowned with signal success," etc., calling upon the rebels to end their "unnatural rebellion." [6] Then he retreated aside to Wilmington on the seacoast, hoping to receive reinforcements. This ruinous error let Greene in behind him. Cornwallis' next mistake was a decision to go north into Virginia and cooperate with Generals Phillips and Arnold.

Arnold had been in Virginia since the last of December, 1780, when Clinton sent him thither with a few troops and vessels. He seemed to bear a charmed life, ravaged at will, advanced to Richmond, chased Governor Jefferson into hiding, and made the air of the state aromatic with clouds of smoke from burned tobacco warehouses. Washington sent Steuben to fight him but the Prussian chiefly wrangled with the Virginians. As he wrote afterwards in abandoned poverty:

"I shall always regret that circumstances, perhaps, induced me to undertake the defense of a country where Cæsar and Hannibal would have lost their reputation, and where every farmer is a general, but where nobody wishes to be a soldier." [7]

Herein lies, perhaps, the secret of Washington's military genius: he won where Cæsar and Hannibal would have failed. But Steuben's difficulties were appalling, and he was not rich enough to pay his own way as Lafayette did. The value of American money at that time is shown in a letter of Steuben's telling of the problem of raising cavalry:

"The Assembly have passed a law limiting the price of horses for the cavalry at five thousand pounds, a price inadequate to the purchase of the meanest horse. Very indifferent horses, which have been impressed, have been valued from twenty to thirty thousand pounds and upwards." [8]

He could not buy hacks at $150,000 apiece! And he needed three hundred. They had cost $150 before. Light Horse

Harry Lee while praising Arnold's brilliance was shamed at the supineness of Virginia before him.[9]

The degradation of seeing Arnold, of all men, making himself at home in Virginia with no one to oppose him was almost unendurable to Washington. The French alone could save his native state, but they were inert. Suddenly his hopes were raised. Providence sent a gale in January to disperse and disable the British blockading fleet off Newport. The French fleet did not dare come out entire, but Admiral Destouches sent three ships under de Tilly to cut Arnold off from the sea. Washington was disgusted because the whole fleet did not go, and began to criticize the allies more and more recklessly. He hastened Lafayette south with all the men he could spare, twelve hundred or so, to cooperate with the three French ships. In his instructions he told Lafayette:

"You are to do no act whatever with Arnold, that directly or by implication may screen him from the punishment due to his treason and desertion, which, if he should fall into your hands, you will execute in the most summary way." [10]

Lafayette won everybody, especially the ladies' auxiliaries, on his way South. He spent his own money and gave promissory notes and displayed every charming trait.[11] But the French ships returned to Newport and Lafayette halted, expecting to be recalled to Washington's side.

There was something about French mistakes that seemed to irritate Washington beyond his usual control. Most uncharacteristically he appears in the rôle of a tactless critic who endangered what good feeling there was between the French and the Americans, leaving it to Rochambeau to play the nobler part. The French thought that they had their reasons for caution in risking their fleets and the right to use their own judgment; and after all, Virginia and Arnold were matters of minor importance to them. Besides, they had all too many excuses for disgust with the Americans. If Rochambeau had done nothing more than quote Washington's words about them there would have been fury. The impartial young Swedish

Count de Fersen described to his father how the patriots looked in foreign eyes:

"The spirit of patriotism only exists in the chief and principal men in the country, who are making very great sacrifices; the rest who make up the great mass think only of their personal interests. Money is the controlling idea in all their actions, they only think of how it may be gained; every one is for himself, no one for the general good. The inhabitants of the coast, even the best Whigs, carry to the English fleet anchored in Gardner Bay provisions of all kinds, and this because they are well paid; they overcharge us mercilessly; every thing is enormously dear; in all the dealings we have had with them they have treated us more like enemies than friends. Their greed is unequalled, money is their God; virtue, honor, all count for nothing to them compared with the precious metal. I do not mean that there are no estimable people of noble and generous character: there are many, but I speak of the nation in general."

Next Fersen was writing to his father:

"There is a coolness between Washington and M. de Rochambeau; the dissatisfaction is on the part of the American General, ours is ignorant of the reason. He has given me orders to go with a letter from him, and to inform myself of the reason for his discontent, to heal the breach if possible, or if the affair be more grave to report to him the cause." [12]

The conduct of Rochambeau throughout the alliance was marked by a magnanimity quite equal to Washington's and in some instances more unshaken. Contrasting him with another French general, the Baron de Vioménil, who might have broken with the Americans, Fersen says:

"The Baron is very quick and high-tempered; he has not the precious sang-froid of M. de Rochambeau, who was the only man capable to command us here, and to maintain the perfect harmony which has existed between two nations so different in their manners and their language, and who, at bottom, have no love for each other. There were never any disputes between our two armies during the period we were together, but there were often just causes of complaint on our side. Our allies have not always conducted themselves well towards us, and the time we have passed with them has not taught us to love or esteem them. M. de Rochambeau himself has not always had reason to praise them; notwithstanding which his conduct was always the same. His example had its effect on the army, and the severe orders he gave restrained everybody and enforced that rare discipline which was the admiration of all America and of the English who witnessed it. The wise, prudent and simple conduct of M. de Rochambeau has done more to conciliate America to us than the gain of four battles would have done." [13]

Washington's wrath was the more embarrassing to Washington, as to the French, from the fact that he was absolutely helpless unless the French sent him money, men, and ships. He had to pack his former aide, John Laurens, off to France with a despairing prayer to the King. While he was at it, he asked Laurens to bring him from France

"A travelling Razor case with every thing compleat . . . a best pocket Reconnoiterer—or Telescope . . . a good Saddle, bridle & furniture (excluding Pistols) fit for a republican General   A Watch string

$$\left.\begin{array}{l}\text{"2 Doz}^n \text{ dishes sized} \\ \text{4 doz}^n \text{ Soup} \\ \text{8 doz}^n \text{ shallow}\end{array}\right\}\text{Plates}\left\{\begin{array}{l}\text{of Tin or something} \\ \text{very light for the Field."} \end{array}\right.$$ [14]

To the King, Laurens was instructed to explain that a young nation in revolution inevitably made mistakes in money, paper, credit, and that the American soldiers and people must have cash; otherwise, one more "feeble and expiring effort in the next campaign" would put a "period to our opposition." A naval superiority was vital. More French troops were "extremely desirable." [15]   To Franklin Washington wrote concerning "the present infinitely critical posture of our affairs." [16] Then he set out for Newport to make a personal appeal to Rochambeau. If it had not been for a certain Irish tailor he might never have reached the French general.

Hercules Mulligan is a name of impossible sound. Once invented it would seem impossible to forget. Yet it is not remembered, though, if there had been no Hercules Mulligan, George Washington might have met the fate he tried to contrive for Benedict Arnold. He might have been captured as Charles Lee was, and General Prescott; and he might have been sent to England on a fleet frigate to join his friend, Laurens, the ex-President of Congress, now domiciled in London Tower. It would have been a bad time to be caught.

Hercules Mulligan was once denied a place in the Hall of Fame because he was "a mythical person," but he was a very real Irishman, born in Coleraine in 1740, and brought to America at the age of six. When he grew up he became a clothier and tailor in New York, a fashionable tailor, with a capacious ear for gossip. In 1779 he got word to Washington of a plot to seize him in time to thwart it. In 1781 he warned Washington that Clinton was going to send three hundred dragoons to intercept him on his way to Newport. Washington took another road. Benedict Arnold suspected Mulligan of being one of Washington's spies and had him arrested and court-martialled, but was unable to convict him. Washington took his first breakfast in New York with Mulligan in 1783.[17]

In April, 1781, Washington wrote to Governor Livingston of New Jersey:

"Intelligence has been sent to me, by a gentleman living near the enemy's lines, who has an opportunity of knowing what passes among them, that four parties had been sent out with orders to take or assassinate your Excellency, Governor Clinton, myself, and a fourth person, whose name is not known. . . . I shall take such precautions on the occasion, as appear to me necessary."[18]

Governor Livingston wrote to Joseph Reed that he believed him to be the fourth.[19]

Leaving camp, March 2nd, 1781, Washington rode away to Newport and reached there without mishap in four days, receiving royal homage on the way, and reviewing the legion of the Duc de Lauzun at Lebanon. At Newport the French Admiral Destouches, who had temporarily succeeded the dead de Ternay, took him in his barge to the French flagship, where he met a cluster of generals. Landing again he rode through a lane of smart French soldiers three deep on either side. That night the streets were "grandly illuminated," says Ezra Stiles, who adds that he was "received as a Marshal of France." [20] But he never received the title, though Rochambeau was instructed to give the honors of that grade to "M. le général Vasingthon." [21]

For the grand illumination, the town gave candles to those who were too poor to buy them. Thirty boys preceded Washington down the street with tall candles and when he reached his door he turned and thanked them. "This was glory enough for the young patriots." [22] Newport was crowded with French noblemen, who would play big rôles in the far-off French revolution. Here was the Vicomte de Noailles, in whose regiment Napoleon would dawn as a junior officer; Berthier, who would be his military adviser; the Duc de Lauzun, who would say to the executioner at the guillotine, "We are both Frenchmen; we shall do our duty"; Comte Dumas, who would shine at Waterloo, and many another. [23] They were all idolaters of this new-world giant, "this Atlas," says the Chevalier de Silly. "We had not eyes enough to see him with." [24] On the second night they gave him as magnificent a ball as they could. Washington's partner was the beautiful Miss Margaret Champlin. The French officers decorated the ballroom and paid the great dancer the last compliment of taking the instruments from the musicians and playing the opening tune themselves.

There was a vast amount of kissing in those days and Newport may have respected the custom of North Carolina of which an officer wrote: " 'Tis customary for the gentlemen after the Jigg to Kiss their Partners, and nothing but that could have induced me to dance the Jiggs." [25] It was Miss Champlin's privilege to choose the music for her dance and she felicitously (perhaps a little maliciously) selected "A Successful Campaign." [26] The music of the old tune is so gay that merely playing it and imagining the tall Washington stepping out to it somehow makes him live again beyond the power of words.

Washington took pleasure in all the grandeurs and graces and nobody carried them off better. But he was not happy with Rochambeau and, according to the Duc de Lauzun, the military situation "was perfectly disagreeable to him and he did not hide the fact." Rochambeau's requests as to the appointment of certain officers he would not grant.[27] Suddenly, as if to oblige him, the whole French fleet stood out to sea on the way to the Chesapeake. Washington sent word to Lafayette to push on south and take Arnold. But the British admiral, Arbuthnot, also went south, and now Washington had his doubts.

He made his way slowly back to camp, leaving Newport March 13th, 1781. In Bristol, maidens scattered flowers and evergreens in his path. At Providence, the children flocked about him with torches and tried to clasp his hand. The Comte Dumas says that they called him Father and "crowded in front of us so as to hinder our advance. General Washington, softened, stopped for some moments, and pressing my hand, said to me:

" 'We may be beaten by the English; that is the chance of war; but here is the army that they will never conquer.' " [28]

He danced at a grand military ball in Providence, but had to decline an invitation to Boston. The expenses of the trip were $19,848½ in continental money, plus £68.12.0 "where paper w^d not pass." [29] When he reached New Windsor camp he was greeted with a complaint signed by seven field officers because Lafayette's aide, Gimat (which Washington spelled "Jamat"), and Major Galvan (who afterward committed suicide over a love-affair with an American coquette) had received commissions and commands. Washington complained in turn:

"The best meant endeavors to promote the service is subject to, and often meets with, the most unfavorable constructions." [30]

He was so disgusted that he decided to recall Lafayette from the South, but events changed his mind. He was still sure that inscrutable Providence would win the war against the unmentioned but ever-active and usually successful Satan, yet he expected now to meet the fate of Moses and die before the Promised Land was reached:

"Our affairs are brought to an awful crisis, that the hand of Providence, I trust, may be more conspicuous in our deliverance. The many remarkable interpositions of the divine government, in the hours of our deepest distress and darkness, have been too luminous to suffer me to doubt the happy issue of the present contest; but the period for its accomplishment may be too far distant for a person of my years, whose morning and evening hours, and every moment (unoccupied by business), pants for retirement, and for those domestic and rural enjoyments, which in my estimation far surpass the highest pageantry of this world." [31]

It was a dismal world he lived in when his sole hope lay in a vague deity that tormented him for the purpose of theatrical displays of its power and kindliness. He was still sullen over the French, his real redeemers, and wrote to Joseph Jones a long letter with a line and the word "Private" alongside this lengthy paragraph:

"It is a misfortune which seems to attend all our measures to do things unreasonably—or rather to neglect the critical moment to do them.—Had the French Commanders at Rhode Island complied (in the first instance) with my request to send the whole Fleet, and a detachment from their Land force to Virginia, the destruction of Arnold's Corps must inevitably have been compleated during the debilitated state of the British Fleet.—The enterprize now is bold and precarious—rendered more so by an unfortunate, and to me unaccountable delay of twenty four hours in their quitting Newport after it was said they were ready to Sail.—The wind & weather being as favourable to them, and as adverse to the enemy in Gardners bay, as the powers of the Air could devise.—but it ought to be *our policy to make the most of their assistance without disgusting them by our censures*, or reminding them of their mistakes. . . . The critical situation of affairs in Virginia, and North Carolina produces anxious moments, and we wait impatiently for decisive acc[ts]—God grant they may be favourable to us—but the face of things is much changed since my first proposing the Expedition to Portsmouth; at that time the French were decidedly superior in their Navy—now they are unquestionably inferior." [32]

On the next day he wrote to William Fitzhugh: "It is to be lamented, greatly lamented," that the French had not sent their fleet when he proposed it.[33]   That also was "in confidence." On the 28th, when he wrote to Lund, he was still fuming:

"It was unfortunate—but this I mention in confidence—that the French Fleet detachment did not undertake the enterprize now upon, when I first proposed it to them—the destruction of Arnolds Corps would then have been inevitable," etc.

He followed this with pleasant questions about home:

"How many Lambs have you had this Spring?—How many Colts are you like to have?—Is your covered ways done?—what are you going about next?—Have you any prospect of getting paint and oyl?—are you going to repair the Pavement of the Piaza?—is any thing doing, or like to be done with respect to the wall at the edge of the Hill in front of the House?—Have you made good the decayed Trees at the ends of the House, or the Hedges, so^{ed}—Have you made any attempts to reclaim more Land for Meadow?—&c. &c.—An Acc^t of these things would be satisfactory to me, and infinitely amusing in the recital, as I have these kind of improvements very much at heart— As soon as you can conveniently do it after receipt of this letter give me a list of the number and kind of Mares I possess.—the number of Colts from 4 years old (inclusive) to those of this spring with the ages—colour—kind—and sexes—Mrs Washington (from report only, I believe) has taken a fancy to a Horse belonging to Mr James Cleveland, brother to the one had from him before (and wch I think a fine horse)—if you can get him in the way of barter, provided he is as handsome, and as fine a horse as represented—& the colour of the set she drives—I shall be very well pleased with your doing it.—She joins me in best wishes for you Mrs Washington, and Milly Posey." [34]

Now this letter fell into British hands and Clinton decided to publish the criticisms of the French for manifest reasons. He gave it to Rivington who printed it April 4th, 1781, in his *Gazette*.   He did not publish Washington's bucolics as to the lambs and colts, but only his grumbling at the allies.

In the meanwhile Washington anxiously waited to hear what the whole French fleet would do to Arnold.   Letters from Lafayette were brave statements of discouraging truths.   On

March 25th he wrote that the French and British fleets were engaged. He could hear a furious cannonade for three hours. The action must have been bloody but Lafayette could not even guess which side had won.[35] Two days later the Chevalier de la Luzerne ended the suspense: "I lament the ill success of an expedition which, if it had succeeded, would have," etc. But "the contest has been highly honorable." [36] Destouches wrote that he had won but had been unable to pursue and decided to return to Newport.[37]

Rochambeau offered to march to New York and combine forces, but Washington decided that such a movement would be premature and declined the offer.[38] To Congress he wrote that the New York Line was likely to follow the example of the Pennsylvania and New Jersey Lines if their sixteen months' pay were not at once attended to.[39] To John Laurens in Paris he wrote that Cornwallis had driven Greene out of North Carolina into Virginia; he had ordered Lafayette and Wayne with the reconstructed Pennsylvania Line to reinforce Greene, "but how either can march, without money or credit, is more than I can tell." He put this phrase in cipher, also a long and frantic outcry in cipher:

"The world are disappointed at not seeing Arnold in Gibbets; and, above all, because we stood in need of something to keep us afloat, till the result of your mission is known; for, be assured, my dear Laurens, that day does not follow night more certainly, than it brings with it some additional proof of the impracticability of carrying on the war without the aids you were directed to solicit. As an honest and candid man, as a man whose all depends on the final and happy termination of the present contest, I assert this, while I give it decisively as my opinion, that, without a foreign loan, our present force, (which is but the remnant of an army,) cannot be kept together this campaign, much less will it be increased and in readiness for another. . . .

"We cannot transport the provisions from the States in which they are assessed to the army, because we cannot pay the teamsters, who will no longer work for certificates. It is equally certain, that our Troops are approaching fast to nakedness, and that we have nothing to cloathe them with; that our Hospitals are without medicines and our sick without nutriment except such as well men eat; That all our public works are at a stand, and the artificers disbanding. But why need I run into the detail, when it may be declared in a word, that we are at the end of our tether, and that now or never our deliverance must come." [40]

None of the darkest of the dark hours was darker than April, 1781. Maryland had joined the Confederation at last after forcing Virginia to surrender her claim to vast Western lands; but this left Washington's own claims in a dubious position. Congress had ceased to print money in March, just before Robert Morris became The Financier with no finances. Finances were now in utter collapse. Pennsylvania could not pay her assemblymen their wages.[41] There was graft and misery in the hospitals. Of four directors, two were dismissed and one was tried and acquitted.[42] The final director was Dr. John Cochran, who succeeded Dr. William Shippen in February, 1781. Dr. Shippen had said that more brave men "fell a sacrifice to the neglect and iniquity in the medical department than by the sword of the enemy." [43] Congressman Thornton had written:

"Want of Fidility, Honour, and Humanity, in the Drs and averice in the Suttlers, has Slain ten Soldiers to the Enemies one, and will Soon prevent every man of Common Sense from putting his Life and Fortune in the Power of Such as Destroy both without pity or mercy." [44]

Dr. Cochran found the hospitals in such horrible condition that he gave the last sheets on his own bed to the wounded and pawned his personal credit for supplies. Some of the surgeons had not received a shilling of pay in two years and could get no public clothing. The convalescent soldiers had to beg for food on the streets. "Destitution paralyzed, and very nearly extirpated, the hospitals during the greater part of the war." [45] There was an eternal lack of remedies. France, the one resort, sent medicines as everything else.

To Washington's other discontents a most unusual chagrin was added now. He was caught gossiping behind the back of his friends—a thing everybody does but dreads to be caught at. He had been missing Lafayette and had written to say that while he could not recall the troops he would welcome Lafayette himself, and he could turn the troops over to Steuben:

"It was with great reluctance I could resolve upon seeing you separated from head-quarters. My friendship for you makes me desirous of having you near me, and there will occur frequent occasions in cooperative measures in which it would be of the greatest utility I should have it in my power to consult you."

Again he wrote:

"I therefore not only repeat the offer . . . but accompany it with a wish, that you may return." [46]

This appeal accompanied a most embarrassing explanation, for Lafayette had written:

"A letter from you, relating to the delays of the French, makes a great noise at Philadelphia. Indeed, it gives me pain on many political accounts." [47]

To this Washington had to answer, acknowledging that he had written a confidential letter to Lund:

"I can neither avow the letter, as it is published by Mr. Rivington, nor declare that it is spurious, because my letter to this gent[n] was wrote in great haste, and no copy of it taken. . . . That the enemy fabricated a number of Letters for me formerly is a fact well known; that they are not less capable of doing it now, few will deny. As to his asserting, that this is a genuine copy of the original, he well knows that their friends do not want to convict him of a falsehood, and that ours have not the opportunity of doing it, though both sides are knowing to his talents for lying." [48]

Next, as Washington must have foreseen, came a letter from Rochambeau quoting his letter to Lund, and rebuking Washington with a noble dignity. Worse yet, he pointed out that Washington had not told the exact facts: the letter he spoke of writing to urge the French fleet to sail had not been written until six days after the three ships sailed, and had not been received until ten days after. He added:

"I only state these facts to call to your mind these dates, which I beg you to verify by your correspondence, that you may be entirely persuaded, that there will never be the least delay in what concerns the troops whom I command, in the execution of your orders, as soon as I shall receive them." [49]

Washington ate humble pie with little relish but meekly. It must have irked him especially since he had written glowing praises to Destouches for his battle with the British. In his natural desire to evade entire responsibility for the letter to Lund, he avoided any direct denial, yet he also avoided mentioning the fact that he had written even more forcefully to other people than to Lund. In any case, there is a certain malicious delight in watching the good and the great squirming in embarrassments more frequent in more petty lives:

"I assure your Excellency, that I feel extreme pain at the occasion of that part of your letter of the 26th instant, which relates to an intercepted letter of mine published by the enemy. I am unhappy that an accident should have put it in their power to give to the world any thing from me, which may contain an implication the least disagreeable to you, or to the Chevalier Destouches. . . . The enemy have fabricated whole letters for me, and even a series of letters; and it is not improbable they may have given a different turn to some of my expressions in the present instance. It would however be disingenuous in me not to acknowledge, that I believe the general import to be true. . . . Whatever construction it may bear, I beg your Excellency will consider the letter to a private friend, a gentleman who has the direction of my concerns at home, totally unconnected with public affairs, and on whose discretion I could absolutely rely. No idea of the same kind has ever gone to any public body. . . . My letter however was written in haste, and might have been inaccurately expressed. I have lately learnt, (though not officially,) that the cause of the delay I have alluded to was a want of supplies for the fleet. Impressed with a real esteem for and confidence in the Chevalier Destouches, I heard this circumstance with satisfaction. With this explanation, I leave the matter to his candor and to yours, and flatter myself it will make no impressions inconsistent with an entire persuasion of my sincere esteem and attachment." [50]

Rochambeau accepted this as handsomely as was to be expected and the incident was closed, leaving Washington to brood in idleness like Prometheus chained to the rock. Washington had, as Æschylos said, "too much leisure." He had, in fact, time to resume the compilation of his diaries, which he had ignored for almost exactly six years. His last entry was on June 19th, 1775, the day that he was handed his commission as commander-in-chief of the army besieging the town of Boston. Now, on May 1st, 1781, he was in cooperation with a French lieutenant-general, and all Europe was at war or in a state of armed neutrality. Yet he had fewer soldiers with him than then. At Boston he had found 16,000 effectives. Now he had not half the number, perhaps not a quarter. His diary opens:

"I begin, at this Epoch, a concise Journal of Military transactions &ca. I lament not having attempted it from the commencement of the War, in aid of my memory—and wish the multiplicity of matter which continually surround me and the embarrassed State of our affairs which is momently calling the attention to perplexities of one kind or another may not defeat altogether, or so interrupt my present intention, and plan, as to render it of little avail."

He reviews the state of affairs lugubriously:

"Instead of having Magazines filled with provisions, we have a scanty pittance scattered here and there in the different States. Instead of having our Arsenals well supplied with Military Stores, they are poorly provided, and the Workmen all leaving them . . . we are daily and hourly oppressing the people—souring their tempers—and alienating the affections. Instead of having the Regiments compleated to the new establishment and which ought to have been so by the   of agreeably to the requisitions of Congress, scarce any State in the Union has, at this hour, an eighth part of its quota in the field and little prospect, that I can see, of ever getting more than half. In a word—instead of having everything in readiness to take the Field, we have nothing and instead of having the prospect of a glorious offensive campaign before us, we have a bewildered and gloomy defensive one—" [51]

In addition to the woes of the South, he had to record that, in the north of New York, starvation would probably compel the evacuation of Fort Schuyler, and a mutiny was threatened.

There was grave danger of an invasion of British and Indians from that quarter. He "directed the Q. M. Gl. to send 50 Barls. of flour and the like qty. of salted Meat immy. up," but there were only 24 barrels in store. At West Point there was meat for only two days. He sent General Heath to make a personal appeal to all the eastern governors. Colonel Greene's command on the Croton was attacked, the Colonel killed and several soldiers "inhumanly murdered."

He writes to his spies, the two Culpers, "C—Senr" and "C—Junr," and they send him information of the British movements. Clinton is despatching 2,000 men somewhere, leaving him only 4,000 regulars, but Washington dares not attack unless he can get French help. Yale makes him a Doctor of Laws. Harvard had made him one five years before, but Ezra Stiles wrote:

"We cannot add to the Accumulation of Glory which shines around the Name of Washington; and which none but himself thinks unmerited. But we are ambitious of the honor of enroll[g] his Name in our Register & Archives, among those whose literary Merits entitle them to the highest academical Dignities." [52]

Of course, Washington made a polite acknowledgment. [53]

In May, Admiral Destouches was supplanted by the Comte de Barras, who arrived in a frigate and asked for an interview with Washington. Rochambeau's son, the Vicomte de Rochambeau, also returned from his errand to France, bringing the news that the King was sending a big fleet under the Comte de Grasse and a convoy of supply ships. Word came also from de Grasse that he had a force "sufficient to fulfil the offensive plans" but could not arrive before July 15th and must leave by the middle of October, since he was cooperating with the Spanish. [54]

Washington appointed Weathersfield, Connecticut, as the place for a conference and reached there May 19th, 1781, two days ahead of the French. But de Barras did not accompany Rochambeau, since the ubiquitous Admiral Arbuthnot had reappeared off Newport and threatened the French fleet with attack. A profound disagreement at once endangered the pleasant relations between Rochambeau and Washington. The Frenchman could not see the American's plan for an attack on New York, and pleaded for an expedition to Virginia to relieve "the poor Marquis" *le garçon*, Lafayette, who was trying to fend off Arnold, Phillips, and Cornwallis. He argued that it was a mistake to let England occupy the very centre of the continent.[55]

Washington insisted that the detachments Clinton was making to Virginia weakened New York so that it could be easily taken; furthermore, that an attack on the city would tend to delay or recall those detachments and thereby help in the defence of Virginia. Rochambeau would not be persuaded until he had sent a courier to de Barras to ask if he would not make a voyage to Chesapeake Bay. But de Barras refused, since the British fleets had been reinforced. Rochambeau had to give in and affix his signature to Washington's plan.[56] He regretted this the more since certain despatches from Germain had been captured by a privateer, revealing the new British plan to conquer the South and confine Washington's contemptible force to the North for later destruction.[57] Once overborne, Rochambeau repeated to Washington his earlier assurance, "You are to do with me what you will," and devoted himself to the carrying out of Washington's plans. A message was drawn up to be sent to de Grasse by a fast frigate asking his cooperation in the attack on New York.

In a private letter to de Grasse, however, Rochambeau, though he mentioned the agreement to attack New York, reminded him that d'Estaing had failed to get over the bar into the harbor, painted a picture of the distresses of Virginia and gave it as his own private opinion that an attack on Cornwallis there was far the best step.[58] This letter doubtless influenced de Grasse in the decision he took it upon himself to make, and confirms the credit due to Rochambeau. At Weathersfield, however, he was meek and subordinate and conformed to Washington's plans for the New York campaign. It was arranged that de Barras should go to Boston as a safer port than Newport and be ready to join de Grasse as soon as he reached the coast. This would release Rochambeau's army from the task of protecting the fleet at Newport, and Rochambeau agreed to march his whole army at once to New York.

Washington evidently doubted that the French would ever attain the real naval superiority without which the expedition to Chesapeake Bay would be of little avail, and indeed it is one of the wonders of history that they obtained it just when they did and held it just long enough. He therefore barely entertained the idea of a southern march as a vague possibility.

In view of the praise heaped upon him for his final decision to march south it is necessary to remember that he would not listen to the plan when Rochambeau pressed it and that he made the following entry in his diary, giving the many reasons why such a plan was impracticable, none of which reasons was justified in the eventual performance:

"22d. Fixed with Count de Rochambeau upon plan of Campaign—in substance as follows—That the French Land force (except 200 Men) should March as soon as the Squadron could Sail for Boston—to the North River—and there, in, conjunction with the American, to commence an operation against New York (which in the present reduced State of the Garrison it was thought would fall, unless relieved; the doing which w[d] enfeeble their Southern operations, and in either case be productive of capital advantages) or to extend our views to the Southward as circumstances and a Naval superiority might render more necessary and eligable.—The aid which would be given to such an operation in this quarter.—the tardiness with which the Regiments would be filled for any other.—the insurmountable difficulty and expence of Land transportation—the waste of Men in long Marches (especially where there is a disinclination to the Service—objections to the climate &ca.) with other reasons too numerous to detail, induced to this opinion." [59]

His diary and his letters emphasize this profound hallucination, for he denied the appeals of the Governors of South Carolina and Virginia, describing the distress of the South and "pressing my repairing thither." He answered "that no relief c^d be given from this army till we had acquired a Naval superiority and c^d transfer Troops by Water." [60]   He wrote to Greene that he could not come south because of "the inevitable loss of men from so long a march . . . and the difficulty, I may say impossibility, of transporting the necessary baggage, artillery, and stores by land." [61]   Yet when they went, they went by land and very smoothly.

Rochambeau left him on May 23rd, 1781, and he set himself to his letter-writing, preparing despatches to the four New England governors, "calling upon them in earnest and pointed terms, to compleat their Continental Battalions," and to hold their militia ready to march at a week's notice. On his return to New Windsor he received a letter from young Laurens saying that the French ministry did not approve an attack on New York, also that the King could not lend any more money, but would give six million livres for the purchase of supplies, the balance to be at Washington's orders. This had a magnificent sound, but a livre was only a franc and, as Robert Morris wrote, it boiled down to almost nothing, and it was the final gift. Morris insisted that a national bank was the only thing the British would fear. [62]

Now Congress rose in wrath because the King not only dealt direct with Washington but put the money at his disposal. The dread of royal power awoke, and it was alleged that the King was buying up Washington. Since Arnold had been purchased everybody was suspect, and Germain wrote that he thought Washington could be bribed to end the rebellion if he were given a chance to join the British army and share in the plunder of the Spanish colonies! [63]   The storm over the King's six million livres was stilled by Luzerne, who pointed out that the words "or some other person" were included in another letter. Washington was glad enough to be relieved of the responsibility.

When Rochambeau went back to Newport he found great opposition to his plans. Among his officers dissension and personal ambition played the parts they played in the American army. De Barras particularly disliked the idea of subjecting himself to de Grasse, who was of a later commission; he was eager for independent action for his own glory, such as an attack on Newfoundland.[64] After two councils of war the French made certain changes in their plans and decided to leave de Barras at Newport with four hundred of Rochambeau's men and a thousand militia. The Duc de Lauzun was chosen to carry this news to Washington, though he was reluctant to inform Washington that the plans agreed on had been reviewed and modified by a council of French officers. But he obeyed his orders and delivered to Washington a letter from Rochambeau, which was, he says, "written badly with much embarrassment!"[65]

"It threw Washington into such a rage that he would not answer. It was only on the third day, and then out of regard for me, that he gave me an answer, a very cold one, in which he said that he held to the plan that he had signed."[66]

Rochambeau accepted the rebuke and made ready to march. The Marquis de Chastellux sided with Washington against Rochambeau and took great credit for his victory over his chief in a letter to Luzerne. The British intercepted it and published it as a proof of strife among the French. Rochambeau seeing it sent for Chastellux, showed him the letter, and "then threw it into the fire, and left him a prey to his own reflections."[67] In his later calm, Washington wrote to Chastellux politely stating that Chastellux had misunderstood his ideas, asking him to rectify the mistaken impression that Washington presumed to disapprove of the French councils of war, and expressing his "high sense of the obligation" conferred on America by the French resolution to stay in Newport.[68]

Washington was always diplomat enough to cast oil on troubled waters, but he was consumed with impatience at the resistance to his plans, and saw in a prompt attack on New York the only answer to the wild appeals from the south. An odd instance of the fortunes of war was the effect upon Clinton of a letter that Washington wrote to Lafayette explaining the results of the Weathersfield conference, saying that he could not march south because of the waste of troops on so long a march, and announcing his intention to attack New York. He said that he could not say more because Lafayette had no cipher, and "my letters have been frequently intercepted of late." [69] This letter was itself intercepted and with it a number of others: one to Major Tallmadge concerning his spies in New York; one to Lund saying that he expected the British to burn Mount Vernon but hoped that the stock could be driven out of reach; and one to a dentist, Dr. Baker, in Philadelphia with this intensely personal appeal:

"Sir, A day or two ago I requested Col° Harrison to apply to you for a pair of pincers to fasten the wire of my teeth.—I hope you furnished him with them—I now wish you would send me one of your scrapers, as my teeth stand in need of cleaning, and I have little prospect of being in Philadelp^a soon.—It will come very safe by the Post—& in Return, the Money shall be sent so soon as I know the cost of it.—"

Another was a letter to Jacky Custis describing the prolonged illness of Martha:

"Dear Custis, (On Saturday last I returned from a Conference held with the Count de Rochambeau at Weathersfield, and found Mrs Washington very unwell, as she had been for five or Six days preceeding, & still continues)—Her complaint was in the Stomach, billious, and now turned to a kind of Jaundice; but she is better than she has been.—though still weak & low.—As she is very desirous of seeing you—and as it is ab^t the period for her returning to Virginia, I should be glad, if it does not interfere with any important engagements, if you could make her a visit.—That you may not be alarmed, & on that acc^t use unnecessary speed, I think it incumbent on me to add, that I do not conceive that she is in any kind of danger. . . . The States this way, are miserably slow in sending in their recruits for the Army, and our supplies come in equally tardily—"

Another one of Clinton's captures that comes to us from oblivion in the opening of his papers is this little note from Martha in her characteristic hand and spelling. She wrote it perhaps on her sick bed, and she makes an amusing slip in her effort to handle the tricky third person—as well as in other dark phases of grammar:

"M Washington will be glad to know if the Cotton for the counter-pins was wove—and whitend,—how many yards was there of it, how many Counterpins will it make—she desired milly Posey to have the fine peice of linning made white how is Betty has she been spinning,—all winter—is charlot done the worke I left for her To do" [70]

Martha was still "low and weak" on June 17th, according to a letter Washington wrote to Joseph Webb enclosing "my Measure for a pair of draw-Boots (Horse-skin) to be made of the Leather Manufactured at your Works." [71]   Six days later Washington wrote to St. Clair, "Mrs. Washington is in a fair way of recovering." [72]   The very next day he wrote in his diary for June 24th, 1781:

"Joined the Army at its encampment at Peekskill.   Mrs. Washington set out at the same time for Virginia—but with an intention to Halt at Philadelphia if from information and circumstances it was not likely she should remain quietly at Mt. Vernon.

"A Letter from Count de Rochambeau informs me that he shall be with his first division at Newtown on the 28th. where he proposed to assemble his force and march in Brigades while the Duke de Lauzens Legion continued to move on his left flank." [73]

Rochambeau had left Newport on June 10th, 1781, and paused at Providence till June 18th, before he moved on.   He cheered the countryside with the rapid progress of his smart and extremely well-conducted army.   The Baron Cromot du Bourg found Washington impressive and affable, though not so awe-inspiring as he expected, but his manners were "those of one perfectly accustomed to society, quite a rare thing cer-tainly in America." [74]   On that march went also the Comte Guillaume de Deux-Ponts, as his name was literally trans-lated from the original Wilhelm von Zweibrücken.   He and his brother, Christian, served with Rochambeau.   He describes the French disappointment at the small number of their allies:

"They told us at Newport that the American army had 10,000 men. It has 2500 or 3000 men, and that is not much of a lie for the Americans." [75]

This was only one more of Washington's unwelcome humiliations. In spite of all his prayers and struggles, he wrote to Congress:

"I am not stronger at this advanced period of the Campaign than when the Army first moved out of their Winter Quarters." [76]

There was something ridiculous about it. He had more officers than he had men for, more generals than he could provide with commands. He had to write to the idle St. Clair that there was no place for him. He had been compelled to appoint Major-Generals Heath and Stirling "to the Command of Wings, which are in fact no more than Divisions, and which also have their Maj[r] Generals attach[d] to them.

"There wou[d] be an indelicacy as you very justly observe in sending you to Virginia at present because you must necessarily supercede the Marquis de la Fayette, who has had much trouble, and who appears to be just now reaping the fruits of his labours; I can therefore only advise you to remain in Pensilvania awhile longer" [77]

Lafayette had been kept busy in Virginia. General Phillips died and was succeeded in command by Benedict Arnold, whose first communication to Lafayette was returned with scorn, a refusal to deal with him and a promise to say why if he wanted to know.[78] Lafayette was having the familiar troubles, no troops, desertions, no food, no clothes. But he was brave and cheerful and Anthony Wayne was with him. He was afraid of Cornwallis, from whose military genius he said he was "taking lessons." His own principle of action was:

"While the enemy were anxious to fight, not one gun was fired, but the moment they declined coming to action we made it our business to force them to partial engagements followed by general retreats." [79]

Some say that his conduct was superbly clever. Colonel J. F. Mercer, who was with him, said that his movements were "silly & misjudged" and if Cornwallis had shown more energy, "the Marquis's army wou^d have been broken & dispers^d, & Lord Cornwallis wou^d have escap^d the catastrophe at York." [80] Lafayette wrote to Luzerne that he was terrified by his youth and inexperience and the troops he had to handle. Steuben bothered him: "*Le Baron est si unpopular.*" He would rather be debarrassed of Lord Cornwallis than of a third of his army; but he was a very polite enemy: "*nous faisons la guerre en gentlemen.*" But "*Mon dieu,* why haven't we a fleet here? . . . If the French army could fall from the clouds into Virginia and be supported by a squadron we should do some very good things . . . *me voici pour longtems en Virginie; lord Cornwallis est si attachant!*" [81]

If Cornwallis was keeping Lafayette on the jump he had reduced Clinton to frenzy, for Clinton had not meant that he should advance into Virginia and he made no secret of his dismay at the time, or afterwards, during the famous and voluminous Clinton-Cornwallis controversy that followed.

But all Washington knew was that Greene was getting nowhere in the Carolinas, Cornwallis was getting everywhere in Virginia, and he could accomplish nothing toward the conquest of New York.

XLVIII

HE IS FORCED TO GO SOUTH

THE campaign against New York is a long story of banquets, reviews, skirmishes, reconnaissances sometimes under fire, surprises that did not surprise, and a general beating about the bush with no result whatever. To trace it upon a map would be arduous and fruitless.[1]

The French noted Washington's "sang froid" in danger. He and Rochambeau slept under a hedge and had to escape across a stream in open boats with their horses dragged after, swimming.[2] In one quick march from White Plains in July, 400 Frenchmen dropped from the heat.[3] The Duc de Lauzun ordered to surprise a fort in a night attack found that General Lincoln had alarmed it unintentionally and the Frenchman had to rescue him from destruction after heavy loss in a panic of flight. Washington, coming belatedly to the rescue, greeted Lauzun with joy, then spent three days and nights with him on an exhausting reconnaissance during which they had nothing to eat but the fruit they found on the trees.[4] Everywhere there was frustration and the Tories rejoiced. An intercepted letter of Germain's expressed his satisfaction at being told that there were more Americans in his Majesty's service than in that of the colonies.[5] The colonists ridiculed this, though it was perilously close to the truth. Rivington's *Gazette* published such taunts as this:

"July 11.—The rebel chiefs are put to their trumps to keep their party alive, under the increasing diffidence of the people after so many repeated impositions. The current lie lately minted at New Windsor, New York, to bring out the militia *once more to the Shambles,* is that the French fleet from the West Indies is soon to appear off New York, from which it is added, the British *are preparing to run away.* And

FRENCH OFFICERS
(From B. J. Lossing's Life of Washington)

thus they are promised, if they will rise, plunder and victory without fighting and bloodshed. . . .

"George! George! the paralytic state of your cause is too manifest to deceive a people who have bought wisdom at the expense of their *fortunes* and *blood* . . . murderer of Andre! murderer of those Americans who sought liberty, but have lost their lives in your baneful projects and services, by trusting to the never to be forgotten false and bloody orders of 1776." [6]

In polar contrast were the sketches of Washington by enthusiastic Frenchmen. A French chaplain, the Abbé Robin, was quite overwhelmed by his appearance, by his career, by his genius:

"As if his faculties were aggrandized by difficulties, he never has more resources than when he seems to have no more . . . economical, abstemious for himself, prodigal for the public cause. . . . His aspect in all places, is that of a benevolent God: old men, women, children, all run to see him pass. . . . This cold people . . . is inflamed by him, and the first songs that emotion has dictated to them have been written to celebrate Washington." [7]

Commissary-General Claude Blanchard was invited to dinner with him and dined under a tent at a table loaded with plenty, including "some pie, a kind of tart, greatly in use in England and among the Americans." Everything was "put upon the table at the same time." There was the usual incessant drinking of toasts. A few days later he makes this observation:

"There was a clergyman at this dinner who blessed the food and said grace after they had done eating and had brought in the wine. I was told that General Washington said grace when there was no clergyman at the table, as fathers of a family do in America. The first time that I dined with him there was no clergyman and I did not perceive that he made this prayer yet I remember that on taking his place at table, he made a gesture and said a word, which I took for a piece of politeness, and which was perhaps a religious action. In this case his prayer must have been short; the clergyman made use of more forms. We remained a pretty long time at table. They drank twelve or fifteen healths with Madeira wine. In the course of the meal beer was served and grum, rum mixed with water." [8]

Never was Washington more thwarted than by the sight of New York. He did not need to be restrained from self-destruction as when he had wanted to attack Boston in rowboats. He was slowly convinced that only a far larger force than his could dream of assault on that fortified city. Rochambeau had realized this from the first, knowing more of sieges, and he wrote to de Grasse, earnestly imploring 5,000 more French troops:

"These people here are at the end of their resources. Washington has not half the troops he counted on; I believe, though he is hiding it, that he has not 6000 men. M. de la Fayette has not 1000 regulars with the militia to defend Virginia. . . . This is the state of affairs and the great crisis at which America finds itself; and especially in the Southern states just now. The arrival of M. le Comte de Grasse can save her, all the means we have at hand avail nothing without his help and the naval superiority that he can secure." [9]

This appeal led de Grasse to take on board his ships more than 3,000 French troops collected in San Domingo, and to this reinforcement, the freedom of America owes much. Once more Rochambeau, while explaining Washington's desire to attack New York, got home his own obsession:

"The southwesterly winds and the distressed state of Virginia will probably lead you to prefer Chesapeake Bay, and it is there that we think you can render the greatest services, aside from the fact that you are only two days from New York."

Rochambeau told Washington frankly what he had written to de Grasse, and Washington, of course, was glad of extra men from anywhere. The situation had changed from the time when Lafayette cut in two the number of French troops because it was not possible to send many to America without rousing American suspicion. Now they had American lethargy to off-set. The Spanish Admiral Solano, for whom the French troops had been sent to San Domingo, graciously said that he would not need them until time for a winter campaign in the West Indies. The Comte de Grasse borrowed a part of the army for two months only. At Rochambeau's request he also borrowed at Havana 1,200,000 livres. He reminded Rochambeau:

"Though this whole expedition has been concerted only on your demand and without warning to the ministries of France and Spain, I believe myself authorized to take some responsibility on my own shoulders for the common cause. But I should not dare to change the whole plan of their project by the transplantation of so large a body of troops." [10]

He borrowed 3,500 men, however, also artillery, and he had from 25 to 29 ships. He asked for the presence of the squadron of de Barras, to whom he offered the exquisite courtesy of independent command. De Barras yielded reluctantly, expressing a fear that he would have to face two British fleets. Nevertheless, he promised to make for Chesapeake bay. [11]

In view of all these facts it is dishonest to deny the French the whole initiative in the Yorktown triumph, and nothing more can be claimed for Washington than that, when at last he was utterly baffled before New York and learned of de Grasse's approach, he acted with superb energy. From the south came frantic appeals. R. H. Lee, who was then and since accused of complicity in the Conway Cabal, besought him to come to Virginia. Governor Jefferson had resigned, no successor was yet elected, and the next in power was a British captive. Even the last printing press in the state had been captured. He hoped that "the arts of wicked men" had not marred Washington's friendship for him, but warned him of the danger:

"It would be a thing for angels to weep over, if the goodly fabric of human freedom which you have so well labored to rear, should in one unlucky moment be levelled with the dust. There is nothing I think more certain than that your personal call would bring into immediate exertion the force and the resource of this State and its neighboring ones, which directed as it would be will effectually disappoint and baffle the deep laid schemes of the enemy. . . . Our country is truly Sir in a deplorable way, and if relief comes not from you it will probably come not at all—I have heard it reported in this country that Gen. Wayne dislikes being commanded by the Marquis—if this should be unhappily true, the consequences will be obvious to you."

He enclosed the copy of a letter he had written to Congress-man James Lovell—of all people!—urging that Washington be "possessed of Dictatorial powers," both federal and Virginian.[12] To this Washington stubbornly replied on July 15th:

"I am fully persuaded, however, (upon good military principles,) that the measures I have adopted will give more effectual and speedier relief to the State of Virginia, than if I was to march thither with dictatorial powers, at the head of every man I could draw from hence, without leaving the important posts on the North River quite defence-less, and these States open to devastation and ruin."

He insisted, he was "morally certain," that if properly sup-ported he would bring about "the fall of New York, or a with-drawal of the Troops from Virginia." Yet he confessed that, though he was "left last Winter with a force so much reduced as to be scarcely able to garrison West point; . . . not half the men which were required to be with the Army, as recruits for the Continental Batt^{ns}, by the first day of Jany last are yet arrived—and of those asked by me from the Militia not one is come."[13] He repeated what he had told so many others, that he would lose half his men on the march to Virginia. On July 30th he was still writing the same thing to Lafayette.[14] Two weeks later he made entry in his Diary that word had come from de Barras of the sailing of de Grasse with his fleet for Chesapeake bay and his anxiety "to have every thing in the most perfect readiness to commence our operations in the mo-ment of his arrival as he should be under a necessity from particular engagements with the Spaniards to be in the West Indies by the Middle of October." Suddenly he yielded under a confessed compulsion:

"Matters having now come to a crisis and a decisive plan to be determined on, I was obliged, from the shortness of Count de Grasse^s promised stay on this Coast, the apparent disinclination in their Naval Officers to force the harbour of New York and the feeble compliance of the States to my requisitions for Men, hitherto, and little prospect of greater exertion in the future, to give up all idea of attacking New York; and instead thereof to remove the French Troops and a detachment from the American Army to the Head of Elk to be transported to Virginia for the purpose of co-operating with the force from the West Indies against the Troops in that State." [15]

This was written in the calm of night, but we have a striking picture of the blind fury with which he welcomed the news that was to mean deliverance to his country and his own last battle of the war. It just chanced that Thomas Pickering and Robert Morris called on Washington that afternoon. They found him "striding to and fro in such a state of uncontrolled excitement that he did not seem to notice their presence. They immediately withdrew. In a short half-hour they were sent for, and found him clothed with his usual serene dignity. . . . He referred to the scene . . . apologizing for his extraordinary appearance told how he had hoped for months to carry out his great plans agreed on with French commanders only to have them thwarted. Calmly he told, though tossing like a suppressed volcano within—in slow and measured phrase, how bitterly and utterly he had been disappointed . . . exclaimed

" 'I wish to the Lord the French would not raise our expectations of a co-operation, or fulfil them.' "

He described his plan of attack on New York in cooperation with the Comte de Grasse. On that morning he had just had word that de Grasse was not coming to New York at all, but going to the Chesapeake. At the same time Washington learned that Clinton had been reinforced from England.

"Resentment, indignation, and despair had burst upon him. His hopes were blasted, and he felt that the cause was lost and his country ruined."

Before that day was ended he formed the great plan to go south, called in Pickering and told him to set the whole machinery in motion to expedite the march of half his army.[16] Once he was over his storm he beamed, as always. He wrote to de Grasse that "it had been judged expedient to give up for the present the enterprise against New York, and turn our attention towards the south." He was inclined to favor Charleston as the first point of recovery, for he could not be sure that Cornwallis would still be in Virginia.[17]   At this time he did not know that Cornwallis had begun to fortify Yorktown.

He wrote a circular letter to the states that he had to change his plan.   He consigned to General Heath half his troops and the perilous northern command, with instructions to protect West Point at all hazards.[18]   He wrote to Robert Morris to try to secure "a month's pay in specie" for his men as they had shown signs of discontent and the northern regiments did not like southern service.   With a touch of French by contagion he added:

"I make no doubt that a *douceur* of a little hard money would put them in a proper temper." [19]

Robert Morris managed it.   He raised $30,000 in cash.   He borrowed $20,000 of it from Rochambeau! promising to return it by the first of October.   And he kept his word.   For John Laurens arrived in time with two and a half of the King's six million livres, and Morris paid Rochambeau out of that! Thus the French King was allowed to repay the money borrowed from himself.   Clever people, those Americans!   They not only took all the cash from those innocent Frenchmen, but have since taken most of the credit as well.

Washington had now two new anxieties.   He was afraid that Cornwallis would get out of Virginia and that the English fleets would capture de Grasse or de Barras, or both.   He wrote to Lafayette that he was "distressed beyond expression" and hoped that he would do all in his power to prevent Cornwallis' escape by land.   "May that great felicity be reserved for you." [20]   He had word from Lafayette that Cornwallis had gone up the York river to York and was throwing up fortifications.   Lafayette wrote gaily that one of his spies, who was a servant of Lord Cornwallis, had been unable to send full details because "His Lordship is so shy of his papers, that my honest friend says he cannot get at them." [21]

Washington took every precaution to guard against the discovery of his march-off to the last moment. He had French kitchens built in New Jersey, had a camp laid out. He had letters written to be intercepted. The story is told that he went so far in his ruses as to sacrifice a Baptist preacher. According to Lossing, Washington summoned the ardent young clergyman, a Mr. Montagnie, and asked him to carry a despatch to Morristown, directing him to cross the river at King's Ferry and go to Haverstraw by way of the Ramapo Pass:

"Montagnie, knowing the Ramapo Pass to be in possession of the Cow-boys and other friends of the enemy, ventured to suggest to the commander-in-chief that the upper road would be the safest.

" 'I shall be taken,' he said, 'if I go through the Clove.'

" 'Your duty, young man, is not to talk, but to obey!' replied Washington, sternly, enforcing his words by a vigorous stamp of his foot. Montagnie proceeded as directed, and, near the Ramapo Pass, was caught. A few days afterward he was sent to New York, where he was confined in the Sugar House, one of the famous provost prisons in the city. The day after his arrival, the contents of the dispatches taken from him were published in Rivington's *Gazette* with great parade, for they indicated a plan of an attack upon the city. The enemy was alarmed thereby, and active preparations were put in motion for receiving the besiegers. Montagnie now perceived why he was so positively instructed to go through the Ramapo Pass, where himself and dispatches were quite sure to be seized. When they appeared in Rivingon's *Gazette*, the allied armies were far on their way to the Delaware. Montagnie admired the wisdom of Washington, but disliked himself to be the victim."

Lossing had this story from the lips of a Mr. Pierson who had it "from the lips of Mr. Montagnie himself." It may be true, but it is worth noting that Thomas B. Montanye, a well-known Baptist clergyman, and the only one of the name at that period, was only twelve years old at the time, and did not become a Baptist until 1788, when he was converted by the Reverend John Gano, who converted Washington also, ac-

cording to certain affidavits.[22]   There is, therefore, good reason
to doubt that Washington was cruel enough to have sent such
a messenger to such a doom.   But Boudinot tells in his *Journal*
a convincing story of how Washington talked to a British sym-
pathizer, pretending to trust him, filling his ears with an
elaborate lie for Clinton's consumption and begging him not to
breathe it, knowing that it would be carried to Clinton at once.[23]

Whether or not he fooled Clinton, Washington kept his own
troops guessing, and Surgeon Thacher says that bets ran high as
to whether they were going to occupy the camp ostentatiously
laid out in New Jersey or steal a march on the enemy and go
to Virginia.[24]   They soon realized the truth and gloated over
Clinton's imagined anxiety.

But Clinton had not been so anxious of late; for, on August
11th, 1781, three thousand Hessian reinforcements had reached
him from overseas, a number almost equal to Washington's
whole army.   Their arrival had been promptly learned by
Washington and had driven the final nail in Rochambeau's
argument that the siege of New York could never succeed.

Why Clinton had not come forth from New York to attack
Washington all this while, and why he did not rush forth as
soon as the seasick Hessians were on their land legs, was never
explained to the satisfaction of anybody but Clinton, who asserted that the thing was impossible, though "there is a set
of discontented animals here, some of the Military that are
determined to criticize *all I do*." [25]   In his unpublished history
of the war, Clinton explained that even with the reinforcements, his total effectives were under 10,000, and that the
"indispensable Deduction" for manning the various forts, reduced "my acting Army to at most 4000."   He emphasized his
positive orders to Cornwallis not to go beyond the boundaries
of South Carolina, his permission to go into North Carolina,
and his dismay when Cornwallis invaded Virginia.   He blamed
the loss of the Revolution, indeed, upon Cornwallis' abandonment of the Carolinas.[26]   Cornwallis said he left the Carolinas
for fear that Greene would "hem me in among the great rivers,

and by cutting off our subsistence, render our arms useless."[27]
When Washington struck off south, Clinton was not uneasy because he was sure that the British had the naval superiority and Washington would be unable even to feed his troops.

Great praise has been given to Washington for the secrecy of his departure from the environs of New York and his complete deception of Clinton. As a matter of fact, the Hessian Lieutenant-Colonal von Wurmb gave Clinton ample warning, having learned from his spies that preparations to supply Washington with food and forage had been made all across New Jersey, also that a French officer of distinction had instructed his American mistress to meet him in Trenton.[28] But Clinton says that, while he was surprised to learn that Washington had taken so many of his men, he had thought it probable that he would send a detachment, and in either case, he was helpless:

"I will not pay Mr. Washington's Understanding so bad a Compliment as to suppose he thought it necessary to deceive me, whatsoever Deceptions Policy might have required with respect to his own people; for he too well knew I was in no Capacity to intercept his March to the Southward, whenever he pleased to make it. . . . To have landed such a handful in the Jersies (supposing I had every requisite naval support and Assistance) in face of Works only seven Miles distant from his Camp at Chatham, is an absurdity which I am persuaded that Officer never suspected me capable of and consequently could have no Inducement to guard against as he might have met me (had he chosen it) with four times the number I could have possibly thrown on Shore; if I had had Boats to have landed my whole force at once."[29]

Clinton's only device now for recalling Washington from joining the attack on Cornwallis was to attack the defenseless northern seacoast towns or to make a dash for Philadelphia, which he longed to repossess. He decided first to crush de Barras's fleet and recapture Newport. Admiral Graves consented, but he was not ready. Clinton actually had his men on transports when he learned on August 28th, 1781, that de Barras had left Newport. Thus Graves' delay had "lost an opportunity of making the most important attempt that had offered the whole war." [30]   Next Clinton decided that the thing to do was to go to the rescue of Cornwallis.   The whole Council unanimously agreed.   But he did not go.   Van Tyne says "In the William L. Clements Library there are minutes of a council of war held by Clinton for six weeks preceding the capitulation at Yorktown, which show Clinton holding out against every one of his officers in the policy which led straight to the surrender and the loss of America." [31]

Yet in his Narrative Clinton wrote:

"I lament, and ever shall, that those exertions could not have been made in time. . . . I have every reason to think we should have had most complete success." [32]

The minutes of the meetings of the councils also show that the naval officers made many difficulties, required much time for repairs and caused delays for which Clinton ought not to be blamed—nor perhaps the naval officers, since they had their orders concerning the West Indies.[33]

While Clinton and his colleagues were debating what to do, counting upon a naval superiority that was no longer certain, promising Cornwallis reinforcements and giving him explanations for unavoidable delay, Washington was hastening on his long march.[34]

He and Rochambeau rode ahead, to Philadelphia, to assure transportation from the Head of Elk down Chesapeake Bay, and to expedite "Ordnance, Stores &ca."   They reached the town August 30th, 1781.   Washington stopped at the City Tavern and paid his respects to Congress.   There was a banquet, of course, and the toasts were echoed by salvos from the ships on the river.   The streets were illuminated.[35]   But the troops were glum and mutinous and had to be bribed with back pay in part.

On Sunday he wrote letters.   On Monday and Tuesday the French troops passed in review in their dazzling white uniforms.   Deux-Ponts said of Congress: "The thirteen members took off their thirteen hats at each salute of the flags and of the officers, and that is all I saw that was respectful or remarkable." [36] Those thirteen members represented thirteen rival nations and the day was far off when they should become one. On September 4th Luzerne gave a sumptuous feast and "healths were drunk in rapid succession." The next day Washington, finding "everything in a tolerable train here," hastened on to prepare the embarkation at the Head of Elk. Passing through Chester he was met by a despatch from de Grasse, who had arrived in Chesapeake Bay on August 30th, 1781, and had found no one there, nothing done. [37]

Never was Washington more thunderstruck with joy. He ran to greet Rochambeau, calling the news, and waving his hat. [38] The French officers were, says Deux-Ponts, "as much surprised as they were touched by the joy very true and very pure of General Washington.

"Naturally cold and of a demeanor grave and noble . . . his features, his expression, his whole carriage were changed in an instant. He cast off the quality of the arbiter of North America and was content for a moment with that of a citizen happy in the welfare of his country: a child whose every wish had been granted, could not have revealed a livelier emotion." [39]

Lauzun says: "I have never seen a man moved by a greater or sincerer joy." [40] Washington had waited long enough for this day. He threw off all doubts. His letters glow. He wrote de Grasse, saying that he counted on a personal interview "almost as soon as this will reach your hand." He was in great haste. He said that if transport were not ready at the Head of Elk he would march the bulk of his troops by land. He hinted that Cornwallis must not be let slip. He wrote to Lafayette of his "infinite satisfaction" and the "additional pleasure in finding, that your ideas on every occasion have been so consonant to my own, and that by your military dispositions and prudent measures you have anticipated all my wishes." [41] His spirits soared and did not fall. Eight days later he was writing to General Lincoln:

"Every day we now loose is comparatively an age . . . Hurry on then, my Dear Gen[l], with your Troops on the wing of Speed." [42]

At the Head of Elk he found the lack of boats he expected, but he says in his Diary, "I wrote many letters to Gent[n] of Influence on the Eastern Shore, beseeching them to exert themselves in drawing forth every kind of Vessel which would answer for this purpose." [43] In the first boats available, Washington and Rochambeau sent out the Bourbonnais grenadiers and chasseurs and Lauzun's infantry, also Colonel John Lamb's regiment of artillery and other American troops. Head winds and calms alternated to delay them. Lauzun paused at Annapolis before proceeding, and it was not until September 25th, 1781, that the artillery reached the James river.[44] Baltimore was illuminated for Washington on September 8th, and there "I rec[d] and answered an address of the Citizen's." [45]

Good luck was on a holiday and it crowned Washington's bliss with a glimpse of Mount Vernon. Homesickness had been one of his most gnawing torments for six years and four months —ever since he rode away on May 4th, 1775. Now, knowing that he could steal a little time without delaying the plodding troops, he galloped off for home in the early morning of September 9th, 1781, and rode with all his might, though it was a Sunday, to "my own Seat at Mount Vernon." He took with him only his servant Billy, and his new favorite, his aide, Colonel David Humphreys.[46] He reached home late at night, startling Martha, who had not been warned of his visit. The great news flew about the plantation and the next morning his slaves flocked to the mansion, to look "sorrowfully upon a face so changed by the storms of campaigns and the mighty cares which had burdened his mind during more than six years of absence." [47]

He spent hours with the manager of his estates, then made ready for Rochambeau and Chastellux, who arrived with their suites the next day. On the 11th a great feast was given for the neighbors. Among his delights was the presence of a short stepladder of four little step-grandchildren, all of them born since his departure. Two of them would become his own children by adoption, for their father Jacky Custis, now twenty-eight, was impelled to go to war as his step-father's aide-de-camp, and so trotted off to an unforeseen death.

For the time, Washington was spared the knowledge of this, as of the fact that on the very night of his arrival at Mount Vernon, "one or more volunteers in the service of Hell" broke into the State House at Philadelphia and totally defaced the portrait that Peale had painted for the state in 1778.[48]

He was spared yet a while also the knowledge that Benedict Arnold, withdrawn from Virginia on account of illness, had joined Clinton and on September 6th sacked the town of New London, thirteen miles from Arnold's own birthplace, and burned many houses, slaughtered many soldiers.[49] The motive for this vandalism was, of course, Clinton's wish to decoy Washington from the south. But he was never to be diverted from his purposes by such measures. Three blessed days he allowed himself at Mount Vernon, where he wrote to the Marquis on the 10th:

"We are thus far, my Dear Marquis, on our way to you. . . . Should there be any danger as we approach you, I shall be obliged if you will send a party of Horse towards New Kent Court House to meet us. With great personal regard & affection, I am, my Dear Marquis, Your Most Obed^t Servt.

Go. WASHINGTON.

"P. S. I hope you will keep Lord Cornwallis safe, without Provisions or Forage until we arrive. Adieu." [50]

On the 12th he was off again. Martha bade him good-by and doubtless let her only son go with all the misgivings a mother knows in times of war. Washington had gone through six years of war without a scratch. Camp fever got Jacky in one month. On the 15th Washington was in Williamsburg, where the Marquis awaited him. As he approached the town, he encountered Lieutenant-Colonel St. George Tucker, surprised him by calling his name, shook hands with him and introduced him to Rochambeau, then, says St. George Tucker, in a letter little known:

"At this moment we saw the Marquis, riding in full speed from the town, and, as he approached General Washington, threw his bridle on his horse's neck, opened both his arms as wide as he could reach, and caught the General round his body, hugged him as close as it was possible, and absolutely *kissed him from ear to ear* once or twice as well as I can recollect with as much ardour as ever an absent lover kissed his mistress on his return. I was not more than six feet from this memorable scene." [51]

This letter was written in Tucker's old age, and would be strongly suspect, but it chances that on the very day of the occurrence he wrote to his wife:

"Amidst the late gloom the dawn of Happiness now appears, and the smiling prospect of Peace begins to be discovered. Can you assign a reason, my Fanny, why my style in several of my late letters so often breaks out into bombast? I wish I could avoid what I so cordially condemn; but I find that I am imperceptibly led from the exultation of mind, which I have for a fortnight experienced, to burst out into a turgid manner of writing which I condemn no less in myself than in others. I will endeavor to drop it, though my Fanny is the only person to whom I address myself. . . .

"I wrote you yesterday that General Washington had not yet arrived. About four o'clock in the afternoon his approach was announced. To my great surprise he recognized my features and spoke to me immediately by name. Gen. Nelson, the Marquis, &c., rode up immediately after. Never was more joy painted in any countenances than theirs. The Marquis rode up with precipitation, clasped the General in his arms, and embraced him with an ardor not easily described. The whole army and all the town were presently in motion . . . men, women, and children seemed to vie with each other in demonstrations of joy, and eagerness to see their beloved countryman. His quarters are at Mr. Wythe's (George Wythe, signer of the Declaration of Independence) house. Aunt Betty has the honor of the Count de Rochambeau to lodge at her house. We are all alive and so sanguine in our hopes that nothing can be conceived more different than the countenances of the same men at this time and on the first of June."

It is not often that vivid legends can be so exactly authenticated. Stories more often grow in the manner astonishingly indicted in a rumor that must have added a tang all its own to Washington's exultation. Arnold's successful devastation at New London has been mentioned. By the time the news reached Washington at Williamsburg it had grown to the form that St. George Tucker gave it in his letter of September 14th:

"By what channel I know not—but we heard from York yesterday that the British had received an account there of an attack made on West Point, in which they were repulsed with the loss of fifteen hundred men—among whom was the infamous Arnold, who fell before those works on which he would have been executed, had not Fate too partially decreed him the death of a soldier instead of that of a traitor. I do not know that any confidence is to be placed on this story. In telling it, therefore, it would not be proper to consider it as any thing more than vague report; yet I received it from Andrews, who, you know, is in the Governor's family, and possesses his unlimited confidence." [52]

This is an unusually striking case of the unreliability of un-documented rumor, and the irresistible tendency to dramatize it. It satisfied a hunger of the soul to represent Arnold sinking in his own gore as he failed to conquer the fortress he had failed to betray. Arnold still is a great disappointment to the yearning for well-constructed lives, well-rewarded and well-punished deeds. It would probably have marred Washington's felicity insufferably to have learned that Arnold died a hero's death at the foot of a bastion. He still hoped to fit him with a halter.

Washington had promised to see the Comte de Grasse in a few days, but the Comte had been called out to sea on important business. Six days after his arrival off Cape Henry, his greeting by Lafayette's representative, and the landing of the troops he brought, a frigate left outside on sentry duty sighted sail. De Grasse thought at first that this was de Barras's fleet; but it was Admiral Graves, who marched by in challenging array. If de Grasse had been timid or weak, the high hopes of Washington would have been a mockery. But on the very September 5th when he received the tidings of de Grasse's arrival in Chester, de Grasse went forth to close with the British. His fleet was under sail in less than three-quarters of an hour. He cut his cables and stood out to sea with splendid and most unusual energy for any admiral. For five days the armadas thundered and shifted for the weather gage. Then Graves felt his fleet "too mutilated" and decided to return to New York. As de Grasse returned to the Bay, he saw a fleet awaiting him. This time it was de Barras, who had slipped into harbor without loss while de Grasse was keeping Graves busy.[53] The French had bravely won that all important "naval superiority" on which everything depended. How long could they hold it against England's humiliated admirals and her far-swarming, inexhaustible fleets?

On the 17th of September, Washington boarded a little boat captured from the British and sailed to the flagship, the stupendous 110-gun behemoth, *Ville de Paris*, presented to the King by the city of Paris. Custis is the dubious authority for a plausible story that the tall de Grasse, when he sighted the taller Washington, seized the giant, kissed him on both cheeks and cried:

"My dear little General."

The American officers could not control their mirth and Knox laughed till his fat sides shook.[54] The laughter ended in a prolonged contest. Washington wanted de Grasse to move up the river and shut Cornwallis off from escape. De Grasse, having tasted British blood, wanted more. He is said to have thought that he might even chase the British into New York harbor and blockade them there. But Washington and Rochambeau had their way and de Grasse magnanimously consented to play a humble rôle. The generals left the ship on September 18th and were so detained "by hard blowing and contrary Winds" that it took them four days to reach Williamsburg. It took them six days more to begin the march to Yorktown, where, on September 28th, 1781, the French troops drove in the first British pickets.

It was forever fortunate, to the United States at least, that de Grasse yielded to the plea of the landsmen. If he had gone out, Cornwallis might have made his way to Clinton by land or have been reinforced by Clinton and the British fleet, as he so nearly was.

Only seven months later, the marvellous battleship, *Ville de Paris,* was a riddled hulk; and the Admiral de Grasse was the prisoner of Admiral Rodney, in the Battle of the Saints, April 12th, 1782, which ended the brief supremacy of the French navy.

Curiously, de Grasse's hopes of victory were largely ruined on that day by Captain the Honorable William Cornwallis, brother of the Earl in whose disgrace he had so large a share. Curiously again, de Grasse would not surrender to Captain Cornwallis but waited for Admiral Hood's final broadside before he struck.[55] Hood also had taken part in this Battle off the Chesapeake, of which the British historian, Captain W. M. James, C. B., R. N., has written:

"The North American campaign of 1781 is of eternal interest, for the indirect outcome of the operations was the birth of the United States of America. The period of hostilities down to the battle off the Chesapeake was the period of labour. After that battle, which was, indeed, little more than a skirmish, British opposition to the wishes of the Colonists melted away.

"Yorktown has often been described as one of the 'decisive battles of the world,' but it was the naval skirmish off the Chesapeake that was decisive. . . . Cornwallis may have been too impetuous, Clinton may have been weak in not giving definite orders to Cornwallis, Germain may have been more wrong-headed than ever, but, allowing all that, the victory in the end was to the holder of the sea line of communications. From the day Clinton divided his forces on the American seaboard the success of the campaign depended on the sea forces.

"From the day de Grasse appeared in the Western Atlantic the British operations were doomed, if the Frenchman was a leader of skill and determination. . . . Graves was not the man for such critical times. At no period in her history has England so felt the want of a first-class sea-commander in the vital area."[56]

XLIX

YORKTOWN

NOTHING in Washington's military career shows the kindliness of his heart and his indifference to personal autocracy more poignantly than an overlooked little memorandum that he ordered destroyed.

While Cornwallis was shackled and nagged by Clinton's minute instructions usually too late, Washington had given Greene every support in his power, but never sent him an order —only praise and sympathy.[1] Greene had undergone appalling hardships with men dropping from famine and so naked that they tied clumps of moss to their shoulders and hips to keep the muskets and cartridge boxes from chafing the skin.[2] Yet Greene had done superb work in cooperation with Sumter, Lee, Marion, Pickens, Colonel Washington, and others. On hearing that his idol, George Washington, was coming south, Greene wrote to Knox with only partial cynicism:

"We have been beating the bush, and the General has come to catch the bird." [3]

Washington, however, proved his affection secretly. Realizing that by going south he automatically superseded Greene in command and robbed him of his independence, he tried to soften the blow by a personal message sent with a letter of congratulation following Greene's success at Eutaw Springs.[4] He even went so far as to say that he was saving Greene from being superseded by Rochambeau! Not wishing to have the message run the risk of capture or publication, he instructed Colonel Lewis Morris to memorize it and destroy it. This is the message:

"Col. Morris will inform General Greene in the sincerest manner that there are but two motives which can possibly induce Genl. W— to take the command to the southward: one, the order of C— to repair thither; the other, the French army going there. In the last case Count R— would command if Genl. W— did not go in person. General Washington wishes, not only from his personal regard to Genl. Greene, but from principles of generosity and justice, to see him crowned with those laurels which from his unparalleled exertions he so richly deserves."—*Memorandum to Col. Lewis Morris, to be destroyed as soon as he has committed them to memory.* 6 October. 1781.[5]

Fortunately Colonel Morris disobeyed the order and thus preserved one of the most delicate masterpieces of tact and tenderness in the history of military command. It is difficult to imagine any of the other great generals even thinking of such a courtesy. While many of such actual deeds of Washington's are lost to view, wide fame has been given to less worthy deeds that he never did. Thus a fascinating story is told that, long before he started south, he realized what an ideal trap Yorktown made for Cornwallis, wrote a letter addressed to Lafayette, and got it intercepted by Clinton. In this he alleged a hope that Cornwallis "would fortify either Portsmouth or Old Point Comfort, *for, were he to fix upon Yorktown,* from its great capabilities of defence, he might remain there snugly and unharmed, until a superior British fleet would relieve him with strong reinforcements, or embark him altogether."

This has the authority of Washington's own adopted son, G. W. P. Custis, who adds:

"This fated letter quieted the apprehensions of the British commander-in-chief as to the danger of his lieutenant, and produced those delays in the operations of Sir Henry that tended materially to the success of the allies and the surrender of Yorktown." [6]

As a prototype of the delicious stratagem by which Br'er Rabbit got himself put in the briar patch, this story has its charm. But Custis was only six months old at the time and his adopted father's letters are always turning up to discredit the reminiscences of his namesake's anecdotage. In the first place, Cornwallis was hardly the man to take his ideas from Washington's carefully pretended fears. In the second, as early as May 24th, 1781, he had received advice from Clinton, written in April, to fortify the York river and find a good naval base for the British fleet. Later Clinton had sent him an intercepted letter of Washington's to Lafayette. But this letter of May 31st, 1781, which has already been cited, did not mention Cornwallis or York, Portsmouth, or Old Point Comfort. It stated the plain fact that Washington intended to attack New York. Clinton, in his letter of alarm to Cornwallis, announced that Washington would have 20,000 men besides militia and probable French reinforcements, against Clinton's 10,931. Clinton, therefore, had urged Cornwallis to send him all the troops he could spare and to fortify himself at York to guard the Chesapeake in cooperation with a British fleet. Clinton preferred York to "the sickly port of Portsmouth." But Cornwallis from the first had disapproved of Yorktown, and had written on June 30th, 1781:

"It far exceeds our power, . . . to make safe defensive posts there and at Gloucester."

Nevertheless, he obeyed orders, though reluctantly, and Germain's interference added further confusion.[7] Finally, as has been shown, Washington was present at Yorktown almost as unwillingly as Cornwallis. At that, he might have been too late; for if the impetuous Marquis had not been in one of his unusually conservative moods, the battle might have been concluded before Washington got there. It might have been a French victory in appearance as it eventually was in fact.

While Washington was still in Philadelphia, de Grasse had landed Saint Simon's 3,200 troops and they had joined Lafayette at once in Williamsburg. Lafayette had more than 4,000 men. De Grasse wanted to add 1,800 marines and attack Cornwallis at once. The French, with Lafayette's Americans, had already more than 9,000 against the hemmed-in 7,000 of

Cornwallis. But Lafayette realized the risk of defeat and, knowing that Washington was on the way, opposed the hottest arguments of the French, who were impatient to do the job and be gone.[8] Cornwallis was also tempted to attack, but after careful reconnoitering decided that his chance of cutting through was small, so he fell back on York and began to fortify. He also was restrained by deference to a superior, for he believed that Clinton would soon come south with reinforcements and take command. Even when Washington arrived he brought with him only 2,000 Americans and 4,000 Frenchmen, under a French lieutenant-general.

There is confusing discrepancy in the various official estimates of numbers at Yorktown, but it is roughly correct to say that the army under Washington was made up of 5,500 Continentals, and 3,500 militia or 9,000 Americans, and 7,000 French regulars.

Nobody denies that the French navy played an essential rôle in the victory. It drove off a great British fleet before Washington arrived; it helped to surround Cornwallis; it prevented Clinton from bringing reinforcements, and it transported the invaluable heavy siege artillery. De Grasse had with him 28 ships of the line and 6 frigates; de Barras had 8 ships of the line. De Grasse had on board his fleet 19,000 seamen, and de Barras about 5,000, besides some French troops under General de Choisy.

In other words, the French force at Yorktown was not, as is usually stated, 7,000 to the American 9,000, but 31,000 to 9,000. The French were 3 to 1, and it was their overwhelming number that broke Cornwallis' resistance so soon. Nor should it be overlooked that the Americans largely wore French clothes and French shoes, used French weapons and French ammunition. French loans had fed them. Washington had had to borrow French flour to save his men from hunger and French money to save them from mutiny.

Observe the names in the line of battle, too. Most of them are so foreign that the American, unable to pronounce them and unwilling to try, blandly refuses to remember that they were there. In effect, he denies their existence. Yet at the time they were of vital importance. Directories are usually dull reading, but even to the fairly well-read American, not to mention the solely schoolbook-bred, there should be drama or at least music in the list of the conquerors of Cornwallis.

The Americans formed the right wing: the Continentals in three divisions under three major-generals; Lincoln, an American, Lafayette, and Steuben, a German by birth but officially a Frenchman. In Lafayette's division were noticeable: his former aide Gimat, Lieutenant-Colonels Hamilton of the West Indies, and Laurens of South Carolina, and Colonel Hazen with a regiment of Canadians, mostly French-Canadians. Steuben's and Lincoln's divisions were largely American, but with a large admixture of foreign born, including Wayne's Scotch, Irish and German Pennsylvanians. Knox was American, but Colonel Moylan was Irish and "Colonel Armand," really the Marquis de Rouérie, was French. The chief of engineers was the French Chevalier du Portail. In the militia was the German-born General Weedon.

The left wing was commanded by Lieutenant-General Rochambeau. His aides were the Swedish Count de Fersen, Marquis de Vauban, Marquis de Damas, Chevalier de Lameth, and Baron de Clozen, MM Dumas and de Lauberdière. There were four major-generals, the Baron and the Vicomte de Vioménil, the Chevalier de Chastellux and the Marquis de Saint Simon; and Brigadier-General de Choisy. Among the officers were the Marquis de Laval, the brothers Deux-Ponts, Marquis de Custine, the Vicomtes de Noailles and de Pondeux, Marquis d'Audechamp and Marquis de Rostaing. The artillery was commanded by d'Aboville, and the Duc de Lauzun had his own legion. Among others were the Comte de Charlus, Berthier, who was later a marshal under Napoleon, de Fleury, whose bravery has been spoken of, the Vicomte de Rochambeau, Commissary Blanchard, the Baron d'Ezbeck, de Bressolles, d'Anselme, d'Espeyron. The regiments wore such ring-ing names as Bourbonnois, Soissonnois, Saintonge, Royal Deux-Ponts, Agénois, Gâtinois, Touraine.[9]

Hardly one American in a hundred thousand has ever heard of these, yet all of them crossed the sea and risked their lives for his country. Just to mention their names is a little reparation of neglect.

> Time hath, my lord, a wallet at his back
> Wherein he puts alms for oblivion,
> A great-sized monster of ingratitudes:
> Those scraps are good deeds past, which are devour'd
> As fast as they are made, forgot as soon
> As done.

After one dip in the wallet to lift for a moment's view the aliens who gave Washington his one great, effective victory, their names may be dropped back into forgetfulness. But the French succeeded in surprising, if only for the moment, the respect of the Americans. A Virginia militia colonel solemnly wrote that they were "very different from the ideas formerly inculcated in us of a people living on frogs and coarse vegetables. Finer troops I never saw." [10] That was more than the French would say of the American militia. The Duc de Lauzun, who was assigned to the attack on Gloucester over the river, was disgusted with the innkeeper general, Weedon; not because he was an innkeeper but because he was "a coward and a sloth." Washington offered to order Weedon not to interfere with the duke, but Lauzun said that since he was subordinate he would obey his superior whoever he was.[11]

The amazing willingness of the French aristocrats to accept posts inferior to these peasants speaks worlds, not only for their tact, but for their pure devotion to the cause. Rochambeau solved the matter by sending over Brigadier-General de Choisy, who was senior to Weedon. Choisy denounced Weedon's militia for cowards when they failed him in an attack.[12]

One day Lauzun met a pretty woman, who begged him to flee since the terrible Tarleton was near and had said he wanted "to shake hands with the French duke." Lauzun said

he was eager to oblige him. Almost at once Tarleton appeared
with all his men, far outnumbering the legion. Yet Lauzun
went to meet him. Tarleton raised his pistol; his horse
threw him. Lauzun dashed forward and captured the horse,
but Tarleton was carried off wounded and his men broke.[13]
To reinforce Choisy, Washington borrowed six hundred marines from de Grasse.[14] The siege abounded in skirmishes
about the outskirts. Colonel Scammell of New Hampshire, the
man who could always make Washington laugh, was killed in
one foray.

A word as to the situation that Washington found before
him: The western shore of Chesapeake bay is slashed into a
fringe by slanting rivers. The villages of York and Gloucester
faced each other across a mile-wide sheet of water. Cornwallis
occupied both villages and had some ships and sailors on the
river. He had built a strong line of works around Yorktown,
which had no commanding positions but was lifted thirty
feet or so above the river level. In his line of works he had
ten redoubts, sixteen batteries, with 65 guns, none of them
heavy. He had an outer line of defences, trenches, redoubts,
also frigates moored to sweep the flanks with fire. Across
the river, Gloucester was somewhat similarly fortified. He
took advantage of the many creeks flowing into the York, the
deep ravines, the marshy ground, and "the wild little glens
that gash the bluff." Cornwallis was harshly blamed for the
surprising readiness with which he abandoned his outer works
on the approach of the enemy, who occupied them thankfully
at once after reconnoitering and spending a night in bivouac.

Washington slept at the foot of a mulberry tree with the
roots for pillow. A slip from it grown huge was pointed out
a hundred years later.[15] Legendary trees live long.

The next day the allies took their posts in a long half-moon
about Cornwallis. On the morning of September 30th the
besiegers were amazed to find the whole exterior line of
works evacuated. They moved in and began to strengthen
them under British fire. Pickering tells a somewhat jarring

story concerning Washington's ignorance of military terms and incidentally gives a picture of the positions assumed by the armies after they had sat down to the investment of York. Washington had asked Pickering to accompany him on a reconnaissance, and Knox thus accosted him:

" 'Colonel Pickering, the General thinks we ought to move and encamp nearer to the enemy's works: What is your opinion?'

"I answered instantly, expressing precisely all the following ideas, and I am sure, nearly in these words:

" 'The duties of troops at a siege are severe. Those off duty ought to be so situated as to take their rest in security. We must look for repeated sallies from the enemy, and if any of them are made in great force, they will beat the guards of the trenches, and compel them to retreat! If the camp be near, the soldiers will not have time to rouse from sleep and to recollect themselves, before the enemy will be upon them. Shot from the enemy's outworks, reaches where we now are. For these reasons I think we are near enough.'

" 'Well, but we must invest the place,' said General Washington. This remark, I confess, surprised me: while in a moment I replied:

" 'The object of an investment is to prevent the besieged from receiving succour, or making their escape. The American Army now extends so as to command the ground from York river, below the town, round to the morass on our left. Above the town, the French army commands the ground from the morass to the river. Duke Lauzun's legion and General Weedon's brigade of Virginia militia are at Gloucester Point, opposite to Yorktown; and Count de Grasse, with his fleet, commands the mouth of the river. No passage is open except that up the river; and Lord Cornwallis will not attempt to escape by marching into the heart of the country. So I think, sir, the place is completely invested already.'

"The General made no further observation; and the troops continued on the ground they then occupied. This was the seventh year of the war; and twice, I believe, the besieging of the enemy in New York had been contemplated; yet it seems apparent, from the facts just stated, that General Washington had not then formed any distinct idea of the investment of a fortified place.   Some twelve years before, when a captain in the militia of Massachusetts, I had read two or three books on fortifications and the conducting of sieges." [16]

It seems incredible that Washington should not have known the technical term "investment," but he had a poor head for proper names and unusual words.   There is confirmation of Pickering in the fact that in his diary Washington speaks of "the Investiture of the Enemy," which would refer, of course, only to their uniform.   Wayne used the same word in a letter to Reed,[17] but he also was a fantastic stylist.

Cornwallis had not foreseen a regular siege and relied on the British navy and his superior, Clinton, to save him.

To one who stands on the edge of the wide water at York-town, and feels an east wind pressing the ripples to shore there comes a certain revocation of the dead, who must have spent hours staring into the haze there for the ever-triumphant British sails to swoop forward.   Behind the besieged the malicious host of the hated French and the despised rebels burrowed closer and closer.   Among them crashed the round shot and bursting shell from the great guns.   There were nearly two thousand Germans huddled up with Cornwallis and five hundred or more American loyalists—southern Tories, who must have been doubly anxious, having gone through the fearful treachery and butchery of the guerilla raids in the South where both sides disgraced the name of man and sullied the black chronicles of war.

Cornwallis had few high officers; not a major-general, and only one brigadier, O'Hara; only two colonels, and very small numbers and resources for any long investiture—the word was good enough for Washington.

Washington was in a hurry.   He feared the arrival of the British fleet.   He feared the departure of the French, the on-

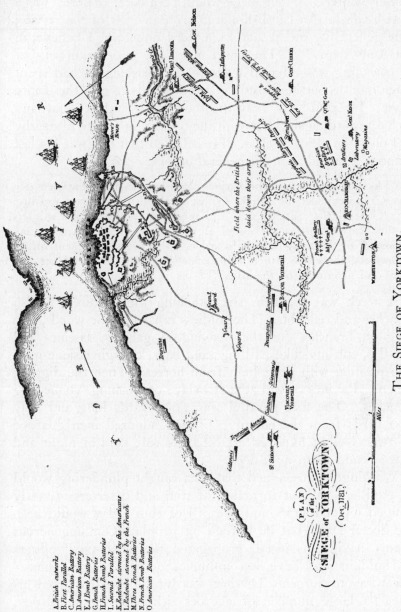

A. British outworks
B. First Parallel
C. American Battery
D. American Battery
E. A Bomb Battery
G. French Batteries
H. French Bomb Batteries
I. Second Parallel
K. Redoubt stormed by the Americans
L. Redoubt stormed by the French
M. Three French Batteries
N. French Bomb Batteries
O. American Batteries

PLAN of the
SIEGE of YORKTOWN
(Oct. 1781)

Miles

THE SIEGE OF YORKTOWN.
(From Sparks' *Life of Washington*.)

coming winter.   A long siege would be a bore.   "Bore" was a
newish word.   An English officer wrote in 1781 of the service,
"the generallity call it a *Bore*, a word unknown, I believe, in
the Am^n Army." [18]   The word may have been unknown, but
the meaning was infernally familiar.   Washington had spent
seven months outside Boston in 1775-6, only to gain the empty
town.   He could not bear the thought of such a delay and
such a reward, again, now with the country in a state of apathy
and only the allies restless.   He believed that this was his last
chance.   He said so in his general orders:

"The advanced season and various conditions render it indispensably
necessary to conduct the attacks against York with the utmost rapidity.
The General therefore expects and requires the officers and soldiers
of this army to pursue the duties of their respective departments and
stations with the most unabating ardor.   The present moment offers,
in prospect, the epoch which will decide American Independence, the
glory and superiority of the allies." [19]

A week was spent in strengthening the captured British
trenches and redoubts.   The soldiers ransacked the woods, ripping off branches for the weaving of gabions, fascines and
hurdles, cutting stakes, filling sand bags, dragging siege-guns
into position with little help from horses.   Then the digging
began.   Ravines saved the trouble of making connecting
trenches.   The first parallel was 2,000 yards long and only
600 yards from the enemy.   Fifteen hundred men guarded
by twenty-eight hundred attacked the soft sand at night and
dawn found them neck-deep.

Washington threatened that men caught plundering would
be punished without formality of trial and deserters instantly
hanged.   Good straw and one gill of rum a day would keep
the doctor away, but he warned his people: "Our ungenerous
enemy having, as usual, propagated the small-pox" officers
and soldiers must have no communication with the neighbors.[20]
According to Surgeon Thacher, Cornwallis expelled from his
lines "a large number of negroes sick with the small-pox,
probably for the purpose of communicating the infection to

our army." [21] Possibly he expelled them for the purpose of not communicating the infection to his own men.

On October 9th, says Dr. Thacher, Washington "put the match to the first gun, and a furious discharge of cannon and mortars immediately followed, and Earl Cornwallis has received his first salutation." [22] Governor Nelson had a home in Yorktown. It is still there, though the Governor asked Lafayette to shoot it to pieces lest it shelter the enemy.[23] By October 11th fifty-two cannon were battering Yorktown down.

There are many anecdotes of these days. Steuben, the only officer on the American side who had ever seen a siege, played an important part. On the night of October 11th, he and Wayne were together when a British shell came their way. Steuben, being a wise soldier, threw himself into a trench; Wayne, being another, followed suit, but landed on Steuben's back. Steuben commented, overshoulder:

"I always knew you were brave, . . . but I didn't know you were so perfect . . . you cover your general's retreat in the best possible manner." [24]

Washington, however, is quoted by Dr. Thacher as rebuking his brave and devoted aide, Colonel Cobb. Solicitous for the safety of his chief, who was standing in an exposed situation and watching the attack on the redoubts, Cobb urged:

"Sir, you are too much exposed here, had you not better step a little back?"

"Colonel Cobb," replied his Excellency, "if you are afraid, you have liberty to step back." [25]

This sounds so crassly uncharacteristic of Washington that we must believe he smiled when he said it, as he must have smiled when, on another day, a chaplain standing near him had his hat covered with sand from a shot that struck at his feet. Much agitated, he took off his hat and showed it to Washington, who replied "with his usual composure:

" 'Mr. Evans, you had better carry that home and show it to your wife and children.' " [26]

One other word is reported from him, of no importance except for its plausibility and its dialect. Watching the attack on the redoubts through an embrasure, he turned to Knox and said: "The work is done, and *well* done." Then he turned to his black shadow and said:

"Billy, hand me my horse." [27]

The second parallel, at 300 yards from the enemy, split the remaining distance and was run the night of October 11th. Washington wrote in his Diary the next day:

"This business was conducted with the same secresy as the former and undertaken so much sooner than the enemy expected (we should commence a second parallel) that they did not by their conduct and mode of firing, appear to have had any suspicion of our Working parties till day light discovered them to their Picquets. . . .

"14th. The day was spent in compleating our parallel, and maturing the Batteries of the second parallel. The old batteries were principally directed against the Abattis and salient angles of the enemys advanced redoubts on their extreme Right and left to prepare them for the intended assault for which the necessary dispositions were made for attacking the two on the left and,

"At half after Six in the Evening both were carried; that on their left (on the Bank of the River) by the Americans and the other by the French Troops. The Baron Viomenil commanded the left attack and the Marq^s de la Fayette the Right on which the light Infantry were employed." [28]

This attack was made the occasion of a famous race between the French and the American heroes and it gave the hungry Alexander Hamilton a brief chance to show his military fire, though he had to fight his own fellow-officers first. The attack under Vioménil was led by Guillaume Deux-Ponts. On his part, Lafayette had promised the lead to the brave Major Gimat, his ex-aide. But Alexander Hamilton chanced to be field officer of the day, and he demanded the privilege as his right. When Lafayette tried to keep his promise to Gimat, Hamilton went over his head to Washington in an ardent letter. Washington could easily have repaid Hamilton's former insults, but he proved his magnanimity by giving him the priceless privilege, even at the cost of overruling Lafayette. [29]

According to another account, Lieutenant-Colonel Francis Barber was the man whom Hamilton edged out of the post of command—not of danger, for he was not hurt, while both Gimat and Barber were wounded, along with twenty-three others—nine were killed. According to a third account, Hamilton stole the glory from the brave Muhlenberg, who was really his chief, and was also wounded in the attack.[30] It was not Hamilton's fault that he was not honored with a wound. He was so short that he could not climb the palisade and, asking a soldier to kneel, stepped on his back and bounded over the parapet.[31] Since Hamilton wrote the official account of the attack, and with all his brilliant literary skill, he managed to make most of the glory his own.

In 1802, in his newspaper, the New York *Evening Post*, Hamilton denied a tradition "that General Lafayette, with the approbation or connivance of General Washington, ordered me . . . to put to death all those of the enemy who should happen to be taken in the redoubt; and that, through motives of humanity, I forebore to execute the order. Positively and unequivocally" he denied it.[32]

From a sickbed in Paris, Lafayette wrote to thank him. Hamilton accused Reverend William Gordon of originating the tale and, indeed, according to that chronicler:

"The marquis said to gen. Washington—'The troops should retaliate on the British, for the cruelties they have practised.' The General answered—'You have full command, and may order as you please.' The marquis ordered the party to remember New London, and to retaliate, by putting the men in the redoubt to the sword after having carried it. . . . Col. Hamilton, who conducted the enterprise with much address and intrepidity, in his report to the marquis, mentioned, to the honor of his detachment—'that, incapable of imitating examples of barbarity, and forgetting recent provocations, they spared every man that ceased to resist.' "[33]

This was one more reason why Hamilton loathed the Reverend Dr. William Gordon, who had previously accused Hamilton of advising Washington to overthrow Congress.

Among the wounded on this night was Captain Stephen

Olney, to whom we owe the statement that, before the assault, the regiment was paraded and addressed by Washington, who ordinarily did not deliver battlefield orations. Captain Olney says:

"I thought then that His Excellency's knees rather shook, but I have since doubted whether it was not mine." [34]

The capture of the two redoubts within a minute of each other was dazzling war, and Washington expressed his delight in General Orders next day, thanking his men "for the spirit and rapidity with which they advanced to the attacks assigned them, and for the admirable firmness with which they supported them, under the fire of the enemy, without returning a shot.

"The General reflects with the highest degree of pleasure on the confidence which the troops of the two nations must hereafter have in each other. Assured of mutual support, he is convinced there is no danger which they will not cheerfully encounter—no difficulty which they will not bravely overcome." [35]

In his Diary he said:

"The bravery exhibited by the attacking Troops was emulous and praise worthy. Few cases have exhibited stronger proofs of Intripidity, coolness and firmness than were shown upon this occasion." [36]

He noted that "since the Investiture of York" the Americans had lost 2 officers, 1 sergeant, and 20 "R & F" killed, and 8 officers, 1 sergeant and 56 "R & F" wounded—a total loss of 88. The French had lost 2 officers killed and 7 wounded, but far more rank and file; 50 being killed and 127 wounded—a total loss of 186.

All this while there had been a dramatic exchange of letters between Cornwallis and Clinton, and one must imagine the dashing couriers, the fleet frigates, the perilous rushes through the hostile lines, the anxious readings. Cornwallis had received from Clinton a letter dated September 24th:

"At a meeting of the General and Flag Officers held this day, it is determined, that above five thousand men, rank and file, shall be embarked on board the King's ships, and the joint exertions of the navy and army made in a few days to relieve you, and afterwards co-operate with you. The fleet consists of twenty-three sail of the line, three of which are three deckers. There is every reason to hope we start from hence the 5th October. . . . At a venture, without knowing whether they can be seen by us, I request, that if all is well, upon hearing a considerable firing towards the entrance of the Chesapeak, three large separate smokes may be made parallel to it; and, if you possess the post of Gloucester, four." [37]

Cornwallis answered that same night:

"I have ventured these last two days to look General Washington's whole force in the face in the position on the outside of my works, and I have the pleasure to assure your Excellency, that there was but one wish throughout the whole army, which was, that the enemy would advance. I have this evening received your letter of the 24th, which has given me the greatest satisfaction. I shall retire this night within the works, and have no doubt, if relief arrives in any reasonable time, York and Gloucester will be both in possession of his Majesty's troops. I believe your Excellency must depend more on the sound of our cannon than the signal of smokes for information; however, I will attempt it on the Gloucester side.—Medicines are wanted." [38]

On October 2nd he had a letter from Clinton saying that "necessary repairs of the fleet will detain us here to the 5th of October." In Clinton's history he tells how he "kept 5000 Select Troops ready in Transports" and how frantically he tried to hasten the repairs of the ships, supplying them with army lumber and ammunition. He describes his "mortification" at the Admiral's reports of further delay until the 8th, and next, until the 12th. Finally, "notwithstanding all our Anxiety & Efforts . . . it was the afternoon of the 19th before the Fleet was fairly at Sea." He tells how carefully he worded his letters to Cornwallis to avoid encouraging him "by trusting too much to our Punctuality . . . to let slip an opportunity of effecting something by himself." [39]

Clinton's letter of September 30th reached Cornwallis on the 10th of October:

"Your Lordship may be assured that I am doing every thing in my power to relieve you by a direct move, and I have reason to hope, from the assurances given me this day by Admiral Graves, that we may pass the bar by the 12th of October, if the winds permit, and no unforeseen accident happens: . . . I shall persist in my idea of a direct move, even to the middle of November, should it be your Lordship's opinion that you can hold out so long; but if, when I hear from you, you tell me that you cannot, and I am without hopes of arriving in time to succour you by a direct move, I will immediately make an attempt upon Philadelphia by land, giving you notice, if possible, of my intention. If this should draw any part of Washington's force from you, it may possibly give you an opportunity of doing something to save your army; of which, however, you can best judge from being upon the spot."

Cornwallis answered on the 11th:

"I have only to repeat what I said in my letter of the 3d, that nothing but a direct move to York river, which includes a successful naval action, can save me. . . . With such works on disadvantageous ground, against so powerful an attack we cannot hope to make a very long resistance."

On the 15th he wrote "in cypher" with patriotic self-sacrifice:

"My situation now becomes very critical; we dare not shew a gun to their old batteries, and I expect that their new ones will open tomorrow morning; experience has shewn that our fresh earthen works do not resist their powerful artillery, so that we shall soon be exposed to an assault in ruined works, in a bad position, and with weakened numbers. The safety of the place is, therefore, so precarious, that I cannot recommend that the fleet and army should run great risque in endeavouring to save us." [40]

On the 16th he attempted a forlorn and desperate sortie, but was driven back in. As Washington wrote to Congress: "They had only time to thrust the points of their bayonets into four pieces of the French and two of the American artillery, and break them off; but the spikes were easily extracted."

The British shells were nearly expended, sickness was torturing and slaying faster than the relentless enemy, whose smothering bombardment Washington described:

"The whole of the batteries kept up an incessant fire, the Cannon at the Ambrazures of the enemy, with a view to destroy them, the Shells into the Enemy's Works, where by the information of deserters they did much execution.

"The French battery on the left, by red hot shot, set fire to (in the course of the Night) the Charon frigate and 3 large Transports which were entirely consumed." [41]

Cornwallis now decided to play his last trick, and try to cut his way through the circle. He could not hope to break the line before Yorktown, but he thought he might surprise the weaker forces in front of Gloucester, where Colonel Simcoe knew a secret path to the rear.[42] Once through, he could hasten north along the peninsula, and perhaps reach Clinton at New York. Or they might meet at Philadelphia. They might do many things disastrous to the Americans. Light Horse Harry Lee, who admired Cornwallis as a great general, praised the plan:

"This bold conception bespoke the hero, and was worthy of its author. Nor can it justly be deemed so desperate as was generally conceived. Washington could not possibly in time seize the northern and southern route; and without availing himself of horses, he never could overtake his foe." [43]

Lee describes what friendship Cornwallis would have found among the loyalists in Maryland, and in Pennsylvania. By a roundabout route he could have reached the Carolinas again and played havoc with Washington's hopes. He got one division across the river in the night; the boats were returning for the second.

"But Providence had decreed otherwise: a furious storm suddenly arose, and forced the returning boats down the river considerably below the town. Day appeared before the boats reached their destination, and the forenoon was occupied in bringing back the division which had passed." [44]

If Cornwallis was anxious about Clinton, Washington was no less anxious about de Grasse. This was a naval war, indeed. Boudinot, who was close to Washington, tells of a trick he played on the British to hasten their collapse:

"The French Troops brought out by Count De Grasse, were absolutely necessary to compleat the line of Circumvallation, and perfect the siege— about 2 days before the Capture. The Count sent word to Genl Washington that he should within 48 Hours withdraw those Troops & that he must provide accordingly—This was in effect raising the Siege. Genl Washington remonstrated ag^t it in vain. He sent the Marquiss La Fayette on Board the Fleet to dissuade Count de Grasse from so ruinous a measure. he obstinately presisted, and said his orders were positive & not discretionary.

"Genl Washington finding that nothing but storming the enemies lines would prevent the raising of the Siege, and that would unnecessarily occasion the loss of great numbers on both sides, to avoid which he fell on the following expedient—He sent out Col Hamilton with some other officers with a Flag of Truce on some business—They were met half way by a number of British officers, They carried with them something to eat and drink In Conversation they mentioned to the British Officers. their concern for them as Gent^n & Soldiers that the American Army had determined to Storm their lines.—that the American Soldiery & Country People were so exasperated at the Conduct of the British to the Southward, that they could not answer for the Consequences. as they did not think they could be restrained by authority and Discipline—That they knew Genl Washington's humane Temper, and his wish to avoid the unnecessary shedding of blood. That in Case of a Capitulation the same Terms the British gave to our Troops at Charles Town, with the addition of the Officers wearing side Arms & being immediately sent on their parole into New York they believed might be obtained. That they did not wish their names to be mentioned &c &c Within a few Hours after their return proposals for surrendering on Terms were sent out, and the capitulation took place—Count De Grasse remained several days (notwithstanding the Positive Nature of his Orders) to enjoy the pleasure of the surrender, the rejoicings &c &c." [45]

Whether Cornwallis could have or should have held out longer is a point on which admirers and critics differ completely. It is certain that if he had delayed a week more that region would have been the scene of as fierce and bloody a battle by land and sea as one could wish. But Cornwallis crumbled with his fortress, on which such fire was concentrated that he could not repair the damage or build an abatis or fire a single gun. His officers agreed that a few hours more of bombardment would destroy the works beyond hope of defending them against an assault. He made his great decision:

"Under all these circumstances, I thought it would have been wanton and inhuman to the last degree to sacrifice the lives of this small body of gallant soldiers, who had ever behaved with so much fidelity and courage, by exposing them to an assault, which from the numbers and precautions of the enemy could not fail to succeed." [46]

Washington knew how it felt to make that decision; he had ended his first campaign as a young officer with a surrender. His Diary for October 17th, 1781, says:

"About ten o'clock the Enemy beat a parley, and Lord Cornwallis proposed a cessation of Hostilities for 24 hours, that Commissioners might meet at the house of a Mr. Moore (in the rear of our first parallel) to settle terms, for the surrender of the Posts of York and Gloucester. To this he was answered, that a desire to spare the further effusion of Blood would readily incline me to treat of the surrender of the above Posts, but previous to the meeting of Commissioners I wished to have his proposals in writing and for this purpose would grant a cessation of hostilities two hours. Within which time he sent out A letter with such proposals (tho' some of them were inadmissible) as led me to believe that there would be no great difficulty in fixing the terms. Accordingly hostilities were suspended for the Night and I proposed my own terms to which if he agreed Commissioners were to meet to digest them into form.

"18th. The Commissioners met accordingly; but the business was so procrastinated by those on their side (a Colo. Dundas and Major Ross) that Colo. Laurens and the Viscount De Noailles who were appointed on our part could do no more than make the rought draft of the Articles which were to be submitted for Lord Cornwalliss. consideration.

"19th. In the Morning early I had them copied and sent word to Lord Cornwallis that I expected to have them signed at 11 o'clock and that the Garrison would March out at two o'clock, both of which were accordingly done." [47]

"Both of which were accordingly done" is all that Washington says in his Diary of this peak of his military career. Fortunately there were other witnesses. Cornwallis tried to make as good terms as Burgoyne had made. By an astounding coincidence he chose the exact anniversary of Burgoyne's surrender for sending a drummer out on a parapet to beat a "parley" and an officer to wave a white handkerchief. The officer came forward, was blindfolded and taken to the presence of Washington. Cornwallis wanted especially to see that the loyalists with him were not subjected to the perils of reprisal for their fidelity to the King. So he stipulated at first:

"That the garrisons of York and Gloucester shall be prisoners of war, with the customary honours. And, for the conveniency of the individuals which I have the honour to command, that the British shall be sent to Britain, and the Germans to Germany, under engagement not to serve against France, America, or their allies, until released or regularly exchanged. That all arms and public stores shall be delivered up to you; but that the usual indulgence of side-arms to officers, and of retaining private property, shall be granted to officers and soldiers, and that the interest of several individuals, in civil capacities and connected with us, shall be attended to." [48]

Washington would not grant conditions wrung from Gates and never kept. He refused to send the foreigners home, but promised to march them "to such parts of the country as can most conveniently provide for their subsistence; and the benevolent treatment of the prisoners, which is invariably observed by the Americans, will be extended to them." That "invariably" was dismally droll in view of some of his earlier comments on the subject. He offered the surrendering army the same "honors" as were granted to the garrison at Charleston. Officers' side arms and property were "indulged." He would not commit himself as to the Tories.

Cornwallis asked as a last favor that his sloop *Bonetta* be lent to him to carry dispatches to Clinton "with such soldiers as I may think proper to send as passengers in her . . . and that no person may be punished or molested for having joined the British troops."

In the terms finally agreed upon, he was permitted to borrow the sloop, but as to the punishment of natives for joining the British troops, the decision was: "This article can not be assented to, being altogether of civil resort." [49]

Under threat of a renewal of battle Cornwallis signed reluctantly at 11 o'clock on the morning of October 19th, 1781. One of the articles of the capitulation directed the troops to march out with "colors cased, and drums beating a British or German march." This meant, says Knox, in writing to his wife, "the charmer of my soul," that they were not permitted to unfurl their colors or play Yankee Doodle.[50] This was a bit of revenge for John Laurens, who had surrendered at Charleston and had been refused desired honors. When the British surrendered they played an old tune, "The World Turned Upside Down." [51] Strangely, Cornwallis was by title in command of the Tower of London in which John Laurens' father was now imprisoned.

Thinking of everything, Washington had written to de Grasse on the 17th:

"I should be anxious to have the honor of your Excellency's participation in the treaty, which will according to present appearance shortly take place. I need not add how happy it will make me to welcome your Excellency in the name of America on this shore, and embrace you upon an occasion so advantageous to the interests of the common cause, and on which it is so much indebted to you. Should naval reasons deprive me of this happiness, by requiring your Excellency's presence on board, I entreat that you will be pleased to appoint an officer to represent you, and take charge of the capitulation to be signed by your Excellency." [52]

He asked de Choisy in Gloucester to select the place for the grounding of the arms.[53]

The supreme instance of Washington's unwillingness to claim the center of the stage, or to strut, or even take his manifest rights, was his refusal to accept the sword of victory. He selected his dear friend, Knox, for the recipient, but, on second thought, realized how sweet it would be to General Lincoln, who had surrendered his sword at Charleston, to take a British sword. Knox agreed with him.[54]

At three o'clock the British moved out of their works into the mile-long alley formed by the French and American troops. Washington headed his line, Rochambeau his. Cornwallis was absent, he pleaded illness—feigned it, they say; though a general of his quality might well have been sincerely sick to death at being ordered into a trap and left there by his own nation until he was released by the man he had chased across New Jersey and pursued in vain the other way across, not quite five years before. He sent out his sword by his only other general, O'Hara. The British and Hessians considered it a lesser disgrace and perhaps a more logical gesture to surrender to their old enemies the French. Adjutant-General, the Comte de Dumas, rode out in front of O'Hara to lead the British to their place.

"Where is General Rochambeau?" said O'Hara.

"On our left," Dumas answered, "at the head of the French line."

O'Hara then spurred his horse toward Rochambeau, but Dumas galloped ahead, and placing himself in front of Rochambeau, pointed to Washington opposite, saying:

"You deceive yourself; the commander-in-chief of our army is to your right."

He led the way, but when O'Hara offered the sword, Washington checked him, saying, according to Dumas:

"Never from such good a hand (*jamais d'une aussi bonne main*)."

This part of the surrender is never given in the American accounts, which represent O'Hara on foot, doffing his hat to Washington and murmuring an apology for his chief's illness. As he offered the sword, Washington motioned him to Lincoln, who took it and handed it back at once. Conway says that Washington said coldly to O'Hara, "Pass on!"[55]

The troops then marched through the two lines to the field where they grounded their arms in a circle of French hussars. The German Von Seybothen wept as he shouted to his weeping soldiers the command:

"Streckt das Gewehr und legt Patrontaschen und Säbel ab!" [56]

There were many Germans on the American side, too; in Lauzun's Legion, and in the French regiments, and the Comte de Deux-Ponts was really Prinz von Saarbruck-Zweibrücken with German troops in his Legion.[57] Much was said of the horror of hireling Hessians on the British side, but there was no audible opposition to using them as deserters or to employing other German mercenaries on the patriot side. One of the Germans says that the French were very good to them and ringed them round to protect them from the plundering of the American soldiers, who were not allowed to visit them.[58] In general there was great good feeling and the farmers flocked in to sell the prisoners food for their hard money.

Of course, Washington was gracious to his captive general and feasted him well. Even in England, Fox and others rejoiced and this story was published of Washington:

"When Lord Cornwallis dined with General Washington for the first time, Rochambeau, being asked for a toast, gave *The United States*. Washington gave *The King of France*. Lord Cornwallis, simply, *The King*; but Washington, putting that toast, added, *of England*, and facetiously, *confine him there, I'll drink him a full bumper*, filling his glass till it ran over." [59]

Dr. Thacher tells a melancholy story:

"On one occasion, while in the presence of General Washington, Lord Cornwallis was standing with his head uncovered, his Excellency said to him politely, 'My Lord, you had better be covered from the cold'; his Lordship, applying his hand to his head, replied, 'it matters not, Sir, what becomes of this *head now*.'" [60]

But Congress took a sudden grisly interest in that head, remembering the cruelties practiced by the British troops in the Southern campaign and forgetting the rivalling cruelties of the patriots. Congress planned to order Washington to hang Cornwallis. Boudinot tells of the fight to save Washington no less than Cornwallis from such infamy:

"Mr Duane & Myself opposed it with all our powers. as contrary to all good faith, having entered into a Capitulation with him, after the facts committed, & having knowledge of them.—That it would Expose our Commander in Chief to the necessity of resigning his Command or forfeiting his Honor & Reputation &c &c &c. The debate continued several Day's and with great difficulty we succeeded in putting a negative on it, by a small Majority" [61]

There was a similar struggle in 1865 to save Robert E. Lee and Jefferson Davis from the halter, and all the repulsive history of that ugly period was foreshadowed and crudely outdone in this. Even Washington had his savage capabilities and it was not long before the King of France had to make a personal appeal to keep Washington and Congress from putting to death in reprisal an innocent young British officer chosen by lot.

For the splendor of riding to Congress with the news of the triumph Washington selected the devoted Tench Tilghman and recommended his merits to the generosity of Congress.[62] Tilghman rode hard and clattering into the town after midnight, roused President McKean with the tidings. The newspapers of the day told how the German watchman who led Tilghman to the right door, went his way waking the town from its famous somnolence with the cry:

"Basht dree o'glock, und Gorn-val-lis isht da-ken!" [63]

Boudinot adds this pathetic touch:

"When the messenger brought the News of this Capitulation to Congress, it was necessary to furnish him with hard money for his expenses, There was not a sufficiency in the Treasury to do it, and the Members of Congress, of which I was one, each paid a Dollar to accomplish it." [64]

Nevertheless, Congress voted him "a horse properly caparisoned, and an elegant sword," voted thanks to all concerned, two stands of captured colors to Washington, and two field-guns to Rochambeau.[65] The shipping and the sailors surrendered by Cornwallis were turned over to the French, since the Americans had not a vessel there. They kept the rest.

Perhaps Washington took a hint from the vote of Congress that the flags and guns were not considered his but Congress's to give away; for, after he had spent ten days on his official report, he sent it to Congress in the care of David Humphreys, together with a number of battle flags—but by no means all—taken from the captured regiments. Through the country Humphreys galloped with a small escort, and reaching Philadelphia, November 3rd, was met by the City troop and escorted to the State House, "where he laid the standards at the feet of Congress."[66]

This ignored and beautiful scene was Washington's Roman tribute to the majesty of the Republic and its Congress. Later, Washington wrote to Humphreys from Philadelphia: "I am detailed here."[67] Always he was meekest and least grasping in his greatest hours.

Congress, of course, decreed a day of thanksgiving. A committee had been appointed on September 15th for that purpose, but it had preferred to wait till the suspense was over, as if to see if Providence should earn the honor. When the lavish mercy was made known, the Presbyterian, Dr. Witherspoon, presented a glowing proclamation, which was adopted and the date set for December 13th, 1781.[68] Washington himself, in his General Orders for October 20th, paid an unusually fervid tribute to conspicuous Providence. The French King not only ordered the Te Deum to be sung in France, but instructed Rochambeau to have it celebrated in his army.[69] This order was signed by Louis XVI, with no forewarning of what this Revolution would mean to him and his Queen and the Dauphin, upon whose birth America congratulated him.

In England, King George had written to Lord North on November 3rd, 1781, in blissful ignorance of the black tidings on the way:

"I feel the justness of our cause; I put the greatest confidence in the valour of both Navy and Army and above all in the Assistance of Divine Providence: the moment is certainly anxious; the dye is now cast whether this shall be a Great Empire or the least dignified of the European States." [70]

It was Sunday, November 25th, when the news reached Germain, who carried it to Lord North, who took it, said Germain, "As he would have taken a ball in his breast. For he opened his arms exclaiming wildly as he paced up and down the apartment . . .

" 'Oh God! it is all over!' " [71]

It is all over! If it only had been! But there were two years of war yet to come, and for Washington new burdens of tribulation, new anxieties. Even at this time, he was uncertain of his success, and afraid of his own people, of the allies, of the enemy. He begged de Grasse to cooperate in the recapture of Charleston. De Grasse, having more than kept his promises to the Americans, had earlier promises to keep with the Spaniards in the West Indies. He declined and has incurred unreasonable odium since. Then Washington asked him to transport troops for the recapture of Wilmington, North Carolina. He consented, then withdrew the consent, for fear that the British might prevent his return to San Domingo. And they might have done it. Clinton left New York with the fleet, October 19th, and arrived on the 24th only to find that he had nobody to relieve. As Professor Wilbur C. Abbott says:

"Over the whole of the English effort to conciliate or conquer the rebellious colonies, may be placed one epitaph, 'Too late'." [72]

If Admiral Graves had been a Nelson or a Farragut, he might even then have gone in and destroyed the French fleet huddling in the river. But he turned back to New York. Then de Grasse sailed away, leaving Washington to the problems of further war.

Persecutors of loyalists alone showed energy. Poverty of spirit, apathy, greed of gain resumed their sway. Washington had to do his utmost to save his poor soldiers from being starved to death by Congress, and at the same time to save Congress from being lynched by the mutinous soldiers. It had been more than three years since Washington had fought a battle. There would be two years more of battle only with his countrymen before peace came. In the war he now waged with his people and their representatives and their loyalties to their thirteen little dominions, he achieved some of his greatest and most lasting victories.

He had to plead with them, be diplomatic, wheedle, exhort. He could not or would not fight them openly. The long exasperation of this helplessness may explain an apocryphal anecdote that is well found even if unsound. It is told that soon after the surrender he took one of his black slaves to a retired spot in the woods near Yorktown and with his horsewhip made him dance. George Morgan comments:

"It was as if the great man had said: 'Now, you rascal! It's your turn. For seven long years have I busied myself in bloody contention. I have marched, I have fought, I have beaten the haughtiest of humankind—and now, sir, I'm going to gad *you!*'" [73]

But if the incident occurred, perhaps his mind might be more accurately read as justifying itself thus:

"For six years I have been the slave of everybody else, unable to command or punish anybody. Here is somebody I own and can command and punish."

Among the witnesses of the surrender at Yorktown was a young man emaciated with dysentery, supported to the field for a last and a first glimpse of military grandeur.

It was Jacky Custis. He had gone to the wars. They took him to Eltham, home of his aunt. Washington sent Dr. Craik to care for him, and summoned Jacky's wife and children and mother, Martha, to hurry down from Mount Vernon.

Washington was sent for on November 5th and, mounting his horse at midnight, rode the thirty miles to Eltham, arriving with the dawn to be told by Dr. Craik that there was no hope. He flung himself on a bed in grief. Jacky had been a son to him, his only hope of an aide in peace. He had poured out great love upon the boy and his loss was bitter. He had to rouse himself to comfort Martha and Jacky's wife, weeping by the deathbed. To the young widow with four children about her knees, he said:

"From this moment I adopt the two youngest as my own." [74]

The curious statement has often been piously made that Providence denied Washington children so that he might the better act as the Father of his Country. But the translator of the "Travels of the Marquis de Chastellux," probably John Kent, said:

"I had the pleasure of passing a day or two with Mrs. Washington, at the General's house in Virginia, where she appeared to me to be one of the best women in the world, and beloved by all about her. She has no family by the General, but was surrounded by her grand children, and Mrs. Custis, her son's widow. The family were then in mourning for Mr. Custis, her son by a former marriage, whose premature death was subject of public and private regret. . . . The General was uncommonly affected at his death, insomuch that many of his friends imagined they perceived some change in his equanimity of temper, subsequent to that event." [75]

Another bitter loss he must have felt when he found time to go to Fredericksburg a week later to see his mother and his sister, Betty. He went humbly on foot to his mother and this, according to Custis, was his greeting:

"She bid him welcome by a warm embrace, and by the well-remembered and endearing name of George—the familiar name of his childhood; she inquired as to his health, remarked the lines which mighty cares and many toils had made in his manly countenance, spoke much of old times and old friends, but of his glory not one word." [76]

The story is often repeated. The awe-smitten chroniclers even express wonder that she called him by his first name! By what other name could a mother call her boy? It is added that, though she often spoke of Washington as a good son, and in his early life obedient, she never spoke a word of him as the deliverer of his country.[77]

If the day of the surrender was the gleaming zenith of the war for him, the nadir must have been that lonely day when his mother welcomed him kindly as a prodigal but carefully forebore to mention the triumph that made him the most conspicuous and important man in the world then, and perhaps since.

Let us put this among the legends better disbelieved. So many histories are false that the building of Mary Washington into a Gorgon may well be one of them.

Washington was being abandoned by everybody. His son, Jacky, was gone; his mother was remote, troubled perhaps by the cancer that later gnawed her life away. Lafayette was in haste to be off to Europe.

But Washington could dance and he danced at Fredericksburg, November 12th, though it was only a week since Jacky's death. His mother astounded the neighbors and Washington's French companions by entering the room on her son's arm, and accepting the homage of the throng, with her own magnificence. Then she confessed that "it was high time for old folks to be in bed, and retired, leaning as before on the arm of her son." [78]

Washington returned to revel in the dance. Mrs. Willis, one of the Gregory girls, later paced a minuet with him. He danced also with the sixteen-year-old Maria Mortimer.[79] In the shank of the evening he "went down some dozen couple in the contre dance with great spirit and satisfaction." [80]

The next day found him at Mount Vernon for two more days. He wrote a long letter of farewell to Lafayette, who sailed from Boston, just before Christmas. He paid Lafayette a tribute of homage and of devotion and ended his letter with "a tender of my ardent Vows for a propitious voyage, a gracious reception from your Prince, an honorable reward for your services, a happy meeting with your lady and friends, and a safe return in the spring to, my dear Marq⁵, your affectionate friend."

Even in this letter he impressed upon Lafayette the absolute necessity of a naval superiority for France's sake and America's:

"It follows then as certain as that night succeeds the day, that without a decisive naval force we can do nothing definitive, and with it every thing honorable and glorious. A constant naval superiority would terminate the war speedily; without it, I do not know that it will ever be terminated honorably." [81]

Mingling affection with statecraft, and war with real estate, he wrote a long and canny letter to a rival bidder for a piece of land he wanted, and tried to stop expensive competition.[82]

To Congress he sent a letter of thanks for its resolutions and took "a particular pleasure in acknowledging, that the interposing hand of Heaven . . . has been most conspicuous and remarkable." [83]

But to Nathanael Greene he wrote the next day that he was hastening to Philadelphia to "attempt to stimulate Congress . . .

"My greatest Fear is, that Congress viewing this stroke in too important a point of Light, may think our Work too nearly closed, & will fall into a state of Languor & Relaxation to prevent this Error I shall employ every Means in my Power—and if unhappily we sink into that fatal mistake no part of the Blame shall be mine.

"Whatever may be the Winter politics of European Courts it is clearly my opinion, that our Grand object, is to be prepared in every point for War—not that we wish its Continuance, but that we may be in the best Situation to meet every Event." [84]

This was wise and hopeful but there was more prophecy in the letter he had written a fortnight earlier to the Governor of Virginia, on whose soil his life began and his battles with the English ended:

"I will candidly confess to Your Excellency, that my only apprehension (which I wish may be groundless) is, lest the late important

Success, instead of exciting our exertions, as it ought to do, should produce such a relaxation in the prosecution of the War, as will prolong the calamities of it." [85]

They were prolonged and many, but from now on what had begun as a Civil War between the English subjects of the King, at home and overseas, continued as the first civil war between Americans. It would be hard to find among them all a man who could have taken Washington's place, endured so patiently the torments he endured, or builded out of such chaos an edifice, for all its flaws, so magnificent as the United States. His fiftieth year seemed to mark only the early forenoon of his tremendously busy, infinitely effective day.

AFTERWORD

This biography began blithely as a one-volume study of certain neglected phases of Washington's career and character. It seems doomed to go on forever and forever, piling up tomes of increasing bulk and diminishing scope.

The fault is really Washington's for living so vast and various a life of such unrivalled significance in so many fields. Further blame is due to those who keep turning up important documents and revising earlier attitudes. Perhaps one should not mention those who persist in propagating venerable errors and mossy traditions as sacred documents and insist upon filling the minds of the young with ancient lies for their dear benefit.

It is unsafe to offend watchdogs, therefore it is not altogether unpleasant. I think it is even an honorable duty. I have been peculiarly delighted to find that many children who have somehow got hold of my book have said that it taught them to love Washington for the first time, by ridding him of the offensive handicaps of the cherry-tree and other priggish inventions.

But I still encounter innumerable grown-ups who take a patriotic pride in denouncing this biography while boasting their innocence of having read it. This is a kind of Irish bull of criticism and rather picturesque. With a few conspicuous exceptions, those who have read it have recognized at least the author's profound admiration and affection for nearly everything in Washington's life except the fables that cluster about him.

My first volume barely managed to get Washington through his first thirty years. The second, though much larger, hardly compassed fifteen years. This third volume, still longer, is strained to embrace four years. I might seem to be working out the exact formula of Achilles and the hare, but the worst is over now.

I am not, alas, one of those strong characters who are able to say No to thousands of picturesque or significant deeds and utterances of the hero, and deny them publication. I look with envy on authors who are gifted with the power to write more or less brilliant one-volume biographies of enormous men, and I falter in awe before those who can serenely put forth what are fashionably called "evaluations"—and in even humbler awe before those who can review these evaluations and point out their errors.

An evalution of Washington, or even a brief account of his life, is like a transcontinental railroad map. It shows nothing of the scenery, emphasizes one route in straight black lines, represents connecting roads by thin threads and deletes the others altogether. It distorts everything that it indicates and omits infinitely more than it includes. Still, such maps are both convenient and indispensable, and I do not mean to underrate them.

Fortunately there is no lack of them. There are at least a thousand published biographies of Washington, ranging from one in my possession that is no bigger or thicker than a thumb, to fat five-volume works. There is a biography for every taste, from those who treat Washington as a heaven-sent Messiah to those who treat him as a stupid old bore. Since there is no law compelling anybody to read this work of mine and no effort to pass such a law, or to suppress the thousand other available accounts, I am going on with this one, recommending its more violent opponents to seek their pasturage elsewhere and continuing to do my utmost to find out all I can about the actual Washington and to publish as much of it as accurately as I can, until somebody passes a law against it—and, perhaps, even after that.

The more I study Washington the greater and better I think him, yet I am not trying to prove him great or good. I am trying solely to describe him as he was and let him speak for himself. He was a man of such tremendous undeniable achievement that he does not need to be bolstered with propaganda, protected by a priestcraft of suppression, or celebrated by any more Fourth of July oratory.

He was a man of such eagerness for eventual justice and of such mercy even to his enemies, that his own example, if such a plea were necessary, would authorize my intense concern to be just to those who came in conflict with him. So far as I can discover, there has never been an effort made to deal fairly with Conway, Charles Lee, Gates, and others who stood in Washington's path. They have been labelled as scoundrels and gibbeted with the summary justice of Judge Lynch.

In these pages, for the first time, I think, the notorious Conway has a day in court. When I read his manuscript letters in the New York Historical Society collection, I was astounded to find how human he was, how wise and well-justified in many respects, and how shabbily treated, whatever his mistakes and misdeeds. A few writers had recognized that he was rather the tool than the guiding spirit of the Conway Cabal, but had overlooked what the manuscripts and letters only recently published disclose: that he never wrote the famous phrase Washington accused him of writing, was brave in battle and eager to serve in any capacity.

I have been unable to learn just what he did to make Washington hate and pursue him with such uncharacteristic relentlessness, but I have tried to be fair with him—as with General Horatio Gates, whose multitudinous letters in the New York Historical Society library still await much-needed publication. The study of these and of the Society's published volumes of the papers of General Charles Lee, has led me to write of both men in a tone much different from that to be found in the standard works.

One of the most picturesque figures in history, General Charles Lee, had faults of such number and brilliance that it is really unnecessary to be so unjust to him as practically all published history is. His alleged treason at Monmouth, has been, I think, outrageously assumed and magnified ridiculously. I have not attempted to plead for him (or for anyone else more than the documents disclose), but I am tempted to believe that Elias Boudinot, who knew Lee well, was not far wrong in believing that he was touched with insanity. Boudinot's privately published *Journal* gives astonishing evidences in that direction, and Lee's conduct after his court-martial closely resembles that of a paranoiac. This theory, if true, earns for Lee a sense of profound pity—if indeed anybody ever lived who did not deserve profound pity. In any case, Lee seems to have suffered acutely from delusions of grandeur and persecution. Washington had the grandeur without the delusions, and he was not denied persecutions of reality and of exquisite torment.

Charles Lee undoubtedly wavered in his loyalty—as did the vast majority of Americans; but evidence that he ever did anything of treasonable effect, is woefully incomplete and contradictory.

Since Washington was a land-holder, a plutocrat, a farmer, a money-lender, a manufacturer, an exporter and many other things, it was necessary to pay a certain attention to economic and financial matters during this period, and to emphasize the fact that while he was working and fighting without pay and skirting the edge of personal bankruptcy, and while his few devoted officers and soldiers and their families were going naked and hungry, the country in general did not suffer, and many classes grew rich.

The graft and profiteering of the times was stupendous, and it is unjust to Washington as well as to truth, to conceal any longer the fact that the generation of Americans which coincided with the Revolution, was far from being the supremely virtuous race its descendants have been pleased to pretend. I had either to suppress Washington's innumerable denunciations or do something to justify them. Offensive as this material will perhaps appear to certain types of patriot, I regret that I could publish only a slight skimming of the vast cauldron of corruption, greed and selfishness.

If the Americans of that time had been what their posterity imagines, or anything like it, they would have driven the British into the sea in a few weeks and set up a government of ideal beauty immediately. Because they were what they were and were not what they were not, poor Washington was never able to put up a real fight, never able to secure a real army, never able to give his military abilities a real test, but was compelled to spend most of his time running away from a lazy enemy or keeping at a safe distance while he sent out heartbreakingly vain appeals for food, money, old clothes, soldiers, helpful legislation, the deferment of mutual jealousies, some unity of action.

The meekness with which he endured, while denouncing, the evils of his masters, the people, gives him a saintliness unique among great soldiers and creators of nations. But he cannot be understood unless the truth is told about his environment.

Yet I have tried to deal fairly also by the public and by the soldiers, for it seems to me to be the height of folly to expect people to be angels, philosophers or heroes and revile them for falling short of perfections. There was such confusion of conditions then that only posterity could say which people were right and which were wrong, and even that decision has only the value of posterity's own virtue. Posterities alter in every respect and we find an almost rhythmic change of opinion in historians themselves. Our own sufficiently faulty and rebuked generation is posterity to the forefathers and we shall be the forefathers to a later. As we do not expect reverence from our posterity, we need not offer it to our ancestry.

It is perhaps useless to protest that when I speak of the thievery, cowardice, cruelty and laziness of certain individuals or classes or periods, I am not setting myself up as their judge in a superior court, but merely trying to describe them in relation to certain standards. I am not presuming to condemn men for running away from battles, stealing other men's money or reputations, or telling lies about them, but merely picturing their actions as they affected Washington, who had to win the war with what materials he found and build a nation while he restrained its centrifugal forces.

The more I read of the American Revolution the more difficult I find it to understand how it ever could have succeeded. I can hardly believe that it did. As a matter of fact it never did succeed in the way it was meant to at the beginning; and its results were not at all what they were expected to be at the end of it.

But the more I study it, the more I marvel at Washington's greatness and patience and his genius. He was not at all the Washington that is taught in the schools. He was far greater than that bland miracle-worker. He was infinitely human, incessantly guessing wrong, making innumerable false prophecies, countless mistakes, losing his temper, regaining it, being coerced into defeats and dragged away from them, driven into victories in spite of himself and driving others to heights they could not otherwise have attained. I find him eternally fascinating and various; and that is why it is so hard for me to deal briefly with him.

It is out of style to give much space to battles nowadays, but I have given a great amount of space to them, for many reasons. In the first place, this volume concerns a warrior in a war and the war was partly won by battles. Then, it is important to see Washington in the field and in camp; and in both places there is need of large revision in the usual descriptions of him. Finally, battles had a distinct economic and institutional importance. When a battle was won or lost, money rose or fell, with all the social consequences of that influence; political hopes and ideas were also fundamentally altered by the prospects of failure or success.

The Revolutionary War has waited a hundred and fifty years for its "Now it can be told!" for a frank and honest discussion in the same spirit that was attained concerning the

World War within ten years of its close. It is high time that the whole truth should be revealed for its own good sake, and for many other sakes, and though I have neither the space nor the wit for such work, I have given unusual space here not only to the hard lot of the private soldier, good and bad, and of the officers, good and bad, but to camp and hospital and prison horrors, and to the hideous cruelty of graft and inefficiency.

I have made what use I could of all the diaries and letters I could find of officers, soldiers and citizens, and these change the classic pictures materially. The pathos of the individual soldier's lot comes out with appealing and amazing vividness from some of these illiterate writings, and it was difficult indeed to omit, as I had to, all but a phrase or two here and there.

Since it has been my lot to know a good deal of the drudgery of a soldier's life without tasting any of the splendor, I have been particularly interested in the camp life, the paper-work, organization and tactical details which meant so much to Washington's career and his success.

The reader of this volume will feel that the author of it has a very low opinion of the majority of the Americans contemporary with Washington. This is true, and if there were room for more evidence there would be evidence of a still lower opinion—an opinion almost as low as Washington's own.

A few soldiers, a few statesmen, a few devoted men did all the work, suffered all the hardships, and saved the country in spite of itself, while the majority ran away or kept aloof, grew fat and looked on. That was Washington's infinitely repeated declaration, and it is an insult to his memory to conceal it longer.

I have tried to document everything that is offered as the truth, and to indicate what is doubtful. Where I have found fault with a legend or a tradition I have told why. Many biographers prefer to ignore popular anecdotes as if they were beneath the dignity of history, but where the public cherishes beliefs about famous characters, those beliefs should be confirmed or corrected. Washington is peculiarly the victim of legend, and nearly everything the public knows about him is untrue. I have given, therefore, no little space to a discussion of such familiar questions as "Did he swear at Monmouth? Did he pray at Valley Forge? Did he write Washington's Prayer?" and the like. The immense popularity of such riddles gives them a right to attention.

The list of books consulted and quoted will show whether or not I have neglected either the original sources or the results of their study by the eminent scholars who have so much altered the old methods of regarding these times and people. The notes give in each case the source of the authority and, as far as possible, a fair statement of opinions contrary to my own.

I have taken full advantage not only of the documents heaped up by Edmund C. Burnett, in his *Letters of Members of the Continental Congress*, but of his own wisdoms gleaned from them.

Luckily for me, Mr. William L. Clements not only expended the great sums necessary to the purchase and importation and salvation of the Clinton, the Germain and other invaluable documents, but granted me the hospitality of his home and his treasures. There was an almost uncanny delight in sitting up nights reading Sir Henry Clinton's unpublished manuscript history of the war, and seeing Washington through his eyes, and Germain's and Howe's; and in spending days in handling the memoranda and the letters of these men and their correspondents. I have been further provided with a great number of photostats, and permitted to reproduce Clinton's interesting map of the Battle of Monmouth and to quote freely from documents.

Research for which I had neither the time nor the ability fell to my advantage in the scholarship and the generosity of other students of those manuscripts, Professor Claude H. Van Tyne, Randolph G. Adams and Miss Jane Clark, to whom I am more obliged than I can say. Miss Clark has graciously allowed me to quote from her unpublished study of Burgoyne's campaign.

It has been my good fortune, too, to live near the Huntington Library and to enjoy the courtesy of Mr. Leslie E. Bliss, and Mr. Robert O. Shad, and especially of Captain R. E. Haselden, curator of the manuscripts. To Mr. Willard O. Waters I am obliged not only for certain research but for reading the proofs and catching a number of errors.

When I acknowledge a kindness in granting me the access to material, I do not, of course, mean to include any responsibility for the use or misuse I have made of it, or imply any liability for my own opinions or errors.

I must again express my gratitude for the freedom with which the vast riches of the Library of Congress have been opened to inspection; for access to the splendid collections of the New York Public Library, the New York Historical Society, the Virginia State Library, the J. Pierpont Morgan Library, and the gatherings of Dr. Rosenbach.

The interesting and convincingly lifelike frontispiece of this volume has been published only once before, I believe, and then last year. I am indebted to ex-Senator Joseph S. Frelinghuysen for the privilege of reproducing it here. It is the work of Charles Willson Peale, who painted it from life during the Revolution. It was originally obtained from the artist by Judge Robert S. Goldsborough, at whose home, "Maple Grove," near Easton, Md., Peale lived in December, 1779. After the painting had hung there for a hundred and forty-eight years, Senator Frelinghuysen purchased it from the heirs of the Goldsborough estate and it now hangs in his collection of American historical paintings at Far Hills, New Jersey. The portrait is 19½ x 24. It has never been cleaned and is still in its original wooden frame.

The index was prepared, as before, by Mr. O. S. Wadleigh, and Mr. J Dale Eunson once more merits acknowledgment for his care in the transcription of old manuscripts, and blurred photographs, and in the difficult proof reading. I am again, and more than ever, grateful for my wife's tireless aid, enthusiasm and keen-eyed zest for accuracy.

APPENDIX I

NOTES AND REFERENCES

CHAPTER I

1. Sparks, *Correspondence of the American Revolution*, I, p. 317.
2. *Familiar Letters of John Adams and His Wife*, p. 265, April 26, 1777.
3. John Adams, *Works*, I, p. 267.
4. Samuel McCoy, *This Man Adams*, p. 87.
5. John Adams, *Works*, X, pp. 165, 166.
6. Letters of Ebenezer Huntington, *American Historical Review*, V, p. 725.
7. Quoted by General John B. Gordon in his *Reminiscences*, p. 134, when speaking of R. E. Lee and his Washingtonian care not to let his military needs exceed his constitutional bounds.
8. Ford, *Writings*, V, p. 140.
9. Ford, *Writings*, V, p. 145.
10. Gaine's *Mercury*, Feb. 3, 1777. Cited by Moore, *Diary of the Revolution*, I, p. 367.
11. Smythe's Diary, Moore, op. cit., I, p. 399.
12. E. A. and G. L. Duyckinck, *Cyclopædia of American Literature*, I, p. 455.
13. *Tagebuch des Capt. Wiederholdt*, p. 32.
14. Wiederholdt, op. cit., p. 33.
15. *Virginia Folk-lore About George Washington*, by J. S. Wise (Publications of the Sharon, Mass. Hist. Soc., No. 4, April, 1907), p. 15. Captain Wise had these reminiscences from old aunts of his stepmother.
16. Ford, *Writings*, V, p. 145. Letter to Morris, Clymer and Walton, Jan. 1, 1777.
17. E. J. Lowell, *The Hessians*, p. 290. It should be remembered, however, as Lowell notes, that the Hessian was helpless from ignorance of the language and the special hostility of the people, while the English had only to lay off their red coats to pass as citizens. The Americans chiefly deserted to go home, though a disgracefully large number went over to the British army, some of the more humorous of them deserting back to the rebel lines as soon as they had acquired a rifle and a warm uniform. There are many works in German and English proving how cruelly the Hessians have been misjudged.
18. Force, *American Archives*, 5th Series, III, p. 1613. See also Volume II of this work, p. 546. All historians agree that Washington was given the power if not the name of Dictator. Most of them say that he received the dubious gift on December 27th, 1776. But December 12th was the date on which Congress adjourned in Philadelphia to meet in Baltimore, and "Resolved that, until the Congress shall otherwise order, General Washington be possessed of full power to order and direct all things relative to the department and to the operations of war." Force, op. cit., p. 1606.
19. *Familiar Letters of John Adams*, p. 255. April 6, 1777.
20. Ford, *Writings*, VI, p. 197. Letter to J. P. Custis, Nov. 14, 1777. Esti-

mates as to the number and effectiveness of American privateers may be found
in G. W. Allen's *Naval History of the American Revolution*, I, p. 46, J. R.
Speare's *History of the United States Navy*, p. 30, and E. E. Hale's *Naval History of the American Revolution*, in Winsor, *Narrative and Critical History of America*, VI, ch. vii.

21. Force, op. cit., p. 1513.

22. Force, op. cit., p. 1514. Ford, *Writings*, V, p. 145 n.

23. Edwin M. Stone, *Life and Recollections of John Howland*. In the *Pennsylvania Magazine of History and Biography*, XX, p. 515, is a vivid picture of this scene giving Washington's words as recalled by a Sergeant R——, but the account being dated 1832 can hardly be accepted as accurate.

24. Ford, *Writings*, V, pp. 141, 143 n.

25. Wm. Gordon, D.D., *History of the . . . Independence of the U. S. A.*, II, p. 155. Gordon's history "can no longer be accepted as an authority in American history," says Prof. O. G. Libby in an article in the *American Historical Review*, VII, p. 697 (in which he accuses Ramsay of being also an unscrupulous plagiarist from whom Gordon had also plagiarized according to an earlier article by Prof. Libby in the Report of the American Historical Association, 1899, I, p. 367). Still, on occasion, Gordon may be relied on for a picturesque detail, whether stolen or honestly acquired by the research he is known to have made, for we have his letters to and from Washington and others.

CHAPTER II

1. Wm. Gordon, D.D., *History of the . . . Independence*, II, p. 131.

2. W. S. Stryker in *The Battles of Trenton and Princeton*, gives in an Appendix the British and Hessian statements, pp. 328, 319, 334, 400, 398, 424, 426. In his unpublished history of the war, Clinton says that he warned Howe against such a string of posts. His manuscript is at the William L. Clements Library, where is also in the Germain MSS. a long paper called "Hints for the Management of an Intended Enquiry" into the conduct of Howe, whose negligences are scathingly analyzed.

3. General Joseph Reed, in W. B. Reed's biography, I, p. 286. James Wilkinson in his *Memoirs*, I, p. 135 n., says of Roche de Fermoy, "This man, like De Woedtke, turned out a worthless drunkard, although he wore the Croix de St. Louis." Of Hausegger he says that he "did not acquit himself with reputation and was afterwards cashiered." Alexander Graydon, still a prisoner in the British lines, tells in his *Memoirs*, p. 218, how "Houssacker" brought word of the hopelessness of Washington's position after the second battle of Trenton and advised his fellow-captives to mix with the British and change sides. Stryker, op. cit., p. 259, speaks of "the very questionable manner" in which Roche de Fermoy left his post. Humphrey Nickerson, *The Turning Point of the Revolution*, p. 146, states that de Fermoy was found asleep at his post with no orders given, when St. Clair made his retreat from Ticonderoga in July, 1777, and adds that "he may have been a rascal and was certainly grossly incompetent."

4. E. M. Stone, *Life and Recollections of John Howland*, p. 73. B. J. Lossing, *Field-Book of the American Revolution*, II, p. 63, had the anecdote of the scratched arm from Howland's own lips.

5. Ford, *Writings*, V, p. 147.

6. Stryker, op. cit., pp. 265 n., 265.

7. Lossing, op. cit., II, p. 233 n. Stryker gives the name of the murdered

clergyman as Rosbrugh. V. L. Collins in his *President Witherspoon*, II, p. 94, gives it as Rosborough and says that he was killed "under the misapprehension that they were settling scores with the President of the College of New Jersey."

8. F. S. Drake, *Life and Correspondence of Henry Knox*, p. 38.

9. Gordon, op. cit., II, p. 156. Wilkinson, *Memoirs*, I, p. 135.

10. Only the day before, the soldiers of General Mifflin's brigade had shown themselves so indifferent to alarm signals that he had issued a brigade order beginning: "His Excellency Gen. Washington having last night, by Express, ordered the Brigade to be held in readiness to march in the Night, or early this morning, at a minute's notice. The Commanding Officer, in obedience to orders, directed the Brigade to be paraded at two o'clock, but was surprised to find very little Attention paid to the Drums. Had the enemy advanced towards this Town at that time, the Army here might have been, to their eternal Disgrace and the Ruin of their Country, made Prisoners of War." Stryker, op. cit., p. 432.

11. W. B. Reed, *Life and Correspondence of Joseph Reed*, I, p. 286.

12. Reed, op. cit., p. 287.

13. S. G. Fisher, *The Struggle for American Independence*, I, p. 566. Gordon, op. cit., p. 156.

14. Henry Belcher, *The First American Civil War*, II, p. 203.

15. Wilkinson, op. cit., I, p. 138.

16. William Swinton, *Campaigns of the Army of the Potomac*, p. 283, cf. Col. G. F. R. Henderson, *Stonewall Jackson*, II, p. 485.

CHAPTER III

1. Trumbull's account of the picture is given in his *Autobiography* (1841), p. 167. This painting now hangs at Yale University.

2. G. W. Greene, *Life of General Nathanael Greene*, I, ch. xiii.

3. Ford, *Writings*, V, p. 148.

4. C. C. Felton, in *Proceedings, Massachusetts Historical Society*, 1855-1858, p. 335, tells of visiting Princeton, seeing the room where the council was held and in another home "the little round table" at which Washington and the officers sat. He heard there the story that the candle was left burning and as it burned out left traces still preserved.

5. W. S. Stryker, *The Battles of Trenton and Princeton*, document 94, p. 446. The anecdote of Scott is given without naming the authority in *The Magazine of American History*, XIII, p. 504.

6. Wm. B. Reed, *Life and Correspondence of Joseph Reed*, I, p. 287.

7. J. T. Goolrick, *Life of Hugh Mercer*, p. 51. The order of march and the rank of various officers is given variously in various accounts. H. C. Cameron in *American Historical Review*, IV, p. 732, claims to have been the first to call attention to the masterly arrangement of these troops geographically.

8. John Howland, later President of the Rhode Island Historical Society, was in that march with Col. Hitchcock's brigade, and was one of those who stayed the six weeks, then marched home. His vivid story is given in full in Edwin M. Stone's *Life and Recollections of John Howland*, p. 75. It was previously given in Andrew Sherburne's *Memoirs*, p. 301.

9. Stryker, op. cit., document 88, p. 438.

10. J. F. Watson, *Annals of Philadelphia*, II, p. 313, selections from the diary of "Mrs. M. M., a widow lady of respectable character, of tory feelings and prejudices—dwelling at Burlington, New Jersey."

11. Edwin Knott Hopson, Jr., *Captain Daniel Neil,* p. 13, a very brief but very scholarly biography.

12. James Wilkinson, *Memoirs,* I, p. 141 n., says, "I have always been staggered as to the fact of a British brigade having halted at Maidenhead, the night of the 2d of January, when Lord Cornwallis lay at Trenton, only six miles distant, with the intent to engage; yet it is so recorded in British and American history, though the inhabitants of that village now deny the assertion."

13. F. S. Drake, *Life and Corres. of Henry Knox,* p. 37.

14. Sir Henry Clinton's MS., *An Historical Detail of Seven Years Campaigns in North America,* ch. iii, p. 75. (William L. Clements Library.)

15. Wilkinson, op. cit., I, p. 149, says that he believes the story of Erskine's cry was told to Colonel Fitzgerald by Cornwallis' officers when Washington "made a pretext for sending a flag to Brunswick" from Pluckemin. "He was courteously received, and introduced to most of the general officers, who spoke freely of the trick General Washington had played on them, and the race they had run, as they had made a forced march from Trenton to Brunswick— such was their alarm for the safety of their magazine. I ascribe to that visit, though with diffidence, the report of Sir William Erskine's having objected to Lord Cornwallis's postponement of his attack at Trenton, the evening of the 2d; indeed if my recollection does not deceive me, when on hearing the firing in the morning, Lord Cornwallis inquired what it could be, Erskine replied, 'My Lord, it is Washington at Princeton.' The recital of Captain Leslie's death, and the respect with which his body had been treated, affected General Leslie so sensibly, that he retired to a window and shed tears; and when Colonel Fitzgerald returned, he sent his acknowledgments to General Washington."

CHAPTER IV

1. Journal of Captain Thomas Rodney, no. 88 in the Appendix to W. S. Stryker, *The Battles of Trenton and Princeton,* p. 438.

2. The spaniels are described by Wilkinson, who saw them himself, *Memoirs,* I, p. 141.

3. C. H. Van Tyne, *England and America,* p. 132.

4. There is no clear and complete account of this brief but extremely complex affair, and I have had to clarify it as best I could from the mixed and contradictory documents, most of which are contained in the appendix to Stryker's *The Battles of Trenton and Princeton.* I have also made use of Wilkinson's *Memoirs,* E. N. Hopson, Jr.'s, *Captain Daniel Neil,* T. J. Wertenbaker's *The Princeton Battle Monument,* William C. Armstrong's *The Battles in the Jerseys, The Saint Clair Papers,* Drake's *Life of Knox,* Goolrick's *Life of Mercer,* Reed's *Life of Reed,* Greene's *Greene,* Carrington's *Battles of the Revolution* and *Washington the Soldier,* Custis' *Recollections,* Stedman's *American War,* Belcher's *First American Civil War,* Fortescue's *History of the British Army,* as well as Irving, Bancroft, Fisher, Trevelyan, and other standard works.

5. Wertenbaker, op. cit., p. 82.

6. Wilkinson, op. cit., I, pp. 141, 144.

7. V. L. Collins, *A Brief Narrative of the Ravages of the British and Hessians* (Princeton University Library, 1906), p. 43, "General Mercer did not ask for quarter, but fought on till so sorely wounded that he was left for dead." George Lewis, in whose arms he died, told him of the American indignation at his being wounded after he surrendered, to which Mercer replied, "The tale . . .

is untrue, George. My death is owing to myself." G. W. P. Custis, op. cit., p. 183 n.

Gaine's *Mercury*, Jan. 13, 1777. See Frank Moore's *Diary of the Revolution*, I, p. 372 n. The author of this article states that General Mercer "when he was taken up by our people, asked how many the numbers were who had thus attacked him, and upon being told, he cried out with astonishment, 'My God; is it possible? I have often heard of British courage, but never could have imagined to find such an instance as this.'

"Another account says, that the 17th regiment just before they charged the rebels, deliberately pulled off their knapsacks and gave three cheers; then broke through the rebels, faced about, attacked, and broke through a second time. Colonel Mawhood then said, it would be prudent, as they were so few, to retire; upon which the men, one and all, cried out, 'No, no; let us attack them again'; and it was with great difficulty their colonel could induce them to retreat; which at length they performed in the utmost order.

"To the honor of this brave regiment, both as soldiers and as men, not one of them has ever attempted to plunder, nor encouraged it in others."

These boasts from the British side are probably as true, and quite as impartial, as the anecdotes of American tradition. General Mercer's surprise at British courage is in itself surprising since he was himself a surgeon at the battle of Culloden and came to America to escape the persecutions.

8. Wertenbaker, op. cit., p. 96. Hopson, op. cit., p. 21.

9. Stryker, op. cit., pp. 284, 455. Sparks, *Writings*, IV, p. 556. Howe wrote that though he could not contradict the account of the cruel treatment, "I can aver my abhorrency of the barbarity . . . the heat of action will sometimes produce instances that are only to be lamented."

10. *Account of Sergeant R——*. Penn. Mag. of Hist. & Biog., XX, p. 517.

11. Rev. Wm. Gordon, *History of the Independence*, II, p. 157.

12. Custis, op. cit., p. 190.

13. H. P. Johnston, *Yale and Her Honor-Roll in the American Revolution*, p. 60. E. M. Stone, *John Howland*, p. 78. E. M. Avery, *History of the United States*, VI, p. 55.

14. Custis, op. cit., p. 187.

15. Ford, *Writings*, V, p. 148.

16. *Annual Register* for the year 1777, p. 19.

17. George Inman, *Narrative of the Revolution*, Penn. Mag. of Hist. & Biog., VII, p. 242. Wilkinson, op. cit., I, p. 145, says, "They fled in disorder, not toward Maidenhead, as is stated by all historians, but up the north side of Stoney Brook, over fields and fences, without regard to roads, and inclining towards Pennington." A British sergeant Sullivan stated that Mawhood took a lower road to Maidenhead, "missed our brigade and passed by us unobserved in the morning, joined us in the afternoon, after we crossed the river near Princetown." *Penn. Mag.*, XXXII, p. 56.

18. Fortescue, op. cit., III, p. 203. Howe's orders are given in the *Kemble Papers* (N. Y. Hist. Soc., 1883), I, p. 434.

19. Wilkinson, op. cit., p. 146, says that he had this account in 1796 from David Harris himself.

20. Thomas Jones, *History of New York*, II, p. 471.

21. This story is told by Pickering, later adjutant-general, in his letter on Washington's generalship, reproduced in *Tyler's Quarterly*, VII, July, 1925, p. 38. Pickering had it from Major Hoops. In this same letter, Pickering quotes St. Clair's story of Washington's disappearance.

22. F. S. Drake, *Life of Knox*, p. 40.

23. Edward Everett Hale, in his *Memories of a Hundred Years*, I, p. 148, says that Jared Sparks told him the story when Hale was in Harvard, a pupil of Sparks. Sparks did not give Hale the name of the captain, but adds that "a courteous correspondent tells me that the officer in command lived to old age and often repeated the anecdote. It was Captain Varnum of the Massachusetts Line. . . . It was Mercer's advance upon this bridge . . . that brought on the battle."

24. B. J. Lossing, *Field Book of the Revolution*, II, p. 238, says that Kelly was captured by the British, but Stryker, op. cit., p. 289, says that he brought his prisoner into the American lines.

25. Custis, op. cit., p. 186.

26. Thomas Olden's diary, Stryker, op. cit., p. 287 n.

27. Wilkinson, op. cit., p. 148.

28. From a letter in the Rosenbach collection, published in the company's pamphlet, *1776 Americana*.

29. Custis, op. cit., p. 187.

30. Stryker, op. cit., p. 292. His figures, carefully compiled, differ materially from the first hasty reports of Washington as given in his letter to Congress.

31. W. B. Ganoe, *The History of the U. S. Army*, p. 37.

32. Ford, *Writings*, V, p. 149. In this report Washington says that he could not bring off the brass cannon. Other accounts say that he did.

33. Ganoe, op. cit., p. 37.

CHAPTER V

1. G. W. P. Custis, *Recollections*, p. 137. Custis brands as an "absurdity" the story that Washington's mother was a royalist, but admits that she doubted the success of the rebellion. Ramsay, a contemporary, in his biography of Washington, p. 2, makes her a royalist. B. J. Lossing, *Mary and Martha*, p. 58 n., describes "some absurd fictions" about Mary and her home in Fredericksburg, including one about a visit that Washington paid to her, when she looked up from her work in the garden to say laughingly, " 'Well, George, haven't they caught you?' His reply was to hand her a bag of silver." Lossing points out that Mary did not move to Fredericksburg till 1775 and that Washington was not in that town, nor in Virginia, until 1781, when he passed through with foreign officers.

2. Mrs. Roger A. Pryor, *The Mother of Washington*, p. 257.

3. B. J. Lossing, *Washington a Biography*, II, p. 394 n. H. C. Cameron, *Am. Hist. Rev.*, IV, p. 733. Lodge, *The Life of George Washington*, I, p. 183, says "Frederick the Great is reported to have said." Woodrow Wilson, *Life of Washington*, p. 193, says evasively, "Men loved to tell afterwards how Frederick the Great had said that it was the most brilliant campaign of the century." Norman Hapgood, *Life of Washington*, I, p. 172, says, "Frederick is reputed to have," etc. See also E. M. Avery, *A History of the United States*, VI, p. 56, S. G. Fisher, *The Struggle for American Independence*, I, p. 569 n., G. M. Wrong, *Washington and his Comrades* (Chronicles of America), p. 105. Even the careful Stryker, *The Battles of Trenton and Princeton*, p. 464, quotes the fabled praise without question. Sidney Hayden, *Washington and his Masonic Compeers*, 2d ed. 1886, p. 148, says that Frederick "who was at the head of Masonry in Continental Europe sent him an elegant sword."

4. E. J. Lowell, *The Hessians*, p. 52.

5. Friedrich Kapp, *Friedrich der Grosse und die Vereinigten Staaten von Amerika*, p. 27 n. May 9, 1777. Kapp's book speaks frequently of *"Der Hass Friedrichs gegen England"* and *"seine Erbitterung gegen England,"* pp. 37, 38, 39. He describes Frederick's elusive relations with the Americans and his keen interest in Virginia tobacco.

6. Kapp, op. cit., p. 41.

7. J. H. Latané, *A History of American Foreign Policy*, p. 14.

8. Kapp, op. cit., p. 13: "Noch heute glaubt man in Amerika allgemein—so schnell bemächtigt sich der Mythus populärer Gestalten—dass Friedrich seiner Anerkennung Washington's durch Uebersendung eines Ehrendegens Ausdruck verliehen habe; ja selbst wissenschaftliche Zeitschriften wiederholen gläubig diese Fabel, die sich, wie es scheint, auf die Thatsache stützt, dass der preussische Waffenschmied Theophilus Alte in Solingen Washington einen selbstgearbeiteten schönen Säbel mit einer bewundernden Inschrift schenkte."

In his *Der Soldatenhandel deutscher Fürsten nach Amerika*, Kapp shows that Frederick should never have been credited with readiness to recognize American independence, "when he really was not ready to do anything of the kind." The fable of the sword was further dispelled by Moncure D. Conway, *Century Magazine*, April, 1901, who says that Carlyle told him that in all his researches he found no incident or phrase as a basis for the story of the sword. See also Leland Haworth, *American Historical Review*, IX, p. 476. But nothing seems to check its vitality.

Edward J. Lowell, *The Hessians*, p. 54, even thinks that Kapp overestimates in his *Friedrich der Grosse*, p. 71, the beneficial effect on the American cause of the delay Frederick caused in the shipment of Hessians. J. G. Rosengarten, *Frederick the Great and the U. S.* (a paper read before the Pennsylvania-German Society, Oct. 25, 1904), Lancaster, Pa., 1906, sums up the story of Frederick and America.

Concerning the sword see also Sparks, *Writings*, XI, p. 169 (Ford, *Writings*, XIII, p. 269), and Washington's letter of September 12, 1796, to John Quincy Adams, then at The Hague, describing the "curious affair" of the mysterious blade, of which he says, "It has my name engraved thereon and the following inscription, translated from the Dutch, 'Condemner of despotism, Preserver of Liberty, glorious Man, take from my Son's hands, this Sword, I beg you. A. Solingen.'"

Washington thought it and the inscription Dutch and credited it to Amsterdam.

9. Kapp, *Friedrich der Grosse*, p. 38. Lord Mahon, *History of England*, VI, p. 87, says that "Frederick . . . had no especial love or care for the North American cause; indeed it is scarcely mentioned in his most familiar letters, unless for a sorry jest on the name of General Howe: *Nous entendons parler du General Howe dont chaque chien en aboyant prononce le nom.*" (A Voltaire, le 17 Juin 1777.) The story of the portrait sent by Frederick is cited from the New Jersey *Journal* in Frank Moore's *Diary of the Revolution*, II, p. 309.

10. Heinrich Dietrich von Bülow, *Militärische und vermischte Schriften* (Leipzig, 1853), p. 52.

11. Charles Botta, *History of the War of Independence*, translated by G. A. Otis, I, p. 429.

12. Horace Walpole, *Correspondence*, III, p. 73.

13. Horace Walpole, *Memoirs of George II*, I, p. 347. See volume I of this work, p. 120.

14. Horace Walpole, to Sir Horace Mann, April 3, 1777.

15. Nicholas Creswell, *Journal*, pp. 181, 180.
16. Morris and Hooper are cited by Bancroft, *History of the United States*, IX, p. 256.
17. Frank Moore, *Songs and Ballads of the American Revolution*, p. 156.

CHAPTER VI

1. Wm. Gordon, *History of the . . . Independence*, II, p. 157, says that Knox urged Morristown, "while Greene had already set off in that direction." George W. Greene, *Life of Nathanael Greene*, 1840, says that Greene "had already anticipated Washington's happy decision to establish his quarters at Morristown." But F. V. Greene, *General Greene*, p. 65, says "To what extent Greene participated in planning these movements it is impossible to say." F. S. Drake, *Life of Henry Knox*, p. 40, says "Knox recommended the march to Morristown, which he had observed to be a good position. . . . His earnest importunities prevailed." For St. Clair's claim see Appendix II.

2. James Wilkinson, *Memoirs*, I, p. 149. Adjutant-General Pickering wrote in 1824, "Here, too, the happy expedient was suggested by St. Clair." (Tyler's *Quarterly*, July, 1925, p. 38.) W. H. Smith, *The St. Clair Papers*, I, p. 42; "Again St. Clair's quick perception and information proved useful to Washington. In passing to the northward in the beginning of the campaign, St. Clair's route lay through Morristown . . . he had thereby an opportunity to see some part of those hills which were afterwards of so great use . . . St. Clair described Morristown and its vicinity to General Washington as a place where an army could be cantoned. He quickly decided, and the army had orders to take the route towards that place, and St. Clair was left with a rear-guard to destroy the bridges, the last of which was barely effected when the enemy appeared and fired upon the Americans."

3. Ford, *Writings*, V, p. 149.
4. Sir George Otto Trevelyan, *The American Revolution*, III, p. 321. W. S. Stryker, *The Battles of Trenton and Princeton*, p. 303.
5. Ford, *Writings*, V, p. 151.
6. Ford, *Writings*, V, p. 154.
7. Wilkinson, op. cit., I, p. 150.
8. Ford, *Writings*, V, p. 171. B. J. Lossing, *Washington, a Biography*, II, p. 399 n.
9. Edwin Knott Hopson, Jr., *Captain Daniel Neil*, pp. 26-30.
10. E. C. Burnett, *Letters of Members of the Continental Congress*, II, p. 378. See also p. 585, and III, p. 162, *Journals of Congress*, Aug. 24, 25, 1780.
11. Sparks, *Writings*, IV, p. 308 n., says that this attack was really the idea of the New York Convention, which sent along a committee to carry out its ideas, with which Washington merely fell in. Later they wrote to Washington and criticized the conduct of the unhappy expedition.
12. Ford, *Writings*, V, p. 153.
13. Ford, *Writings*, V, p. 155.
14. Maj. Gen. Wm. Heath, *Memoirs*, p. 113. This book was ridiculed at the time, according to W. C. Ford (*Am. Hist. Rev.*, XXIII, p. 278), who describes it as the "earliest printed autobiography after the War," and states that Heath was charged with publishing it "to promote an election to office. . . . He attained rank without distinction, and grew corpulent in inaction and performance . . . his book was greeted by smiles on all sides. It was impossible

to misinterpret such a delightful piece of vanity. Its historical value shrinks before its personal quality." Throughout the book Heath quaintly refers to himself as "Our General."

15. Ford, *Writings*, V, pp. 174, 178.
16. Ford, *Writings*, V, p. 191.
17. Ford, *Writings*, V, p. 206 n.
18. Ford, *Writings*, V, p. 214.
19. Ford, *Writings*, V, p. 217.
20. Sparks, *Correspondence of the American Revolution*, I, p. 336.
21. Allen French in *The Day of Concord and Lexington* describes Heath's activities and achievements on that great day.

CHAPTER VII

1. John Adams, *Works*, III, p. 70 n.
2. Holt, *Journal*, Oct. 19, 1775, quoted in Frank Moore's *Diary of the Revolution*, I, p. 153. On May 28, 1777, Washington himself wrote to Congress, "We are told government offered the prisoners they took to the India Company." Ford, *Writings*, V, p. 396.
3. Hinkhouse, *The Preliminaries of the American Revolution as seen in the English Press*, p. 162.
4. W. Massey, *History of England During the Reign of George III*, Vol. II, p. 230, cited by W. B. Donne, *Correspondence of George III*, II, p. 65.
5. W. Bodham Donne, *The Correspondence of King George the Third with Lord North*, II, pp. 54, 55.
6. George Ives, *A History of Penal Methods*, p. 263.
7. Lord Mahon (Earl Stanhope), *History of England from the Peace of Utrecht to the Peace of Versailles* (5th Ed.), III, p. 318.
8. Adams, *Works*, III, p. 91.
9. Ford, *Writings*, VI, p. 466. Letter to Congress, April 10, 1778.
10. *The Annual Register*, 1781, XXIV, pp. 143, 322.
11. G. T. Crook, *The Complete Newgate Calendar*, IV, pp. 153, 156.
12. Crook, op. cit., IV, p. 264. Oddly enough, Lord Ellenborough's younger brother, Thomas Law, came to America in 1793 and married Elizabeth (Eliza) Parke Custis, eldest child of Jacky Custis. The marriage was unhappy and she left him, resuming her maiden name. See Edith Tunis Sale's *Old Time Belles and Cavaliers*, p. 228, where it is erroneously stated that Law was a nephew of Lord Ellenborough. Law is frequently mentioned in Washington's diaries of the period.

CHAPTER VIII

1. E. C. Burnett, *Letters of Members of the Continental Congress*, II, p. 243.
2. Ford, *Writings*, V, p. 202.
3. Burnett, op. cit., pp. 243, 292.
4. *New York Gazette*, February 10, 1777, cited in Moore, *Diary of the American Revolution*, I, p. 383.
5. Ford, *Writings*, V, p. 235 n. From the accusation of encouraging perjury Washington clears himself and repeats his statement that many were forced to take the oath of royal allegiance, in his letter to Congress, Feb. 5, 1777:
"From the first institution of civil government, it has been the national policy

of every precedent State to endeavor to engage its members to the discharge of their duty by the obligation of some oath . . . I have often thought the States have been too negligent in this particular, and am more fully convinced of it from the effect General Howe's excursion has produced in New Jersey. An oath is the only substitute that can be adopted to supply the defect of principle. By our inattention in this article, we lose a considerable cement to our own force, and give the enemy an opportunity to make the first tender of the oath of allegiance to the King. Its baneful influence is but too severely felt at this time. The people generally confess they were compelled to take protection, and subscribe the *Declaration,* yet it furnishes many with arguments to refuse taking any active part; and further they allege themselves bound to a neutrality at least. Many conscientious people, who were well-wishers to the cause, had they been bound to the States by an oath, would have suffered any punishment rather than have taken the oath of allegiance to the King; and are now lost to our interest for want of this necessary tie. Notwithstanding the obligations of the *Association,* they do not conceive it to have the same effect as an oath." Ford, *Writings,* V, p. 222.

6. Henry Belcher, *The First American Civil War,* II, p. 211.

CHAPTER IX

1. Edward McCrady, *History of South Carolina in the Revolution, 1775-1780,* Chapter XIV. See also the defence of Washington by H. L. Osgood, *American Historical Review,* VII, p. 167.

2. N. W. Stephenson, *The Day of the Confederacy* (Chronicles of America Series), p. 30.

3. Dr. Herbert Friedenwald, *The Continental Congress, Report of American Historical Association,* 1894, p. 233.

4. Ford, *Writings,* V, p. 211 n.

5. Sparks, *Writings,* IV, p. 337.

6. Gen. Emory Upton, *The Military Policy of the United States,* p. 27.

7. Ford, *Writings,* V, p. 201.

8. Ford, *Writings,* V, p. 159.

9. *William and Mary Quarterly,* IV, p. 104.

10. Ford, *Writings,* V, p. 309.

11. W. C. Ford, *Orderly Books of the Revolution,* No. 1, *Orders of Major-General Heath* (Privately Printed), p. 5.

12. W. C. Ford, *General Orders Issued by Major-General Israel Putnam* (Privately Printed), p. 44.

13. Ford, *Writings,* V, pp. 256, 342.

14. Ford, *Writings,* V, p. 343.

15. Ford, *Writings,* V, p. 251.

16. Ford, *Writings,* V, p. 302.

17. C. H. Van Tyne, *England and America,* p. 131.

18. C. H. Van Tyne, *The American Revolution,* p. 134.

19. *Magazine of American History,* VII, p. 137.

20. Ford, *Writings,* V, p. 254.

21. Sparks, *Correspondence of the Revolution,* I, p. 361.

22. Ford, *Writings,* V, p. 327.

23. Ford, *Writings,* V, p. 206.

24. Ford, *Writings,* V, p. 242 n.

25. Ford, *Writings*, V, p. 276.
26. Ford, *Writings*, V, p. 286.
27. Ford, *Writings*, V, p. 302.
28. Ford, *Writings*, V, p. 372.
29. Ford, *Writings*, V, p. 323.
30. Ford, *Writings*, V, p. 323 n.
31. Ford, *Writings*, V, p. 222.
32. Ford, *Writings*, V, p. 421.
33. Ashbel Green, *Life*, p. 88.
34. Nicholas Creswell, *Journal*, p. 203.
35. Green, op. cit., p. 92.
36. V. L. Collins, *President Witherspoon*, II, p. 19.
37. E. C. Burnett, *Letters of Members of the Continental Congress*, II, p. 339.
38. B. H. Wise, *Memoir of General John Cropper*, p. 11.
39. Cited by Frank Moore, *Diary of the American Revolution*, I, p. 444.
40. Ford, *Writings*, V, p. 256.
41. Ford, *Writings*, V, p. 262 n.   J. C. Ballagh, *Letters of R. H. Lee*, I, p. 269.
42. Col. Matlack in *Military Papers of General John Cadwalader*, Penn. Mag., XXXII, p. 163.
43. Fortescue, *History of the British Army*, III, p. 204.
44. Ford, *Writings*, V, p. 263 n.
45. Sparks, *Writings*, IV, p. 338. The version in the text follows that of the original without Sparks' improvements. (See Henkel's Catalog, p. 31, No. 677, Dec. 15, 16, 1891.)

CHAPTER X

1. Ford, *Writings*, V, p. 351.
2. W. C. Ford, *General Orders Issued by . . . Putnam*, pp. 5, 23, 34, 83.
3. Private Somerville, *Autobiography*, pp. 288-9, cited by George Ives, *A History of Penal Methods*, p. 154.
4. Sir Charles Napier, *Remarks on Military Law*, p. 160, cited by Ives, op. cit., p. 149. Surgeon Thacher, *Military Journal*, p. 182, gives his own vivid sensations on seeing American soldiers flogged. He also describes the ordeal of the gauntlet and the bayonet.
5. Wm. Cobbett, *Advice to a Young Man*, par. 44, cited by G. D. H. Cole, *The Life of William Cobbett*, p. 30.
6. G. D. H. Cole, op. cit., p. 151.
7. Major W. A. Ganoe, *History of the U. S. Army*, pp. 129, 174, 262.
8. F. A. Shannon, *The Organization and Administration of the Union Army, 1861-1865*, I, pp. 175, 227.
9. Ford, *Writings*, I, pp. 303, 411.
10. C. K. Bolton, *The Private Soldier Under Washington*, p. 170 n.
11. Ford, *Writings*, V, p. 307.
12. Ford, *Writings*, VI, p. 350.
13. Henry Whiting, *Revolutionary Orders of General Washington*, p. 39.
14. Whiting, op. cit., p. 64.
15. Ford, *Writings*, IX, p. 127.
16. Bolton, op. cit., pp. 171-6.
17. *Orderly Book of Major William Heth* (Virginia Historical Collections, XI, new series, p. 347).

18. Captain B. H. Liddell Hart, *Great Captains Unveiled,* p. 111.
19. *Huntington Papers* (Conn. Hist. Soc. Coll.), XX, p. 301.
20. *Letters of Ebenezer Huntington,* Am. Hist. Rev., V, p. 721.
21. *Huntington Papers,* p. 48.
22. Ella Lonn, *Desertion During the Civil War* (Am. Hist. Assn., 1929), pp. V, 124, 147, 226-236 et passim.

CHAPTER XI

1. *Diary of James Allen, Esq., of Philadelphia.* Penn. Mag. of Hist. & Biog., IX, p. 283.
2. E. C. Burnett, *Letters of Members of the Continental Congress,* II, p. 300. John Adams, *Works,* I, p. 263.
3. Ford, *Writings,* V, p. 192.
4. Ford, *Writings,* V, p. 273.
5. Burnett, op. cit., II, p. 311. Elbridge Gerry to Joseph Trumbull: "He is considered by Congress as a brave and deserving Officer, and had it been possible to have proceeded in the line of Succession in appointing officers would undoubtedly have been promoted. This cannot be done with° giving great Dissatisfaction to the States that had no officers in the army in the beginning of the War; who claim a Right to their proportion, agreable to the Number of Men wch. they furnish for the Service, of Major and Brig. Generals . . . I think General Arnold will meet a timely promotion."
6. Sparks, *Writings,* IV, p. 344.
7. Ford, *Writings,* V, p. 270 n.
8. Ford, *Writings,* V, p. 350.
9. Ford, *Writings,* V, p. 168.
10. *Lee Papers,* II, pp. 358, 357.
11. Ford, *Writings,* V, p. 240 n.
12. *Lee Papers,* II, p. 358. February 10, 1777.
13. Dr. Rush's Diary cited by Burnett, op. cit., II, pp. 263, 269, 299. *Journals of Congress,* Feb. 21, 1777.
14. Ford, *Writings,* V, pp. 266, 267 n. G. H. Moore, *Treason of Charles Lee,* p. 106.
15. *Journal of Elias Boudinot* (Privately Printed), p. 74.
16. *Lee Papers,* II, p. 361.
17. *Magazine of American History,* III, p. 450.
18. Moore's work, published in 1860, is also reproduced in Vol. IV of the collection of *Lee Papers* published by the New York Historical Society, together with three other Lee biographies. John Fiske in his "Charles Lee, The Soldier of Fortune," *Essays Historical and Literary,* I, p. 85, believes that Lee's scheme throws light on Howe's later movements, and finds nothing good in Lee's character; but Howe always looked to Philadelphia, which Lee declared worthless, and Fiske makes Lee a more perfect villain than facts warrant.
19. *Lee Papers,* II, p. 394.
20. J. C. Ballagh, *The Letters of R. H. Lee,* I, p. 266. In Howe's letter to Germain, July 16, 1777 (*Correspondence of King George III,* edited by Sir John Fortescue, III, p. 462), Howe speaks of preferring to go up the Delaware but then, as always, his whole purpose was to attack Philadelphia, whose capture Lee wisely said would be of no final value.
21. Burnett, op. cit., II, p. 316.

22. Ford, *Writings*, VII, p. 117. See also Thomas Balch's *Les Français en Amérique*, p. 68 (or in T. W. Balch's translation, *The French in America*, p. 78). Doniol in his enormous work, *Histoire de la participation de la France*, etc., devotes a whole chapter to *Du Coudray et Ses Intrigues* (II, p. 353), and says that his American dreams were as ambitious as De Broglie's. He quotes Lafayette's estimate of him as "a mischief-maker (*brouillon*), a good officer, but vain to insanity." Lafayette says that his death by drowning in Sept., 1777, was "Perhaps a happy accident." (II, p. 317.)

23. F. S. Drake, *Life of Knox*, p. 42. Noah Brooks, *Henry Knox*, p. 91.

24. Burnett, op. cit., II, p. 404. See *Journal of Congress* and biographies of the three generals.

25. John Adams, *Works*, I, p. 265.

CHAPTER XII

1. Ford, *Writings*, V, p. 250. February 23, 1777, to Joseph Reed.
2. Ford, *Writings*, V, p. 266.
3. Sparks, *Writings*, IV, pp. 546-8-9.
4. Gardner W. Allen, *A Naval History of the American Revolution*, I, p. 83. Charles Martyn, *Artemas Ward*, p. 226 n. Charles H. Walcott has written a privately printed monograph, *Sir Archibald Campbell*.
5. Cushing, *Writings of Samuel Adams*, IV, p. 340. E. C. Burnett, *Letters of Members of the Continental Congress*, II, p. 209.
6. C. Stedman, *History of the American War*, I, p. 169.
7. Ford, *Writings*, V, p. 255.
8. Ford, *Writings*, V, p. 258. Sparks, *Writings*, IV, p. 334.
9. Ford, *Writings*, V, p. 257 n.
10. Sparks, *Writings*, IV, p. 350. Ford, *Writings*, V, p. 274.
11. Burnett, op. cit., II, p. 302.
12. Sparks, *Writings*, IV, pp. 559, 560.
13. Sparks, *Writings*, IV, p. 460. Ford, *Writings*, V, p. 430.
14. *Lee Papers* (New York Hist. Soc. Coll.), II, p. 371.
15. W. W. Atterbury, *Elias Boudinot* (read before the Huguenot Society, Feb. 15, 1894), p. 5.
16. Elias Boudinot, *Journal of Historical Recollections*, p. 9.
17. Boudinot, op. cit., pp. 19, 24, 47, 68.
18. P. M. Ashburn, *A History of the Medical Department of the U. S. A.*, p. 20.
19. MS. Letter, April 9, 1778, Benjamin Rush to General Gates, N. Y. Hist. Soc. Coll.
20. H. E. Brown, *The Medical Department of the U. S. A.*, p. 46.
21. Brown, op. cit., p. 46.
22. See the quotations from the *Freeman's Journal* and the *Connecticut Journal* for January, 1777, concerning the abominable mistreatment of prisoners, cited in Moore's *Diary of the American Revolution*, I, pp. 374-8, and for an instance of kindliness on a British prison ship, a citation from the New Hampshire *Gazette*, November 2, 1779, in Moore's work, II, p. 219. There is a large literature about the horrors of British prison ships. In chapter XVIII of Allen, op. cit., II, is an unusually fair and full account of the whole subject of military as well as naval prisoners. A reference to a subscription taken up for American

prisoners in England is found in Ashbel Green's *Life*, p. 79. He says, "it were criminal to withhold" it.

23. G. W. Allen, op. cit., II, p. 655.

24. Cited in E. F. de Lancey's notes to Thomas Jones, *History of New York* (N. Y. Hist. Soc. Coll), I, p. 705.

25. Cited by de Lancey, op. cit., I, p. 706.

26. Rivington's *Gazette*, June 9, 1781. Cited by Moore, op. cit., II, p. 435.

27. R. H. Phelps, *Newgate of Connecticut*, p. 53. This is a fairly complete history of the Simsbury Mines.

28. Ford, *Writings*, V, p. 294.

29. Ford, *Writings*, IV, p. 309. To Gent—Gen. Howe, July 30, 1776. Sparks, *Writings*, IV, p. 23. Howe's answer is on p. 512.

30. Sparks, *Writings*, IV, p. 141. Ford, *Writings*, IV, p. 477.

31. Ford, *Writings*, V, p. 167.

32. Ford, *Writings*, V, p. 170 n.

33. Ford, *Writings*, V, p. 311.

34. Sparks, *Writings*, IV, p. 558.

35. Ford, *Writings*, V, p. 423.

36. At a conference of the American Historical Society in 1908, on "Research in American Colonial and Revolutionary History," Professor C. H. Van Tyne mentioned a need that has not yet been met: "The subject of prisoners of war and of their treatment, of the prisons themselves, of the exchange of prisoners with the enemy, of the parole system, and of the mutual recriminations of English and Americans will give ample opportunity for a critical use of the sources and for a display of impartiality and justice in dealing with prejudiced testimony."

37. [Alex. Graydon] *Memoirs of a Life*, pp. 240, 222.

CHAPTER XIII

1. Ford, *Writings*, V, pp. 195, 499 n. See also Vol. II, p. 533 of this work.

2. Ford, *Writings*, X, p. 132. An excellent study of the aides is to be found in Berthold Fernow's "Washington's Military Family," *Magazine of American History*, VII, p. 81. A still better is found in Chapter V of John C. Fitzpatrick's *The Spirit of the Revolution*.

3. Ford, *Writings*, V, p. 247 n.

4. Unpublished letter from Washington to St. Clair, April 10, 1778, in the Huntington Library.

5. Unpublished letter from James McHenry, Dec. 13, 1798; in the Huntington Library.

6. W. S. Baker, *Itinerary of General Washington*, p. 69.

7. A. H. Vandenberg, *The Greatest American, Alexander Hamilton*, p. 243. This work is hardly more than a hymn of adoration to Hamilton. For a decidedly different view of him supported by infinite documentation see Claude G. Bowers' superbly realistic *Jefferson and Hamilton*.

8. M. L. Davis, *Memoirs of Aaron Burr*, I, p. 79.

9. James Parton, *Life of Aaron Burr*, p. 84. See also Samuel H. Wandell and Meade Minnigerode's *Aaron Burr*, I, p. 60.

10. Hamilton, *Works*, IX, p. 232. In his note, the editor, Henry Cabot Lodge, says that it "would have been perfectly justifiable to have destroyed or suppressed this letter altogether, for it was written by Hamilton when he was very

angry, and had lost control of himself, so that the opinions here expressed do not in the least represent his real feeling about Washington, for whom he had the deepest reverence and affection, either at this or at any other time." Both of these statements are open to doubt, but Lodge objects to the action of Hamilton's son in publishing only part of the letter: "He should have given all or nothing." So Lodge publishes it entire.

11. David Meade, *Meade Family History*, Wm. & Mary Quarterly, XIII, p. 97.

12. Cited by H. J. Ford, *Alexander Hamilton*, p. 56. The passage from Fitzpatrick is op. cit., pp. 67-74. See also F. S. Oliver, *Alexander Hamilton*, pp. 70, 73. "It is beyond question that the messages to Congress, and the correspondence with British generals, which impressed Europe with the dignity and power of the American leader, were mainly the work of Hamilton's mind. The official correspondence of Washington during this period had a wide audience and a great celebrity, and while we must acknowledge the credit due to his secretary in the vigour, the logical arrangement, the lucidity and the stateliness of these documents, we are no less bound to beware of the absurd explanation which has depicted the commander-in-chief as a kind of puppet. It is a favourite device of a certain class of commentators upon great men to attribute their excellences always to someone else, and Hamilton has not altogether escaped this indiscreet tribute, either during his life or subsequently. But certainly he never sought it, nor gave the least colour to the legend. Washington was not the readiest of writers, but he held his opinions in a vice; and we may safely assume that if his vivacious secretary had happened upon any occasion to set forth his own views and not those of his chief, the despatch containing them would have been rewritten before it was signed. It is not unfair, however, nor is it any derogation from the splendid character of the commander-in-chief, to say that Hamilton began by writing to his instructions, and ended by divining, interpreting and anticipating his thoughts. . . .

"In the following year we find for the first time murmurs against the undue influence exercised by Hamilton upon the mind of Washington. The charge was maintained till the end of his days, and in later years became one of the chief cries of the Democratic party."

13. Ford, *Writings*, I, p. 219. See Vol. I of this work, p. 292.

14. P. L. Ford, *The True George Washington*, p. 76. By "Sim's" is meant Thomas Simes' *Military Guide* according to Colonel O. L. Spaulding, Jr., in an article on "The Military Studies of George Washington," *American Historical Review*, XXIX, p. 675.

15. F. V. Greene, *General Greene*, p. 16. F. S. Drake's *Knox*, p. 12.

16. Bishop Meade, *Old Churches of Virginia*, I, p. 295.

17. Everett T. Tomlinson, "Winters at Morristown," in N. Y. *World*, Feb. 20, 1927. See also letter from Colonel Fitzgerald in K. M. Rowland's *Charles Carroll of Carrollton*, I, p. 201, and the letter from Arnold, in Sparks' *Correspondence*, I, p. 359.

18. Letter of March 8, 1777, cited in J. G. Palfrey's *Life of William Palfrey*, Sparks' American Biography, new series, VII, p. 424.

19. G. W. P. Custis, *Recollections*, p. 138.

20. Mrs. A. H. Wharton, *Martha Washington*, pp. 112-118.

21. Frank Moore, *Diary of the Revolution*, I, pp. 446, 477.

CHAPTER XIV

1. Cited in Frank Moore's *Diary of the Revolution*, I, p. 407.
2. In a letter from England quoted by the Penn. *Evening Post*, May 15, 1777, cited in Moore, op. cit., I, p. 442.
3. Sir G. O. Trevelyan's *The American Revolution*, I, p. 250, and there is much about Rigby in Vol. I of this work, and throughout *The Correspondence of King George III*.
4. C. Stedman, *The American War*, I, p. 284.
5. Ford, *Writings*, V, p. 321.
6. Ford, *Writings*, V, p. 371.
7. W. W. Henry, *Patrick Henry*, I, p. 518.
8. J. T. Adams, *New England in the Republic*, p. 19.
9. Elias Boudinot, *Journal*, p. 54. See also Rev. G. F. Tuttle, *"Washington at Morristown,"* Harper's Magazine, February, 1859, cited by Lossing, *Life of Washington*, II, p. 415 n.
10. Ford, *Writings*, V, pp. 310-311.
11. Wm. Nelson, *The American Newspapers of the 18th Century as Sources of History* (Reports Am. Hist. Assn., 1908, I, p. 220).
12. G. W. P. Custis, *Recollections*, pp. 294-9. Reverend Ashbel Green, who knew Rivington well and "dealt with him pretty largely," is also authority for this fact (*Life*, p. 45), and it explains why, after the evacuation of New York, he was enabled to continue in business. Even Dr. Witherspoon was unaware of Rivington's true position and "gibbeted him in a pamphlet." W. L. Stone, in J. G. Wilson's *Memorial History of New York* (IV, p. 140), mentions that "It has been said and believed that Rivington, after all, was a secret traitor to the crown, and in fact the secret spy for General Washington. Be this, however, as it may, etc." According to Wm. Nelson, op. cit., p. 219, Hugh Gaine tried to play both sides by publishing a Tory paper in New York and a patriot edition in New Jersey. Dr. Green's *Life*, picturesque and valuable as it is in many phases of American life during a long period, seems to be generally unknown. It is not mentioned by Winsor or in Channing and Hart's *Guide* nor even in the extensive bibliographies of the American Historical Association. See also H. P. Johnston, "The Secret Service of the Revolution," in *Magazine of American History*, VIII, p. 96.
13. Ford, *Writings*, V, p. 385 n.
14. C. E. Godfrey, *The Commander-in-Chief's Guard*, p. 39. See also G. W. P. Custis, *Recollections*, ch. VII. Lossing, *Field Book of the Revolution*, II, p. 120 n., gives information obtained from Custis and others, also a picture of the banner of the Guard.
15. Ford, *Writings*, V, p. 349.
16. Custis, op. cit., p. 259.
17. Ford, *Writings*, V, p. 333.
18. Communicated to the author in a letter from Mr. Harlan F. Burket.
19. Ford, *Writings*, V, p. 397.
20. Sparks, *Writings*, IV, p. 461.
21. Ford, *Writings*, V, p. 411 n. See also Alexander Hamilton's account, *Works*, IX, p. 76.
22. Graydon, *Memoirs*, p. 247.
23. Ford, *Writings*, V, p. 436.
24. Stedman, op. cit., p. 284.

APPENDIX I

25. Nicholas Creswell, *Journal*, pp. 251, 254, 255, 256.

26. Mrs. Henry Champion, *American Flag*, in *Journal of American History*, I, no. 1, p. 13, tells the Ross story and quotes an entry of a draft on the Treasury, May, 1777, "Pay Betsey Ross £14, 12s. 2d. for flags for fleet in Delaware river." Mrs. Champion also gives reasons for dismissing the coat of arms as the source.

27. G. E. Hastings, *Francis Hopkinson*, pp. 257, 466.

28. In a letter to me, Mr. Ballard Thruston sums up the startling results of his deep research. They completely discredit the Betsy Ross legend, and show that the Stars and Stripes were intended for the navy while "Washington and the Board of War agreed upon an entirely different design for the army to carry as national colors." Mr. Thruston's investigations in the correspondence between Washington and the Board of War from 1779 to 1783 proved that it was impossible to obtain the materials for the colors in this country and they were ordered from France. But "the materials did not arrive and the colors were not made until the winter of 1782-3. Those colors were in the hands of the Field Commissary of Military Stores in March 1783, but so far nothing has been found to show that they were ever distributed to the army."

CHAPTER XV

1. Lieutenant-Colonel O. P. Robinson, *The Fundamentals of Military Strategy*, p. 56.

2. *Annual Register* for 1777, XX, pp. 47-49. See Trevelyan's *American Revolution*, III, ch. XXIV, for a very full statement of English fears that the loss of American liberty meant the end of British freedom.

3. C. H. Van Tyne, *The War of Independence, American Phase*, p. 381. "Military experts have assumed that this was the aim of the British Government and its generals. In all the available correspondence as to the aim of the campaign, not a sentence makes any such proposal."

The quotations from Major General Robertson are taken from his cross-examination before the House of Commons as reported in *The Detail and Conduct of the American War*, 3rd ed. (London, 1780), p. 102. He adds: "Hudson's river actually divides the northern from the southern provinces; the northern produce cattle which are wanted in the southern, and they again wheat which is wanted in the northern; our possessing that river would almost cut off all communication between them. It is a great object, and would greatly distress them."

4. *Detail and Conduct of the American War*, p. 135.

5. T. J. Huddleston, *Gentleman Johnny Burgoyne*, p. 110.

6. F. E. Chadwick, *Sea Power: the Decisive Factor in our Struggle for Independence*, American Hist. Ass'n Reports, 1915, p. 173. C. H. Van Tyne, op. cit., p. 371, says: "It must be accredited to that 'sluggard in war,' General Gates, that with no gentle methods he placed Arnold in charge of that work despite Congress itself."

7. A. T. Mahan, *The Major Operations of the Navies in the War of American Independence*, p. 25.

8. Ford, *Writings*, VI, p. 231. Dec. 2, 1777.

9. Jane Clark, *Responsibility for the Failure of the Burgoyne Campaign*, MS.

10. Lord Fitzmaurice, *Life of William, Earl of Shelburne*, 2nd ed., I, p. 247. Historic MSS. Commission, Knox MSS., VI, p. 277. Hoffman Nickerson, *The*

Turning Point of the Revolution, pp. 94-98, 464-5. He is in sharp dispute with Channing (*History of the U. S.,* III, pp. 247-250), who scouts the story of the mislaid orders of Germain to Howe and denies that "the authorities in England had in mind any permanent conquest of the Hudson Valley by Burgoyne." E. B. de Fonblanque, *Rt. Hon. J. Burgoyne,* p. 233 n. Sir John Fortescue, *History of the British Army,* III, p. 210.

11. *Detail and Conduct of the American War,* pp. 102, 105.
12. Ford, *Writings,* V, pp. 458, 471 n.
13. *Detail and Conduct of the American War,* p. 60.
14. Ford, *Writings,* VI, p. 2.
15. Ford, *Writings,* V, p. 521.
16. E. C. Burnett, *Letters of Members of the Continental Congress,* II, p. 413.
17. Ford, *Writings,* V, p. 490.
18. *St. Clair Papers,* I, p. 429.
19. *St. Clair Papers,* I, p. 437.
20. Burnett, op. cit., II, p. 435.
21. *Huntington Papers,* p. 66. John Chester to Joshua Huntington.
22. *Familiar Letters of John Adams and his Wife,* p. 292.
23. Burnett, op. cit., II, p. 437. Lovell's Letter. See also W. C. Ford, *Journals of Congress,* Aug. 1, 2, 3, 1777.
24. Ford, *Writings,* VI, p. 3.
25. Ford, *Writings,* VI, p. 17.
26. Ford, *Writings,* V, p. 504.
27. Ford, *Writings,* V, p. 493.
28. See Sparks, *Correspondence,* II, p. 515. "An Indian scout of ours returned this morning, and brought with them five prisoners. The enemy, not knowing we had Indians in our service, were decoyed, thinking them their own." General Carrington, himself an Indian fighter and a martyr to later Congressional injustice, says in his *Washington the Soldier,* p. 172:

"General Burgoyne had no sympathy with the British policy which ordered the hire of Indian allies. The following declaration stands to his perpetual credit, and should appear in every volume that may ever be published which refers to his campaign in America. His words were these: 'The Indian principle of war is at once odious and unavailing, and if encouraged, I will venture to pronounce its consequences will be sorely repented by the present age and be universally abhorred by posterity.' And afterwards, in the presence of the Earl of Harrington, when St. Luc claimed that 'Indians must fight their own way, or desert,' Burgoyne answered: 'I would rather lose every Indian than connive at their enormities.' And still another incident is to be noticed, especially as it places before the reader a very characteristic utterance of General Gates, his adversary in that campaign. The latter wrote to General Burgoyne as follows: 'The miserable fate of Miss McCrea, massacred by Indians, was peculiarly aggravated by her being dressed to receive her promised husband, but met her murderers instead, employed by you. Upward of one hundred men, women and children, have perished by the hands of ruffians to whom it is asserted you have paid the price of blood.' To this, the gallant general replied: 'I would not be conscious of the acts you presume to impute to me, for the whole continent of America; though the wealth of worlds was in its bowels, and a paradise upon its surface.' "

29. *Pickering's Journal,* cited by Ford, *Writings,* V, p. 502 n.
30. Lossing, *Field Book of the Revolution,* II, p. 212 n.
31. Ford, *Writings,* V, p. 503.

32. Clinton's MS., *An Historical Detail*, p. 79. (Clements Library.)
33. *Clinton Papers*, July 6, 1777. (William L. Clements Library.)
34. Clinton's MS., *An Historical Detail*, p. 79.
35. Ford, *Writings*, V, p. 515.
36. Ford, *Writings*, V. p. 517 n.
37. Ford, *Writings*, V, pp. 518 n., 519 n.
38. Ford, *Writings*, V, p. 521.
39. Ford, *Writings*, VI, p. 13.
40. This letter was published with different spelling in *Magazine of American History*, VII, p. 136. It is included in none of the collections and was sold at an auction at the Anderson Galleries, New York, December 18th, 1928.
41. Ford, *Writings*, V, p. 520 n.
42. *Knox MSS. Various Collections*, VI, p. 133, cited by G. H. Guttridge, *Lord George Germain in Office, 1775-1782*, Am. Hist. Rev., XXXIII, p. 31.

CHAPTER XVI

1. W. C. Ford, *Journals of Congress*, VIII, July 31, 1777. Scharf & Westcott, *History of Philadelphia*, I, p. 343.
2. *Journals of Congress*, VIII, Aug. 8, Aug. 4, 1777.
3. Sparks, *Writings*, V, p. 16.
4. It is Ganoe, *History of the U. S. Army*, p. 42, who calls attention to the astonishing reasons given for commissioning Lafayette. He adds: "Nowhere in the history of the Revolution did our lawmakers intimate by the slightest token that there existed such a thing as military technic or efficiency. Family, caste, friendship, favor and politics seemed to be the determining factors in awarding splendid commissions. Arnold, the most brilliant divisional commander of the war, was passed over time after time by incompetents until he finally responded to ill treatment with treason."

The history of the Comte de Broglie's ambition and of De Kalb's and Lafayette's relations with him, is treated in Doniol's *La Participation de la France*, in Kapp's *Leben des Amerikanischen Generals Johann Kalb*, Thomas Balch's *Les Français en Amérique*, Bernard Faÿ's *L'esprit révolutionnaire en France et aux Etats-Unis*, in Charlemagne Tower's *The Marquis de La Fayette in the American Revolution*, and other works. Lafayette's story is also told in his own *Mémoires de ma main*, in George Morgan's *The True La Fayette*, H. D. Sedgwick's *La Fayette*, Brand Whitlock's *La Fayette*, and fantastically poeticized in Joseph Delteil's *Lafayette*.
5. Tower, op. cit., I, p. 184, gives a facsimile of this letter.
6. Lafayette, *Mémoires, Correspondance et Manuscrits*, I, p. 227.
7. Doniol, op. cit., II, p. 416. Lafayette, op. cit., I, p. 89.
8. Lafayette, op. cit., I, p. 158.
9. Delteil, op. cit., pp. 46, 49-51.
10. Sparks, *Writings*, V, p. 455. Lafayette, op. cit., I, pp. 19, 21.
11. Ford, *Writings*, VI, p. 39.
12. Ford, *Writings*, VI, p. 41 n.
13. Humphrey Nickerson, *Turning Point of the Revolution*, ch. vii, gives an excellent and unbiased account of this battle.
14. *Mag. of Am. History*, III, p. 580. Nickerson, op. cit., pp. 118, 196, 208.
15. Letter to Gov. Clinton, July 21, 1777, *Mag. of Am. Hist.*, VII, p. 135, not in Ford or Sparks. See I. D. Butler's *Deficiencies in our History* (an address to

the Vermont Hist. and Antiquarian Society, Montpelier, 1846), p. 13. See also
J. B. Wilbur's *Ira Allen, Founder of Vermont.* This book gives a fresh and
important history of the whole subject. There is much about the New York
side of the controversy in C. Morgan's *Documentary History of the State of New
York*, Vol. IV, pp. 529-1035.

16. *Journals of Congress*, VIII, August 20, 1777.
17. Ford, *Writings*, VI, p. 45.
18. *Journals of Congress*, August 21, 1777.
19. *Journals of Congress*, August 23, 1777.
20. *Journals of Congress*, August 22, 1777.
21. Ford, *Writings*, VI, p. 49 n.
22. *Valley Forge Orderly Book of General George Weedon*, pp. 17-19.
23. Ford, *Writings*, VI, p. 52.
24. Ford, *Writings*, VI, p. 80.
25. *Familiar Letters of John Adams and his Wife*, p. 323.
26. *Weedon's Valley Forge Orderly Book*, p. 34.
27. Weedon, op. cit., pp. 31-33.
28. Weedon, op. cit., p. 38.
29. Weedon, op. cit., p. 46.
30. C. F. Adams, *Cavalry in the War of Independence*, Mass. Hist. Soc. Proc.,
April-June, 1910, Vol. XLIII, serial IV, p. 562. Lafayette, who was present,
says that Washington "exposed himself very independently" and the next morning "admitted that a petty traitor could have destroyed him" (*Mémoires*, I, p.
21).
31. Ford, *Writings*, VI, p. 147.
32. Ford, *Writings*, VI, p. 56 n.
33. *Journals of Col. James Montresor* (N. Y. Hist. Soc. Coll., 1881), p. 436.
34. Belcher, *The First American Civil War*, II, p. 236 n.
35. Ford, *Writings*, VI, p. 67.
36. M. I. J. Griffen, *The Catholics and the American Revolution*, I, p. 242.
37. Muhlenberg, *Life of Muhlenberg*, p. 30.
38. Burnett, *Letters of Members of the Continental Congress*, II, p. 352 n.
39. Montresor, op. cit., p. 518.
40. *Memoir of Col. Benjamin Tallmadge* (ed. by H. P. Johnston), p. 28.
Henry Lee, *Memoirs of the War*, p. 83. Lee gives Howe 18,000 men.
41. Ford, *Writings*, VI, p. 191. See also pp. 227 n., 237 n.
42. Montresor, op. cit., p. 429.
43. *Howe's Narrative*, p. 60. Kemble Papers (N. Y. Hist. Soc. Coll., 1883),
I, p. 125. Clinton MS. *An Historical Detail.*

CHAPTER XVII

1. Bowen and Futhey, *Sketch of the Battle of Brandywine* (Bulletin of Hist.
Soc. of Pa., I, No. 7). Robert Bruce, *Brandywine*, p. 22. W. W. MacElree,
Along the Western Brandywine. The ford named from John Chads, who had
a ferry there, is variously spelled Chadd's, Chad's, and Chads's.
2. *Weedon's Valley Forge Orderly Book*, pp. 91, 104, 118. Muhlenberg,
Life of General Muhlenberg, p. 116.
3. Ford, *Writings*, VI, p. 67 n.
4. Bowen and Futhey, op. cit., p. 9. Cornwallis was at the lower fork of the
creek about the time Knyphausen reached Kennett Square and seems to have fired

a signal from there, for otherwise unexplained cannon balls have been found there.

5. Sullivan's letter to Washington, October 24, 1777. Sparks, *Writings*, V, p. 458.

6. Sparks, *Writings*, V, p. 459.

7. Muhlenberg, op. cit., p. 92.

8. Henry Lee, *Memoirs of the War*, p. 88 n.

9. *Bland Papers*, I, p. 67, cited by W. B. Reed, *Life & Corres. of Joseph Reed*, I, p. 309.

10. Sparks, *Writings*, V, p. 459. MacElree, op. cit., p. 139, says that Speare, "or Spicer as he is sometimes called . . . whether drunken patriot, wily spy, or tavern hero, unquestionably saved the Battle of Brandywine for the British." He quotes Washington as saying the same thing in his letter to Sullivan a month later; but in that Washington refers to "the Major's rank, reputation, and knowledge of the country." Neither Pennsylvania nor New Jersey claims him.

11. This anecdote seems to deserve acceptance as history. See *A Sketch of Squire Thomas Cheyney*, by John Hickman, p. 31 (published in the bulletin of the Penn. Hist. Soc., cited above, with Joseph Townsend's *Some Account of . . . the Battle of Brandywine*). Townsend also testifies to Cheyney's mission, p. 10. See the *Reminiscence* of Elizabeth W. Smith, printed in a *Memoir of General Persifor Frazer*, and reprinted in the *Penn. Mag. of Hist.*, XLVI, p. 40. The Squire suffered persecution afterward for his action and his patriotic sentiments. See also Lossing, *Field Book*, II, p. 381 n. Bruce, op. cit., p. 27.

12. Sparks, *Writings*, V, p. 460.

13. W. A. Ganoe, *History of the U. S. Army*, p. 42.

14. Greene's own words, G. W. Greene, *Life of Greene*, II, p. 462.

15. This story of Brown and Washington has excellent authority. W. Darlington, *Proceedings of Historical Society of Penn.*, I, pp. 18, 58, 59, cited by Greene, op. cit., II, p. 461.

16. Townsend, op. cit., pp. 21-26.

17. H. B. Carrington, *Washington the Soldier*, p. 188. MacElree, op. cit., p. 145, cites Lafayette's comment: "When in line of battle it became necessary for a regiment to assume a position to the right, without breaking ranks, instead of filing simply to the right, the left began a never-ending countermarch." *Mémoires*, I, p. 20.

18. Col. F. C. Hooton, *The Battle of Brandywine, with Its Lines of Battle*, p. 7.

19. *Journals of Captain John Montresor* (N. Y. Hist. Soc. Coll., 1881), p. 449.

20. *Journal of Ebenezer Elmer*, Penn. Mag., XXXV, p. 105.

21. *Revolutionary Services of Capt. John Markland*, Penn. Mag., IX, p. 105.

22. *Orderly Book of Capt. John Nice*, Penn. Mag., XVI, p. 360.

23. B. H. Wise, *Memoir of Gen. John Cropper*, p. 6.

24. T. C. Amory, *Major General John Sullivan*, p. 48.

25. W. C. Ford, *Journals of Congress*, Vol. VIII, Sept. 9, 1777.

26. Ford, *Writings*, VI, p. 68 n. The ford which Washington calls Jones's was really Jefferis', about 6 miles from Chad's. Bowen and Futhey, *Sketch of the Battle of Brandywine*, p. 8.

27. G. W. Greene, op. cit., II, p. 462.

28. J. T. Goolrick, *Life of Hugh Mercer*, p. 75.

29. Muhlenberg, op. cit., p. 99. It is to be noted, however, that Weedon's *Orderly Book* contains on September 13, 1777 (p. 45), a statement that "The Gen! takes the earliest opportunity to return his warmest thanks to the Officers & Sold.rs

of Gen! Weedons Brigade engag'd in the late Action for their Spirited & Soldierly behaviour, A Conduct so worthy under so many disadvantages cannot fail of establishing to themselves the highest Military reputation."

30. Charlemagne Tower, *La Fayette in the Revolution*, I, p. 230.
31. Lafayette *Mémoires*, I, pp. 25, 62 n.
32. Lafayette, *Mémoires*, I, pp. 101, 103.
33. Drake, *Knox*, p. 47.
34. Ford, *Writings*, VI, p. 69. C. Henry Kain (*Military and Naval Operations on the Delaware River in 1777*, p. 178) says: "It is worthy of note that this is the only report that Washington ever made upon the Battle of Brandywine." He states that Washington wrote it, but it is in Pickering's hand.
35. Pickering's letter in *Tyler's Quarterly*, VII, p. 30.
36. *Clinton Papers*, Letter to Gen. Carpenter, Jan., 1778. (W. L. Clements Library.)
37. Ford, *Writings*, VI, p. 74 n.
38. The Deputy Adjutant-General's figures. *Kemble Papers*, I, p. 135. Howe's report to Germain is given in full in Dawson's *Battles of the U. S.*, I, p. 281. John Fiske (*American Revolution*, 1896, I, p. 326), after putting the American loss at "a little more than a thousand," says, "rolls afterward captured at Germantown showed that the British loss considerably exceeded that figure," which would make Howe's loss about three times his official report. Fiske not only fails to give his authorities, but neglects to specify the fact that those alleged rolls put Howe's loss at two thousand. This was fantastic, and Fortescue naturally prefers "the evidence of Howe's casualty list to that of these apocryphal rolls." It is quite probable that the rolls "found on the dead officer" were rebel propaganda forgery, enormously exaggerating the British losses and cutting the total force down. Fortescue, *History of the British Army*, III, p. 218 n.

R. H. Lee (J. C. Ballagh, *Letters of R. H. Lee*, I, p. 322) gave Howe's loss as "between 2 & 3000 . . . Our loss in killed & wounded scarcely comes up to 500." This is as trustworthy as the British rumor that Howe "killed 1400, and took 400 Prisoners," *Kemble Papers*, I, p. 133.

These apocryphal rolls are reproduced in the *Penn. Mag.*, IV, p. 121, and they put the British loss in killed and wounded at 1,976. But they prove far too much on the wrong side, for they give Howe's total force at Brandywine as only 10,280. Having lost a fifth of this in one brief battle, where did he get the "superiority in numbers" that Fiske gives him at Germantown (op. cit., I, p. 329), despite all the detachments he had to make? Fiske even dares to say: "Nothing can be more absurd than the careless statement, so often made, that the Americans were 'routed' at the Brandywine."

This is amazing, since Lafayette said, "the rout became complete," and describes the efforts necessary to check the stampede twelve miles from the battlefield. Greene said he "found the whole of the troops routed," and so did many others.

Knyphausen in his report says that the British loss was 622, which slightly exceeds Howe's estimate, but roughly confirms it.

39. *Major André's Journal*, I, p. 88, says, "We took this day eleven pieces of ordnance, five French brass guns, three Hessian, and three American." Lowell, *The Hessians*, p. 199.
40. John Marshall, *Life of George Washington*, II, p. 306.
41. *Familiar Letters of John Adams and His Wife*, p. 300.
42. Hamilton, *Works*, IX, p. 100.
43. Graydon, *Memoirs*, p. 272.
44. Thomas Paine, *Works* (Patriots' Ed.), III, p. 2. The Crisis, V.

45. Cited by Jones, *History of New York*, I, p. 197.
46. Howe's Report reproduced by Belcher, *First American Civil War*, II, p. 248.
47. Burnett, *Letters of Members of the Continental Congress*, II, p. 519.
48. Ford, *Writings*, VI, p. 72.
49. Marquis de Chastellux, *Travels in North America* (London, 1787), I, p. 242.

There is no space to take up here the second battle of Brandywine that raged among the historians and biographers. Bancroft in his history managed to arouse a constant succession of resentments at his injustices. He was superior to the necessity for giving his authorities and blandly proceeded to destroy reputations as he went along. He was occasionally forced to modify his condemnations by documents and arguments that he could not withstand. His account of this battle assailed Greene, as well as Sullivan, with such injustice that G. W. Greene and T. C. Amory counterattacked with deadly effect. See G. W. Greene's *Life of Greene*, the preface to Volume II and the Appendix, pp. 417, 459, 469, 470. Bancroft answered hotly and was again refuted. In Winsor's *Narrative and Critical History*, VI, pp. 418-19, and VIII, p. 478, there is very cogent proof of Bancroft's unfairness and unreliability. S. G. Fisher's *The Legendary and Myth-Making Process in Histories of the American Revolution*, makes Bancroft out little better than a more ponderous Weems. G. W. Greene, however, has been found guilty of altering the very letters he quotes in a manner that almost outsparks Sparks.

CHAPTER XVIII

1. *Weedon's Valley Forge Orderly Book*, p. 47.
2. Weedon, op. cit., p. 61.
3. *Familiar Letters of John Adams and His Wife*, p. 303.
4. Ford, *Writings*, VI, pp. 78, 79 n.
5. *Huntington Papers* (Conn. Hist. Soc.), XX, p. 363.
6. Ford, *Writings*, VI, p. 74.
7. Montresor, *Journals* (N. Y. Hist. Soc. Coll.), p. 451.
8. Baker, *Itinerary of General Washington*, p. 90.
9. Col. Bentalou, *Pulaski Vindicated*, cited in Sparks' Life of Pulaski, *American Biography*, new series, IV, p. 419.
10. Pickering's *Journal*, cited by Baker, op. cit., p. 90.
11. *Tyler's Quarterly*, VII, p. 30.
12. *Journals of Congress*, Sept. 17, 1777.
13. Reed, *Life of Reed*, I, p. 312 n.
14. Hamilton, *Works*, IX, p. 101.
15. John Adams, *Works*, II, p. 439.
16. Sparks, *Writings*, V, p. 72.
17. Sparks, *Writings*, V, p. 74.
18. Sparks, *Writings*, V, p. 74 n. Sparks, *Correspondence of the American Revolution*, I, p. 437.
19. Montresor, op. cit., pp. 457, 459.
20. C. Henry Kain, *Military & Naval Operations on the Delaware in 1777* (City History of Philadelphia, 1910), p. 180. This is a valuable monograph on the river battles, as is Gen. Wm. S. Stryker's *The Forts on the Delaware in the Revolutionary War*.
21. Marquis de Chastellux, *Travels in America*, p. 206.

22. W. A. Ganoe, *History of the U. S. A.*, p. 44, gives the British 6,000. F. V. Greene, *The Revolutionary War*, p. 89, gives them "fewer than 9,000."

23. F. S. Drake, *Life of Henry Knox* (Letter to Gen. Artemas Ward), p. 53. Ford, *Writings*, VI, p. 91 n.

24. Ford, *Writings*, VI, pp. 197, 227 n., 237 n.

CHAPTER XIX

1. Pickering's Journal, cited by Baker, *Itinerary of General Washington*, p. 95. *Diary of Lieut. James McMichael*, Penn. Mag., XVI, p. 153.

2. *Major André's Journal*, I, p. 106.

3. Wilkinson's *Memoirs*, I, pp. 362-63: "It was too widely extended for strict concert, and too complicated for precise co-operation, on which the success of the enterprise essentially depended; nor can I believe that the composition, equipments, and numerical force under General Washington, warranted the expectation of the capture of the army under Sir William Howe; yet the principal of the attack evinced the wisdom of the projector, and, although it *could not* be so successful as at Trenton, it produced the most salutary effects to the country. It reminded Sir William Howe of the scenes of Trenton and Princeton, taught him to respect his antagonist, and inspired him with fear of an enemy whom he had despised. It forced him into Philadelphia, straitened his quarters, and *put him on the defensive;* and no more important consequences could have been produced, by the most sanguinary victory, short of an absolute conquest."

Capt. von Münchäusen, *Journal und Relationen* (Penn. Mag. XVI, p. 201, also XXIII, p. 486), a Hessian on Howe's staff: "Everybody acknowledges that Washington's project was well conceived. Through his able spies, he was fully aware of our position. He knew that on account of our having sent away some of our detachments, our defense was entirely in one line . . . we could without breaking this line, send no regiments to the place where he might attack us."

Scharf & Westcott, *History of Philadelphia*, I, p. 354: "The country was rough and broken; the converging lines were six or seven miles apart; the only communication was by couriers; yet all the divisions were expected to co-operate, to attack simultaneously, to be within supporting distances of each other at critical stages of the battle, and each division was to accomplish something which was to be necessary to the success of each of the other divisions. . . . Battles are not fought by any such clock-work system nowadays, even with the telegraph, the railroad, and a perfected signal service."

Gen. B. T. Johnson, *General Washington*, p. 169: "The plan was fatally defective. It proposed to march green troops twelve miles in the night. None but veterans can make such a movement. The darkness disorganizes the command, and destroys the control of field and company officers over the troops. File-closers become powerless. And after such a march with such troops, four separate attacks in front, both flanks and rear to be made by four separate commands at the same instant of time, were impossible. It was impracticable, as the result showed. But Washington, knowing the value of vigor and enterprise in war, that surprise and the unexpected are wonderful forces in attack, hoped to repeat the exploit of Trenton."

C. F. Adams, in his *Washington and Cavalry* (Proc. Mass. Hist. Soc., May, 1910), p. 570: "An audacious conception, it was well planned by Washington, and came near being a brilliant success. Unfortunately, there was . . . no possibility of quick communication on the field." He quotes the plan as "conclusive evidence of the absence of any current conception of either the organization of cavalry or its use in field work." Adams positively scarifies Washington's military errors. In the Dec., 1910, issue of the Proc. Mass. Hist. Soc., p. 234, he made a further attack.

4. It is reproduced as the frontispiece of *Weedon's Valley Forge Orderly Book.*

5. B. H. Liddell Hart, *A Greater than Napoleon,* p. 56.

6. Weedon, op. cit., p. 72. The same plan in slightly different spelling is given as endorsed by Washington in the *Penn. Mag.,* XXVI, p. 387.

7. *Münchäusen's Journal,* Penn. Mag., XVI, p. 201. Also, *Penn. Mag.,* I, p. 13.

8. Henry Lee, *Memoir of the War,* p. 96.

9. Sparks, *Writings,* V, p. 470. Scharf & Westcott, *History of Philadelphia,* I, p. 357 n.

10. *Germain Papers* (W. L. Clements Library).

11. *Detail and Conduct of the American War,* p. 188. Howe's Report is reproduced by Belcher, *The First American Civil War,* II, p. 274. It was said that Howe was warned by a countryman, but the warning was perhaps more vague than is generally assumed, for the only account of it is given by the Hessian Captain Ewald, who had earned the gratitude of an American "by no means a Tory," whose property he protected from pillage. This man out of gratitude called on Ewald and, departing, said, "My friend, be on your guard tonight and tomorrow." Ewald passed the hint along, and says that Col. von Wurmb sent out a special patrol; but Knyphausen seems not to have been impressed, for in his report to his Landgrave he said he knew nothing of the attack until a patrol of Hessian chasseurs ran into about 300 men (Armstrong's) a mile beyond the outposts beyond a bridge over the Wissahickon. Under von Wurmb the Hessians fought for the bridge, lost it, won it again, and so held off the militia. Knyphausen went to the aid of the British left, but the Hessians took no other part in the battle except for von Wurmb's fine work in holding off with 300 chasseurs Armstrong's whole force, which left twenty dead when it retreated. See E. J. Lowell, *The Hessians in the Revolutionary War,* p. 201. Armstrong reported a loss of "not quite 20," and said he was held off by "a superior body of the enemy." He does not say superior in numbers. See Carrington, *Battles of the Revolution,* p. 390. Fortescue, *History of the British Army,* III, p. 271.

General Richard Fitzpatrick of the British army, whose recently discovered letters were published in the N. Y. *Times* in 1926 says in the Nov. 7th issue, p. 7, "We were surprised indeed in every sense of the word for we had not above two hours' notice of their advancing and then gave no credit to it . . . the advance corps were for above two hours entirely unsupported." He gives Musgrave the glory of saving the day with "about a hundred."

12. William Johnson, *Life of Greene,* I, p. 83. See Sparks' *Life of Count Pulaski, American Biography,* New Series, IV, p. 421.

13. John C. Fitzpatrick, *Spirit of the Revolution,* p. 77.

14. G. W. Greene, *Life of Greene,* II, pp. 474, 476. Bancroft, *History of the United States,* IX, p. 426, collected these criticisms of Greene and enraged G. W. Greene into a fierce controversy over his sneering tone. The charges and replies are reproduced at length in the Appendix to Greene's second volume. Conway's criticism of Greene is quoted in a later chapter on the Conway Cabal. Lafayette's remark is in his *Mémoires,* I, p. 29.

15. K. M. Rowland, *Charles Carroll of Carrollton,* I, p. 228.

16. Sullivan's letter to M. Weare, Oct. 25, 1777, cited in Sparks, *Writings,* V, p. 464, also in T. C. Amory's *Life of Sullivan,* p. 58.

17. Letter of Col. John E. Howard, cited by Sparks, *Writings*, V, p. 468.

18. C. J. Stillé, *Wayne and the Pennsylvania Line*, p. 96. Amory, op. cit., p. 59.

19. Watson, *Annals of Philadelphia*, II, p. 58.

20. General Hunter's *History of the 52nd British Regiment*, cited by Stillé, op. cit., p. 97.

21. Thomas Paine, *Works* (Patriots' Ed.), III, p. 271. Letter to Benjamin Franklin, May 16, 1778.

22. Clinton MS. cited in W. Sargent's *Life of André*, p. 114.

23. Fortescue, *Correspondence of George III*, III, p. 508.

24. Paine, op. cit., III, p. 270.

25. Pickering's Letter. *Tyler's Quarterly*, July, 1925, p. 31.

26. *Memoir of Col. Benjamin Tallmadge*, p. 32.

27. Watson, op. cit., II, p. 49.

28. Chastellux, *Travels in America*, II, p. 210.

29. John Marshall, *Life of George Washington*, II, p. 323. See also Johnson, *Greene*, I, p. 85.

30. Amory, op. cit., p. 60. Contemporary account of the Battle of German-town, *Penn. Mag.*, XI, p. 331.

31. Sparks, *Writings*, V, pp. 467-68.

32. Watson, op. cit, II, p. 49. E. J. Lowell, *The Hessians*, p. 202. Gen. Armstrong in command of this militia wrote a report (Dawson, *Battles of the United States*, I, p. 329), in which he describes his artillery work from the "Horrenduous" high ground on either side of the Wissahickon against the Hessians, who, according to him, outnumbered his men and drove them off. They did not discover the general retreat until an hour afterwards, so, by a quirk of unimportance, they were "last on the ground."

33. Belcher, *First American Civil War*, II, p. 265. Fortescue, *History of the British Army*, III, p. 223.

34. Johnson, op. cit., I, p. 87.

35. H. M. Muhlenberg, *Life of General Muhlenberg*, p. 114, citing Hubley's *Anecdotes of the Late War*.

36. Amory, op. cit., p. 61.

37. *Memoir of Col. Benjamin Tallmadge*, p. 32.

38. Custis, *Recollections*, p. 196.

39. Howe's Report to Germain is given in full in Dawson, op. cit., I, p. 330. Belcher, op. cit., II, p. 275.

40. William Gordon, *History of the . . . Independence*, II, p. 234. G. W. Greene also repeats this story in his biography of Greene, I, p. 480. C. F. Adams' comments are in the Mass. Hist. Soc. Proc., Dec., 1910, p. 237. He includes in his condemnation the story that Greene lost a curl of his own and laughed at a captain whose wig was shot off.

41. Stille, op. cit., p. 96.

42. Paine, op. cit., III, p. 269.

43. Watson, op. cit., II, p. 38.

44. *Kemble Papers* (N. Y. Hist. Soc. Coll., 1883), I, p. 137. Fortescue, *History of the British Army*, III, p. 222 n.

45. Gordon, op. cit., II, p. 234.

46. *Münchäusen's Journal*, Penn. Mag., XXIII, p. 483.

47. Weedon, op. cit., p. 67.

48. Letter from Capt. Matthew Irwin, Oct. 6, 1777, offered at an auction of

Patrick Henry Papers by Stan V. Henkels, Dec. 20, 1910. See Catalogue No. 1021, p. 79.

49. Ford, *Writings*, VI, pp. 96, 100 n., 127.
50. Ford, *Writings*, VI, p. 99.
51. Ford, *Writings*, VI, p. 113.
52. Lafayette, *Mémoires*, I, p. 36.
53. Ford, *Writings*, VI, p. 101.
54. Ford, *Writings*, VI, p. 106.
55. Letter to Joseph Whipple, Nov. 21, 1777, cited in Winsor's *Narrative and Critical History of America*, VI, p. 421 n.

CHAPTER XX

1. Ford, *Writings*, VI, p. 178.
2. Ford, *Journals of Congress*, Oct. 8, 1777, IX, p. 785.
3. MS. Letter to Gates, Nov. 21, 1777. N. Y. Hist. Soc. Coll.
4. The capitulation itself is in the Archives of Montreal. A photograph of it shows it to be written in badly spelled French, much weathered. The word is not, as all histories say, "assassination" but "lassassin," the first time and "lassassinat" the second. The writing is so bad that an early reading of the word as "assault" is not inexcusable. Why Stephen made his statement in 1776 and not before is mystifying.
5. Stephen went back to Virginia as a farmer. He had written to a prospective officer early in 1777: "I was nothing in a Military way: in less than a year I was a Col-Brigadier-Major General. Had not my attachment to the Interests of America been superior to all Scrupolosity—I would have now been poking at home about the mill" (*Penn. Mag.*, XV, p. 243). Stephen's rise had been rapid but his fall still faster. He went back and poked at home about his mill until Arnold's raid on Virginia in 1781, when he came out in his farm clothes riding a sorry horse and directing the retreat. (George Morgan, *Patrick Henry*, p. 305.) Patrick Henry wrote and asked for his daughter's hand in marriage to a friend, Captain A. G. Dandridge (*Va. Mag. of Hist. & Biog.*, XI, Oct., 1903, p. 216). Stephen took some part in the Virginia Convention of 1788. (H. B. Grigsby, *The History of the Va. Fed. Convention of 1788* with notes by R. A. Brock, Va. Coll., 1890, I, p. 36.) It is Brock who recalls the astonishing fact that Stephen first proposed a strong navy, I, p. 214 n. See S. M. Hamilton, *Letters to Washington*, V, p. 87 n. Stephen died in 1791.
6. This letter, which turned up too late for inclusion in its chronological place, was addressed to Captain Van Swearingen, May 15, 1761. See also S. M. Hamilton, *Letters to Washington*, III, pp. 201, 202, referring to Stephen's demagogic electioneering promises of reform, easy money, etc.
7. *Weedon's Valley Forge Orderly Book*, Nov. 20, 1777, p. 136.
8. MS. Letter in J. Pierpont Morgan library.
9. Ford, *Writings*, VI, p. 161, Nov. 1, 1777.
10. Ford, *Writings*, VI, p. 223, Nov. 26, 1777. See *Journals of Congress*, Dec. 1, 1777, p. 982.
11. Sparks, *Writings*, V, p. 82 n. Ford, *Writings*, VI, p. 98 n.
12. Ford, *Writings*, VI, p. 158. Nov. 1, 1777.
13. *Valley Forge Orderly Book*, in which other similar citations can be found. The same passages are in other orderly books, notably General Muhlenberg's, published in the *Penn. Mag.*, XXXV.

14. Kate M. Rowland, *Life of Charles Carroll of Carrollton*, I, p. 231.
15. Ford, *Writings*, VI, p. 111.
16. See C. Henry Kain, *The Military & Naval Operations on the Delaware in 1777* (City Hist. Soc. of Philadelphia, 1910), p. 192. See also W. S. Stryker, *The Forts on the Delaware in the Revolutionary War.* (Privately printed.)
17. Ford, *Writings*, VI, p. 216.
18. Ford, *Writings*, VI, p. 221.
19. MS. letter to Gates, Nov. 27, 1777. N. Y. Hist. Soc. Coll.

CHAPTER XXI

1. Thomas Paine, *Works* (Patriots' Ed.), III, p. 18.
2. MS. letter, April 9, 1778. N. Y. Hist. Soc. Coll.
3. MS. letter to Gates, Nov. 27, 1777. N. Y. Hist. Soc. Coll. See E. C. Burnett, *Letters of Members of the Continental Congress*, II, pp. 571, 593.
4. *Orderly Book of General Muhlenberg* (Penn. Mag., XXXV, pp. 80, 84, Oct. 15, 1777). In the *Valley Forge Orderly Book* the spelling is quite different. Muhlenberg, *Orderly Book*, p. 84.
5. James Wilkinson, *Memoirs*, I, p. 323.
6. W. S. Baker, *The Engraved Portraits of Washington*, p. 12.
7. Pickering and Upham, *Life of Timothy Pickering*, II, p. 109.
8. Ford, *Journals of Congress*, Nov. 6, 1777, IX, p. 870.
9. *Journals of Congress*, Nov. 4th and 5th, 1777, IX, pp. 861-67.
10. *Journals of Congress*, Nov. 1, 1777, IX, p. 855.
11. Henry Belcher, *First American Civil War*, II, p. 347.
12. Alice M. Baldwin, *New England Clergy and the Revolution*, p. 161.
13. Maj.-Gen. Phillips in a letter to Clinton, June 14, 1778, says: "We have considered ourselves as passengers, under the sanction and virtue of a Treaty, not prisoners." (Historical MS. Commission, Am., MSS. I, p. 267.) V. L. Collins, *President Witherspoon*, II, pp. 33, 34, quotes President Witherspoon's approval of the scheme to take advantage of Burgoyne's impatient statement that the public faith had been broken in not giving the officers the promised quarter; he said: "We have here the declared opinion of one of the parties, that the public faith is broken by the other. . . . Therefore we have reason to conclude that . . . General Burgoyne will not heed it on his. He would act the part of a fool if he did. . . . His folly . . . is our good fortune."

Dr. Witherspoon therefore advocated, says his biographer, a course "that posterity very generally has marked as a blot on the history of the young republic."

14. J. T. Adams, *The Burgoyne Expedition*, an article in the North American Review, Oct., 1927, p. 380. J. W. Fortescue, *A History of the British Army*, III, pp. 241-43, speaks of it as a "sordid story of meanness, cowardice and ill-faith." He says that Burgoyne could march out "a bare 3,500 men fit for duty . . . all that were left of the seven thousand who had started from Canada." He credits Gates with "from eighteen to twenty thousand men." He describes how a militia colonel bayoneted a defenceless British corporal, how a boy of fourteen "wantonly shot dead" a British officer and was tried and "commended," and how, when the officer was buried in the Anglican church, a mob plundered and wrecked the church during the funeral. Of effort to encourage deserters and enlist them, he says that "by this contemptible conduct Congress defeated its own object. . . . In vain Washington and other of the American generals remonstrated, with all the indignation of gallant officers and honourable men."

15. Ford, *Writings*, VI, pp. 225, 175, 190.

16. E. J. Lowell, *The Hessians . . . in the Revolutionary War*, p. 190. R. W. Pettingill, *Letters from America, 1776-79*, pp. 134, 143. "Four to five officers lie together in a hole when they can hardly turn over." "Private soldiers without straw or blankets." "The pretty Boston girls were entirely neutral," p. 145. Their money was paid to them in worthless paper.

17. Sparks, *Writings*, V, pp. 346, 347.

18. From the facsimile published in E. B. de Fonblanque's *Rt. Hon. J. Burgoyne*, opp. p. 328. See also Ford, *Writings*, VI, p. 411.

19. Ford, *Writings*, VI, p. 412 n.

20. Sparks, *Correspondence of the American Revolution*, II, p. 96 n.

21. Henry Lee, *Memoirs of the War*, p. 582.

22. Ford, *Writings*, VI, pp. 154, 156 n.

23. Hamilton, *Works*, IX, p. 106.

24. Hamilton, op. cit., IX, pp. 111, 112, 115.

25. Hamilton, op. cit., IX, p. 120.

26. Sparks, *Correspondence of the American Revolution*, II, pp. 31, 38.

27. Ford, *Writings*, VI, p. 212.

28. Ford, *Writings*, VI, pp. 231, 233 n.

29. *Journals of Congress*, IX, Nov. 24, 1777.

30. Ford, *Writings*, VI, p. 197. Charles C. Moore (*The Family Life of Washington*, p. 99) says that the privateer was not finished. The other account is in W. C. Ford's *Correspondence and Journals of S. B. Webb*, II, pp. 4, 5.

31. G. W. Greene, *Greene*, I, p. 227, II, p. 179. Drake, *Knox*, p. 71.

32. Congressman Harnett, Nov. 13, 1777. Burnett, op. cit., II, p. 547. The complete text of the Articles of Confederation is given in Ford, *Journals of Congress*, IX, p. 907.

33. A. M. Schlesinger, *New Viewpoints in American History*, pp. 184, 195.

34. Max Farrand, *Framing of the Constitution*, p. 51. Farrand, *The Fathers of the Constitution*, p. 54.

35. W. S. Stryker, *The Forts on the Delaware*, p. 24 n.

36. In Appendix I of *Marins et Soldats français en Amérique*, the Vicomte de Noailles describes some of these officers. Thomas Balch, *Les Français en Amérique, 1777-83*, discusses them more briefly. Though they were all eligible to the Society of the Cincinnati and request was made of the French Government to send a list, many of them were not to be traced. The expenditure by Pulaski of $50,000 is mentioned by his paymaster, Baldesque, in W. T. R. Saffell's *Records of the Revolutionary War*, pp. 34-36.

37. R. G. Adams, *Germain Papers*, William L. Clements Collection.

38. Henry Lee, *Memoirs of the War*, p. 105 n.

39. *Diary of Dr. Albigence Waldo*, Dec. 12, 1777. Penn. Mag., XXI, p. 305.

40. W. B. Reed, *Life of Reed*, I, p. 354.

41. Ford, *Writings*, VI, p. 245 n.

42. *Journals of Congress*, Dec. 16, 1777.

43. *Penn. Mag.*, XXI, p. 53.

44. Joseph S. Walton, *George Washington in Chester County* (Proc. Chester Co. Hist. Soc., 1898), p. 3. *Journals of Congress*, Dec. 19, 1777.

45. Joseph S. Walton, op. cit., pp. 3-5.

46. *Penn. Mag. of History*, XXXV, p. 299.

47. *Familiar Letters of John Adams and His Wife*, p. 322.

48. *Journals of Congress*, Dec. 14, 1777, Nathanael Greene wrote, "General Conway has been a great incendiary in our army. He was lately made a major-

general, which he obtained by the most dirty artifice." G. W. Greene, *Life of Greene*, II, p. 31.

49. Henry Dearborn, *Journal*, Dec., 1777, p. 13.

50. *Diary of Dr. Albigence Waldo*, Penn. Mag., XXI, pp. 306-311.

51. Ford, *Writings*, VI, pp. 257-262.

CHAPTER XXII

1. Henri Doniol, *Histoire de la participation de la France A l'Établissement des États-Unis d'Amérique*, III, p. 264.

2. Vicomte de Noailles, *Marins et Soldats français en Amérique*, p. 361.

3. *Deane Papers* (N. Y. Hist. Soc.), I, p. 380.

4. Charlemagne Tower, *The Marquis de La Fayette in the American Revolution*, I, p. 262. Doniol, op. cit., III, pp. 219, 221. Du Buysson, who came over as a companion and relative of Lafayette's, displays the French genius for misspelling foreign names and calls Conway "Mr. de Convoite" first, and next, "Mr. de Canoite," just as he refers to an even more familiar name first as "Vasington," then as "Wasington":

"Mr. de Convoite, brigadier-major, is detested by the officers of his brigade and regarded with jealousy (*jalousé*) by all the generals, even by Vasington, because he has kept his brigade at work and instead of letting it rest idle in camp, has made it maneuver and instructed it himself."

Du Buysson knew whereof he spoke for when he found that Congress would not give him a commission—

"I put a shirt in my pocket and offered my service to Mr de Canoite, brigadier-major, who was admitted to have the best instructed and most disciplined brigade. He received me marvellously. He gave me a mattress in his tent and permitted me to serve as a volunteer in his brigade."

5. Ford, *Writings*, VI, p. 121.

6. Ballagh, *Letters of R. H. Lee*, I, p. 337.

7. Kate M. Rowland, *Life of Charles Carroll of Carrollton*, I, p. 228.

8. Sparks, MSS. LII (pt. 3), p. 127. Cited by L. C. Hatch, *The Administration of the American Army*, p. 27.

9. Edward Channing, *History of the United States*, III, p. 290.

10. James Wilkinson, *Memoirs of My Own Times*, I, pp. 330, 331.

11. See Vol. II of this work, p. 506. Stirling's grandson, W. A. Duer, in his *William Alexander, Earl of Stirling*, p. 185, accuses Wilkinson of being grossly inaccurate and so contradictory and inconsistent in its particulars as to refute itself. He accuses Wilkinson of fabricating a letter to Stirling, which was not found among his papers. But Wilkinson's other documents are extant and seem accurately quoted.

12. Ford, *Writings*, VI, p. 279. Lossing, *Field Book of the Revolution*, II, p. 338 n., believes that Wilkinson's object in mentioning Conway's letter was "to sound Lord Stirling, through his aid." But it sounds a trifle complicated and there is nothing to confirm it.

13. Ford, *Writings*, VI, p. 180.

14. Wilkinson, op. cit., I, p. 384.

15. MS. letter, Nov. 28, 1777. Gates Papers in N. Y. Hist. Soc. Coll. See Sparks, *Writings*, V, p. 485.

16. Wilkinson, op. cit., I, p. 375.

17. MS. in N. Y. Hist. Soc. Coll.

18. Ford, *Writings*, VI, p. 278.

19. MS. letter in N. Y. Hist. Soc. Coll.

20. Ford, *Writings*, VI, p. 362.

21. MS. letter, in N. Y. Hist. Soc. Coll, Feb. 19, 1778.

22. Wilkinson, op. cit., I, p. 408.

23. Wilkinson, op. cit., I, p. 388.

24. MS. letter, Feb. 22, 1778. N. Y. Hist. Soc. Coll.

25. Wilkinson, op. cit., I, p. 405.

26. Ford, *Writings*, VI, p. 268 n. Sparks, *Writings*, V, p. 203, attacks Conway for the "remarkable" assertion that he "never applied for the appointment of major-general, when there are letters of an anterior date from him to Congress, in which he not only applies, but insists." But Conway does not say he never applied for the promotion to major-general; he distinctly says he never applied for the post of inspector-general.

27. Ford, *Writings*, VI, p. 270 n.

28. E. C. Burnett, *Letters of Members of the Continental Congress*, III, pp. 23, 69.

29. MS. letter to Gates, Nov. 11, 1777. N. Y. Hist. Soc. Coll.

30. Ford, *Writings*, VI, p. 277.

31. Sparks, *Writings*, V, p. 494.

32. Sparks, *Writings*, V, p. 503.

33. Burnett, op. cit., III, pp. 60, 52. It seems that Conway's ambition was exaggerated in the report, but Colonel Jedediah Huntington wrote of him: "his Intrigue is Infinite and his Ambition unbounded, I don't think anything will satisfy him short of the chief Command . . . & I can't help believing the honest and well meaning Part of Congress have been imposed upon and duped by a Cabal which I am confident is in and about them . . . we might with great Propriety tell Congress that we consider the late Promotions as an ingenious Intimation that they wish we would Leave the Service. but lest the Cause should suffer by such a Step we shall perhaps do no more than remonstrate." *Huntington Papers* (Conn. Hist. Soc.), p. 390.

34. Sparks, *Writings*, V, p. 511.

35. H. J. Ford, *Alexander Hamilton*, p. 98.

36. J. H. Smith, *Our Struggle for the Fourteenth Colony*, II, p. 482. See also W. C. Ford, *Penn. Mag.*, XX, p. 90. "The plot which has passed into history as the Conway Cabal originated some time before Conway had anything to do with it. . . . There is not enough evidence to prove that Gates was a party to any scheme having a definite purpose to supplant Washington." He asserts that other officers used Gates for their own advancement and Congressmen encouraged them to "an actual plot to advance Gates even at the expense of removing Washington."

CHAPTER XXIII

1. Döhla, *Tagebuch eines Bayreuther Soldaten*, p. 44.

2. Thacher, *Military Journal*, p. 166.

3. Quoted by Rush in his Diary, E. C. Burnett, *Letters of Members of the Continental Congress*, II, p. 263. See also S. Weir Mitchell, *Historical Notes of Dr. Benjamin Rush*, 1777, Penn. Mag., XXVII, p. 140.

4. John Adams, *Works*, IX, p. 542.

GEORGE WASHINGTON

5. Adams, op. cit., III, p. 92.

6. W. C. Ford, *Statesman and Friend*, Correspondence of John Adams with Benjamin Waterhouse, p. 81.

7. Paul Leicester Ford (*Atlantic Monthly*, May, 1895) claimed that Rush was a genuine adversary of Washington's and as a result of his immense burrowing in early records was convinced that if more truth were known great numbers of the fathers were guilty of attacks upon Washington:

"Yet not merely have these been forgotten, but the very descendants of the men who were bitterest in their attacks upon him have most carefully avoided reviving the facts, and have actually taken every means in their power to suppress and destroy all proofs of such antagonism. As an instance of this, the biographies of Samuel and John Adams, of Elbridge Gerry, of Jonathan and John Trumbull, and of Richard Henry Lee, as well as such materials as exist concerning James Lovell, William Williams, Daniel Roberdeau, and Francis Lightfoot Lee, are either silent or absolutely deny that these several men were concerned in the attempt to remove Washington from the command of the army at one of the most critical moments of the revolution." Jonathan Trumbull, *Vindications of Patriots of the American Revolution*, p. 10.

This statement naturally incensed the descendants of the men mentioned and fierce denials were not lacking. Jonathan Trumbull and J. G. Woodward, op. cit., describe their controversy with P. L. Ford and declare his documentation weak. Some of the societies of descendants still constitute themselves guardians of the whole period from too inquisitive approach.

8. Burnett, op. cit., III, p. 21.

9. Letter to William Plumer, March 28, 1813. *Proc. Mass. Hist. Soc.*, XLVIII, p. 508.

10. *July 4, 1776*, A Catalogue of Autographs and Documents (Rosenbach Coll.), p. 42.

11. Eugene E. Prussing, *The Estate of George Washington, Deceased*, p. 162. C. H. Callahan, *Washington, the Man and Mason*, p. 317, says, "Of all men, he probably enjoyed the most intimate acquaintance with the Commander-in-chief."

12. MS. in Library of Congress, Washington Papers, I, p. 520. Sparks gives it (*Writings*, V, p. 493), with his usual corrections, and spells out the names of Lee, Mifflin, and Gates, which Craik gave as R. H. L. G-L M-n, and G-s.

13. The letter is given in full in Sparks, *Writings*, V, p. 495.

14. W. W. Henry, *Patrick Henry*, I, p. 546.

15. Ford, *Writings*, VI, p. 452.

16. Ford, *Writings*, VI, p. 454. Washington must have been cruelly wounded by Rush's activity, but that did not prevent him from giving Rush full sway in his own field as a surgeon. At this time the Reverend Dr. Gordon, who was collecting material for a history, wrote to Washington and asked him about the old project to make Charles Lee commander-in-chief and the more recent movement to replace him with Gates, and he gives Washington's reply:

"I have attended to your information and remark, on the supposed intention of placing General L. [*meaning Lee*, before captivation] at the head of the army; whether a serious design of that kind had ever entered into the head of a member of Congress or not, I never was at the trouble of inquiring. I am told a scheme of that kind is now on foot by some, in behalf of another gentleman—but whether true or false, whether serious, or merely to try the pulse, I neither know nor care; neither interested nor ambitious views led me into the service—I did not solicit the command, but accepted it after much entreaty, with all that diffidence which a conscious want of ability and experience equal to the discharge of so important a trust, must naturally create in a mind not quite devoid of thought; and after I did engage, pursued the great line of my duty, and the object in view (as far as my judgment could direct) as pointedly as the needle to the pole. So soon then as the public get dissatisfied with my services, or a person is found better qualified to answer her expectation, I shall quit the helm with as much satisfaction, and retire to a private station with as much content, as ever the weary pilgrim felt upon his safe arrival in the Holy-land, or haven of hope;—and shall wish most devoutedly that those who come after may meet with more prosperous gales than I have done, and less difficulty. If the expectation of the public has not been answered by my endeavours, I have more reasons than one to regret it; but at present shall only add, that a day may come when the public cause is no longer to be benefited by a concealment of our circumstances; and till that period arrives, I shall not be among the first to disclose such truths as may injure it."

William Gordon, *History of the . . . Independence*, II, p. 305. Gordon sent this letter with others to the London Monthly Magazine, which printed it July, 1800. It is reproduced in the *Magazine of American History*, XIII, p. 487. This letter is not found in either Sparks or Ford.

When Washington became President he made Rush Director of the Mint, a post he held for fourteen years. His influence in medicine during the Revolution was unluckily great, according to Colonel Ashburn:

"By virtue of his social and professional prominence, his position as teacher and his facile pen, Benjamin Rush had more influence upon American medicine and was more potent in the propagation and long perpetuation of medical errors than any man of his day. To him, more than to any other man in America, was due the great vogue of vomits, purging, and especially of bleeding, salivation, and blistering, which blackened the record of medicine and afflicted the sick almost to the time of the Civil War." Colonel P. M. Ashburn, *A History of the Medical Department of the United States Army*, p. 19.

17. Jan. 27, 1778. Burnett, op. cit., III, p. 56.
18. Sparks, *Writings*, V, pp. 497, 499.
19. Ford, *Writings*, VI, p. 354.
20. E. C. Burnett, op. cit., III, p. xxxiii.
21. Kate M. Rowland, *The Life of George Mason*, II, p. 474.
22. Letter of Feb. 1, 1778. See *Mag. of American History*, xviii, p. 188.
23. William Dunlap, *History of . . . New York*, II, p. 133.

The story that Washington escaped ousting by one vote began early, however, for Rivington's *Royal Gazette* of Dec. 19, 1778, refers to it, though bunglingly: "About twelve months ago a motion for superseding General Washington was carried by only one voice." Frank Moore, *Diary of the American Revolution*, II, p. 106.

Elbridge Gerry, a great admirer of Gates, and accused of complicity in the Cabal, wrote to General Knox (Burnett, op. cit., III, p. 74) that he knew nothing of any "plan being formed to injure the reputation of, or remove from office, the gentleman hinted at in your favour of January the 4th."

Eliphalet Dyer wrote (Burnett, op. cit., III, p. 122):

"Be assured there is not the most distant thought of removing Genll. Washington, nor ever an expression in Congress looking that way, is a Tory lye from the beginning."

The Rev. William Gordon says that Samuel Adams was so much suspected by the soldiers that officers lay in wait for him and "would have handled him so as to have endangered his life," if he had not avoided the ambush. But Adams wrote that Hancock "could vindicate me against a Report . . . that I have been called to Account and severely reprehended at a Boston Town Meeting for being in a Conspiracy against a very great Man." (Burnett, op. cit., III, p. 264.)

But John Howland (E. M. Stone, *Life of John Howland*, p. 92) told that when he was a barber and dressed General Gates' hair, Samuel Adams once came in and discussed the plot to remove Washington and resented their inability to convert Congressman Ellery to the scheme. Gates talked freely but Adams tried to hush him up. Howland thought that Samuel Adams was afraid of Washington's popularity but not active in "Gates's scheme."

24. Burnett, op. cit., III, p. 164.

25. Burnett, op. cit., III, p. 42.

26. W. B. Reed, *Life and Correspondence of Joseph Reed*, I, p. 343 n.

27. MS. letter, Nov. 27, 1777, in N. Y. Hist. Soc. Coll.

28. MS. letter, Nov. 27, 1777, in N. Y. Hist. Soc. Coll. See Sparks, *Writings*, V, p. 484.

29. Burnett, op. cit., II, p. 570 n.

30. MS. letter, N. Y. Hist. Soc. Coll., Nov. 21, 1777.

31. William Johnson, *Life and Correspondence of Nathanael Greene*, I, p. 154. Greene himself wrote to his brother:

"A horrid faction has been forming to ruin his Excellency and others. Ambition how boundless! Ingratitude how prevalent! But the factions are universally condemned. General Mifflin is said to be at the head of it. And it is strongly suspected that General Gates favors it. Mifflin has quarreled with the General because he would not draw the force off to the southward last summer, and leave the New England States to themselves before the enemy's object was ascertained. It was uncertain whether he intended to go up the North River, to Newport, or to the southward. The General thought it his duty to take a position to give the earliest support to either. Mifflin thought Philadelphia was exposed by it, and went there and raised a prodigious clamor against the measure, and against me for advising it. But the General, like the common father of all, steadily pursued the great Continental interest without regard to partial objects and the discontents of individuals. This faction has been the offspring of that measure. See upon what a monstrous principle the General is persecuted." G. W. Greene, *Life of Greene*, II, p. 30.

32. [Graydon] *Memoir of a Life*, p. 278.

33. Burnett, op. cit., III, p. 79 n. Mifflin was certainly outspoken enough in a letter he wrote to Sharpe Dulany protesting against an accusation of being one of the Cabal. This letter, dated Feb. 1, 1778, was included in the Z. T. Hollingsworth Collection sold at Anderson's Galleries, New York, Nov. 28, 1928 (catalogue 2201). In the course of it Mifflin says to Dulany:

"I am told that my old acquaintance Mr. Dulany has charg'd me with a Design of ruining General Washington and of setting up General Gates in opposition to him & that Mr. Dulany has further injured me by the most opprobrious term of 'damnd Rascal.' As a friend to my Country I have spoken my sentiments on public matters. . . . I love and esteem General Washington and know him too well to ever wish for a Change. I love my Country & for her Sake deprecate the idea of such a Change. But I have seen & amongst my friends have said that General Washington's judgment on Military Points was too frequently counteracted by what I believed a dangerous influence. I have quoted Long Island & Mount Washington as Instances of that Influence and have lamented that the General did not consider the great value of his own private Judgment—a Judgment universally admitted & admired."

34. *Tyler's Quarterly*, July, 1925, pp. 25-29.

35. Pickering and Upham, *Life of Timothy Pickering*, II, p. 69. Pickering's letter to his brother-in-law protesting against naming a baby "George" as a proof that he "idolized" either George III or George Washington, is given on p. 71.

36. T. Pickering, *Review of the Correspondence between the Hon. John Adams and the late Wm. Cunningham, Esq.*, pp. 121-24.

37. *N. Y. Hist. Soc. Coll.*, 1878, p. 434. Letter of Feb. 2, 1778.

38. Ford, *Writings*, VI, p. 356 n., Feb. 2, 1778.

CHAPTER XXIV

1. "An officer, an eye-witness, has told me, that . . . some, while on duty as sentinels, have doffed their hats to stand in, to save their feet from freezing." J. F. Watson, *Annals of Philadelphia*, II, p. 84.

2. "General Washington mentioned it to me, when at his table, June 3, 1784." Dr. William Gordon, *The History of the . . . Independence*, II, p. 278.

3. G. W. P. Custis, *Recollections*, p. 209.

4. Gordon, op. cit., II, p. 279.

5. J. C. Young, *Marse Robert*, by his personal attendant, the ex-slave, William Mack Lee, Collier's Weekly, March 12, 1927, p. 19.

6. F. A. Shannon, *The Organization and Administration of the Union Army, 1861-65*, I, pp. 94-95.

7. This was told to me by officers of the regiment.

8. W. C. Ford, *Journals of Congress*, Dec. 20, 1777, IX, pp. 1043, 1046.

9. W. C. Ford, *Journals of Congress*, Dec. 31, 1777, IX, p. 1072.

10. J. S. Walton, *George Washington in Chester County*, p. 6.

11. *Mémoires de ma Main*, I, p. 35.

12. Winthrop Sargent, *Life of Major André*, p. 116 n. Thacher, *Military Journal*, p. 126.

13. Ford, *Writings*, VI, p. 267. Marshall, *Life of Washington*, II, p. 433. He says the total of the army was over 17,000. See also Hatch, op. cit., p. 93, T. W. Bean, *Washington at Valley Forge*, p. 2.

14. Lossing, *Field Book*, II, p. 333, gives a map and description of the arrangement.

15. Duponceau MS. cited by Kapp, *Life of Steuben*, p. 120.

16. W. G. Sumner, *The Financier and Finances of the Revolution*, II, p. 128.

17. Drake, *Knox*, p. 55.

18. Ford, *Writings*, VI, p. 379.

19. Ford, *Writings*, VI, p. 381 n. Drake, op. cit., p. 56.

20. Ford, *Writings*, VI, p. 436.

21. *Valley Forge Orderly Book*, March 13, 1778.

22. Henry Woodman, *Valley Forge*, p. 75.

23. Sumner, op. cit., I, Ch. VII. Galloway's evidence in *Detail & Conduct of The War*, p. 122. Ford, *Writings*, VI, p. 450.

24. Ford, *Journals of Congress*, Dec. 10, 1777, IX, p. 1014.

25. John F. Watson, *Annals of Philadelphia*, II, p. 322.

26. Scharf & Westcott, *History of Philadelphia*, I, pp. 373-75.

27. Ford, *Writings*, VI, pp. 347 n., 348 n.

28. Beveridge, *Life of John Marshall*, I, p. 116. See also Marshall, *Life of Washington*, II, p. 434.

29. Woodman, op. cit., p. 63.
30. Ford, *Journals of Congress*, March 7, 1778, X, p. 229.
31. Ford, *Writings*, VI, p. 406.

CHAPTER XXV

1. John C. Fitzpatrick, *Spirit of the Revolution*, p. 88.
2. *Journals of Captain John Montresor* (N. Y. Hist. Soc., 1881), p. 457.
3. *Weedon's Valley Forge Orderly Book*, p. 300.
4. John C. Fitzpatrick, *George Washington's Accounts of Expenses*, pp. 52, 53.
5. Harold Kellock, *Parson Weems of the Cherry Tree*, pp. 83-85.
6. Mason L. Weems, *Life of Washington*, p. 169.
7. Washington's death is minutely described by Tobias Lear in *Letters and Recollections of George Washington*. His will is reproduced in Ford, *Writings*, XIV, and with great scholarship in Eugene E. Prussing's *The Estate of George Washington, Deceased*.
8. Weems, op. cit., p. 227.
9. Weems, op. cit., p. 183.
10. Rev. E. C. M'Guire, *The Religious Opinions and Character of Washington*, p. 158.
11. Rev. William J. Johnson, *George Washington the Christian*, p. 105.
12. Benson J. Lossing, *Field Book of the Revolution*, II, p. 336 n.
13. W. S. Baker, *Itinerary of George Washington*, p. 122.
14. L. C. Barnes, *The John Gano Evidence* (Bulletin of William Jewell College, Sept. 15, 1926, Series No. 24, No. 1), p. 5. There is a biographical notice of Gano in W. B. Sprague's *Annals of the American Pulpit*, VI, p. 62; and in J. M. Cramp's *Baptist History*, p. 560. *The Literary Diary of Ezra Stiles* has frequent references to this popular evangelist.
15. Since this quotation might bring embarrassment upon the clergyman, his name is omitted from this acknowledgment of his courtesy and interest in the truth.
16. John F. Watson, *Annals of New York*, p. 305.
17. John C. Fitzpatrick, *The Diaries of Washington*, IV, p. 252.
18. Watson, *Annals of Philadelphia*, II, p. 61. Watson, *Annals of N. Y.*, p. 304.
19. M'Guire, op. cit., Appendix. Johnson, op. cit., p. 89. Johnson's book reproduces the painting in the Presbyterian Hospital.
20. Sparks, *Writings*, XII, p. 410.
21. These and many other such citations are given with their sources in the splendidly documented book by John E. Remsburg, *Six Historic Americans*, pp. 109-10. This work contains an immense amount of evidence concerning the religious beliefs of Paine, Jefferson, Washington, Franklin, Lincoln, and Grant.
22. Sprague, op. cit., V, p. 394. See also William L. Stone, in *Magazine of American History*, XIII, p. 597, where the full letter is given.
23. Remsburg, op. cit., p. 120.
24. Cited in Rev. Bird Wilson's *Memoir of Bishop White*, pp. 189, 193, 197.
25. M'Guire, op. cit., p. 141. M'Guire makes a few excerpts from the Diaries to prove that Washington went to church. There are no citations from the Sundays when he did not.
26. Bishop Meade's *Old Churches, Ministers and Families of Virginia*, II, pp. 242-55.

27. See Vol. II of this work, p. 47. Also Vol. I, ch. xxx.

28. M'Guire, op. cit., p. 343.

29. For an extended discussion of these Prayers, see Vol. I of this work, Appendix II.

30. Ford, *Writings*, X, p. 254. A searching exposure of the composition of the Prayer is given by Franklin Steiner in *The Truth Seeker*, July 23, and Dec. 31, 1927; and by W. H. Whittiken in the issue of July 27, 1929.

31. Ford, *Writings*, X, p. 261 n.

32. W. C. Ford, *Journals of Congress*, March 16, 1776, IV, p. 209.

33. Ford, *Writings*, IV, p. 83 n.

34. Ford, *Journals of Congress*, Nov. 1, 1777, IX, p. 855.

35. *Valley Forge Orderly Book*, Dec. 17, 1777, p. 159.

36. Ford, *Writings*, VII, pp. 28, 29 n.

37. Ford, *Writings*, VI, p. 105 n.

38. John Joseph Henry, *Campaign Against Quebec*, p. 41.

39. I. N. Arnold, *Life of Benedict Arnold*, gives all of these citations with their sources. See pp. 115, 118, 330, 394, 406, etc. See Humphrey Nickerson, *The Turning Point of the Revolution*, p. 278.

40. E. B. de Fonblanque, *Life of Burgoyne*, Appendix F, p. 490.

41. Ervin Chapman, D.D., *Latest Light on Abraham Lincoln*, II, frontispiece. This was specially painted for the work, in the course of which, on p. 554, the extreme "chasteness" of Lincoln's conversation is emphasized. This is in strange contrast with the evidences to the contrary in Beveridge's *Life of Lincoln*, Vol. I.

42. J. F. Rhodes, *History of the United States*, IV, p. 215. The biographies of Lincoln by Lamon and Beveridge and others discuss these matters at length, and Remsburg, op. cit., has brought together great numbers of arguments on both sides.

43. S. E. Forman, *Our Republic*, p. 685.

44. C. S. Olcott, *Life of William McKinley*, II, p. 109. J. F. Rhodes, *The McKinley and Roosevelt Administrations*, p. 106. Randolph G. Adams, *A History of the Foreign Policy of the United States*, p. 277. C. A. & Mary Beard, *The Rise of American Civilization*, p. 375.

45. Jefferson's *Syllabus . . . of the Doctrines of Jesus*, given in a letter to Dr. Benjamin Rush, April 21, 1803, *Works*, X, p. 381. *The Morals of Jesus* is reproduced in facsimile at the end of Vol. XX. See also his many letters to Priestley, John Adams, Edward Douse, etc. See also Randall's *Life of Thomas Jefferson*, III, pp. 553-60.

46. Franklin in a letter to Ezra Stiles, March 9, 1790, *Literary Diary* (F. B. Dexter), III, p. 387, outlines his views on religion. Bernard Faÿ in his recent *Franklin, The Apostle of Modern Times*, based on "innumerable documents unknown to former biographers," including "between 600 to 900 unpublished letters," says p. vi, "These documents of Franklin's private life enable me to show that he was a follower of the seventeenth century English Pythagoreans. He believed in metempsychosis, and in a supreme Deity, who was surrounded with innumerable inferior gods, with Christ for one of His prophets."

47. Albert J. Beveridge, *Abraham Lincoln*, I, p. 539. He completely discredits Father Chiniquy's accounts of Lincoln's religious enthusiasm and describes the disgust of Lincoln's intimates at such claims.

CHAPTER XXVI

1. Watson, *Annals of Philadelphia*, II, p. 321.
2. *Penn. Mag.*, XXI, p. 304.
3. G. W. Greene, *Life of Nathanael Greene*, I, p. 542.
4. C. O. Paullin, *Out-Letters of the Continental Marine Committee and Board of Admiralty*, II, p. 227.
5. Ford, *Writings*, VI, p. 275 n.
6. *Valley Forge Orderly Book*, Feb. 4, 1778.
7. *Detail and Conduct of the American War*, p. 122. A startling picture of the cosmopolitan nature of Washington's army is shown in B. F. Stevens' *Facsimiles of MSS. in European Archives Relating to America*, No. 2094, a letter from Galloway, March 25, 1778, enclosing "An account of the Number of Deserted Soldiers, Gallymen &c from the Rebel Army and fleet, who have come into Philadelphia and taken the Oath of Allegiance, with a particular account of the Places in which they were Born.

Total Soldiers to this day	1134
Of which were born in England	206
"　　"　　"　　"　　" Scotland	56
"　　"　　"　　"　　" Ireland	492
"　　"　　"　　"　　" Germany	88
"　　"　　"　　"　　" America	283
"　　"　　"　　"　　" Canada	4
"　　"　　"　　"　　" France	5
	1134
Total Gallymen &c to this day	354
Of which were born in England	69
"　　"　　"　　"　　" Scotland	22
"　　"　　"　　"　　" Ireland	157
"　　"　　"　　"　　" Germany	16
"　　"　　"　　"　　" America	75
"　　"　　"　　"　　" France	15
	354"

This shows that only one in four was American born.

8. Belcher, *The First American Civil War*, II, p. 345 n.
9. H. A. Muhlenberg, *Life of General Muhlenberg*, p. 125.
10. Woodman, *History of Valley Forge*, pp. 51, 66.
11. These instances and numberless others of interest are found in *Weedon's Valley Forge Orderly Book*, pp. 180, 184, 197, 231, 232, 235, 236, 257, 281; John Whiting's *Revolutionary Orders*, pp. 84, 86, 93; *The Orderly Book of General Edward Hand*, Penn. Mag., XL, p. 222, and Saffell's *Records of the Revolution*, p. 373.
12. Ford, *Writings*, VI, pp. 445, 478.
13. *Huntington Papers* (Conn. Hist. Soc. Coll., XX), p. 395, Jan. 16, 1778.
14. *Tables of Organization*, Revised April, 1925, General Service Schools, Fort Leavenworth, Kansas.
15. G. W. Greene, op. cit., II, pp. 47, 49, 53.

16. MS. N. Y. Hist. Soc., Dec. 14, 1777. Lafayette to Gates.

17. Charlemagne Tower, *The Marquis de La Fayette in the American Revolution*, I, p. 265, Jan. 6, 1778. Lafayette, *Mémoires*, I, p. 144.

18. Lafayette, op. cit., I, p. 73.

19. G. W. Greene, op. cit., II, p. 27.

20. Letter to Gouverneur Morris, Feb. 2, 1778. Cited by Tower, op. cit., II, p. 479.

21. Ford, *Writings*, VI, pp. 289, 289 n.

22. Lafayette, op. cit., I, p. 154. MS. letter, March 11, 1778. N. Y. Hist. Soc. Coll.

23. MS. letter, April 2, 1778. N. Y. Hist. Soc. Coll.

24. The value of Steuben's famous instruction has rarely been questioned, but later in the war, Colonel Mercer insisted that his system was all wrong. Mercer pointed out the astonishing fact that while the British were learning from the Americans the use of open order formation and bush fighting, the Americans were dragged back to the Prussian close-order system. (Gaillard Hunt, *Fragments of History*, p. 50.)

This is odd, too, in view of the scorn and ridicule heaped on Braddock and his troops in his day, and since, by all Americans. On the other hand, Fortescue in his *History of the British Army* insists that the bad habits the British Army learned in America unfitted it for future battles on European soil (III, pp. 535-39).

This is only another instance of the great biological or other law that nations in contact exchange diseases, vices, follies, but not their virtues, if any. The first gift of newly discovered America to Europe was said to be the venereal plague of the 15th Century. From the Revolution the British took back wrecked strategical principles that caused them to be defeated by the French for a long while with great regularity. The French, as a result of American contagion, lost all sense of subordination and turned their monarchy upside down in a Revolution of their own. In the present century America is chiefly known abroad in all directions as the disseminator of the cocktail, jazz, immodesty and tyranny of women.

Steuben was sent to America by Beaumarchais, that sly and witty librettist, whose influence on American destinies can never be sufficiently appreciated because of the mixture of his motives and the gay cynicism of so many of his acts. It is hard for a comedian to get solemn persons to take seriously one who takes nothing seriously. It is difficult to know what to call Steuben. The Germans call him Friedrich Wilhelm von Steuben, the French who sent him over called him de Steuben. Benjamin Franklin in his letter of introduction to Washington calls him Baron de Steuben. Washington writes the name Steuben. He signed himself "Steuben." He was not a Prussian born but had fought France as a soldier for Frederick the Great in the Seven Years' War. Released from the Prussian army he visited Paris and met the Comte de Saint Germain, the Minister of War (whose name almost duplicated that of the British Lord Germain). Beaumarchais coerced him into going and furnished him with liberal money, so that he did not have to ask the American commissioners for it. Nor did he ask them to promise him military preferment, in view of the trouble already fomented by the crowd of foreigners in America. See Beaumarchais' letter of Dec. 6, 1778, quoted by J. B. Doyle, *Fr. Wm. von Steuben*, p. 45.

25. Kapp, *Steuben*, p. 655.

26. Kapp, op. cit., pp. 114, 119.

27. G. W. Greene, op. cit., I, p. 568.

28. Kapp, op. cit., p. 236.

29. Ford, *Writings*, VI, p. 288 n. Fitzpatrick, *Spirit of the Revolution*, p. 128. Robert W. Chambers in historical notes to his Revolutionary novel, *The Painted Minx*, points out the great elegance and variety in the uniforms of many of the organizations. In this field as in others his scholarship is profound and it is important to remember that not all the soldiers were always shabby.

30. C. J. Stillé, *Anthony Wayne*, p. 154, July 12, 1778, to Richard Peters, of the Board of War.

CHAPTER XXVII

1. Ford, *Writings*, VI, p. 272.
2. W. C. Ford, *Life and Correspondence of S. B. Webb*. In this work, II, pp. 19-85, Mr. Ford has given perhaps the only clear account of this whole complex and obscure subject of the handling of prisoners and the years of dispute while the captives pined. Much of the correspondence between Howe and Washington is reproduced in full.
3. Hamilton, *Works*, IX, p. 129.
4. Ford, *Writings*, VI, pp. 398-405.
5. Ford, *Journals of Congress*, March 18, 1778, X, p. 266.
6. Ford, *Writings*, VI, p. 459.
7. Ford, *Journals of Congress*, April 10, 1778, X, p. 329.
8. Ford, *Journals of Congress*, April 10, 1778, X, p. 334. In the preface to *Letters of Members of the Continental Congress*, III, p. x, Dr. E. C. Burnett describes this lately unearthed drama.
9. Ford, *Writings*, VI, p. 466.
10. Ford, *Writings*, VI, pp. 479-80.
11. Burnett, op. cit., III, p. 255.
12. Ford, *Journals of Congress*, May 15, 1778, XI, p. 502.
13. Ford, *Writings*, VII, p. 17.
14. Ford, *Writings*, VI, pp. 472-89, 489 n.
15. *The Journal of Elias Boudinot*, pp. 77-81. W. S. Baker, *Itinerary of General Washington*, p. 124 n., says that Lee could not have arrived till May 20th, 1778.
16. Ford, *Journals of Congress*, Feb. 3, 1778, X, p. 114.
17. Lossing, *Field Book of the Revolution*, II, p. 352 n.
18. W. S. Stryker, *The Battle of Monmouth*, p. 14.
19. John Fiske, *Essays Historical and Literary*, I, p. 86.

CHAPTER XXVIII

1. Andrew Dunlap, Jan. 21, 1778, in Rev. Lewis Lampman's *Leonard Bronk*, p. 8.
2. *Valley Forge Orderly Book*, p. 244, March 1, 1778.
3. W. T. R. Saffell, *Records of the Revolution*, p. 362. As late as May 31, 1778, Washington was asking for "as many women of the army as can be prevailed on to serve as nurses . . . for which they will be paid the usual price."
4. Ford, *Writings*, VI, p. 355.
5. Ford, *Writings*, VI, p. 355 n.
6. John C. Fitzpatrick, *Accounts of Expenses*, p. 53. *Spirit of the Revolution*, p. 95. Concerning the charge for Martha's expenses see Lossing's *Field Book of the Rev.*, I, p. 576 n.

7. Duponceau MS., Kapp, *Life of Steuben*, p. 120.

8. Duponceau MS., Kapp, *Life of Steuben*, p. 121.

9. Lossing, *Mary & Martha Washington*, p. 168.

10. The reference to Scammel is given by Watson, *Annals of Philadelphia*, II, p. 61. Concerning Scammel see also Henry Lee, *Memoirs*, p. 496, Lossing, Field Book, I, p. 430. The anecdote of the stump-cutter is given in the *Magazine of American History*, XVI, p. 202.

11. A. J. Beveridge, *John Marshall*, I, pp. 118, 132.

12. E. P. Chase, *Our Revolutionary Forefathers, the Letters of François Marquis de Barbé-Marbois*, p. 114.

13. *The Military Journal of George Ewing*, p. 35.

14. New York *Mirror*, January 11, 1834, quoted from "a gentleman well known for his veracity," cited in the *Magazine of Am. Hist.*, XI, p. 80.

15. H. C. Lodge, *Life of Washington*, II, p. 392.

16. Mrs. A. H. Wharton, *Colonial Days and Dames*, p. 97.

17. Michael J. O'Brien, *Washington's Irish Friends*, Journal of the American Irish Historical Society, XXV, pp. 347-349.

18. *Diary of Col. Allen McLane*, Penn. Hist. Soc. Coll., I, p. 141, cited by M. J. O'Brien, op. cit., p. 349.

19. Ewing's *Journal*, pp. 35, 44.

20. Francis von A. Cabeen, *The Society of the Sons of St. Tammany of Philadelphia*, Penn. Mag. XXV, p. 434, sets the first appearance of Tammany in 1683 when he made his mark opposite the name "Tammanens." He was gradually elevated to local sainthood and May first allotted to him. His festival spread widely and a bucktail was worn in the hat on May first, while persons in Indian disguise rushed into ballrooms, with war whoops and war dances and then took up a collection. In 1772 a society was formed in Philadelphia in his name for social and benevolent purposes. Among the charter members were many men who later turned Tory, Galloway, William Franklin, Duché, also many staunch rebels.

21. Ewing's *Journal*, pp. 44-47.

22. Geo. C. D. Odell, *Annals of the New York Stage*, I, p. 194.

23. Ford, *Writings*, II, p. 101. See Vol. I, p. 415 of this work.

24. Ford, *Writings*, VI, p. 413.

25. Ford, *Writings*, VI, p. 389 n.

26. Ford, *Writings*, VI, p. 390.

27. Ford, *Writings*, VII, p. 41.

28. Ford, *Writings*, VII, p. 27. May 26, 1778.

29. There is an enormous mass of material concerning the Americans abroad. The *Silas Deane Papers* alone fill five captivating volumes published by the N. Y. Hist. Soc. One could spend a lifetime in the biographies and works of Franklin, John Adams, Arthur Lee and others. See also Sparks', *The Diplomatic Correspondence of the American Revolution*, the monumental tomes of Doniol, the sprightly biographies of the *Figaro* Beaumarchais, by Loménie and later authors including several recent American and English books about him; Kapp's and other works on Frederick the Great; innumerable isolated letters; and recent works on American diplomacy. The archives of European nations are still bulging with hundreds of thousands of documents from which somebody constantly drags out new treasures. R. H. Lee's attacks are in Ballagh's *Letters of R. H. Lee*, II, pp. 123, 198. See D. J. Hill, *Am. Hist. Rev.*, XXI, p. 709; also XX, p. 671. Bernard Fay's *Franklin* points out how Franklin "inveigled France into the Revolutionary War," and how one of his American

colleagues not only came within an ace of preventing the alliance but "kept London in touch with what was going on," pp. vii, 415-499. Fay points out the immense advantage Franklin found from his Masonic connections. Louis XVI was a Mason, as was Washington.

30. Ford, *Journals of Congress*, May 2, 1778, XI, p. 418. Brand Whitlock, *La Fayette*, I, p. 133. David Ramsay, *History of the American Revolution*, I, p. 68, Lafayette *Mémoires*, I, p. 75.

31. John Whiting, *Revolutionary Orders of General Washington*, p. 77. *Valley Forge Orderly Book*, p. 307.

32. Wharton, *Martha Washington*, p. 126.

33. This account of the celebration is taken chiefly from a letter by an eyewitness published in the New Jersey *Gazette*, May 13, 1778. It is given in full in Frank Moore's *Diary of the Revolution*, II, p. 49. See also Sparks' *Writings*, V, p. 357 n.

34. Elijah Fisher's Diary, included in Carlos E. Godfrey's *The Commander-in-Chief's Guard*, p. 275.

CHAPTER XXIX

1. Cited by E. F. De Lancey, notes to Thomas Jones, *History of New York* (N. Y. Hist. Soc.), I, p. 716. Galloway's attacks on Howe fill his pamphlets, as in *A Reply to the Observations of Sir Wm. Howe*, p. 108.

2. Galloway, op. cit., p. 6. In Winthrop Sargent's *Life of André*, p. 167, is given André's elaborate description of the fête, concerning which there is no lack of description in many works, notably Scharf and Westcott's *History of Philadelphia*, which contradicts (I, p. 379) the incessant statement that Peggy Shippen (later Mrs. Benedict Arnold) and her two sisters took part. Though their names were on the programme and their dresses made, their father was persuaded by the Quakers that the Turkish costumes provided for them were unseemly, and he thwarted their "dancing fury" by keeping them at home.

3. Scharf & Westcott, op. cit., I, p. 381.

4. Ford, *Writings*, VII, p. 15. Conway's letter, dated August 9, 1777, is given in Henkel's Catalog, No. 1183, Jan. 16, 1917, p. 103.

5. C. F. Adams, *Cavalry in the War of Independence*, Proc. Mass. Hist. Soc., April-June, 1910, pp. 547-576. See also Vol. II of this work, pp. 447-449.

6. Clinton MS. cited by Sargent, op. cit., p. 164 n. A detailed account of the Barren Hill affair is given in Charlemagne Tower's *The Marquis de La Fayette in the American Revolution*, I, pp. 325-342. Watson, *Annals of Philadelphia*, II, pp. 61-2, tells of the men who warned Lafayette. C. E. Godfrey, *The Commander-in-Chief's Guard*, p. 276. Lafayette, *Mémoires*, I, p. 47.

7. Letter to Gouverneur Morris, May 29, 1778. Ford, *Writings*, VII, p. 31.

8. Sargent, op. cit., pp. 167, 177. Howe left Mrs. Loring in America according to H. Belcher, *The First American Civil War*, II, p. 146, "leaving on American shores Calypso inconsolable for the departure of her Ulysses." When Howe reached England he somehow faced down his embattled critics in the ministry, leaving his actions in America to mystify history. He saw no further action in the field but occupied important military posts at home, was made a full general in 1793 and in 1795 became Earl Howe on the death of his brother, the Admiral, who also resigned in 1778 but was caught by the French naval advance, saved Newport and refused to serve further. In his later years, however, he became one of England's most glorious admirals, rivalling Nelson in fame.

9. Sir Henry Clinton, *An Historical Detail of Seven Years Campaigns in North America* (William L. Clements Coll.), pp. 99-103.

10. W. L. Stryker, *The Battle of Monmouth*, p. 105.

11. Letter to Henry Laurens, April 30, 1778. Ford, *Writings*, VI, p. 509.

12. Ford, *Writings*, VII, p. 43.

13. Sparks, *Correspondence of the American Revolution*, II, p. 100.

14. Charles Francis Adams, op. cit., p. 572.

15. Sparks, *Correspondence of the American Revolution*, II, p. 53.

16. Ford, *Writings*, VI, p. 422. Pulaski's value as "the organizer of the American cavalry" is described by Eugene Pivány in his *Hungarian-American Hist. Collections* (Budapest, 1927), p. 20. He emphasizes the value also of his fellow countryman, "Kowácz." Washington accepted "Mr. Kovatch" but warned Pulaski against "a fondness for introducing foreigners into the Service." At Washington's recommendation Congress commissioned "Kowatz" a Colonel. Pulaski's Legion by Oct., 1778, had 330 officers and men. Pulaski was killed at the siege of Savannah in 1779 and Kowácz at Charleston five months earlier.

17. Ford, *Writings*, VI, p. 507.

18. Hamilton, *Works*, IX, p. 148.

19. Burnett, *Letters of Members of the Continental Congress*, III, p. 174.

20. Ford, *Writings*, VII, p. 32.

21. G. W. Greene, *Life of Greene*, II, p. 79.

22. Ford, *Writings*, VII, p. 60.

23. H. B. Dawson, *Battles of the United States*, I, p. 396.

24. Letters to Germain, May 23, June 5, 1778. Ford, *Writings*, VII, p. 53 n.

25. See Dawson, op. cit., I, p. 396, and nearly every other modern historian.

26. C. J. Stillé, *Anthony Wayne*, p. 137.

27. Scharf and Westcott, op. cit., I, p. 385.

28. Ford, *Writings*, VII, p. 69.

29. Ford, *Writings*, VII, p. 69 n.

30. Ford, *Writings*, p. 72 n.

31. Stillé, op. cit., p. 143.

32. Godfrey, op. cit., p. 279.

33. Hamilton, *Works*, IX, p. 141. Lafayette, in his *Mémoires*, I, p. 51, gives his side of the story very briefly.

34. Ford, *Writings*, VII, p. 75 n.

35. Johann Heusser's MS. *Journal* cited by Stryker, op. cit., p. 93.

36. *André's Journal*, II, p. 10.

37. Stryker, op. cit., p. 80.

38. G. W. P. Custis, *Recollections*, pp. 311-320.

39. Stryker, op. cit., p. 109, tells this story very differently, omitting Washington altogether and saying that General Maxwell granted Howell leave and sarcastically congratulated him on escaping hot work, whereupon Howell remained to fight, and reached the tavern the next day in time to speak to his brother before he died. But the story in the text is given by Daniel Agnew in the detailed *Biographical Sketch of Governor Richard Howell, of New Jersey*, Penn. Mag., XXII, p. 225. Agnew tells of Howell's further activities in secret service for Washington. He was elected Governor of New Jersey eight times and received Washington in the triumph of 1789.

40. Von Eelking's "Hulfstruppen," cited by J. W. de Peyster, *The Battle of Monmouth*, Mag. of Am. Hist., II, p. 413. See Thomas Anburey, *Travels*, II, p. 220.

41. C. F. Adams, op. cit., p. 579.

42. Clinton, op. cit., pp. 104, 105.

43. *Lee Papers*, III, p. 10. This is Lee's testimony at the trial. The details of this battle are extraordinarily complete—more than complete in fact, for they are full of contradictions. The court-martial of Lee brought out much testimony and numberless letters and newspaper articles were written at the time. The court-martial proceedings are given in full in the *Lee Papers*, III. They were also published separately in 1864. When referred to in these notes the edition of the *Lee Papers* by the N. Y. Hist. Soc. is indicated.

44. Stryker, op. cit., p. 115.

45. Henry Lee, *Memoirs*, p. 113. Gen. H. B. Carrington, *Battles of the American Revolution*, p. 419, has a minute description.

46. Stryker, op. cit., p. 111. *Lee Papers*, III, p. 83. Dr. Griffiths' testimony.

47. Jomini, *Précis de l'Art de la Guerre*, cited by Stryker, op. cit., p. 102.

CHAPTER XXX

1. *Lee Papers*, III. The present account of the battle is largely compiled from the minute and voluminous, and often contradictory, testimony brought out at the court-martial of General Lee. Though these proceedings were published separately in 1778 by John Dunlap and again in 1864, they are also reproduced entire in the New York Historical Society's four-volume compilation of the *Lee Papers*, which includes practically everything by or concerning Lee, including his subsequent letters and articles. The references herein to the court-martial testimony are simply given under the page reference to this edition. William S. Stryker, Adjutant-General of New Jersey, made a long and thorough study of this battle and, after his death, it was edited by Wm. Starr Myers, and published under the title, *The Battle of Monmouth*. References to this are simply given as Stryker.

2. *Lee Papers*, III, p. 179.

3. *Lee Papers*, III, p. 95.

4. Stryker, op. cit., p. 175.

5. Ford, *Writings*, VII, p. 77.

6. B. C. Steiner, *The Life and Correspondence of James McHenry*, pp. 1-18.

7. *Lee Papers*, III, p. 78.

8. *Lee Papers*, III, p. 231.

9. *Lee Papers*, III, pp. 79, 68.

10. Stryker, op. cit., p. 175.

11. *Lee Papers*, III, pp. 72, 79.

12. *Lee Papers*, III, p. 80.

13. *Lee Papers*, III, p. 68.

14. *Lee Papers*, III, p. 80.

15. Written in McHenry's copy of Marshall's *Life of Washington*, III, p. 473. Quoted in *Magazine of American History*, III, p. 363. Harrison's testimony is in *Lee Papers*, III, p. 75.

16. F. S. Oliver, *Alexander Hamilton*, p. 53. Lodge, *Life of Washington*, I, p. 236, says "with a deep oath, tradition says."

17. Custis, *Recollections*, p. 413.

18. *Lee Papers*, III, p. 28. Fiske, *Essays, Historical and Literary*, I, p. 91, quotes an eye-witness, a sergeant, as remembering that Washington said, "My God! General Lee what are you about?"

19. General H. B. Carrington, *Washington the Soldier*, p. 234, gives a full

treatment of this matter and decides that Washington was not profane. The place where Lafayette stated, in 1825, that Washington swore has been variously given, but the important thing is that he was not on the spot at the battlefield. See Dawson, *Battles of the U. S.*, I, p. 408. Lafayette in his *Mémoires* made no reference to an oath, and his biographer, Tower, *The Marquis de La Fayette in the American Revolution*, I, p. 384, indicates only that Washington showed "very evident astonishment." George H. Moore was so incensed at the thought that Washington could ever have sworn during his whole life that he attacked every alleged instance in a work called *Libels on Washington with a Critical Examination Thereof* (printed by the author, N. Y., 1889). The only testimony he admits is Jefferson's "by God" story during the Presidency, to which he grants "some color of authenticity." Thomas Balch, *Papers relating chiefly to the Maryland Line*, p. 105, quotes a Captain Thomas Washington as saying that Lee said, " 'Sir, these troops are not able to meet British Grenadiers.' " 'Sir,' said General Washington, much excited, 'they are able and by G-d they shall do it.' "

Edward Everett Hale, in his *Memories of a Hundred Years*, I, p. 169, says he heard in conversation that when Washington asked Lee at Monmouth why such a column was retiring, Lee said that the American troops would not stand the British bayonets. Washington replied:

" 'You damned poltroon, you have never tried them!' "

On p. 170, note, Hale quotes a story by an eye witness as "From a note by Dr. (A. A.) Woodhull": David Breading, temporary aide to General Maxwell, was sent to report Lee's action to Washington. "The General said: 'Young man, can you lead me to General Lee?' Breading replied that he could. The General said: 'Lead on, and I will follow.' They went at furious speed, and found General Lee. Washington said:

" 'Why have you acted thus?' and swore at him in no mild terms. My granduncle, David Breading, narrated this to me, himself being the actor."

20. *Lee Papers*, III, p. 12. Lafayette's exact words in his *Mémoires de ma main*, I, p. 52, are: "*Vous savez, lui dit Lee, que tout ceci état contre mon avis,*" and adds: "Whereupon Washington sent him to the rear and formed seven or eight hundred men with cannon with whom M. de Lafayette charged himself with checking the enemy."

21. *Lee Papers*, III, p. 78.

22. *Lee Papers*, III, p. 81.

23. *Lee Papers*, III, p. 64.

24. *Lee Papers*, III, p. 112.

25. *Lee Papers*, III, p. 147.

26. *Lee Papers*, III, p. 156.

27. *Lee Papers*, III, p. 159.

28. *Lee Papers*, II, p. 437.

29. *Lee Papers*, III, p. 191.

30. *Lee Papers*, III, pp. 14, 38, 47.

31. *Lee Papers*, III, pp. 223, 214. Long after the battle Colonel Jackson, hearing that his conduct had been criticized, demanded a court-martial and was exonerated. The testimony at that trial concerns this battle and is included in the *Lee Papers*.

32. Sir Henry Clinton's MS., *Historical Detail of Seven Years Campaigns* (Wm. L. Clements Coll.), I, pp. 104, 110.

33. Col. John Laurens' letter to his father, June 30, 1778. *Lee Papers*, II, p. 433.

34. *Lee Papers*, III, p. 63.
35. *Lee Papers*, III, p. 53.
36. *Lee Papers*, III, p. 73.
37. *The Journal of Elias Boudinot*, p. 81.
38. *Lee Papers*, III, p. 62.
39. *Lee Papers*, III, p. 200.
40. *Lee Papers*, III, pp. 114, 75.
41. Custis, op. cit., pp. 218, 292.
42. *Lee Papers*, III, p. 75. The battle ground is difficult to visualize. General F. V. Greene, *The Revolutionary War*, p. 146 n., says that Sparks' map of Monmouth is "very defective in topography and otherwise. It was copied into Lossing, Irving and other histories and was probably the cause of much of the difficulty expressed by various writers as to understanding the battle of Monmouth." He praises the map given in Avery's *History of the U. S.*, based on U. S. Geological Survey. Its only fault is that it is too small to be clear. I have preferred to include Clinton's own map. There is an excellent map in Carrington's *Battles of the Revolution*. Tower's *La Fayette*, I, p. 368, gives a French sketch with notes. In André's *Journal*, II, p. 12, his map is given.
43. *Lee Papers*, III, pp. 81, 75.
44. *Lee Papers*, III, p. 157.
45. *Lee Papers*, III, p. 137.
46. Stryker, op. cit., p. 205.
47. McHenry, *Magazine of American History*, III, p. 359.
48. F. Kapp, *Life of Steuben*, p. 161.
49. Kapp, op. cit., p. 160.
50. *Lee Papers*, III, p. 94.
51. Johnson, *Life of Greene*, I, p. 106.
52. Stryker, op. cit., p. 212.
53. *Kemble Papers* (N. Y. Hist. Soc., 1883), p. 154.
54. Stryker, op. cit., p. 207.
55. C. J. Stillé, *Anthony Wayne*, pp. 148-150.
56. Stedman, *The American War*, II, p. 21.
57. Stryker, op. cit., p. 218.
58. McHenry, *Mag. of Am. Hist.*, III, p. 359.
59. Stryker, op. cit., p. 225.
60. Lafayette *Mémoires*, I, p. 53.
61. *Lee Papers*, III, p. 120. See De Peyster, *Mag. of Am. Hist.*, II, p. 410.
62. Custis, op. cit., p. 224.
63. Stryker, op. cit., pp. 188-192, sums up the evidence. See C. H. Van Tyne, *England and America*, p. 21. The extent to which Custis allowed his fancy to go is seen in the anecdote in his *Recollections*, pp. 286, 287. In his notes to Custis, *Recollections*, p. 226, B. J. Lossing says that Alexander Hamilton's widow told him that she often saw Captain Molly, and that she was a red-headed Irish girl.
64. Mason L. Weems, *Washington*, p. 101.
65. James Thacher, *Military Journal*, p. 136. Dr. J. D. Schoepff, surgeon of the Anspach-Bayreuth troops, wrote a pamphlet which Dr. J. R. Chadwick published as *The Climate and Diseases of America*, in which he makes many striking observations including the fact that "the American troops, although they fight in a climate to which from youth up they have been accustomed, invariably suffer from the inclemencies of the weather, the insalubrity of the swamps, and the fatigues of the campaigns, quite as much as, and even more

than, the royal European troops. When our soldiers have been sickly, theirs
have been doubly so." (p. 10). "The battle near Monmouth . . . was remarkable from one circumstance which has not its parallel in the history of the New
World; without receiving a wound, fifty-nine men fell on our side solely from
the extraordinary heat." (p. 12).

66. Dawson, op. cit., pp. 415, 417.
67. Stryker, op. cit., p. 262.
68. Ford, *Writings*, VII, p. 87. In this letter to Gates, Washington puts his
losses at 7 officers and 52 rank and file killed, 17 officers and 120 men wounded.
69. Lowell, *The Hessians*, p. 213.
70. Stryker, op. cit., p. 258.
71. *Lee Papers*, II, p. 465.
72. Stedman, op. cit., pp. 21-23.
73. Rev. James Murray, *An Impartial History of the Present War*, II, p. 457.

CHAPTER XXXI

1. Ford, *Writings*, VII, p. 83.
2. Stryker, *The Battle of Monmouth*, p. 235, citing Edward Hand's *Orderly
Book*.
3. Ford, *Writings*, VII, p. 88.
4. *Lee Papers* (N. Y. Hist. Soc.), II, p. 435.
5. *Lee Papers*, II, p. 437.
6. *Lee Papers*, II, p. 437.
7. *Lee Papers*, III, pp. 1, 2.
8. *Lee Papers*, II, p. 452.
9. C. J. Stillé, *Life of Anthony Wayne*, p. 145.
10. *Lee Papers*, II, p. 457.
11. *Lee Papers*, II, p. 472.
12. *Lee Papers*, II, p. 475.
13. *Lee Papers*, II, p. 479.
14. Ford, *Writings*, VII, p. 283.
15. Ford, *Writings*, VII, p. 503.
16. *Lee Papers*, III, pp. 255 n., 258 n.
17. *Lee Papers*, III, p. 208.
18. Gen. B. T. Johnson, *General Washington*, p. 204.
19. *Lee Papers*, III, p. 228.
20. *Lee Papers*, III, p. 229.
21. *Lee Papers*, III, p. 230.
22. *Lee Papers*, III, p. 236. Dr. Rush's letter is in the *Penn. Mag.*, XXIX,
p. 18.
23. *Lee Papers*, III, p. 237.
24. *Lee Papers*, III, p. 238.
25. *Lee Papers*, III, p. 250.
26. *Lee Papers*, III, p. 253.
27. *Lee Papers*, III, p. 254.
28. *Lee Papers*, III, p. 283.
29. *Lee Papers*, III, p. 285.
30. S. G. Fisher, *The Struggle for American Independence*, II, p. 192.
31. *Lee Papers*, III, p. 292.
32. *Lee Papers*, III, p. 293.

33. Ford, *Journals of Congress*, XII, p. 1195.

34. *Lee Papers*, III, pp. 278, 302. There is much about the picturesque Miss Franks in Scharf & Westcott's *History of Philadelphia*, II, pp. 900-3. See Max J. Kohler's monograph, *Rebecca Franks, An American Jewish Belle of the Last Century* (privately printed, 1894). He credits her with a poem really written by Jonathan Odell.

35. *Lee Papers*, III, p. 294.

36. *Lee Papers*, III, p. 448.

37. *Lee Papers*, III, p. 401. Dec. 19, 1779.

38. *Lee Papers*, IV, p. 37.

39. *Lee Papers*, IV, p. 31. In a letter to Dr. Rush, Sept. 26, 1779, he says: "You and many others accuse me of want of religion, there never was a greater mistake—to convince you I send you my proem, from Cicero de legibus—I am perswaded that no Society can exist without religion, and I think the Christian; unincumbered of its sophistications, is the most excellent and [of course] of a divine nature as comprehending the most divine system of which but at the same time, I own, I quarrel with the tediousness and impertinence of the liturgies of the various sects, which so far from being the support are the ruin of all religion—as to the dogmas they are many of 'em not only absurd but impious as they are dishonourable to the Godhead or visible ruler and moderator of the infinity of worlds which surround us I therefore cannot help esteeming myself the [champion] vindicator rather than the Denyer and Blasphemer of the Almighty—" *Lee Papers*, III, pp. 373-4.

In his project for an ideal state, a military colony, he says: "I speak to men and soldiers, who wish and are able to assert and defend the rights of humanity; and, let me add, to vindicate the character of God Almighty, and real christianity, which have been so long dishonoured by sectarists of every kind and complexion; catholics, church of England men, presbyterians, and methodists. I could wish, therefore, that the community of soldiers (who are to be all christians) should establish one common form of worship, with which every member must acquiesce, at least in attendance on divine worship, and the observation of the prescribed ceremonies; but this so contrived as not to shock any man who has been bred up in any of the different sects. For which reason, let all expositions of the scripture, and all dogmas, be for ever banished. Let it be sufficient that he acknowledges the existence, providence, and goodness of God Almighty; that he reverences Jesus Christ: but let the question never be asked, whether he considers Jesus Christ as only a divine person, commissioned by God for divine purposes, as the son of God, or as God himself. These sophistical subtleties only lead to a doubt of the whole; let it be sufficient therefore that he believes in God, in his providence, and in the mediation of Jesus Christ, whether a real God, or only a divinely inspired mortal; for which reason, to prevent the impertinence and ill consequences of dogmatising, no professional priests of any sort whatever shall be admitted in the community. But still I am of opinion, that a sacred order, or hierarchy, should be established, and in the following manner: that this hierarchy are not to be expositors of the divine law, which ought to be understood by every member of common capacity; but as the servitors, or administrators of the solemn ceremonies to be observed in the worship of the Supreme Being, of his Son, or missionary." *Lee Papers*, III, p. 325.

40. *Lee Papers*, III, p. 397.

41. Anne Cary Morris, *The Diary and Letters of Gouverneur Morris*, II, p. 492.

42. *Lee Papers*, IV, p. 35.

43. John Marshall, *Life of Washington*, III, p. 28.

44. Henry Lee, *Memoirs*, pp. 575, 114, 115.

45. Gen. B. T. Johnson, op. cit., pp. 203, 199.

46. H. B. Dawson, *Battles of the United States*, I, p. 410. Gen. H. B. Carrington, *Washington the Soldier*, p. 230.

The extremes to which partisans will go in their attachment to a theory are exemplified in the descriptions of this retreat. In his excellent and carefully documented work, *Battles of the United States*, pp. 410-11, Henry B. Dawson somehow permits himself first to accuse Lee of guilt and treason and of actually cooperating with Clinton in the protection of Clinton's army, and then to say: "In the retreat of General Lee, *per se*, there can, probably, be but little to condemn, beyond its disorderly character. It is, doubtless, true that the detachment was in great danger; and that a retreat (or, as General Lee termed it, 'a retrograde movement') was as necessary to secure it from actual capture by Sir Henry Clinton, as to secure the safety of General Knyphausen's division."

The befuddlement this implies in the traitor and in his purchaser, Clinton, is as great as that of the historian trying desperately to prove a point.

Gen. F. V. Greene, *The Revolutionary War*, p. 145, speaks of the fruits of Washington's toil "all in danger of being lost by the combined incapacity, cowardice and treason of this damnable Charles Lee."

Yet even Hamilton praised Lee's intrepidity.

General Carrington, *Washington the Soldier*, p. 230, thinks that Lee was "overestimated" as an officer, and "knew nothing of handling a large command, or combined commands. Before the Battle of Monmouth, if then, he had never been under fire in the lead of American troops. He was cool enough and brave enough at Monmouth, to retreat with his division. . . . He was unequal to the command."

John Fiske, *Essays Historical and Literary*, I, pp. 89-93, first describing Washington's "terrific outburst of wrath," which never took place, and picturing Lee as a "cowardly and trembling culprit," which he certainly never was, accuses Lee merely of "trying to discredit and supplant Washington." He does not think the explanation "quite so simple," as "collusion with Clinton." But neither explanation of such a retreat could be called simple or sensible.

General Bradley T. Johnson, *General Washington*, pp. 198-203, after regretting Washington's "incomprehensible" habit of appealing to councils of war, and referring to his trust of Lee as something "which does no credit to his judgment of men," states that Lee foresaw American success at Monmouth with Lafayette in the war and "that he alone could insure disaster. With a rout of the army and a probable capture of its commander, the Board of War would be revived, the command would devolve on him, and, in conjunction with the mercenary traitors in Congress, the *débris* of resistance could be surrendered, the terms of the British commissioners accepted, the Union restored, and he secure his dukedom, with vast possessions from the confiscated estates of the rebels. Of his own personal knowledge he knew what a princely estate Mount Vernon was, for he had been entertained there; and it would furnish a delightful haven for an old soldier battered by many wars and buffetted by various fortunes."

This certainly does not lack completeness, but its foundation is not even suggested. He says, "There is no evidence that either Washington or Lafayette had the faintest idea of the length and breadth and height and depth of Lee's turpitude." There is also no evidence whatsoever that Lee had any designs on becoming the Duke of Mt. Vernon.

47. Rivington's *Gazette*, January 23, 1779, cited by Frank Moore, *Diary of the Revolution*, II, p. 120.

48. Spark's *Life of Charles Lee*, though published separately, is reproduced in full in the *Lee Papers*, IV.

49. S. G. Fisher, op. cit., II, p. 185.

50. Henry B. Dawson, op. cit., I, pp. 143-150; and *Major-General Israel Putnam, a Correspondence, passim.* This later work contains both sides of a controversy he held with the editor of the *Hartford Daily Post*, who attacked Dawson and glorified Putnam. The praises of Putnam are celebrated in the biography by his aide, David Humphreys, and in F. L. Humphreys' biography, *Life and Times of David Humphreys.*

51. Ford, *Writings*, VI, p. 427 n., VII, p. 31.

52. *N. Y. Hist. Soc. Coll., 1881*, p. 136. The story of Putnam's lisp is given in I. Q. Leake's *Life of General John Lamb*, p. 262 n.

53. H. P. Johnston, *Correspondence and Public Papers of John Jay*, I, p. 181.

54. For the cooperation of Morris with Washington in ousting Conway, see Sparks, *Life and Writings of Gouverneur Morris*, I, pp. 167, 177. Conway's appeal to Gates is in the N. Y. Hist. Soc. Coll. MS. letter, May 7, 1778.

55. Sparks, *Writings*, V, p. 372.

56. Sparks, *Writings*, V, p. 373 n.

57. E. C. Burnett, *Letters of Members of the Continental Congress*, III, p. 278. June 7, 1778.

58. [Alex. Graydon] *Memoir of a Life*, p. 279 n.

59. Major Garden, *Anecdotes of the Revolutionary War*, I, pp. 430-1.

60. Letter from Gen. Samuel Patterson to Cæsar Rodney, July 6, 1778, in Stan. V. Henkel's Catalog, No. 694. The Washington-Madison Papers, to be sold Dec. 6, 7, 1892, p. 238.

61. Sparks, *Writings*, V, p. 517.

62. Vicomte de Noailles, *Marins et soldats français*, p. 361. In the N. Y. Hist. Soc. Coll. is a MS. letter from Gates, apparently to Conway, dated January 2, 1779.

63. *Lee Papers*, III, p. 265. In a letter to Gates, Dec. 18, 1778 (*Lee Papers*, III, p. 278), Lee says, "Inclos'd is a paper on the subject of poor Conway's case—get it put in the Boston Papers if you can. I know not who wrote it, tho' the world is pleas'd to lay it to me." Jared Sparks, *Life of Charles Lee*, ch. xiii, *Lee Papers*, III, p. 320.

64. Graydon, *Memoirs*, p. 279.

65. *A Reprint of the Reed and Cadwalader Pamphlets* (1863). See also H. W. Smith, *Nuts for Future Historians to Crack*, and W. H. Stryker, *The Battles of Trenton and Princeton*, where these slanders against Reed are aired and answered.

CHAPTER XXXII

1. Elijah Fisher's Diary in C. E. Godfrey's *The Commander-in-Chief's Guard*, p. 280.

2. W. C. Ford, *The Journals of Congress*, XI, July 7, 1778.

3. B. C. Steiner, *The Life & Correspondence of James McHenry*, p. 22.

4. James Parton, *Life of Aaron Burr*, pp. 104, 136, 138. M. L. Davis, *Memoirs of Aaron Burr*, pp. 129-30.

5. Ford, *Writings*, VII, p. 97.

6. Ford, *Writings*, VII, p. 98.
7. Ford, *Writings*, VII, p. 100.
8. Ford, *Writings*, VII, p. 101 n.
9. Ford, *Writings*, VII, p. 104.
10. Ford, *Writings*, VII, p. 104.
11. Chevalier de Pontgibaud, *A French Volunteer of the War of Independence* (R. B. Douglas trans.), p. 57.
12. Ford, *Writings*, VII, p. 161. Letter to Gen. James Nelson, Aug. 20, 1778.
13. H. A. Muhlenberg, *Life of General Muhlenberg,* p. 159, citing Gen. Hand MS.
14. Ford, *Writings*, VII, p. 107.
15. Ford, *Writings*, VII, p. 114 n.
16. Capt. W. M. James, *The British Navy in Adversity*, p. 101.

CHAPTER XXXIII

1. Capt. W. M. James, *The British Navy in Adversity*, pp. 6, 75.
2. James, op. cit., pp. 16-18.
3. W. E. H. Lecky, *The American Revolution* (Woodburn), p. 347.
4. *Historians History of the World*, XX, p. 631. Lord Mahon, *History of England*, VI, pp. 146, 230. James, op. cit., p. 90.
5. G. M. Trevelyan, *History of England*, p. 556.
6. G. W. Greene, *Life of Nathanael Greene*, II, p. 94.
7. Greene, op. cit., II, p. 95.
8. Ford, *Writings*, VII, p. 137.
9. Ford, *Writings*, VII, p. 130.
10. Ford, *Writings*, VII, p. 127 n.
11. Ford, *Writings*, VII, p. 128 n.
12. Ford, *Writings*, VII, p. 127.
13. Charlemagne Tower, *The Marquis de La Fayette in the American Revolution*, I, p. 432. Lafayette, *Mémoires*, I, p. 54, says that d'Estaing could have cut off and captured 1,500 Hessians if Sullivan had not asked him to wait.
14. Ford, *Writings*, VII, p. 156 n. Tower, op. cit., I, ch. xiv, gives a judicial account of these disputes, defending the French from the aspersions of American historians. T. C. Amory in his *Life of John Sullivan* defends Sullivan less impartially.
15. James, op. cit., pp. 102-107.
16. Amory, op. cit., p. 77. Vicomte de Noailles *Marins et soldats français en Amérique*, p. 43 n., says that this protest in the national archives of France is signed by 19 generals.
17. Tower, op. cit., I, p. 477.
18. Laurens' letter to Washington. Ford, *Writings*, VII, p. 169 n.
19. Tower, op. cit., pp. 481, 484. Lafayette, *Mémoires*, I, p. 190.
20. Ford, *Writings*, VII, p. 173.
21. Ford, *Writings*, VII, p. 167.
22. Ford, *Writings*, VII, p. 166 n.
23. G. W. Greene, op. cit., II, p. 125.
24. Amory, op. cit., p. 82. Fortescue, *History of the British Army*, III, p. 258 n. H. B. Carrington, *Battles of the American Revolution*, p. 454.
25. Henri Doniol, *La Participation*, etc., III, p. 409. Vicomte de Noailles,

op. cit., p. 46. *Magazine of American History*, XV, p. 95. Carrington, op. cit., p. 455. G. W. Greene, II, op. cit., p. 125. Mrs. Mercy Warren, who knew whereof she spoke, wrote in her *American Revolution*, II, p. 104:

"A squabble soon after the fleet arrived at Boston, between some French and American sailors, heightened the uneasiness. But the most respectable people, disposed to view with a favorable eye, and to place the utmost confidence in their untried allies, all censure was hushed; and a discreet silence in the more prudent, prevented or counteracted all invidious observations from the less candid."

26. Ford, *Journals of Congress*, Oct. 17, 1778, XII, p. 1021.
27. Tower, op. cit., p. 395.
28. From a letter cited by Ford, *Writings*, VII, p. 200 n.
29. Tower, op. cit., II, p. 10. Lafayette, *Mémoires*, I, p. 207.
30. Ford, *Writings*, VII, p. 198.
31. Ford, *Writings*, VII, pp. 206, 207 n.
32. Tower, op. cit., II, pp. 34-5. Twenty years later Lafayette changed his mind about this duel and made a note that Carlisle was right. Lafayette, *Mémoires*, I, p. 59, and note.
33. Ford, *Writings*, VII, pp. 261-4.
34. Tower, op. cit., II, p. 41.
35. Lafayette, *Mémoires de ma main*, I, p. 61, says that Washington, after his meetings with Doctor Cochran, returned to camp "with heart oppressed and tears in his eyes" and that their final parting was "very tender, very painful. In accusing this great man of insensibility, his enemies concede only his tenderness for M. de Lafayette."

CHAPTER XXXIV

1. *Simcoe's Military Journal*, p. 84.
2. Cited by H. B. Dawson, *Battles of the United States*, I, p. 452.
3. Ford, *Writings*, VII, p. 204.
4. H. B. Dawson, op. cit., I, p. 458.
5. Edward Field, *Diary of Col. Israel Angell*, p. 26.
6. C. E. Godfrey, *The Commander-in-Chief's Guard*, p. 283, 286.
7. Lewis S. Patrick, *Washington's Headquarters at Fredericksburg*, p. 13.
8. Godfrey, op. cit., p. 283.
9. Clinton MS., *An Historical Detail* (Wm. L. Clements Coll.), p. 133.
10. Hatfield's *History of Elizabeth*, p. 471, cited by W. S. Baker, *Itinerary of General Washington*, p. 145.
11. Ford, *Writings*, VII, 280.
12. Ford, *Writings*, VII, 208.
13. Ford, *Writings*, VII, p. 209.
14. Samuel W. Pennypacker, *George Washington in Pennsylvania*, Penn. Mag. XXVIII, p. 266.
15. Ford, *Journals of Congress*, Sept. 8th, 1778, XII, p. 889.
16. Ford, *Writings*, VI, p. 433. To James Bowdoin, March 17, 1778.
17. *American State Papers*, XII, p. 16. Cited by Gen. Emory Upton, *The Military Policy of the United States*, pp. 20, 34.
18. Galloway's computation in B. F. Stevens' *Facsimiles of MSS*. No. 2079. Van Tyne, *England and America*, p. 152, puts the number at 260,000.
19. Ford, *Writings*, VII, p. 303.

20. Ford, *Writings*, VII, p. 299 n. Letter to Thomas Nelson, March 15, 1779.
21. Ford, *Writings*, VII, p. 297.
22. Cited by W. S. Baker, *Itinerary of General Washington*, p. 147.
23. Frank Moore, *Diary of the Revolution*, II, p. 114.
24. Ford, *Writings*, VII, p. 301.
25. *Official Letters of Major-General James Pattison* (N. Y. Hist. Soc., 1875), p. 10.

CHAPTER XXXV

1. Jared Sparks, *Life of Washington*, p. 293.
2. Ford, *Writings*, VII, p. 309 n.
3. F. D. Stone, *Philadelphia Society One Hundred Years Ago*, Penn. Mag., III, p. 376.
4. Letter to Jeremiah Wadsworth, Jan. 2, 1779.
5. Ford, *Writings*, VII, p. 457.
6. Ford, *Writings*, VII, p. 282. To Joseph Reed, Dec. 12, 1778.
7. Ford, *Writings*, VII, p. 214.
8. Ford, *Writings*, VII, p. 150.
9. Penn. Mag., XXIX, p. 59.
10. W. C. Ford, *Journals of Congress*, II, pp. 105, 106. J. B. McMaster, *Old Standards of Public Morals*, Am. Hist. Ass'n Reports, 1905, I, p. 60.
11. Ford, *Journals of Congress*, XII, p. 1261.
12. Ford, *Journals of Congress*, Sept. 13, 1779, XV, pp. 1052-1062; Gaillard Hunt, *Journals of Congress*, XVI, pp. 263-264, Mar. 18, 1780.
13. McMaster, op. cit., p. 60. *Life of Ashbel Green*, p. 70.
14. Pictures of the money are given in B. J. Lossing's *Field Book of the Revolution*, I, p. 317. R. V. Harlow, *Aspects of Revolutionary Finance*, Am. Hist. Rev., Oct., 1929, p. 50, says, "Among the most striking aspects of Revolutionary money was the lack of anything approaching security."
15. Stone, op. cit., p. 386.
16. W. W. Jennings, *History of Economic Progress*, p. 196. See also W. G. Sumner, *The Financier and Finances of the Revolution*, I, pp. 61, 62, 74.
17. Thomas Paine, *Works* (Patriots' Edition), III, pp. 6, 7.
18. C. H. Van Tyne, *American Revolution*, p. 241.
19. Jared Sparks, *Life of Washington*, p. 307.
20. M. D. Conway, *George Washington and Mount Vernon* (L. I. Hist. Soc., 1889), pp. 316-321, letters dated Dec. 18, 1778, and Sept. 14, 1779.
21. Thomas Jones, *History of New York* (N. Y. Hist. Soc.), II, p. 323. W. A. Duer, *Life of Wm. Alexander, Earl of Stirling*, p. 262.
22. J. Hammond Trumbull, *A Business Firm in the Revolution*, Mag. of Am. Hist., XII, p. 17.
23. Trumbull, op. cit., p. 20. G. W. Greene in his *Life of Greene*, III, p. 518, mentions this partnership but says nothing of its secrecy.
24. Trumbull, op. cit., pp. 23, 24. May 14th, 1779.
25. Trumbull, op. cit., p. 26. April 11, 1780.
26. Trumbull, op. cit., p. 27.
27. Trumbull, op. cit., p. 28.
28. F. V. Greene, *General Greene*, p. 299.
29. Ford, *Writings*, XI, pp. 52 n, 52.
30. Report of the committee, Rosenbach Catalogue, "1776 Americana," number 167.

31. W. G. Sumner, *The Financier and the Finances of the Revolution*, I, p. 266.

32. Sumner, op. cit., II, p. 298.

33. Sumner, op. cit., I, p. 80. That depreciation was a form of taxation was well recognized at the time. Franklin thought it the best kind of tax. Franklin, *Works*, VII, p. 292, VIII, p. 151, IX, p. 231, cited by R. V. Harlow, op. cit., p. 62. Gouverneur Morris wrote to Washington to that effect October 26, 1778. Sparks, *Life of Gouverneur Morris*, I, p. 175. He lamented that "this tax has fallen heavy on those, who have served and continue to serve their country." See also in the footnote, Washington's camplaint that a secret memorial intended to be kept from his knowledge had been submitted to Congress.

34. Ford, *Writings*, VII, p. 417.

35. Sumner, op. cit., I, p. 95.

36. J. B. McMaster, op. cit., p. 58.

37. Stone, op. cit., III, p. 380. Watson, *Annals of Philadelphia*, II, p. 299.

38. Tyler, *Literary History of the American Revolution*, II, p. 63.

39. J. S. Moore, *The Convention of 1788*, pp. 3, 4.

40. *Letters on the Occupation of Boston*, p. 231.

41. Lossing, op. cit., I, p. 319.

42. Charles J. Bullock, *The Finances of the U. S. from 1775 to 1789* (Bulletin of Univ. of Wisconsin, pp. 131, 138).

43. Ford, *Writings*, VII, p. 388.

44. Ford, *Writings*, VII, p. 412.

45. *Proc. Mass. Hist. Soc.*, 1871, p. 56. Letter to Lund Washington, May 29, 1779.

46. Ford, *Writings*, VII, p. 451.

47. Ford, *Writings*, VII, p. 455.

48. Ford, *Writings*, VII, p. 505.

49. Sumner, op. cit., I, p. 71.

50. R. V. Harlow, op. cit., pp. 48, 49.

CHAPTER XXXVI

1. Mrs. A. H. Wharton, *Martha Washington*, p. 127. Mrs. Wharton in her excellent biography confuses Washington's camp at Fredericksburg, New York, with the Virginia town, and says: "Although the General had been as near home as Fredericksburg, Virginia, during the autumn, he does not seem to have had time for one day's rest and refreshment at Mount Vernon."

2. Scharf & Westcott, *History of Philadelphia*, I, p. 397.

3. See Volume II of this work, p. 328.

4. Cited by W. S. Baker, *Itinerary of General Washington*, p. 149.

5. Cited by Frank Moore, *Diary of the Revolution*, II, p. 250.

6. W. S. Baker, *The History of a Rare Washington Print*, Penn. Mag., XIII, p. 257. Mr. Baker believed that the portrait was forever lost but in the *Am. Hist. Ass'n Report*, 1896, I, p. 195, C. H. Hart states that Peale relined and restored the picture so that the vandalism is "barely visible."

7. W. J. Potts, *Du Simitière*, Penn. Mag., XIII, p. 359.

8. A. S. Bolles, *Pennsylvania, Province and State*, II, p. 45, cited by H. J. Ford, *Alexander Hamilton*, p. 73. Concerning the Black List and the execution of Roberts and Carlisle, see C. H. Van Tyne, *The Loyalists in the American Revolution*, pp. 269-271.

9. B. C. Steiner, *James McHenry*, p. 20.

10. Steiner, op. cit., p. 25.

11. G. W. Greene, *General Greene*, II, p. 168.

12. Dr. James Thacher, *Military Journal*, p. 155.

13. *Diary of David Meade Randolph*, William and Mary Quarterly, Oct. 1912, p. 135.

14. An eye-witness writing to the *Penn. Packet*, March 6, 1779. Cited by Frank Moore, op. cit., II, p. 133.

15. F. S. Drake, *Life and Correspondence of Henry Knox*, p. 60.

16. Thacher, op. cit., p. 156.

17. G. W. Greene, op. cit., II, p. 89.

18. G. W. Greene, op. cit., I, p. 377.

19. G. W. Greene, op. cit., II, p. 161.

20. Thacher, op. cit., p. 157.

21. Thacher, op. cit., p. 158.

22. B. J. Lossing, *Mary and Martha Washington*, p. 185.

23. Ford, *Writings*, VII, p. 328.

24. Ford, *Writings*, VII, p. 448.

25. Ford, *Writings*, VII, p. 327, 328 n.

26. Sparks, *Correspondence of the Revolution*, II, p. 239.

27. H. P. Johnston, *Correspondence and Public Papers of John Jay*, I, p. 183.

28. Justin Winsor, *Narrative and Critical History of America*, VI, p. 446. See a letter from Tudor severely criticizing Washington's military blunders, written Dec. 13, 1816, *Mass. Hist. Soc. Proc.*, 1912, p. 416. Sullivan referred to this speech in what Winsor (op. cit., VI, p. 446) calls one of his "oily, fussy letters." Sparks, *Corr. of the Rev.*, II, p. 366.

29. MS. letter, N. Y. Hist. Soc. Coll. Mar. 1, 1779.

30. H. P. Johnston, op. cit., I, p. 196.

31. Ford, *Writings*, VII, p. 393.

32. H. P. Johnston, op. cit., I, p. 204.

33. MS. letter, N. Y. Hist. Soc. Coll., June 9, 1779.

34. Ford, *Writings*, VIII, p. 3.

35. Ford, Writings, VIII, p. 18.

36. Hezekiah Niles, *Principles and Acts of the Revolution*, p. 511.

CHAPTER XXXVII

1. Germain to Clinton, August 28, 1779, cited by Ford, *Writings*, VIII, p. 40 n.

2. W. M. James, *The British Navy in Adversity*, p. 163.

3. H. P. Johnston, *The Storming of Stony Point*, p. 28.

4. Historical MS. Commission, *American MSS.*, I, p. 434.

5. H. P. Johnston, op. cit., p. 43.

6. Letter to Eden. Johnston, op. cit., p. 55.

7. Johnston, op. cit., p. 55.

8. Clinton to Haldimand, Sept. 9, 1779, cited by Johnston, op. cit., p. 143.

9. Capt. Allen McLane, *Journal*, cited by Johnston, op. cit., p. 199.

10. Ford, *Writings*, VII, p. 486.

11. Ford, *Writings*, VII, p. 487.

12. Johnston, op. cit., p. 87. Ford, *Writings*, VII, p. 494.

13. *Historic Letters, West Chester Normal School*, p. 18.

14. Johnston, op. cit., p. 95.
15. Ford, *Writings*, VIII, pp. 33, 48.
16. Dawson, *Battles of the United States*, I, pp. 546, 553.
17. Alexander Hamilton, *Works*, IX, p. 174.
18. Stedman, *The American War*, II, p. 151.
19. Ford, *Writings*, VIII, p. 51.

CHAPTER XXXVIII

1. Ford, *Writings*, VII, p. 296. Letter to Benjamin Harrison.
2. W. W. Henry, *Patrick Henry*, II, p. 25. Letter of March 13, 1779.
3. W. C. Ford, *Journals of Congress*, Sept. 17, 1779, XV, p. 1084.
4. Henry, op. cit., I, p. 583. The story of George Rogers Clark is most accurately told by Prof. James Alton James, *The Life of George Rogers Clark*, based upon a thorough study of manuscripts and correcting many misstatements of earlier writers.
5. Ford, *Writings*, VIII, p. 4.
6. Ford, *Writings*, VIII, p. 121.
7. James, op. cit., p. 165.
8. Ford, *Journals of Congress*, Sept. 24, 1779, XV, p. 1096.
9. New light has been shed on this dark and complex history by J. B. Wilbur's *Ira Allen, Founder of Vermont*, and by John Pell's *Ethan Allen*, both disclosing Washington's relations with this neglected statesman and his brother.
10. E. B. O'Callaghan, *The Documentary History of New York*, IV, p. 975.
11. Dr. James Thacher, *Military Journal*, p. 142, speaks of Butler's "eternal infamy" and tells of a Tory who kept a vow to wash his hands in his father's heart's blood, and also killed and scalped his mother, brothers and sisters; of another who exterminated his own family, etc. Lossing and others accept these stories at full value.
12. John Marshall, *Life of Washington*, III, p. 72 n. Andrew Macfarland Davis in his chapter on "The Indians and the Border Warfare of the Revolution" and the Critical Notes (Winsor's *Narrative and Critical History*, VI, p. 664) describes the immense exaggerations and the probable facts. W. L. Stone, *Life of Joseph Brant*, also relieves Brant and other Indians of much unjustified slander.
13. A. C. Flick in *New Sources on the Sullivan-Clinton Campaign in 1779*, The Quarterly Journal of the N. Y. State Hist. Ass'n, July, 1929, publishes several letters of Butler's, notably one to his chief, General Haldimand in which he says: "I ever have and always shall use my utmost endeavours to restrain the Indians from acts of cruelty & indiscriminate vengeance which both as a man & an officer I hold in abhorrence" (p. 216).
14. A. C. Flick, op. cit., pp. 195-210.
15. Ford, *Writings*, VII, p. 339.
16. Unpublished letters to General Clinton, Dec. 31, 1778, January 19, 1779, Jan. 25, May 28, June 10, 1779, in Catalogue of Geo. H. Richmond, pp. 35, 37, 39, 41.
17. Flick, op. cit., p. 193.
18. Ford, *Writings*, VII, p. 356.
19. Ford, *Writings*, VII, p. 356 n.
20. O. E. Rising, *A New Hampshire Lawyer in General Washington's Army*, p. 22.

21. Ford, *Writings*, VIII, p. 8. August 15, 1779.
22. Ford, *Writings*, VII, p. 460.
23. Rising, op. cit., p. 107.
24. Col. Hubbey's *Journal* quoted by Rising, op. cit., pp. 76, 83. Rev. William Gordon, *History of . . . the Independence*, III, p. 21, is very contemptuous of Sullivan's conduct. T. C. Amory in his *Life of Sullivan*, of course, justifies his every act.
25. W. L. Stone, op. cit., II, p. 25.
26. Ford, *Journals of Congress*, Oct. 14 and Oct. 20, 1779, XV, pp. 1170, 1191.
27. Thomas Jones, *History of New York during the Revolution* (N. Y. Hist. Soc.), II, p. 334 n.
28. Jones, op. cit., II, p. 334.
29. Letter to the N. Y. *Gazette*, Sept. 16, 1779, cited by Frank Moore, *Diary of the Revolution*, II, p. 219.
30. *Proc. N. J. Hist. Soc.*, II, p. 31.
31. Stone, op. cit., II, p. 217.
32. S. J. Drake, *The Aboriginal Races of North America*, p. 609.
33. A. M. Davis, op. cit., p. 668.
34. Ford, *Writings*, VIII, p. 140 n.
35. Amory, op. cit., p. 157.
36. Ford, *Writings*, VIII, p. 225 n.
37. Ford, *Writings*, VIII, p. 139.
38. Ford, *Writings*, VII, p. 499 n.
39. B. F. Stevens, *Facsimiles of MSS. in European Archives*, No. 1616.
40. *Historic Letters, West Chester Normal School*, p. 11.
41. Ford, *Writings*, VIII, p. 198. Sparks, *Writings*, VI, p. 198 n.
42. Ford, *Journals of Congress*, June 22, 1779, XIV, p. 758.
43. Ford, *Writings*, VIII, p. 3.
44. Upton, *Military Policy of the U. S.*, p. 40.
45. Ford, *Writings*, VIII, p. 138.

CHAPTER XXXIX

1. W. C. Ford, *Correspondence and Journals of S. B. Webb*, II, pp. 232, 245. H. P. Johnston, *Yale and her Honor-Roll in the American Revolution*, pp. 113, 114.
2. Ford, *Writings*, VIII, p. 161 n.
3. Ford, *Writings*, VIII, p. 147.
4. Ford, *Writings*, VIII, p. 155.
5. Ford, *Writings*, VIII, pp. 157 n, 160.
6. *Revolutionary Army Orders*, Nov. 10, 1779, Va. Hist. Mag., Oct. 1913, p. 379.
7. Thacher, *Military Journal*, p. 177.
8. Ford, *Writings*, VIII, p. 187.
9. *The Huntington Papers*, Conn. Hist. Soc. Coll., XX, p. 437.
10. Thacher, op. cit., p. 180.
11. Thacher, op. cit., p. 181.
12. Gaine's *Mercury*, Feb. 7, 1780, cited by Frank Moore, *Diary of the Revolution*, II, p. 258.
13. Moore, op. cit., II, p. 254.

14. Cited by W. B. Reed, *Life of Joseph Reed*, II, p. 190.

15. B. J. Lossing, *Field Book of the Revolution*, I, p. 310. Emory McClintock's *Topography of Washington's Camp of 1780* has a very full description of Morristown.

16. Ford, *Writings*, VIII, p. 172.

17. Reed, op. cit., II, p. 191.

18. Mary Gay Humphreys, *Catherine Schuyler*, p. 168.

19. Humphreys, op. cit., p. 188.

20. George Bancroft, *History of the U. S.*, X, p. 179.

21. Ford, *Writings*, VIII, p. 215 n.

22. W. C. Ford, *Journals of Congress*, XV, p. 1344.

23. G. W. Greene, *Historical View of the Revolution*, p. 160.

24. The figures as to the taxes are given in *Journals of Congress*, XV, p. 1053. See also XVI, pp. 35, 244.

25. Ford, *Writings*, VIII, p. 170.

26. W. G. Sumner, *The Financier and the Finances of the Revolution*, I, p. 36.

27. Charles Chauncey to Richard Price, *Mass. Hist. Soc. Proc.*, 1903, p. 320.

28. Hunt, *Journals of Congress*, XVI, p. 112, XVII, p. 539.

29. Ford, *Writings*, VIII, pp. 241, 246 n.

30. Ford, *Writings*, VIII, p. 224 n to Schuyler, March 22, 1780.

31. Thacher, op. cit., p. 184.

32. *Simcoe's Military Journal*, p. 131.

33. Thacher, op. cit., p. 189.

34. Sir Henry Clinton, MS., *An Historical Detail*, I, p. 218.

35. G. W. Allen, *Naval History of the Revolution*, II, p. 543.

CHAPTER XL

1. Sparks, *Writings*, VI, p. 150. Dec. 29, 1778.

2. Sparks, *Writings*, VI, p. 148.

3. Sparks, *Correspondence of the American Revolution*, II, p. 247. Charlemagne Tower, *The Marquis de La Fayette in the American Revolution*, II, pp. 50, 51.

4. Brand Whitlock, *La Fayette*, I, p. 179.

5. Whitlock, op. cit., p. 189. H. D. Sedgwick, *La Fayette*, pp. 106-112. Lafayette, *Mémoires*, I, p. 65, forgetting the third person, which he had taken as a "mantle" of egoism, says: "I had the honor of being consulted by all the ministers, and, what was better, kissed by all the women. The kisses ceased the next day. But I kept the confidence of the cabinet."

6. Sparks, *Writings*, VII, p. 492. Lafayette, op. cit., I, p. 65.

7. Doniol, *Histoire de la participation*, etc., IV, p. 233.

8. Doniol, op. cit., IV, p. 236 n.

9. Doniol, op. cit., IV, p. 239 n.

10. Sparks, *Writings*, VI, p. 551.

11. Charlemagne Tower, op. cit., II, p. 70. Cf. Sparks, *Writings*, VI, p. 549.

12. Tower, op. cit., II, p. 80.

13. Ford, *Writings*, VII, p. 359.

14. Ford, *Writings*, VII, p. 481.

15. Ford, *Writings*, VIII, p. 48.

16. E. P. Chase, *Our Revolutionary Forefathers*, The Letters of François, Marquis de Barbé-Marbois, pp. 113-118.

17. Ford, *Writings*, VIII, pp. 65-73, 85.
18. Ford, *Writings*, VIII, p. 217.
19. Sparks, *Correspondence of the American Revolution*, II, p. 441.
20. Lafayette, *Mémoires*, I, p. 259.
21. Sparks, *Writings*, VII, p. 29.
22. Ford, *Writings*, VIII, p. 264 n.
23. Ford, *Writings*, VIII, p. 275.
24. Ford, *Writings*, VIII, p. 280.
25. The suspicion expressed by Ford, *Writings*, VIII, p. 281 n, that Arnold turned over to Clinton the proclamation, which Clinton sent to Germain, is proved by Arnold's own cipher letter quoted in Chapter XLII.

CHAPTER XLI

1. C. H. Van Tyne, *French Aid before 1778*, in Am. Hist. Rev., XXXI, p. 40. He speaks of "That early secret aid which furnished almost ninety per cent of the munitions of war which made the very continuance of military resistance possible during 1776 and which made the victory at Saratoga even conceivable." (P. 20.) See Orlando W. Stephenson on *The Supply of Gunpowder in 1776*, Am. Hist. Rev., XXX, pp. 271-281. "If it had not been for the great quantities of powder obtained by importations from France before the Saratoga campaign, the Revolution would have broken down long before that time."
2. These are Alexander Hamilton's figures. See W. G. Sumner, *The Financier and the Finances of the American Revolution*, II, pp. 127-133. See also C. J. Bullock's *Finances of the U. S.*, 1775-1789 (Univ. of Wis.), ch. V, for a somewhat modified estimate.
3. Gen. Emory Upton, *The Military Policy of the U. S.*, p. 47.
4. Ford, *Writings*, VIII, p. 288. May 27, 1780.
5. Ford, *Writings*, VIII, p. 293.
6. Ford, *Writings*, VIII, p. 333.
7. Ford, *Writings*, VIII, p. 301.
8. Ford, *Writings*, VIII, p. 344 n.
9. Ford, *Writings*, VIII, pp. 344, 352.
10. From a cipher letter sent by Vergennes to Lafayette but intercepted by the British. See *Am. Hist. Rev.*, VIII, p. 507.
11. Cited by C. H. Van Tyne, op. cit., p. 20 n.
12. Ford, *Writings*, VIII, p. 285.
13. Ford, *Writings*, VIII, p. 417.
14. Ford, *Writings*, VIII, p. 304.
15. Ford, *Writings*, VIII, p. 317.
16. Ford, *Writings*, VIII, p. 323 n.
17. Ford, *Writings*, VIII, p. 323 n.
18. Ford, *Writings*, IX, p. 138. See also p. 113.
19. See Sumner, op. cit., II, p. 21, D. R. Dewey, *Financial History of the U. S.*, p. 54, E. L. Bogart, *The Economic History of the U. S.*, pp. 83, 113.
20. Ford, *Writings*, VIII, p. 337. For Washington's comments on the controversy between the bankers and Joseph Reed, see Ford, *Writings*, VIII, p. 331.
21. Ford, *Writings*, VIII, p. 380. See W. C. Ford, *Letters of Joseph Jones*, pp. 27-28, for a strong attack on Greene's stewardship. See Greene's letter to Biddle, Reed's *Life of Reed*, II, p. 469, G. W. Greene's *Life of Greene*, II, p. 287, Hamilton's *Works*, IX, p. 194, 195 n.

22. G. W. Greene, op. cit., II, p. 207.

23. Greene, op. cit., II, p. 208.

24. Emory Upton, op. cit., p. 53.

25. Greene, op. cit., II, p. 344.

26. *Am. Hist. Rev.*, XX, p. 374. This and other letters translated here were found by Mr. W. G. Leland in Paris (p. 341). They were not seen by Doniol or Charlemagne Tower.

27. Gaillard Hunt, *Journals of Congress*, XVII, pp. 508, 510. June 13, 14, 1780.

28. J. A. Stevens, *The Southern Campaign, 1780*, Mag. of Am. Hist., V, p. 255. This article is a glowing defence of Gates' conduct.

29. Ford, *Writings*, VIII, p. 356. See Ford, *Letters of Joseph Jones*, p. 19.

30. Col. Otho H. Williams, *A Narrative of the Campaign of 1780*. Appendix B in Wm. Johnson's *Life of Greene*, I, p. 494.

31. Fortescue, *History of the British Army*, III, p. 323, gives Cornwallis 1500 regulars, and less than 500 militia, and Gates "thrice that number of militia" and "no more regular troops than Cornwallis, and those of inferior quality." Dawson, *Battles of the U. S.*, I, p. 614, gives Gates 4100 men and Cornwallis 2117 men and 122 officers.

32. H. J. Eckenrode, *The Revolution in Virginia*, p. 210.

33. John Marshall, *Life of Washington*, III, p. 197.

34. Alexander Hamilton, *Works*, IX, pp. 204, 203.

35. James Wilkinson, *Memoirs*, I, p. 406.

36. Ford, *Writings*, VIII, p. 440.

37. Ford, *Writings*, VIII, p. 475.

38. *Mag. of Am. Hist.*, V, p. 309. Here are given many of Gates' letters and his orders on this campaign. See also Ford, *Writings*, VIII, p. 422 n., and MSS. N. Y. Hist. Soc. Coll.

39. Ford, *Writings*, VIII, pp. 494, 497.

40. John Austin Stevens, op. cit., V, pp. 255 and 425, makes the best answer to Gates' critics among historians. Henry Lee, *Memoirs*, p. 190, praises Gates in every respect.

41. Ford, *Writings*, IX, p. 11.

42. Ford, *Writings*, IX, p. 15.

43. *Mag. of Am. Hist.*, V, p. 283.

44. MS. letter, Gates Papers, N. Y. Hist. Soc. Coll.

45. Ford, *Writings*, X, p. 62. Here Washington refers in a letter of Aug. 11, 1782, to the fact that he had not had an answer to his letter of March 18th to Gates. In Gates' letter of Aug. 17, 1780 (Ford, *Writings*, X, p. 63 n.), however, Gates says that General Lincoln informed him of Washington's offer of a command.

46. Alexander Garden, *Anecdotes of the Revolutionary War*, I, p. 350.

47. Ford, *Writings*, X, p. 63 n.

48. J. C. Fitzpatrick, *The Diaries of Washington*, IV, p. 184, May 26th, 1791.

49. Ford, *Writings*, VIII, p. 339.

50. Hunt, *Journals of Congress*, XVII, p. 704. Aug. 7th, 1780.

51. W. C. Ford, *Correspondence of S. B. Webb*, II, p. 290.

52. W. C. Ford, *Corr. of S. B. Webb*, II, p. 291.

53. W. C. Ford, *Corr. of S. B. Webb*, II, pp. 300-307.

54. Ford, *Writings*, VIII, p. 233 n.

CHAPTER XLII

1. Brand Whitlock, *La Fayette*, I, p. 22.
2. The letter is cited by H. D. Sedgwick *La Fayette*, p. 378. Whitlock, op. cit., II, p. 140. Part of it is omitted in the 1838 edition of Lafayette's *Mémoires*, V, p. 275. It is given in full in M. McDermot Crawford's *Madame de La Fayette and her Family*, p. 318. See Whitlock, pp. 139-144, for his activities in removing what he described in a letter to Washington as the "intolerable despotism" to which Protestants were subjected. Whitlock, I, p. 292, says of the court of France and La Fayette's religious reforms: "Men there, like most men in those days, like La Fayette himself, while nominally Roman Catholics, were in reality deists, when they were not atheists. But such a movement might excite the opposition of the clergy, even the atheists among them."
3. MS. letter, July 7, 1779, N. Y. Hist. Soc. Coll.
4. This poem is given in full in Winthrop Sargent's *Loyalist Poetry of the Revolution* (privately printed), pp. 1-12. A biographical sketch is on p. 199. The ascription of this poem to Odell is not quite impregnable (see G. W. Greene, *Greene*, II, p. 237 n.), but it is generally accepted as his and M. C. Tyler has no doubt in the matter, *Literary History of The American Revolution*, ch. XXIX. Concerning Odell there is some brilliant writing in Vernon L. Parrington's *The Colonial Mind*, p. 255.
5. Sparks, *Writings*, VII, p. 521. Winthrop Sargent, *Life of Major André*, p. 259.
6. Sargent, *Loyalist Poetry*, p. 50.
7. Randolph G. Adams, Article on Arnold, *Dictionary of American Biography*, I, p. 365.
8. Wm. L. Clements Collection. Beginning with Vol. XXIV, p. 258, the Penn. Mag. published a *Life of Margaret Shippen*, wife of Benedict Arnold, by Lewis Byrd Walker, in which it is stated that her father was really a neutral rather than a Tory. Washington dined at Edward Shippen's house in 1774 when Peggy was 15. She wrote: "Nobody in America could revere his character more than I did." (XXIV, p. 414.)
9. Sir John Fortescue, *The Correspondence of King George*, III, V, p. 415. Lord North to the King, March 26th, 1782: "P. S. The Warrant for Mrs. Arnold's pension, which is enclosed, has been drawn in pursuance of His Majesty's orders."
10. J. B. Wilbur, *Ira Allen*, I, p. 153. John Pell's *Ethan Allen* proves beyond doubt Ethan Allen's eagerness to make Vermont a British province, quoting Allen's own writings. See pp. 190, 194, 199, 211, 216, 222, 225, 233.
11. Wilbur, op. cit., I, p. 196.
12. C. J. Stillé, *Anthony Wayne*, p. 236. See also John Austin Stevens' castigation not only of Arnold but of I. N. Arnold's biography of him, *Mag. of Am. Hist.*, IV, p. 190.
13. Jared Sparks, *Benedict Arnold* (Library of Am. Biog.), III, p. 158.
14. Barbé-Marbois, *Complot d'Arnold*, cited by Sparks, op. cit., p. 145, *Mag. of Am. Hist.*, IX, p. 189. See Sargent's *André*, p. 266.
15. *Mag. of Am. Hist.*, IX, p. 189.
16. M. L. Davis, *Memoir of Aaron Burr*, I, p. 220.
17. Richard Rush, *Occasional Productions*, p. 79, a transcript from Lear's Diary.
18. R. J. Adams, *The Clinton Papers*, p. 27.

19. Sir Henry Clinton, MS. *An Historical Detail* (Clements Coll.), II, p. 43.
20. Sargent, *André*, p. 279.
21. G. M. Philips, *Historic Letters from the Coll. of the West Chester State Normal School*, p. 25.
22. MS. letter to Gov. Thos. Lee, Sept. 18, 1780, Emmett Coll., N. Y. Public Library.
23. *Am. Hist. Rev.*, XX, p. 369.
24. Sparks, *Writings*, VII, p. 519.
25. Ford, *Writings*, VIII, p. 403 n.
26. Rochambeau, *Mémoires*, I, p. 248, cited by Doniol, *La Participation, etc.*, IV, p. 375 n.
27. Doniol, op. cit., IV, p. 380.
28. Lafayette, *Mémoires*, I, p. 365.
29. Ford, *Writings*, VIII, p. 427.
30. Ford, *Writings*, VIII, p. 435.
31. Ford, *Writings*, VIII, p. 444 n.
32. Sparks, *Arnold*, p. 186.
33. *Mag. of Am. Hist.*, IX, part 2, p. 308.
34. Rev. Wm. Gordon, *History of the . . . Independence*, III, p. 128.
35. J. W. Stuart, Life of Jonathan Trumbull, Sen. (Boston 1859).
36. Letters of de Fersen, *Mag. of Am. Hist.*, III, pp. 303, 305.
37. Doniol, op. cit., IV, p. 383.
38. I. Q. Leake, *Memoir of General John Lamb*, p. 258.
39. Sparks, *Writings*, VII, p. 531. André's autographs show that he spelled his own name without an accent. Earlier historians spelled it with a grave accent, which is impossible. His father was born in Switzerland but the original name was probably Andrée. See Sargent, *Life of André*, p. 1.
40. Sparks' letters to Tallmadge and Tallmadge's replies are reproduced in the *Mag. of Am. History*, III, pp. 747-756, and in the *Public Papers of George Clinton (ed. Hugh Hastings)*, VI, p. 259. Sparks quotes from these letters in his *Life of Arnold*. See also H. P. Johnston, *Memoir of Benj. Tallmadge.*
41. *Mag. of Am. Hist.*, III, p. 755, *Public Papers of George Clinton*, p. 263. Tallmadge's letter was written Feb. 17th, 1834.
42. Rush, op. cit., p. 82.
43. There are many first-hand accounts of most of these crowded scenes, and less contradiction than one usually finds. There is some conflict as to who went to breakfast while Washington inspected the fort, the time and place of his receipt of the news. Fenimore Cooper, who is believed to have talked with Lafayette of the scene, mentions Washington's tears as he turned the papers over to Lafayette and Knox. I. N. Arnold's *Arnold* is documented and as fair as could be expected. The whole story, with a wealth of detail, excerpts from nearly all the authorities, photographs of the scenes and a carefully traced map of André's wanderings, is found in William Abbatt's *The Crisis of the Revolution*. Jared Sparks made minute investigations in the documents and among still living witnesses. His letters of inquiry to Tallmadge show how carefully Sparks worked up the material for his biographies of Arnold and Washington. The Appendix to Vol. VII of his *Writings of Washington* contains many documents. H. P. Johnston's *Memoir of Col. Benjamin Tallmadge* is rich in humanity. Winthrop Sargent's *André* is the result of deep research.
44. Joseph Nash was the soldier who related this incident as his own experience. *Mag. of Am. Hist.*, XI, p. 260.
45. I. N. Arnold, op. cit., p. 299.

46. Thacher, *Military Journal,* p. 215.

47. Hamilton, *Works,* IX, p. 207.

48. Tower, op. cit., II, p. 167.

49. M. L. Davis, *Memoir of Aaron Burr,* I, p. 219.

50. I. N. Arnold, op. cit., p. 320. See Sir George Otto Trevelyan, *George the Third and Charles Fox,* I, p. 289 n.

51. W. B. Reed, *Life of Reed,* II, p. 275 n.

52. I. N. Arnold's *Arnold* carries their lives through to the end and gives many of their letters. L. B. Walker, *Life of Margaret Shippen,* Penn. Mag., XXIV, gives many letters, Arnold's will, and the letters of Mrs. Arnold's father concerning Arnold's tangled affairs.

CHAPTER XLIII

1. I. Q. Leake, *Memoir of Gen. John Lamb,* p. 263.

2. Lafayette told Wade this in 1824, Wm. Abbatt, *The Crisis of the Rev.,* p. 45 n.

3. Ford, *Writings,* VIII, p. 450.

4. Abbatt, op. cit., pp. 45, 46.

5. Ford, *Writings,* VIII, p. 450 n.

6. Ford, *Writings,* VIII, p. 451.

7. Smith's own account, cited by Abbatt, op. cit., p. 47.

8. Hamilton, *Works,* IX, p. 206.

9. G. W. Greene, *Greene,* II, pp. 227, 228.

10. C. J. Stillé, *Wayne,* p. 236.

11. Stillé, op. cit., p. 234.

12. Tallmadge's letter to Sparks, *Mag. of Am. Hist.,* III, pp. 753, 756.

13. Ford, *Writings,* VIII, p. 458.

14. Thacher, *Military Journal,* p. 222.

15. Ford, *Writings,* VIII, p. 455.

16. Ford, *Writings,* VIII, p. 455 n.

17. Ford, *Writings,* VIII, p. 499.

18. *Penn. Mag.,* XXV, p. 370. The version in Ford, *Writings,* VIII, p. 493, is slightly different.

19. Ford, *Writings,* VIII, p. 494 n.

20. In a letter to Madame Tessé, *Mémoires,* I, p. 371, Lafayette says that the discovery of the plot was due to *"une combinaison de hasards incroyables."* Cited by Charlemagne Tower, *The Marquis de La Fayette in the Am. Rev.,* II, pp. 164-166.

21. Henry Lee, *Memoirs,* p. 395. The story of Sergeant Champe told at length in Lee's *Memoirs* has been severely criticized. Jefferson called the whole work "an historical novel" (Randall, *Life of Thomas Jefferson,* III, p. 661), but aside from certain confused details of incident and chronology, it is unquestionably true and is confirmed by Washington's letters. Sargent in his *André,* p. 451, tells the story that Lee's manuscript was "in a very undigested form," being delivered to the publishers at a time when Lee was "in duress." In the editing the contradictions slipped in. Sparks, *Writings,* VII, pp. 545-549, gives Lee's correspondence with Washington on this subject and explains the probable origin of the discrepancies.

22. Washington's letter was written Oct. 20, 1780, nearly three weeks after André's execution. Ford, *Writings,* IX, p. 4. Lee, *Memoirs,* p. 408.

23. Gaillard Hunt, *Journals of Congress,* XVIII, p. 950. Oct. 18th, 1780.

24. See Thacher, op. cit., p. 228. Abbatt, op. cit., p. 60.

25. Jared Sparks, *The Life and Treason of Benedict Arnold*, p. 284.

26. Alex. Hamilton's Letter to John Laurens, *Works*, IX, p. 218. André's theatrical activity and his engaging personality have been recently presented with great charm in the historical novel, *The Painted Minx*, by Robert W. Chambers, whose vivid romantic imagination is always careful to ground itself on most thorough and conscientious research in a period on which he is an authority. In G. C. D. Odell's *Annals of the N. Y. Stage*, I, p. 188, it is stated that a scene painted by André was preserved until 1821. It is highly praised in Sargent's *André*, p. 153.

27. Abbatt, op. cit., p. 46 n. Sparks, *Writings*, VII, p. 533.

28. Abbatt, op. cit., p. 47. Sparks, *Writings*, VII, p. 534.

29. Abbatt, op. cit., p. 47. Sparks, *Writings*, VII, p. 534.

30. Sparks, *Writings*, VII, p. 539.

31. *Mag. of Am. Hist.*, III, p. 753.

32. The Cow-Chace is published in full in Sargent's *André*, p. 236, and Lossing's *Field Book of the Revolution*, II, p. 878. Wm. Johnson, *Greene*, I, p. 204, says, "Wayne did not sit in the board of officers . . . perhaps from considerations of delicacy; . . . the wounds of the pen last longer than those of the sword." Johnson is unusually hostile to André. See Thomas Boyd, *Mad Anthony Wayne*, p. 172.

33. See Greene, *Greene*, II, pp. 234, 5, for Greene's cross-examination of André. Sparks, *Writings*, VII, p. 535, for the paper drawn up by André.

34. Kapp, *Steuben*, p. 289.

35. Johnson, *Greene*, I, p. 210. G. W. Greene, his grandson, says, p. 235, "a tear, say our family traditions, dimmed his eye." The findings of the court are given by Abbatt, p. 62.

36. Thacher, op. cit., p. 224.

37. Abbatt, op. cit., p. 62 n.

38. Sparks, *Writings*, VII, p. 539.

39. Greene, *Greene*, II, p. 237. This is on the authority of Barbé-Marbois, who doubtless made up the dialogue from Greene's account.

40. Sparks, VII, p. 540. Johnson in his *Greene*, I, p. 207, denounces this charge and even accuses André of being responsible for the arrest of these patriots.

41. Gen. Robertson's letter, cited by Abbatt, op. cit., p. 67 n.

42. *Simcoe's Military Journal*, p. 294.

43. *Simcoe's Military Journal*, pp. 293, 294.

44. Thomas Jones, *History of New York during the Revolutionary War*, pp. 375, 382.

45. Fortescue, *History of the British Army*, III, p. 336.

46. *Public Papers of George Clinton*, VI, p. 403. Letter of Nov. 11, 1780. There is much about Washington's secret service system in the *Mag. of Am. Hist.*, VIII, pp. 95-105.

47. Sparks, *Writings*, VII, p. 541.

48. Sparks, *Writings*, VII, p. 542.

49. Sparks, *Writings*, VII, p. 543.

50. Hamilton, *Works*, IX, p. 208.

51. Hamilton, *Works*, IX, p. 209. In this long letter Hamilton gives a very vivid account of André's execution and philosophizes on the ugliness of war.

52. Bowman's letter to Tallmadge, cited by Abbatt, op. cit., p. 52. His statement differs slightly from that in Thacher's *Military Journal*. There are many

descriptions of André's execution, the most picturesque being that of Capt. Van Dyk.

53. This account is given in full in a pamphlet published in 1892 by the Washington Association of New Jersey, *George Washington, an Address . . . by Rev. David R. Frazer*, also *Letters Relating to the Execution of Major Andre*.

54. Abbatt, op. cit., p. 73 n.

55. Abbatt, op. cit., p. 75

56. *Memoir of Col. Benj. Tallmadge*, p. 57.

57. A facsimile of this letter is given by R. G. Adams, *The Clinton Papers*, p. 28. See also Sparks, *Writings*, VII, p. 537.

58. Hamilton, *Works*, IX, pp. 216, 219.

59. Ford, *Writings*, VIII, p. 473 n. To Rochambeau.

60. Stanhope, *History of England*, VII, p. 72.

61. Sir H. Clinton, *MS. An Historical Detail*, W. L. Clements Coll., II, p. 43.

62. R. G. Adams, op. cit., p. 34.

63. London *Public Advertiser* reproduced in Rivington's *Gazette* and cited by Moore, *Diary of the Revolution*, II, pp. 393, 398.

64. Sir G. O. Trevelyan, *George III and Charles Fox*, I, p. 293.

65. Abbatt, op. cit., p. 79.

66. Sargent, *André*, p. 183. Sargent says he had the story from a member of the woman's family.

CHAPTER XLIV

1. Doniol, *La participation de la France*, IV, p. 397.

2. H. P. Johnston, *Correspondence and Public Papers of John Jay*, I, p. 449.

3. Wm. Abbatt, *The Crisis of the Revolution*, p. 80. Ford, *Writings*, VIII, p. 474 n.

4. See Tallmadge's letter of Sept. 17, 1822, to Pickering. H. P. Johnston, *Memoir of Col. Benj. Tallmadge*, pp. 135, 136.

5. I. Q. Leake, *Life and Times of General John Lamb*, p. 264.

6. Henry Whiting, *Revolutionary Orders of General Washington*, pp. 138, 145, Nov. 16 and Dec. 8, 1780.

7. W. H. Smith, *The St. Clair Papers*, I, p. 106 n.

8. Ford, *Writings*, VIII, pp. 470, 471.

9. Ford, *Writings*, VIII, p. 495 n. See IX, p. 9, for his instructions to Greene.

10. Ford, *Writings*, VIII, p. 493 n. See E. C. Burnett, *Letters of Members of the Continental Congress*, IV, pp. xi, xii. Whiting, op. cit., pp. 147, 149, 176.

11. Ford, *Writings*, VIII, pp. 502-507.

12. Marquis de Chastellux, *Travels in North America*, translated by an English Gentleman, with notes (1787), pp. 113-131.

13. James Thacher, *Military Journal*, p. 199.

14. Chastellux, op. cit., pp. 136-139, 352.

15. Lafayette, *Mémoires, correspondance et manuscrits*, I, p. 381. See Tower, *La Fayette*, II, p. 172.

16. Ford, *Writings*, IX, p. 17.

17. Ford, *Writings*, IX, p. 36 n.

18. Ford, *Writings*, IX, p. 56.

19. Ford, *Writings*, IX, p. 45. To Gouverneur Morris, Dec. 10, 1780.

20. Ford, *Writings*, IX, p. 51.

21. Ford, *Writings*, IX, p. 76.

22. Ford, *Writings*, IX, p. 74 n. See Clinton's *Private Intelligencer*, repro-

duced in the *Mag. of Am. Hist.*, X, pp. 412-14. The spy who betrayed Washington's plan says in this letter, "When I was at the highlands I spent a night with Parsons, and another with General Stark. I am on the best of terms with them both. The latter with his family stayed a night at my house since." See also F. L. Humphreys, *Life and Times of David Humphreys*, I, pp. 187-197. Heath's *Memoirs*.

23. See C. Stedman, *The American War*, II, p. 257, Mahon, *History of England*, VII, pp. 45, 49, R. G. Adams, *A History of the Foreign Policy of the United States*, pp. 45, 83, C. H. Van Tyne, *The American Revolution*, pp. 313-9, *The Cambridge History of the British Empire*, I, p. 716.

24. This letter dated December 15, 1780, not given in the collections, is found in W. P. Palmer's *Calendar of Virginia State Papers*, I, p. 402.

25. Fortescue, *History of the British Army*, III, p. 353.

26. W. C. Ford, *Correspondence and Journals of S. B. Webb*, II, p. 331.

27. Friedrich Edler, *The Dutch Republic and the American Revolution* (Johns Hopkins Univ. Studies), pp. 183-189. This is a thorough study of the whole activity of Holland in the war.

28. Included in the *Military Papers of Gen. John Cadwalader*, Penn. Mag., XXXII, p. 171. This letter is given somewhat differently in Ford, *Writings*, VIII, p. 466.

29. Ford, *Writings*, IX, p. 63.

30. Ford, *Writings*, IX, p. 76. To James Duane, Dec. 26, 1780.

31. The Duc de Lauzun, *Mémoires*, p. 351, says, "*Je sus la mort de M. le Chevalier de Ternay, que l'on dit mort de chagrin.*" In the English edition, p. 196, Scott Moncrieff translates this, "who had died, it was said, of a broken heart."

32. Ford, *Writings*, IX, p. 83 n. To Col. Brodhead, Dec. 29, 1780.

CHAPTER XLV

1. Ford, *Writings*, IX, p. 91. Letter to New England States.

2. This estimate of numbers is based on the fact that 1,250 men were discharged and 1,150 furloughed. Detailed accounts of the mutiny are given in *The Letter-Book of Lieut. Enos Reeves*, Penn. Mag., XXI, p. 72, C. J. Stillé's *Anthony Wayne and the Pennsylvania Line*, *The St. Clair Papers*, I, pp. 110, 533-570, Reed's *Reed*, L. C. Hatch, *Administration of the American Revolutionary Army*, Chapter VII, the biographies of Lafayette, and letters of his discovered in France and transcribed by W. G. Leland for the *Am. Hist. Rev.*, XX, p. 582. See Sparks, *Corr. of the Am. Rev.*, III, pp. 192, 198.

3. Stillé, op. cit., p. 240.

4. Stillé, op. cit., pp. 174, 229. For details of this embroilment with Washington, see W. H. Smith, *St. Clair Papers*, I, p. 108. He accuses Wayne of fomenting the difficulty instead of allaying it, as Sparks says; and he gives St. Clair credit for stilling the tempest.

5. Hatch, op. cit., p. 125.

6. Stillé, op. cit., p. 240.

7. Stillé, op. cit., p. 242.

8. Lieut. Reeves, op. cit., p. 74.

9. Lieut. Reeves, op. cit., p. 75.

10. Translated from the letters transcribed by W. G. Leland, *Am. Hist. Rev.*, p. 582.

11. Ford, *Writings*, IX, p. 89.
12. Ford, *Writings*, IX, p. 91.
13. Ford, *Writings*, IX, p. 112.
14. Ford, *Writings*, IX, p. 95.
15. Ford, *Writings*, IX, p. 92.
16. Ford, *Writings*, IX, pp. 91, 92 n.
17. Ford, *Writings*, IX, pp. 89, 102 n.
18. Clinton MS., *An Historical Detail* (Wm. L. Clements Coll.), II, p. 89. His "Private Intelligencer," the Original Secret Record, is published in the *Mag. of Am. Hist.*, beginning, X, p. 327. These documents contributed by Dr. T. A. Emmett with introduction and notes by E. F. De Lancey give an appalling view of the ease with which Clinton kept himself informed as to Washington's affairs, the minuteness of his intelligence, and the number of his informers.
19. Reed, *Reed*, II, p. 329.
20. Ford, *Writings*, IX, pp. 119, 122, 123 n. See Hatch, op. cit., p. 136, of the opposing sentiments of those who criticized Reed for his concessions and those who approved them. See also Reed's *Reed*, II, pp. 333-335.
21. Ford, *Writings*, IX, p. 118. Sparks, *Writings*, VII, Appendix X, gives correspondence.
22. MS. letter in the Huntington Library, January 21st, 1781.
23. Henry Whiting, *Revolutionary Orders of General Washington*, p. 169, Jan. 30, 1781. See also p. 139. His request for power to increase the number of lashes is in Ford, *Writings*, IX, p. 126, Feb. 3, 1781.
24. Dumas, *Souvenirs*, cited by Thomas Balch, *Les Français en Amérique*, p. 117. Dumas's exact words are somewhat un-Washingtonian: "*Allons, mes enfants, du courage; c'est moi qui vais vous conduire, puisque c'est mon devoir de tenir le gouvernail.*"

CHAPTER XLVI

1. Cited by W. P. Baker, *Itinerary of General Washington*, p. 207.
2. Ford, *Writings*, IX, p. 161.
3. *Mémoires de M. le duc de Lauzun* (Paris, 1822), p. 353. *Memoirs of the Duc de Lauzun* (translated by C. K. Scott Moncrieff), p. 197.
4. Ford, *Writings*, IX, p. 116.
5. Hamilton, *Works*, IX, p. 226.
6. Lafayette, *Mémoires, correspondance et manuscrits*, I, p. 385.
7. Ford, *Writings*, IX, p. 53.
8. Hamilton, *Works*, IX, p. 224.
9. Ford, *Writings*, IX, p. 131.
10. James Wilkinson, *Memoirs*, I, p. 854.
11. Henry Lee, *Memoirs*, p. 501 n.
12. Hamilton, *Works*, IX, pp. 232-6.
13. Hamilton, *Works*, IX, p. 238.
14. B. C. Steiner, *The Life and Correspondence of James McHenry*, p. 35.
15. Cited by H. J. Ford, *Hamilton*, p. 119.
16. Lafayette, op. cit., I, p. 423. April 18, 1781.
17. Ford, *Writings*, IX, p. 227 n.
18. Ford, *Writings*, IX, p. 226.
19. Ford, *Writings*, IX, p. 230.
20. Ford, *Writings*, IX, p. 377.
21. Ford, *Writings*, IX, p. 245.

22. Hamilton, *Works*, IX, p. 243.

23. Hamilton, *Works*, IX, p. 245.

24. M. D. Conway, *George Washington and Mount Vernon* (L. I. Hist. Soc.), p. xlii. See Volume I of this work, p. 223.

25. Ford, *Writings*, X, p. 137.

26. Ford, *Writings*, IX, p. 182.

27. M. D. Conway, *Barons of the Potomack*, p. 81, *George Washington and Mount Vernon*, p. xliii, also Volume II of this work, p. 45.

28. *The Virginia Calendar of State Papers*, I, pp. 455, 502, gives letters from Lewis and his partner, Charles Dick, complaining of the galling ingratitude and of "being meanly cheated (pardon the Expression) out of two years Services." Lewis wrote to the Treasurer of Virginia:

"I expected to have received by Mr Dick, the money I have advanced for the Public Gunn factory at Fredericksburg, for which he had a warrant on the Treasury. No man is a better judge of the loss I must at any rate sustain, by not receiving my money than you are, most part of it was advanced as early as July, and without such advance the factory must have been discontinued, as no money could be had at the Treasury, or so little that the business must have suffered greatly. had I suffered that factory to have stoped, I know the public would have condemned me for it, allthò' I should not have been blameable, as the cause would have been the want of money. You may remember that I was desired to borrow all the money I could for the use of the State. I think I procured between thirty & Forty thousand pounds, seven Thousand of which I lent the State, being all that I had at that time on hand. by these advances I have distressed myself greatly, and at this time am not able to pay the collector my Taxes, and continue my business in the usual manner. I shall be greatly obliged to you to send me the money by Mr James Maury who has the Warrant can it be expected that the State can be well served, when its best Friends are used in the manner I have been treated."

29. Mrs. V. M. Fleming, *The Kenmore Mansion*.

30. Conway, *Barons of the Potomack*, p. 84.

31. Ford, Writings, IX, p. 174.

32. Eckenrode, *The Revolution in Virginia*, pp. 236-260.

33. Ford, *Writings*, IX, p. 20.

34. Lafayette, *Mémoires, correspondance et manuscrits*, I, p. 428. April 23, 1781.

35. Ford, *Writings*, IX, p. 238.

36. Ford, *Writings*, IX, p. 236.

37. *Virginia Calendar of State Papers*, I, pp. 441, 589.

38. Gen. Emory Upton, *The Military Policy of the United States*, p. 57.

CHAPTER XLVII

1. Ford, *Writings*, IX, p. 181 n.

2. Clinton's infatuation for Philadelphia, which Charles Lee said was of no importance, is shown in his letters disapproving Cornwallis' plans against Virginia. See Cornwallis' *Answer*, pp. ix, 82, 106, 203, 264.

Charlemagne Tower, *Essays Political and Historical*, p. 129, calls Cornwallis "the early friend of America, the most earnest and the ablest of the British generals," speaks of "the uprightness of his personal character" and describes the "dormant commission" with which he returned to America in 1778, with authority to assume command in America in the event of the death or retirement of Sir Henry Clinton. This played an important part in increasing the old rivalry between them. Cornwallis was a peer and Clinton was not; this increased Clinton's resentment and caused him to treat Cornwallis with extreme harshness. Tower asserts that "Cornwallis was forced, against his own military judgment and by the express direction of his commanding officer, into the disastrous situation which led to his capture."

3. J. Watts de Peyster, *The Affair at King's Mountain*, Mag. of Am. Hist., V, pp. 401-423. In this article he gives a critical review of the many false accounts of this battle. See S. G. Fisher, *The Struggle for American Independence*, II, pp. 342-366. Fisher tells the story of the Southern campaigns with much clarity. Henry Lee devotes most of his *Memoirs* to the events in which he took a great part. His work is almost unique in the honesty and fairness with which he concedes the merits of his opponents and the faults of his fellow-countrymen.

4. Lee, *Memoirs*, pp. 237, 583. See also *Mag. of Am. Hist.*, X, p. 506.

5. Lee, *Memoirs*, pp. 250-296. Ganoe, *History of the U. S. Army*, p. 75.

6. Cornwallis, *Answer to . . . the Narrative . . . of Clinton*, p. 47.

7. Kapp, *Steuben*, p. 691. *Letter to Knox*, Feb. 4, 1784.

8. Sparks, *Correspondence of the American Revolution*, III, p. 293.

9. Lee, *Memoirs*, pp. 297-314.

10. Ford, *Writings*, IX, p. 151.

11. Gilbert Chinard, *Lafayette in Virginia* (Institut Français de Washington), p. viii. In this edition of unpublished letters Lafayette is seen in a most captivating light.

12. Letters of De Fersen. *Mag. of Am. Hist.*, III, pp. 371, 372.

13. De Fersen, *Mag. of Am. Hist.*, III, p. 446.

14. MS. in the Congressional Library, January 30, 1781.

15. Ford, *Writings*, IX, pp. 102-109.

16. Ford, *Writings*, IX, p. 109 n.

17. Morgan J. O'Brien, *Hercules Mulligan*, Journal of the Am. Irish Hist. Soc., XXVI, pp. 96-104. Washington refers to Mulligan's warning in his letter to Lafayette, Ford, *Writings*, IX, p. 166.

18. Sparks, *Writings*, VII, p. 471.

19. Reed, *Reed*, II, pp. 337, 338 n.

20. F. B. Dexter, *The Literary Diary of Ezra Stiles*, II, p. 522.

21. Vicomte de Noailles, *Marins et soldats français en Amérique*, pp. 149, 150.

22. *Newport Illustrated*, p. 36, cited by W. S. Baker, *The Itinerary of General Washington*, p. 209.

23. See Vicomte de Noailles, op. cit., Thomas Balch, *Les Français en Amérique*, etc. S. A. Drake, *Nooks and Corners of the New England Coast*, p. 394.

24. Cited by W. S. Baker, op. cit., p. 210.

25. *The Letter Book of Lt. Enos Reeves*, Penn. Mag., XXI, p. 381.

26. J. C. Fitzpatrick, *Spirit of the Revolution*, p. 173.

27. Duc de Lauzun, *Mémoires*, p. 352.

28. Dumas, *Souvenirs*, cited by Thomas Balch, op. cit., p. 122 n. This anecdote of the children is assigned by Irving, Bancroft and others to his earlier ride to Hartford, but see W. S. Baker, op. cit., p. 211.

29. Baker, op. cit., p. 213.

30. Ford, *Writings*, IX, pp. 185, 204.

31. Ford, *Writings*, IX, p. 192.

32. MS. letter in the Huntington Library, March 24, 1781.

33. Ford, *Writings*, IX, p. 190.

34. This letter is taken from the Clinton papers in the W. L. Clements Collection.

35. Sparks, *Correspondence of the Revolution*, III, p. 272.

36. Sparks, *Correspondence of the Revolution*, III, p. 273.

37. Ford, *Writings*, IX, p. 191 n.

38. Ford, *Writings*, IX, p. 205.

39. Ford, *Writings*, IX, p. 208.

40. Ford, *Writings*, IX, p. 211.

41. *St. Clair Papers*, I, p. 544 n. See Ford, *Writings*, IX, p. 280, letter to Col. Crawford, June 9, 1781, of Washington's concern for his lands.

42. Col. P. M. Ashburn, *A History of the Medical Department of the U. S. Army*, p. 20.

43. C. H. Van Tyne, *The War of Independence, American Phase*, p. 281.

44. E. C. Burnett, *Letters of Members of the Continental Congress*, II, p. 188.

45. General John Cochran, *Medical Department of the Revolutionary Army*, Mag. of Am. Hist., XII, pp. 241-260.

46. Ford, *Writings*, IX, pp. 223, 224.

47. Ford, *Writings*, IX, p. 225 n.

48. Ford, *Writings*, IX, p. 225.

49. Ford, *Writings*, IX, p. 232 n.

50. Ford, *Writings*, IX, p. 231.

51. J. C. Fitzpatrick, *The Diaries of George Washington*, II, p. 205.

52. F. B. Dexter, op. cit., II, p. 531.

53. Sparks, *Writings*, VIII, p. 45.

54. Ford, *Writings*, IX, p. 282 n. *Diaries*, II, p. 254. Governor Trumbull's account of Washington's visit to Weathersfield is given in W. C. Ford, *S. B. Webb*, II, p. 340. Washington neglected to mention that he went to church, but Trumbull says that he did and that the text was, "Blessed are the poor in spirit, for theirs is the Kingdom of Heaven."

55. Doniol, *La Participation*, IV, pp. 628-656, gives the details of Rochambeau's arguments and rebukes American historians for their failure to do him justice and their ascription of the plan to Washington. Thomas Balch, *Les Français en Amérique*, p. 128 n., also asserts that Rochambeau deserves the greater part of the credit.

56. See Sparks, *Writings*, VIII, p. 517.

57. Sparks, *Writings*, VIII, p. 519.

58. Rochambeau, *Mémoires*, II, p. 277, cited by Sparks, *Writings*, VIII, p. 76.

59. Fitzpatrick, *Diaries*, II, p. 217.

60. Fitzpatrick, *Diaries*, II, p. 225.

61. Ford, *Writings*, IX, p. 266. See also pp. 273, 274, 277 n., 304.

62. Letter to Clinton, *Public Papers of George Clinton*, VII, p. 427.

63. R. G. Adams, *The Germain Papers*, p. 43.

64. Fitzpatrick, *Diaries*, II, p. 254. August 14, 1781.

65. The letter is given in Ford, *Writings*, IX, p. 268, with Washington's answer.

66. Lauzun, *Mémoires*, p. 358.

67. Rochambeau, *Mémoires*, I, p. 274, cited by Sparks, *Writings*, VIII, p. 60 n.

68. Ford, *Writings*, IX, p. 269 n.

69. May 31, 1781. The letter is among the Clinton papers in the Wm. L. Clements collection. R. G. Adams, *Clinton Papers*, p. 24, believes that this letter convinced Clinton of Washington's intention to attack him in New York.

70. All of these letters are found in the Clements collection.

71. Ford, *S. B. Webb*, II, p. 342.

72. *St. Clair Papers*, I, p. 552.

73. Fitzpatrick, *Diaries*, II, p. 229.

74. Baron Cromot du Bourg's *Journal*, reproduced in the *Mag. of Am. Hist.*, IV, pp. 293-297, gives details of this march over the terrible roads. Thomas Balch, op. cit., p. 124 n., states that he has positive evidence that this Journal was undoubtedly written by Cromot de Bourg. The march is more briefly described by Comte G. de Deux-Ponts, whose work *Mes Campagnes d' Amérique*, is published both in French and English under the title *My Campaigns in America*, by S. A. Green.

75. Deux-Ponts, op. cit., pp. 35 n., 117 n. Rochambeau, in a letter to Ségur (Doniol, IV, p. 637), said that Washington had only "a handful of men" (*une poignée de monde*)—not 4,000 under arms.

76. Ford, *Writings*, IX, p. 324. Aug. 2, 1781.

77. *St. Clair Papers*, I, p. 552. The text is copied from the original in the Huntington Library.

78. Tower, *The Marquis de La Fayette*, II, p. 339.

79. G. Chinard, *Lafayette in Virginia*, p. 25. July 10, 1781.

80. Gaillard Hunt, *Fragments of Revolutionary History*, p. 51, a long and interesting letter concerning the whole campaign.

81. Translated from W. G. Leland's *Letters from Lafayette to Luzerne*, Am. Hist. Rev., XX, pp. 604-5.

CHAPTER XLVIII

1. Details of these complex maneuvers may be found in Washington's Diaries and Letters, the memoirs of the French concerned, Otto Hufeland's *Westchester County During the American Revolution*, etc., Scharf's *History of Westchester County*, Vol. II, Moore's *Diary of the American Revolution* (on the skirmishes at Kingbridge and Tarrytown), Heath's *Memoirs*, Thomas Balch, *Les Français en Amérique*, etc.

2. Balch, op. cit., pp. 145-8, citing Rochambeau and Cromot du Bourg.

3. Cromot du Bourg, *Journal*, Mag. of Am. Hist., IV, p. 296.

4. Lauzun, *Mémoires*, pp. 360-363.

5. Ford, *Writings*, IX, p. 349. *Pennsylvania Packet*, Aug. 2, 1781, cited by Moore, op. cit., II, p. 458. C. H. Van Tyne, *The Loyalists in the American Revolution*, p. 172, quotes Rivington's statement in January, 1780, that the New York loyal militia amounted to 5,855 men.

6. Rivington's *Royal Gazette*, July 14, 1781, cited by Moore, op. cit., II, p. 456.

7. Abbé Robin, *Nouveau Voyage dans l'Amérique Septentrionale* (1782), p. 62.

8. Claude Blanchard, *Journal*, p. 118.

9. Doniol, *La Participation*, IV, p. 647.

10. Doniol, op. cit., IV, p. 650.

11. Doniol, op. cit., IV, p. 653.

12. J. C. Ballagh, *The Letters of Richard Henry Lee*, II, pp. 233, 235.

13. Ford, *Writings*, IX, p. 305.

14. Ford, *Writings*, IX, p. 321.

15. Fitzpatrick, *Diaries*, II, p. 254. This is in striking conflict with the account given in many of the histories. Even Major Ganoe, in his *History of the U. S. Army*, says, p. 76:

"Washington secretly decided to bottle up Cornwallis. He collected in that country between the Bronx and Dobb's Ferry, the French from southern New England and the Americans from the Highlands, as if to lay siege to New York. Then he marched to Sandy Hook, having written to the various governors of his contemplated attack on New York. He was well on his way to Philadelphia before his intentions were suspected."

16. Octavius Pickering and Charles W. Upham, *Life of Timothy Pickering*, II, p. 54.

17. Ford, *Writings*, IX, p. 336. This letter was signed jointly by Washington and Rochambeau.

18. Ford, *Writings*, IX, pp. 352, 343.

19. Ford, *Writings*, IX, p. 355.

20. Ford, *Writings*, IX, p. 358.

21. Ford, *Writings*, IX, p. 336 n.

22. B. J. Lossing, *Field Book of the Revolution*, II, p. 213 n. He says that Mr. Pierson also told a woman the story and she made a novel of it. Lossing had similar evidence for his story of the prayer at Valley Forge. There is a biography of Montanye in Sprague's *Annals of the American Pulpit*, VI, p. 265. He seems to be the man upon whom this questionable legend was fashioned.

23. Elias Boudinot, *Journal*, p. 41.

24. James Thacher, *Military Journal*, p. 262.

25. A MS. by Clinton written for some unknown correspondent, published in *New York City during the American Revolution* (Mercantile Library Ass'n, N. Y.), p. 182.

In his controversies with Cornwallis he enlarged the arguments in his *Narrative*, London, 1783. Cornwallis wrote *An Answer to that Part of the Narrative*, etc., London, 1783, publishing many letters. To this Clinton replied with *Observations on Some Parts of the Answer of Earl Cornwallis*, etc., containing letters and papers, London, 1783. Clinton's unpublished history in the Wm. L. Clements collection and a mass of letters in his and the Germain Papers increase the documents. I have had the privilege of consulting many of them in manuscripts and in copious photostats, but the subject is too involved and too remote from Washington's personal interests to be fully developed here.

26. Clinton MS., *An Historical Detail* (Wm. L. Clements Coll.), II, p. 185.

27. Cornwallis, *Answer*, p. 51.

28. E. J. Lowell, *The Hessians*, p. 262.

29. Clinton MS., *An Historical Detail*, II, p. 250.

30. Clinton, *Narrative*, p. 17.

31. C. H. Van Tyne, *England and America*, p. 145.

32. Clinton, *Narrative*, p. 34.

33. All these minutes are in the Clements collection. They show the naval officers raising one serious problem: if they transported Clinton's troops to the Chesapeake and received orders to sail for the West Indies at once, what would then become of the troops? Clinton says he offered to bring them back by land, and emphasizes the fact that he had no command over the navy and could not presume to make demands. See Capt. W. M. James, *The British Navy in Adversity*, pp. 296-7.

34. His Diaries give the day-by-day details. Baker's *Itinerary of General Washington* gives more, and there is a graphic article by John Austin Stevens, *The Route of the Allies from King's Ferry to the Head of Elk*, in the Mag. of Am. Hist., V, p. 1.

35. *Pennsylvania Packet*, Sept. 1, 1781, cited by Baker, op. cit., p. 236.

36. Deux-Ponts, *My Campaigns in America*, pp. 43, 126.

37. Doniol, op. cit., IV, p. 656. Fitzpatrick, *Diaries*, II, p. 258. James, op. cit., p. 288.

38. Doniol, op. cit., IV, p. 673.

39. Deux-Ponts, op. cit., pp. 43, 126.

40. Lauzun, op. cit., p. 367.

41. Sparks, *Writings*, VIII, pp. 155-7.

42. Sparks, *Writings*, VIII, p. 159. The original in the J. Pierpont Morgan Library naturally differs from Sparks' version.

43. Fitzpatrick, *Diaries*, II, p. 259. John Austin Stevens, op. cit., *Mag. of Am. Hist.*, V, p. 19, says that these letters have never been published and have not been discovered in spite of a thorough search for them.

44. I. Q. Leake, *Life of John Lamb*, p. 277.

45. Fitzpatrick, *Diaries*, II, p. 260.

46. F. L. Humphreys, *Life and Times of David Humphreys*, I, p. 221.

47. B. J. Lossing, *Mary and Martha Washington*, p. 208.

48. *Freeman's Journal*, Sept. 12, 1781, cited in Report of the Am. Hist. Ass'n, 1896, I, p. 194.

49. C. B. Todd, *The Massacre at Fort Griswold*, Mag. of Am. Hist., VII, p. 161.

50. Fitzpatrick, *Diaries*, II, p. 260.

51. W. C. Bruce, *John Randolph of Roanoke*, I, p. 45.

52. *Mag of Am. Hist.*, VII, p. 212.

53. This indecisive yet most decisive engagement is formally described in the reports of both de Grasse and Graves, in the *Mag. of Am. Hist.*, VII, pp. 288 and 367. Capt. W. M. James, *The British Navy in Adversity*, p. 290, gives a vivacious account of this battle with graphic illustrations, and a frank statement of British blunders that lost a great opportunity.

54. G. W. P. Custis, *Recollections*, p. 236.

55. James, op. cit., ch. XX.

56. James, op. cit., p. 298.

CHAPTER XLIX

1. F. V. Greene, *The Revolutionary War*, p. 265.

2. Ganoe, *History of the U. S. Army*, p. 76.

3. Drake, *Knox*, p. 68.

4. Ford, *Writings*, IX, p. 377.

5. Ford, *Writings*, IX, p. 378 n.

6. G. W. P. Custis, *Recollections*, p. 233.

7. Cornwallis, *Answer*, pp. 101, 115, 163, 123. See Fortescue, *History of the British Army*, III, p. 396, on the "tangle of contradictory orders."

8. Doniol, *La Participation*, IV, p. 660. Thomas Balch, *Les Français en Amérique*, p. 159. H. P. Johnston, *The Yorktown Campaign*, p. 100.

9. H. P. Johnston, op. cit., p. 109. This book is an encyclopædia for Yorktown.

10. Letter by Colonel Fontaine, Oct. 26, 1781, cited by Johnston, op. cit., p. 178.

11. Lauzun, *Mémoires*, p. 369.

12. Balch, op. cit., pp. 164, 168, 181.

13. Lauzun, op. cit., p. 373.

14. Ford, *Writings*, IX, p. 371 n.
15. Washington Irving, *Life of Washington*, IV, p. 328. See *Mag. of Am. Hist.*, VIII, p. 205. Cromot du Bourg, *Journal*, Mag. of Am. Hist., IV, p. 445, gives a minute technical account of the siege from an engineer's standpoint. The *Campaigns* of Deux-Ponts gives other details.
16. Timothy Pickering, letter of July 29, 1824, *Tyler's Quarterly*, VII, p. 33.
17. Fitzpatrick, *Diaries*, II, p. 262. Reed, *Life of Reed*, II, p. 367.
18. *Letters of Robert Biddulph, 1779-1783*, Am. Hist. Rev., XXIX, p. 106.
19. *Orderly Book of the Siege of Yorktown*, Sept. 30.
20. *Orderly Book of the Siege of Yorktown*, Oct. 1.
21. James Thacher, *Military Journal*, p. 276.
22. James Thacher, op. cit., p. 274.
23. G. W. P. Custis, op. cit., p. 336.
24. Friedrich Kapp, *Steuben*, p. 457.
25. Thacher, op. cit., p. 276.
26. Thacher, op. cit., p. 271.
27. Lossing, *Field Book of the Revolution*, II, p. 519 n.
28. Fitzpatrick, *Diaries*, II, pp. 265, 266.
29. Henry Lee, *Memoirs*, p. 501 n. Lee says he had the story from Hamilton.
30. Barber's name was given by Hamilton's son in his biography. See H. J. Ford, *Alexander Hamilton*, p. 125. See also J. C. Connolly, *Francis Barber*, Journal of the Am. Irish Hist. Soc., 1927, p. 232. Johnston, op. cit., p. 147. General Muhlenberg's claim seems to be well established by his biographer, pp. 271-277. The fact that Hamilton wrote the report gave him his grip on fame.
31. I. Q. Leake, *Life of John Lamb*, p. 279.
32. *Mag. of Am. Hist.*, VII, pp. 363, 366. Of Hamilton's share in the founding of the paper, see Allan Nevins, *The Evening Post*, p. 17.
33. Wm. Gordon, D.D., *The History of the . . . Independence* (1794), III, p. 258. For Hamilton's clash with Dr. Gordon during the war see Appendix IV.
34. A. M. McCrillis, *Captain Stephen Olney*, The Minute Man, Dec., 1926, p. 314.
35. *Orderly Book of the Siege of Yorktown*, p. 42.
36. Fitzpatrick, *Diaries*, II, p. 266.
37. Cornwallis, *Answer to Sir Henry Clinton's Narrative*, p. 197.
38. Cornwallis, op. cit., p. 199.
39. Clinton MS., *An Historical Detail* (Wm. L. Clements Coll.), II, pp. 270-271.
40. Cornwallis, op. cit., pp. 202-205.
41. Ford, *Writings*, IX, p. 382. To Congress, Oct. 16, 1781. Fitzpatrick, *Diaries*, II, p. 264.
42. *Simcoe's Military Journal*, p. 253. See also J. C. Döhla, *Tagebuch eines Bayreuther Soldaten*, p. 146, in which there is much about the heaviness of the bombardment.
43. Lee, op. cit., p. 504.
44. Lee, op. cit., p. 506.
45. *Journal of Elias Boudinot*, p. 37.
46. Cornwallis, op. cit., p. 211. Letter to Clinton.
47. Fitzpatrick, *Diaries*, II, p. 268.
48. Cornwallis, op. cit., p. 216.
49. The articles are given in full in Johnston, op. cit., p. 187.
50. Letter of Oct. 19, 1781, Drake, *Knox*, p. 70.
51. Johnston, op. cit., p. 155.

52. Ford, *Writings*, IX, p. 384 n.

53. Ford, *Writings*, IX, p. 386 n.

54. E. M. Lindley, *Montpelier*, Mag. of Am. Hist., XVI, p. 128.

55. The account of Dumas is given by Balch, op. cit., p. 183. See Conway, *George Washington and Mount Vernon*, p. xli.

56. J. C. Döhla, op. cit., p. 152. He makes many perhaps natural blunders, such as saying that at Washington's side were Gates and Greene. Popp, in his *Journal*, puts Greene and Sumter at Washington's side, *Penn. Mag.*, XXVI, p. 248. Henry Lee, who was an eye witness of the surrender, gives a lively account of it, *Memoirs*, pp. 512-3. See also Thacher's *Military Journal*, pp. 279-80.

57. J. G. Rosengarten, *American History from German Archives*, pp. 32-34. See also Döhla, op. cit., p. 151, and Popp's *Journal*, Penn. Mag., XXVI, pp. 41, 245.

58. Döhla, op. cit., p. 152.

59. *The Universal Magazine*, London, Feb., 1782, cited in *Mag. of Am. Hist.*, XVI, p. 591.

60. Thacher, op. cit., p. 292.

61. Boudinot, op. cit., p. 59.

62. Ford, *Writings*, IX, p. 388.

63. Cited by Johnston, op. cit., p. 158 n.

64. Boudinot, op. cit., p. 38.

65. Gaillard Hunt, *Journals of Congress*, XXI, Oct. 29, 1781, p. 1081.

66. F. L. Humphreys, *David Humphreys*, I, pp. 234-6. The author complains of the oblivion to which this significant and beautiful ceremony has been consigned, and the deplorable mistreatment of a painting showing the scene that was given to Yale College.

67. Humphreys, op. cit., I, p. 245, an elsewhere unpublished letter of December 11, 1781.

68. V. L. Collins, *President Witherspoon* (Princeton Univ. Press), II, p. 65. *Journals of Congress*, XXI, p. 1076.

69. M. I. J. Griffin, *Catholics and the American Revolution*, I, pp. 290, 291.

70. Fortescue, *The Correspondence of King George III*, V, p. 297.

71. Wraxall, Sir N. W., *Historical Memoirs of My Own Time*, II, p. 100.

72. Wilbur C. Abbott, *New York in the Am. Rev.*, p. 188.

73. George Morgan, *Patrick Henry* (1929), p. 309.

74. Custis, *Recollections*, pp. 254-5. Custis was, of course, the youngest of the children. Washington wrote to Lafayette, Nov. 15th: "I arrived at Eltham, (the Seat of Colonel Bassett,) time enough to see poor Mr. Custis breathe his last. This unexpected and affecting event threw Mrs. Washington and Mrs. Custis, who were both present, into such deep distress, that the circumstance of it, and a duty I owed the deceased in assisting at his funeral rites, prevented my reaching this place till the 13th." Ford, *Writings*, IX, p. 406.

75. Chastellux, *Travels in North America* . . . with notes by the translator (1787), I, p. 194 n.

76. Custis, op. cit., p. 142.

77. Edith Tunis Sales, *Old Time Belles and Cavaliers*, p. 49. Mrs. Roger Pryor, *The Mother of Washington*, p. 174, protests against the growth of the traditions concerning Mary Washington's temper and cites several dubious anecdotes of her fierce sternness.

78. Custis, op. cit., p. 143.

79. Mrs. Pryor, op. cit., p. 311.

80. Custis, op. cit., p. 144.

81. Ford, *Writings*, IX, pp. 405-409.
82. Ford, *Writings*, IX, p. 410.   To Benjamin Dulany, Nov. 15, 1781.
83. Ford, *Writings*, IX, p. 409.
84. Ford, *Writings*, IX, p. 408 n.   The spelling is from the original in the J. Pierpont Morgan library.
85. MS. letter in the Huntington Library, Oct. 27, 1781, to Governor Nelson.

APPENDIX II

WHO SUGGESTED THE STROKE AT PRINCETON?

Everybody agrees that the march to Princeton from Trenton saved Washington's army and thereby the American cause from destruction. The credit for the ingenuity that extricated the army is of consequent importance.

Since Washington made the decision and accepted the risks he has full right to high credit for a military stroke of unsurpassed brilliance. But it is amazing to see how the cloud of biographers differ in the detail of the origin of the idea. This conflict extends to nearly every phase of his career.

Some historians go so far as to declare or imply that Washington fully expected when he crossed the Delaware to make the night-march to Princeton. His own words belie such a theory. Others insist that he had made up his mind before sunset to move out at midnight. But this again is belied by his own statement that it was not until nightfall that he learned of Cornwallis' great superiority in numbers. Cornwallis' actual superiority was only 5,500 to 5,000, but naturally in the dusk they seemed more numerous than they were, as hostile armies have a habit of seeming.

Washington was dismayed at his situation and called a council of war to help him out of it. At that council the famous maneuver was suggested and acted upon with the most feverish haste, and a confusion which only Cornwallis' fatuity failed to turn into disaster.

Bancroft (IX, p. 246), says that Washington had the plan in mind before he crossed the Delaware. Stryker and others say that he had it in mind before he took his post behind the creek. There is a fundamental contradiction between these views. Dr. Gordon (II, p. 156) says the plan was Washington's. Marshall (II, p. 252) says that Washington formed the bold design. Washington Irving (ch. XLVI, 1856 ed., vol. II) says that Washington "revolved in his mind" the plan and laid it before the council.

General H. B. Carrington, *Battles of the American Revolution* (p. 286), says that Washington "had matured a plan of escape" and proposed it to a council that "promptly endorsed" it. In his *Washington the Soldier* (p. 152), Carrington implies that Washington had planned to surprise Brunswick and had a reconnaissance made of the roads in December. Lossing, *Field Book* (II, p. 233), says that Washington proposed the plan. In his *Washington, a Biography* (II, p. 385), he says, "In that darkest hour the mind of Washington received light."

Fiske, *The American Revolution* (I, p. 242), says that when Cornwallis "called his antagonist an old fox, he did him no more than justice. In his union of slyness with audacity, the movement which Washington now executed strongly reminds one of 'Stonewall' Jackson." Trevelyan, *The American Revolution* (III, p. 132), says, Washington "rapidly thought out a scheme." General B. T. Johnson, *General Washington* (p. 153), represents Washington as not only originating the plan but having to fight for it against an unwilling group of officers, whom he finally overawed by opening the door and showing that the ground had frozen.

In his *Trenton,* pp. 271, 273, and an article in the *Magazine of American History* (VIII, p. 550), Stryker says that Reed or General Dickinson were both far more likely to have proposed the march than St. Clair, but, after careful investigations, gives all the glory to Washington. "It is certain that the great chieftain knew what he was about, and did not deliberately put himself in a trap that day, and then despairingly ask his general officers to get him out of it. Nor can it be supposed that General Washington left it until eleven o'clock at night before he at least thought of what orders he must give six hours thereafter."

In his appendix (p. 442), he quotes Private Lardner's letter, written, however, long years after, declaring that "the thought of the movement that night originated entirely with Washington—solely his own manœuvre." To back this assertion, Lardner declares that he himself with three other men had been "posted as a patrole on this very road," with which Washington "must have been made acquainted or the patroles would not have been placed there." But a patrol should have been there in any case as a safeguard. If Cornwallis had had the road patrolled as common military caution required, Washington would have been discovered as soon as he set out.

Unfortunately, the story that the idea was not Washington's can not be smothered by assumptions that he ought to have, hence, must have, thought of the most brilliant step in his military life. That a council was held is not denied by anybody. The best that Stryker will allow St. Clair is that since he was in St. Clair's tent, Washington may have courteously asked his opinion.

Sparks, in his *Life of Washington* (p. 215), simply says that a council was called "and a bold resolution was adopted." This is perhaps as much as can be said without danger of contradiction, though Washington himself annuls the allegations that he had premeditated the plan for some time. Frederick D. Stone, in *Winsor's History* (VI, p. 377), credits the council with the decision. J. T. Goolrick, in his biography of *General Hugh Mercer,* attributes the suggestion to Mercer. Alexander Hamilton, in his funeral oration on Greene in 1789 (*Works,* VIII, p. 67), assigned to Greene "a portion of the praise which is due as well to the formation as to the execution of the plans." But F. V. Greene, *General Greene* (p. 66), says that "something must be allowed to the warmth of eulogy in a funeral oration upon a most intimate friend." Greene's grandson, George Washington Greene, in his biography (I, p. 303), as shown in the text, gives all the credit to St. Clair.

Wilkinson, who was in Trenton at the time, says in so many words (*Memoirs* I, p. 140), that Washington asked advice, and was inclined "to hazard all on a general engagement," that St. Clair suggested the maneuver which Washington "adopted" and that St. Clair got the idea from having "fallen on the road which led to the Quaker bridge," while examining the ground along the Assanpink. Pickering, later adjutant-general, said that St. Clair proposed it. (Tyler's *Quarterly,* July, 1925, p. 37). But then Pickering in this astonishing review denied Washington practically every claim to military ability. S. G. Fisher, *The Struggle for American Independence* (I, p. 566), favors St. Clair.

St. Clair alone laid direct claim to it and said in his *Narrative:*

"The General summoned a council of the general officers at my quarters, and, after stating the difficulties in his way, the probability of defeat, and the consequences that would necessarily result if it happened, desired advice. I had the good fortune to suggest the idea of turning the left of the enemy in the night, gaining a march upon him, and proceeding with all possible expedition to Brunswick. General Mercer immediately fell in with it, and very forcibly pointed out its practicability and the advantages that would necessarily result from it, and General Washington highly approved it, nor was there one dissenting voice in the council." (W. H. Smith, *The St. Clair Papers*, I, p. 36).

Bancroft said sarcastically (p. 246), that, after Washington had proposed his plan, and "Mercer forcibly pointed out the advantages of the proposal; Saint Clair liked it so well, that in the failing memory of old age he took it to have been his own." But Bancroft was always at war with every reputation save Washington's.

Washington never definitely claimed to have originated the plan, but he gave nobody else the honor, and in any case he very definitely puts aside any pretense of having it in mind before nightfall for he wrote to Congress three days later:

"In this situation we remained till dark. . . . Having by this time discovered, that the enemy were greatly superior in number, and that their intention was to surround us, I ordered, etc." (Ford, *Writings*, V, p. 147.)

In his biographical introduction to his edition of *St. Clair's Papers*, W. H. Smith made a strong plea for St. Clair. In the *Magazine of American History* (VIII, p. 538), H. P. Johnston, reviewing the work, strongly controverted Smith. He seems, however, to juggle over-deftly with important facts. In the same volume, p. 550, General Stryker ridiculed Smith's claims for much the same reasons that he reproduced in his volume on *The Battles of Trenton and Princeton.*

The comments of Johnston and Stryker actually boil down to the belief that it was impossible for Washington to have got himself into a trap unintentionally. But this is rather a religious than an historical method of argument. It is very strongly contradicted by Washington's career, which abounded in traps.

On page 680 of the same volume, W. H. Smith answered both Johnston and Stryker, and with keen logic exposed their manifest contradictions. He asks pertinently why Washington held a council of war at all if he knew just what to do; he points out that, while Washington did not indeed give St. Clair credit for proposing the midnight march to Princeton, "Washington's despatches were generally meagre, and personal mention the exception. . . . He does not refer to the important suggestions made to him by Colonel Reed during the day, nor the council held at St. Clair's quarters in the evening, and yet the fact that such council was held is as well established as any other event in history."

He quotes General Greene's statement concerning the debate over retreat or attack, and the advocacy of each, "when a voice was heard saying . . . 'Let us take the new road through the woods and get in the enemy's rear by a march upon Princeton.'" Smith emphasizes Washington's own words, "In this situation we remained till dark. . . . Having by this time discovered that the enemy were greatly superior in number, and that their design was to surround us, I ordered all our baggage to be removed silently to Burlington." Smith also notes that it was not until after midnight that Colonel Reed sent the order to Putnam to meet the baggage train. Only after the position was taken up does Reed say "it was *resolved* to make a forced march."

In spite of all the eminent authorities who find unbearable the very thought of Washington's being caught in a net, there is reason to believe that St. Clair's imagination turned a tragic plight into one of the most superb and important moves in military history. In reaching this conclusion it is not necessary at all to accuse Washington of blind folly. It is only necessary to remember what indisputably happened. When he returned to Trenton, he could not move at all because his army was disintegrating. He rashly promised a bounty for six weeks more of service, but the men insisted on seeing the hard money. He could not stir until it came from Philadelphia where Robert Morris procured it by begging from house to house on a New Year's morning. By the time the money had arrived and he had called his troops together from outlying villages, the British were on him. His advance posts did not hold as he hoped. Cornwallis poured into Trenton with far more men than Washington had dreamed of encountering.

Now and now only, as Washington himself states—"having by this time discovered that the enemy were greatly superior to us"—did he find himself not only unable to attack with his unreliable militia, but apparently unable even to retreat with safety since the river was impassable and the roads to the rear almost as wet. He called the council of war, and the officers hung between hopeless retreat and hopeless attack when an inspired voice proposed the magnificent solution. The ground froze suddenly. He got his baggage off on one road and stole out on another, waking his men from sleep for the march.

Every general has been saved by the advice of obscurer generals, Napoleon no less than others. A supplementary answer to Johnston's and Stryker's denials of St. Clair's right to the glory is seen in the fact that they claim too much. They also ridicule St. Clair's claim to suggesting the Morristown march and include that too in Washington's complete original plan.

But Washington himself admits, as is shown later, that he had originally set his heart on Brunswick, had no idea of the Morristown move and took it "by the advice of my officers." Great wisdom has been attributed to Washington in selecting Morristown for the winter, but he says more than once that he went there only for a few days.

It can be argued, then, that somebody, most probably St. Clair, suggested to Washington both the Princeton and the Morristown moves. But the peril and the responsibility for success or failure were Washington's and it takes wisdom to recognize wisdom. In the words of his namesake, George Washington Greene, the grandson of General Nathanael:

"None but great men know how to take counsel." *Historical View of the American Revolution*, p. 247.

Whether Washington first thought of the stratagem or not, he carried it out with such amazing skill and such dramatic success that he made it his own and earned the laurels flung to him from all quarters as a military genius of the first order.

APPENDIX III

A WORD FOR HOWE

"He is such an unintelligible gentleman, that no rule of interpretation can possibly be found out by which to unravel his designs," wrote young Alexander Hamilton.[1]

"It is impossible to discover the designs of an enemy who has no design at all," wrote John Adams. "An intention that has no existence, a plan that is not laid, cannot be divined." [2]

Howe was "extremely fond of liquors and intoxicated the greatest part of his time," says the Tory Judge Jones, who describes him further as "feasting, gunning, banqueting, and in the arms of Mrs. Loring . . . lolling in the arms of his mistress, and sporting his cash at the faro bank." [3]

An English punster on the name of the river proposed that Howe be elevated to the peerage as "Baron Delay Warr." [4]

"The success of the Americans is not owing to their strength or bravery, but to the astonishing conduct of the British forces, to the *lenteur* and *timidité* of the British General," wrote the French Major Du Portail in a letter captured by the British.[5]

An Englishman wrote, "Had he been consigned to his grave, instead of being sent to America, many a stream of blood, many a million of treasure, and a long series of dishonour had been saved to this country." [6]

"There was something so inexplicable in all these transactions, that men of sense stood amazed at their unparalleled absurdity. . . . Never was there so great inability shewn by any Commander," wrote Galloway, the Tory. "Blunder upon blunder is incessantly rising in its view, and as they rise, they increase in magnitude . . . he had carried his military farce too far. . . . Never was an enemy more perfectly in the power of another, than the Rebel army had lately been in that of Sir William Howe. . . . As if determined to give the Congress and New States opportunity and time sufficient to reinforce their armies, he pursued the very measures which Washington himself would have advised for that purpose. . . . Blunders so gross . . . that their possibility almost exceeds the utmost extent of our belief. Blunders as fatal to this kingdom, as their cause is inexplicable." [7]

The dubious patriot, General Charles Lee, who spent much time with Howe, wrote of him:

[1] Hamilton, *Works*, IX, p. 87, to Gouverneur Morris, July 6, 1777.
[2] *Familiar Letters of John Adams and his Wife*, p. 283.
[3] Thomas Jones, *History of New York*, I, pp. 168, 171, 176.
[4] Jones, op. cit., I, p. 197.
[5] Jones, op. cit., I, p. 190.
[6] *Royal Register*, VIII, p. 166. Cited by Jones, op. cit., I, p. 241.
[7] John Galloway, *Letters to a Nobleman on the Conduct of the War*, 1779, pp. 57, 66, 68, 71, 74, 90, 92.

"Friendly candid good natur'd brave and rather sensible than the reverse . . . He is naturally good humour'd and complacent, but illiterate and indolent to the last degree unless as an executive Soldier, in which capacity He is all fire and activity, brave and cool as Julius Cæsar. . . . He shut his eyes, fought his battles, drank his bottle, had his little Whore, advis'd with his Counsellors, receiv'd his orders from North and Germain, one more absurd than the other, took Galoways opinion, shut his eyes, fought again. . . . I am more struck with the admirable efficacy of Blunder—it seem'd, to be a tryal of skill which Party shou'd outdoe the other, and it is hard to say which play'd the deepest strokes." [8]

In everything said against Howe, Washington is dragged along and their indissoluble union is linked in the joint cynicism of a British writer in 1778:

"Any other General in the world than General Howe would have beaten General Washington; and any other General in the world than General Washington would have beaten General Howe." [9]

This is the inevitable consequence of such wholesale damnation. Since Howe was so bad, Washington must have been equally contemptible not to have whipped him. If the lazy Howe and his hireling Hessians always won against the heroes, the heroes must have had their faults, too. When a man has been so brilliantly, so unanimously and so completely abused as Howe has been for a century and a half, there is small profit in adding a stone to the cairn. That he was a genius when he chose to be there is no denying. His battle plans are models in every respect except pursuit. He must have had reasons aside from mere indolence for his failures. For one thing, says Captan James, "We should remember in his favour that he was fighting with one hand behind his back, that he was not only a general conducting a campaign, but also a Peace Commissioner." [10]

The extent of dissension in England is little realized. The Whigs with pride and impunity carried on a war against Government that brought upon the Tories in America persecution, confiscation, dungeons and death. Captain John Montresor, an engineer with Howe, made long lists of the reasons for British failure in America. Among his multitude were these:

"Factions in both Houses of Parliament—Debates previous to Execution—Correspondence from members to rebels—Not a sufficient number of Troops at first. . . . Not but ¼ as many Engineers as the Enemy. . . . Burke corresponded with Franklin and avowed it—Fox declared that had he been in America he would be the first that would have taken up arms in its defence." [11]

Finally it should never be forgotten that the task confronting Howe or any other general was so enormous as to be impossible even with half-way opposition from his enemy to meet the half-way support at home. He could win victories only if he left his conquests without garrison. The ruthless Napoleon

[8] *Lee Papers*, II, pp. 397-9. Letter to Dr. Benjamin Rush, June 4, 1778.

[9] This was given as "the opinion of the Marquis de la Fayette" in a letter signed "An Old Soldier" reproduced in the *Gentleman's Magazine*, 1778, p. 368, from Lloyd's *Evening Post*, Aug. 17, 1778. The whole letter is given in W. C. Ford's *The Spurious Letters Attributed to Washington*, p. 153.

[10] Captain Wm. M. James, C.B., R.N., *The British Navy in Adversity*, p. 51.

[11] *Journals of Capt. John Montresor* (N. Y. Hist. Soc. Coll., 1881), pp. 139-40, 138.

smashed himself and his grand army in the Russian wastes and there was something in the American task to take the heart out of a man and drive him to liquor or love or faro.

Howe wrote to Carleton that he was going to attack Philadelphia and could not help Burgoyne. Germain, forgetting Howe's inability to begin a campaign early, never told him that Burgoyne counted on him as a vital aid, until much later when he wrote that, after Howe had finished his conquest of Philadelphia, he might join Burgoyne. To Howe's campaign against Philadelphia Germain gave formal approval but only half the reinforcements Howe declared to be necessary.[12]

In the second place Howe wrote to Carleton that Burgoyne could whip Americans as easily as he could. He did not realize that it was the wilderness that was whipping Burgoyne, and that the Americans were merely allies. After all the difficulties he himself had encountered in finding horses, forage, wagons, and laborers enough to move him out of Boston and New York with the fleet at hand, Howe should have realized that Burgoyne, cutting the way for his artillery through jungles of trees, with an enemy felling more of them across every path, would be in greater need of cooperation the farther he got.

But he did not realize this, and that is all there is to it. History is packed with instances of people who forget or fail to imagine, and everyday life is made up of so little else that great triumphs are always awaiting those who occasionally remember, sometimes realize, once in a while imagine, and fairly often employ plain common sense.

Howe's delay in getting out of the harbor of New York was not his own fault. The fleet was not his to command. It was commanded by his elder brother. Furthermore, he was deceived not only in his hopes of heavy reinforcements from England, but in his reliance on Tory promises. The loyalists, like the rebels, talked large and delivered small. Two New York Tories promised to raise 6,000 men for Howe, almost as many men as Washington had. They raised eleven hundred, mostly foreigners.[13] Congress knew how Tory Pennsylvanians were, especially the Quakers. Howe was deluded into believing that his appearance in that quarter would raise immense numbers of them. Practically none appeared.

The mystery of his so-called "abandonment" of Burgoyne and the tantalizing riddles of his conduct are cleared up and disclosed to be rational according to his lights, in a letter he wrote to Lord Germain on July 16, 1777. The King was so interested that he copied Howe's words in his own writing for his own files:

"MY LORD—By the movement of the Enemy's Army in Jersey . . . he seems to point at preventing a junction between this and the Northern Army, which will no farther affect my proceeding to Pensilvania, than to make a small change in the distribution of the Troops. For if the Enemy should cross the North River before I sail from hence, or should approach it so near as to give me a prospect of reaching Philadelphia before him, I shall in either case strengthen Sir Henry Clinton still more . . . he will then have sufficient force to act on the defensive against the whole Rebel Army; . . . If G. Washington should march to the defence of Pensilvania, I shall on such Event order them to join me in that Province: the Enemy's movements taking this turn, I apprehend

[12] Germain to Howe, March 3, 1777. Sir John Fortescue, *History of the British Army*, III, p. 209.

[13] Fortescue, *History of the British Army*, III, p. 206.

General Burgoyne will meet with little interruption otherwise than the difficulties he must encounter in transporting Stores and provisions for the Supply of his Army.

"On the other hand if G. Washington should march with a determination to force G. Burgoyne, the Strength of G. Burgoyne's Army is such as to leave me no room to dread the event; but if M^r. Washington's intention should only be to retard the approach of G^l Burgoyne to Albany; he may soon find himself exposed to an attack from this quarter and from G^l Burgoyne at the same time, from both of which, I flatter myself, he would find it difficult to escape." [14]

It was early in July that Howe began to stuff his troops into the transports. New York harbor was hot but bad weather outside prevented his sailing until July 23rd. It was the weather not Howe that Washington should have blamed for that nerve-racking delay. It was clever of Howe, in any case, to wear out Washington's men and keep them on the jump by moving a few ships up the river or the sound while he waited for a good sea breeze.

Expecting a voyage of no more than three weeks, forage for that time only was shipped. Land was not made for forty days and so many of the horses died or were thrown overboard to die that his cavalry action later was seriously hampered.[15] The dearth of horses was one of Howe's chief excuses for all his inaction.

When he reached Delaware Bay July 31st. he found that his brother, the Admiral Lord Howe, was unwilling to take his ships up the river since a naval officer who had cruised there for months warned him that it was not feasible as the rebels had filled it with obtructions.[16] It was also found that the tides were perilous and the banks too marshy for easy landing or healthy encampment. The naval officers refused to put Howe ashore.

John Fiske insists that Howe's excuse for not landing was "trumped up and worthless," but Sir John Fortescue says he greatly doubts "whether Mr. Fiske ever cast eye over" the highly technical explanations of the naval officers.[17] Fiske was doing his utmost to fasten the guilt of treason on Charles Lee and establish the fantastic theory that Howe's movements "would be inexplicable to-day except as the result of the wild advice of the marplot Lee." [18]

But Lee's paper is of no help whatever in explaining Howe's movements, since, to repeat, Lee ridiculed the importance of Philadelphia and urged a landing in Maryland, which Howe never touched. Howe went straight to the Delaware and found conditions that thwarted him. The wisdom of the naval refusal to attempt a landing there is confirmed by Hoffman Nickerson, the historian of Burgoyne's expedition, who says:

"Having myself experienced the fierce tides in the lower Delaware which led Howe's naval officers to advise quitting that river and trying the Chesapeake, I am more than willing to believe that these tides and not Lee's plan at all persuaded Howe to move by the Chesapeake as he finally did." [19]

[14] Fortescue, *Correspondence of George III*, III, p. 462.

[15] E. E. Curtis, *The Organization of the British Army in the American Revolution*, p. 126.

[16] James, op. cit., p. 64. Channing, *History of the United States*, III, p. 251 n.

[17] Fortescue, *History of the British Army*, III, 214 n., citing Fiske.

[18] Fiske, *The American Revolution*, I, pp. 314, 320.

[19] Hoffman Nickerson, *The Turning Point of the Revolution*, Appendix V, p. 463.

The naval officers carried him off and made for Chesapeake Bay. Contrary winds fought the ships so persistently that the fleet made less than fifteen miles a day. It took twenty-four days to cover three hundred and fifty miles—five times as long as passenger ships now require for crossing the ocean. The ships of to-day are in constant touch with the land, but Washington had three weeks and more of further frantic suspense.

This digression as to Howe's motives and at least partial excuses seems necessary, if for no other reason, at least as a means of saving Washington's face. If Howe had been the "fool" that Hamilton called him [20] or the idiot that most of the historians have pictured, Washington was an inferior imbecile or he would have crushed him instantly, instead of learning by experience what a rattlesnake of danger this torpid Howe could be. The rattlesnake also is lazy and does not pursue, yet is not to be disregarded.

The last word in justification of Howe is a might-have-been. At Brandywine, he crushed the Americans so badly that a ruthless pursuit might have destroyed them, and by a direct march caught Congress unready for flight. With Philadelphia in his hands, he could have sent Clinton up the Hudson while he marched overland. The army of Gates would have had to break up and divide to escape from the triple threat. Burgoyne would have come through and Gates' great host might have joined Washington's in the British prison camps. If Burgoyne had not surrendered, France would never have entered the war. If France had not sent her soldiers and her fleets, Cornwallis would never have been trapped.

Considering these possibilities—and possibilities are all that a strategist has to gamble on—Howe might easily have been hailed as one of the greatest generals of all time, and Washington forgotten as one of the countless futile rebels. If Howe had had the genius of pursuit, all these things might have been added unto him.

It has been said that Howe prolonged the war for the sake of the higher pay than he would have had on a peace-footing, but even Galloway, who tore him to pieces with such keen arguments, dismisses the charge with the statement that "the love of money is the least of all his passions," and while his favorites grew rich from plunder, he gained little. But Galloway insists that Howe protracted the conflict out of loyalty to the enemies of the ministry, "the dark and heinous conspiracy of the Faction with which the General was connected." [21]

Light Horse Harry Lee found Howe's inactions "wonderful." His Memoirs edited by his grandson Robert E. Lee show the characteristic Lee chivalry and are marked by a fairness to the enemy all too infrequent in American history. He denies that Howe lacked courage, was indolent, or too friendly to the American cause. That, in Lee's eyes, would have been treason to England, and he adds, "Traitors are not to be found among British generals." Still he admits that Howe's failures to press his advantages "involve an inquisitive mind in a perplexity not easy to be untangled." [22]

He was a gambler who often won but never quite broke the bank. It has been too easy for rival officers and for historians in libraries to call him a dithering idiot. If he had played out one hand more, there would have been different history to write, and his name would have stood glorious there. Being

[20] Hamilton, *Works*, IX, p. 84.
[21] [Joseph Galloway] *A Reply to the Observations of Lt. Gen. Sir Wm. Howe* (London 1780), pp. 111-113.
[22] Henry Lee, *Memoirs of the War*, edited by R. E. Lee, p. 109.

a Whig and a liberal, if he had conquered America, there is no telling what changes he would have made in England when he went back as another Cæsar.

In the Clinton Papers at the Clements Library is a summing up of Howe's American campaign in the hand of the secretary of Clinton, who doubtless dictated the words:

"Had Sir Wm. Howe Fortified the Hills round Boston, he could not have been disgracefully driven from it: Had he pursued his Victory at Long Island, he had ended the Rebellion: Had he landed above the lines at New York, not a man could have escaped him: Had he fought the Americans at Brunswick he was sure of victory: Had he coöperated with the Northern Army, he had saved it, or had he gone to Philadelphia by land, he had ruined Mr. Washington and his Forces; But, as he did none of these things, had he gone to the D——l, before he was sent to America, it had been a saving of infamy to himself and indelible dishonour to this Country."

This may serve as the worst possible epitaph for Howe's achievements. It may be a little unfair as to his motives.

Mark Antony, according to tradition, might have conquered Rome but for Cleopatra's abandonment of him in the sea-battle at Actium. Howe had his own Cleopatra, Mrs. Loring, the beautiful gambler who lost three hundred guineas a night without a qualm.[23] While such infatuations may distress the historian they cannot be ignored in the quest for explanations. It was said in England that Howe's sea-voyage "made the Americans a present of Burgoyne's army," and of the French alliance. It was said that he "played at bo-peep with the rebels" and his voyage to Chesapeake Bay was called "circumbendibus."[24]

One explanation of such a ridiculous error is as good as another, and for the sake of the record it may be well to include the explanation that was made to John Bernard, the actor, when he visited America in 1797. He says that the reason for the "perverse and fatal" voyage was "that Mrs. Loring, being at this time in as critical a condition as the country, required the benefit of sea-air, and her wish was law!"[25]

[23] E. F. DeLancey, notes to Thomas Jones, *History of New York during the Revolutionary War* (N. Y. Hist. Soc.), II, p. 424.

[24] *The Detail and Conduct of the American War*, p. 27

[25] John Bernard, *Retrospections of America*, pp. 60-1. In an anonymous pamphlet *Historical Anecdotes*, published in London in 1779 and consisting of letters from New York, there is a letter dated January 25, 1778, stating (p. 43), "A great deal has been placed to the account of the General's fondness for, and attachment to, Mrs. L——g; who is beyond compare the Greatest Woman in the world; to whom all Men must pay their court, if they hope for Preferment. She is, however, far advanced in her pregnancy, and was left at New York. But then the General has found another Desdemona at Philadelphia, even the pretty Miss ——, who is now his Excellency's flirt." Belcher, however (*First American Civil War*, II, p. 261), says that Mrs. Loring was established at Philadelphia "in a convenient house" belonging to James Logan, called "Stenton, . . . a fine mansion in the best eastern colonial style." Stenton, which served Howe as headquarters for a time, is just south of Germantown, and the famous historic mansion is further described in Scharf & Westcott's *History of Philadelphia*, I, p. 161, II, p. 872, and in Watson's *Annals of Philadelphia*, I, p. 476, II, pp. 39, 480.

Bernard met Washington and revered him, yet he tells how he was amused as much as startled by the "disclosure" that American independence, which "every one supposes was owing to George Washington, with some support from his countrymen, and a little assistance from the French," was really owing to "a female patriot, the beautiful and fascinating Mrs. Loring." Seeing the country's affairs "veering like an unruddered vessel, into the suction of a whirlpool, she conceived the noble enterprise of their rescue, by exerting all her arts and charms to entrap the affections and influence the counsels of that modern Antony—Sir William Howe."

How long must she wait for her statue to adorn the Hall of Fame? She is still exiled from the knowledge, not to say the gratitude, of her countrymen, while Betsy Ross, who did nothing worth mentioning, smiles from innumerable walls?

APPENDIX IV

THE PACIFISTS AND REVEREND MR. DUCHÉ

Like all other stout soldiers, Washington was never in so inhospitable a mood toward peace proposals as just after a defeat.

He had dealt roughly with the tender efforts of Lord Drummond towards conciliation, and he needed all his self-control to restrain his impatience when a delegation of Quakers, having already called on Howe, called at Pennypacker's Mill on October 7th, 1777, with an exquisitely untimely testimonial concerning the ungodliness of war. The Quakers were in particularly bad odor at this time. They were being exiled, beaten and stoned. Guns were fastened to them and they were forced to march. They retaliated by expelling the "Free Quakers" who took up arms with the rebels. Their devotion to peace cost them a million dollars. With a recrudescence of the old Massachusetts frenzy against them, John Adams lashed them now in a letter to his wife:

"We have been obliged to attempt to humble the pride of some Jesuits, who call themselves Quakers, but who love money and land better than liberty and religion. The hypocrites are endeavoring to raise the cry of persecution, and to give this matter a religious turn, but they can't succeed . . . American independence has disappointed them, which makes them hate it. Yet the dastards dare not avow their hatred to it, it seems." [1]

They had been putting Washington into quandaries since 1756 when he was whipping drafted deserters and found six Quakers among his conscripts. [2]

In the Revolution he saw his best general, Greene, expelled from the church for fighting. He had just lost two battles, largely because of Quaker aloofness from the cause, and a number of Quakers had been shipped to Virginia as dangerous conspirators. General Armstrong described the visitation:

"We lost a great part of yesterday with a deputation of Quakers . . . seeking in the world only peace, truth, and righteousness, with equal love to all men, &c. And asking, in a dark manner, his aid for their brethring in exile, &c. . . . The General gave them their dinner and ordered them only to do penance a few days at Pott's grove, until their beards are grown." [3]

Washington, who had never loved Pennsylvania since it was a rival nation to Virginia, now wrote a letter to the President of the Council of the state, a tart letter, too. Though Pennsylvania had no less than 30,000 voters the interest in the conflict was so small that in 1778 less than 200 votes were cast for the assemblyman. [4] Though invaded, the state had turned out only twelve hundred men, though its quota was four thousand.

---

[1] *Familiar Letters of John Adams and His Wife*, p. 305. For the Quaker side, see C. F. Holder, *The Quakers in Great Britain and America*, pp. 558-60.

[2] See Volume I of this work, p. 309.

[3] Scharf and Westcott, *History of Philadelphia*, I, p. 359.

[4] [J. Galloway] *Letters to a Nobleman on the Conduct of the War*, p. 21.

Washington demanded that the Governor draft at least half of the men capable of bearing arms and he made odious comparisons with New York's "noble resistance" and New Jersey's success in repelling all but raids without a Continental regiment:

"It is a matter of astonishment to every part of the continent, to hear that Pennsylvania, the most opulent and populous of all the States, has but twelve hundred militia in the field."

He declared that if he could get the men promised he could hold the forts along the Delaware and starve Howe out of Philadelphia. The Continental quota was not even a third full. Bounty could no longer be afforded and he advised the draft as it was already enforced in New England and Virginia. As a result of this fierce letter ridiculing the presence of only twelve hundred Pennsylvania men in the field four months later there were "between sixty and one hundred men under General Lacey" and practically nobody to check British raiders between the Delaware and the Schuylkill rivers. On March 27th, 1778, Washington was able to write that the state quota "has never been above half kept up, and sometimes I believe there has not been a single man. General Lacey has not now above seventy." [5]

From now on to the end of the war this steady dwindling of the army went on relentlessly, each campaign seeing fewer men than the one before. Only the hardships increased as the war proceeded with a sickening public lethargy that justifies W. G. Sumner in saying:

"On the whole, if we compare the American war of independence with the struggle of the Dutch for independence, or with that of the Southern States in 1861, the sacrifices of the Revolutionary war must be considered trivial." [6]

It is not to be wondered then that some of the best hearts in America, especially those in whom love for the mother-country was inextinguishable, should have despaired and, despairing, been persuaded that further resistance was not only hopeless but murderous.

Among these was the timorous parson, Jacob Duché, who had opened the first Continental Congress with prayer. The delegates had been swept away by his fervor. John Adams wrote, "I never heard a better prayer." [7] From that first Congress Washington had written of independence that "no such thing is desired by any thinking man in all North America." [8] Many full-blooded American thinkers had seen nothing to convert them from his opinion of that date. After the Declaration of Independence, Duché, unconvinced but obedient, omitted the name of the King from the official prayers at his church and on July 8, 1776, was made chaplain to the second Congress. He did not relish the post and three months later resigned on the grounds of ill health, refusing even the money due him and asking that it be paid to the widows and orphans of Pennsylvania officers.

When Howe entered Philadelphia Duché promptly restored the King to the prayers, yet he was one of the first to be thrown into jail. The British denounced him as a Judas and a traitor to his church as well as to his anointed king. The chill of the cell seems to have frozen in one night what ardor the

[5] Ford, *Writings*, VI, p. 117. (Oct. 17, 1777); p. 289 n. (Feb. 12, 1778); p. 451 (Mar. 27, 1778).
[6] W. G. Sumner, *The Financiers and the Finances of the American Revolution*, II, p. 148.
[7] *Familiar Letters of John Adams and His Wife*, p. 37.
[8] Ford, *Writings*, II, p. 444.

defeats of the rebels had left in him, and he recanted, was released, returned to his pulpit, and again restored the King to the prayers—all of which must have been bewildering to the deity whom he so variously implored.

On October 8th he decided to redeem Washington's soul and tell him just how to save the country. He wrote a long letter, and entrusted it to Mrs. Anne Ferguson of Graeme Park to deliver to Washington, in whom its piety awakened a dreadful rage. The letter burned his hands like a smoking grenade and he made haste to toss it over to Congress as a "ridiculous, illiberal performance," adding that he had desired the bearer of it, "if she should hereafter by any accident meet with Mr. Duché, to tell him I should have returned it unopened, if I had had any idea of the contents; observing at the same time, that I highly disapproved the intercourse she seemed to have been carrying on, and expected it would be discontinued." [9]

Just two years before Duché had sent to Washington a sermon dedicated to him with a letter saying, "My Prayers are continually for you, and the brave Troops under your command." Washington answered with natural cordiality.[10] Duché's new letter began with a request that before Washington read even the second sentence, he should retire and "weigh well its important contents."

He then went on to explain how he had been swept away by the torrent of rebellion and coerced into preaching and praying for the success of armed opposition. Threatened with violence, he had been forced either to shut up the churches or quit "using the petitions for the royal family." Then came "the fatal declaration of independency" and his appointment to the chaplaincy of Congress, which he "rashly accepted," thinking the declaration really only "an Expedient . . . thrown out in terrorem, in order to procure some favourable terms." Shocked by Congress' refusal to treat with the Peace Commissioners, he saw that "independency was the idol, which . . . rather than sacrifice . . . they would deluge their country in blood." He then resigned.

Now "in the language of truth and real affection," he addressed Washington, feeling sure that he also had never expected such extremes. "Your most intimate friends at the time shuddered at the thought of a separation from the mother country; and I took it for granted, that your sentiments coincided with theirs." He drew a picture of the blight upon the land:

"A Degeneracy of Representation—confusion of councils—Blunders without number. The most respectable characters have withdrawn themselves, and are succeeded by a great majority of illiberal and violent men."

Duché went down the line naming names with scorn, whacking many a head, and winding up with language uncomfortably like opinions that Washington himself often uttered confidentially:

"Are the Dregs of a Congress, then, to influence a mind like yours? These are not the men you engaged to serve . . . Most of them elected by a little low Faction . . . 'Tis you, Sir, and you only, that support the present Congress

[9] Ford, *Writings*, VI, p. 115.

[10] W. C. Ford gives all the correspondence in his privately printed *The Washington-Duché Letters* in which he gives also an account of Mrs. Ferguson's activities on p. 26, concerning whom see *Penn Mag.*, XXXIX, p. 257. There is much about Duché in Hastings, *Life and Works of Francis Hopkinson*, also in the *Penn. Mag.*, II, p. 58. M. C. Tyler's *Literary History of the American Revolution*, II, p. 287. Sabine's *Loyalists of the American Revolution*, I, p. 388. Sparks' *Writings of Washington*, V, pp. 476-482.

. . . turn to the Army. The whole world knows, that its very existence depends upon you, that your Death or Captivity disperses it in a moment . . . what have you to expect from them? Have they not frequently abandoned even yourself in the hour of extremity? Have you, can you have the least confidence in a sett of undisciplined men and officers, many of whom have been taken from the lowest of the People, without Principle, without Courage. Take away those, that surround your Person, how very few are there, that you can ask to sit at your Table?"

He explained why France could not fight England, giving reasons that had persuaded Washington also to ridicule the hope of French intervention. Then he appealed to Washington as the one man who could remove the bar to peace. He implored Heaven to inspire him to this great deed, "thus immortalizing yourself as Friend and Guardian of your Country." He called on Washington to persuade Congress to rescind "the hasty and ill-advised declaration of Independency," to recommend the immediate cessation of hostilities and the appointment of Gentlemen to confer with his Majesty's Commissioners.

Finally he said that, if Washington agreed with him and found his advice rejected by Congress, he ought then to "Negotiate for America at the Head of your Army . . . With the most ardent Prayers for your spiritual as well as temporal welfare, I am Your obed^t. and sincere Friend and Servant."

This quotation, though incomplete, would be overlong if it were not of value in revealing Washington's character and also as an evidence of the antiquity of much contemporaneous talk of wars to end war, disarmament and eternal peace by conference, and by force if necessary.

Practically everything in his letter had been said by Washington himself, yet the mere reading of it so far from converted him that it both infuriated and terrified him. He cried, "Get thee behind me, Parson!" He did not want to be found with such a leprous document in his possession. He did not want to be suspected of entertaining any such loathsome opinions. He fired the letter off to Congress at once. Perhaps he smiled as he imagined those politicians whom he admired little and loved less as they read what Duché said of them.

It is not surprising that they were not in the least flattered by being called degenerate dregs from low factions. John Adams wrote his wife:

"Mr. Duché, I am sorry to inform you, has turned out an apostate and a traitor. Poor man! I pity his weakness and detest his wickedness." [11]

Henry Laurens called the letter a "Rascally epistle from the Ir-Revd. Jacob Duche." The North Carolina delegates called him "the first of villains." Congressman Folsom of New Hampshire wrote: "See what a Judas was a Chaplin to Congress." [12]

One of the most indignant men was Francis Hopkinson, ardent patriot and brother-in-law of Duché, to whom he wrote:

"What Infatuation could influence you to offer his Excellency an Address fill'd with gross Misrepresentations, illiberal abuse & sentiments unworthy of a Man of Character. . . . You have by a vain and weak Effort attempted the Integrity of one whose Virtue is impregnable to the Assaults of Fear or Flattery: . . . Would not the Blood of the Slain in Battle rise against such Perfidy?" [13]

Hopkinson sent this to Washington with a request that he forward it to

[11] *Familiar Letters*, p. 320.
[12] E. C. Burnett, *Letters of Members of the Continental Congress*, pp. 526, 527, 538.
[13] Hastings, op. cit., p. 271.

Duché, and accompanied it with a letter strongly disclaiming similar opinions. Washington answered:

"I will endeavor to forward it to him, but I imagine it will never be permitted to reach his Hands. I confess to you, that I was not more surprised than concerned, at receiving so extraordinary a letter from Mr. Duché, of whom I had entertained the most favorable opinion, and I am still willing to suppose, that it was rather dictated by his fears than by his real Sentiments; but I very much doubt whether the great numbers of respectable characters, in the State and the Army on whom he has bestowed the most unprovoked and unmerited abuse, will ever attribute it to the same cause, or forgive the Man, who has artfully endeavored to engage me to sacrifice them to purchase my own Safety.

"I never intended to make the letter more public, than by laying it before Congress. I thought this a duty, which I owed to myself; for, had any accident have happened to the Army entrusted to my command, and it had ever afterwards have appeared, that such a letter had been wrote to and received by me, might it not have been said, that I had in consequence of it betrayed my country? And would not such a correspondence, if kept a secret, have given good grounds for the suspicion? I thank you for your favorable sentiments, which you are pleased to express of me, and I hope no act of mine will ever induce you to alter them." [14]

In January, 1778, Washington returned Hopkinson's letter to him, having never found an opportunity of conveying it, and having never made its contents public.

To finish with Duché, it may be said that, dazed by the reception of his message of sweetness and light, he sailed for England on the same ship with Cornwallis. In 1783 he wrote to Washington a pathetic letter protesting that he was "one who ever was and wishes still to be your sincere friend, who never *intentionally* sought to give you a moment's pain," and asked his forgiveness, protesting that he wrote when he "looked upon all as gone." He had no thought "to advise an act of base treachery, my soul would have recoiled from the thought; not to surrender your army, or betray the righteous cause of your country, but, at the head of the army, *supporting and supported by them,* to negotiate with Britain for our constitutional rights."

He begged Washington to help him out of his banishment. "Your liberal, generous mind, I am persuaded, will never exclude me wholly from your regard for a mere political error." He was well received, well paid and well treated in England "but unalterable affection to my native country" urged his return. He had appealed to the State of Pennsylvania for mercy.

To this Washington replied with his usual generosity and his usual reluctance to meddle in other jurisdictions:

"I have received your letter of the 2d of April, and, reflecting on its contents, I cannot but say that I am heartily sorry for the occasion which has produced it. Personal enmity I bear none to any man. So far, therefore, as your return to this country depends on my private voice, it would be given in favor of it with cheerfulness." [15]

But the Pennsylvania laws against refugees were not rescinded for several

[14] Cited by A. H. Quinn, *The Spirit of Independence,* Scribner's Magazine, July, 1926. This transcription is more exact than the one in Ford's *Washington-Duché Letters,* p. 28.
[15] Ford, *The Washington-Duché Letters,* p. 38.

years and it was not till 1792 that this pathetic renegade was permitted to creep home, aged and paralyzed. He lodged with Bishop White, his old classmate, and called on Washington, who greeted him cordially; and, says Bishop White, "manifested generous sensibility, on observing, in the limbs of Mr. Duché, the effects of a slight stroke of paralysis." [16]

In 1798 he was buried by the side of his wife in Philadelphia, the capital of the Republic, "under the Presidency," says Moses Coit Tyler, "of that very General whom, in its dark days, he had exhorted to betray both himself and it to the enemy." [17]

This accusation of treason is repeated by practically all the historians, though Duché's letter of explanation makes plain what would be evident to any mind not influenced by war psychology, that he had no thought of treachery, unless it be treachery to advise a man to arbitrate a quarrel whose development has abandoned its original cause. He never meant what he seemed at the time to mean: that Washington should lead his army against Congress. He meant only that he should stay at its head until the British made fair terms.

While it is a trifle out of sequence, it is astonishing to record that Duché's supposed request that Washington march against Congress with his army was alleged two years later as a request of Hamilton's—and by another clergyman. The otherwise incredible story is told by Hamilton in a letter to his friend, John Laurens, describing his effort to run down the original inventor of the slander. Hamilton also had written with disgust of Congress and used Duché's word, "degeneracy," but could not, of course, have proposed what he was accused of:

"The Cabal have reported that I declared in a public house in Philadelphia that it was high time for the people to rise, join General Washington, and turn Congress out of doors? I am running the rogues pretty hard. Dana was the first mentioned to me. He has given up Dr. Gordon, of Jamaica Plains. You well remember the old Jesuit. He made us a visit at Fredericksburg, and is writing the history of America. The proverb is verified,—'There never was any mischief, but had a priest or a woman at the bottom.' . . . I have written to Gordon, and what do you think is his answer?—he will give up his author if I will pledge my honor 'neither to give nor accept a challenge, to cause it to be given or accepted, nor to engage in any encounter that may produce a duel.' . . . I have ridiculed the proposal, and insisted on the author, on the principle of unconditional submission. What the Doctor's impudence will answer, I know not." [18]

Dr. Gordon answered evasively and Hamilton wrote to him three months later:

"The unravelment of the plot in the ridiculous farce you have been acting, proves, as I at first suspected, that you are yourself the author of the calumny."

Gordon turned the papers over to Washington, who informed him that he regretted his bringing such a disagreeable business before him, and that Colonel Hamilton was amenable for his own conduct. [19]

Washington himself had occasion in later years to be annoyed by Gordon's

---

[16] A. Wilson, *Memoir of Bishop White*, p. 58.

[17] M. C. Tyler, op. cit., II, p. 293.

[18] Hamilton, *Works* (Federal ed.), IX, p. 175. See also pp. 122, 169, 175, 189.

[19] Ford, *Writings*, VIII, p. 259.

pryings. Hamilton's idea of a good clergyman was probably Washington's own, based on the Virginian type. Hamilton thus recommended a chaplain, Doctor W. Mendy, to Anthony Wayne:

"He is just what I should like for a military parson, except that he does not drink. He will fight, and he will not insist upon your going to heaven whether you will or not. He tells me there is a vacancy in your brigade. I should be really happy if, through your influence, he can fill it. Pray take care of the good old man." [20]

Hamilton probably summed up his religious predilections, and perhaps Washington's in the ideal wife he asked John Laurens to find for him. Among her qualifications he said:

"As to religion a moderate stock will satisfy me. She must believe in God and hate a saint." [21]

[20] Hamilton, *Works,* IX, p. 201.
[21] Ibid., p. 187.

APPENDIX V

THE SPURIOUS LETTERS

While the Americans were concocting spurious anecdotes of a semi-divine Washington, it amused the British propagandists to invent an opposite. When one of Washington's bodyguard was hanged for plotting to assassinate him in 1776, the British manufactured an outrageously untrue but minutely imaginative account of an effort to kidnap Washington while he was visiting a certain girl he was alleged to be keeping in a New York dive. They interpolated an indecent passage about a washerwoman's girl and the "antidote to love, Sukey," in a perfectly innocent letter from Benjamin Harrison.[1]

Now they put forth a most elaborate volume called "Letters from General Washington to several of his Friends in the Year 1776," and published in London in May or June, 1777, by the same J. Bew who published the false story of the assassination plot.[2] The letters were alleged to have been written by Washington and they indicated that he had been dragged into the war reluctantly, had never ceased to doubt its success, and abhorred the thought of independence.

Though the imitation of his style was clumsy and the incidents described never took place, the preference of the public for works of fiction kept them alive in spite of his denials of their authorship. When he was at the depth of his unpopularity as President they were brought out to be used against him. And in 1927 one of them was much published in American newspapers as a genuine document. Even if Washington had not denied and denounced them, the same methods of historical criticism that discredit other popular stories of him would expose these.

On January 2nd, 1778, R. H. Lee wrote to Washington:

"The arts of the enemies of America are endless, but all wicked as they are various. Among other tricks they have forged a pamphlet of Letters entitled 'Letters from Gen. Washington to several of his friends in 1776.' The design of the Forger is evident, and no doubt it gained him a good Beef Steak from his Masters—I would send you this pamphlet if it were not too bulky for the Post, as it might serve to amuse your leisure hours during the inaction of Winter."[3]

[1] See Vol. II of this work, pp. 402, 290.

[2] While various editions of the *Spurious Letters* are available, Mr. Worthington C. Ford has given them complete, with a learned introduction and notes, in his privately printed brochure, *The Spurious Letters Attributed to Washington*, Brooklyn, 1889. The text of this pamphlet differs somewhat from the version he included in his edition of the *Writings of Washington*. The genuine letter to Martha, dated June 23, 1775, is cited by Charles Moore, *The Family Life of Washington*, p. 128.

[3] J. C. Ballagh, *The Letters of Richard Henry Lee*, I, p. 371.

To this Washington replied on February 15th, 1778:

"The enemy are governed by no principles that ought to actuate honest men; no wonder then, that forgery should be amongst their other crimes. I have seen a letter published in a handbill at New York, and extracts from it republished in a Philadelphia paper, said to be from me to Mrs. Washington, not one word of which did I ever write. Those contained in the pamphlet you speak of are, I presume, equally genuine, and perhaps written by the same author. I should be glad, however, to see and examine the texture of them, if a favorable opportunity to send them should present." [4]

In the preface to the forgeries it was stated that among the prisoners taken at Fort Lee was Washington's old servant, "Billy," who "had been left there on account of an indisposition which prevented his attending his master"; and that he had with him a small portmanteau containing a few stockings and shirts, an almanac in which Washington had kept a diary, "two letters from his lady, one from Mr. Custis, and some pretty long ones from a Mr. Lund Washington, and in the same bundle with them, the first draughts, or foul copies, of answers to them."

These letters showed Washington to be "a very different character from what they had supposed him. I never knew a man so much to be pitied . . . They contain also . . . a deal of information not to be had anywhere else." [5]

This last, at least, was true. It was also true that Washington had a body servant, Billy, whom he remembered affectionately in his will. But Billy was never captured nor was any portmanteau of letters. Washington did write his diary in almanacs, but he gave up keeping one on June 19th, 1775, when he took command, and did not resume until May, 1781, when he began a new one, saying, "I lament not having attempted it from the commencement of the War." [6]

Throughout the spurious letters there appear little touches that indicate an acquaintance with Washington, such as only an American who had known him could probably have possessed. Hence, some former friend either wrote the forgeries or collaborated in them. Along with the realistic touches are many that give away the writer's ignorance of known facts. The style in general is worlds away from Washington's own manner. Mr. W. C. Ford picks out among the most striking false notes, historical and literary allusions such as Washington almost never made:

"The reader of Washington's letters cannot fail to notice how few are the references to matters of history, and how seldom there is any evidence of an acquaintance with even the writings generally understood at that time." [7]

First published in London, the letters were shipped to New York and reprinted in haste. The letter addressed to Martha was printed as a handbill for easier distribution and soon appeared in Philadelphia.

In both of the surviving letters to Martha known to be his and found in Martha's desk, he begins, "My dearest." One ends, "I am with the most unfeigned regard, my dear Patsy, your affectionate." The other ends, "Yr entire George Washington." But in the spurious letters he begins, "My Dearest Life and Love," and ends, "Your most faithful and tender Husband," and never calls her "Patsy" as he does in his own.

[4] Ford, *Writings*, VI, p. 377.
[5] *Spurious Letters* (Ford ed.), p. 6.
[6] *Washington's Diaries* (Fitzpatrick), II, p. 205.
[7] *Spurious Letters*, p. 61 n.

For the sake of comparison the letter he really wrote to Martha, just as he rode away from Philadelphia on June 23rd, 1775, to take command at Boston, is printed in a parallel column with a portion of the spurious letter. The false letter is about 2,000 words long, the real about 140. The other extant letter of his of June 18th, 1775, notifying her of his nomination as commander-in-chief, is 580 words long, but written with the most simple fervor as to a wife, with nothing of the oratorical and didactic propaganda built up, for evident purposes, in the false letter:

WASHINGTON'S LETTER

Philadelphia, June 23, 1775

MY DEAREST:

As I am within a few minutes of leaving this city, I could not think of departing from it without dropping you a line, especially as I do not know whether it may be in my power to write again till I get to the camp at Boston. I go fully trusting in that Providence, which has been more bountiful to me than I deserve, and in full confidence of a happy meeting with you some time in the fall.

I have not time to add more as I am surrounded with company to take leave of me. I retain an unalterable affection for you, which neither time nor distance can change. My best love to Jack and Nelly, and regards to the rest of the Family, . . . with the utmost truth and sincerity.

Yr entire

G. WASHINGTON

THE SPURIOUS LETTER
To the Hon. Lady Washington, Etc.

24 June, 1776

MY DEAREST LIFE AND LOVE,

You have hurt me, I know not how much, by the insinuation in your last, that my letters to you have lately been less frequent, because I have felt less concern for you. The suspicion is most unjust;—may I not add, it is most unkind? Have we lived, now almost a score of years, in the closest and dearest conjugal intimacy to so little purpose that, on an appearance only of inattention to you, and which you might have accounted for in a thousand ways more natural and more probable, you should pitch upon that single motive which alone is injurious to me? I have not, I own, wrote so often to you as I wished and as I ought. But think of my situation, and then ask your heart, if I be *without excuse*. . . .

Why do you complain of my reserve? Or, how could you imagine that I distrusted either your prudence or your fidelity? . . .

I beg to be affectionately remembered to all our friends and relations; and that you will continue to believe me to be

Your most faithful and tender Husband.

G. W.

In the course of the long forgery there are various things that give it away; for example, on June 24th, 1776, he once more begs Martha to consent to inoculation and warns her that "till you have had the smallpox, anxiously as else I should wish for it, I never can think of consenting to your passing the winter here in quarters with me." He says that if she will only be inoculated she can afterwards go to Philadelphia and be safe from Lord Dunmore's raids near Mount Vernon.

The joke of it is that Martha, after joining him in Cambridge, Massachusetts, on December 11th, 1775, had gone on to New York with him, and stayed there in his headquarters until she left for Philadelphia with him on May 21st, 1776. While he conferred with Congress, she was inoculated. We have a letter from him to John Augustine Washington speaking of her being in her "thirteenth day, and she has very few pustules." He left her there on June 5th and went back to New York, while she did not set out for Mount Vernon until August. Yet in the forged letter of June 24th he is begging her to be inoculated and telling her that afterward she may come to Philadelphia. In a forged letter to Lund, dated July 8th, 1776, he begs Lund to try to persuade her to be inoculated.

Similar ridiculous errors could be found all through the spurious letters, to prove that they were composed at a distance and in fundamental ignorance of everything except a few details. In his real letters to his stepson, Washington always begins, "Dear sir" or "Dear Custis." Knowing how fond he was of the boy, the forger rather naturally begins, "My Very Dear Jack."

The purpose of the forgery sticks out everywhere, for, though he is writing to his own family, every letter is a lecture on his political opinions, and every political opinion is not only contrary to his real opinion, but treasonable in a commander-in-chief. The publication of the letters tended, therefore, to convince the readers that he was compelled to be a hypocrite; that while he was a rebel he loved his king; that his one hope was to be reconciled to him; and that Congress was a foolish body that would not give him the supreme power he wanted.

Since these letters appeared in America during the renewed peace advances of the British, what influence they had was to weaken resistance and give the policy of surrender the prestige of Washington's name. Furthermore, since he was fighting a cabal, they tended to prove him insincere, telling the public one thing and his wife another. For example, he is made to write to Martha:

"Suffice it that I say, what I have often before told you, that, as far as I have the controul of them, all our preparations of war, aim only at peace . . . The only true interest of both sides is reconciliation: . . .

"Pity this cannot be accomplished, without fixing on me that sad name, Rebel. I love my King; you know I do: a soldier, a good man cannot but love him. How peculiarly hard then is our fortune to be deemed traitors to so good a King! But, I am not without hopes, that even he will yet see cause to do me justice: posterity, I am sure, will." [8]

Though he had gone to Philadelphia in June to urge the Declaration of Independence, he is made to write to Lund on July 15th, 1776:

"It is a pity, methinks, that Congress had not had better information on this subject: if they had, it is to be presumed, they would not have precipitated the declaration for independency, so as to preclude all possibility of negotiation." [9]

Other remarks are calculated to stir up rancor. He is made to say of his warm friend, Patrick Henry:

"No doubt, Henry is, in many respects, the unfittest man in the State for Governor of Virginia. He has no property, no learning, but little good sense, and still less virtue or public spirit; but he is the idol of the people." [10]

Imagine Washington writing these words:

"A thousand considerations determine me to strain every nerve to prevent the

[8] *Spurious Letters*, p. 75.
[9] Ibid., p. 100.
[10] Ibid., p. 113.

army's being under any other control whilst I live.   Let a persuasion of the necessity of this, if occasion should arise, be seasonably urged in my native state; and in the mean while, let some more than ordinary pains be taken to make me popular." [11]

The real Washington glows and grows in magnanimity by his immense differences from this cheap parody of him.   One rejoices to note the contrast, too, between his actual letters with their pell-mell syntax, dashes, and bad spelling, and the stilted pedantry of these forgeries, which do to him even more than Jared Sparks did in his revisions.

The question rises, Who was the forger?   The London *Monthly Review* of 1796 said that they were "forged, undoubtedly, by a Mr. V——, then a young Episcopal clergyman, who came from New York, in order to make his fortune *here*, in the character of a *Loyalist*."   Mr. Worthington C. Ford, in his edition of the *Spurious Letters*, says that he would "dislike to believe, except on the plainest proof, that one in Holy Orders could stoop so low as to utter forged papers with a view to deliberately injure the reputation of another man." [12] But Reinach, in his *Short History of Christianity* (p. 178), describes the persecution of Dreyfus on forged evidence as clerical work, and Guignebert in his *Christianity, Past and Present* (p. 249), after describing the almost innumerable forgeries used for various purposes, often most cruel, speaks of "the fabrication of documents" as a "characteristic industry."

The man "V——" in question would be the Reverend John Vardill, who was known to have "wielded a ready pen in the service of his masters."   It is not impossible that he collaborated in this work.   Washington thought the author was someone who had knowledge of the family life at Mount Vernon.   Colonel Tench Tilghman wrote from Valley Forge to his father on April 24th, 1778, that Washington "suspects Jack Randolph for the author." [13]   Randolph, because of loyalist sympathy, left Virginia in November, 1775, at a time when Washington was probably known to be urging Martha to be inoculated.   His son, Edmund Randolph, sided with the rebels and was taken into Washington's family.   His letters to his father may have let slip bits of information of which he made such awkward use as he could.   There is no positive proof of Randolph's authorship, but it is not improbable that he at least aided in their composition.

Washington made no effort to deny them publicly at the time, unwisely letting scornful silence be his answer.   During his Presidency when he was undergoing the most ferocious abuse from the opponents of the Jay Treaty, the spurious letters were revived to prove that he had always been a fanatic lover of England, even during the Revolution.   A new edition was brought out for his torment, and he bestirred himself to denounce the imposition.

The difficulty of scotching a lie, particularly a lie about Washington, is seen in the reappearance of quotations from these spurious letters in recent years. They will probably keep coming back eternally, like comets.

[11] *Spurious Letters*, p. 116.
[12] Ibid., p. 29.
[13] Ibid., p. 32.

BOOKS CONSULTED AND QUOTED

Abbatt, William, The Crisis of the Revolution, being the story of Arnold and André, New York, 1899.

Abbott, Wilbur C., New York in the American Revolution, New York, 1929.

Adams, Charles Francis, Cavalry in the War of Independence, Proc. Mass. Hist. Soc., April-June, 1910, Boston, 1910.

Adams, James Truslow, The Burgoyne Expedition, North American Review, October, 1927.

Adams, James Truslow, New England in the Republic, 1776-1850, Boston, 1926.

Adams, John, Familiar Letters to His Wife, New York, 1876.

Adams, John, Works, with a Life of the Author, 10 volumes (edited by Charles Francis Adams), Boston, 1850-56.

Adams, Randolph G., The Papers of Lord George Germain, William L. Clements Library, University of Michigan, Bulletin No. 18, Ann Arbor, 1928.

Adams, Randolph G., The Headquarters Papers of the British Army in North America, Wm. L. Clements Library, University of Michigan, Bulletin No. 14, Ann Arbor, 1926.

Adams, Randolph G., History of the Foreign Policy of the United States, New York, 1926.

Allen, Gardner W., A Naval History of the American Revolution, 2 volumes, Boston and New York, 1913.

Allen, James, Diary of, Philadelphia Counsellor-at-Law, 1770-78 (Penn. Mag. of History and Biography, Volume IX), Philadelphia, 1885.

American Historical Association, Annual Reports, Washington, 1889, ——

American Historical Review.

American Irish Historical Society, Journal, New York.

Amory, Thomas C., The Military Services and Public Life of Major-General John Sullivan, Boston, 1868.

Anburey, Thomas, Travels Through the Interior Parts of America, 1776-81, Boston and New York, 1923.

André's Journal, 2 volumes (privately printed), Boston, 1903.

Annual Register, London, 1777, ——

Anonymous, Epistles Domestic, Confidential, and Official from General Washington (a reprint of the Spurious Letters, with others, including a letter from Timothy Pickering, quoting a denial by George Washington of their authorship, New York, 1796).

Armstrong, William C., The Battles in the Jerseys (New Jersey Society of the Sons of the American Revolution), 1916.

Arnold, Isaac N., The Life of Benedict Arnold, Chicago, 1880.

Ashburn, Colonel P. M., History of the Medical Department of the United States Army, Boston and New York, 1929.

Atterbury, Reverend W. Wallace, Elias Boudinot: Reminiscences of the American Revolution (Paper read before the Huguenot Society, Feb. 15, 1894).

Austin, Mary S., Philip Freneau, New York, 1901.

Avery, Elroy M., History of the United States and Its People, 7 volumes, Cleveland, 1904-10.

Baker, William S., The Engraved Portraits of Washington, Philadelphia, 1880.

Baker, William S., Itinerary of General Washington from June 15, 1775, to December 23, 1783, Philadelphia, 1892.

Balch, Thomas, Les Français en Amérique, Paris, 1872.

Balch, Thomas, The French in America, 1777-83 (translated by T. W. Balch), Philadelphia, 1891.

Balch, Thomas, Papers Relating Chiefly to the American Line, Philadelphia, 1857.

Baldwin, Alice M., New England Clergy and the American Revolution, Durham, N. C., 1928.

Ballagh, James Curtis, Letters of Richard Henry Lee, 1762-94, 2 volumes, New York, 1911.

Bancroft, Aaron, An Essay on the Life of George Washington, Worcester, Mass., 1807.

Bancroft, George, History of the United States, 10 volumes, Boston, 1848.

Barnes, L. C., The John Gano Evidence (Bulletin of William Jewell College, Sept. 15, 1926, series No. 24, No. 1), Liberty, Missouri.

Bean, Theodore W., Washington at Valley Forge one Hundred Years Ago, Norristown, Pennsylvania, 1876.

Beard, Charles A., and Mary R., The Rise of American Civilization, New York, 1927.

Belcher, Henry, The First American Civil War, 1775-78, 2 volumes, New York, 1911.

Beveridge, Albert J., Abraham Lincoln, 2 volumes, Boston and New York, 1928.

Beveridge, Albert J., The Life of John Marshall, 4 volumes, Boston and New York, 1916.

Blanchard, Claude, The Journal of, Commissary of the French Auxiliary Army, etc. (translated from a French MS., by William Duane, and edited by Thomas Balch), Albany, 1876.

Bogart, Ernest Ludlow, Economic History of the United States, New York and London, 1916.

Bolton, Charles Knowles, The Private Soldier Under Washington, New York, 1902.

Botta, Charles, History of the War of the Independence, 2 volumes (translated by George Alexander Otis), New Haven, 1842.

Boudinot, Elias, Journal of Historical Recollections of American Events During the Revolutionary War, Philadelphia, 1894.

Bowen, John S., and Futhey, J. Smith, A Sketch of the Battle of Brandywine (Bulletin of the Historical Society of Pennsylvania, Volume I, No. 7), Philadelphia, 1846.

Bowers, Claude G., Jefferson and Hamilton, Boston and New York, 1925.

Boyd, Thomas, Mad Anthony Wayne, New York, 1929.

Brown, Harvey E., The Medical Department of the United States Army, 1775-1873, Washington, 1873.

Bruce, Robert, Brandywine (privately printed), Oneida County, New York, 1922.

Bruce, William Cabell, John Randolph of Roanoke, 1773-1833, 2 volumes, New York and London, 1922.

Bullock, Charles J., Finances of the United States from 1775 to 1789, with Especial Reference to the Budget (Bulletin of Wisconsin University Press), Madison, Wisconsin, June, 1895.

Bülow, Dietrich von, Militärische und Vermischte Schriften, Leipzig, 1853.

Burnett, Edmund C., Letters of Members of the Continental Congress, Aug. 29, 1774-Dec. 31, 1779, 4 volumes, Washington, 1921.

Butler, James Davie, Deficiencies in our History (an Address to the Vermont Historical and Antiquarian Society), Montpelier, 1846.

Butterfield, C. W., Washington-Irvine Correspondence, Madison, Wis., 1882.

Cadwalader, General John, Military Papers of (Pennsylvania Magazine of History and Biography, XXXII), Philadelphia, 1908.

Calendar of the Correspondence of George Washington with the Officers, 4 volumes, Library of Congress, Washington, 1915.

Calendar of the Washington Manuscripts in the Library of Congress. Compiled under the direction of Herbert Friedenwald, Ph.D., Washington, 1901.

Calendar of Virginia State Papers, Richmond, 1890.

Callahan, Charles H., Washington the Man and the Mason, Washington, 1913.

Cambridge History of the British Empire, The, Volume I, The Old Empire, From the Beginnings to 1783, New York, 1929.

Campbell, John, Minutes of a Conspiracy against the Liberties of America, Philadelphia, 1865.

Carrington, General Henry B., Battles of the American Revolution, 1775-1781, New York, Chicago, New Orleans, 1877.

Carrington, General Henry B., Washington the Soldier, New York, 1899.

Chadwick, French E., Sea Power: The Decisive Factor in our Struggle for Independence (American Historical Association Reports, 1915), Washington, 1917.

Chambers, Robert W., The Painted Minx, Woman's Home Companion, 1929.

Champion, Mrs. Henry, American Flag—The Emblem of Liberty (Journal of American History, I, No. 1), New Haven, 1907.

Channing, Edward, and Hart, Albert Bushnell, Guide to the Study of American History, Boston, 1897.

Channing, Edward, History of the United States, 6 volumes, New York, 1909.

Chapman, Ervin, Latest Light on Abraham Lincoln, 2 volumes, New York, Chicago, Toronto, 1917.

Chase, E. P., Our Revolutionary Forefathers: Letters of Marquis de Barbé-Marbois, New York, 1929.

Chastellux, Marquis de, Letters—Travels in North America in 1780-82, London, 1787.

Chinard, Gilbert, Lettres Inédites de Beaumarchais, de Mme de Beaumarchais et de leur fille Eugénie, Paris, Baltimore, 1929.

Chinard, Gilbert, Lafayette in Virginia. Unpublished Letters, The Johns Hopkins Press, Baltimore, 1928.

Clark, Jane, Responsibility for the Failure of the Burgoyne Campaign, MS.

Clinton, George, Public Papers of (Introduction by Hugh Hastings), 8 volumes, State of New York, 1899.

Clinton, Sir Henry, An Historical Detail of Seven Years' Campaigns in North America, from 1775 to 1782, 3 volumes, Unpublished MS. in the Wm. L. Clements Library.

Clinton, Sir Henry, Narrative of Lieutenant-General, Relative to his Conduct during part of his Command of the King's Troops in North America, London, 1783.

Clinton, Sir Henry, Observations on Some Parts of the Answer of Earl Cornwallis to Sir Henry Clinton's Narrative, London, 1783.

Cole, G. D. H., The Life of William Cobbett, New York, 1924.

Collins, F. A., New York in the Revolutionary Days, New York Herald Tribune, May 16, 1926.

Collins, V. L., A Brief Narrative of the Ravages of the British and Hessians, Princeton University Library, 1906.

Collins, V. L., President Witherspoon, a Biography, 2 volumes, Princeton, 1925.

Conkling, Margaret C., Memoirs of the Mother and Wife of Washington (New edition, revised and enlarged), Auburn, New York, 1853.

Conway, Moncure D., Barons of the Potomack and the Rappahannock, New York, 1892.

Conway, M. D., George Washington and Mount Vernon (Memoirs of Long Island Historical Society, Volume 4), Brooklyn, 1889.

Cornwallis, Earl, Answer to Sir Henry Clinton's Narrative of the Campaign in 1781, Philadelphia, 1866.

Corwin, Edward S., French Policy and the American Alliance of 1778, Princeton University Press, 1916.

Cramp, J. M., Baptist History, Philadelphia.

Cresswell, Nicholas, Journal of, 1774-77, New York, 1924.

Curtis, Edward E., The Organization of the British Army in the American Revolution, Yale University Press, 1926.

Custis, George Washington Parke, Recollections and Private Memoirs of George Washington, New York, 1860.

Davis, Matthew L., Memoirs of Aaron Burr, 2 volumes, New York, 1855.

Davis, Matthew L., The Private Journal of Aaron Burr, 2 volumes, New York, 1838.

Dawson, Henry B., Battles of the United States by Sea and Land, 2 volumes, New York, 1858.

Dawson, Henry B., Gleanings from the Harvest-Field of American History, part 4, Morrisania, New York, 1865.

Dawson, Henry B., and "Selah," Major-General Israel Putnam, A Correspondence, on this Subject, with the Editor of "The Hartford Daily Post," Morrisania, New York, 1860.

Deane Papers, The., 5 volumes, New York Historical Society Collections, 1886-90, notes and translations by Charles Isham, New York, 1887-91.

Delteil, Joseph, Lafayette, New York, 1928.

Detail and Conduct of the American War, London, 1780.

Deux-Ponts, Count William De, My Campaigns in America: A Journal kept by (translated and with an introduction and notes by Samuel Abbott Green), Boston, 1868.

Dewey, Davis Rich, Financial History of the United States, London and New York, 1924.

Dexter, Franklin B., The Literary Diary of Ezra Stiles, 1769-95, 3 volumes, New York, 1901.

Dictionary of American Biography. See Johnson, Allen.

Döhla, Johann Conrad, Tagebuch eines Bayreuther Soldaten, Bayreuth, 1913.

Doniol, Henri, Historie de la participation de la France à l'établissement des Etats-Unis D'Amérique, 5 volumes, Paris, 1886-92.

Donne, W. Bodham, Correspondence of George III with Lord North, 1768-83, 2 volumes, London, 1866.

Doyle, Joseph B., Frederick William Von Steuben and the American Revolution, Steubenville, Ohio, 1913.

Drake, Francis S., The Life and Correspondence of Henry Knox, Boston, 1873.

Drake, Samuel A., Nooks and Corners of the New England Coast, New York, 1875.

Drake, S. J., The Aboriginal Races of North America (fifteenth ed.), New York, 1880.

Duer, William A., The Life of William Alexander, Earl of Sterling (New Jersey Historical Society), New York, 1847.

Duyckinck, Evert A., and George L., Cyclopædia of American Literature, 2 volumes, New York, 1856.

Eckenrode, H. J., The Revolution in Virginia, Boston and New York, 1916.

Edler, Friedrich, The Dutch Republic and the American Revolution, The Johns Hopkins Press, Baltimore, 1911.

Egerton, H. E., Causes and Character of the American Revolution, Oxford Clarendon Press, 1923.

Ewing, George, The Military Journal of, 1754-1824 (privately printed), Yonkers, N. Y., 1928.

Farrand, Max, The Fathers of the Constitution, The Chronicles of America Series, Volume 13, New Haven, 1921.

Farrand, Max., The Framing of the Constitution, New Haven, 1923.

Fay, Bernard, L'Esprit Revolutionnaire en France et aux Etats-Unis, Paris, 1925.

Fay, Bernard, Franklin, The Apostle of Modern Times, Boston, 1929.

Fisher, Sydney George, Legendary and Myth-making Process in Histories of the American Revolution, Am. Phil. Soc., Philadelphia, 1912.

Fisher, Sydney George, The Struggle for American Independence, 2 volumes, Philadelphia and London, 1908.

Fiske, John, The American Revolution, 2 volumes, Boston and New York, 1896.

Fiske, John, Essays Historical and Literary, New York, 1902.

Fitzpatrick, John C., Diaries of George Washington, Published for the Mount Vernon Ladies' Association of the Union, 4 volumes, Boston, 1925.

Fitzpatrick, John C., George Washington's Accounts of Expenses, etc., Boston and New York, 1917.

Fitzpatrick, John C., The Spirit of the Revolution, New Light from Some of the Original Sources of American History, Boston, 1924.

Fleming, Mrs. V. M., The Kenmore Mansion (privately printed by the Kenmore Ass'n), Fredericksburg, Virginia, 1924.

Flick, A. C., New Sources on the Sullivan-Clinton Campaign in 1779, Quarterly Journal of the New York State Historical Association, July, 1929.

Fonblanque, Edward Barrington de, The Right Honorable John Burgoyne, London, 1876.

Force, Peter, American Archives, 4th & 5th Series, Washington, 1837-1853.

Ford, Henry Jones, Alexander Hamilton, New York, 1920.

Ford, Paul Leicester, Orderly Books of the Revolution, No. 2., Orderly Book of the "Maryland Loyalists Regiment," June-October, 1778 (privately printed), Brooklyn, 1891.

Ford, Paul Leicester, The True George Washington, Philadelphia, 1896.

Ford, Worthington C., General Orders Issued by Major-General Israel Putnam, (privately printed), Brooklyn, 1893.

Ford, Worthington C., Letters of Joseph Jones of Virginia, 1777-87, Washington, 1889.

Ford, Worthington C., and Hunt, Gaillard, Journals of the Continental Congress, 1774-1789, 25 volumes, Washington, 1907.

Ford, Worthington C., Orderly Books of the Revolution, No. 1, Orders of Major-General Heath, May-October, 1777, Brooklyn, 1890.

Ford, Worthington C., The Spurious Letters Attributed to Washington, Brooklyn, 1889.

Ford, Worthington C., Statesman and Friend, Correspondence of John Adams with Benjamin Waterhouse, 1784-1822, Boston, 1927.

Ford, Worthington C., The Washington-Duché Letters (privately printed), Brooklyn, 1890.

Ford, Worthington C., Life of George Washington, 2 volumes, Boston, 1899.

Ford, Worthington C., The Writings of George Washington, 14 volumes, New York, 1889-93.

Ford, Worthington C. See George Washington, Ledger A.

Ford, Worthington C., The Correspondence and Journals of Samuel Blackley Webb, 3 volumes, New York, 1893.

Forman, S. E., Our Republic, A Brief History of the American People, New York, 1924.

Fortescue, Sir John, The Correspondence of King George the Third, 6 volumes, New York, 1927-8.

Fortescue, Hon. J. W., History of the British Army, 11 volumes, New York, 1915.

Franklin, Benjamin, Complete Works (edited by John Bigelow) 10 volumes, New York, 1887-88.

Frazer, Reverend David R., George Washington: An Address Delivered, Feb'y 22d, 1892, before the Washington Association of New Jersey, also, Letters Relating to the Execution of Major André, Presented by Mrs. Herbert Gray Torrey, at the same meeting.

French, Allen, The Day of Concord and Lexington, Boston, 1925.

Freneau, Philip, Poems relating to the American Revolution, with introduction by E. A. Duyckinck, New York, 1865.

(Galloway, J.), Letters to a Nobleman in the Conduct of the War. London, 1779.

(Galloway, J.), Reply to the Observations of Lieut. Gen. Sir Wm. Howe, London, 1780.

Ganoe, Major W. A., History of the United States Army, New York, 1924.

Garden, Alexander, Anecdotes of the Revolutionary War, 2 volumes, Charleston, 1822.

Gates Papers, New York Historical Society Collections.

Germain, Lord George, Hints for the Management of an Extended Enquiry, Germain MS., in the possession of the Wm. L. Clements Library, Ann Arbor, Michigan.

Godfrey, Carlos E., The Commander-in-Chief's Guard, Washington, 1904.

Goolrick, John T., The Life of General Hugh Mercer, New York, 1906.

Gordon, General John B., Reminiscences of the Civil War, New York, 1903.

Gordon, William, History of the Rise, Progress and Establishment of the Independence, 3 volumes, New York, 1794.

(Graydon, Alexander), Memoirs of a Life Chiefly Passed in Pennsylvania, Harrisburg, 1811.

Green, Ashbel, and Jones, Joseph H., The Life of Ashbel Green, V. D. M., New York, 1849.

Greene, Francis Vinton, General Greene, New York, 1897.

Greene, Francis Vinton, The Revolutionary War and the Military Policy of the United States, New York, 1911.

Greene, George Washington, Life of Maj.-Gen. Nathanael Greene, 3 volumes, New York, 1878.

Greene, George Washington, Historical View of the American Revolution, Boston, 1865.

Griffin, Martin I. J., The Catholics and the American Revolution, Volume I (privately printed), Ridley Park, Pennsylvania, 1907.

Grigsby, Hugh Blair, The History of the Virginia Federal Convention, with a Biographical Sketch of the Author and Illustrative Notes, Edited by R. A. Brock (Collections of the Virginia Historical Society, New series, IX), Richmond, 1890.

Hale, Edward Everett, Memories of a Hundred Years, New York, 1904.

Hamilton, Alexander, Works of (Federal edition, edited by Henry Cabot Lodge), 12 volumes, New York and London, 1904.

Hamilton, Stanislaus Murray, Letters to Washington and Accompanying Papers (Society Colonial Dames of America), 5 volumes, Boston, 1898.

Hapgood, Norman, George Washington, New York, 1901.

Harland, Marion, More Colonial Homesteads, New York, 1899.

Harland, Marion, The Story of Mary Washington, Boston, 1892.

Hart, Captain B. H. Liddell, Great Captains Unveiled, Boston, 1927.

Hart, Captain B. H. Liddell, A Greater Than Napoleon, Scipio Africanus, Boston, 1927.

Hastings, George E., Life and Works of Francis Hopkinson (Univ. of Chicago Press), Chicago, 1926.

Hatch, Louis Clinton, The Administration of the American Revolutionary Army, New York, 1904.

Hayden, Sidney, Washington and his Masonic Compeers, New York, 1867.

Heath, William, Memoirs of Major General William Heath, Boston, 1798.

Henderson, Colonel G. F. R., Stonewall Jackson and the American Civil War, 2 volumes, New York, 1913.

Henry, John Joseph, Campaign Against Quebec (privately printed), Lancaster, 1812.

Henry, William Wirt, Life, Correspondence and Speeches of Patrick Henry, 3 volumes, New York, 1891.

Hickman, John, Sketch of Squire Thomas Cheyney (Bulletin of Hist. Society of Pennsylvania, Vol. I, No. 7), Philadelphia, 1846.

Hinkhouse, Fred Junkin, Preliminaries of the American Revolution as seen in the English Press (Columbia Univ. Press), New York, 1926.

Historical Anecdotes, Civil and Military: in a Series of Letters, written from America in the years 1777 and 1778, London, 1779.

Historical Manuscripts Commission, Report on American Manuscripts in the Royal Institution of Great Britain, 4 volumes, London, 1904-9.

Historical Manuscripts Commission, Report on the MSS. of Mrs. Stopford-Sackville of Drayton House, Northamptonshire, Volume II, London, 1910.

Holder, Charles Frederick, The Quakers in Great Britain and America, New York, Los Angeles and London, 1913.

Hooton, Colonel F. C., Battle of Brandywine with its Line of Battle (privately printed), Harrisburg, 1900.

Hopson, Edwin Nott, Jr., Captain Daniel Neil, New Jersey Society Sons of the American Revolution, 1927.

Hudleston, F. J., Gentleman Johnny Burgoyne, Indianapolis, 1927.

Hufeland, Otto, Westchester County During the American Revolution (privately printed), New York, 1926.

Humphreys, Frank Landon, The Life and Times of David Humphreys, 2 volumes, New York, 1917.

Humphreys, Mary Gay, Catherine Schuyler, New York, 1897.

Hunt, Gaillard, Fragments of Revolutionary History, Brooklyn, 1892.

Hunt, Gaillard. See W. C. Ford, Journals of the Continental Congress.

Huntington, Ebenezer, Letters of, 1774-1781 (American Historical Review, V), New York, 1900.

Huntington, Joshua & Jedediah, Correspondence of the Brothers, During the Period of the American Revolution (Collections of the Connecticut Historical Society, Volume XX), Hartford, 1923.

Inman, George, Narrative of the Revolution (Penn. Magazine of History and Biography, VII), Philadelphia, 1883.

Irving, Washington, Life of George Washington, 5 volumes, New York, 1856.

Ives, George, A History of Penal Methods, New York.

James, James Alton, The Life of George Rogers Clark (Univ. of Chicago Press), Chicago, 1928.

James, Captain W. M., The British Navy in Adversity, London and New York, 1926.

Jameson, J. Franklin, The American Revolution Considered as a Social Movement, Princeton University Press, 1926.

Jay, John, Correspondence and Public Papers of, 1763-1781 (edited by H. P. Johnston), 4 volumes, New York, 1890.

Jefferson, Thomas, Writings, 20 volumes (Memorial Edition), Washington, 1905.

Jennings, W. W., History of Economic Progress in the United States, New York, 1926.

Johns Hopkins University Studies, Baltimore.

Johnson, Allen, editor, Dictionary of American Biography, 2 volumes, New York, 1928-9.

Johnson, General Bradley T., General Washington, New York, 1897.

Johnson, William, Sketches of the Life and Correspondence of Nathanael Greene, 2 volumes, Charleston, 1822.

Johnson, William J., George Washington the Christian, New York, Cincinnati, 1919.

Johnston, Henry P., The Secret Service of the Revolution (Magazine of American History, VIII), New York and Chicago, 1882.

Johnston, Henry P., Memoir of Colonel Benjamin Tallmadge, New York, 1904.

Johnston, Henry P., The Storming of Stony Point, New York, 1900.

Johnston, Henry P., Yale and Her Honor Roll in the Revolution (privately printed), 1888.

Johnston, Henry P., The Yorktown Campaign and the Surrender of Cornwallis, 1781, New York, 1881.

Jones, Thomas, History of New York During the Revolutionary War, 2 volumes, New York Historical Society, 1879.

Journal of American History, 1907, ——

Kain, C. Henry, Military and Naval Operations on the Delaware in 1777, Philadelphia, 1910.

Kapp, Friedrich, Friedrich der Grosse und die Vereinigten Staaten von Amerika, Leipzig, 1871.

Kapp, Friedrich, Leben des Amerikanischen Generals Johann Kalb, Stuttgart, 1862.

Kapp, Friedrich, Soldatenhandel deutscher Fürsten nach Amerika, Berlin, 1874.

Kapp, Friedrich, The Life of Frederick William von Steuben, New York, 1859.

Kellock, Harold, Parson Weems of the Cherry Tree, New York, 1928.

Kemble, Lieutenant-Colonel Stephen, Journal of (New York Hist. Society Colls., 1883-4), New York, 1884-5.

Kohler, Max J., Rebecca Franks, an American Jewish Belle of the Last Century (privately printed), New York, 1894.

Lafayette, Mémoires, correspondance et manuscrits du Général Lafayette, Publiés par sa famille, 6 volumes, Paris, 1838.

Lampman, Reverend Lewis, Leonard Bronk (paper read to Greene County, New York, Bar Association), 1911.

Latané, John H., A History of American Foreign Policy, Garden City, New York, 1927.

Lauzun, Mémoires de M. le duc de, Paris, 1822.

Lauzun, Memoirs of the Duc de (translated by C. K. Scott Moncrieff), New York, 1928.

Leake, Isaac Q., Memoir of the Life and Times of General John Lamb, Albany, 1850.

Lear, Tobias, Letters and Recollections of George Washington, New York, 1906.

Learned, M. D., & Grosse, C., Tagebuch des Captain Wiederholdt, New York.

Lecky, W. E. H., The American Revolution, 1763-1783 (edited by J. A. Woodburn), New York and London, 1926.

Lee, Henry, Memoirs of the War in the Southern Department of the United States, a new edition, with Revisions and a Biography of the author by Robert E. Lee, New York, 1869.

Lee, Richard Henry, Letters, 2 volumes (James Curtis Ballagh, ed.), New York, 1911.

Lee Papers, 4 volumes, Coll. of the New York Historical Society, New York, 1872-5.

Little, Shelby, George Washington, New York, 1929.

Lodge, Henry Cabot, Life of George Washington, 2 volumes, Boston and New York, 1920.

Lonn, Ella, Desertion during the Civil War, New York, 1928.

Lossing, Benson, J., The Pictorial Field Book of the Revolution, 2 volumes, New York, 1851-2.

Lossing, Benson J., Life of George Washington, 3 volumes, New York, 1860.

Lossing, Benson J., Mary and Martha, the Mother and Wife of George Washington, New York, 1886.

Lowell, Edward J., The Hessians in the Revolution, New York, 1884.

MacElree, Wilmer W., Along the Western Brandywine (privately printed), West Chester, Pa., 1909.

Mackelfresh, Captain C. H., Some Infantry Phases of Stream Crossings, U. S. Infantry Journal, December, 1928.

Magazine of American History, New York, 1877-91.

Mahan, A. T., Major Operations of the Navies in the War of American Independence, 1913.

Mahon, Lord, History of England from the Peace of Utrecht to the Peace of Versailles, 1713-1783, 7 volumes, London, 1858.

Marshall, John, The Life of George Washington, 5 volumes, Fredericksburg, Virginia.

Martyn, Charles, The Life of Artemas Ward, The First Commander-in-Chief of the American Revolution, New York, 1921.

Massachusetts Historical Society, Proceedings.

Maurice, Maj.-Gen. Sir Frederick, An Aide-de-Camp of Lee, Boston, 1927.

McClintock, Emory, Topography of Washington's Camp of 1780, A paper read before the Washington Association of New Jersey at their meeting, February 22, 1894.

McCoy, Samuel, This Man Adams, New York, 1928.

McCrady, Edward, The History of South Carolina in the Revolution, 1775-1780, New York, 1901.

McCrillis, A. M., Captain Stephen Olney, The Minute Man, December, 1926.

McIlwaine, H. R., Official Letters of the Governors of the State of Virginia, 3 volumes, Richmond, 1927-9.

McMaster, John Bach, History of the People of the United States, 8 volumes, New York and London, 1915.

McMaster, John Bach, Old Standards of Public Morals, Report of Am. Hist. Ass'n., 1905, Washington, 1906.

Meade, Bishop, Old Churches, Ministers, and Families of Virginia, 2 volumes, Philadelphia, 1897.

Meade, David, Meade Family History (Wm. and Mary College Quarterly, Vol. XIII), Richmond, Virginia, 1905.

M'Guire, Reverend E. C., The Religious Opinions and Character of Washington, New York, 1836.

Minnigerode, Meade. See Wandell.

Montresor Journals, The (edited and annotated by G. D. Scull), N. Y. Hist. Soc. Collections, 1881), New York, 1882.

Moore, Charles, The Family Life of George Washington, Boston, 1926.

Moore, Frank, Diary of the American Revolution, 2 volumes, New York, 1860.

Moore, Frank, Songs and Ballads of the American Revolution, New York, 1865.

Moore, George H., Libels on Washington with a Critical Examination Thereof (printed by the author), New York, 1889.

Moore, George H., The Treason of Charles Lee, New York, 1860.

Moore, J. Staunton, The Convention of 1788, An Address at the Westmoreland Club, Richmond, Virginia, February 22, 1908.

Morison, S. E., Sources and Documents illustrating the American Revolution, 1764-1788, Oxford, 1923.

Morgan, Christopher, Documentary History of the State of New York, 4 volumes, Albany, 1849.

Morgan, George, The True Patrick Henry, Philadelphia, 1907.

Morgan, George, The True LaFayette, Philadelphia, 1919.

Muhlenberg, General, Orderly Book of (Pennsylvania Magazine, XXXV), Philadelphia, 1911.

Muhlenberg, Henry A., The Life of Major-General Peter Muhlenberg, Philadelphia, 1849.

Murray, Rev. James, An Impartial History of the Present War in America, 2 volumes, London, 1778.

Nelson, William, The American Newspapers of the Eighteenth Century as Sources of History (Report of the Am. Hist. Ass'n., 1908, I), Washington, 1909.

New Jersey Historical Society, Collections.

New York City during the American Revolution (Mercantile Library Ass'n.), New York, 1861.

New York Historical Society, Collections, New York, 1869, ——

New York State Historical Association, Proceedings, New York, 1901, ——

New York State Historical Association, Quarterly Journal, Geneva.

Nevins, Allan, The American States During and After the Revolution, 1775-89, New York, 1924.

Nickerson, Hoffman, The Turning Point of the Revolution, Boston and New York, 1928.

Niles, Hezekiah, Principles and Acts of the Revolution in America, New York, Chicago and New Orleans, 1876.

Noailles, Vicomte de, Marins et Soldats Français en Amérique, 1778-1783, Paris, 1903.

O'Brien, Michael J., Washington's Irish Friends, Journal of American Irish Historical Society, XXV.

O'Callaghan, E. B., The Documentary History of the State of New York, 4 volumes, Albany, New York, 1849.

Odell, George C. D., Annals of the New York Stage (Columbia Univ. Press), 4 volumes, New York, 1927-8.

Olcott, Charles S., The Life of William McKinley, New York, 1916.

Oliver, Frederick Scott, Alexander Hamilton, New York, 1925.

Orderly Book of the Siege of Yorktown, . . . (now first printed from the Original MSS.), Philadelphia, 1865.

Paine, Thomas, Life and Works (The Patriots' Edition, 10 volumes), New Rochelle, 1925.

Palfrey, J. G., Life of William Palfrey (Sparks' American Biography, New Series, VII), Boston, 1846.

Parrington, Vernon Louis, Main Currents in American Thought, The Colonial Mind, 1620-1800, New York, 1927.

Parton, J., The Life and Times of Aaron Burr, New York, 1858.

Paullin, Charles Oscar, Out Letters of the Continental Marine Committee and Board of Admiralty, 1776-80, 2 volumes, New York, 1914.

Pell, John, Ethan Allen, Boston, 1929.

Pennsylvania Magazine of History and Biography.

Pettingill, R. W., Letters from America, 1776-1779, Boston and New York, 1924.

Phelps, Richard H., Newgate of Connecticut, Hartford, 1892.

Philips, George Morris, Historical Letters from the Collection of the West Chester State Normal School, Philadelphia, 1898.

Pickering, Timothy, Review of the Correspondence between the Hon. John Adams and the late Wm. Cunningham, Esq., Salem, 1824.

Pickering, Octavius, and Charles W. Upham, Life of Timothy Pickering.

Piványi, Eugene, Hungarian-American Historical Collections, Budapest, 1920.

Pontgibaud, The Chevalier de, A French Volunteer of the War of Independence (translated and edited by Robert B. Douglas), Paris, 1898.

Prussing, Eugene E., The Estate of George Washington Deceased, N. Y., 1927.

Pryor, Mrs. Roger A., The Mother of Washington, New York, 1903.

Quinn, A. H., The Spirit of Independence, Scribner's Magazine, July, 1926.

Ramsay, David, History of the American Revolution, London, 1793.

Ramsay, David, The Life of George Washington, New York, 1807.

Randall, Henry S., The Life of Thomas Jefferson, 3 volumes, New York, 1858.

Rayner, J. L., and Crook, G. T., The Complete Newgate Calendar, 5 volumes (privately printed), London, 1926.

Reed, William B., The Life and Correspondence of Joseph Reed, 2 volumes, Philadelphia, 1847.

Reed and Cadwalader Pamphlets, a Reprint of, 1863.

Remsburg, John E., Six Historic Americans, New York, 1906.

Rhodes, James Ford, History of the Civil War, 1861-1865, New York, 1923.

Rhodes, James Ford, History of the United States from the Compromise of 1850, 8 volumes, New York, 1893, ——

Rising, Oscar E., A New Hampshire Lawyer in General Washington's Army, Geneva, New York, 1915.

Robin, M. L'Abbé, Nouveau Voyage dans L'Amérique Septentrionale, en l'Année 1781, Paris, 1782.

Robinson, Lieut.-Col. Oliver Prescott, The Fundamentals of Military Strategy, Washington, 1928.

Rosengarten, J. G., American History from German Archives (Pennsylvania-German Society), Philadelphia, 1904.

Rosengarten, J. G., Frederick the Great and the United States (Pennsylvania-German Society), Philadelphia, 1906.

Rowland, Kate Mason, Life and Correspondence of Charles Carroll of Carrollton, 2 volumes, New York, 1898.

Rowland, Kate M., The Life of George Mason, 2 volumes, New York, 1892.

Rush, Benjamin, The Life and Character of Christopher Ludwick, Philadelphia, 1831.

Rush, Richard, Occasional Productions, Philadelphia, 1860.

Sabine, Lorenzo, Loyalists of the American Revolution, 2 volumes, Boston, 1864.

Saffell, W. T. R., Records of the Revolutionary War, Baltimore, 1894.

Sale, Edith Tunis, Old Time Belles and Cavaliers, Philadelphia, 1912.

Sargent, Winthrop, The Life and Career of Major John André, Boston, 1861.

Sargent, Winthrop, Loyalist Poetry of the Revolution, Philadelphia, 1857.

Sawyer, Joseph Dillaway, Washington, 2 volumes, New York, 1927.

Scharf, J. Thomas, and Westcott, Thompson, History of Philadelphia, 1609-1884, 3 volumes, Philadelphia, 1884.

Scharf, J. Thomas, History of Westchester County, 2 volumes, Philadelphia, 1886.

Schlesinger, Arthur Maier, New Viewpoints in American History, New York, 1925.

Schoepff, Johann David, Climate and Diseases of America During the Revolution (translated by J. R. Chadwick), Boston and New York, 1875.

Sedgwick, Henry Dwight, LaFayette, Indianapolis, 1928.

1776 Americana, a Catalogue, Philadelphia, 1926.

Shannon, Fred Albert, The Organization and Administration of the Union Army, 2 volumes, Cleveland, 1928.

Sherburne, Andrew, Memoirs of a Pensioner of the Navy of the Revolution, second edition, Providence, 1831.

Simcoe, Lieut.-Col. J. G., Military Journal, New York, 1844.

Smith, Horace W., Nuts for Future Historians to Crack, Philadelphia, 1856.

Smith, Justin H., Our Struggle for the Fourteenth Colony, 2 volumes, New York, 1907.

Smith, William H., The St. Clair Papers, 2 volumes, Cincinnati, 1882.

Sparks, Jared, Correspondence of the American Revolution, 4 volumes, Boston, 1853.

Sparks, Jared, The Diplomatic Correspondence of the American Revolution, 12 volumes, Boston, 1829.

Sparks, Jared, The Life and Treason of Benedict Arnold, Library of American Biography, Volume III, New York, 1835.

Sparks, Jared, Life of Charles Lee, Library of American Biography, Volume VIII, Boston, 1846.

Sparks, Jared, The Life and Writings of Gouverneur Morris, 3 volumes, Boston, 1832.

Sparks, Jared, Life of Count Pulaski, Library of American Biography, Volume IV, Boston, 1845.

Sparks, Jared, The Life of George Washington, Boston, 1844.

Sparks, Jared, The Writings of George Washington, 12 volumes, Boston, 1834.

Spears, John R., A History of the United States Navy, New York, 1908.

Sprague, William B., Annals of the American Pulpit, 9 volumes, New York, 1866-9.

Squires, W. H. T., The Days of Yester-Year, Portsmouth, Va., 1928.

Stedman, C., History of the American War, 2 volumes, London, 1794.

Steiner, Bernard C., The Life and Correspondence of James McHenry, Cleveland, 1907.

Steiner, Franklin, The Truth Seeker, July 23, December 31, 1927.

Stephenson, Nathaniel W., The Day of the Confederacy (Chronicles of America, 50 volumes), Yale University Press, 1921.

Stevens, B. F., Facsimiles of Manuscripts in European Archives Relating to America, 1773-1783, 25 volumes, London, 1889-1898.

Stevens, B. F., The Campaign in Virginia, 1781, An Exact Reprint of Six Rare Pamphlets on the Clinton-Cornwallis Controversy, 2 volumes, London, 1888.

Stiles, Ezra, The Literary Diary of (edited by F. B. Dexter), 3 volumes, New York, 1901.

Stillé, Charles J., Major-General Wayne and the Pennsylvania Line, Philadelphia, 1893.

Stone, Edwin M., The Life and Recollections of John Howland, Providence, 1857.

Stone, William L., Life of Joseph Brant, 2 volumes, Albany, N. Y,. 1865.

Stryker, William S., The Battle of Monmouth, Princeton University Press, 1927.

Stryker, William S., The Battles of Trenton and Princeton, Boston and New York, 1898.

Stryker, William S., Forts on the Delaware in the Revolutionary War, Trenton, 1901.

Stuart, J. W., Life of Jonathan Trumbull, Sen., Boston, 1859.

Sumner, William Graham, The Financier and the Finances of the American Revolution, 2 volumes, New York, 1891.

Swinton, William, Campaigns of the Army of the Potomac, New York, 1882.

Tables of Organization, Infantry and Cavalry Divisions, Revised April, 1925, General Service Schools Press, Ft. Leavenworth, Kansas, 1925.

Thacher, James, Military Journal During the Revolutionary War, Boston, 1827.

Thurston, Lieut. B. E., River Crossings, Tactical Problems and Methods, U. S. Infantry Journal, January, 1929.

Tomlinson, Everett T., Winters at Morristown, New York World, February 20, 1927.

Tower, Charlemagne, Essays Political and Historical, Philadelphia and London, 1914.

Tower, Charlemagne, The Marquis de La Fayette in the American Revolution, 2 volumes, Philadelphia, 1926.

Townsend, Joseph, Some Account of the British Army (Bulletin of the Historical Society of Pennsylvania, Volume I, No. 7), Philadelphia, 1846.

Trevelyan, George Macaulay, History of England, New York, 1926.

Trevelyan, Sir George Otto, The American Revolution, 3 volumes, New York, 1908.

Trevelyan, Sir George Otto, George the Third and Charles Fox, 2 volumes, New York, 1921.

Trumbull, John, Autobiography, New York, 1841.

Trumbull, Jonathan, and Joseph Gurley Woodward, Vindications of Patriots of the American Revolution, Connecticut Society of the Sons of the American Revolution, 1896.

Tyler, Moses Coit, Literary History of the American Revolution, 1763-1783, 2 volumes, New York and London, 1897.

Tyler's Quarterly Historical and Genealogical Magazine, Edited by Lyon G. Tyler, Richmond.

Upham. See Pickering.

Upham, W. P., Letters Written at the Time of the Occupation of Boston, from the Historical Collections of the Essex Institute, Salem Press, 1876.

Upton, Maj.-Gen. Emory, The Military Policy of the United States, Washington, 1904.

Vandenberg, Arthur Hendrick, The Greatest American, Alexander Hamilton, New York, 1921.

Van Tyne, Claude H., The American Revolution, 1776-1783, New York and London, 1905.

Van Tyne, Claude H., England and America, New York, 1927.

Van Tyne, Claude H., The Loyalists in the American Revolution, New York, 1902.

Van Tyne, Claude H., The War of Independence, American Phase, Boston and New York, 1929.

Virginia Historical Society Collections, Richmond.

Virginia Magazine of History and Biography, Richmond.

Virginia State Papers, Calendar, Richmond.

Walker, Lewis Byrd, Life of Margaret Shippen, Wife of Benedict Arnold, Pennsylvania Magazine of History and Biography, XXIV-XXVI, 1900-2, Philadelphia.

Walpole, Horace, Letters of (selected and edited by Charles Duke Yonge), 2 volumes, New York, 1890.

Walpole, Horace, Memoirs of the Last Ten Years of the Reign of George II, Edited by Lord Holland, London, 1847.

Walter, James, Memorials of Washington and of Mary, his Mother, and Martha, his Wife, from Letters and Papers of Robert Cary and James Sharples, New York, 1887.

Walton, Joseph S., George Washington in Chester County (Proceedings, Chester Co., Historical Society), 1898.

Wandell, Samuel H., and Minnigerode, Meade, Aaron Burr, 2 volumes, New York, 1925.

Ward, S. A., Journals and Letters of Samuel Curwen, 1775-1784, New York, 1842.

Warren, Mrs. Mercy, History of the Rise, Progress and Termination of the American War, 3 volumes, Boston, 1805.

Washington, George, Diaries. See Fitzpatrick.

Washington, George, Ledger A. From the Original in the Library of Congress, with Introduction by W. C. Ford, Mass. Hist. Society, 14 copies only, Boston, 1922.

Washington, George, Ledger B, MS. Library of Congress.

Washington, George, MSS. at Library of Congress, Huntington Library, N. Y. Public Library, J. Pierpont Morgan Library and private collections.

Washington, George, Writings. See Ford, Sparks.

Watson, John F., Annals and Occurrences of New York City and State in the Olden Times, New York, 1846.

Watson, John F., Annals of Philadelphia and Pennsylvania in the Olden Time, 2 volumes, Philadelphia, 1857.

Weedon, General George, Valley Forge Orderly Book of, New York, 1902.

Weems, Mason L., The Life of George Washington; with Curious Anecdotes, Equally Honorable to Himself and Exemplary to his Young Countrymen, Philadelphia, 1837.

Wharton, Anne Hollingsworth, Colonial Days and Dames, Philadelphia, 1895.

Wharton, Anne Hollingsworth, Martha Washington, New York, 1897.

White, William, Memoir of the Life of (Bird Wilson, editor), Philadelphia, 1839.

Whiting, John, Revolutionary Orders of General Washington, New York, 1844.

Whitlock, Brand, La Fayette, 2 volumes, New York, 1929.

Wilbur, James Benjamin, Ira Allen, Founder of Vermont, 1751-1814, Boston and New York, 1928.

Wilkinson, James, Memoirs of My Own Times, 3 volumes, Philadelphia, 1816.

William and Mary Quarterly, Williamsburg.

Williams, Henry Smith, Historians' History of the World, 27 volumes, London and New York, 1926.

Wilson, Bird, Memoir of the Life of the Right Reverend William White, D.D., Philadelphia, 1839.

Wilson, James Grant, The Memorial History of the City of New York, 4 volumes, New York, 1892-3.

Winsor, Justin, Narrative and Critical History of America, 8 volumes, Boston and New York, 1889.

Wise, Barton Haxall, Memoir of General John Cropper (Virginia Historical Collections, Vol. XI), 1892.

Wise, J. S., Virginia Folk Lore about Washington, Publications of Sharon Historical Society, No. 4, April, 1907.

Woodburn, James Albert. See Lecky.

Woodman, Henry, The History of Valley Forge, Oaks, Pennsylvania, 1920.

Woodward, W. E., George Washington, the Man and the Image, New York, 1926.

Wraxall, Sir N. William, Baronet, Historical Memoirs of My Own Time, 2 volumes, London, 1815.

Wright, Colonel J. W., Pickering's Letter of Washington, Tyler's Quarterly Historical and Genealogical Magazine, July, 1925.

Wrong, George M., Washington and his Comrades (Chronicles of America), New Haven, 1921.

Young, J. C., "Marse Robert" by his personal Attendant, the ex-slave, William Mack Lee, Collier's Weekly, March 12, 1927.

INDEX

811